After
Gettysburg

★ *After* ★
Gettysburg

Cavalry Operations in the Eastern Theater
July 14•1863 to December 31•1863

Robert J. Trout

Foreword by Eric J. Wittenberg and J. David Petruzzi

After Gettysburg:

Cavalry Operations in the Eastern Theater from July 14, 1863 to December 31, 1863

Robert J. Trout

Copyright © 2011 Robert J. Trout

ISBN: 978-0-9794035-7-6
974035-7-x
Printed in U.S.A.
First Edition

Cover design by James Zach

Eagle Editions Ltd.
Post Office Box 580
Hamilton MT 59840 USA
www.eagle-editions.com

Contents

Foreword

Time and again, historians of the American Civil War point to the June 9, 1863, battle at Brandy Station, Virginia, as the "turning point" in the ability of the cavalry of the Federal Army of the Potomac to stand as equals with the vaunted Confederate mounted arm. Until January of that year, Federal commanders parsed out most of their cavalry regiments to infantry headquarters as bodyguards, couriers and escorts – in general, serving as little more than well-mounted lackeys. When Army of the Potomac commander Maj. Gen. Joseph Hooker reorganized the cavalry into its own corps in February 1863, the seed for a cohesive Federal mounted fighting force was planted.

No battle or campaign of the war has been as intensely studied or written about than Gettysburg. The Gettysburg Campaign (generally identified as beginning with the Brandy Station battle and lasting until July 14, when Robert E. Lee successfully escaped across the Potomac River with his battered Army of Northern Virginia) has been the subject of seemingly infinite micro-studies. In recent years, the participation of the cavalry of both armies during the campaign has been the subject of notable scrutiny, in particular by these authors. Wittenberg's *The Battle of Brandy Station: North America's Largest Cavalry Battle* (History Press, 2010) contains the most recent scholarship on the brawl that raged across the plains northeast of Culpeper Court House. Both Wittenberg and Petruzzi, in books and articles, have extensively covered the movements and battles of the horsemen of both armies during the balance of the campaign. Our *Plenty of Blame To Go Around: Jeb Stuart's Controversial Ride to Gettysburg* (Savas Beatie, 2006) and (with Michael F. Nugent) *One Continuous Fight: The Retreat and Pursuit of Robert E. Lee's Army of Northern Virginia, July 4-14, 1863,* (Savas Beatie, 2008) are detailed narratives of the exploits of the blue and gray cavalry before and after the main battle. The latter is the first comprehensive study of the nearly two dozen battles and skirmishes (fought primarily by the cavalry) during the retreat from Gettysburg.

Among all that has been written of America's Civil War, however, one enormous void has existed in the scholarship: that of the period following the Gettysburg Campaign to the end of the 1863 calendar year. Although the period contains both the Bristoe Station and Mine Run Campaigns, the period has been the subject of just a handful of small books and few scholarly articles, probably because there was no major infantry battle involving the entirety of the main armies. That's a shame, because there was plenty of fighting and plenty of strategic maneuvering by both sides that have not been examined in any detail by a modern scholar.

Historian Robert J. Trout has finally filled that void. His new study of the intense fighting that filled the fall of 1863 admirably fits the bill. Trout, renowned as the authority on the Army of Northern Virginia's horse artillery and on Maj. Gen. J. E. B. Stuart's staff, has taken a novel approach to these actions. Trout rightly recognized that the bulk of the fighting in the fall of 1863 was done by the mounted arms of both armies, and his study focuses on the cavalry. That's not to say that the infantry is neglected—it is not neglected at all. However, without the exploits of the horse soldiers, the infantry actions likely would not have occurred.

Included in Trout's detailed examination of these events are the cavalry engagements at Brandy Station of August 1 and October 11, 1863, the fight at Culpeper Court House of September 13, the fight at Jack's Shop on September 22, and the so-called "Buckland Races" on October 19. Also addressed is the infantry battle at Bristoe Station on October 14, where Lt. Gen. A. P. Hill's Corps of the Army of Northern Virginia suffered a severe and embarrassing defeat, and the Mine Run campaign of November 27-December 2, 1863. These actions are covered in detail here for the first time. Such colorful and interesting characters as J.E.B. Stuart, Alfred Pleasonton, Judson Kilpatrick, and John S. Mosby fill these pages. At last, the gap in the history of the Civil War in the Eastern Theater has been filled.

We cannot recommend Robert J. Trout's new book to you in stronger terms. If you have an interest in the war in the Eastern Theater in 1863, this book is indispensable and must have a place on the bookshelf of every serious student of the Civil War.

Eric J. Wittenberg
Columbus, Ohio
J. David Petruzzi
Brockway, Pennsylvania

Acknowledgments

This book could not have been completed without the assistance of numerous historians and researchers, many of them authors in their own right, who provided me with material, recommendations, and assessment throughout my work on the manuscript. Mentioning their names seems little compensation for all that they contributed to the final product.

Patricia Walenista combed the libraries at the Museum of the Confederacy, the Virginia Historical Society, and the Library of Virginia for Confederate soldiers' letters, diaries, and reminiscences. She also waded through an untold number of microfilms to locate newspaper accounts of events during the period in question. Her editing skills helped in the final preparation of the manuscript.

Horace Mewborn graciously gave me access to his vast library of cavalry material and assisted in going through reams of papers to locate useful information that I would not have had otherwise. A full day of his time was given in finding, copying, and stapling diaries, letters, articles, telegrams, and reminiscences. He also opened his home to my wife and me during our stay. Finally, he read the final product and offered sage advice in several areas.

Thomas Nanzig supplied me with a vast array of Federal resources including regimental histories, letter collections, diaries, and reminiscences. Many of these sources would have been missed without his willingness to search out and share the material. His observations after reading the manuscript were greatly appreciated.

James Nolan took time to locate and copy numerous pages relating to men who fought in New York cavalry regiments. He was always willing to answer questions, run down obscure facts, and search libraries for material.

Robert F. O'Neill gave freely of his collection of newspaper articles focusing on the Michigan cavalry. On reading the manuscript, he provided insight that assisted greatly in improving it.

Bryce Suderow kindly gave of his time to send packages and emails of newspaper articles, diaries, casualty statistics, and other material he gathered from various repositories that proved invaluable in constructing the story of the cavalry during this period. Additionally, he applied his discerning eye to the manuscript and helped in its final editing.

Ted Alexander also read the manuscript and made suggestions and corrections for which I am grateful.

A host of librarians and historians at various institutions across the country gave of their resources and expertise. I wish to thank John Coski (Historian and Director of Library & Research, Museum of the Confederacy), Mark Bowden (Coordinator for Special Collections, Burton Historical Collection, Detroit Public Library), Karen L. Jania (Reference Archivist, Bentley Historical Library, University of Michigan), Amanda Demeter (Library Assistant, Dept. of Special Collections, University of California at Santa Barbara Library), Wakefield Harper and Matthew Turi (Southern Historical Collection, Louis Round Wilson Special Collections Library, The University of North Carolina at Chapel Hill), Jonathan Dembo and Maurice C. York (Special Collections Department, J. Y. Joyner Library Room, East Carolina University), Rebecca Ebert (Stewart Bell Jr. Archives, Handley Regional Library), Suzanne Hahn (Director, Reference Service, Indiana Historical Society), Sharon Carlson (Western Michigan University Archives and Regional History Collections, Western Michigan University), Terry Foster and Thomas E. Buffenbarger (Research Center Division, United States Army Military History Institute), Christine M. Beauregard (Senior Librarian, Manuscripts & Special Collections, New York State Library), Elizabeth B. Dunn (Research Services Librarian, Rare Book, Manuscript, and Special Collections Library, Duke University), Kelly Sizemore and Chris Kolbe (Archives Research Services, Library of Virginia), and E. Lee Shepard (Vice President for Collections, Virginia Historical Society).

Finally, once more and for always, my wife Judy, tirelessly helped in finding, copying, coordinating, reading, critiquing, and doing all the little things that allowed me to work on and complete this project. How she endures, I will never know but am eternally thankful that she does.

Robert J. Trout
March 7, 2011
Myerstown, PA

Introduction
Sabers Blue and Gray

Historians invariably cite the June 9, 1863, cavalry battle at Brandy Station as the opening of the Gettysburg campaign and the July 14, 1863, crossing of the Potomac River by the Army of Northern Virginia as its close. Although the Confederates drew a collective sigh of relief to be once again on the soil of Virginia, Gen. Robert E. Lee, that army's commander-in-chief, understood that the army still had some marching to do to be really safe. A raging Shenandoah River prevented Lee from taking his army back to the Rappahannock River, where he began his campaign, and placing it once again between Richmond and the Army of the Potomac. Until he did, the initiative still lay with the Federal army's commander, Maj. Gen. George G. Meade.

Although both sides sought a respite from the fray to heal and regain strength, that goal remained elusive, especially for the cavalry. The mounted arm of both armies had been active since the beginning of the campaign, testing each others' mettle in the day long brawl at Brandy Station on June 9 and then moving or fighting almost daily thereafter. The fact that on July 14 the Potomac now flowed between them meant little. Every trooper, North and South, knew he could not expect any meaningful period of rest any time soon.

Along the river's southern shore, the gray troopers settled into their roles as pickets and the army's first line of defense. Their commander had prepared them well to fulfill these duties. Maj. Gen. J. E. B. Stuart had made significant contributions to the Confederate war machine very early in his career. From his first command as a lieutenant colonel of several companies that became part of the First Virginia Cavalry, Stuart demonstrated a signal ability to grasp what functions cavalry could and should perform, a knack for training it to accomplish those tasks, remarkable leadership skills, and an offensive mindset so crucial in a cavalry commander. Early in the war, Stuart revealed a talent for reconnaissance and counter-reconnaissance in the prosecution of which he showcased his tireless vigilance and aggressive nature. He also recognized that cavalry could make a significant contribution to the army only if concentrated under a central command and not scattered throughout the army. As events proved, this gave the Confederates a considerable advantage over their foe in the first year of the war. As a result, the Confederate cavalry's early successes in the eastern theater of the war can be directly linked to Stuart.

As part of his vision of what cavalry could accomplish Stuart gathered around him a coterie of officers who, for the most part, could boast of many talents in their own right. On the brigade level, Wade Hampton, Fitzhugh Lee, William H. F. "Rooney" Lee, and William E. "Grumble" Jones were solid leaders, although Jones's ongoing feud with Stuart hampered both men. Over the course of the campaign just concluded, Beverly H. Robertson's inefficiencies rose to the surface. To get the most out of Robertson's brigade, its commander would have to go. Before his wounding at Gettysburg, Albert G. Jenkins did little to distinguish himself during the march north. Furthermore, his brigade demonstrated a lack of the professionalism and capability possessed by Stuart's brigades. However, for whatever length of time the brigade remained under Stuart's control, it needed to perform when called upon and show that it could be counted on, which it did at Gettysburg. Jenkins's replacement, Col. Milton J. Ferguson was steady if not overly talented. John R. Chambliss, who led "Rooney" Lee's Brigade in the wake of that officer's wounding at Brandy Station, proved that he could be counted on and performed well enough to warrant having his own brigade in the future. Other officers, like Laurence S. Baker, Matthew C. Butler, James B. Gordon, Lunsford L. Lomax, Thomas L. Rosser, Williams C. Wickham, and Pierce M. B. Young waited in the wings ready to take center stage when called.

The Confederate trooper at this stage of the war faced an increasingly confident adversary and the usual shortages of everything needed to fight him. Unfortunately, the situation would not improve. From the war's commencement, the gray cavalry could boast of horses and men who could ride them anywhere their leaders ordered them to go. Weapons proved more difficult to obtain, and the South never managed to put its mounted forces on an even footing with the Federal cavalry in this crucial category. The Southern cavalry that fell under Stuart's command received excellent training for the most part and coupled with their superior horses and horsemanship dominated, though never cowed, their Northern foes until June 9, 1863.

Indeed, the battle of Brandy Station elevated the Federal cavalry's self-perception and forced the Confederate cavalry to recognize that its days of supremacy were over. In the weeks that followed, Stuart's squadrons found their enemy willing and able to stand hoof to hoof with them on any field they chose. The path to parity with the Southern cavaliers had been a rocky one. The blue troopers' woes began at the commencement of the war. While their southern counterparts had been born with a horse under them, or so it seemed, many of the northern boys, especially those from the cities, were new to the saddle and learned riding, care of their mounts, and cavalry drill simultaneously. For many of the officers, the situation was the same. However, training could and eventually did overcome such problems. What truly hampered the blue troopers centered on leadership and organization. No Stuart emerged, or rather, was permitted to emerge from the prewar officer corps.

Talented men existed but politicians with agendas of their own and close-minded, shortsighted officers in key positions who could not grasp what cavalry could contribute beyond guard and escort duty hampered the promotion of such men. These stumbling blocks, along with the belief that the war would end before any significant number of cavalry regiments could be raised and trained, meant that little was done to prepare to meet the Southern horse on anything like an equal footing. Once the war stretched beyond the few months it had been prophesied to last and the Confederate cavalry began to make its presence felt in earnest, the Federal high command scrambled to put regiments in the field. Once this was accomplished, another problem arose – how to use those regiments. Instead of forming brigades, the regiments were scattered throughout the army at the whim of the infantry generals to whom they were assigned. As a result, the blue troopers could not meet the Confederates as a unified force and thus were always at a disadvantage. Regrettably, this lack of leadership and organization continued to be an Achilles heel until late in 1862.

The appointment of Maj. Gen. Joseph Hooker to the command of the Army of the Potomac signaled an end to the Federal cavalry's second-rate status. While Hooker himself failed to defeat Robert E. Lee's army at Chancellorsville, the change he brought to the organization of the cavalry arm created the initial impetus that eventually would be felt on the field of Brandy Station and beyond. Only the lack of a visionary commander would hold back the blue horsemen from becoming all they could be. The man selected to lead the new mounted force, Maj. Gen. George Stoneman, failed to take advantage of the opportunity given to him and fell from favor after Chancellorsville. His replacement, Maj. Gen. Alfred Pleasonton, had risen rapidly through the ranks from the beginning of the war. Many negative things have been written about Pleasonton and while a number of them are true, an accurate assessment of his career has yet to be made. His critics claim that he was a narcissist of the first rank and a behind-the-scenes manipulator capable of almost any act that would assist him in reaching his goals, all of which revolved around improving his position and furthering his career. They accuse him of leading the cavalry mostly from army headquarters, providing little inspiration for his men, seeking credit for any successes, sacrificing the careers of others to secure his goals, and covering up his failures by any possible means. However, even if true, and reasonable doubt exists as to the veracity of a number of these charges, such shortcomings can be laid at the boots of many generals on both sides. Jealousy and ambition fueled Pleasonton's enemies just as they did Stuart's. For these reasons, what Pleasonton accomplished as commander of the Federal cavalry remains difficult to ascertain. Hopefully, what follows will assist in clarifying his achievements as commander-in-chief of Meade's mounted arm.

The three divisions of the Federal Cavalry Corps boasted at least two outstanding leaders and one whose career has been viewed as controversial, though no one would deny his tenacity as a fighter. Brig. Gen. John Buford brought a steady head and hand to his command. A hero of the recent battle at Gettysburg, Buford's contributions to the cavalry arm of the service were much more than his gallant stand on the first day's battle for which history remembers him most. His men trusted and admired him and would follow him anywhere. Like Buford, Brig. Gen. David McMurtrie Gregg had demonstrated his capabilities in the Gettysburg campaign, fighting Stuart to a standstill in a cavalry action east of the main battlefield. Like Buford, Gregg's men had confidence in and respected him for his steady leadership and imperturbable nature even in the midst of trying circumstances. Brig. Gen. Hugh Judson Kilpatrick certainly demonstrated that he could fight cavalry with the best of them. He has come down in history as "Kil-Cavalry," unjustly as events will show, because of the used-up condition of his horses. Kilpatrick's troopers, who called him "Old Kil," understood that he would lead them from the front and demand of them nothing he did not demand from himself. Kilpatrick's successes throughout 1863 confirmed that he deserved the command of one of Pleasonton's divisions. Talented men, like George A. Custer, Henry E. Davies, Thomas C. Devin, William Gamble, John Irvin Gregg, John B. McIntosh, and Wesley Merritt commanded many of the brigades. They stood on equal footing with their counterparts dressed in gray.

The Federal cavalry trooper, much maligned by their adversaries during the first year and a half of the war, ably demonstrated throughout the Gettysburg campaign that they could no longer be ridden around, through, or over. The days of easy victories by their Southern brethren dissipated along with the smoke of the battles at Brandy Station, Aldie, Middleburg, Upperville, and Gettysburg. Always better armed than their foe, the "School of Hard Knocks" had graduated its first class of veterans who could now put those arms to effective use under leadership that rivaled that of the Confederacy, at least on a division, brigade, and regimental level.

Of importance is an understanding of the duties of the cavalry. Just what did cavalry do on a daily basis? The grand charges of cuirassed-clad men thundering down on infantry squares bristling with bayonet walls disappeared soon after Waterloo. The rifled musket meant doom to any mounted soldier foolish enough to venture such an attack. However, some of the duties that Napoleon's cavalry performed still lay within the functions of the Federal and the Confederate mounted arms. Reconnaissance and counter-reconnaissance or screening lay at the core of cavalry operations. Without the proper execution of these vital functions an army commander's plans might be seriously or completely compromised. Delaying actions, whether conducted in the advance to hold an enemy in place until a larger force could be brought to the front or in the retreat to hold off an aggressive enemy's pursuit, could best be performed by a force with the ability to move quickly and strike hard. Cavalry and horse artillery rather than infantry and mounted artillery were much more suited to this role. Pursuing a beaten enemy and not permitting it to rally also fell under the cavalry's responsibilities. Raiding behind enemy lines to cause damage to lines of supply and communication required the swift movement that only cavalry could deliver. Of course, with both sides performing these duties the clash of arms inevitably occurred and the side that emerged victorious had a better opportunity of completing its mission. In the pages that follow these duties and the encounters they precipitated will be explored. Hopefully, a better understanding of cavalry operations and of this particular period of the war will emerge.

Chapter One

From the Potomac to the Rappahannock

Rain fell in torrents. Generals Robert E. Lee and James Longstreet sat on their horses beside the pontoon bridge that spanned the raging Potomac River at Falling Waters. The end of the Army of Northern Virginia's long retreat from Gettysburg lay at hand. The sanctuary of the "Old Dominion" beckoned Lee's plodding columns. In the flickering glow of a handful of torches, the weary troops made their way across the river to safety. Lee, overcome with fatigue, turned over the operation to Longstreet and rode into the darkness. Through the long night, Lee's "Old War Horse" kept vigil, watching regiment after regiment slog over the bridge. The army's transport, mirroring the infantry, struggled through the pouring rain, the calf-deep mud, and the blackness of the night to reach the crossing. The grim circumstances worsened when a wagon, loaded with wounded, missed the end of the bridge and plunged into the dark, turbulent waters. Miraculously the men were saved and the crossing continued.[1] For all, the wretched night passed ever so slowly, leaving behind haunting memories that lasted a lifetime.

With the dawn, Lee returned to relieve Longstreet and to watch the last of his legions gain the Potomac's southern bank. He agonized over the swaying bridge, worrying that it might give way before his men were safely across. An audible sigh of relief escaped Lee when the bulk of the rear guard passed over and he again gave way to his own weariness. Maj. Gen. J. E. B. Stuart, Lee's cavalry chief, who sat nearby, offered a cup of coffee, which Lee gratefully drank down. He returned the cup and remarked that nothing had ever refreshed him so much.[2]

For Lee's infantry the long grueling campaign ground almost to a halt once they stood again on Virginia soil. What had begun rife with high expectations ended on the ridge south of Gettysburg and left Lee, the army, and the Confederate nation contemplating what-might-have-been. Lee's foot soldiers had given all they had to give. Now as they settled into their camps around Bunker Hill and Darkesville along the Valley Pike, they sought to gain an understanding of what had happened, recover their strength, and prepare for what must inevitably come – a continuation of the strife once Maj. Gen. George G. Meade thrust his Army of the Potomac across its namesake river. Until that happened Lee and his men could do little more than wait, which, considering the state of the army, was a pleasant recourse.

Except Brig. Gen. William E. "Grumble" Jones's Brigade that crossed on the 12th, Stuart's troopers had been some of the last Confederates to cross the river.[3] Once on southern soil, Stuart sent Wade Hampton's Brigade, under Col. Laurence S. Baker, who assumed command when Hampton fell wounded on July 3, to guard the river crossings from Falling Waters to Hedgesville. Fitzhugh Lee's Brigade, William H.F. "Rooney" Lee's Brigade, commanded by Col. John R. Chambliss in Lee's absence, Beverly H. Robertson's Brigade, and Albert G. Jenkins's Brigade, led by Col. Milton J. Ferguson after Jenkins's wounding at Gettysburg, rode through Martinsburg on the night of July 14 and camped along the road between that place and Leetown where the men, "Found the citizens very obliging and we could obtain an abundance of provisions."[4] The next day Robertson's Brigade rode on to cover the crossings of the Shenandoah River. Jones's Brigade marched through Leetown to Smithfield on the 13th, remaining there the next day. The other brigades stayed encamped around Leetown.[5] Stuart, his preparations made, settled down at "The Bower," home of Adam Stephen Dandridge, to await the enemy's next move.[6]

North of the river Lee's counterpart, Meade, faced enemies other than those dressed in gray. With complete victory and seemingly an end to the war in sight, the fact that the Confederate army escaped him baffled some and greatly enraged others. Never mind the condition of Meade's men, their extraordinary efforts at Gettysburg, their sacrifice, and their body numbing fatigue, Meade had allowed an opportunity to win the war trickle through his fist because he could not or would not throw the final punch. Gazing at Lee's entrenched position before Williamsport, Meade had envisioned a Pickett's Charge in reverse and decided not to send his men to test Lee's resolve to fight again on Northern soil in the hope of snatching victory from defeat. Through Maj. Gen. Henry W. Halleck, the army general-in-chief, President Abraham Lincoln expressed his disappointment in a telegram to Meade.

> WASHINGTON, D.C., July 14, 1863 — 1 p.m.
> Major-General MEADE,
> Army of the Potomac:
>   The enemy should be pursued and cut up, wherever he may have gone. This pursuit may or may not be upon the rear or flank, as circumstances may require. The inner flank toward Washington presents the greatest advantages. Supply yourself from the country as far as possible. I cannot advise details, as I do not know where Lee's army is, nor where your pontoon bridges are. I need hardly say to you that the escape of Lee's army without another battle has created great dissatisfaction in the mind of the President, and it will require an active and energetic pursuit on your part to remove the impression that it has not been sufficiently active heretofore.[7]

For Meade, Lincoln's "dissatisfaction" proved the final straw and he responded.

HEADQUARTERS ARMY OF THE POTOMAC,
July 14, 1863 — -2.30 p.m. (Received 3.10 p.m.)
Maj. Gen. H. W. HALLECK,
General-in-Chief:
>   Having performed my duty conscientiously and to the best of my ability, the censure of the President conveyed in your dispatch of 1 p.m. this day, is, in my judgment, so undeserved that I feel compelled most respectfully to ask to be immediately relieved from the command of this army.[8]

Meade's resignation failed to move Lincoln to appoint another army commander. Meade stayed at his post and the pursuit of Lee across the Potomac became the Federal army's next concern.

The Northern cavalry rode and fought most of the 14th. The divisions of Brig. Gen. John Buford and Brig. Gen. Hugh Judson Kilpatrick followed Lee's retreating army to Williamsport and Falling Waters, colliding with the Confederate rear-guard.[9] At Falling Waters, Capt. Peter A. Weber, leading Companies B and F of the Sixth Michigan, belonging to Brig. Gen. George A. Custer's brigade of Kilpatrick's division, charged ahead, surprising the Confederates and mortally wounding Maj. Gen. James J. Pettigrew before being driven back with considerable loss, including Weber, who was killed. A second charge resulted in most of the remaining troopers being captured. The rest of Custer's brigade then came up. Companies C and H of the Fifth Michigan charged, freed the prisoners, and captured 52 of the enemy. Buford arrived to supported Custer. In sharp fighting that followed, the blue cavalry added to its laurels by taking over 1,000 prisoners, three battle flags, and one cannon, captured by a squadron from the Eighth New York of Col. William Gamble's brigade, Buford's division.[10] Nevertheless, frustration reigned. Buford reported that some of his troopers viewed the pontoon bridge being cut away on the Maryland side and swinging to the Virginia side of the river.[11] Pvt. John R. Morey of the Fifth Michigan, writing home, expressed the feelings of many of his fellow troopers, "I had hoped that we would capture the whole of Lee's army. But they have evaded us . . . ."[12]

In an effort to support Buford and Kilpatrick in their pursuit, Brig. Gen. David McM. Gregg's Second Brigade under Col. Pennock Huey had also made its way first to Williamsport and then to Falling Waters, but arrived at both places too late to participate in any of the fighting, thus surpassing in disappointment their fellow cavalrymen of the other divisions. The brigade encamped for the night at Falling Waters.[13]

The 14th also saw the first Federal efforts to follow Lee across the Potomac. Early in the afternoon, Brig. Gen. Henry M. Naglee, commanding at Harpers Ferry, ordered a reconnaissance south of the river along the road from Bolivar Heights to Charles Town. Fifty men from the First Connecticut under Maj. Charles Farnsworth were assigned the task. About two miles from Harpers Ferry, the Connecticut cavalry's advance guard of 18 men under Capt. Erastus Blakeslee ran into Confederate pickets from the Twelfth Virginia, Jones's Brigade, and sent them scurrying.[14] At the same time, the Twelfth's commander, Col. Asher W. Harman, who had only just recovered from the wound he suffered during the Brandy Station fight on June 9, just had ridden out with a squad of six men to check his picket posts. Caught in the rout, Harman, unhorsed, fell prisoner to the rapidly advancing Federals.[15] Farnsworth came up and joined Blakeslee in the pursuit, which soon got out of hand. The strung out Federal cavalry ran into the charging Confederate reserve. The tables turned quickly and after a saber and pistol melee the Connecticut boys raced back toward Bolivar Heights. Gobbled up were Maj. Farnsworth, whose horse had been shot from under him, one lieutenant, and a number of men and horses.[16]

Later that same day, after the Twelfth Virginia had re-established its picket line, Brig. Gen. David McM. Gregg, reached Harpers Ferry with Col. John B. McIntosh's and Col. John Irvin Gregg's brigades, crossed the pontoon bridge at Harpers Ferry about 4:00 in the afternoon, and pushed out along the Charles Town road.[17] This time the Twelfth Virginia offered only token resistance before dashing back to Charles Town. Col. Gregg prepared to swing his regiments toward Shepherdstown in the hope of "carrying out fully the plan of sweeping the road between Winchester and Martinsburg."[18] But before he could begin, he received a message from the Federal cavalry's commander-in-chief, Maj. Gen. Alfred Pleasonton, informing him that, "The enemy has crossed the Potomac. You will endeavor to ascertain what direction he has taken, and his intentions. Harass him as much as you can. You will keep up communication with these headquarters through Harpers Ferry. I send you Colonel Huey's brigade."[19] However, when the promised reinforcements did not arrive, Gregg chose to proceed no further and pulled back to Bolivar Heights to camp for the night.[20]

Somewhat frustrated by his withdrawal, Gregg determined to have another go at Shepherdstown on the 15th even though Huey had not yet arrived.[21] Pushing out along the Harpers Ferry/Charles Town Road, Gregg's leading brigade under Col. J. Irwin Gregg reached Halltown and halted. The First Maine drew the job of scouting toward Charles Town and dutifully rode out. About a mile south of Halltown, Confederate vedettes from the Sixth Virginia, Jones's Brigade, that had replaced the Twelfth, offered a very brief resistance before pulling back to their main force, which brought the enemy advance to a standstill.[22] Neither Private John C. Donahue of the Sixth nor Corporal George M. Neese of Capt. Roger P. Chew's Battery of horse artillery, the battery arriving to bolster the gray skirmishers, thought much of the Federal offensive. Ten minutes of long range sniping at Chew's two guns disturbed Neese not at all. He awaited larger game and when the bluecoats formed two companies in the road for a mounted attack, Neese dropped a shell among the ranks, breaking up any thought of a charge. Donahue credited Chew's two guns with ending the small skirmish.[23] The First Maine eventually withdrew to Halltown where Maj. Joseph C. Kenyon of the Eleventh New York, who commanded elements of his own regiment and the Thirteenth Pennsylvania, relieved the New Englanders. The boys from Maine then followed the division toward Shepherdstown.[24]

Gen. Gregg had not delayed his entire command at Halltown while the First Maine scuffled with the enemy. He had turned westward with the main column and, putting Col. Gregg's brigade once again in the lead, made his way toward Shepherdstown, scooping up Confederate stragglers along the way. Approaching the target about noon, Col. Gregg ordered two squadrons of Maj. William H. Fry's Sixteenth Pennsylvania forward. Fry charged through the town, encountering no opposition. The Sixteenth then scouted a little beyond the town before returning and picketing south of the village.[25] With the town secure, Gen. Gregg viewed his mission for the day accomplished. He did issue one more order. Lt. Col. William E. Doster's Fourth Pennsylvania received the assignment to defend the Winchester Road while the rest of the division made camp in and around Shepherdstown. Doster moved out through the Sixteenth's pickets and advanced four miles south to Walper's Crossroads, encountering only a handful of Confederates along the way. Once in possession of the crossroads, Doster threw out vedettes on all the roads. His entire command stayed there until 11:00 that night when three squadrons withdrew to Shepherdstown. The remainder of the regiment was relieved the next morning. Doster's foray down the Winchester Road seemed routine. However, a prisoner revealed that 500 Confederate cavalry lay nearby with another large force off to the left near Charles Town. Doster may have wondered if holding Shepherdstown would be as easy as taking it.[26]

The lack of resistance Stuart offered Gregg on the 15th could be attributed to the Federal position at Harpers Ferry. Meade's cavalry had easy access to the Potomac's south bank. Any attempt by Stuart to hold the line along the river from Shepherdstown to Harpers Ferry would have been impractical. Another reason centered on the fact that, except for Jones, who was encamped near Summit Point, Stuart's brigades had further to ride and did not reach the vicinity of Charles Town until the 15th.[27] Furthermore, Robert E. Lee had not expected to hold the line of the Potomac for any length of time. He knew that the Federal troops would use the bridge at Harpers Ferry as soon as Meade desired. Lee wanted to take up a position in Loudoun County and confront any advance by Meade there. However, the Shenandoah River proved impassable, frustrating Lee's move.[28] Lee needed to buy time and meet any of Meade's thrusts south of the Potomac from Harpers Ferry as close to the river as possible. Those first thrusts came from Meade's cavalry.

John Buford's brigades spent the 15th marching from their bivouacs near Bakersville to Harpers Ferry, Sandy Hook, Knoxville, and then to Berlin, Maryland. The brigades moved their camps to Petersville on the 16th and camped there throughout the next day.[29] Kilpatrick's division not only changed its location but also its commander, temporarily. On the 15th, Kilpatrick handed command over to Custer and went on leave.[30] Having just taken command of the Michigan Brigade on June 28, Custer, as the ranking brigade officer, now took the reins of the division that consisted of his own brigade and that of Col. Edward B. Sawyer. The gamble of promoting the young and inexperienced captain had paid off thus far. Custer had performed well during the limited time he had had with his brigade. Now Kilpatrick's absence provided an opportunity to shine as a division commander.

In his first act as commander, Custer carried out orders to march for Berlin. He led his brigades via Williamsport and Hagerstown, encamping for the night at Boonsborough. Early on the 16th, he roused his men and rode through Rohrersville and Crampton's Gap to Berlin. Here the Second Brigade bivouacked, but before dark the First Brigade trotted off to Harpers Ferry and encamped for the night in the yard of the ruined arsenal.[31] Custer had executed his first orders with alacrity. However, sitting north of the Potomac, his chances of colliding with the enemy appeared remote for the immediate future. In contrast, south of the river the blue cavalry stood to horse, ready for anything Stuart might throw at them.

The 16th dawned quietly. Encamped around Shepherdstown, Gregg's division passed the morning waiting for Huey's brigade to arrive. South of Shepherdstown along the road to Winchester, the Tenth New York, Col. Gregg's brigade, relieved its brother regiment, the Fourth Pennsylvania. The Sixteenth Pennsylvania was no longer on the Winchester road, having withdrawn through Shepherdstown the previous evening and out the Charlestown road where it had stopped and thrown out a picket line.[32] Col. Gregg, concerned for his command's horses, dispatched Col. Charles H. Smith with his First Maine out the Winchester Pike in search of forage. The regiment proceeded unconcernedly, as Smith knew that elements of the Tenth New York guarded the road between two to four miles beyond Shepherdstown.[33] Scarcely had the boys from Maine stretched out their column along the road when a lone courier galloped over a wooded ridge some half to three quarters of a mile to the front and raced toward Smith. Reining in his lathered horse, the rider informed the colonel that the enemy had driven in the Tenth's pickets and had continued to advance rapidly. Smith looked down the pike and quickly grasped the importance of the rising ground ahead.[34] Seizing it became his top priority, and he ordered his men forward at the gallop.

Nearing the height, Smith found the Tenth New York's two squadrons struggling to protect their wounded and their led horses and hold the enemy, which turned out to be Brig. Gen. Fitzhugh "Fitz" Lee's Brigade supported by Col. John R. Chambliss's Brigade. The fight had begun several miles from Shepherdstown near Walper's Crossroads. Col. James H. Drake's First Virginia, Lee's Brigade, initiated the contest by charging the Federal outposts. Backed by the other regiments of the brigade, Drake had little trouble in routing the Tenth, sending it careening back along the Winchester Pike. The gray troopers received two checks that briefly slowed their advance, but nothing the New Yorkers did could stop it. In the retreat, Lt. John T. McKevitt of the Tenth's Company G suffered a severe wound.[35]

Drake succeeded in reaching the ridge before Smith, who disputed possession as soon as the leading elements of his regiment arrived on the summit. At the head of his men, Drake charged the enemy only to receive a mortal wound. Confused by the loss of their commander, the Confederates fell back, leaving the wood and ridge in Federal hands. Except for a mounted company formed in a column of fours in the road below the crest, the First Maine now spread out dismounted skirmishers through the wood along the ridge on both sides of the road and opened a brisk fire. However, the odds favored Fitz Lee who responded in kind by ordering up his sharpshooters and artillery. Galloping forward, Lt. John J. Shoemaker with two guns of Capt. Marcellus N. Moorman's Battery of horse artillery unlimbered and opened fire. Guns from both the First Stuart Horse Artillery under Capt. James Breathed and the Second Stuart Horse Artillery led by Lt. Charles E. Ford soon joined in the fray.[36]

Smith knew trouble when he saw it. His lone regiment and the men from the Tenth New York that rallied to him could scarcely hope to hold out against two brigades and several guns. Feeding in his men slowly until nearly all were engaged, Smith could only watch as the gray cavalry stretched its lines toward his flanks. The First Maine's casualties began to mount. Lt. Col. Stephen Boothby and Lt. George E. Hunton suffered wounds while encouraging their men. Despite gallant resistance, Smith saw his line being forced back. To cover its withdrawal, he turned to his mounted reserve and ordered it forward. Charging through the wood, it scattered Lee's sharpshooters and reached the enemy's artillery before withdrawing. Smith used the time gained to reform his line about 200 yards rear of his previous position, supported by three squadrons of the Fourth Pennsylvania and a section of guns from Capt. Alanson M. Randol's Battery E, First U. S. Artillery commanded by Lt. Ernst L. Kinney that Col. Gregg had dispatched to aid the hard-pressed Mainers. With these reinforcements, minus the men from the Tenth New York that withdrew and joined their regiment on the Martinsburg road, Smith stabilized his line along a stonewall that extended on both sides of the road.

Encouraged by his success, Fitz Lee renewed his attack, his gunners regaining their pieces and pounding the Federals with shot, shell, and canister. The Confederates charged forward, often coming to within 50 yards of the wall, only to be thrown back. Throughout the afternoon, the fighting raged. The Sixteenth Pennsylvania replaced the First Maine, its ammunition all but exhausted, along the wall, but the pressure of Lee's assaults forced Smith to send four of his companies back into the fray. Col. Gregg, who had ridden forward with the reinforcements and assumed command, managed to stabilize his line even though Lee made repeated assaults against the Federal center. Late in the day, a threat in the form of Col. Milton J. Ferguson's Brigade appeared on the Federal right along the Martinsburg road. Fortunately for Gregg, the Confederates swung to the right to link with Fitz Lee's left and while only lightly engaging the Tenth New York, maintained a heavy fire and participated in several charges against Gregg's main line on the Winchester Pike. Late in the afternoon, Gen. Gregg dispatched the First Pennsylvania to bolster Col. Gregg's defense. He then rode forward with the remainder of McIntosh's Brigade and deployed it on the left of Col. Gregg's weary troopers where it played little part in the action of the day. As darkness brought an end to the fighting, Gen. Gregg, his troopers entirely out of ammunition and rations, pulled back to Shepherdstown. At one point during the withdrawal some mules in the supply train stampeded, making a number of the troopers' horses unmanageable, causing some confusion, and forcing a number of men to dismount and retreat on foot. At midnight, Gregg ordered his division to Harpers Ferry. Elements of the Tenth New York were the last to leave the town.[37] Casualties for the mostly dismounted engagement numbered about 100 on each side.[38]

Fitz Lee's, Chambliss's, and Ferguson's brigades did not follow Gregg's weary troopers toward Harpers Ferry, being more than eager to bid them farewell. Withdrawing to their former camps, the Confederates sought the opportunity to take a breath themselves. Fitz Lee pulled back his men to Walper's Crossroads for the night.[39]

While Gregg fought, the remainder of Meade's army replenished its supplies from depots at Berlin and Sandy Hook. Those men who required shoes and clothing could draw them. Orders to cook three days' rations and prepare "to continue the march at the earliest moment practicable" showed everyone that the lull would be brief.[40] Buford's division continued to refit throughout the 16th and Custer's moved from its bivouac near Boonsborough toward Berlin.

The morning of the 17th did not see a renewal of the contest south of the Potomac. Content to leave each other alone for a time, the cavalry of both sides set themselves to other tasks. One that occupied Pleasonton that day centered on reinforcements for his battle-weary divisions. He scratched off an order to Col. Sir Percy Wyndham stationed in Washington. Since his wounding at Brandy Station on June 9, Wyndham had charge of the capital's cavalry forces and the remount depot. Now Pleasonton requested that all those men who belonged with the Army of the Potomac's cavalry be forwarded to their commands immediately. Wyndham scrambled to explain that of the 3,000 men under his command about half had already rejoined the army at Frederick. Another 600 under Col. Charles R. Lowell of the Second Massachusetts guarded the Alexandria Railroad and would join the army when it arrived in that vicinity. The other men were sick, disabled, or unequipped. Wyndham closed his correspondence with the hope that Pleasonton would accept his explanation. That the head of Meade's cavalry had been completely unaware that 1,500 men had rejoined his divisions shows just how much he was in the dark concerning his command.[41]

Informed or not, Pleasonton could issue orders and did so, sending Gregg's division to Sandy Hook to acquire food, ammunition, and forage. Pleasonton cautioned Gregg to "get your command in readiness to move as soon as possible. Keep your pickets and scouts well out in the direction of Charlestown [sic], Leetown, and Shepherdstown."[42] Buford's division remained at Berlin, the men still drawing rations and resting.[43] Custer's division drew the short straw. He led his own

Second Brigade across the Potomac at Berlin. The First Brigade, under Col. Edward B. Sawyer of the First Vermont, left its camp in the arsenal yard at Harpers Ferry and rode down river to the pontoon bridge at Berlin where it linked up with the Second Brigade. Now Custer swung south through Lovettsville and Wheatland to Purcellville where the division encamped for the night. From there, he sent Maj. Crawley P. Dake's Fifth Michigan forward to seize Snickers Gap.[44] Clashing with elements of Brig. Gen. William E. "Grumble" Jones's Brigade, the Fifth managed to secure the gap and capture a few prisoners after a loss of two wounded.[45]

Custer's crossing of the river and his securing of Snicker's Gap set the stage for Meade's next move. Meade's orders for the army's infantry reflected his desire to move quickly to get a jump on Lee. He pushed the Third Corps across the Potomac at Harpers Ferry and then over the Shenandoah to the valley of the Sweet Run where it camped. The Fifth Corps also crossed and camped near Lovettsville. The rest of the army received orders to cross on the 18th.[46] With Lee screened by the Blue Ridge and the Shenandoah River, running at flood stage, Meade took the initiative from the Confederate commander, who would now have to play catch-up to counter Meade's maneuvers.

Meanwhile Fitz Lee's Brigade, along with the Twelfth Virginia, Jones's Brigade, left their camps about 8:00 in the morning and rode for Leetown, arriving about three hours later. The Twelfth returned to its camp four miles from Charles Town on the Berryville road at 2:00 in the afternoon, having made a fruitless roundtrip.[47] The remainder of Stuart's men sat idle in their camps or did picket duty. Once Gregg withdrew from Shepherdstown, the pressure the Federals had been exerting south of the Potomac and west of the Shenandoah lessened significantly. The Confederate cavalry, unable to cross the latter river, could not discover Custer's or the Federal infantry's movement southward. Ignorance proved a temporary boon, allowing the gray troopers to rest and gather strength. The officers and men uttered no complaints when the suspension of hostilities stretched into the following day. Stuart himself welcomed the break. Writing on the 18th from his headquarters at "The Bower" to his beloved wife, Flora, he remarked that it was the first day he had without a brush with the enemy.[48]

Stuart did not take the entire day off, however. He sent a note to his commander that drew a quick response. Lee had heard rumors and wanted some confirmation, expressing concern over a report that the enemy occupied Snicker's Gap and threatened Ashby's Gap. If such moves had occurred, he would have to march the army farther up the Valley. Lee ordered Stuart to discover the composition of the enemy's force.[49]

If Stuart attempted to fulfill Lee's wishes over the following days, no record of it survives. The majority of the Confederate cavalry held firmly to its camps from the 18th to the 22nd. Certainly, the flooded Shenandoah contributed to Stuart's lack of enterprise on this occasion, although the task assigned may have already been performed before Lee's order reached his cavalry chieftain. The portion of the Sixth Virginia that had been left behind at Ashby's Gap when Robertson and Jones rode north during the Gettysburg campaign could have brought the news of the Federal army's movements to Stuart and Lee when it withdrew across the river.[50]

While most of Stuart's cavalry lounged in camp on the 18th, Col. Laurence S. Baker's Brigade, guarding the upper Potomac crossings, faced a rambunctious enemy around Hedgesville. Brig. Gen. William W. Averell's cavalry, under the overall command of Brig. Gen. Benjamin F. Kelly, executed an intrepid crossing of the Potomac on flat boats and clashed with Baker's vedettes late on the 17th, taking 17 prisoners and chasing the remnants to within three miles of Martinsburg. Pulling back, the Federals settled in at North Mountain Station to await developments.[51]

On the 18th, Averell again moved forward, meeting Baker's troopers between Hedgesville and Martinsburg and capturing another 14 men. On the morning of the following day, the blue cavalry advanced on Martinsburg, driving the enemy pickets back. About noon, Baker sent in reinforcements and Averell received orders to withdraw.[52] With portions of Lee's infantry nearby, Baker could only be driven so far. Both Baker and Kelly undoubtedly knew this and the skirmishing meant little, except to those who participated in it.

Farther down the Potomac, Meade continued to march his army across the river. The 18th saw the Third and Fifth corps, which had crossed on the 17th, move south toward Hillsborough. The Second Corps crossed at Harpers Ferry while the First and Eleventh Corps and the Reserve Artillery passed over on the pontoon bridge at Berlin. The Sixth Corps received orders to follow the Eleventh across the river, if time permitted, but otherwise to cross on the morning of the 19th. Only the Twelfth Corps would remain north of the Potomac, but it was to hold itself in readiness to follow the Second Corps.[53]

Pleasonton's cavalry had a full day as well. While the Fifth Michigan held on firmly at Snicker's Gap until after dark, the other regiments of Custer's division spent the day resting at Purcellville, shoeing horses and preparing for the next leap southward. Later in the day, the First West Virginia of Sawyer's brigade relieved the Fifth Michigan from its guard duty in the gap. Custer, ever alert, sent out scouts toward Chester Gap and Front Royal.[54] On the 19th, Custer led his newly shod division through Snickersville and Bloomfield to Upperville, bivouacking there for the night.[55]

Buford's division crossed the river at Berlin between the headquarters' train of the army and the Eleventh Corps. It proceeded toward Purcellville but night caught it spread out along the road. In the lead, Brig. Gen. Wesley Merritt's brigade trotted to near Hillsborough before going into camp.[56] Gamble's brigade bivouacked at 10:00, three miles beyond Lovettsville.[57] Col. Thomas C. Devin's brigade encamped one mile outside Lovettsville, but somewhere along the way managed to lose Private William D. Foote of the Ninth New York who was reported as captured by the enemy.[58] The division marched south on the 19th; passing through Wheatland, Purcellville, Philomont, and Union and drawing rein for the night near Upperville.[59]

Pleasonton had special duties in mind for Gregg's division, which stayed in camp all day. The orders he sent on the 18th directed Gregg to place one of his brigades as rear guard for the army, allowing the Twelfth Corps to pass through Harpers Ferry ahead of it, before riding on to Purcellville. Once there the brigade commander was to report to Pleasonton's headquarters.[60] Gregg selected Col. John B. McIntosh's brigade for this duty. McIntosh reported that he followed the Twelfth Corps to Purcellville, arriving there on the 20th. After reporting to Pleasonton, the brigade marched for Hillsborough where it bivouacked until July 22nd, performing the very important duty of protecting the army's vast supply trains, and then picketed the river road toward the Shenandoah.[61]

Pleasonton took Col. Pennock Huey's and Col. J. Irvin Gregg's brigades of Gen. Gregg's division out of the army's advance as well. The brigades moved through Knoxville to Berlin to cross the river. They could not do this until the evening of the 19th, riding on to Lovettsville.[62] After that, Pleasonton sent the brigades through Leesburg to Manassas Junction, and assigned them to guard duty along the Orange & Alexandria Railroad.[63]

Meade's columns slogged on toward the Rappahannock on the 19th and 20th. Names familiar to the officers and men of the Army of the Potomac became targets for the days' marches - Snickersville, Upperville, Ashby's Gap, Bloomfield, Union, Rectortown, Aldie, Middleburg, Philomont, and Goose Creek. By the 20th, Meade expected his headquarters to be established near Union.[64] The blue tide surged forward with nary a Confederate in sight to oppose it.

Though hidden behind a river and a mountain chain, Meade's maneuvering did not go unnoticed. Robert E. Lee had expected his adversary to use the bridges at Harpers Ferry and other crossings farther down the Potomac in an attempt to gain an advantage over the Confederate army still encamped in the Valley. He was not surprised when Meade did just that. By the 18th, Lee determined to move elements of his army to counter Meade. Longstreet received orders on the 19th at Bunker Hill to proceed to Millwood with the goal being the possession of Ashby's Gap. Lee informed Stuart that if the situation permitted Lee wanted the cavalry across the Blue Ridge, fronting Washington, and interposed between Longstreet and the enemy.[65]

Leaving his camps on the morning of the 20th, Longstreet arrived at Millwood later in the day to find the Shenandoah impassable and the enemy in possession of the far bank, an indication of their occupation of Ashby's Gap. The following day Longstreet trekked south toward Front Royal, hoping to cross the river there and seize Manassas Gap and Chester Gap before the Federals.[66] A. P. Hill's Corps did not move until the 21st when it followed in Longstreet's wake, leaving Lt. Gen. Richard S. Ewell's Corps in the Valley to continue to destroy the Baltimore and Ohio Railroad and deal with Kelly's force, trying to defend it.[67]

Unable to comply with Lee's orders to cross the Shenandoah with a major portion of his command, Stuart dispatched Robertson's Brigade to cover Longstreet's advance. By the evening of the 20th, Lee, acknowledging Stuart's inability to carry out his previous orders, had another mission for his cavalry chief.

A rumored force of the enemy threatened part of Ewell's command. Lee ordered Stuart to be alert for an attack emanating from Harpers Ferry and to go himself the following morning to cooperate with Ewell should the rumor prove true. It didn't. That allowed the remainder of the Southern horse to enjoy the quiet of camp life a little longer.[68]

The respite ended abruptly on the 21st with orders to cook three days rations.[69] Once again, rumors ran rampant. Capt. Richard H. Watkins took time to write his wife, Mary, that his regiment, the Third Virginia, had orders to cook rations and prepare to move out on the 22nd. He reported, "Rumor says that we go towards Richmond, that the enemy is advancing on the south side of the James River. Others have it that we return to Pennsylvania." Watkins added, "I do not trouble myself with either. When the order comes to march, I expect to be ready to go will try to do my duty . . .."[70] Indeed, that was all Stuart could ask from any of his men.

Stuart left Baker's Brigade in the Valley to bring up the rear of Ewell's column when it moved to join the army. Jones's Brigade stayed in place to guard the lower Shenandoah and then follow the army across the river. The Twelfth Virginia picketed Key's Ferry on the 22nd and pulled back to Rippon the next day. Its outpost line stretched from that place to the Martinsburg road. Portions of the Twelfth did not leave until the morning of the 24th, rejoining the regiment near Strasburg that evening.[71]

Fitz Lee's, Chambliss's, and Ferguson's brigades rode away from their camps near Leetown early on the morning of the 22nd and forced marched through Millwood in an effort to reach Manassas Gap and hold it, in order to protect the army's flank. Thwarted in this effort by both the swollen Shenandoah and the fact that the Federals already possessed the gap, the brigades trotted south, camping near Front Royal.[72]

For several days, the Federal cavalry north of the Potomac had kept a wary eye on Stuart's cavalry in and around Shepherdstown, seeking to divine its intentions. On the 19th, Col. Andrew T. McReynolds of the First New York, stationed at Sharpsburg, Maryland, had reported Stuart's activity and suggested the possibility of another raid.[73] A copy of the report forwarded to Meade elicited no response but may have contributed to Meade's decision on the 20th to halt his army's progress south "until the information received from the cavalry renders it certain what the movements of the enemy are."[74] Any information Meade expected to learn from his cavalry while it stayed east of the Shenandoah would be of little benefit, but to send it over the river ran the risk of possible destruction. Yet, Meade chose to do just that. However, he also had another stratagem.

If the reconnaissance over the Shenandoah achieved little or nothing, the gaps in the Blue Ridge became crucial because from them the enemy's movements beyond the river could be observed. To seize these vital points Meade also turned to his cavalry. Part of Custer's division already held Snicker's Gap, but Ashby's Gap, Manassas Gap, and Chester Gap must be occupied before the Confederates pushed over the river. If Lee managed to cross the Shenandoah opposite the gaps, he could not advance any farther if Meade's forces held them. The Federal infantry could continue its march south virtually unopposed while Lee struggled to gain a foothold east of the Shenandoah.

As the rest of Gregg's division marched toward Manassas Junction from the 20th to the 24th, McIntosh's brigade dutifully rode into Purcellville on the 20th and reported to Pleasonton. A difficult assignment awaited it. The brigade turned around and trotted for Harpers Ferry where it drew supplies before crossing the Shenandoah and scouting toward Charles Town. Unsupported, McIntosh knew that a collision with Stuart's cavalry in any strength could be fatal. However, Stuart had departed. The absence of Confederates provided the kind of valuable information Meade required, but while the success of McIntosh's foray told Meade where the Confederates were not, he still did not have knowledge of where they were. The gaps held the answers to his questions about Lee's forces.[75]

On the 20th, Custer's division rode from Upperville for Ashby's Gap. Custer threw forward the Fifth Michigan under Maj. Crawley P. Dake backed by Lt. Alexander C. M. Pennington's Battery M, Second U. S. Artillery. Dake dismounted most of his men and advanced on foot. Lt. Col. Elijah V. White's Thirty-fifth Virginia Battalion and portions of Robertson's Brigade, then in possession of the gap, offered what resistance they could, which proved to be very little. A mounted company or two from the Fifth charged up the road, scattering the remnants of the opposition, and the bluecoats soon were greeted with an unobstructed view of the Shenandoah River and beyond. Custer then sent Col. Charles H. Town with his own First Michigan and the Sixth Michigan to secure the gap. Sawyer's brigade accompanied Custer's brigade but served mostly as observer before returning to Upperville for the night.[76] The division held the gap until the evening of the 23rd.[77]

John Buford's brigades left their camps on the morning of the 20th and trotted into Rectortown.[78] From there, Buford dispatched Merritt to take and hold Manassas Gap and Gamble to do the same at Chester Gap. The former reached Linden Station on the Manassas Gap Railroad that night. The latter encamped at "Oak Hill" near Piedmont Station, a squadron of the Twelfth Illinois going on picket. Devin rode on to Salem with the division's wagon train.[79] At 5:00 in the afternoon Buford sent a report to Pleasonton detailing his progress and posing the question, "Where shall I go next?" Pleasonton had no ready answer to that question. A circular sent out by Meade confirmed that the Federal commander still lacked the information he required to put his army in motion. For the moment, Buford and everyone else would sit and wait until the cavalry or some other source gave Meade what he needed.[80]

The 21st dawned with both Lee and Meade once more groping for each other as they had in the Gettysburg campaign. Eager to gain a foothold over the Shenandoah, Lee waited to hear from Longstreet. Early in the morning Lee's "Old War Horse" marched his troops from their camps around Millwood to Front Royal. He hoped to cross the river there and seize Manassas Gap or Chester Gap or both.

Meade already possessed Snicker's and Ashby's, but his army stood stagnant because he could not be sure where Lee was. All that changed when reports began to arrive at Meade's headquarters.

Capt. Lemuel B. Norton, Chief Signal Officer, reported from Snicker's Gap at 9:00 in the morning that a large body of infantry had been passing through Millwood for two hours and that a general's headquarters had been seen at Millwood. The message reached Meade an hour and a half after it was sent, giving the Federal commander the first evidence of what Lee's intentions might be. The seizure of Manassas Gap and Chester Gap now became paramount, and Meade must have felt somewhat reassured when he received news from Buford that Merritt would be entering Manassas Gap and Gamble would occupy Chester Gap before the end of the day. The question became, would that be soon enough?[81]

Merritt moved forward into Manassas Gap and took two Confederate officers prisoner. They stated that Lee had not crossed the Shenandoah but remained near Bunker Hill and Winchester. Frustrated that he could learn no more, Merritt rode out of the gap toward the river. More prisoners fell into his hands. Ominously, these were from the Seventeenth Virginia Infantry of Brig. Gen. Montgomery D. Corse's brigade that Longstreet had hurried forward to take both gaps. Upon crossing the river at Front Royal, Corse sent Col. Arthur Herbert's Seventeenth Virginia to Manassas Gap. With the rest of his brigade, Corse and several batteries marched for Chester Gap. Merritt reported that, according to his prisoners, he faced a full division at least 10,000 strong with a large wagon train on the other side of the river. Expressing confidence that he may not have felt, Merritt wrote that he could hold his position "against all odds."[82]

Meanwhile, Gamble departed his camps at "Oak Hill" about 7:00 in the morning and headed toward Chester Gap. Around 3:30 in the afternoon when he reached a position about a mile short of the gap, his skirmishers ran into Confederate outposts. Without hesitating, Gamble threw six squadrons, led by one from the Eighth New York, and Lt. Edward Heaton's Battery B/L, Second U. S. Artillery at the enemy and drove them to the crest of the gap. There he collided with cavalry, infantry, and artillery and soon realized that his mission could not be accomplished against such odds, especially when it was discovered that Heaton's ammunition was faulty. Only one in 12 rounds would explode. After pulling back about a mile and a half, Gamble settled for guarding the crossroads where the road from the gap divided, one fork leading to Barbee's Cross Roads and the other to Little Washington.[83]

Merritt met with his own setback. At 9:00 that evening he reported clashing with the Confederates at the west end of Manassas Gap. The First U. S. Cavalry's scout toward Front Royal failed to even make it out of the gap much less to Front Royal and the river. A follow-up reconnaissance in force by the First, Second, and Fifth U. S. Cavalry stalled at the west end of the gap as well. Merritt admitted he could learn nothing further and became convinced that he faced more than one regiment. He decided not to withdraw but to hold what he could of the gap and await developments.[84]

Dawn of the 22nd brought fresh orders to Meade's idle infantry corps. The Third and Fifth corps marched to reinforce Merritt at Manassas Gap while the First Corps moved to White Plains to support the Third and Fifth. The Second Corps trekked to Paris to assist in holding Ashby's Gap, while the Twelfth Corps camped at Snickersville to aid the cavalry holding Snicker's Gap. The Sixth Corps and Reserve Artillery marched to Rectortown on the Aldie Pike. The Eleventh Corps stayed put but made preparations to move at a moment's notice. Buford was to hold Manassas Gap as long as possible and keep an eye on Chester Gap as well.[85]

All of Meade's maneuvering came to naught. By the night of the 21st, Longstreet had pushed enough troops over the Shenandoah to secure both Manassas Gap and Chester Gap. Pickett's Division, Hood's Division, now under Brig. Gen. Evander M. Law, and McLaws's Division crossed the river, strengthened the Confederate hold on the gaps, and with Robertson's Brigade of cavalry in the lead began to march toward Culpeper Court House.[86] On the 22nd, Longstreet even felt bold enough to launch an offensive in an attempt to capture some of Gamble's cavalry and artillery at the eastern terminus of Chester Gap. Gamble could do nothing to stop the Confederate juggernaut that poured out of the gap.[87] Meade had taken steps to reinforce the cavalry holding three gaps but had not sent infantry to Chester Gap. That omission was his plan's undoing.

Reports of the breakthrough arrived at Buford's headquarters by mid-afternoon on the 22nd. Gamble told of a seven hour-long effort to contain the Confederates that began about 10:00 in the morning and did not end until after 5:00 in the afternoon when five regiments of enemy infantry forced his withdrawal. He admitted to not only losing the gap but the road to Sperryville and Culpeper as well. With a final word of warning that Confederate troops in great numbers were pushing rapidly toward Culpeper, Gamble closed with the hope that "our army will act accordingly." The Eighth New York drew guard duty once again as the exhausted brigade bedded down for the night.[88] Buford dutifully passed word of Longstreet's success up the chain of command to Pleasonton and told his commander that he intended to withdraw Merritt from Manassas Gap to Orleans. However, over three hours later Merritt had yet to receive the order. In his 6:00 dispatch, he indicated that he still held the eastern end of the gap thanks to his artillery, which kept the enemy in check, and gave no intention that he would fall back.[89] Whether Buford ever sent the orders to withdraw or Merritt felt duty bound to hold until relieved is not known, but Merritt's persistence resulted in Meade's and Lee's infantry clashing the following day.

By the night of the 22nd, Robert E. Lee must have been satisfied that he had retaken some if not all of the initiative from Meade. With Longstreet trudging toward Culpeper, Hill in the process of crossing the Shenandoah, and Ewell about to leave Winchester to rejoin the army, Lee only needed to use the speed of his men to reach the familiar lines along the Rappahannock and Rapidan rivers ahead of the Federal army. Once there he could really rest his men and either plan to strike at

Meade again or await his adversary's next move.

For Meade the day must have brought the realization that Lee had managed to escape him once more. To counter the breakthrough at Chester Gap the Federal commander issued new marching orders for the following day – the First Corps to Warrenton, the Second to Markham's Station on the Manassas Railroad, the Third through Manassas Gap to attack the enemy moving through Front Royal and Chester Gap, the Fifth to support the Third, the Sixth to Rectortown with a division at White Plains, the Eleventh to New Baltimore, and the Twelfth to Paris. The cavalry received no orders in this communication.[90] With these maneuvers, Meade intended to intercept a portion of Lee's army and perhaps cripple it.[91] The shifting of the corps to Warrenton and New Baltimore put Meade in position to move south should the attack at Manassas Gap fail.

Brig. Gen. John H. H. Ward's brigade of the First Division of the Third Corps joined Merritt's cavalry at Manassas Gap between 4:00 and 5:00 on the morning of the 23rd. A few hours later, the entire First Division arrived and began to form in support of Ward. The rest of the corps stood at hand should one division not be enough. Initially, the Confederates had only Brig. Gen. Ambrose R. Wright's Brigade, under the command of Col. Edward J. Walker, to oppose this vast host. The action commenced about 2:00 in the afternoon. Ward quickly drove back Walker, secured Wapping Heights, and threatened to push on to Front Royal. Then reinforcements in the form of Lt. Gen. Richard S. Ewell with Maj. Gen. Robert E. Rodes's Division arrived and brought the Federals to a halt. However, Ewell, recognizing that Meade intended to contest further crossing of the Shenandoah at Front Royal, withdrew up the Page Valley to Luray, leaving Meade in possession of the gap the following morning. [92]

The majority of the Federal cavalry spent the 22nd out of touch with its adversaries. The boredom of gap guarding with no enemy in sight ended for Custer's command early in the day with orders to proceed to Amissville. Leaving Ashby's Gap sometime in the afternoon, with five regiments and two batteries of artillery, Custer marched only about five miles, reaching Piedmont Station on the Manassas Gap Railroad where he camped for the night. He met no enemy on the way other than a dozen soldiers trying to drive off a herd of cattle and sheep near Upperville. He captured the animals but not the would-be herdsmen.[93] The next day he moved on to Amissville, arriving about 5:00 in the afternoon. Near this place, he captured two drunken stragglers from Fitz Lee's Brigade. In their inebriated state, the two men gave little information that Custer accepted as worthwhile. However, one of the men mentioned that his company had picketed Gaines' Cross Roads three days earlier. As a precautionary measure, Custer sent the First West Virginia toward the crossroads.[94]

Maj. Charles E. Capehart led his regiment out along the road. He and his men had been riding most of the day and the weary troopers could not have welcomed the added duty. The possibility of a late day skirmish probably added to their discomfort. Almost immediately after leaving Amissville, Capehart ran into infantry pickets and drove them to within a half mile of the crossroads where resistance stiffened. A charge failed to dislodge the Confederates. Pulling back, Capehart established his outposts three quarters of a mile from his destination, having suffered two casualties.[95] Custer sent off a report to Pleasonton at 8:30 that evening, stating that he intended to "annoy the enemy tomorrow morning as much as it is in my power to do."[96]

Meanwhile, Buford's division concentrated at Barbee's Cross Roads for what turned out to be a two-day break from the hostilities. In Gamble's brigade, the Twelfth Illinois saddled up for a scout on the morning of the 23rd, returning after two hours. They repeated the exercise the next day to confirm the position of Confederate pickets and then returned to camp.[97] Devin's brigade arrived on the 23rd.[98] Only Merritt's brigade managed to inflict any damage on the enemy. Relieved by Ward's infantry at Manassas Gap early in the morning, Merritt led his men along the Blue Ridge toward Markham with orders to observe the area near Chester Gap where the First U. S. Cavalry captured about 50 Confederates after a brief skirmish. Merritt then rode on to join Buford.[99]

Most of Gregg's division continued to guard various points along the railroad west and south of Manassas Junction. Huey's brigade picketed all the way to Thoroughfare Gap and New Baltimore. A portion of Col. Gregg's brigade trotted along the railroad toward Warrenton Junction while their brethren lounged in camp. At 3:00 in the morning, McIntosh rode for Snickersville and Ashby's Gap to relieve two of Custer's regiments still on guard at those points.[100]

During these days, the Confederate cavalry also spent time in the saddle. Stuart with Fitz Lee's, Chambliss's, and Ferguson's brigades had forded the Shenandoah below Front Royal at "Island Ford" on the 22nd and by the next day had reached Chester Gap, although the troopers had to use a by-path over very rough terrain to achieve their goal. The forced march continued until the three brigades encamped near Gaines' Cross Roads on the night of the 23rd, holding the Rock's Ford road and the Warrenton Turnpike.[101]

The two brigades in the Valley set themselves in motion as well. Jones's Brigade pulled back from the Shenandoah and encamped near White Post on the night of the 22nd, having concluded its mission of guarding the lower Shenandoah against possible Federal crossings. It remained there throughout the next day, cooking rations, resupplying from its wagons, and preparing to follow Longstreet's and Hill's columns across the river at Front Royal.[102]

Ewell made a final attempt at capturing Kelly's force, still stubbornly protecting the Baltimore and Ohio Railroad between Martinsburg and Hedgesville. He failed, though Kelly was forced to retreat. Ewell then turned south and marched up the Valley toward Winchester. On the 23rd, Baker's Brigade, which had performed its role well, withdrew from Martinsburg, still acting as Ewell's rear guard, and began the long journey to rejoin Stuart.[103] That rendezvous would not come soon. As Ewell and Baker marched, part of the Federal cavalry stirred itself.

At dawn on the 24th, true to his word, Custer set out from Amissville for

Newby's Cross Roads with five regiments and two batteries to annoy whatever enemy he might encounter. A mile and a half from the crossroads, the leading elements of the Fifth Michigan captured two men who claimed that Longstreet's Corps occupied the crossroads. Alerted to the danger ahead, Custer quickly realized that his single regiment near Gaines' Cross Roads might need assistance. After dispatching two regiments and a battery to aid the First West Virginia, Custer pushed ahead with the First, Fifth, and Sixth Michigan and Pennington's Battery M, Second U. S. Artillery. When within a mile of Newby's, the advance guard encountered enemy infantry pickets, dismounted, and deployed as skirmishers. Companies E, H, K, and L of the Fifth Michigan, along with three or four companies of the Sixth, slowly drove forward until they reached the main enemy line that stretched out along a ridge. Reaching the top of the ridge, the Michiganders took advantage of available cover and opened up a steady fire on the enemy. Companies D and I of the Fifth deployed on the right to prevent being outflanked.[104] Lt. Robert Clark with one section of the artillery deployed on a crest to the left of the road, supported by the First Michigan, and opened fire.[105]

Custer's early morning assault did not come as a complete surprise to the Confederates moving south through the crossroads toward Culpeper Court House. Two cavalrymen on their way to have their horses shod at Amissville found the road full of Federals and galloped back to the crossroads where they informed Brig. Gen. Henry L. Benning, commanding a brigade in Brig. Gen. Evander M. Law's Division of Longstreet's Corps, of the danger that lay about a mile to the east. Standing near Benning when the two troopers delivered their startling news, Col. William C. Oates of the Fifteenth Alabama Infantry of Col. James L. Sheffield's Brigade, also of Law's Division, overheard the report and volunteered to make a reconnaissance.[106]

Oates pushed forward and almost immediately became engaged. Back at the crossroads, Benning, hearing nothing but the sharp exchange of skirmisher fire, concluded that no serious threat existed and after receiving word from A. P. Hill that he would relieve Oates, moved on. Scarcely a half-mile down the road, shells arcing over his men alerted Benning that Oates faced more than just skirmishers, but despite this, he continued his march until he reached the ford of the Hazel River. Here another message from Hill arrived, ordering Benning to wait for Hill's artillery. On the heels of this message, a lieutenant galloped up with a third, directing Benning to follow the officer and strike the rear of the enemy. Taking his brigade of Georgians and the Fourth Alabama Infantry of Sheffield's Brigade, Benning marched off.[107]

Even before Benning arrived, Custer recognized that he had bitten off a bit more than he could chew and decided to withdraw, as the Confederates his men already faced began to move around the Fifth Michigan's left flank. He pulled back behind his rear guard, consisting of two troops of the Sixth Michigan under Col. George Gray, two troops of the Fifth Michigan commanded by Capt. Smith H. Hastings, and a section of Battery M led by Lt. Carle A. Woodruff, and retreated

32

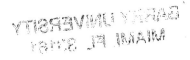

slowly toward Amissville. The rear guard soon found itself in danger when Benning's men erupted from a concealed position and drove Gray's troops, who led the retreat, back on Hastings and Woodruff, effectively cutting the rear guard off from Custer.[108] Gray's momentary rout startled and turned the team of Woodruff's leading gun, almost upsetting the piece. Gray ordered Woodruff to cut the traces and abandon the piece. Determined not to lose his charges, the scrappy lieutenant unlimbered instead and opened fire with canister.

While Gray attempted to rally his men, Capt. Hastings rode up to Woodruff and repeated Gray's command. Again, Woodruff refused to leave his guns behind at which point Hastings offered his services. Dismounting his men, he ordered some to fight in support of the lone artillery piece while others assisted the artillerymen, along with ten battery horses, to move the second gun across a stretch of marshy ground to the left of the road where it opened fire. Then Woodruff returned with the horses for the first piece and alternately shifted his guns one piece at a time to the left, keeping up a continuous fire, until he outflanked the enemy infantry. After about two hours of fighting and heavy labor, Woodruff and Hastings reunited with a greatly relieved Custer, all of whose efforts to succor his rear guard had failed. Gray came trotting in later in the day, having taken another route to safety.[109]

The Confederates were frustrated over the lost opportunity. His guide and local citizens had assured Benning that the Federals could not reach Amissville by any other route than the one he guarded. Confident that his trap would prove successful, he did all he could to bring it off successfully. The initial assault routed Gray's leading elements and almost carried the day, but the determined resistance of Woodruff and Hastings and perhaps a feeling of overconfidence that the enemy had nowhere else to go may have led Benning to conserve his men in the hope of reducing casualties. In the end, he left the battlefield with a handful of prisoners and marched back to the ford.[110]

During the time Custer clashed with the enemy at Newby's Cross Roads, the other divisions of the Federal cavalry maintained the status quo of the previous day. The infantry would not be so lucky. Now well aware that Lee had slipped past him and would soon occupy the old lines along the Rappahannock and Rapidan rivers, Meade prepared marching orders. He targeted Warrenton and Warrenton Junction as the goals for the various corps and planned to have his headquarters at the former on the 25th. Like Benning, whose report revealed his disappointment on the Federals' escape from his trap, Meade's own frustration over opportunities lost came through in his use of the words "the following movements . . . will take place immediately" in the circular. All the corps commanders were ordered to ". . . move their troops and trains to the points designated with the utmost dispatch, making forced marches . . ." and "each corps commander will bivouac his corps for the night at such point as he may select as best adapted to carry out these instructions."[111] Had such a sense of urgency permeated all of Meade's orders since crossing the Potomac, Lee may not have been able to reach Culpeper Court House so easily if at all.

The Confederates also experienced a day in motion as the race to the Rappahannock continued. At 3:00 in the morning, after a satisfyingly nutritious breakfast of blackberries, Pvt. Lawson Morrissett of the Fourth Virginia mounted his horse and along with his fellow troopers rode away from their camp five miles north of Gaines' Cross Roads. Their companions in the Third Virginia saddled up at 6:00 and followed. The other regiments of Fitz Lee's, Chambliss's, and Ferguson's brigades fell in line. Stuart accompanied the column, which halted for several hours about a half-mile from the crossroads while the leading regiment, the Second Virginia, skirmished lightly with the enemy. Nothing came of the action and although Stuart heard the artillery firing from the direction of Newby's Cross Roads, he arrived there too late to be of any assistance to Benning's infantry. The troopers moved on, camping near Rixeyville for the night.[112]

Robertson's Brigade completed its mission in advance of Longstreet's Corps and established a picket line along the south bank of Rappahannock at Kelly's Ford.[113] Baker's Brigade marched with Early's Division of Ewell's Corps up the Valley and by the evening of the 24th camped five miles south of Strasburg.[114] By the time Jones's Brigade reached Front Royal, it found Chester Gap blocked by the enemy and turned back, riding behind Early's Division up the Valley and encamping at Strasburg with Early.[115]

After shrugging off Custer's feeble attack, Longstreet's and Hill's infantry pushed on toward Culpeper Court House without further annoyance. Lee now had two corps south of the Rappahannock with Ewell marching unimpeded to join him. Without fighting a major engagement, Lee had crossed the Shenandoah and placed his army in position to occupy the same lines it held before the northern invasion. His report showed no sign of the relief he must have felt.

Notes:

1.   James Longstreet, *From Manassas to Appomattox*, (Philadelphia: J. B. Lippincott, 1896.

2.   Reprint, Secaucus, New Jersey: The Blue and Gray Press, 1984), 429-430.

3.   John Esten Cooke, *Robert E. Lee*, (New York: G. W. Dillingham Co., Publishers, 1899), 334. John Carroll Donahue Diary, Sixth Virginia Cavalry, Accession #28589, Reel 519, Library of Virginia (hereafter cited as LV).

        McDonald states that the crossing took place on the 13th. William N. McDonald, *History of the Laurel Brigade* (No city: Published by Mrs. Kate S. McDonald, 1907. Reprint, Arlington, Virginia: R. W. Beaty, Ltd., 1969), 164.

        The Twelfth Virginia had not accompanied Jones's Brigade north, instead doing picket duty near Harpers Ferry. McDonald, *History of the Laurel Brigade*, 164-165; Edward G. Longacre, *The Cavalry at Gettysburg*, (Rutherford: Fairleigh Dickinson University Press, 1986), 267.

4.   Diary of Thomas William Brown Edwards, Edwards Family Papers 1863-1900, Accession #28733, LV.

5.   Donahue Diary.

        According to one source, the Fifth North Carolina, Robertson's Brigade, with only 147 men mounted and fit for duty, arrived at Millwood opposite Ashby's Gap on the 17th and found everything quiet. The regiment still occupied this position when Stuart ordered Robertson to cover Longstreet's march on the 19th. The Fourth North Carolina, which probably accompanied the Fifth, numbered only 78 officers and men. *North Carolina Presbyterian*, August 8, 1863.

        Lt. Col. William R. Carter of the Third Virginia recorded that his regiment encamped at Newcommer's Mill on Opequon Creek, which was on the road to Leetown from Martinsburg. Since Stuart reported that all his brigades, save Baker's and Jones's, moved back to Leetown, it follows that all camped for the night somewhere on the road from Martinsburg to Leetown. *The War of the Rebellion: The Official Records of the Union and Confederate Armies* (Harrisburg, PA: National Historical Society, 1971), series 1, vol. 27, 705 (hereafter cited as *O.R.*); Diary of William Richard Carter, Accession #39390, Reel 2644, LV.

6.   W.W. Blackford, *War Years With Jeb Stuart* (New York: Charles Scribner's Sons, 1945), 235.

        The Dandridge family had played host to Stuart and his staff in October 1862 before and after Stuart's Chambersburg Raid.

7.   *O.R.*, series 1, vol. 27, part 1, 92.

8.   *Ibid.*, 93.

9.   According to one source, the fighting at Williamsport amounted to nothing more than Company A, First Ohio, under Capt. Noah Jones, then acting as Kilpatrick's headquarters guard, which had been rushed ahead of the division, watching the last of Stuart's regiments cross the river. A few of the Confederates dismounted and opened a fire that lasted until the Federal artillery arrived and dispersed them. Samuel L. Gillespie, *A History of Company A, First Ohio Cavalry, 1861-1865* (Washington C.H. Ohio: publisher unknown, 1898), 166; Historical Data Systems' American Civil War Research Database at, <www.civilwardata.com> August 22, 2009, (hereafter cited as HDSACWRD).

        A second source stated that the Fifth Michigan charged through Williamsport without encountering any opposition, reached the river, drew fire from Confederate artillery on the other side, which was replied to by an accompanying battery, and returned through the town, riding downriver. John R. Morey Diary, John R. Morey Papers, Microfilm mf363 c, Bentley Historical Library, University of Michigan (hereafter cited as BHL/UM).

10. *O.R.*, series 1, vol. 27, part 1, 937, 990; Gillespie, *Company A, First Ohio Cavalry*, 169; Jasper B. Cheney Diary, Civil War Times Illustrated Collection (hereafter cited as CWTIC), U. S. Army Military History Institute, Carlisle Barracks, PA (hereafter cited as USAMHI); Abner B. Frank Diary, Civil War Miscellaneous Collection (hereafter cited as CWMC), USAMHI; John Inglis Diary, 1863, John Inglis Papers, 1862-1911, SC22716 Box 1 Folder 1, New York State Library (hereafter cited as NSL); John B. Kay to Dear Parents, July 16, 1863, John B. Kay Papers, Microfilm mf468 c, BHL/UM; Victor E. Comte to Dear Elise, July 16, 1863, Victor E. Comte Papers, Microfilm mf365 c, BHL/UM; *Detroit Free Press*, July 21, 1863.

Kilpatrick actually claimed to have captured over 1,500 prisoners and two cannon. His report, reprinted in the Northern press, eventually found its way into the Richmond papers and came under the scrutiny of Robert E. Lee, who disputed it. He argued that no organized body of men fell into enemy hands, only stragglers. As to the two guns, they had been abandoned due to a lack of horses. He stated bluntly, "No arms, cannon, or prisoners were taken by the enemy in battle … The number of stragglers thus lost I am unable to state with accuracy, but it is greatly exaggerated in the dispatch…" *O.R.*, series 1, vol. 27, part 1, 990-991.

11. *O.R.*, series 1, vol. 27, part 1, 929.

12. John R. Morey to Dear Parents, July 16, 1863, John R. Morey Papers, Microfilm mf363 c, BHL/UM.

13. *O.R.*, series 1, vol. 27, part 1, 971; Thomas Covert to My Dear Wife, July 27, 1863, Covert Collection, USAMHI.

14. *O.R.*, series 1, vol. 27, part 2, 204-205 and part 3, 679 and 813.

A portion of the First Connecticut Cavalry, Companies A, B, and E commanded by Maj. Farnsworth, was attached to the Middle Department, consisting of the Eight Corps under Maj. Gen. Robert C. Schenck and was stationed at this time at Harpers Ferry.

15. *O.R.*, series 1, vol. 27, part 2, 205; George Baylor, *Bull Run to Bull Ru or Four Years in the Army of Northern Virginia*, (Richmond: B.F. Johnson Publishing Company, 1900. Reprint, Washington , D.C.: Zenger Publishing Co., Inc. 1983), 151; .

Two accounts credit the First New Jersey with Harman's capture. One claimed that the Federals did not know that Harman had been cut off from his regiment. Only after his nephew, Lt. Lewis Harman, the adjutant of the Twelfth Virginia, appeared under a flag of truce, inquiring after his uncle did the Federals begin a search and find the colonel hiding in the tall grass. A third version confirms that Harman was found later and made a prisoner, inferring that the Connecticut cavalry did not actually capture the colonel. William P. Lloyd, *History of the First Regiment Pennsylvania Reserve Cavalry*, (Philadelphia: King & Baird, Printers, 1864), 64; Henry R. Pyne, *The History of the First New Jersey Cavalry*, (Trenton: J. A. Beecher, Publisher, 1871), 167;

16. *New Haven Daily Palladium*, July 28, 1863.

As usual, both sides disagreed on both the number of men engaged and the number of casualties. Capt. Blakeslee admitted to the loss of Maj. Farnsworth and 24 men out of the 50 he had. He stated that his men faced 200 of the enemy. Lt. George Baylor of the Twelfth recorded that the number of captured Federals totaled 32 men, including Farnsworth and a lieutenant, along with 31 horses. There were also a number of killed and wounded. He recalled that the Federals had the 200 men while his side had the 50. *O.R.*, series 1, vol. 27, part 2, 205; Baylor, *Bull Run to Bull Run*, 151.

A Connecticut newspaper gives the loss as 24 but then lists 25 names as prisoners, none of them being a lieutenant. *New Haven Daily Palladium*, July 28, 1863.

17.   *O.R.*, series 1, vol. 27, part 1, 917; William Brooke Rawle, *History of the Third Pennsylvania Cavalry*, (Philadelphia: Franklin Printing Company, 1905), 259, 286; Harold Hand, Jr., *One Good Regiment: The Thirteenth Pennsylvania Cavalry 1861-1865*, (No city: Trafford Publishing, 2000), 71; Isaac H. Ressler Diary, CWTIC, USAMHI; Jonah Yoder Diary, Ronald D. Boyer Collection, USAMHI.

18.   *O.R.*, series 1, vol. 27, part 1, 959.

19.   *Ibid.*, vol. 27, part 3, 691.

20.   Yoder Diary; Rawle, *Third Pennsylvania Cavalry*, 259 and 286.

21.   The brigade had fallen back from the river to Boonsborough and camped there the night of the 15th. Apparently, Pleasonton's order of the 14th had yet to reach Huey who only began to march on the 16th, did not cross the river until 1:00 in the afternoon, and then rested for two hours before starting to meet Gregg at Shepherdstown. *O.R.*, series 1, vol. 27, part 3, 691; Thomas Covert to My Dear Wife, July 27, 1863, Covert Collection USAMHI.

22.   The Sixth Virginia had ridden to Charles Town after dark on the 14th, encamping at about midnight. Donahue Diary.

23.   George M. Neese, *Three Years in the Confederate Horse Artillery* (New York: The Neale Publishing Co., 1911. Reprint, Dayton, Ohio: Press of Morningside Bookshop, 1983), 199-200; Edward P. Tobie, *History of the First Maine Cavalry 1861 - 1865* (Boston: Press of Emery & Hughes, 1887), 181; Donahue Diary; *O.R.*, series 1, vol. 27, part 1, 980.

   Col. Charles H. Smith of the First Maine stated in his report that he encountered a superior force, drove it over a mile, and fought it for two hours. This does not appear to have been the case as all other sources indicate that the skirmish lacked the intensity Smith gave it.

   A Confederate source recorded that Jones called up his entire brigade when the Federals reached within a mile of Halltown. William H. Arehart, "Diary of W. H. Arehart," *The Rockingham Recorder* 1 (December, 1947): 3, 213.

24.   *O.R.*, series 1, vol. 27, part 1, 978; Thomas West Smith, *The Story of a Cavalry Regiment: "Scott's 900," Eleventh New York Cavalry* (Chicago: W. B. Conkey Company, 1897), 109-110; Tobie, *First Maine Cavalry*, 181.

25.   Ressler Diary; Yoder Diary; George D. Bayard, Owen Jones, John P. Taylor, *History of the First Regiment Pennsylvania Reserve Cavalry* (Philadelphia: King & Baird, Printers, 1864), 65; *O.R.*, series 1, vol. 27, part 1, 978.

26.   *O.R.*, series 1, vol. 27, part 1, 984.

27.   Thomas William Trussell Diary, First Virginia Cavalry, Eleanor S. Brockenbrough Library, Museum of the Confederacy (hereafter cited as MOC); Jasper Hawse Diary, The Handley Library, Winchester, Virginia (hereafter cited as HL); Carter Diary; Diary of Lawson Morrissett, Fourth Virginia Cavalry, Eleanor S. Brockenbrough Library, MOC; Donahue Diary; Neese, *Three Years in the Confederate Horse Artillery*, 199.

28.   *O.R.*, series 1, vol. 27, part 2, 324.

29.   *Ibid.*, part 1, 929; Civil War Diary of George H. Chapman, Indiana Historical Society (hereafter cited as IHS); Cheney Diary; Frank Diary.

30.   *O.R.*, series 1, vol. 27, part 1, 1004.

31.   Victor E. Comte to Dear Elise, July 16, 1863; Victor E. Comte Papers, Microfilm mf365 c, BHL/UM; Rev. Louis N. Boudrye, *Historic Records of the Fifth New York Cavalry, First Ira Light Guard* (Albany: S. R. Gray, 1865), 73; Morey Diary.

32.   Yoder Diary
        Yoder stated that after the Tenth relieved his regiment, the Sixteenth Pennsyl-
vania, it proceeded back into Shepherdstown and turned to the right. Coming from
south of the town this would have put the Sixteenth on either the road leading to
Charles Town or the one to Harpers Ferry. Since he reported that his regiment was
involved in the fighting it would seem more likely that it was picketing along the
Charles Town Road and became involved on the left flank of the fighting.
        Huey probably did not arrive until after most of the fighting had ended and does
not appear to have been engaged at all.
33.   Maj. M. Henry Avery, commanding the Tenth, had placed Maj. Alvah D. Waters with
        Companies H and L, under command of Captains William Peck and George Van-
        derbilt, and Companies C and G, under command of Lieutenants Benjamin F. Sceva
        and John T. McKevitt, on the Winchester Pike. A squadron, under Captain John G.
        Peirce, took position on the Dam No. 4 road. Avery and the remaining three
        squadrons picketed the Martinsburg road. *O.R.*, series 1, vol. 27, part 1, 982.
34.   The ridge and wood were on the property of Dr. Vincent Butler, whose home,
        "Mount Pleasant," stood nearby. Dr. Butler's name is often given as Boteler or con-
        fused with Alexander R. Boteler, whose home, "Fountain Rock," stood about a mile
        and a half closer to Shepherdstown. James C. Holland, ed., *Military Operations in Jef-
        ferson County Virginia (Now West Virginia) 1861-1865* (Henry Kyd Douglas Camp, No.
        199, Sons of Confederate Veterans, 2004), 11; information supplied by Susan M.
        Collins, curator of the Jefferson County Museum in Charles Town, WV.
35.   *O.R.*, series 1, vol. 27, part 1, 982.
        During one of the brief stands made at the reserve post, Capt. Peck lost Lt. John
        T. McKevitt of Company G, shot through a lung, and seven other men missing and
        wounded, three of whom later died in the hospital.
36.   The exact number of guns the Confederates had in the action is unknown. Only Shoe-
        maker's section can be verified. Evidence for additional guns comes from several
        sources. Lt. George W. Beale recalled the guns firing singly, by section, and all to-
        gether. This would indicate more than Shoemaker's section. Lt. Robert T. Hubard,
        Jr., of the Third Virginia gave the number as four. Federal sources also credit the Con-
        federates with more than two guns, one source claiming as many as eight guns. The
        First and Second Stuart Horse Artillery batteries were attached to the brigades of Fitz
        Lee and Rooney Lee (Chambliss) and would have been the batteries to accompany
        these brigades into the battle. Breathed could only have had one section in the fight
        as Lt. Francis H. Wigfall stated in a letter dated July 18, 1863, that his section had
        been without ammunition since crossing the Potomac. *The Richmond Times Dispatch*
        stated that Fitz Lee had only three guns. John J. Shoemaker, *Shoemaker's Battery*
        (Gaithersburg: Butternut Press, no date), 49; Lewis T. Nunnelee, *History of a Famous
        Company of the War of Rebellion (So Called) Between the States*, MOC, 91; Lt. Robert T.
        Hubard Jr., *The Civil War Memoirs of a Virginia Cavalryman*, ed. Thomas P. Nanzig
        (Tuscaloosa: The University of Alabama Press, 2007), 105; G. W. Beale, *A Lieutenant
        of Cavalry in Lee's Army* (Baltimore: Butternut and Blue, 1994), 122; Tobie, *First Maine
        Cavalry*, 185; Francis Halsey Wigfall to Miss Louise Wigfall, July 18, 1863, Louis T. Wig-
        fall Family Papers, MMC-3183, Manuscript Division, Library of Congress (hereafter
        cited as LC); *O.R.*, Series 1, Vol. 27, part 1, 978. *Richmond Daily Dispatch*, July 18, 1863.
37.   Tobie, *First Maine Cavalry*, 181-185; Carter Diary; Robert J. Trout, *Galloping Thunder*:

The Stuart Horse Artillery Battalion (Mechanicsburg: Stackpole Books, 2002), 321, 715; *O.R.,* series 1, vol. 27, part 1, 978, 980-982, 984-985; *Richmond Daily Dispatch*, July 18, 1863; *Richmond Whig*, July 27, 1863; *Daily Morning News*, August 5, 1863; *Philadelphia Weekly Times,* April 1, 1882.

The Thirteenth Pennsylvania of Col. Gregg's brigade was not engaged, being on picket duty near Halltown. Hand, Jr., *One Good Regiment*, 71.

38.   Gregg reported his loss at 8 enlisted men killed, 4 officers and 68 enlisted men wounded, and 1 officer and 10 enlisted men missing. A second official accounting gives the loss as 8 enlisted men killed, 8 officers and 64 enlisted men wounded, and 24 enlisted men missing. The correspondent of the *New York World* wrote that the Federals lost between 300 and 400 with over 100 killed, which are grossly inflated numbers. Fitz Lee's report of the action, if he submitted one, is missing, but contemporary newspaper sources state Confederate casualties numbered between 75 and 100 with no prisoners. Lt. Col. William R. Carter of the Third Virginia put his brigade's losses at 11 killed, 27 wounded, and 9 missing. *O.R.,* series 1, vol. 27, part 1, 193 and 960; *Richmond Daily Dispatch* (quoting the *New York World*); *Richmond Whig*; Carter Diary.

39.   Carter Diary.

Presumably, Chambliss withdrew to Walper's Crossroads with Lee. Nothing is known of Ferguson's disposition on the night of the 16th-17th, but he probably moved back along the Martinsburg road and camped.

40.   *O.R.,* series 1, vol. 27, part 3, 713.

41.   *Ibid.,* 717; Edward G. Longacre, *Jersey Cavaliers: A History of the First New Jersey Volunteer Cavalry, 1861-1865* (Hightstown: Longstreet House, 1992), 152.

42.   *O.R.,* Series 1, Vol. 27, part 3, 713.

Pvt. Yoder of the Sixteenth Pennsylvania of Col. Gregg's brigade recorded that his regiment stayed at Harpers Ferry, as did Pvt. Lucas of the First Pennsylvania of Col. McIntosh's brigade. Yoder Diary; Dona Bayard Sauerburger, ed., *I Seat Myself to Write You a Few Lines: Civil War and Homestead Letters from Thomas Lucas and Family* (Bowie, Maryland: Heritage Books Inc., 2002), 162.

43.   *O.R.,* Series 1, Vol. 27, part 3, 929.

One source stated that his regiment, the Eighth New York, crossed the Potomac on this day. Cheney Diary.

44.   *Ibid.,* part 1, 1001 and 1004; Morey Diary; Horace K. Ide, Edited and additional material by Elliott W. Hoffman, *History of the First Vermont Cavalry Volunteers in the War of the Great Rebellion* (Hightstown: Longstreet House, 1992), 126; Gillespie, *Company A, First Ohio Cavalry*, 170; Boudrye, *Fifth New York Cavalry*, 73; *Detroit Free Press*, August 2, 1863.

45.   The only unit from Jones's Brigade that crossed the Shenandoah on the 17th would appear to have been the Thirty-fifth Virginia under Lt. Col. Elijah V. White. However, when White reached the gap, he found it already in the possession of the enemy and withdrew. What force Dake skirmished with at the gap is unknown although a possible solution lies in a report filed on July 14, 1863, by Col. Charles R. Lowell of the Second Massachusetts. Lowell's regiment was attached to the Department of Washington and on July 10 made a scout to Ashby's and Snicker's gaps.

During the expedition, Lowell clashed with two companies of the Fourth North Carolina under Capt. Lewis A. Johnson at Ashby's Gap. Lowell also skirmished with elements of the Sixth and Twelfth Virginia at Snicker's Gap. These few companies undoubtedly remained in the vicinity as one source stated and then fought with Dake's Fifth Michigan before White's arrival. Dake reported that the 12 prisoners he took came from Jones's Brigade, undoubtedly from the Sixth or possibly the Twelfth Virginia.

Finally, a communication from Robert E. Lee to Stuart dated July 18, 1863, stated that Stuart previously had informed Lee about elements of the Sixth Virginia being at Ashby's Gap.

John E. Divine, *35th Battalion Virginia Cavalry* (Lynchburg: H.E. Howard, Inc., 1985), 37; Louis H. Manarin, *North Carolina Troops 1861 – 1865 – A Roster, Volume II Cavalry* (Raleigh: North Carolina Office of Archives and History, 2004), 264 and 369; James McLean, *California Sabers: The 2nd Massachusetts Cavalry in the Civil War* (Bloomington: Indiana University Press, 2000), 44-45; Frank L. Klement, ed., "Edwin B. Bigelow: A Michigan Sergeant in the Civil War," *Michigan History* 38 (1954): 3, 223; *O.R.,* Series 1, Vol. 27, part 1, 1039-1040, part 2, 999 and 1001, and part 3, 1020.

46. *O.R.,* Series 1, Vol. 27, part 3, 714, 718.
47. Arehart, "Diary of W. H. Arehart," 213-214.
48. Stuart probably meant since Gettysburg. J. E. B. Stuart to My Darling Wife [Flora Stuart], July 18, 1863, James Ewell Brown Stuart Papers, 1851-1968, Mss1ST923d, Microfilm reel C621, Virginia Historical Society (hereafter cited as VHS).
49. *O.R.,* Series 1, Vol. 27, part 3, 1020.
50. *Ibid.*

Lee instructed Stuart to have the Sixth withdraw south along the mountain. The men may have risked a crossing of the Shenandoah at Berry's Ferry on the road from Ashby's Gap to Millwood.

51. *Ibid.,* part 2, 281.
52. *Ibid.,* part 2, 210, 281; Henry Woodbury Moore and James Washington Moore, *Chained to Virginia While Carolina Bleeds* (Columbia, South Carolina: Henry Woodbury Moore, M. D., 1996), 160.
53. *O.R.,* Series 1, Vol. 27, part 3, 718.
54. *Ibid.,* part 1, 1001; Morey Diary; Klement, ed., "Edwin B. Bigelow," 223.
55. Morey Diary; Boudrye, *Fifth New York Cavalry,* 73-74.
56. Chapman Diary; Inglis Diary; Samuel L. Gracey, *Annals of the Sixth Pennsylvania Cavalry* (Lancaster, Ohio: Vanberg Publishing, 1996), 192.

Merritt wrote his Gettysburg campaign report on the 18th while near Petersville, Maryland, indicating his brigade's starting point for the day's march. *O.R.,* Series 1, Vol. 27, part 1, 943.

57. Frank Diary; Samuel M. Blackwell, Jr., *In the First Line of Battle: The 12th Illinois Cavalry in the Civil War* (Dekalb: Northern Illinois University Press, 2002), 115; Abner Hard, M.D., *History of the Eighth Illinois Cavalry Regiment Illinois Volunteers, During the Great Rebellion* (Dayton: Morningside Bookshop, 1996), 266.
58. Newel Cheney, *History of the Ninth Regiment, New York Volunteer Cavalry, War of 1861 to 1865* (Jamestown: Martin Merz & Son, 1901), 123; Committee on Regimental History, *History of the Sixth New York Cavalry (Second Ira Harris Guard), Second Brigade – First Division – Cavalry Corps, Army of the Potomac, 1861 to 1865* (Worchester: The Blanchard Press, 1908), 151.
59. *O.R.,* Series 1, Vol. 27, part 1, 929; Chapman Diary; Cheney Diary; Frank Diary; Inglis Diary.

From July 16 to August 1, Cheney's entries are one day early, meaning, for example, that he recorded events that happened on the 18th as having happened on the 17th. All of his locations and other information are accurate. Only his dating is in error.
60. *O.R.,* Series 1, Vol. 27, part 3, 720; Yoder Diary; Ressler Diary.

61.   *O.R.,* Series 1, Vol. 27, part 3, 968; Rawle, *Third Pennsylvania Cavalry,* 325; Longacre, *Jersey Cavaliers,* 169.

62.   Ressler Diary; Yoder Diary; Smith, *"Scott's 900,"* 110; Hand, Jr., *One Good Regiment,* 71.

     Two of the above sources confirmed that the Sixteenth Pennsylvania and the Eleventh New York encamped at Lovettsville on the night of the 19th. Presumably, the remainder of Gregg's brigade did the same. Huey's brigade probably camped nearby. Ressler Diary; Smith, *Eleventh New York Cavalry,* 110.

     Pvt. Alvin N. Brackett wrote on the morning of the 19th from Harpers Ferry that he expected to move momentarily and follow the Eleventh Corps. The First Maine did not cross the river until the 20th. Alvin N. Brackett to Dear Brother, July 19, 1863, Alvin N. Brackett Letters, Gregory A. Coco Collection, Harrisburg Civil War Roundtable Collection (hereafter cited as HCWRTC), USAMHI; Tobie, *First Maine Cavalry,* 188.

63.   *O.R.,* Series 1, Vol. 27, part 1, 960, 983, and part 3, 720.

     The itinerary for the two brigades can only partly be constructed. Col. Gregg's left Lovettsville on the 20th, rode through Leesburg, crossed Goose Creek, and camped for the night. The next day, it passed through Centreville and encamped south of Bull Run. The 22nd saw the brigade reach Bristoe Station. Ressler Diary; Yoder Diary; Tobie, *First Maine Cavalry,* 188-189.

     Huey's brigade followed much the same route and timetable. Captain Willard Glazier, *Three Years in the Federal Cavalry,* (New York: R. H. Ferguson & Company, Publishers, 1874), 301.

     Just exactly who or what these brigades were to guard against with Lee's army on the far side of the Shenandoah is unknown. One possible answer is that the railroad needed to be rebuilt so it could be used as a supply line in the upcoming movement against Lee. Another possibility is Maj. John S. Mosby, although sending two brigades of the army's cavalry for such duty, appears to be excessive.

64.   *O.R.,* Series 1, Vol. 27, part 3, 726.

65.   *Ibid.,* part 2, 324, 362, and part 3, 1026.

66.   *Ibid.,* part 2, 362, 449.

67.   *Ibid.,* part 2, 449 and 609.

68.   *Ibid.,* part 3, 1027.

69.   Carter Diary; Morrissett Diary; Donahue Diary.

     Preparations may have begun on the previous day. Pvt. William H. Arehart recorded in his diary that his regiment, the Twelfth Virginia, Jones's Brigade, received orders to shoe its horses and turn most of its wagons over to the brigade. Arehart, "Diary of W. H. Arehart," 214.

70.   Richard Henry Watkins to Mary Watkins, July 21, 1863, Richard Henry Watkins Papers, 1861-1865, Mss1W3272a1-355, VHS.

71.   Arehart, "Diary of W. H. Arehart," 215.

72.   *O.R.,* Series 1, vol. 27, part 2, 707; Carter Diary; "Reminiscences of the War" by W. A. Curtis, Box 4 of 4, Folder - Reminiscences Undated, Confederate Veteran Papers, William R. Perkins Library, Duke University (hereafter cited as WRP/DU).

     Edwards wrote that his regiment, the Ninth Virginia, and presumably his brigade, Chambliss's, camped six miles from Millwood on the road to Front Royal. Edwards Diary.

     Hawse recorded that his regiment, the Eleventh Virginia, encamped near Berryville on the 21st. Hawse Diary.

73.   *O.R.,* Series 1, vol. 27, part 3, 728.

74.   *Ibid.*

75.   Though McIntosh recorded that he proceeded to Hillsborough and drew supplies from Harpers Ferry, he failed to state where he crossed the river. Gen. Gregg reported that McIntosh rejoined the brigade at Warrenton, having been detached at Harpers Ferry. This seems to indicate that the brigade probably crossed the river there. Additionally, how many regiments of the brigade accompanied McIntosh over the river is unconfirmed. According to the historian of the Third Pennsylvania, his regiment picketed the road from Hillsborough to the Shenandoah on both the 20th and the 21st. The First Pennsylvania encamped at Hillsborough at noon on the 21st and remained there until the 23rd. *Ibid.*, part 1, 960 and 968; Rawle, *Third Pennsylvania Cavalry*, 325; Lloyd, *History of the First Regiment Pennsylvania Reserve Cavalry*, 67-68.

      Exactly when McIntosh's report reached Meade is unknown. However, it could not have been on the 20th since McIntosh only arrived at Purcellville on that date. The next morning he had to turn around and ride for Hillsborough and Harpers Ferry before crossing the river to perform his mission. In all probability, the report did not arrive until sometime on the morning of the 21st. Sauerburger, ed., *I Seat Myself to Write You,* 163.

76.   *O.R.*, Series 1, vol. 27, part 1, 1004 and 1017; Morey Diary; Hoffman, *First Vermont*, 127; Boudrye, *Fifth New York Cavalry*, 74; *Supplement to the Official Records of the Union and Confederate Armies* (hereafter cited as *Supp. to O.R.*); Wilmington, NC: Broadfoot Publishing Company, 1994), part 1, vol. 5, 287; Divine, *35th Battalion Virginia Cavalry*, 37; *Fayetteville Observer*, September 14, 1863; *Detroit Free Press*, August 2, 1863.

      An individual, signing his name only as P. W. A., accused Robertson of incompetence for losing the gap, but Capt. Lewis A. Johnson, Company A, Fourth North Carolina, replied, claiming that Robertson's entire command numbered only about 200 men and even with the addition of Lt. Col. Elijah V. White's Thirty-fifth Virginia Battalion, numbering about 150 men, to have attempted to make a stand against the overwhelming numbers of the enemy would have been "worse than madness." *Fayetteville Observer*, September 14, 1863.

77.   *O.R.*, Series 1, vol. 27, part 1, 1017.

78.   The division had camped at various locations with Gamble's brigade south of Union about three miles from Upperville, probably near Panther Skin Creek and Devin's brigade near Upperville. Merritt's brigade also camped somewhere in this same area. Chapman Diary; Cheney Diary; Frank Diary; Inglis Diary.

79.   *O.R.*, Series 1, vol. 27, part 1, 929; Chapman Diary; Cheney Diary; Frank Diary; Inglis Diary; W. N. Pickerill, *History of the Third Indiana Cavalry* (Indianapolis: Aetna Printing Co., 1906), 86; Gracey, *Annals of the Sixth*, 193.

      The brigade continued to guard the wagon train, marching to Warrenton on the 24th and the next day encamping two miles south of the town. On the 26th, the Sixth New York marched to Bealeton Station while the rest of the brigade marched to Liberty. On the 27th, the brigade united at Rappahannock Station. The Sixth New York picketed from the Station to Sulphur Springs, also known as White Sulphur Springs and Lee's White Sulphur Springs, on the 28th and the next day from Beverly Ford to Sulphur Springs, relieving the Seventeenth Pennsylvania. The 30th saw the Sixth picketing at Lee's Ford. Two companies, F and H, pursued an unknown force of Confederate cavalry through Union Mills but did not succeed in catching them. The Ninth New York relieved the Sixth on the 31st. The Sixth arrived back at camp after 10:00 in the evening, received rations and ammunition, and was prepared to move out at midnight. *History of the Sixth New York Cavalry*, 152-153.

Note: No Union Mills near Lee's Ford or Sulphur Springs could be found.

80. *O.R.*, Series 1, vol. 27, part 3, 729 and 730.
81. *Ibid.*, part 3, 733-735.
82. *Ibid.*, part 2, 362 and part 3, 735.
83. *Ibid.*, part 1, 937; Chapman Diary; Cheney Diary; Frank Diary.
     One source reported Gamble's casualties as one killed, six wounded, and a number missing. Hard, *Eighth Illinois Cavalry*, 267.
84. *O.R.*, Series 1, vol. 27, part 1, 945.
85. *Ibid.*, part 3, 739-740.
86. Manarin, *North Carolina Troops*, 265 and 369
87. *O.R.*, Series 1, vol. 27, part 2, 362.
88. *Ibid.*, part 3, 741; Chapman Diary; Cheney Diary; Frank Diary.
89. *O.R.*, Series 1, vol. 27, part 3, 742.
90. *Ibid.*, part 3, 745-746.
91. *Ibid.*, part 1, 118.
92. *Ibid.*, 489-490, part 2, 449-450, 626-627; Longstreet, *From Manassas to Appomattox*, 431-432.
93. Morey Diary; Gillespie, Company A, *First Ohio Cavalry*, 171.
     One source estimated the cattle as numbering 1,200 head, which, if true, would have been a significant loss to Lee's army. *New York Herald*, July 26, 1863.
94. *O.R.*, Series 1, vol. 27, part 3, 753-754; Morey Diary; Gillespie, Company A, *First Ohio Cavalry*, 171.
     The two men Custer captured could not have been guarding the crossroads three days past. Fitz Lee's brigade did not cross the Shenandoah until the morning of the 22nd. After a forced march, Lee's Brigade along with Chambliss's and Ferguson's brigades camped below Gaines' Cross Roads the night of the 23rd, holding the Warrenton Turnpike that ran through Amissville. *O.R.*, Series 1, vol. 27, part 2, 707.
95. *O.R.*, Series 1, vol. 27, part 1, 1003, 1020.
     Custer recorded the loss as six or seven wounded.
     The enemy Capehart encountered probably came from Brig. Gen. Henry L. Benning's brigade that was encamped at Flint Hill. The Fourth Alabama from Brig. Gen. Evander M. Law's brigade was also present. *O.R.*, Series 1, vol. 27, part 2, 418.
96. *O.R.*, Series 1, vol. 27, part 1, 1002.
97. Frank Diary.
98. Cheney, *Ninth Regiment, New York Volunteer Cavalry*, 124.
99. *O.R.*, Series 1, vol. 27, part 1, 930 and 945; Pickerill, *Third Indiana Cavalry*, 86.
100. *O.R.*, Series 1, vol. 27, part 1, 930, 968, 979, and part 3, 756; Ressler Diary; Yoder Diary; Thomas Covert to My Dear Wife, July 23, 1863, Covert Collection, USAMHI; Smith, "*Scott's 900*," 111; Hand, Jr., *One Good Regiment*, 71.
     A squadron of the First Pennsylvania relieved the Seventh Michigan in picketing Ashby's Gap. Lloyd, *History of the First Regiment Pennsylvania Reserve Cavalry*, 68.
101. *O.R.*, Series 1, vol. 27, part 2, 707; Carter Diary; Curtis "Reminiscences".
     Pvt. Lawson Morrissett of the Fourth Virginia recorded in his diary that his regiment, and undoubtedly Fitz Lee's entire brigade, marched with Flint Hill on its left, meaning they took the Sandy Hook/Little Washington road, and camped five miles from Gaines' Cross Roads, probably near Little Washington. Morrissett Diary.
102. Donahue Diary.
     Hawse recorded that his regiment, the Eleventh Virginia, encamped along the

Opequon Creek on the 22nd and near Kernstown on the following day. The brigade probably was spread out between White Post and the Opequon. Hawse Diary.

103. One source stated that Baker's Brigade withdrew on the 22nd. It is possible that a portion of the brigade left on the night of the 22nd and the rest the following day. *O.R.,* Series 1, vol. 27, part 2, 449; Manarin, *North Carolina Troops,* 4; Donald A. Hopkins, *The Little Jeff: The Jeff Davis Legion Cavalry, Army of Northern Virginia* (Shippensburg: White Mane Books, 1999), 165.

104. One company of the Fifth Michigan was sent to the left to guard a road and did not participate in the fighting, and Companies M and G had been assigned to support Pennington. Morey Diary; Klement, ed., "Edwin B. Bigelow," 224.

105. *O.R.,* Series 1, vol. 27, part 1, 1003; *Chicago Tribune,* July 28, 1863; *Detroit Free Press,* Aug. 2, 1863.

106. This is the same Col. Oates who in the future would gain immortality for his gallant struggle with Col. Joshua L. Chamberlain for possession of Little Round Top that had taken place at the battle of Gettysburg.

107. *O.R.,* Series 1, vol. 27, part 2, 418-419.
     Note: The Hazel River is also known as the Aestham River. To avoid confusion, the former will be used throughout this work.

108. Gray narrowly escaped serious injury or death during Benning's first attack. The horse in front of Gray went down and Gray's mount stumbled over it, tossing its rider to the ground. Before Gray could regain his feet, a large portion of the squadron ran over him. Only the fact that many of the horses were unshod saved him. *Chicago Tribune,* July 28, 1863; *Grand Rapids Daily Eagle,* August 8, 1863.

109. *O.R.,* Series 1, vol. 27, part 1, 1002-1004, part 2, 418-419; Morey Diary; *Chicago Tribune,* July 28, 1863; *Richmond Daily Dispatch,* August 4, 1863; *Detroit Free Press,* August 2, 1863; Walter F. Beyer and Oscar F. Keydel, eds., *Deeds of Valor: How American Heroes Won the Medal of Honor* (Detroit: The Perrien-Keydel Company, 1906), 256-257.
     In his report, Custer stated that he captured the servant of Stuart's medical director. The individual Custer referred to in this instance is unknown. Surgeon Talcott Eliason had begun the campaign as Stuart's medical director for it was he who treated Maj. Heros von Borcke after that officer's wounding at Upperville on June 19, 1863. However, in a letter dated July 18, Stuart wrote to his wife, Flora, that Eliason was sick and Dr. John B. Fontaine was acting as medical director. Nevertheless, the servant supplied accurate information concerning Stuart's presence at Gaines' Cross Roads at 9:00 the previous evening. *O.R.,* Series 1, vol. 27, part 2, 707; J. E. B. Stuart to My Darling Wife [Flora Stuart], July 18, 1863, Stuart Papers, 1851-1968, Mss1ST923d, Microfilm reel C621, VHS; Robert J. Trout, *They Followed the Plume* (Mechanicsburg: Stackpole Books, 1993), 101.

110. Custer reported a total loss of 30 killed, wounded, and missing. *O.R.,* Series 1, vol. 27, part1, 1004 and part 2, 419.

111. *Ibid.,* part 3, 759-760.

112. *Ibid.,* part 2, 707; Morrissett Diary; Carter Diary.

113. Manarin, *North Carolina Troops,* 264 and 369.

114. Hopkins, *The Little Jeff,* 165.

115. Donahue Diary.
     Hawse stated that the Eleventh Virginia camped at Fisher's Hill on the 24th. Hawse Diary.

Chapter Two

Stalemate Across the Rappahannock

As anxious as Brig. Gen. George A. Custer had been for his rear guard on July 24, he woke up fresh and ready to renew the contest the following day. Leading his command back toward Gaines' Cross Roads, he encountered no enemy but did glean information from various individuals eager to supply it. What he learned was simply that the Confederates had moved on. Custer assuaged his fighting spirit with the knowledge that the previous day he had, at least according to his informants, "spread great consternation through the entire rebel column extending beyond Gaines' in the direction of Chester Gap." Of course, with his adversaries gone confirmation could not be made. That bothered Custer not at all, but the condition of his men and horses did. With no enemy in sight, he requested that his division "have a little rest until we can forage and ration."[1]

With Lee having escaped him behind the Rappahannock River, Meade spent the 25th solidifying his position in and around Warrenton and Warrenton Junction as some of his corps completed the movements ordered the previous day. Portions of Meade's infantry replaced the cavalry that guarded bridges and railroads, allowing Gregg's and Buford's divisions to shift position. Gen. Gregg's division regrouped at Warrenton Junction, although it took some time to bring all the brigades together. Col. Gregg arrived on the 24th, but McIntosh would only leave Ashby's Gap on the 26th, bivouacking near Middleburg that night. The next day he marched through Salem, Thoroughfare Gap, and New Baltimore, camping at 9:00 in the evening within two miles of Warrenton. Col. Pennock Huey's brigade could only move from Bristoe Station and White Plains when infantry arrived to relieve him of guard duty.[2] Merritt's brigade rejoined Buford and together with Gamble and Devin marched for Orlean where Merritt encamped. The other brigades rode on, took possession of Warrenton, and then marched to Liberty and Fayetteville, picketing the river from Waterloo through Sulphur Springs to Kelly's Ford.[3] Recuperation and refitting became the order of the day throughout the Federal horse, at least for those not watching the enemy across the Rappahannock.

That enemy too sought respite from their labors. Three of Stuart's brigades returned to their old campgrounds in and around Brandy Station; a fourth found itself in foreign territory. Fitz Lee's troopers settled down on the farm of John Minor Botts. Private Lawson Morrissett recorded in his diary that he, "Drew rations, a thing much desired. Loose corn for our horses. First time since left Maryland."[4]

Two squadrons from the Third Virginia, Capt. John A. Chappell's and Capt. William M. Field's, guarded Rixey Ford on the Hazel River.[5] Chambliss's Brigade also occupied a portion of the Botts farm and shared in the outpost duties.[6] Robertson maintained his guard at Kelly's Ford on the Rappahannock. Being from the Valley, Ferguson's Brigade knew little or nothing about the previous goings on along the two rivers. It took position around Sperryville before moving closer to Brandy Station.[7]

For Jones and Baker, still in the Valley, July 25 passed as so many of the previous days – on the march. Baker's troopers left their camp 5 miles south of Strasburg and rode 12 miles before stopping for the day near Mt. Jackson.[8] Jones's Brigade continued up the Valley, ending the day between Mt. Jackson and New Market.[9] Progress proved slow but with the enemy allowing for breathing space, it was at least steady.

All was quiet on the 26th. Lee seemed content to await both Ewell's arrival and Meade's next move. Meade, however, made plans to probe Lee's line of defense along the Rappahannock, sending scouts toward Rappahannock Bridge to ascertain its condition.[10] On the 27th, Buford's division marched to Rappahannock Station. The Third Indiana picketed at Kelly's Ford until 10:00 at night when the Twelfth Illinois relieved it.[11] That same day, elements of Col. J. Irvin Gregg's brigade, also assigned to watch the river below Bealton Station, reported that the bridge at Rappahannock Station had sunk about two feet and was impassable.[12] Undeterred, Meade issued Pleasonton orders to have the cavalry clear the south bank of the enemy as soon as a crossing could be made somewhere along the river and to spread a portion of the cavalry on the army's flank toward Fredericksburg.[13] The crossing, however, assumed priority. Only a rain-swollen river stood in the blue cavalry's way.[14]

Over the next few days rumors snaked their way through both armies and into the newspapers. Some of the stories proved true while others consisted of nothing but smoke and disappeared on the wind. Meade's interest in the bridge at Rappahannock Station drew attention from the Confederates, and the accumulation of materials for the bridge's reconstruction was reported in the Richmond papers, along with the opinion that the Yankee army was very demoralized with several regiments being put under arrest for refusing to cross the river.[15] On the Federal side, a report of Stuart being relieved of his command of the cavalry surfaced in the papers. Fitz Lee was designated his replacement.[16]

Although both armies seemed to be at rest, much was happening behind the scenes. On the 28th, the Federals took steps to relieve a problem that had been haunting them for quite some time. No one had ever doubted the expense of equipping and maintaining a cavalry regiment. However, an understanding of that did not automatically translate into solving the problems inherent in keeping a regiment in the field for long durations. This especially applied to the acquisition and care of horses. With over 30 regiments of cavalry in the Army of the Potomac, finding, training, shipping, and caring for horses should have been a priority from the beginning. The facts showed otherwise. In May 1863, 5,673 horses were issued to the cavalry, followed in June by another 6,327, and another 4,716 in July.[17] This amounted to a remount of all the cavalry in the army every two months.

Recognizing that something needed to be done, the Secretary of War issued the following:

GENERAL ORDERS No. 236. WAR DEPT., ADJT. GENERAL'S OFFICE

Washington, July 28, 1863.

1. A bureau will be attached to the War Department, to be designated the Cavalry Bureau.

2. This bureau will have charge of the organization and equipment of the cavalry forces of the Army, and of the provision for the mounts and remounts of the same.

3. The purchases of all horses for the cavalry service will be made by officers of the Quartermaster's Department, under the direction of the chief of the Cavalry Bureau. Inspections of horses offered for the cavalry service will be made by cavalry officers.

4. Depots will be established for the reception, organization, and discipline of cavalry recruits and new regiments, and for the collection, care, and training of cavalry horses. These depots will be under the general charge of the Cavalry Bureau.

5. Copies of inspection reports of cavalry troops, and such returns as may be at any time called for, will be sent to the Bureau established by this order.

6. The enormous expense attending the maintenance of the cavalry arm points to the necessity of greater care and more judicious management on the part of cavalry officers, that their horses may be constantly kept up to the standard of efficiency for service. Great neglects of duty in this connection are to be attributed to officers in command of cavalry troops. It is the design of the War Department to correct such neglects by dismissing from service officers whose inefficiency and inattention result in the deterioration and loss of the public animals under their charge.

By order of the Secretary of War:

E. D. TOWNSEND,

Assistant Adjutant-General.[18]

This was followed up by a second "General Order" that gave instructions for inspecting horses each month, the categorizing of horses in regards to their condition, the purchasing and requisitioning of horses through the bureau, and the assigning of Maj. Gen. George Stoneman as chief of the Cavalry Bureau.[19]

The problems addressed by these orders were all too apparent to the men sitting astride the horses in the field. Most were well aware that the care of their mounts had much to do with their ability to fight the enemy. Nevertheless, when generals issued orders to ride here or ride there, hold this gap or that crossroads, or scout this road or that village, they never asked about the condition of the men, much less the horses. They expected their orders to be executed promptly. The bureaucrats in Washington had little conception of the conditions in the field and the demands put on men and horses. Their efforts in alleviating a serious problem were commendable, but in the end, horses would be swallowed up by the war, just as surely as men.[20]

Across the Rappahannock, Stuart also took the time to address issues that plagued the efficiency of his command. However, his concern focused on things other than horses.

GENERAL ORDERS NO. 25   HDQRS. CAVALRY DIV., ARMY OF N. VA.
July 29, 1863.

The nondescript, irregular body of men, known as Company Q, which has so long disgraced the cavalry service, and degraded the individuals resorting to it, is hereby abolished. The sick or disabled men, requiring hospital treatment, will be sent, as heretofore, to the general division hospital in Hanover, where they will receive the kindest treatment and care known to the army.

The horses will be kept with the commands to which they belong, forges being put in operation near brigade or regimental headquarters for the unshod. Those horses likely to remain in unserviceable condition for some time will be assembled on Monday in each week, and sent under a good non-commissioned officer to division headquarters, where they will be furnished with the necessary authority to proceed to the camp of disabled horses of the division, established at a suitable place in the rear, under charge of the division quartermaster, whence, as soon as recuperated, they will be returned to the field. The non-commissioned officer will, in all cases, bring back a receipt to each regimental commander for the horses delivered over by him, each horse being described with sufficient minuteness to be readily identified.

Efficient provost guards will be organized without delay, to remain with each train, to prevent the members of the command from be-taking themselves to the trains under any pretense whatever. All such will be arrested, and returned under guard to their command, and should any commanding officer, less than a brigade commander, grant permission for such absence, the officer granting the pass will be forthwith reported to the brigade commander, who will place him in arrest for trial. This guard will also be charged with the preservation of order in the trains, the safety of public and private property, and the prevention of outrage upon, or unlawful seizure of, the property of citizens.

A provost guard will also be organized for duty with each brigade, or detached command, whose general duties will be to prevent straggling and disorders of every kind (to that end being so stationed as to watch vigilantly over the command), and, in battle, to arrest persons going to the rear, recording the names of such for future punishment, and compelling them to return to the front.

No brigade, regiment, or company officer has authority to give permits to be absent beyond the limits of the brigade, which limits will be understood to be 5 miles from brigade headquarters, and brigade commanders will rigidly scrutinize all such permits within those limits.

The major-general commanding is convinced that unless a more sure means of detecting and punishing the guilty and preserving the strength of this command can be devised, all discipline is gone, and with it the efficiency of the cavalry division. By prowess in action, by vigilance on the outpost, and by patient endurance on the march, it has won a name of which its members may be justly proud; but, owing to the inefficiency of a portion of the company officers, and the forgetfulness on the part of many of the men of their high duty and the patriotic resolve which has hitherto been the rule of their action, its members are rapidly diminishing, and its efficiency becoming consequently impaired.

The major-general appeals hopefully to the brigade commanders, regimental officers, and to the men of his division to aid him in arresting this growing evil. He is determined to spare no effort to rescue his command, in which he feels so much pride, from the impending fate. Let the straggler be disgraced in the eyes of all honest and patriotic men; let the artful dodger on the battlefield receive the retributive bullet of his gallant comrade; let every man recognize his duty to his oppressed country as his sole motive, and vengeance on a ruthless invader his constant aim.

By command on Maj. Gen. J. E. B. Stuart
H.B. McClellan
Major and Assistant Adjutant-General[21]

Stuart's concern over the effects of "Company Q" on his command was equaled by his frustration over what he deemed defects in the mode of fighting adopted by his division. He expressed his frustration in a general order:

GENERAL ORDERS NO. 25   HDQRS. CAVALRY DIV., ARMY OF N. VA.
    July 30, 1863.

The major general commanding has endeavored in vain, by oral injunctions, to correct the defects in the mode of fighting pursued by this division, but they have been so steadily on the increase that he is compelled to make their correction the subject of General Orders.

In preparing for action, skirmishers should always be quickly deployed, either mounted or dismounted, according to the nature of the ground; the cavalry column formed into distinct squadrons and regiments, with distinct intervals, which are indispensable; those squadrons in rear of the one engaged taking special care that any confusion which may occur in front shall not extend to them, and, above all, not permitting any retreat of those engaged to break their front, but remain firm and unbroken until ordered into action.

If a squadron engaged becomes broken, and compelled by overwhelming force to retire, its members will take care not to run through the ranks of those in the rear, but will move to the nearest rallying point without confusion, or precipitancy, or noise.

The column in advancing to the charge will move steadily up at a walk, taking the trot when about 200 yards from the enemy, the trot being slow and steady in front, each squadron keeping its formation distinct and well closed. The charge will be delivered against the enemy by squadrons, the gallop being taken when within 50 yards of the enemy's front, and the gait increased instead of diminished as the enemy is neared, so as to give the greatest possible force to the shock against the enemy's column, the rider sitting firmly in the saddle, with his saber wide awake for the thrust. Too much importance cannot be given to the shock of the charge, the furious impact of horse against horse, for in that will consist the success of the charge. The enemy once broken, must be followed vigorously, the officers taking care not to allow the pursuit to lag on account of the accumulation of prisoners and plunder. Plundering in battle is strictly prohibited. The habit taken from the enemy, which is becoming so prevalent, a habit counseled by fear, of charging as soon as within a quarter of a mile of the foe, up to the range of pistol-shot, and there halting to deliver fire, is highly injudicious and entirely destructive of success. The pistol should never be used in a charge, excepting when the enemy is beyond an impassable barrier near at hand, or by a man unhorsed in combat, in which latter case especially it may be made a most effective weapon.

Whenever practicable, an attack should be made on either or both flanks simultaneously with the front attack, but the latter should not be too much weakened for this purpose. All troops are tender about their flanks; and oftentimes, when a real flank attack is impracticable, a mere feint or demonstration pushed boldly toward the flank and rear will strike dismay into the enemy's ranks. An attack of cavalry should be sudden, bold, and vigorous; to falter is to fail. The cavalry which arrives noiselessly but steadily near the enemy, and then, with one loud yell, leaps upon him without a note of warning, and giving him no time to form or consider anything but the immediate means of flight, pushing him vigorously every step with all the confidence of victory achieved, is true cavalry; while a body of men equally brave and patriotic, who halt at every picket and reconnoiter until the precious surprise is over, is not cavalry.

While rashness is a crime, boldness is not incompatible with caution, nay, is often the quintessence of prudence.

The position which the cavalry officers generally take in battle is a subject requiring immediate correction. Though highly creditable to their gallantry, it is highly derogatory to their discretion, and at direct variance with their duty. The following will be hereafter adhered to strictly:

A brigade, regiment, or squadron advancing in line of battle, will have the commander in front sufficiently far to supervise and control its movements; but in columns of squadrons, platoons, fours, or twos, the brigade commander must be in a position sufficiently central to keep his brigade well in hand, and make communication to his colonels easy and intelligible.

The regimental commander will preserve such a location in his column as shall be sufficiently central to control and supervise its movements and check any wavering by prompt support; to order his squadron commanders successively to the charge, and superintend their rallying and return to action. These duties will absorb all his energies and time, and will require the active assistance of the lieutenant-colonel, major, and regimental staff.

The squadron commander will lead his squadron, keeping it together, preserving in his own person coolness and self-possession, but the quickness of an eagle. He will be assisted by the second captain and lieutenants, all striving by precept and example to insure success, remembering that in victory alone is safety and honor. The squadron commander who hesitates to lead his men whenever ordered by his colonel, is a disgrace to his commission; and men who fail or falter in a charge led by their squadron chief, will not be lost sight of in the annals of infamy and disgrace.

Should the charge be repulsed, the skirmishers on the flanks will, instead of retiring with the column, direct a concentrated fire on the advancing column of the enemy, endeavoring to hold it in check till fresh troops move up.

The ambulance corps alone will be allowed to remove the wounded, and all will bear in mind that our first duty to our wounded is to win the victory.

Should any check or confusion occur, the utmost silence will be observed in the ranks, in order that the commands of officers may be distinctly heard and quickly executed. The commands given will be few and to the point.

The major-general commanding appeals not only to the officers but to the men of his division to observe the rules he has laid down for their guidance.

That individuality of action which so strongly characterizes the conduct of our troops in battle, if unguided or misdirected, can but produce confusion. But let the same idea control the mind of every man, let them apply these general principles to the incidents of battle as they arise, and success is certain.

By command on Maj. Gen. J. E. B. Stuart
H.B. McClellan
Major and Assistant Adjutant-General[22]

Whether the decline of the Southern horsemen's fighting qualities could be attributed to the adoption of practices attributed to their Northern brethren as Stuart ascribes is a topic for debate. What is paramount is Stuart's belief that his cavalry had fallen into bad habits and that he felt it necessary to take steps to correct those habits. Events soon to unfold would attest to the impact of the steps he took.

Stuart was not the only officer concerned with the army's mounted arm. Having felt for some time that the cavalry's organization had significant limitations, Robert E. Lee wrote to President Jefferson Davis, suggesting reorganization.[23] The changes Lee put forth would make the single division under Stuart a corps with two divisions commanded by Wade Hampton and Fitzhugh Lee, both of whom would become major generals. The number of brigades would be increased from five to six, but the number of regiments and/or legions in each brigade would be reduced from five or six to four.[24] Promotions to brigadier general for colonels Matthew C. Butler, Williams C. Wickham, Laurence S. Baker, and Lunsford L. Lomax were also suggested. Current brigade commander Brig. Gen. Beverly H. Robertson would be transferred as per his request. How soon these changes could or would be implemented was left to Davis.[25]

On the day when all this paperwork began shuffling behind the opposing lines, Meade sought for an opportunity to get at Lee, but heavy rain in the afternoon erased any thought Meade might have had regarding offensive operations.[26] Nevertheless, the Federal cavalry stood poised to strike when that opportunity arose. Buford's division remained near Rappahannock Station on the 28th, still recovering from the effects of the Gettysburg campaign and waiting on the river to fall, the bridge to be repaired, or pontoons to arrive so that the river could be crossed.[27] Most of his troopers enjoyed a peaceful time in camp, but others, such as the men from the Twelfth Illinois, who picketed Kelly's Ford, carried out the usual duties assigned to cavalry facing the enemy.[28] Kilpatrick's division, still under Custer's command, moved not a muscle other than to ship men whose horses had been declared unfit for further service to Washington for remounts. Custer retained but 1,200 men, which put him out of action until the others returned.[29]

The regiments of Gen. Gregg's division marched to new campsites, performed outpost duty, scouted, or sent out foraging parties.[30] Col. J. Irvin Gregg's troopers still kept a wary eye on the Confederates on the south bank of the Rappahannock, when they could be seen through the deluge, and reported at least 50 men at both Rappahannock Station and Beverly Ford. Conditions at Kelly's Ford and Norman's Ford appeared more favorable with only 5 men observed at the former and 2 at the latter. Information received through unrevealed channels indicated that the Confederates had only one brigade in reserve at Brandy Station.[31] Somehow amidst the day's downpour, the Second New York of Huey's brigade managed to net 15 prisoners.[32] Nevertheless, the rain kept the river high, making it the major obstacle to any movement south.

Across the river, the activities of Fitz Lee's, Chambliss's, Robertson's, and Ferguson's men mirrored their Federal counterparts in that most did little or nothing, other than hope that the river would not fall. Vedettes from various regiments still watched the river crossings, but for the most part the men stayed in camp, except for some who moved their camps to sites that were more favorable. A Richmond paper gave credit to the cavalry for having been so active in the recent campaign, stating that it had been in no less than 19 fights. If the weary troopers paid attention to such things, they may have argued that it felt like more.[33] Baker's and Jones's brigades continued their march to rejoin Stuart near Culpeper Court House. July 26 saw them pass through New Market, over the Massanutten, and through Luray before camping for the night. On the next day they crossed the mountains at Thornton's Gap and encamped near Sperryville just west of Amissville and Custer's outposts.[34]

The presence of these brigades attracted Custer's attention. At 1:00 in the afternoon of the 28th, Custer advised Pleasonton that 3,000 of the enemy's cavalry lay in and about Little Washington just north of Sperryville with pickets only two miles from his own at Gaines' Cross Roads. He bemoaned the fact that his weakened condition prevented him from striking at them, but he soothed his frustration with the knowledge that his supply train had arrived and his men and horses were now being fed.[35] Pleasonton immediately passed Custer's report along to army headquarters and received in turn a suggestion from Meade that one or two brigades be sent to reinforce Custer or replace him since the position he held was an important one. The perceived threat passed before Pleasonton could act when Baker and Jones moved on to Culpeper Court House.[36]

As Baker and Jones rode toward Culpeper to rendezvous with Stuart, other Confederates arrived at the cavalry chieftain's headquarters with prisoners in tow. Sergeant Fountain Beattie of Maj. John S. Mosby's command rode in, bringing with him 141 Federal officers and men along with harnesses, arms, and other equipment.[37] A continual thorn in the enemy's side, Mosby kept things stirred up behind Federal lines. His activities initiated repeated efforts to wipe him out. An expedition including the Sixth Ohio, Huey's brigade, Gregg's division, launched this same day failed to find a single ranger.[38] In the days ahead, Mosby persisted in his activities, and the Federals kept hunting.

July 29 brought more rain. For Lee and Stuart it also brought relief. Ewell arrived at Madison Court House, reuniting all of Lee's army.[39] Baker's and Jones's arrival the previous day gave Stuart six brigades to share the work of guarding the river crossings. Stuart quickly put Jones to use, having him relieve Fitz Lee's Brigade on the Rixeyville road. Fitz Lee pulled back to near Culpeper Court House. Baker's Brigade held to its camp near Culpeper to recuperate.[40] The Confederates had no desire to stir up the enemy, being quite content to maintain the status quo. Watching and only watching was all that Stuart demanded.

Meade wanted more. Buford, ever vigilant and attuned with Meade's desire to strike at the enemy, sent Capt. Alfred McQ. Corrigan with a squadron of the Ninth New York, Devin's brigade, across the Rappahannock at Freeman's Ford, even though the river had risen 15 inches.[41] On the other side, Corrigan divided his force into four parts, leaving a reserve troop at a fork in the road, sending two others toward the Hazel River along different routes, and holding the last at a central position as support for the other two. He discovered the Confederates at Rixey Ford felling trees and prepared to oppose any attempt at crossing. Buford reported Corrigan's findings to Pleasonton the next day, along with the fact that the river at last was falling.[42] Meade also received other good news during the night. His pontoon train finally had arrived at Rappahannock Station. The enterprising engineer in charge, Capt. George H. Mendell, had already picked out a site, stating that only enemy cavalry pickets held the other side.[43]

Because of all the good news, Meade began issuing orders on the 30th in preparation for crossing the Rappahannock. The Twelfth Corps received orders to march for Kelly's Ford and the Second to move to Morrisville to support the Twelfth. A timetable was established that set the crossing for the night of the 31st.[44] The cavalry shifted position only slightly. Gregg's division, minus Huey's brigade, rode for Amissville on the 29th to relieve Custer's division, which it did on the 30th. Custer then withdrew to Warrenton Junction.[45] McIntosh's and Col. Gregg's brigades camped a couple of miles beyond Warrenton on the Waterloo road for the night. The next day at 7:00 in the morning, they set out, crossed the Rappahannock, passed Merritt's Reserve brigade, and reached Amissville. The Sixteenth Pennsylvania, Gregg's brigade, drew outpost duty at Gaines' Cross Roads amidst a heavy downpour.[46] Buford watched the fords near Rappahannock Bridge and telegraphed Pleasonton that all were extremely high due to the rain. Those of Buford's command off duty rested and tended to their horses. They knew that a little water wasn't going to stop Buford.[47] With all the activity around them, some probably guessed that something would happen very soon.

Sometime during the 30th, Jeb Stuart sat down to write his wife, Flora, a letter. He reported his present location and the fact that his command had resumed its familiar role of being the "eyes and ears" of Lee's army. He complained of rain and mud, lamented his inability to bring back black silk for her from his northern excursion, and commented on the health of Maj. Heros von Borcke of his staff, who had been badly wounded at Upperville on June 19. Nowhere did he give any hint that his adversaries intended to pay him a visit anytime soon.[48] His men were equally at ease, resting in their camps. The Third Virginia, Fitz Lee's Brigade, even sent 60 men home to secure fresh horses.[49] The day passed uneventfully.

In comparison, the 31st bustled with activity for at least one of Stuart's brigades. Not surprisingly it turned out to be Fitz Lee's. Along with Lt. Charles R. Phelps's section of Capt. Marcellus N. Moorman's Battery and three guns from Capt. James Breathed's Battery, Lee reacted to scouting reports that came in during the morning by saddling up at 5:00 in the afternoon and riding toward Fredericksburg. Supposedly, Meade threatened to swing around Robert E. Lee's right flank, cross the Rappahannock, and seize the heights above the town. After riding all night, the brigade passed through Salem Church at 8:00 on the morning of August 1 before discovering that all had been a rumor and the enemy was not preparing to cross the river at Fredericksburg. The troopers promptly dismounted and made every effort to catch up on the sleep they had lost.[50]

The scouting reports that drew Fitz Lee's Brigade away from its post near Kelly's Ford had one thing correct. Meade was making preparations to cross, just not at Fredericksburg. John Buford could contain himself no longer and at 6:00 on the morning of August 1 threw 80 men over the Rappahannock, driving away the Confederate vedettes. He reported that the river had risen over three feet during the night, but was falling again. He warned that he could not cross any more of his command without a bridge and lamented that Capt. Mendell had no orders to construct one. Then Buford hunkered down to wait and see if his superiors would take advantage of his aggressiveness.[51]

Meade, however, was not prepared to follow Buford's lead just yet. Throughout the day, he continued to order his infantry corps about: the First to hold and picket the river from near Beverly Ford to Wheatley's Ford, to post a division at Rappahannock Station, to be prepared to cross the river as soon as a second bridge could be built there, and to keep a division at Bealton Station, guarding the railroad from the river to Warrenton Junction; the Second to shift one of its divisions to Elkton; the Third to hold and picket the river from Sulphur Springs to the forks of the river above Beverly Ford; the Fifth to mass near Fayetteville and be prepared to move in any direction; the Sixth to hold the river crossings at Waterloo, guard the river from Waterloo to Sulphur Springs, and protect the supply depot at Warrenton; the Eleventh to occupy Greenwich, Bristoe Station, Brentsville, and a point along Cedar Run four or five miles from the railroad, defending the army's rear; and the Twelfth to remain poised to cross the river at Kelly's Ford and watch the river from Wheatley's Ford to Ellis' Ford.[52]

Pleasonton also sent orders to his cavalry. Custer was to stay at Warrenton Junction to supply and refit. Buford, centered on Rappahannock Station, guarded the river from Kelly's Ford to Sulphur Springs. Two of Gregg's brigades, stationed at Amissville, were to picket from Sulphur Springs through Corbin's Cross Roads to Gaines' Cross Roads. The third, under Huey, received orders to march to Georgetown and from there, to scout and patrol the area all the way to Thoroughfare Gap. Gregg's orders also stated that he was to scout toward Sperryville and Little Washington. Gregg dispatched six companies of the First Pennsylvania, two from the First New Jersey, and two from the First Massachusetts, all from McIntosh's brigade, under Col. Horace B. Sargent of the latter regiment to probe toward the Hazel River beyond Rixeyville. Sargent crossed the river at Hill's Mill, ran into enemy vedettes, and swung northwest. With companies E and F of the First Pennsylvania in front, he attempted to drive toward Culpeper Court House but encountered stiff opposition. After a brief skirmish, Sargent pulled back to the Hazel and crossed at Oak Shade, having confirmed the strong presence of the Confederates. Another patrol led by Maj. Samuel B. M. Young of the Fourth Pennsylvania, Gregg's brigade, reconnoitered toward Little Washington, drove about 100 of Ferguson's cavalry through the village, and captured a private from the Second Virginia, who was on a supply-purchasing mission at the order of Fitz Lee.[53] The evidence suggested that the Confederates were present and not planning to leave in the near future.

As the army maneuvered itself into position, Meade's plan began to unfold. Maj. Gen. Henry W. Slocum, commanding the Twelfth Corps, reported to Meade at 11:00 at night that he had arrived at Kelly's Ford at 6:00 to find 100 troopers from the Fourth North Carolina of Robertson's Brigade holding the opposite side of the river. The Sixty-sixth Ohio Infantry crossed in boats and drove off the Confederates. Federal engineers went to work. The bridge had been finished and a full brigade of infantry had crossed the river. Two more brigades would cross at daylight.[54] Johnny Reb was in for a long day.[55]

John Buford roused his division between 1:00 and 3:00 in the morning but when orders failed to come had to watch them sit around and wait for almost eight hours. Exasperated, he sent portions of Merritt's brigade across the river about 5:00. Company L of the Second United States crossed first, using pontoon boats, and began skirmishing with the enemy. When the engineers finally completed the bridge between 10:00 and 11:00, Buford threw the remainder of his three brigades over the Rappahannock.[56] The Federal advance, consisting of the Sixth New York, Devin's brigade, proceeded only a short distance before encountering Confederate vedettes from Baker's Brigade in the first line of timber.[57] The skirmish lasted only a few minutes until it became clear to Baker's boys that the bluecoats were serious. Retreating rapidly, the thin gray line made for the rest of the brigade in position about a mile to the rear along the base of a hill.[58] Baker brought his regiments into line, placing the Jeff Davis Legion, Phillips Legion, and Cobb's Legion south of the railroad with the latter next to the tracks.[59] The Second South Carolina and the First South Carolina formed up on the north side of the railroad. Capt. James F. Hart's Battery of horse artillery unlimbered further to the left of the First South Carolina.[60]

Hart opened fire, but the blue cavalry pushed forward and overlapped the Confederate line, sending Hart rearward, and leaving Baker to delay the enemy as best he could.[61] As the Federal cavalry advanced in columns of squadrons by brigades, Baker saw that he had no choice but to fall back. To help gain time, Col. Pierce M. B. Young of Cobb's Legion at one point rode forward and began shouting out orders to imaginary troops in the hope that it might delay the enemy.[62] Throwing out skirmishers once again, the gray cavalry about faced and withdrew as slowly as the Federals would permit. Both Baker and Hart made stands on their way back to Brandy Station, but in each instance Buford, with Merritt's brigade on the right, Devin's in the center, and Gamble's, now under Col. George Chapman of the Third Indiana, on the left, outflanked them.[63]

Finally, Baker ordered a retreat to a position about a half-mile beyond the station, hoping to reform on a line between the Kennedy House on the right and the Botts farm on the left. Problems developed during the withdrawal. Hart's Battery came under attack by a Federal mounted column. With its guns limbered, the battery was defenseless. Seeing the danger, Lt. Col. Joseph F. Waring wheeled the Jeff Davis Legion around and, with Cobb's Legion in support, charged into the enemy ranks. The attack repulsed the Federals, and Hart galloped on to the Kennedy House hill. However, a new danger arose when another enemy squadron threatened Baker's right flank before it could take position. The First South Carolina and the Phillips Legion responded, charging into the midst of the blue cavalry and driving it back.[64]

The Kennedy Hill position proved less than ideal. The Orange & Alexandria Railroad traversed through the hill and when Baker finally formed the brigade the First North Carolina, the Second South Carolina, and the Cobb Legion came into line north of the railroad while the First South Carolina, the Jeff Davis Legion, and Phillips Legion formed up on the south side.[65] Skirmishers renewed their contest and squadrons charged with sabers drawn. Initially, Baker's regiments succeeded, only to be once again outflanked and forced to retreat. The scene played out repeatedly, but each time the Confederates retreated further.[66] Hart's Battery took position on the hill north of the railroad cut. Capt. William M. McGregor's Battery, under the capable command of Lt. Charles E. Ford, arrived and unlimbered next to Hart.[67] Despite the charges of the gray cavalry and the firing of the two batteries,

Hart's and Ford's position became increasingly untenable as Buford slowly pushed Baker back past the artillery south of the railroad, uncovering the batteries' right flank. Although the Federals could not get at the guns because of the cut, the cannoneers now became easier targets for the enemy's skirmishers. Nevertheless, the guns maintained their fire. The Ninth New York, Devin's brigade, fronted the Confederate artillery for quite sometime and suffered the effects of 20 shots that fell into its ranks, killing at least one and wounding several others.[68]

Buford wanted those guns and with his usual decisiveness and foresight had already taken steps to overcome the problem of the cut by sending Merritt further north of the artillery position under the cover of some woods. Shortly after Baker fell back, exposing the artillery's right flank, Merritt's brigade emerged from a line of trees on Hart's and Ford's left flank. Hart immediately saw that the guns were doomed unless he could hold off the enemy cavalry and get help from his own. Lt. Ford ordered his men to double load canister, the first time the gunners of McGregor's Battery had ever heard such an order, and to swing the guns around to face the oncoming blue cavalry.[69] Hart's gunners did the same and together both batteries opened a destructive fire that compelled Merritt's troopers to retreat. In the aftermath, Hart and Ford limbered and galloped rearward.[70]

Baker's retreat became a series of stands and charges by his regiments, with the horse artillery taking any position it could to add supporting fire. The withdrawal never became a rout, although there were moments that only Baker's leadership and the courage and determination of his men prevented it. In the swirling chaos a group of gray skirmishers became cut off and did not hear the order to fall back. Several couriers attempted to reach them, but all failed until Sergeant Major Richard T. Fulghum of the First North Carolina rode through the mêlée and delivered the message. The troopers successfully reached their lines and the retreat continued.[71] In an effort to stem yet another of Buford's flanking movements, Baker received a severe wound in his arm and relinquished command to Col. Pierce M. B. Young of Cobb's Legion. Soon after, Young, struck in the chest, left the field, turning command over to Col. John L. Black of the First South Carolina. He too fared no better and suffered a wound in the palm of the hand that compelled him to withdraw. Lt. Col. Thomas J. Lipscomb of the Second South Carolina likewise fell, wounded, leaving Lt. Col. William W. Rich of the Phillips Legion to command the brigade to the end of the fight.[72]

Between 4:00 and 5:00, the brigade took position within a mile and a half of Culpeper.[73] Here it finally received reinforcements.[74] The Twelfth Virginia Infantry of Brig. Gen. William Mahone's Brigade and the Twelfth Mississippi Infantry of Brig. Gen. Carnot Posey's Brigade were thrown out as skirmishers along the edge of a wood about a half a mile beyond the Bell house toward Culpeper and 500 yards across an open plain from the Federal dismounted skirmishers. Buford brought up Lt. Alexander C. M. Pennington's Battery M, Second U. S. Artillery and opened fire. The stalemate lasted only a short time. Then another of Stuart's brigades finally joined the fray. Brig. Gen. William E. Jones with his brigade and Capt. Roger

P. Chew's Battery of horse artillery joined Baker's line near the Bell farm.[75]

Coming from the direction of Rixeyville, Chew found himself on the right flank of Buford's line and hesitated not a moment in taking advantage of it, opening an enfilading fire that damaged one of the Federal guns. Seeing his flank in danger and pressed by infantry and cavalry to his front, Buford began a hasty retreat. Stuart rode in among the infantry skirmishers and gave the order to charge. The Federals now took their turn at holding and retreating, holding and retreating. Near the home of John Minor Botts, a huge cornfield stretched between the house and the railroad. Buford filled the field with dismounted men who fought furiously to hold their position and give time for their comrades to retreat. Chew's Battery raked the field and Stuart sent in his own dismounted skirmishers to drive the Federals out. Buford's withdrawal reached Brandy Station where the pursuit ended as darkness fell. During the fight Chew's Battery took no less than five different positions.[76]

Casualties on both sides reflected the day's hard fighting. Northern newspapers reported Buford's losses as 13 killed, 57 wounded, and 137 missing in Merritt's brigade; 4 killed,13 wounded, and 2 missing in Gamble's Brigade; 5 killed, 23 wounded, and 18 missing in Devin's Brigade; and 2 wounded in Pennington's battery.[77] Confederate losses were given at between 75 and 100 killed and wounded and about 50 prisoners. Every colonel who succeeded to the command of Baker's Brigade throughout the day was wounded. Capt. Edwin W. Branch of the Twelfth Virginia Infantry was killed and Lt. Robert P. P. Burwell of McGregor's Battery suffered a slight arm wound that proved fatal by the end of the month.[78]

The results of Buford's and Baker's brawling much favored the Federal commander. He accomplished his mission of establishing a solid bridgehead south of the Rappahannock and brought back confirmation of the presence of Lee's infantry near Culpeper. The question arises if Stuart could have done anything to prevent Buford's success. This is doubtful. Stuart's brigades were spread out along the Hazel and Rappahannock. Chambliss was encamped below Culpeper Court House and Fitz Lee near Salem Church. Neither of them could have offered any immediate help, and Stuart knew he had infantry to back him up near Culpeper. He seemed willing to trade ground and Baker's men for time. Stuart may have wanted a more rapid withdrawal that would have put less strain on Baker's troopers, but Buford's aggressiveness did not allow for it. By the time Stuart realized that Buford wanted more than just to drive in the Confederate picket line, it was too late to do anything but make a fighting retreat, the speed of which was what Buford and Baker argued about for several miles.

Beyond the speculation lies the fact that Baker had to face the enemy alone for longer than he, and probably Stuart, had anticipated. The gallant courage of the brigade caused Stuart to issue a general order, commending Baker's men and the horse artillery.[79] He also wrote to his wife Flora, stating that he had been with Baker during the entire fight and praising Baker and the brigade.[80] If the cavalry chieftain thought that his general order would appease the men, he greatly underestimated them, or at least those of Hart's Battery, who writing years after the war, still questioned their commander's reasoning.[81]

For Buford, no such questioning existed then or afterward. He received commendations from both the military and public sectors and deserved them.[82] His success broke open the river line and Meade's infantry tramped over the bridges to secure what Buford had bought with the blood and sweat of his men. Maj. Gen. John Newton, commanding the First Corps, reported late in the afternoon that in Buford's wake Brig. Gen. John C. Robinson's Second Division crossed the river along with portions of the Third Division, a force totaling 2,200 men. But Newton had no intention of staying. By morning, he wanted to pull all of his men back except for a strong outpost line. His whole purpose for crossing appeared to be a site-seeing expedition and a testing as to whether the bridge would hold up. At almost the same time, orders came from army headquarters, ordering Slocum to pull the major portion of his command back across the river at Kelly's Ford. The situation changed again late in the evening when Newton requested that another bridge be thrown over the river and asked for reinforcements from another corps.[83] The day closed with all sides trying to catch their collective breaths and wondering what the dawn would bring.[84]

During the final days of July while Meade had prepared for his visit across the river, Mosby continued to create havoc behind Federal lines. On the evening of July 30, the partisan chieftain struck, capturing 29 sutlers' wagons along the road between Germantown and Fairfax Court House that he whisked off toward Aldie. Unknown to the raiders, their first capture just east of Germantown had been reported to Brig. Gen. Rufus King, commanding the Federal forces in the area. He sent out word immediately to his cavalry commander, Col. Charles R. Lowell of the Second Massachusetts, who intercepted Mosby near Aldie, recapturing all of the wagons and scattering Mosby's small force. The setback deterred the intrepid Mosby not in the least and over the next few days he found other ways to harass the enemy and still avoid capture.[85]

The rest of the Federal cavalry carried on with its assigned work. Gen. Gregg kept his finger on the pulse of Ferguson's Brigade whose vedettes faced him at Gaines' Cross Roads and Newby's Cross Roads. He also confirmed that the Confederates had two guns stationed at the Rixeyville crossing of the Hazel River. The First Maine relieved the Sixteenth Pennsylvania, both in Col. Gregg's Brigade, on picket at Gaines' Cross Roads, but not before three enemy troopers gave themselves up to the Keystone Staters.[86] Custer, still refitting near Warrenton Junction, received orders to send out a detachment of men to hunt for guerrillas in the area between the Bull Run Mountains and Blue Ridge. The eight-day expedition began on August 1 and included 100 men from the Fifth and 150 from the Seventh Michigan regiments under the command of Col. William D. Mann of the Seventh. He spent the time chasing Mosby and Lt. Col. Elijah V. White across the countryside, visiting Salem, White Plains, Middleburg, Hopewell, Aldie, Rectortown, Haymarket, and Greenwich, succeeded in capturing about a dozen of Mosby's men, and returned without loss.[87]

Dawn on August 2 found the two foes of the previous day's fighting still staring at each other, waiting to see who would flinch first. Circumstances forced Buford, much against his nature, to take a step backward. He wrote in a dispatch to Pleasonton's headquarters that his men and horses needed water and recorded that he, himself, was "worthless" after the long fight under a relentless sun. He withdrew from his lines near Brandy Station to within a mile of the river, threw out the Eighth New York, Gamble's Brigade, and Ninth New York, the latter later relieved by the Seventeenth Pennsylvania, both from Devin's brigade, as vedettes and allowed his men to get whatever shade and rest they could. Stuart's pickets moved very little in following him, keeping about a mile and a half distant.[88]

Throughout the day, the sun beat down with equal intensity north of the Rappahannock. The men of the First Maine, Col. Gregg's brigade, Gen. Gregg's division, standing watch between Amissville and Little Washington and suffering through the heat like everyone else, yearned for cool weather – a feeling that pervaded both armies.[89] Private Allen L. Bevan of the First Pennsylvania, McIntosh's brigade, encamped near Amissville, speculated, "I think that Meade intends to advance and give Lee battle." [90] Fortunately, speculation did not require marching or fighting and could be done reclining peacefully in the shade. Others had to brave the broiling heat as duty demanded. Custer began to establish an outpost line east to Aquia Creek, using 600 men, presumably newly mounted, for that purpose. Huey still detached from Gregg's division, scoured the country near Georgetown looking for bushwhackers, some of whom had fired on his vedettes.[91] Undoubtedly, every man Custer sent on picket and Huey's entire brigade longed to be in the shade, speculating.

In the heat, Stuart's command did as little as required. Baker's Brigade squatted behind its outposts and tried to pull itself together. A private of the First North Carolina sent a short letter home to assure his family that he had survived another fight on the already bloody fields of Brandy Station. Others of the brigade undoubtedly did the same. Jones and Chambliss remained in support about two miles beyond Brandy Station. The Sixth, Seventh, and Twelfth Virginia stood grand guard all morning a mile back from the station and through the afternoon until 4:00. Nothing happened and they fell back to camp. Chew's Battery, having been without rations for two days, sent out men to search for green apples. On the evening of the 2nd, the battery limbered and rode back to the brigade's wagon park a mile south of Culpeper on the Orange Court House Road to have its horses shod. Robertson's Brigade resumed picket duty near Kelly's Ford. Fitz Lee's Brigade watched the lower Rappahannock from its camp near Salem Church.[92]

Buford roused himself and his men early on the 3rd. Responding to reports from his furthermost outposts that the enemy was advancing with cavalry, infantry, and artillery, he threw out his division and pushed a mile and a half forward until he came up against a strong Confederate picket line. The two battle flags that had been reported now appeared to fly over the Confederate reserves. Buford questioned the young officer who made the report. The man insisted that he had seen several regiments. Not one to take chances, especially with a river at his back, Buford sent out scouting parties, but when they reported nothing unusual, he pulled back to his old position, satisfied that there would be no trouble.[93] A little before noon, Buford received orders from Pleasonton to send a brigade to Kelly's Ford and have it establish outposts in the direction of Stevensburg. Buford dispatched Devin who arrived in the evening. Finding that the infantry had already withdrawn to the north side of the river, Devin did not cross, as Slocum had issued orders that anyone wishing to pass through his lines required his written permission. Pleasonton reacted swiftly, reporting to Meade that Slocum was interfering with his commanders. He stated that Devin's orders to scout toward Stevensburg had been countermanded by Slocum and that such action on the part of other infantry commanders would greatly affect the efficiency of the cavalry. Meade agreed and on the 4th sent an order to Slocum chastising him for holding back Devin and for withdrawing his own command north of the river. Meade further instructed Slocum to send Devin on his mission and to be prepared to support the cavalry should the enemy threaten it.[94]

About noon on the 3rd, Gen. Gregg received orders from Pleasonton, urging him to mount a reconnaissance toward Culpeper. A report had been received that Lee's wagon train was moving toward Orange Court House and that no camp smoke could be seen near Culpeper. Lee had indeed considered a new line of defense and on August 1 had ordered Ewell to have the area about one and a half miles from Orange Court House in the direction of the Rapidan examined by officers as a possible defensive position. Federal signal officers on Watery Mountain now were seeing the results of that survey in the movement of troops.[95] In compliance with his orders, Gregg sent scouting parties out in several directions, including one toward Gaines' Cross Roads. The First Massachusetts, McIntosh's brigade, under Col. Horace B. Sargent pushed to within two miles of Culpeper without encountering any opposition. At that point, it ran into a superior force and withdrew. Maj. Sidney W. Thaxter with a portion of the First Maine, Col. Gregg's brigade, trotted toward Keysville, capturing three members of the Second Virginia, Fitz Lee's Brigade, on the way to rejoin their regiment after separating from it at Winchester. Thaxter also gobbled up four horses, one abandoned limber, and one ambulance before returning. A detachment of the Tenth New York, Gregg's brigade, lead by Lt. Benjamin F. Sceva struck out for Little Washington where it clashed with 20 of the enemy, pushing them back through the hamlet, and capturing four prisoners belonging to the Seventeenth Virginia, Ferguson's Brigade. Capt. Patrick Kane took Company E, Thirteenth Pennsylvania, Gregg's brigade, on a 40 mile jaunt, returning to camp at Amissville without incident. From the information gathered, Gen. Gregg confirmed that the Confederates were indeed falling back.[96]

One hundred troopers from each of Custer's regiments undertook a reconnaissance toward Falmouth, returning by way of Stafford Court House. The excursion may have been a pleasant ride, although, considering the condition of the brigade's horses, the wear and tear on the men and animals may not have been worth the effort. Pvt. Charles H. Johnson of the First Michigan summed up his feeling about the expedition in a letter, "After a ride of 48 hours in the hot sun and only stopping twice to make coffee I do not know wheather [sic] it amounted to any thing . . . ."[97]

The withdrawal of the Confederate infantry over the Rapidan River placed Stuart in a difficult situation, which Robert E. Lee addressed on August 4. He informed his cavalry chief that the corps of Longstreet and Hill would cross the river that day. He cautioned Stuart that if given the chance the Federals would occupy Culpeper once the infantry had gone and suggested that it would be well if Stuart could hold it without sacrificing his men.[98] The probing done by the enemy on the previous day had already alerted Stuart to the threat and early on the 4th, he placed Jones's Brigade just outside of Culpeper along the Rixeyville road.[99] Then, rather than waiting for his adversaries to come calling, Stuart seized the initiative and attacked Buford between 1:00 and 2:00 in the afternoon. With the brigades of Chambliss, Ferguson, and Baker and at least six guns from four batteries of horse artillery under Maj. Robert F. Beckham, Stuart drove back Buford's picket line about 1,500 yards before running up against stiff resistance.[100]

This time Buford had fallen victim to surprise, having sent a dispatch to Pleasonton that morning, reporting all quiet on his front.[101] However, Beckham's artillery fire quickly brought the Federals to life. Roused from its repose by a shell that dropped right in front of its camp, the Sixth Pennsylvania, Merritt's brigade, rapidly deployed two mounted squadrons on the extreme right of the brigade's line. The Eighth New York, Gamble's brigade, also victims of the artillery fire, formed with its brother regiments on the left. Buford stabilized his line and began to push back. Battery B/L of the Second U. S. Artillery under Lt. Edward Heaton opened a galling fire on the lone 12 pounder from Moorman's Battery under Lt. Charles R. Phelps. The accurate fire hit every man serving the gun and so damaged the piece that after the fight it had to be sent back to Richmond for repairs.[102]

The fury of Buford's response bowled Stuart back over all the ground he had taken. Heaton's artillery continued to take its toll, mortally wounding Lt. Breckinridge C. Bouldin, adjutant of the Fourteenth Virginia, Ferguson's Brigade. Even when the Confederates reached their starting point, they could not stop the blue wave, which pushed them 800 yards beyond. Once again, darkness ended the fighting, but not before Stuart learned that the Federals were still in force in his immediate front with infantry encamped across the river. Not being able to drive Buford back over the river, Stuart contented himself with establishing a new picket line and sat down to watch and wait his worthy foe's next move. Stuart's reconnaissance-in-force cost him 6 killed and 18 wounded.[103]

While Merritt and Gamble welcomed Stuart into their camps for a brief visit, Buford's other brigade under Devin occupied itself by sending out two scouting parties from Kelly's Ford toward Stevensburg. The party on the main road ran into a strong force at the crossing of Mountain Run and could go no further. The other party, consisting of a squadron from the Sixth New York and one from the

Third West Virginia, encountered no pickets but did capture a trooper of the Fourth Virginia, Fitz Lee's Brigade, who divulged that Robertson's Brigade held Stevensburg and the position of all of Lee's corps. Devin suggested further scouting expeditions across Ellis' Ford.[104]

Elsewhere, events were less exciting. Custer's time as division commander ended when Kilpatrick returned and resumed his post.[105] The division remained in place around Warrenton Junction and along its picket line from near Kelly's Ford down river toward Fredericksburg. Col. Edward B. Sawyer, commanding the First Brigade, reported that his vedettes had been driven in the night before from the direction of Fredericksburg. The Tenth New York, Gregg's brigade, Gregg's division, almost received some payback at the hands of Ferguson's troopers who attacked the Tenth's outposts near Newby's Cross Roads at 5:00 in the morning, capturing three men. But the prisoners regained their freedom shortly afterward when elements of the Tenth charged and routed the Confederates.[106] Other portions of Gen. Gregg's command, including two squadrons from the Sixteenth Pennsylvania, Col. Gregg's brigade, again probed toward Culpeper during the day and found Jones awaiting them in strength. The Federals pulled back and settled in at Amissville.[107]

While Jones's, Ferguson's, Chambliss's, Robertson's, and Baker's brigades busied themselves in watching or fighting the enemy from Rixeyville to Kelly's Ford, Fitz Lee's troopers spent the day resting in their camps around Salem Church. Lt. Col. William R. Carter of the Third Virginia recorded that he concluded a court of inquiry on the 4th, ably demonstrating the amount of enemy activity the brigade faced. He even undertook a site-seeing excursion to Fredericksburg to view the old battlefield. The Rappahannock flowed quietly here, unmolested, as both sides showed no interest in crossing.[108]

August 5 began with a flurry of activity north of the river. Just after midnight, Gen. Gregg roused McIntosh who in turn shook Col. John P. Taylor of the First Pennsylvania from his blankets and sent him on another scout. The target was again Culpeper via Rixeyville. The First Pennsylvania, supplemented by a contingent from the First Maryland (Union), trotted away from its camp at 3:00 in the morning and reached the river at daybreak. Crossing, Taylor pushed on to Rixeyville where he learned that enemy skirmishers had moved in behind him. However, Taylor could not be turned from his mission that easily and leaving a squadron under Capt. Robert J. McNitt to guard his rear, he rode on to Muddy Run. Here the Federals encountered the Eleventh Virginia, Jones's Brigade, in numbers they could not budge and after an hour of skirmishing withdrew. Taylor did not come away empty handed, having acquired information that Jones's Brigade was encamped two miles beyond Muddy Run. Unfortunately, Taylor did not get there himself and had to rely on what he could learn from the local citizenry.[109]

Stuart was also up early and evidently wondering if he could recover some of the lost ground of the previous day. Buford reported that the Confederates attempted to drive back his outpost line at daylight only to be repulsed after a few shots.[110] Gamble's and Merritt's men rested easy in their camps. Further down stream, Devin took the offensive, sending a scouting party to Ellis' Ford.[111] The heavy rain of the previous night prevented the troopers from crossing the river. Devin also reported that Mountain Run was unfordable. He could not even cross his supply wagons at the Kelly's Ford pontoon bridge because Slocum issued orders that no wagons should be allowed to cross without orders direct from him. Worse, the ford was impractical for wagons, leaving Devin frustrated. He assured Buford that he would resume his reconnaissance missions as soon as the river subsided.[112]

After Col. Taylor's failed foray in the morning, Gen. Gregg bided his time until late in the afternoon. No longer content to sit idle, he dispatched another scouting party toward Culpeper. This time Col. Horace B. Sargent of the First Massachusetts took 300 men from his own regiment and contingents from the First Pennsylvania and the First New Jersey, all from McIntosh's brigade, and rode toward the Hazel River. He arrived near sundown and crossed where Gourd Vine Creek joined the river. As soon as he crossed, troopers from Jones's Brigade barred his way. Perceiving a threat to his left flank if he pushed forward, Sargent shifted to his right and swung south, crossing Muddy Run without opposition. He approached Rixeyville from the south and again ran into more of Jones's outposts three miles from the hamlet. Avoiding further confrontation in the dark, Sargent guided his men to Rixey Ford and crossed at 2:00 in the morning. He concluded that the enemy still held Culpeper in strength but were withdrawing closer to the town.[113]

Like Gregg, Devin abhorred inactivity. As the river fell, he ordered another reconnaissance and sent out two squadrons, one from the Sixth New York commanded by Capt. John Pierce and one from the Third West Virginia under Capt. Everton J. Conger. Pierce first clashed with the enemy at the junction of the Kelly's Ford and the Germanna Plank roads. Outnumbered, Pierce skirmished briefly to reveal the Confederates' strength, losing one horse killed, before falling back and heading toward the Rapidan. Between Pierce and Conger several fords on the Rapidan were visited. At Ely's the enemy held the ford on the north bank but quickly retreated across the ford and into the trees. The two squadrons returned to Kelly's Ford with much more information than the morning patrols.[114]

Except for the brief encounters with probing Federal patrols and the ever-popular picket duty, Stuart's troopers rested in their camps. The seemingly continuous activity of the Federal cavalry, while bothersome, did not appear to be anything of major concern. The strain of the previous weeks of marching and fighting had begun to take a firm grip on both armies. Meade sat in his camp awaiting reinforcements. Washington cautioned him to use the time to recruit his animals, collect forage and provisions, and deal with the guerilla problem. Lee pondered Meade's next move, dealt with the news that the army's rations might have to be reduced, requested arms for 1,700 men who had no weapons, and advised Richmond on how to improve the rail transportation.[115] Even with the armies stagnant, both commanders had work to do. Unlike many of their men, they could not look forward to a rest anytime soon.

Notes:

1.   *O.R.*, Series 1, vol. 27, part 3, 765-766; Morey Diary.
2.   *O.R.*, Series 1, vol. 27, part 3, 768; Ressler Diary; Yoder Diary; Smith, *"Scott's 900,"* 111; Lloyd, *History of the First Regiment Pennsylvania Reserve Cavalry*, 68.

    One source provided evidence that McIntosh or a portion of his command was still at Ashby's Gap as late as 5:00 in the afternoon of the 26th. Sauerburger, ed., *I Seat Myself to Write You*, 164.
3.   *O.R.*, Series 1, vol. 27, part 1, 946; Chapman Diary; Frank Diary; Cheney Diary; Inglis Diary; Cheney, *Ninth Regiment, New York Volunteer Cavalry*, 126; *Chicago Tribune*, July 28, 1863.
4.   Diary of Lawson Morrissett, Fourth Virginia Cavalry, Eleanor S. Brockenbrough Library, MOC.
5.   Carter Diary.
6.   R. L. T. Beale, *History of the 9th Virginia Cavalry in the War Between the States* (Amissville: American Fundamentalist, 1981), 98.
7.   The location of this brigade is muddled to say the least. Three sources state that it accompanied Fitz Lee's and Chambliss's brigades across the Shenandoah through Chester Gap toward the Rappahannock. However, other sources state that the brigade remained in the Valley with Imboden's Brigade near Winchester. The fact that the Fourteenth Virginia's adjutant, Lt. Breckinridge C. Bouldin, was killed in the fight near Brandy Station on August 4 would seem to establish the brigade's presence with Stuart. *O.R.*, Series 1, vol. 27, part 2, 707; Robert J. Driver, Jr., *14th Virginia Cavalry* (Lynchburg: H. E. Howard, Inc., 1988), 25 and 103; J. L. Scott, *36th and 37th Battalions Virginia Cavalry* (Lynchburg: H. E. Howard, Inc., 1986), 6; Jack L. Dickinson, *16th Virginia Cavalry* (Lynchburg: H. E. Howard, Inc., 1989), 32; John Harper Dawson, *Wildcat Cavalry: A Synoptic History of The Seventeenth Virginia Cavalry Regiment of The Jenkins-McCausland Brigade in The War Between the States* (Dayton: Morningside House, Inc., 1982), 27. Hopkins, *The Little Jeff*, 165; Moore and Moore, *Chained to Virginia*, 161.
8.   Donahue Diary.
9.   Hawse wrote that the Eleventh Virginia camped at Rude's Hill. Hawse Diary. *O.R.*, Series 1, vol. 27, part 3, 772.
10.   Gregg's regiments had spent the 25th and 26th picketing the line of the Rappahannock south of Bealton Station, including Beverly, Kelly's, and Norman's fords. Smith, *"Scott's 900,"* 111.
    Cheney Diary; Chapman Diary; Frank Diary.
11.   Merritt's Reserve Brigade encamped near Warrenton. Private Michael Donlon of the Second U. S. Cavalry wrote that he had arrived there the previous night after fighting at Manassas Gap for two days. In his short letter he added that his regiment was saddled and he expected to leave and return to the fighting at any minute. Michael Donlon to Dear Brother, July 27, 1863, Michael Donlon Letters, CWMC, USAMHI. *O.R.*, Series 1, vol. 27, part 3, 772.
12.   At least two regiments, the Sixteenth Pennsylvania and the Tenth New York, did picket duty below Bealton Station on the 26th and may have reported about the bridge. Ressler Diary; Yoder Diary. *O.R.*, Series 1, vol. 27, part 3, 772.
13.   In a letter to Flora on July 30, Stuart mentioned that it was raining every day. A mem-
14.   ber of the Third Indiana Cavalry recorded a severe rain on the night of the 25th/26th. J. E. B. Stuart to My Darling Wife [Flora Stuart], July 30, 1863, Stuart Papers, 1851-

1968, Mss1ST923d, Microfilm reel C621, VHS; Samuel J. B. V. Gilpin Diary, E. N. Gilpin Papers, 1861-1911, Manuscript Division, LC.
15. *Richmond Enquirer*, August 1, 1863.
16. *Chicago Tribune*, July 30, 1863.
17. *O.R.*, Series 3, vol. 3, 1041.
     A communication dated October 30, 1863, gave the numbers 5,073 for May and 6,927 for June. August would see 5,499 horses issued with 5,827 for September, and another 7,036 in October. *O.R.*, Series 1, vol. 29, part 2, 398.
18. *O.R.*, Series 3, vol. 3, 580.
19. *Ibid.*, 580-581.
20. Despite the Cavalry Bureau's efforts over the next few months, the situation remained for the most part unaltered. In a November 15 report written by Maj. Gen. Henry W. Halleck to Secretary of War Edwin M. Stanton, Halleck stated that the War Department could look to remounting all of its 223 cavalry regiments every two months during the next year. The horses required would total 435,000. He cited that the problems the Cavalry Bureau was to have addressed remained and that the primary fault lay with the treatment of the horses by the cavalry soldiers themselves. This, of course, ignored the factors of disease, lack of horseshoes, and a chronic absence of proper feed, none of which could be laid at the boots of the troopers.
     Nevertheless, Halleck's solution was to reassign any trooper to the infantry whose horse suffered, through the soldier's own neglect, and was rendered unfit for service. This also was to be applied to officers who failed to maintain the efficiency of their regiments. While such neglectful officers and men certainly existed in the cavalry service, proving that the neglect was intentional on the part of the officers and soldiers had the potential to tie up military courts everywhere throughout the armies.
     The War Department was attempting to solve an almost insoluble problem. Hard service resulted in attrition of both men and horses. While care for the animals was vital, when on campaign it was at times set aside by men who often ate sparingly, if at all, got little sleep, suffered through all kinds of weather, and put themselves in harms way every day. The circumstances of war dictated that the horses would suffer as well. Washington failed to understand this. *Ibid.*, 1042.
21. *O.R.*, Series 1, vol. 27, part 3, 1049-1051.
22. *Ibid.*, 1054-1055.
23. Stuart had broached this subject with Lee in a communication dated May 27, 1863. Stuart suggested an increase in the number of brigades and the formation of divisions. At that time Lee did not think that such changes were warranted unless additional cavalry regiments could be formed or added to Stuart's command. *O.R.*, Series 1, vol. 25, part 2, 836-837.
24. Because of its assignment to the Valley, Jenkins's (Ferguson's) Brigade would not be included in the reorganization.
25. *O.R.*, Series 1, vol. 27, part 3, 1068-1069.
     On July 30, Baker received a promotion to brigadier general and assumed permanent command of the brigade, Lee having asked for it previously. James B. Gordon became colonel of the First North Carolina, replacing Baker. Manarin, *North Carolina Troops*, 4; Ezra J. Warner, *Generals in Gray* (Baton Rouge: Louisiana State University Press, 1959), 15.
26. Carter Diary; Gilpin Diary.
27. John Inglis to Dear Parents, July 29, 1863; John Inglis Papers, SC22716 Box 1 Folder

1, NSL; Cheney, *Ninth Regiment, New York Volunteer Cavalry*, 126.

    The Eighth Illinois, Gamble's brigade, sent 113 sick and wounded men that had accompanied the regiment until it finally had the opportunity to address their needs to Washington hospitals. Hard, *Eighth Illinois Cavalry*, 267.

28. Chapman Diary; Cheney Diary; Frank Diary; Inglis Diary; Blackwell, *12th Illinois Cavalry*, 117.
29. *O.R.*, Series 1, vol. 27, part 3, 775. Hoffman, *First Vermont*, 127-128; Glazier, *Three Years*, 309-310.
30. Benjamin W. Crowninshield, *A History of the First Regiment of Massachusetts Cavalry Volunteers,* (Boston: Houghton, Mifflin and Company, 1891), 167; Rawle, *Third Pennsylvania Cavalry*, 326; Lloyd, *History of the First Regiment Pennsylvania Reserve Cavalry*, 68; Tobie, *First Maine Cavalry*, 189; Smith, *"Scott's 900,"* 111.
31. *O.R.*, Series 1, vol. 27, part 3, 776.
32. Yoder Diary.
33. Morrissett Diary; Carter Diary; *Richmond Enquirer*, August 1, 1863.
34. Donahue Diary; Hawse Diary; Arehart, "Diary of W. H. Arehart," 215; Hopkins, *The Little Jeff*, 165; Moore and Moore, *Chained to Virginia*, 161; Neese, *Three Years in the Confederate Horse Artillery*, 201.
35. *O.R.*, Series 1, vol. 27, part 3, 775.
36. *Ibid.*, 776; Donahue Diary; Hawse Diary; Hopkins, *The Little Jeff*, 165; Neese, *Three Years in the Confederate Horse Artillery*, 201.
37. *O.R.*, Series 1, vol. 27, part 2, 991.
38. Martin Oviatt Diary, Martin Oviatt Papers, Microfilm 21,640-1P, LC.
39. *O.R.*, Series 1, vol. 27, part 2, 324.
40. Carter Diary; Donahue Diary; Hawse Diary; Hopkins, *The Little Jeff*, 165; Neese, *Three Years in the Confederate Horse Artillery*, 202; David G. Douglas, *A Boot Full of Memories: Captain Leonard Williams, 2nd South Carolina Cavalry* (Camden: Gray Fox, 2003), 249; Moore and Moore, *Chained to Virginia*, 161.
41. Brig. Gen. John Buford to Maj. Gen. Alfred Pleasonton, July 29, 1863, Telegrams Collected by the Secretary of War, Unbound, RG 107, M504, National Archives and Records Administration, (hereafter cited as NARA).
42. *O.R.*, Series 1, vol. 27, part 3, 781-782.

    The rest of Buford's regiments kept to their camps or continued with picket duty. In the afternoon, the Twelfth Illinois returned to picket at Kelly's Ford. Chapman Diary; Cheney Diary; Inglis Diary; Frank Diary.

43. *O.R.*, Series 1, vol. 27, part 3, 782.
44. *Ibid.*, 783-784.
45. Morey Diary; Frederick Bush to Dear Father, August 1, 1863, Christian and Frederick Bush Collection, MS 2004-22, Box 1, Folder 1, Archives of Michigan (hereafter cited as AM).

    Custer took time on the 29th to chastise a local citizen named "Major" Williams. According to one of the Michigan Brigade's troopers, who had escaped from local bushwhackers, Williams had been acting as a scout for the Confederate cavalry. The trooper claimed to have seen him among his captors. Custer sent a portion of the First Michigan to burn Williams's house near Salem in retaliation. *Detroit Free Press*, August 8, 1863.

46. *O.R.*, Series 1, vol. 27, part 1, 983 and 1004; Ressler Diary; Yoder Diary; Rawle, *Third Pennsylvania Cavalry*, 326; Tobie, *First Maine Cavalry*, 189; Smith, *"Scott's 900,"* 111.

    According to two sources, Huey's brigade marched to within a few miles of Warrenton on the 29th and then countermarched to its former campground, this being further east of Warrenton toward Warrenton Junction. The brigade remained here on the 30th, the Sixth Ohio doing picket duty east of the junction at Weaverville. The brigade had lost a large number of horses condemned as being unserviceable, which undoubtedly contributed to its not accompanying Gregg to Amissville. Oviatt Diary; Glazier, *Three Years*, 310-311.

47. Gilpin Diary; Frank Diary; Cheney Diary; Brig. Gen. John Buford to Maj. Gen. Alfred Pleasonton, July 31, 1863, Telegrams Collected by the Secretary of War, Unbound, RG 107, M504, NARA; Blackwell, *12th Illinois Cavalry*, 117-118.

48. J. E. B. Stuart to My Darling Wife [Flora Stuart], July 30, 1863, Stuart Papers, 1851-1968, Mss1ST923d, Microfilm reel C621, VHS.

49. Morrissett Diary; Donahue Diary; Neese, *Three Years in the Confederate Horse Artillery*, 202; Carter Diary.

50. Carter Diary; Trussell Diary; Morrissett Diary; Hubard, *Memoirs*, 106; Shoemaker, *Shoemaker's Battery*, 50; Robert J. Trout, ed., *Memoirs of the Stuart Horse Artillery Battalion: Moorman's and Hart's Batteries* (Knoxville: The University of Tennessee Press, 2008), 61.

51. *O.R.*, Series 1, vol. 27, part 3, 787-788.
   Just what regiment the 80 men belonged to cannot be determined. However, none of the regiments in Gamble's brigade appear to have been involved and Devin's brigade was up river near Fox's Ford. That leaves Merritt's brigade as the most likely to have supplied the troopers. Chapman Diary; Cheney Diary; Frank Diary; Inglis Diary; Cheney, *Ninth Regiment, New York Volunteer Cavalry*, 126.

52. *O.R.*, Series 1, vol. 27, part 3, 788-790, 793-794.
   Elkton was another name for Elk Run.

53. *Ibid.*, 790-792; Oviatt Diary; Sauerburger, ed., *I Seat Myself to Write You*, 165; *New York Herald,* August 4, 1863.

54. *O.R.*, Series 1, vol. 27, part 3, 791.

55. This crossing of the Rappahannock undoubtedly "surprised" Stuart, as had the one on June 9, 1863. But so had the crossings on December 31, 1862, March 17, 1863, April 14, 1863, and April 28, 1863. Other "surprises" lay in the future. Of course, much is made of the June 9 crossing as it has been labeled the beginning of the Gettysburg campaign. For that reason and that reason only has it garnered a significant amount of attention. That the other "surprises" have been almost completely ignored makes the June 9 "surprise" stand out.
   Should Stuart have known about all these crossings before they happened? The answer is no. With a river between opposing forces, it was very difficult to discover an enemy's intentions. Stuart's men could scout an area when no natural obstacles prevented free movement. However, a river poses a number of problems to the normal scouting mission. Even if a scout is undertaken, it might simply result in discovering that the enemy is present in strength on the other side of the fords, as had several Federal patrols already mentioned. Should a ford be crossed, the chances of discovering anything of significance is very small and the danger to the scouting party very great. An individual can achieve greater success, but even he is limited to his observations and his interpretations of them. Scouting may be able to uncover troop locations, supply depots, and the like. What it cannot reveal are plans. This falls into the realm of espionage. Plans to cross a river are usually not divulged to officers and men below a certain rank and the capturing of such men by scouting parties would not necessarily reveal what is really taking place. Expecting Stuart to know

every time the Federals planned to push across the river is unreasonable.

56.   *O.R.*, Series 1, vol. 27, part 1, 931-932, part 3, 819-821; Michael Donlon to Dear Brother, August 8, 1863, CWMC, USAMHI; Chapman Diary; Cheney Diary; Frank Diary.

      An exchange of messages involving Buford, Meade, Mendell, Gouverneur K. Warren, Pleasonton, and Meade's Chief of Staff, C. Ross Smith, shows considerable confusion in the army's higher command. Buford was prepared to cross at Rappahannock Station but could not get the engineers to co-operate. Mendell inquired of Warren if he was to build the bridge for Buford. Warren told Mendell that a bridge had already been laid at Kelly's Ford for Buford's use. Pleasonton told Buford that Buford's orders stated that he was to cross at Kelly's. Buford informed Pleasonton that he would cross at Rappahannock Station as soon as a bridge was laid. Smith informed Buford that Mendell had orders not to throw the bridge across the river at the station until Buford had crossed at Kelly's. How much the delay affected Buford's subsequent actions cannot be determined.

57.   *History of the Sixth New York Cavalry*, 153; *New York Times*, August 8, 1863; *Weekly State Journal,* August 26, 1863.

58.   One source gave the brigade's strength at the beginning of the fight as 800 men. A second stated the brigade strength as 935. Douglas, *A Boot Full of Memories*, 253; Eleanor D. McSwain, ed., *Crumbling Defenses or Memoirs and Reminiscences of John Logan Black, Colonel C. S. A.* (Macon: J. W. Burke Company, 1960), 56.

59.   One source places Cobb's Legion on the far right on the road to Kelly's Ford. *Weekly State Journal*, August 26, 1863.

60.   The source for this alignment does not include the First North Carolina. One source stated that at least two companies, "C" and "F," were acting as skirmishers on the left of the line. Most likely, this regiment had supplied the pickets and the skirmishers that the Federals first encountered. The remainder of the regiment could have been reforming, possibly behind the hill or in support of Hart's Battery, or moving out to the flanks. Samuel Elias Mays, "Sketches from the Journal of a Confederate Soldier," *Tyler's Quarterly Historical and Genealogical Magazine* 5 (1923): 2, 97; *Weekly State Journal*, August 26, 1863.

      In a history of the battery, Hart stated that the brigade's and his first position was on Fleetwood Hill and that the battery took almost the same exact position it held during the battle on June 9. One other source mentions that Hart occupied Fleetwood Hill. This must have been at the start of the fighting, because all other accounts have the cavalry fighting located along the railroad and not on Fleetwood Hill. If Hart unlimbered on Fleetwood Hill at all, it could only have been for a brief time as Buford rapidly pushed along the railroad, driving Baker before him. Hart must have moved up to support Baker very early in the fighting. Trout, ed., *Memoirs*, 219-220; *Weekly State Journal*, August 26, 1863.

61.   Several sources stated that the Confederate artillery opened fire early in the fight, but that Buford's guns were not used to any extent. *Washington Daily Morning Chronicle*, August 6, 1863; *Richmond Enquirer*, August 7, 1863; *New York Times*, August 8, 1863.

62.   Mays, "Sketches," 98; *Weekly State Journal*, August 26, 1863.

63.   *New York Times*, August 8, 1863.

      Chapman assumed temporary command of Gamble's brigade on July 31. Chapman Diary.

64.   Brooks, ed., *Stories*, 189; Hopkins, *The Little Jeff*, 166.

65. McSwain, *Crumbling Defenses*, 57.

66. Brooks, ed., *Stories*, 190.

67. One account indicates that McGregor's Battery may have been with Hart from the beginning or joined him before taking position on Kennedy House hill. George W. Shreve, "Reminiscences in the History of The Stuart Horse Artillery, C. S. A.," Roger Preston Chew Papers, Jefferson County Historical Society, Charles Town, WV.

68. Cheney, *Ninth Regiment, New York Volunteer Cavalry*, 126-127.

69. Trout, ed., *Memoirs*, 220; Shreve, "Reminiscences."

70. According to Shreve's account, McGregor's Battery limbered to the rear, but Hart gave a different version of how his battery retreated.

    Hart stated that all of the Confederate cavalry took position on the east side of the railroad, leaving his battery and McGregor's alone on the west side of the tracks without cavalry support. Once Merritt had been repulsed, Hart felt that his only hope was to gain the east side of the tracks, but to do so would mean the advancing enemy squadrons pursuing Baker's regiments would have to be checked. Seeing Lt. Col. John D. Twiggs of the First South Carolina on the other side of the cut, Hart sent a message to him, asking if Twiggs would turn around and charge the Federal cavalry behind him in an effort to buy enough time for the artillery to limber and reach the railroad crossing to its front near the base of the hill. Twiggs agreed to try, swung his regiment around, and charged. As the South Carolinians thundered down the slope of Kennedy House hill in column of fours, Hart and Ford limbered their guns, galloped forward toward the crossing, and dashed over the tracks in rear of Twiggs who held the enemy in check long enough for the artillery to make its escape.

    Hart's account seems improbable. For Baker to leave his artillery isolated and unsupported against an enemy that had advanced over three miles with troops on both sides of the railroad would have been a terrible error in tactics. Additionally, other crossings existed behind the Confederates, toward Culpeper. The crossing to Hart's front was not his only means of escape.

    Trout, ed., *Memoirs*, 220; Shreve, "Reminiscences."

71. *Weekly State Journal*, August 26, 1863

72. Chris J. Hartley, *Stuart's Tarheels: James B. Gordon and His North Carolina Cavalry* (Baltimore: Butternut and Blue, 1996), 253; Brooks, ed., *Stories*, 190; *Richmond Daily Dispatch*, August 3, 1863; *Richmond Enquirer*, August 4, 1863.

    According to one source, Baker and Young received their wounds near the Kennedy House position, while Black received his near Culpeper Court House when rallying on the infantry line. McSwain, *Crumbling Defenses*, 57-59.

73. *Richmond Enquirer*, August 4, 1863; *Richmond Daily Dispatch*, August 6, 1863; *Richmond Whig*, August 12, 1863.

74. *O.R.*, Series 1, vol. 27, part 1, 932.

    The question arises as to why Stuart failed to bring Chambliss's Brigade into the fight. According to Col. R. L. T. Beale of the Ninth Virginia, the brigade, minus the Fifteenth Virginia, guarding Bank's Ford on the Rappahannock near Salem Church, was encamped near the Botts farm and could have joined Baker in the fight even before the Confederates reached Brandy Station. However, this appears to have been a general statement by Beale, regarding the first location of the brigade upon its return to the area following the Gettysburg campaign. There is evidence that Chambliss had moved his camp before the fight. In a letter dated August 11, 1863, Private John O. Collins of the Tenth Virginia wrote that he was camped six miles below Culpeper Court House and described riding to the battle and going directly into it, driving the enemy back beyond Brandy Station. This explains why Chambliss did not support Baker immediately. It also confirms that Stuart did bring Chambliss into the fight, probably about the same time as Jones. John O. Collins Letter, August 11, 1863, John Overton Collins Papers (Mss1C6944a), VHS; John Fortier, *15th Virginia Cavalry*, (Lynchburg: H. E. Howard, Inc., 1993), 37; Beale, *9th Virginia Cavalry*, 98.

75. Major Daniel A. Grimsley, *Battles in Culpeper County, Virginia, 1861-1865* (Culpeper: Raleigh Travers Green, publisher, 1900), 14, Accession #F232.C9G8 (also Fiche 105 VA: 129 and Fiche 157 Unit 5 VA59), LV; *Weekly State Journal*, August 26, 1863.

   One source stated that Jones arrived at 3:00, but this seems to be too early and does not coincide with other sources. Ada Bruce Desper Bradshaw, Ed., *The Civil War Diary of Charles William McVicar*, (no publisher, 1977), 21.

76. *Ibid.*; Bradshaw, *Diary...McVicar*, 21-22; Grimsley, *Battles in Culpeper County*, 14; Neese, *Three Years in the Confederate Horse Artillery*, 203-204; *Richmond Enquirer*, August 7, 1863; *Richmond Daily Dispatch*, August 11, 1863.

77. *Washington Daily Morning Chronicle*, August 6, 1863; *Philadelphia Press*, August 7, 1863; *New York Times*, August 8, 1863.

   All of these papers reported that the First U. S. Cavalry suffered between five and ten killed. The lower number has been used in these calculations.

78. Robert J. Trout, *The Hoss: Officer Biographies and Rosters of the Stuart Horse Artillery Battalion* (Myerstown: JebFlo Press, 2003), 124; Trout, ed., *Memoirs*, 220; Shreve, "Reminiscences;" *Richmond Whig*, August 3 and August 8, 1863; *Richmond Daily Dispatch*, August 3, 1863; *Washington Daily Morning Chronicle*, August 6, 1863.

   One source gave the number of Confederates captured at 100, including some wounded. *New York Herald*, August 3, 1863.

   Stuart gave an account of his casualties to his wife, Flora, as being 15 mortally wounded or killed, 35 wounded, and 3 or 4 missing. J. E. B. Stuart to My Darling Wife [Flora Stuart], August 2, 1863, Stuart Papers, 1851-1968, Mss1ST923d, Microfilm reel C621, VHS.

79. Brooks, ed., *Stories*, 191.

80. J. E. B. Stuart to My Darling Wife [Flora Stuart], August 2, 1863, Stuart Papers, 1851-1968, Mss1ST923d, Microfilm reel C621, VHS.

81. Trout, ed., *Memoirs*, 220.

82. *O.R.*, Series 1, vol. 27, part 3, 824; *Washington Daily Morning Chronicle*, August 6, 1863; *Philadelphia Press*, August 7, 1863; *New York Times*, August 8, 1863.

83. *O.R.*, Series 1, vol. 27, part 3, 823-825.

84. One regiment that had stayed out of the fight chose to take on another antagonist in the form of the Confederate government. Members of the Fifth North Carolina, then encamped near Culpeper, took the time, while their comrades in arms struggled with the blue cavalry, to compose a letter to North Carolina governor Zebulon B. Vance, requesting that he use his influence to have them recalled home. They cited ill treatment, the lack of opportunity to gain plunder and fresh horses in Pennsylvania and Maryland during the recent northern invasion, the condition of their horses, and the winnowing of their effective strength as a brigade from 1400 to less than 400. They offered that if allowed to return they would not only recuperate but also prevent future raids by Federal forces in the state.

   If Vance attempted to use his position to have the brigade recalled, he failed. The brigade remained with Lee's army, although its commander, Beverly Robertson, did get to go home. The Fourth and Fifth North Carolina became part of Brig. Gen. James B. Gordon's Brigade when the cavalry reorganized. Governor's Papers – Zebulon Baird Vance, 1862-1865, 1877-1879, Box GP 168, Folder 8/1 – 4/63, North Carolina State Archives.

 Some verification concerning the horse situation in the brigade comes from two letters. In the first, Sgt. Abraham G. Jones of the Fifth North Carolina on August 3 stated that he saw about 100 men from the brigade at Orange Court House who had lost their horses during the Gettysburg campaign and confirmed that the brigade lost a great many horses in Pennsylvania. Abraham G. Jones to Dear Ellick, August 3, 1863, Abraham G. Jones Papers, Collection No. 135, East Carolina Manuscript Collection, Joyner Library, East Carolina University (hereafter cited as ECMC/JL/ECU).

 In the second, Pvt. M. P. Person, a farrier in the First North Carolina, wrote on August 18 from North Garden Depot southwest of Charlottesville that 160 horses from his regiment were there trying to be strengthened and healed so they could return to the front. M. P. Person to Dear Father, August 18, 1863, Southgate-Jones Family Papers, Box 1, Folder 1862-1863, WRP/DU.

85. *O.R.*, Series 1, vol. 27, part 2, 988-992; *New York Herald*, August 2, 1863.

86. *O.R.*, Series 1, vol. 27, part 3, 820; Yoder Diary.

 The two guns were from Capt. Roger P. Chew's Battery. Bradshaw, *Diary... McVicar*, 21.

 A dawn scout to the Hazel River by the First Pennsylvania, McIntosh's Brigade, revealed the Confederates still in possession of the opposite bank and taking rapid steps to strengthen their position. The Pennsylvanians chose not to force a crossing, camping instead within visual range of the graycoats. A truce was quickly formed that prohibited any shooting unless either side made an effort to cross. The day passed peacefully. Lloyd, *History of the First Regiment Pennsylvania Reserve Cavalry*, 69.

87. *O.R.*, Series 1, vol. 27, part 2, 992-994; John A. Clark to My Dear Friend, August 10, 1863, Clark-Whedon Papers, James S. Schoff Civil War Collection, Manuscripts Division, William L. Clements Library, University of Michigan (hereafter cited as WLC/UM); John B. Kay to Dear Sister Jennie, August 1, 1863; John B. Kay Papers, Microfilm mf468 c, BHL/UM; George Harrington Diary, Dr. Allan Giddings Collection, 1859-1876, Call No. A-333, Western Michigan University Archives & Regional History Collection, Western Michigan University (hereafter cited as WMUARHC/WMU); Allyne C. Litchfield to My Dear Wife, August 1, 1863, Allyne Cushing Litchfield Papers, James S. Schoff Civil War Collection, Manuscripts Division, WLC/UM.

 Some confusion at brigade headquarters had Mann receiving one set of orders and his second-in-command, Lt. Col. Allyne C. Litchfield, receiving another. While visiting at headquarters, Litchfield had been ordered to take the Seventh toward Stafford Court House and Aquia Creek. Mann cleared up the mess and his orders stood. Allyne C. Litchfield to My Dear Wife, August 1, 1863, Allyne Cushing Litchfield Papers, James S. Schoff Civil War Collection, Manuscripts Division, WLC/UM.

88. *O.R.*, Series 1, vol. 27, part 3, 827; Cheney Diary; Frank Diary; Inglis Diary.

89. Richard Henry Watkins to Mary Watkins, August 5, 1863, Watkins Papers, 1861-1865, Mss1W3272a1-355, VHS; Alvin N. Brackett to Dear Friend Hattie, August 2, 1863, Brackett Letters, Gregory A. Coco Collection, HCWRTC, USAMHI.

90. Allen L. Bevan to Dear Sister, August 2, 1863, Allen L. Bevan Letters, CWMC, USAMHI.

91. *O.R.*, Series 1, vol. 27, part 3, 830.

92. Donahue Diary; William H. Arehart, "Diary of W. H. Arehart," *The Rockingham Recorder* 1 (December, 1948): 4, 271; Bradshaw, *Diary...McVicar*, 22; Cadwallader Jones Iredell to My Dear Mattie, August 2, 1863, Cadwallader Jones Iredell Papers, 363-Z,

Folder 1, Correspondence 1862-1863, Southern Historical Collection, Wilson Library, University of North Carolina at Chapel Hill (hereafter cited as SHC/UNC); Neese, *Three Years in the Confederate Horse Artillery*, 204; Manarin, *North Carolina Troops*, 264 and 369; Carter Diary; Morrissett Diary; Collins Letter.

93. *O.R.*, Series 1, vol. 27, part 3, 831; Chapman Diary; Frank Diary.

94. *O.R.*, Series 1, vol. 27, part 3, 829, 832-834, 839-840; Inglis Diary; Cheney, *Ninth Regiment, New York Volunteer Cavalry*, 128; Charles Elihu Slocum, *The Life and Services of Major-General Henry Warner Slocum*, (Toledo, Ohio: The Slocum Publishing Company, 1913), 122.

  Slocum reported Devin's arrival in a dispatch dated August 2 at 2 P.M. The date appears in parentheses in the Official Records, possibly meaning that the original dispatch had no date and the compiler of the records assigned one or that it could not be read clearly. If this date is taken as accurate it would mean that Devin crossed the river at 11:00 on the morning of the 1st, attacked the enemy along with the rest of Buford's division, sustaining 5 killed, 23 wounded, and 18 missing, recrossed the river after dark, and rode down to Kelly's Ford, arriving late in the evening of August 1 as Slocum reported. This is highly unlikely considering Buford's statement on the condition of his men on August 2. The date on Slocum's dispatch should be August 4. Buford sent Devin on the afternoon of the 3rd, which is confirmed from other sources. He arrived, sent a message to Buford at 7:00, and met with Slocum, who told him to remain north of the river until morning. All of this would seem to confirm that the date of Slocum's dispatch should read August 4.

  Slocum's interference with the cavalry raised the ire of Buford as well. He wrote to Ambrose Burnside that nothing in the army had changed since that officer had left. The Corps commanders still exercised too much caution, a situation with which Buford found no favor. John Buford to My Dear Burn [Ambrose Burnside], August 12, 1863, George H. Stuart Collection, MMC-3248, LC.

95. *O.R.*, Series 1, vol. 27, part 3, 832-833, 1072.

96. *Ibid.*, part 1, 1058 and part 3, 839; Brig. Gen. David McM. Gregg to Maj. Gen. Alfred Pleasonton, August 3, 1863, and Brig. Gen. David McM. Gregg to Lt. Col. Andrew J. Alexander, August 4, 1863, Telegrams Collected by the Secretary of War, Unbound, RG 107, M504, NARA; Hand, Jr., *One Good Regiment*, 71; *New York Herald*, August 17, 1863.

  Huey's brigade continued to patrol east and west of Thoroughfare Gap. Thomas Covert to My Dear Wife, August 3, 1863, Covert Collection, USAMHI.

97. Charles Johnson to Dear Mother, August 5, 1863, Charles M. Johnson Letters, Collection No. Wyles Mss 36, Box 1, Folder 4, Department of Special Collections, Donald C. Davidson Library, University of California at Santa Barbara (hereafter cited as DCDL/UCSB).

98. *O.R.*, Series 1, vol. 27, part 3, 1075.

99. Donahue Diary; Arehart, "Diary of W. H. Arehart," 271; Neese, *Three Years in the Confederate Horse Artillery*, 204-205.

100. *O.R.*, Series 1, vol. 29, part 1, 22; Cheney Diary; Driver, *14th Virginia Cavalry*, 25; Donahue Diary; *Richmond Enquirer*, August 10, 1863.

  Buford reported facing six guns. According to Lt. Francis H. Wigfall of Breathed's Battery they were as follows: two guns came from McGregor's Battery, still led by Lt. Ford, one from Moorman's Battery, the 12-pounder mentioned by Buford, under the command of Lt. Charles R. Phelps, one, a Whitworth also mentioned by Buford, from Breathed's Battery under Lt. Wigfall, and two from Capt. Wiley H. Griffin's Battery.

Another source stated that Stuart had eight guns. Charles R. Phelps, August 10, 1863, Charles R. Phelps Letters (#2920), The Albert H. Small Special Collections Library, University of Virginia (hereafter cited as UV); Francis Halsey Wigfall to Mrs. Louis T. Wigfall, August 13, 1863, Wigfall Family Papers, MMC-3183, Manuscript Division, LC; *Richmond Daily Dispatch*, August 10, 1863.

101. *O.R.*, Series 1, vol. 29, part 1, 21.

102. *Ibid.*, 22; Cheney Diary; Frank Diary; *Washington Daily Morning Chronicle*, August 11, 1863; *Daily Union & Advertiser*, date unknown; New York State Military Museum and Veterans Research Center at, <www.dmna.state.ny.us/historic/mil-hist.htm> December 31, 2009 (hereafter cited as *NYSMMVRC*); Charles R. Phelps, August 10, 1863, Charles R. Phelps Letters (#2920), The Albert H. Small Special Collections Library, UV; Shoemaker, *Shoemaker's Battery*, 50.

   Buford, arguably the best cavalry officer in the Army of the Potomac, was here caught by surprise when on the same side of the river as Stuart, illustrating quite clearly the impossibility of knowing every time the enemy planned to attack. How much more so when a natural boundary stood between the opposing sides.

103. *O.R.*, Series 1, vol. 29, part 1, 22; *Washington Daily Morning Chronicle*, August 11, 1863; *Richmond Daily Dispatch*, August 10, 1863; *Richmond Whig*, August 7, 1863.

104. One source states that two prisoners were taken. *History of the Sixth New York Cavalry*, 154; *O.R.*, Series 1, vol. 29, part 1, 22.

   There are two Barnett's Fords. One is on the Rapidan northwest of Orange Court House and the other is on the Rappahannock downstream from Kelly's Ford. This Barnett's Ford is also known as Ellis' Ford. To avoid confusion Ellis' Ford will be used in all instances referring to the Barnett's Ford on the Rappahannock River.

105. Gillespie, *Company A, First Ohio Cavalry*, 172; *HDSACWRD*, <www.civilwardata.com> August 22, 2009.

106. *New York Herald*, August 10, 1863.

   If the reporter was correct in identifying the men who attacked the Tenth New York as being from Jenkins's (Ferguson's) Brigade then only part of the brigade fought with Stuart in the afternoon.

107. *O.R.*, Series 1, vol. 27, part 1, 1004, and vol. 29, part 2, 5, 33; Ressler Diary; Yoder Diary; Lloyd, *History of the First Regiment Pennsylvania Reserve Cavalry*, 69.

108. Richard Henry Watkins to Mary Watkins, August 5, 1863, Watkins Papers, 1861-1865, Mss1W3272a1-355, VHS; Carter Diary; Morrissett Diary.

109. *O.R.*, Series 1, vol. 29, part 1, 27-29; Lloyd, *History of the First Regiment Pennsylvania Reserve Cavalry*, 69; Grimsley, *Battles in Culpeper County*, 15; *Philadelphia Inquirer*, August 12, 1863.

   Huey's Brigade still patrolled the area around Georgetown and Thoroughfare Gap. Thomas Covert to My Dear Wife, August 5, 1863, Covert Collection, USAMHI.

110. *O.R.*, Series 1, vol. 29, part 2, 6.

   Pvt. Abner B. Frank of the Twelfth Illinois recorded in his diary that he stayed undisturbed in his camp all day. However, Pvt. Jasper B. Cheney wrote that skirmisher fire aroused him at 1:00 in the morning and forced his regiment, the Eighth New York, to retreat under a full moon that lit up the landscape as if it were daytime. One solution to this contradiction would be that Cheney's regiment was camped closer, possibly doing picket duty, to Stuart's lines and withdrew rather than precipitate a fight. Frank Diary; Cheney Diary.

111. Devin's report states that he sent the scouting party to Barnett's Ford, meaning Ellis' Ford as stated above.
112. *O.R.*, Series 1, vol. 29, part 2, 6.
113. *Ibid.*, part 1, 997.
    While the regiments of McIntosh's brigade dealt with the enemy, at least one of Col. Gregg's practiced dealing with the enemy. The men of the Sixteenth Pennsylvania occupied some of their camp time with saber drill. Ressler Diary.
114. *New York Times*, August 11, 1863.
115. Carter Diary; Morrissett Diary; Donahue Diary; *O.R.*, Series 1, vol. 29, part 2, 8, 624-625, 628.

Chapter Three

Stagnation

By the morning of August 6, the cavalry of both sides engaged an adversary that waged war indiscriminately – heat. Officers from Meade's army returning to Washington from Warrenton reported that all activity had ground to a virtual halt. Several cases of sunstroke felled men in the Federal Quartermasters Department and 38 horses succumbed while on a train bound for Alexandria.[1] South of the Rappahannock, soldiers complained about the heat as well.[2] Capt. Richard H. Watkins of the Third Virginia, Fitz Lee's Brigade, wrote that he was "Camped in a clear field without a simple shade tree near us and have been broiling in the hot sun for three or four days (the hottest weather that I have ever felt)."[3] Pvt. John O. Collins of the Tenth Virginia, Chambliss's Brigade, echoed Watkins's thoughts. He complained of the heat and the lack of sufficient food after fighting the enemy and driving him beyond, "Brandy Station where we lay on the field for about ten days the hottest place on earth and where we nearly starved. I never suffered so much for something to eat in my life."[4] The very idea that anyone might consider fighting in such stifling temperatures bordered on the unbelievable. That was probably why John S. Mosby and his partisans ignored the heat and pressed their attacks on Federal supply lines – no one expected it.

Nothing and no one appeared safe with Mosby roaming the countryside. Assistant Surgeon Franklin Grubb of the First Artillery Brigade, newspaper correspondent Lesley G. Morrow, hospital steward Job S. Ullom, and hospital attendants David McWilliams and Jerome Cunningham were caught in Mosby's net three miles below Centreville, along with an ambulance and a sutler's wagon. The two conveyances were emptied where they stood, but the prisoners were taken into the woods, relieved of their boots, saber belts, personal effects, and horses before being released.[5] Others of Mosby's band scooped up 15 to 20 wagons near Fairfax Court House and were in the process of unhitching the horses and looting the drivers when a portion of the Twelfth Illinois, Gamble's brigade, Buford's division, that had been encamped nearby heard the ruckus and interrupted them. All the guerillas escaped, making off with a few horses and some valuables taken from the drivers.[6]

However, Mosby's raids were not without setbacks and consequences. Nine men of his band caught in the Warrenton area were taken to Washington. Dressed in civilian attire and found to be farmers from Fairfax and Loudoun counties, the men faced a growing clamor for their trial as "common highwaymen." A proposed solution to the raids came in the form of a suggestion to arrest all males along the Annandale to Warrenton road capable of bearing arms.[7] Mosby had stirred up a whirlwind, which had been his intention. The cost to the Federals was known. The cost to Mosby's men was yet to be calculated.

The day did not pass entirely peacefully for all of the Federal cavalry thanks to Pleasonton, who ordered Brig. Gen. David McM. Gregg to send out scouting parties toward the Hazel River and Sperryville. Dragging themselves onto their mounts, the men chosen for the duty must certainly have had a few choice words for their commander-in-chief, but orders were orders. The missions only confirmed what already had been established - the Confederates held both positions with a brigade of cavalry near each and showed no intention of going anywhere, especially in the heat. However, the Federal cavalrymen may have garnered some solace from the fact that because of their incursion some of their foes were ordered out to picket Oak Shade and Starke's fords on the Hazel. While not an even exchange, at least a few more graybacks would suffer in the heat, too.[8]

The staring contest continued on the 7th. Federal cavalry vedettes stood within a mile of Chew's Battery stationed on Fleetwood Hill. The camps of Buford's troopers could be seen just four miles away.[9] Other Confederates either watched enemy pickets or the gently rolling waters of the Hazel and the Rappahannock glide by. Men of the First Massachusetts, McIntosh's brigade, Gregg's division, kept an eye on the graycoats near Amissville.[10] With everybody watching everybody, Lee and Meade could be sure of where the other was and, for the most part, knew what the other was up to, which amounted to very little. The heat finally had shut down active operations, although Gregg shifted his division a few miles from around Amissville to Sulphur Springs.[11] The troopers of both armies ordered to stand watch found whatever shade they could, while their companions sat in their camps and enjoyed a day off. Not so the paper shufflers in Washington.

Meade already had been cautioned as to what he should be doing during the period of quiescence. Now the Adjutant General's office issued a general order downsizing the army's transport for personal baggage, mess-chests, cooking utensils, desks, and other such paraphernalia. Undoubtedly, the effort to streamline the army's wagon train sprang from several concerns not the least of which was the supply of horses and mules needed to keep the army mobile. The cavalry received special attention because some of its members insisted on dragging around extra baggage on their horses, causing the animals to break down more rapidly or so ran the bureaucrats' line of reasoning. Officers were admonished that they would be held accountable for the elimination of the practice from their commands.[12]

While officers throughout the army scrambled to comply with the new standards, portions of the Federal cavalry engaged in implementing the suggestion made previously in the newspapers by indiscriminately arresting civilians behind the lines. The matter came to Meade's attention and early on the 8th, his chief of staff, Maj. Gen. Andrew A. Humphreys, sent a communication to Pleasonton inquiring into the practice and ordering all such arrests to cease unless evidence could be produced to confirm the disloyalty of the individual or his connection to those engaged in committing depredations.[13]

Stuart also took steps to conserve his command's horseflesh by issuing an order forbidding the granting of permits allowing troopers to be absent from the ranks if they wanted to take their horses with them. Since the men could not travel very far without their mounts, the order acted both to preserve the horses and keep the men with the army. In addition and as a precaution against those horses that might desire to wander off on their own account, taking their owners with them, Stuart required that roll calls for the men be taken at Reveille, Retreat, and Tattoo, with the results immediately forwarded to regimental adjutants.[14] How effective the order would be, remained to be seen.

A heavy rain on the night of the 7th failed to relieve the troops from the stifling heat.[15] Early the next morning, Buford received orders to withdraw a portion of his command across the Rappahannock, leaving only enough troopers south of the river to hold the Confederates until infantry from the First Corps could come up in support. The new camp was to be at a point closest to the river where water and good grazing could be found. Buford's division had born the brunt of the fighting since the army reached the Rappahannock and the respite was long overdue. The division completed the maneuver on the 9th.[16]

Even amidst his withdrawal, Buford maintained his vigilance. He inspected his outpost line from the Hazel River to Mountain Run, found it four times as long as the Confederate's, and reduced it. He attempted to communicate with Gregg by moving four miles up the Hazel, but with no success. Buford's troopers drew the enemy's fire but did not reply. A similar scout by Devin to Mountain Run failed to uncover any gray cavalry. Buford correctly surmised that Lee had nothing but Stuart's cavalry north of the Rapidan and that Stuart had no disposition to attack.[17]

Indeed, Stuart's troopers contented themselves with the various small tasks of camp life. The brigades still maintained the relative positions they had held for the past several days. The men attended to their horses and equipment, wrote letters, and swapped rumors. Private James A. Jeter of the Ninth Virginia, Chambliss's Brigade, wrote home, "I have seen hard times for the last two months. I have not pulled off my shoes more than two or three times since the 20th of June." He also recounted that his regiment's pickets and those of the enemy were only 200 yards apart, each waiting for the other to start something.[18] And so, both sides maintained their vigilance, in the stifling heat, wondering who would make that first move.

The blue cavalry took the initiative on the 9th when McIntosh, under orders from Gen. Gregg, sent Capt. Benjamin W. Crowninshield and the first squadron of the First Massachusetts across the Hazel River at Welford's Ford in an attempt to link up with Buford's vedettes at Beverly Ford. Lt. George W. Lyon and 16 men of Company I, First Pennsylvania accompanied Crowninshield. The Federals crossed the river and pushed back the Confederate pickets, but within a quarter of an hour, 150 gray troopers arrived and drove Crowninshield back over the river. Lt. Lyon, who had been sent downstream toward Beverly Ford, became cut off and was feared lost. However, the intrepid lieutenant kept his head, led his men through and around the enemy forces intent on capturing him, reached the ford, and crossed the Rappahannock to safety.[19] The venture brought sharp criticism from Gen. Gregg and McIntosh for their superiors. Both repeated to cavalry headquarters their opinion that to place pickets south of the Hazel was too dangerous. Maj. Gen. Andrew A. Humphreys, Meade's chief-of-staff, retorted by asking why only one officer and 16 men were detailed to link with Buford's men at Beverly Ford. Gregg was asked to explain. The matter caused a stir for some time.[20]

Elsewhere, an alert Federal signal officer intercepted a Stuart dispatch, confirming that Lee's cavalry chief had his eyes on the doings north of the Rappahannock. Stuart reported that the enemy's camps had been shifting away from Warrenton and Waterloo toward the railroad. Stuart did not offer his opinion on what the movement meant, leaving the interpretation to Lee. At least one Federal officer, Brig. Gen. Rufus King, worried that Stuart might be planning another raid and cautioned the commanding officer at Fairfax Station to take every precaution to guard his post.[21]

Such a raid was not in the offing. Stuart's regiments had no intention of going anywhere north of the Rappahannock. Fitz Lee's Brigade lay in camp, enjoying Sunday services; Chambliss's Brigade had relocated to the Woodville area to hopefully get some rest; Baker's Brigade kept an eye on Buford at Rappahannock Station; Jones guarded Beverly Ford and vicinity; Robertson watched the Federals at Kelly's Ford; and Ferguson opposed Gregg near Sperryville.[22] Even the newspapers found little to report, but did observe that Stuart's men were always alert and often in line of battle, awaiting an enemy much bolder since the battle at Brandy Station on June 9.[23]

The newspapers also fostered rumors. One intrepid reporter even wrote, with some certainty, that Maj. Gen. John B. Hood had been promoted to lieutenant general and would soon assume the command of Lee's cavalry. According to the source, the report of Stuart being replaced was well received among the cavalry.[24] Stuart caught wind of it and wrote to his wife, Flora, telling her not to believe a word of it. He took it as an attempt to degrade him and had every confidence that his superiors would not replace him.[25] Contrary to the reporter's assertion that the report was well received among the rank and file, a letter to the editor of the *Richmond Daily Dispatch* claimed that the men did not welcome it and, in fact, strongly opposed it. The writer asserted that Stuart's reputation among the regiments had never been higher and that the only rejoicing being done over the rumor was north of the Rappahannock.[26] As most rumors do, this one eventually faded and disappeared when other more serious concerns came to the fore.

One of these concerns involved the equipping of the Confederate cavalry as it struggled to compete with its ever-improving foe. On August 10, Col. John R. Chambliss, commanding Brig. Gen. William H. F. "Rooney" Lee's Brigade, submitted a letter to Col. Alexander R. Boteler, recently attached to Stuart's staff, who, in an effort to increase the cavalry's effectiveness, had requested opinions from various officers.[27]

Col. A. R. BOTELER:

In compliance with your request, I will briefly touch upon those points which in my opinion demand the consideration of our authorities in advancing, recuperating, and promoting the efficiency of the cavalry service, and call attention to the causes that have produced the difference which now exists between its present condition and that of a few months ago. A great disparity exists between the effective cavalry force of the enemy and ours. Especially, in view of the probability that their advantages in this respect may be vastly increased, it is most important that our cavalry be placed upon an equality with theirs. Should it be deemed compatible with the public interest, there is no doubt that at this time, particularly under a proper recruiting system projected in the different counties of our State especially, many valuable acquisitions to our now shattered ranks would accrue to us. Hundreds of details have been made from the cavalry of men to easy places in quartermaster's, commissary, or medical departments, and no orders can force or invoke these detailed men to their commands when their employers declare it incompatible with the public service that they should be ordered back. Their places can be easily supplied by competent, crippled or otherwise, disabled soldiers.

The superiority of the enemy's cavalry armament, coupled with their better ammunition, is a point demanding prompt attention. It is accorded that no arm for mounted service can be compared to the breech-loading carbine. Dismounted fighting with the carbine on the part of the enemy has become very popular, and comprises the best share of their fighting. The inferiority of our armament and ammunition tends to inspire the one not at all and to make bolder the other. It would seem that not a very high degree of mechanical skill is required in perfecting the present Richmond carbine made after Sharps patent, or that it is not impossible to provide a sufficiency of such arms put up in the very best style of manufacture abroad. Encouragement to inventors and experimentalists in perfecting and putting up not only such arms but fixed ammunition, with a view to its preservation in wet weather and under rough handling, will go far toward arresting the wholesale waste and destruction of powder and lead.[28]

The sabers issued by the Department are miserably inferior weapons, estimated at so low a value by the soldier, and really of so little account, that they are soon lost or cast away as worthless. The soldier will prize a good weapon, the quality of which will inspire him with pride for its good keeping and confidence when in contact with his foeman's steel.

The saddles issued by the Ordnance Department are dreaded, ridiculed, and avoided by officers and men, and are used only through necessity, seldom without proving ruinous to the backs of horses. Though samples of the best approved saddles can be had anywhere, it is strange that no trees can be manufactured comparable to the McClellan saddles, when as much time and material is consumed in constructing the miserable apologies issued to the cavalry in imitation of the above-named saddles. It would seem that a board of suitable and enterprising officers would take pleasure in instituting inquiry on this subject and in arresting the useless waste of material in the manufacture of these Confederate saddles.[29]

Other parts of the cavalry soldiers' equipments furnished by the Government might be greatly improved, but are of inferior moment to those already mentioned. Above all other considerations rises the question now causing much dissatisfaction and disorganization in the cavalry, "When am I to get another horse, and how can I buy one at the present prices after I have lost so many without any compensation from the Government?" The provisions of the bill passed by Congress allow payment for those horses only killed in action. I know that a majority of my most efficient men have lost from one to five horses, broken down by the hardships of the service, and a small minority of horses lost in the service are killed in action. It is with great reluctance that an officer can exchange or part with an accomplished and experienced cavalry soldier whom he finds dismounted through such circumstances, and is pecuniarily unable to provide himself forever and ever with horses. The good soldier of this dismounted class of two or more years' experience is too valuable to be parted with, and some provision should be made to supply such men. Although there are many in this service who for various reasons should be transferred to other branches of the service, and there are many infantrymen who are applying for transfers to the cavalry, and such transfers would greatly recruit and strengthen us, still the objections raised by company and field officers of the infantry render such exchange nigh to an impossibility. I would suggest that you call attention not only to the foregoing matter of this paragraph relative to the providing payment for horses lost by being disabled, broken down, exhausted, and left within the enemy's lines, &c., but also to rendering exchange a matter easier to be effected. There is a crying want of veterinary surgeons to be attached to and to accompany the cavalry to provide medicines and proper treatment in the field and camp for such horses. The establishment of a veterinary hospital in some locality secure from cavalry raids, convenient and accessible to the main railroad communications, where cheap sheds or coverings for the winter season might be erected, where surgeons and farriers might be appointed, with the labor of hired negroes to attend to the horses, would greatly enhance the efficiency of the service; would put a stop to straggling and lurking behind with the shadow of an excuse, and effectually hush the discontent arising from the necessity of having to retain invalid horses in the field and of making worthy cavalry soldiers involuntary members of the foot battalion for any length of time.[30]

The chief and main cause of the present dismembered and shattered state of our ranks has been the want of horseshoes and horseshoe nails, forges, and transportation therefore. Provide every soldier with shoe pouches and shoes to put in them, and fewer dismounted men will harass the service. A greater number of blacksmiths should be retained and employed in each regiment.

Drilling is indispensably necessary to rendering troops thoroughly efficient. The force of cavalry now confronting the enemy is so small that every man is on picket or outpost duty for a majority of the time, and the horses are so constantly employed that a horseback drill is dreaded. With increased numbers we would be more upon an equal footing with the enemy and be enabled to withstand the various shocks incident to a service having so small an effective force of cavalry. During the late expedition into the enemy's country many valuable horses were lost owing mainly to the want of shoes, which failed to arrive and be provided before the start. Men became dismounted, separated from their commands, and thus left behind from the impossibility of keeping a pace with the mounted men [had] to find places of safety and to congregate in masses of "Qs." I have hastily drawn attention to the main causes of disorganization and dismemberment in this branch of the service, and in view of the vastly superior resources of the enemy and their superior strength, prompt remedies are imperatively demanded.

I have the honor to be, colonel, your obedient servant,
Jno. R. Chambliss, Jr.,
Colonel, Commanding Lee's Cavalry Brigade[31]

Whether other brigade commanders echoed Chambliss's view of the situation confronting Lee's mounted arm cannot be confirmed, but Col. Boteler dutifully passed Chambliss's observations up the chain of command. The controlling forces in Richmond read and commented on what Boteler submitted and did address some issues, most notably the carbine, saddle, and horse infirmary, to some degree. Other points may have been dealt with as best as the circumstances allowed, but Chambliss's comments indicated an awareness that the decline of the Confederate cavalry had begun. Sadly, for Chambliss and the other men under Stuart, the government did not have the means or the power to stop it.

Though the lack of horses and equipment plagued Stuart's cavalry with increasing frequency, one commander had a solution for the problem – take whatever you need from the enemy. John Mosby's supply problems found resolution in the myriad of Federal supply trains and sutler wagons threading their way to and from the Army of the Potomac's front lines. On August 11, a tempting target made its way along the Little River Turnpike and, despite the efforts of Col. Charles R. Lowell's Second Massachusetts, was scooped up by Mosby, who once again made his escape unscathed. The capture included 19 wagons and their teams, saddles, bridles, harness, and 25 prisoners, except for the latter, just the kind of supplies that the cavalry required.[32]

On August 10, the Army of the Potomac's tri-monthly report was issued stating that Pleasonton's cavalry numbered 12,251 officers and men present. However, only 8,808 were present and fully equipped for duty.[33] Many of the regiments fell far short of their full strength. Pvt. Allen Bevan of the First Pennsylvania, McIntosh's brigade, Gregg's division, explained his regiment's need for recruits in a letter to his sister, "We want 464 men to fill up our Regiment. Company B requires 40 men to make us number 96 men which is the number required to make a full company." He added that three of the regiment's officers and 9 men had been sent back to Harrisburg, the state capital, on recruiting duty.[34]

The August return for Stuart's cavalry showed an aggregate present and absent of 17,681 officers and men, an aggregate present of 9,580, with an effective strength of 8,225, of which 1,333 were dismounted, leaving a mounted total of 6,892 ready for duty.[35] That the Confederate cavalry had 10,789 officers and men who were either not present, still with the army but unable to perform their duty, or dismounted clearly emphasized the problems facing Stuart and his commander. Had a third of those absent been with the army and equipped to fight, Stuart would have at least been able to match numbers with Pleasonton. As it was, the gray troopers were both outnumbered and poorly equipped. Nothing would improve over the coming months.

Besides the absentee problem, Stuart faced a growing desertion rate among the regiments in Ferguson's Brigade. The Valley men had seen hard service since they joined up with the boys from over the mountains. Not as well-schooled in military knowledge and less skilled in the kind of warfare they had recently been called upon to perform, Ferguson's troopers experienced a rising tide of discontent that threatened to engulf the brigade. Back on the 5th of August the first desertion had occurred in the Fourteenth Virginia, but many men from the other regiments of the brigade had already left. Then on the 10th a mass desertion in the Thirty-sixth Virginia Cavalry Battalion occurred. About 50 men simply walked away from their duties in an effort to reach home. Most were caught and returned to the ranks, but the event alerted Stuart to the fact that something needed to be done to address the situation. The men wanted to go home. To preserve the brigade, Stuart was going to have to let them. The question was when.[36]

Another soldier headed home on the 10th. Brig. Gen. John Buford received a leave of absence from the army for ten days in order to return to his home in Kentucky. Buford's family had been stricken with typhoid fever. A daughter, sister-in-law, and father-in-law had succumbed to the disease, and his wife was gravely ill.[37] Buford's loss to the army at this time was not as critical as it would have been a few weeks earlier. The slowing down of operations and the competency of his replacement, Brig. Gen. Wesley Merritt, would help the First Division overcome Buford's absence. Unfortunately, other orders were also issued that complicated the situation.[38]

The same day Buford left, Merritt received orders to turn over all of his brigade's horses and equipment to the staff officers of Buford's division and send his men to Alexandria for the purpose of remounting and refitting. The horses and arms left behind would be used to mount and outfit every able-bodied man in the rest of the division. Merritt immediately telegraphed Pleasonton from his camp on the Paine farm just across the river from Kelly's Ford and requested that he be allowed to accompany his brigade because the officer in command was new and would not be able to see to the outfitting as well as Merritt felt he could. Of course, if Merritt left with his brigade, he would not be able to command the division in Buford's absence. Not until the 15th did Pleasonton issue orders permitting Merritt to go with his men. That left the division under the command of Col. Thomas C. Devin until Buford returned.[39]

The day did not pass without at least one patrol. The Sixth New York, Devin's brigade, thankfully left their outposts in the morning to return to their camp only to trot away from it again on an afternoon scout. Their excursion took them across Mountain Run toward Stevensburg where the Sixth Virginia, Jones's Brigade, formed a line of battle and turned them aside. The Federals trotted down to Ely's Ford on the Rapidan where another force of the enemy confronted them. No one apparently wanted to fight at either place and the Confederates simply watched as the Federals withdrew and crossed the Rappahannock. The 30 mile jaunt confirmed what had already been known, the enemy held Stevensburg and guarded the area between the rivers.[40]

The unrelenting heat held sway over the camps of both armies. One reporter commented that the thermometer for the previous week had varied between 90-100 ° in the shade with no air movement. Men and animals suffered from a lack of water. The men had no spirituous stimulants, vegetables, or sutlers' delicacies to lift their spirits or strength. The list of camp illnesses increased.[41] Men dreamed of home and the comforts it could afford them. The reality was Mosby swooping down on anything with hooves or wheels and a raging sun, neither of which was inclined to grant a respite.

On the night of the 11th a small detachment from Fitz Lee's Brigade crossed the Rappahannock at Smith's Ford and swept through the surrounding country, bagging an enemy lieutenant near Stafford Court House and a mail carrier on the road between Stafford Court House and Falmouth. Satisfied, the party scampered back over the river, reveling in their success as the mail divulged considerable information on Meade's troop dispositions.[42] After being the recipient of so many Federal incursions, Lee's men must have enjoyed their nighttime foray. While it meant little in the overall scheme of things, it certainly must have brought some individual satisfaction to the men who participated in it.

The 12th brought more of the same heat, picket duty, and camp boredom, although a restructuring of Pleasonton's command did cause a minor distraction for those regiments involved. Gen. Meade issued an order disbanding the Second Brigade of the Second Cavalry Division commanded by Col. Pennock Huey, sending the Second New York to the First Brigade, Third Division and the Fourth New York to the Second Brigade, First Division. The remaining three regiments, the First Rhode Island, Sixth Ohio, and the Eighth Pennsylvania, were to be assigned to the two brigades of the Second Division as its commander, Gen. Gregg, saw fit.[43]

Both armies concerned themselves with the local citizenry. The Federals, certain that every able-bodied man between Warrenton and Washington had to be a member of Mosby's band, scoured the countryside and arrested those who appeared to have Southern leanings. The Confederates, distressed over disloyal citizens helping the enemy by acting as guides and providing information, took steps to correct the problem. Raids across the river, usually at night, brought both successes and failures. Twenty men from Capt. George H. Matthews's company of the Third Virginia, Fitz Lee's Brigade, crossed the river on the night of August 11-12 and captured two disloyal citizens and two good horses before returning. A small party of the Fifteenth Virginia, Chambliss's Brigade, had much poorer luck. The men ventured out in the daylight, slipped over the river near Falmouth, ran into a Federal patrol, and were captured.[44]

Rain on the morning of August 13 broke the heat wave as the weather turned somewhat cooler.[45] Nothing of any significance occurred except that the Sixth New York, Devin's brigade, in replacing its brother regiment, the Seventeenth Pennsylvania, on outpost duty along Mountain Run, found the Confederate vedettes "quite saucy."[46] Apparently the cooling rain brought a corresponding rise in aggression. Still, nothing of importance occurred until the following day when elements of Devin's brigade undertook an early morning scouting expedition. The results added nothing new to what was already known. Meanwhile, the Confederates struck, capturing the Vine-Tree signal station atop Watery Mountain near Warrenton and making off with a number of men, 16 horses, several wagons, some telescopes, and camp equipment. The officers managed to escape.[47] The incident failed to rouse the interest of Gen. Pleasonton even though it took place behind the lines of the Sixth Corps. However, the Federal cavalry chieftain did react to something else.

The report of a single scout from Col. William D. Mann's Seventh Michigan, Custer's brigade, stationed at Hartwood Church above United States Ford produced a letter from Pleasonton to Meade's chief of staff in which the Federal cavalry commander urged an immediate increase of both cavalry and infantry on the army's left flank. The scout reported 10,000 infantry from Longstreet's Corps and 5,000 mounted infantry, along with some regular cavalry, all preparing to bridge or ford the Rappahannock and, according to what the scout supposedly learned from the Confederates themselves, to sweep around Meade's flank and drive toward Washington.[48]

Pleasonton's request received some support from another source that insisted that Stuart with 5,000 to 6,000 cavalry was about to launch a raid on Meade's supply lines within the next two weeks. A worried Pleasonton asked for permission to concentrate all of his cavalry not required on the picket lines. He received authority to place the men of each division not on picket or in support of the pickets at a convenient point, holding them in readiness for a general concentration of the cavalry if the situation required.[49] Orders flew about as if on wings and men saddled their horses and prepared to gallop off at a moment's notice. Some infantry commanders were informed that they would be responsible for guarding the river line when the cavalry withdrew. The alert included all transportation in the army, which had to be ready to move to the flanks or the rear as necessary. The troops received three days rations and orders to be prepared to march. Everyone took measures to respond to Stuart the second he set one hoof on the north side of the Rappahannock.[50] The furor boiled over to the 15th. Families of officers and soldiers were ordered out of the area. They could not be permitted to get in the way if the army had to move swiftly.[51]

All this hustle and bustle did not go unnoticed by the Confederates. Reports stated that Federal cavalry appeared on the heights above Fredericksburg; Stafford Court House was evacuated and the quartermaster and commissary stores burned; a Federal cavalry division was camping around Hartwood Church and guarding Bank's Dam; the enemy constantly changed their positions.[52] Despite all this marching and shifting of men and supplies and since the Confederates had no intention of crossing the river in force, Stuart's men simply went on with their daily routine. Pvt. Jones of the Fifth North Carolina, Robertson's Brigade, came off outpost duty at Ellis' Ford, celebrating in the rumor that the Federals were deserting in droves and that everything was quiet and peaceful, at least at his post.[53] On the other hand, George Neese of Chew's Battery wished that the enemy might do something to relieve the boredom he suffered standing watch day after day.[54]

In the end, although the Confederates had done nothing, the false report of a lone scout and Pleasonton's willingness to believe it caused a considerable amount of pointless excitement and maneuvering, not to mention anxiety, for the men of the Army of the Potomac. The troops most affected had been the Federal cavalry, the main body of which had been withdrawn from the right, fronting the Rappahannock and Hazel rivers, and concentrated on the left and in rear of Falmouth.[55] Until the scare dissipated, Meade's army stood to arms, tense and alert.

While the 14th marked the beginning of the majority of the Federal cavalry's movement towards the army's left flank, other mounted units headed to the right for a different reason - to search for Mosby. Capt. George V. Griggs with 120 men of the Second New York, Sawyer's brigade, Kilpatrick's division, with elements of its brother regiment, the First Vermont, trailing behind, trotted through Thoroughfare Gap and marched for Hopewell where a lone enemy vedette managed to evade capture. The column's advanced guard took fire from ambush just on the other side of the mountain. Capt. Griggs dismounted a number of his men and routed the partisans from their camp, capturing horses and equipment. Sending out other search parties, Griggs had the satisfaction of seeing 2 prisoners and 15 to 20 horses rounded up. The Vermonters, meanwhile, expected to encamp and guard the gap for the next week, but the presumed situation along the Rappahannock altered their orders. After gaining their objective, they turned around and marched for Hartwood Church where they found their brigade and Custer's awaiting their arrival.[56]

The Thirteenth Pennsylvania, Gregg's brigade, Gregg's division, mirrored the New Yorkers' successful venture, sending out several parties to feel out the enemy. Capt. John Kline led his men on a charge through Little Washington, chasing off the village's defenders. Capt. Nathaniel S. Sneyd's column rode all the way to Chester Gap, capturing three prisoners and four horses destined for Ferguson's Brigade. The horses immediately replaced worn out ones in Sneyd's troop. A third party under Lt. Lewis McMakin encountered a Confederate officer who managed to escape, hurried along by a few shots from Lt. McMakin. The regiment returned to its camp the morning of the 15th, thoroughly satisfied with its efforts.[57] Greeting the weary men was an order shifting Gregg's brigade to the army's left flank toward Catlett's Station. The march lasted all day, the regiments coming within a mile of the place when they camped for the night.[58] McIntosh moved as well, but stopped near Warrenton. His regiments guarded the roads from that place toward Manassas Junction.[59]

Elsewhere that day, Col. Charles R. Lowell received a telegram from Maj. Gen. Henry W. Halleck's chief of staff, Col. Joseph H. Taylor, that Col. Elijah V. White with 350 of his men infested the area near Dranesville. Lowell was ordered to attack him. Taking his regiment, the Second Massachusetts, Lowell rode off in search of the partisans. Patrolling from Centreville to Aldie and beyond to Goose Creek, Lowell experienced a frustrating four days. He came close to bagging his prey along Goose Creek, but being warned, White melted into the countryside. Rumors placed him here one day and somewhere else the next. Lowell marched hither and thither, rounded up ten men, and returned to Centreville frustrated that he could not come to grips with his elusive foe.[60]

The problem of an enemy that nipped at your heels one minute and then disappeared into the foliage the next continued to irritate if not exasperate Federal commanders throughout Meade's army. Every able-bodied civilian was looked on with both suspicion and contempt. The indiscriminant arrests made a few days earlier had received a sharp rebuke from Meade, but a loophole had been left in the orders. If evidence could be produced, individuals could be taken into custody. The Fifth Michigan, Custer's brigade, Kilpatrick's division, set out early on the 15th for Aquia via Stafford Court House. Its orders permitted the apprehension of all male citizens able to bear arms. That was sufficient enough evidence for 30 men to be arrested. Two hundred men from two of Custer's other regiments, the First and the Sixth Michigan, rode to Falmouth and returned by way of Brooke's Station on the Fredericksburg and Potomac Railroad, and Stafford Court House, looking for guerillas and finding none.[61]

Others also spent the day guarding against men able to bear arms. Maj. Joseph C. Kenyon of the Eleventh New York, Gregg's brigade, Gregg's division, received an order at 9:00 in the morning to report with the regiment to Washington. The troopers mounted up and trotted out. After an all-day march, the men camped at Bristoe Station late in the evening. Following a dawn breakfast of coffee and pork rations, the march resumed. Arriving at Centreville at noon, Maj. Kenyon found 15 sutler wagons needing an escort, Mosby having been active in the area. Taking on this duty, the regiment reached Washington late in the day, only to find that no accommodations awaited them. With this "thank you for your service" the Eleventh ended their connection with the Army of the Potomac.[62]

Lt. Col. William R. Carter of the Third Virginia, Fitz Lee's Brigade, drew the assignment of provost marshal of Fredericksburg on August 16. Given 110 men to assist him, he rode into the town, lamenting, "What a commentary on war and the depravity it generates! That it should require such a force too keep a place once noted for its hospitality and order quiet."[63] If quiet failed to reign in Fredericksburg, elsewhere along the contending lines peace held sway. Troopers from Stuart's various regiments went on or off outpost duty, depending on their schedule. Nothing else stirred south of the Rappahannock to break either the monotony or the routine, although at least some members of the Fourth North Carolina, Robertson's Brigade, encamped near Stevensburg, planned to make the effort. Sgt. William H. Edwards and a few of his compatriots planned a little drinking spree to occupy their time. What they hoped to drink and where they obtained it undoubtedly were military secrets.[64]

For Pvt. John O. Collins of the Tenth Virginia, Chambliss's Brigade, who arrived at Brandy Station with his compatriots thinking he was about to receive some much needed rest from picket duty, the day held an unwelcomed surprise. Confronted with a line of enemy sharpshooters, the regiment went back on duty, forcing Collins to lie down to sleep in line of battle. Uncomfortable, he looked to see what kept him awake and found, "I was laying on yankee bones. I moved my po-

sition and this morning I found myself laying whare [sic] a yankee died[.] I was laying on his hair and other remains[.] [A]fter I got myself out I moved again[.]" One
of Collins's fellow troopers, not so unnerved by the incident, took part of the Federal's leg bone and began to carve a ring out if it. Collins turned from the sight to
enjoy a breakfast of walnuts.[65]

Elsewhere the day passed uneventfully. Not so the 17th. Custer, still watching the enemy's doings along the lower Rappahannock from Falmouth to at least
Richard's Ford, reported that 2,000 Confederate cavalry and eight or ten wagons
passed down river on the south side of the Rappahannock. His suspicions may
have been raised further, when Confederates fired on his men from across the river
at Falmouth. He dispatched a patrol to investigate as much as they could from their
side of the river.[66] Nothing came of it. Had Custer actually seen almost a third of
Stuart's cavalry riding within sight of Federal vedettes, he might well have wondered if the raid was on. However, no such movement took place. The fear of a
raid by Stuart or a movement across the river by Lee continued to make Meade's
army jumpy.

Ever aware of Mosby popping up where he was least expected and never
wanted, patrols were constantly being sent out in various directions to dissuade the
Gray Ghost from practicing his trade. The Sixteenth Pennsylvania and the First
Maine, both of Gregg's brigade, Gregg's division, pulled such duty this day, leaving their camps at Catlett's Station and marching to Hay Market. They returned
via Thoroughfare Gap and Hopewell on the 18th.[67] Other regiments drew the same
task, visiting Salem, New Baltimore, White Plains, Markham, Barbee's Cross Roads,
Orlean, Greenwich, and Gainesville. Seeing Mosby everywhere and worrying
about Lee or Stuart or both crossing the Rappahannock forced the Federal cavalry
to spread itself out over areas that should have been considered secure.[68] Certainly,
when nothing transpired, all were much relieved.

Relief of a different nature lightened every man's heart. A cooling wind
began to blow through both armies. The hot, stagnant air that had engulfed man
and animal for what seemed an eternity, gave way to a gentle northern breeze that
blew throughout the day. Instead of two clashing foes on the ground, two contending fronts battled in the air above. Clouds gathered as night fell and just before
midnight, violent thunderstorms rained torrents of water on the parched earth. The
all-night downpour turned the placid Rappahannock into an impassable barrier to
all movement across it and flooded the lowlands with its overflow.[69]

Although Kilpatrick reported on August 18 that his outpost line was undisturbed, cannonading near Dumfries caused cavalry squadrons to scramble to discover the cause and kept the troopers up until midnight. Endless speculation as to
what the gunfire meant gave the senior officers of the army much to ponder. However, no enemy could be found and the men returned no wiser for all their efforts.
The blame for the uproar eventually focused on a gunboat on the Potomac.[70] The
truth of the matter did nothing for the worn out cavalrymen and their horses sent
out once again on a fruitless chase. Constant vigilance came at a price.

The swollen river prevented excursions into enemy territory for both sides. The only alternative was observation. Captain Joseph Gloskoski, acting signal officer for Pleasonton and the army in general, took his job seriously and carefully listed his observations in his daily report. Casting his glass upon the Confederate positions around Fredericksburg, he noted that no large concentration of troops could be seen except for a single cavalry regiment, one battery, and an infantry force matching that of the cavalry in numbers. The infantry, he reported, was scattered along the river and fired on anything blue that came to their attention on the north bank. He added that the people of Falmouth revealed that only small scouting parties of Confederates had been allowed to cross the river when fordable.[71] No invasion appeared imminent.

The fact that Stuart's cavalry appeared blockaded by a raging river and that the disposition of Stuart's brigades had given no reason to suspect a raid of any kind did not stop the fear of graycoats running amok behind Federal lines from affecting Meade's officers and men. Col. Alfred Gibbs, commanding the One Hundred Thirtieth New York Volunteer Infantry stationed at Manassas Junction, reported that he had been informed that 4,000 Confederate cavalry had left the Shenandoah Valley headed for Hopewell and Hay Market. This caused a whole division of the Eleventh Corps to rush about in preparation to meet the enemy. Gibbs requested cavalry, as he had none.[72] The stagnation along the front lines conjured up phantom Confederates, far outnumbering the real ones led by Mosby and White, in the army's rear. The call for cavalry assistance, first to run down mystery cannonading and now to tangle with enemy cavalry half the size of Pleasonton's entire force played havoc with the blue troopers and their commanders. Galloping here and there debilitated men and horses and ground away at morale. The Federal cavalry had won its spurs at Brandy Station. Would they now be dulled through careless use?[73]

The 19th passed peacefully, although several patrols were conducted. One of Gen. Gregg's regiments, the First Pennsylvania, McIntosh's brigade, occupied itself with scouting around Greenwich and Gainesville, looking for enemy cavalry and finding none.[74] After a jaunt from Catlett's Station through Trent's Store to Dumfries, Garrisonville, and Stafford Court House by three squadrons of the Seventeenth Pennsylvania, Devin's brigade, Buford's division, under Captains Luther B. Kurtz and Weidner H. Spera and Lt. Warren F. Simrell, Merritt reported all quiet in those places.[75] An intercepted signal from Stuart to Lee should have calmed Federal nerves. Stuart reported that he had moved his headquarters to Culpeper Court House because of a lack of forage for his horses.[76] Other than that, the gray cavalry remained quiet.

That quiet permitted the enlisted men and non-commissioned officers of the First North Carolina, Baker's Brigade, of Stuart's command to hold a meeting to deal with a problem that had arisen in the Tarheel State.[77] News from the Western and Eastern fronts had caused a war weariness to settle in parts of the state and brought about a desire for peace in some influential persons. Among these was Editor William W. Holden of the *North Carolina Standard* who began a campaign to end the war. His call for peace negotiations between the two governments received little attention in Richmond, prompting Holden to demand that North Carolina make a separate peace. Confederate deserters, hiding in the mountain counties in the western part of the state, took up the cry and a "civil war" broke out between those loyal to the Confederacy and those advocating peace with the United States. To make matters worse, Federal incursions along the coast caused considerable damage and allowed other Confederate deserters to commit many acts of terror on the defenseless families of soldiers who stayed with their commands on the front lines of the war.[78]

The North Carolinians' meeting was unofficial and did not originate with Stuart, his generals, or the regiment's officers, though the latter were invited to attend. Faced with the fact that many of their own families might already be suffering from the conflict within their home state, the men passed several resolutions addressing the situation back home. They repudiated those in the state who claimed to represent the front line soldiers' wishes for peace by any means other than independence and stated that all such overtures of peace during a time of reverses in the field could only give encouragement to an enemy they faced every day. They claimed for themselves the motto "Victory or Death," and affirmed their confidence in the Almighty's goodness and infinite mercy.[79] As eloquent and patriotic as their statements were, the fact that these men even had to address such a problem while putting their lives in jeopardy each day told much about what was happening far behind the lines among those whose prayers and support they needed. The Confederacy had begun to unravel.

August 20 saw some Confederate cavalry on the march, not across the river in a great raid, but actually in support of a little one by the Confederate States Navy. Col. Thomas L. Rosser, commanding the Fifth Virginia, received orders from his commander, Fitz Lee, to take his regiment on an 82 mile jaunt to Middlesex and Gloucester counties. There, Rosser met with Lt. John T. Wood of the Confederate Navy, who required assistance with a little project he had concocted. On the night of the 22nd, Wood and his men attacked and captured two United States gunboats, *Satellite* and *Reliance*, with the help of Rosser's men. The following night the adventure continued when Wood, taking the gunboats partly manned with 30 of Rosser's men under the command of Capt. Thomas W. Clay, Capt. Fendall Gregory, and Lt. William C. Nunn, maneuvered out into the bay off the mouth of the Rappahannock and captured three transports and their crews. Wood could accomplish little more under the guns of the Federal fleet lying off the coast and landed Rosser's men at Urbana. The regiment returned to its camp near Fredericksburg after sending the prisoners and some of the captured goods to Richmond. Rosser reported no loss except for deserters who left the regiment to return to their homes in the lower counties of Prince George, Surry, Sussex, Southampton, and Princess Anne.[80]

Rosser's movement on the 20th apparently went unnoticed by Federal outposts. However, Kilpatrick did warn his superiors that the enemy was heavily concentrated in and above Fredericksburg. He forwarded a message from Maj. Gen. Gouverneur K. Warren that Fitz Lee with 2,000 cavalry and six pieces of artillery moved near United States Ford. Warren feared a crossing at Blind Ford.[81] The Federal high command seemed determined to repulse an invasion its enemy had no intention of launching.

The alarms persisted. Custer was put on alert to have his brigade stand ready to move at a "moment's notice," and to "observe the greatest vigilance." The brigade's transport was sent to Hartwood Church. Custer's own report of a threat to the right of the army stirred up a hornets' nest of activity and rumor. Gen. Gregg received a warning from Meade that Stuart was reported to be in the Valley with all his cavalry except Fitz Lee. Gregg was to watch the mountain gaps closely. Pleasonton advised that Lee's army was pulling back toward Richmond. Brig. Gen. John W. Geary, commanding the Second Division of the Twelfth Corps stationed near Ellis' Ford, heard from a source that the citizens of Aldie expected Lee to advance through Dumfries toward Washington at anytime. Col. Alfred Gibbs, commanding the Nineteenth New York, way back at Manassas Junction, somehow learned that a heavy force of Stuart's cavalry had crossed the river at United States Ford and that skirmisher fire had been heard near Elk Run. The "raid" turned out to be nothing more than a Federal cavalry unit near Elk Run discharging their carbines for cleaning.[82]

The disease infecting Meade's army originated in the minds of men constantly kept on alert, men who strained every ounce of their energy to fathom Lee's or Stuart's next move. A cloud of dust across the river became a vast troop movement. Picket fire evolved into a major attack. Stuart could be preparing to launch a raid across the Rappahannock and be in the Valley threatening to swoop down on the army's rear through one of the mountain gaps. Lee moved down river in preparation for an offensive and also shifted his army back toward Richmond at the same time. Conflicting reports battled in the minds of generals with the worst of them always winning. The *petite guerre* of the past few weeks had taken its toll. In doing nothing, Meade had surrendered the initiative to Lee who had done nothing to take it and was doing nothing to keep it, although Meade and his generals believed he was or would, soon.

As for Lee, he had his own problems. Desertion plagued his army with no end of it in sight. An amnesty, which Lee thought might have a positive effect, failed when upon reading it men left the army to take advantage of it. Some men actually went home. Others left to join various groups of partisans. Even Mosby's band was suspect, although Lee could not believe that Mosby was aware of it. Almost all the deserters seemed to successfully evade parties sent to bring them back. Lee decided that the only recourse was the strict enforcement of the death penalty.[83]

Stuart also had difficulties. As if the Hood controversy had not been enough, a trooper, who called himself "Cavalryman," wrote to the *Richmond Sentinel* to address the horse issue. His approach differed in that he cited a lack of feed as the real trouble. Claiming that each cavalryman "does not sometimes get eight pounds of corn per week" for his horse and that the horses were "forced to go four and five days without any grain whatever," he chastised the Quartermaster Department for failing to do its job. He went further, stating that men who had to join "Company Q" due to the loss of their horses were often denied rations by the Commissary Department. He told of sitting on outpost duty day and night and of going 86 hours without food for either man or horse.[84] If half of what he wrote was true, then Stuart's cavalry was in worse condition than anyone thought or wanted to admit. That Stuart had been forced to move his own headquarters for lack of forage adds some credence to the soldier's allegations.

Another problem plagued the cavalry, a shortage of clothing, which Stuart raised in a message to Lt. Col. James L. Corley, Lee's Chief Quartermaster. Stuart stated his need and inquired as to what the difficulty might be in addressing it.[85] Corley's response is unknown, but the clothing shortage added to the feed shortage, the arms shortage, the horse shortage, and the manpower shortage surely must have caused Stuart to ponder just how he was expected to meet his foe on the battlefield with any chance of success. Concerning the men under arms and facing that foe, Stuart kept them busy either on picket or in camp. Pvt. John O. Collins of the Tenth Virginia, Chambliss's Brigade, wrote on August 22, "We have to work very hard [.] [W]e have to get up at light and drill till 7:00 then one hour to get breakfast and eat[.] [A]t 8 go out and graze till twelve[.] [C]ome in drill till three then graze till night."[86] Tucked in between may have been another meal, if rations were available.

Because of the lack of numbers in the ranks, all of those fit for duty had been forced to pull extra weight. Pvt. William D. Smith of the Fifth North Carolina, Robertson's Brigade, in camp near Raccoon Ford lamented that those men who lost their horses either in combat or through starvation, the latter he felt was sometimes intentional, pulled no duty and in fact, occasionally received passes to go home to secure another mount while those that took care of their horses, himself included, ended up with all the duty. A cavalryman required a horse to be cavalryman. Without one, a dismounted man was a problem that the army struggled to solve. Some of the men left in the ranks harbored resentment against those who could not contribute their fair share. Unfortunately for Pvt. Smith and others still having a horse, the situation would worsen and they would be called upon for even more.[87]

Back in Richmond, Jefferson Davis, who had just recently dealt with Robert E. Lee's offer to resign from command of the army and who was very cognizant of what Lee and the Confederacy as a whole faced, proclaimed a day of fasting and prayer for the entire nation. On the 21st, the soldiers of Lee's army who were not on the picket line or engaged in other duties necessary to maintain the safety and security of the army attended numerous services held by chaplains of the various commands.[88] While for some, sitting quietly with bowed heads may have been something they were not used to doing, all had ample experience in going without food. The tragedy of Davis's day of fasting was that it was more the norm rather than the exception throughout the army.

Fortunately, the men on the front lines of both armies could enjoy relative peace and quiet. Stories of Lee receiving reinforcements and making plans for crossing the river still rippled through the Federal army, but finally Meade grasped that no attack was being planned and took steps. He ordered that the contemplated movement of one of Gen. Gregg's brigades to the left should be cancelled and that Gregg be so positioned on the right flank as to give early warning should Lee attempt to attack the army's flank via a route between the army and the mountains or by way of the Valley.[89] Some shifting also occurred in Kilpatrick's Division but not to a new location. To rectify a discrepancy in the strengths of his two brigades, Kilpatrick ordered the transfer of the First Vermont from the Sawyer's Brigade to Custer's. Because Col. Sawyer also commanded the First Vermont, his regiment's transfer removed him from command of the brigade. Newly commissioned Col. Henry E. Davies, Jr., of the Second New York, assumed command of the brigade. He had only just joined his regiment. Among his first tasks would be attempting to cope with the partisans.[90]

The guerrillas continued to infect the area between Warrenton and Washington. Federal cavalry patrolled this way and that in a continuous effort to waylay and eradicate Mosby, White, and others, measuring success in the few men they managed to arrest who looked like they might be members of the nefarious bands.[91] Besides the guerilla bands, some of the blue cavalry dealt with other enemies. Sickness from bad drinking water and the stench of rotting horses plagued the men of the Ninth New York, Devin's brigade, Buford's division, in their camp at Catlett's Station. Sgt. John Inglis wrote in a letter to his sister that he felt ill and could barely stand up without falling. His grit came through as he added that he thought he would be better in a day or two.[92] Soldiers face more than enemy bullets and had their courage tested even in camp.

John Buford returned to the army on the 21st. Three members of his family had fallen victim to the fever, but his wife had been spared. One can only imagine the internal battle between grief and joy as he once again took up the reins of command. He was greeted by an order from Meade, who was still not pleased with the number of horses being consumed by his command, further reducing the amount of transportation in the army.[93] Fortunately, there was good news on the horse front, as far as the cavalry was concerned. A large supply of fresh horses had been procured and the number of men at the dismount camp near Alexandria had been reduced from 3,000 to 1,500.[94]

Buford found his command stretched out to and encompassing Kelly's Ford, Waterloo, Orlean, Gainesville, Greenwich, Bristoe Station, Catlett's Station, Bealton, Elk Run, and Dumfries.[95] The day after his arrival, Company C from the Ninth New York, patrolling the road between Union Church and Dumfries, was ambushed by about 30 guerillas, losing three wounded and three captured. Since the road had been patrolled every day, nothing had been expected. When Buford left, the war had been along the river; when he returned he found it within his own lines.[96] That was the bad news. The good news was that all division commanders could report the river line as quiet, except for an enemy cavalry movement on a road paralleling the Bowling Green Road.[97]

The troops observed belonged to Col. Thomas H. Owen's Third Virginia, Fitz Lee's Brigade. On the 22nd, Owen led 200 of his men down to Port Royal and crossed the river at 2:00 on the afternoon of the 23rd. Riding up the other side to Falmouth, Owen encountered no opposition and managed to scoop up three pickets belonging to the Fifth Michigan, Custer's brigade, at the ford where he recrossed the river at 11:00 in the evening. With no men lost, the expedition was a complete success, although to ride so far for so little might have seemed a waste of horseflesh and manpower.[98] Elsewhere within Confederate lines, vedettes stood watch at fords and men rolled over in their sleeping blankets. The latter was the preferred duty.

The Federal cavalry probed and patrolled. Gen. Gregg dispatched scouting parties from the brigade camp near Warrenton toward Little Washington and Barbee's Cross Roads. The former collided with Confederate pickets at Amissville and drove them back on their reserves, which brought the Federals up short. With nothing further to gain or learn, the bluecoats retreated. The other patrol did not fare as well. Lt. William H. Bricker of the Third Pennsylvania, McIntosh's brigade, led his 20 men toward the Chester Gap road, passing through Barbee's Cross Roads without seeing a single enemy. The return trip proved more eventful, when an ambush force of between 25 and 30 men swept out from a wood and scattered Bricker's command, capturing the lieutenant and four other men.[99]

Elsewhere Companies L and M of the Sixteenth Pennsylvania, Gregg's brigade, replaced its brother regiment, the First Maine, on outpost duty near Greenwich. At 2:00 on the morning of August 23, six nervous troopers fired their carbines, bringing out Lt. Isaac H. Ressler and five men from the reserve. After a careful investigation, Ressler concluded that no enemy was present, just a pack of dogs, although they did seem to have Southern leanings.[100]

A follow-up reconnaissance on the 24th, conducted by Maj. Samuel E. Chamberlain of the First Massachusetts, McIntosh's brigade, provided a solution as to the probable identity of the Confederates that shattered Lt. Bricker's patrol. Chamberlain identified the enemy as a Capt. Welch of the Sixth Virginia, Jones's Brigade, who was rumored as being in the area with 30 to 60 men to assist farmers with harvesting their wheat crop.[101] Capt. William R. Welch of the Sixth Virginia could well have been in the area for just that purpose since he was a native of Fauquier County, as were the men of his company.[102] Chamberlain did not have the opportunity to avenge the troopers of the Third Pennsylvania since Capt. Welch and his men had faded into the landscape. Chamberlain returned empty handed.[103] Also returning, was Col. Gregg's brigade, which left its camp near Catlett's Station in the morning, rode through Warrenton, crossed the river, and settled once more into its old camp at Sulphur Springs.[104]

The disappearance of Capt. Welch coincided with the reappearance of John Mosby and his band of merry men. Even as Maj. Chamberlain trotted off toward Barbee's Cross Roads, Mosby situated himself and about 30 of his rangers in a position near Annandale and proceeded to reconnoiter the surrounding area for possible targets. A herd of horses presented itself and Mosby decided to recruit the animals for Confederate service. Unfortunately, troopers of the Second Massachusetts guarded the herd.[105] Mosby arranged his men and struck the Federals at Gooding's Tavern, scattering the bluecoats and capturing over 100 horses. While the fight was of short duration, it proved quite costly for the partisans. Mosby received a wound in his side, the ball passing around and coming out in the back near the spine, and another in the fleshy part of his leg between the knee and thigh, which passed through without causing any severe damage.[106]

Word of Mosby's wounding reached welcoming ears in the Federal army. Speculation ran high as to whether the partisan chieftain would succumb to his injuries. A story about a lady who happened to come upon the wagon supposedly taking the grievously wounded Mosby to Culpeper made the papers. The woman revealed that she saw Mosby prostrate in the back of an open wagon, protected from the sun by an umbrella and having "the ghastly hue of death" upon his face. The papers also reported that the fallen warrior had received two wounds in the chest and another in the back. They were thought to be mortal. Despite this wishful thinking, Mosby's wounds, which received immediate treatment thanks to Surgeon William Dunn, would heal and he would be back in the saddle in four weeks.[107]

While both Stuart and Lee lamented Mosby's wounding, they could celebrate his successes against the rear echelons of Meade's army. Having him and Lt. Col. Elijah V. "Lige" White distract portions of the Federal cavalry from the Rappahannock line helped ease the pressure on Stuart's brigades.[108] This became increasingly important when Stuart received orders from Lee on the 24th to sent Ferguson's Brigade back to the Valley. Maj. Gen. Samuel Jones, commanding the Department of Western Virginia, had experienced some setbacks and required all the troops under his control to rejoin him.[109] Having his numbers reduced could not have pleased Stuart, but he nevertheless issued the order. The men of Ferguson's Brigade, rejoicing at the news that they were going home, began their journey on the 25th. A long ride awaited them, but somehow it didn't matter.[110]

That same day, part of a Federal cavalry brigade also left for a long ride but not homeward. Custer led three of his regiments, the First Vermont and the Fifth and Sixth Michigan, on a 64 mile round trip excursion to King George County and back. The jaunt resulted in a brisk skirmish with elements of the Forty-seventh Alabama Infantry along the road from King George Court House to Port Conway that produced little information and less than a handful of prisoners.[111] In light of Owen's raid across the river on the 22nd and the rumored forthcoming raid by Stuart, Custer's expedition may have been necessary, but its execution exhausted men and horses at a time when Washington was screaming about conserving both.

On the following day, Col. J. Irwin Gregg also wore out some horseflesh, but for a much better reason. Still wondering what lay to his front around Little Washington, he dispatched a portion of the Sixteenth Pennsylvania on a reconnaissance mission toward the hamlet. Arriving at Gaines' Cross Roads, the column split, with one squadron riding on to Flint Hill and the other toward Little Washington. The first advanced for two miles, scattering a handful of the enemy before calling it a day. However, the second squadron, under the command of Capt. Andrew F. Swann, found more of the foe in residence at Little Washington and willing to dispute ownership. The brief scuffle cost the Sixteenth one man wounded and one missing for a reward of eight horses captured. The squadron then returned to camp.[112] For the remainder of the Federal cavalry, the day passed as quietly as it could under the circumstances, although a few of Buford's troopers spent the day patrolling for guerillas near Stafford's Store. They engaged a band led by Jim Tolson, son of old, deaf Ben Tolson, resulting in one horse wounded and some arms and uniforms captured.[113]

Except for the small number of Confederate cavalry stirred up by the Sixteenth Pennsylvania, the 25th and 26th passed peacefully enough for most of Stuart's troopers as they lay stretched out along the river watching their foes on the other side that were stretched out along the river watching them. The ongoing lull allowed some men of the Third Virginia, Fitz Lee's Brigade, to start for home to acquire fresh horses.[114] Presumably some men from other regiments did the same. Most of these probably numbered among the dismounted troopers of the ubiquitous "Company Q" Stuart had ordered out of existence.[115] Circumstances ruled otherwise and while the name may have been buried officially, the "unit" endured, as did the problem of replacing horses lost due to service or disease. With Ferguson's Brigade gone home, Stuart confronted an increasing drain on his manpower, a situation that harbingered ill for the future. The men of the Third Virginia were also concerned about the future, especially what the folks back home perceived it to be.

Like the men of the First North Carolina, Baker's Brigade, those of the Third Virginia felt compelled to address the seemingly growing undercurrent of gloom as expressed in the Richmond newspapers. In a letter written to the *Richmond Sentinel* on August 26, "Trooper" of the Third affirmed the regiment's belief that the Gettysburg campaign was not a defeat but merely a blocking of what Lee wanted to accomplish, that the army had yet to be defeated, and that by "the blessing of God" it would never be defeated. He declared that neither the Pennsylvania campaign nor the fall of Vicksburg should be reasons for despondency and that the army was as enthusiastic as ever in its desire to win independence. To illustrate the patriotism of men true to the cause, "Trooper" pointed out the recent arrival in camp of two new recruits to the regiment, one of whom was Roger A. Pryor, late brigadier general, who lost his command under mysterious circumstances but who still wanted to serve his country, even as a private. The men of the Third welcomed him and called upon others who thus far had avoided service to follow his example.[116]

These tit-for-tat articles, including those attacking Stuart, blaming him for the decline of the cavalry's proficiency, for the loss of horses, and for the poor condition of his men, illustrated the discontent and the decline of morale among the

Confederate cavalry. Beset by enemies from without and within, Stuart tried to cope. He had always had his critics, but his triumphs had kept them at bay. Now those individuals and entities that opposed him began to gather strength. Fortunately, one of them, the *Richmond Whig*, reevaluated its position and published an "Amende," removing the blame from Stuart and placing it on "the authorities." The editor reaffirmed his paper's faith in both Stuart and his troopers and called on "the authorities" to do their duty and help the cavalry return to what it once had been.[117] As if to echo the paper's support, Stuart received word from Gen. Hood, who stated that he would not accept command of the cavalry over Stuart.[118]At least these two controversies apparently had been removed; giving Stuart some much needed peace of mind.[119] For others there was to be no rest of any kind, mental or physical.

If the Federals thought that the wounding of the Gray Ghost would lessen their problem with partisans roaming around in the rear of the army, they were greatly mistaken. Although Mosby's band may not have been quite as active, Lt. Col. "Lige" White picked up the slack on the 27th when he went in search of Federals and found 125 men of the Eleventh New York encamped north of the Potomac opposite Edwards Ferry. Crossing the river at White's Ford with 100 men, White filtered through the enemy's patrols and came suddenly upon the men of the Eleventh who, even though they had fortifications from which to resist, were routed downstream for several miles, losing 2 killed, 2 wounded, and 16 captured, along with 35 horses and mules. The cost to the Confederates was one man wounded.[120]

August 28 dawned with three regiments from Fitz Lee's Brigade saddling up and starting on a march south to counter a supposed advance of the enemy into King William County. While the Third Virginia stayed behind to look after the river outpost line, the other regiments trotted to the rescue. They ventured as far as Bowling Green where they learned that the threat had dissipated. [121] His mission now aborted, Fitz Lee allowed his men to encamp and enjoy a night's sleep. The Little Fork Ranger Company of the Fourth Virginia managed to do better, collecting over 60 watermelons to eat. Whether the tasty treats were donated, purchased, or otherwise obtained cannot be determined.[122]

North of the Rappahannock near Watery Mountain Station Federal cavalry also left their camps on a mission. Col. J. Irwin Gregg received orders to send out scouts to confirm that Brig. Gen. Wade Hampton with 5,000 cavalry had started from Culpeper Court House to make a raid into Maryland. Once again rumor had triggered a response in the Federal high command. Gregg complied and reported that Jones's and Jenkins's (Ferguson's) brigades lay near Sperryville. There was no sign of a movement of 5,000 cavalry toward Maryland or anywhere else.[123] That Ferguson's Brigade had departed three days earlier and none of Gregg's scouts discovered it says something about the thoroughness of their scouting. However, in their defense, the two sides did not come into contact and no prisoners were taken. What was being looked for - a large mass of mounted men that could not have been easily missed - did not include a few vedettes or their supports. Obviously, one gray cavalryman looked much like another, so divining that Ferguson was no longer in their front could not be accomplished through merely looking at the enemy. How long Stuart could hope to keep the move secret remained to be seen.[124]

A scooping up of men and mail near Stafford Court House on the 28th by unknown Confederates infuriated Judson Kilpatrick. Determined to hunt down the perpetrators, he summoned Lt. Col. Allyne C. Litchfield of the Seventh Michigan, Custer's brigade, fresh off of picket duty, and sent him with 150 men from his own regiment and a like number from another of Custer's regiments, the Fifth Michigan, to scour the area between Falmouth and Aquia Creek. Leaving at 3:00 on the morning of the 29th, Litchfield did as ordered but after riding 36 miles, returned with not one prisoner.[125] Whether Kilpatrick fumed in frustration is not recorded, but others shared his exasperation and more.

The palpable fear of Confederate cavalry falling on the rear of the Northern army constantly plagued the blue cavalry's high command. Even the imperturbable John Buford became a victim when on the 29th he passed on word from one of his scouts that Brig. Gen. John B. Imboden with 1,500 cavalry occupied Leesburg and had been there for a week.[126] The scout may have seen elements of White's command, concentrating before crossing the river on the night of the 27th. In any event, it was not Imboden, who was in the Valley trying to contend with problems of his own. Several other scouting parties from Harpers Ferry patrolled the area from Point of Rocks to within one and a half miles of Leesburg and found no enemy. Various commanders from above and below Leesburg sent in conflicting reports, adding to the confusion.[127] Once again the failure to obtain accurate information had stirred up a hornet's nest. Buford even put his division on alert on the 28th with orders to be ready to move on a half hour's notice.[128]

The weight given to Buford's report led Pleasonton to suggest to Maj. Gen. Andrew A. Humphreys's, Meade's chief of staff, that Buford send a brigade to clear out the enemy.[129] In the end, Col. Thomas C. Devin, commanding the division in Buford's temporary absence, received orders to investigate and drive off Imboden. On the morning of August 30, he led his own brigade through Bristoe Station, Gainesville, and Hay Market, arriving at a point within three miles of Aldie at 6:00 in the evening where he camped until 11:00.[130] Leaving his fires burning, he trotted toward Ball's Mill on Goose Creek and eventually reached a point within one and a half miles of Leesburg at 3:00 on the morning of the 31st. Quietly, he put his men in position.

With two squadrons of the Ninth New York placed to guard one of the enemy's lines of retreat and Lt. Edward Heaton's battery of horse artillery so dispersed as to guard the others, Devin's troopers charged into town. Proud of the effort his men had made, Devin wrote in his report, "Had there been any force there we would certainly have dispersed or captured a greater portion of it. As it turned out there were no troops in the town. Imboden had not been there at all. White had left on Saturday from his camp near the town, which we over-hauled."[131]

100

Making the best of a disgusting situation, Devin sent the Ninth New York over Hog-Back Mountain to scour the country for the enemy – any enemy. They proved elusive. The regiment returned and established an outpost line east of Leesburg. Suddenly, a mounted patrol appeared. Capt. Conway W. Ayers in command of the pickets attempted to cut off its retreat with his squadron. Unable to do so, he chased the fleeing men nearly all the way to the Potomac River only to learn that they were a troop of a sister regiment, the Eleventh New York under Capt. Michael A. McCallum that had been out on a reconnaissance. While Devin discovered the identity of his foe, Col. James B. Swain of the Eleventh reported that McCallum encountered 450 enemy cavalry, supposedly from Imboden's command.[132] Even when there was no enemy, there was.[133]

Following the rest of his orders to comb the country for any and all guerillas, Devin sent Col. William Sackett with four squadrons of the Ninth New York through Philmont, Middleburg, White Plains, Thoroughfare Gap, New Baltimore, and Buckland Mills. Devin took the other regiments of the brigade toward Hay Market. At the intersection of the Hay Market and Aldie roads, he sent another squadron of the Ninth New York to scout Blakely's Mills, Harper's bridle path over the mountain, and Hopewell Gap. The rest of his command marched through Hay Market and reached Buckland Mills during the night. By 3:00 on the afternoon of September 2, Devin arrived at Weaverville and encamped. All he had to show for his venture was a handful of prisoners.[134]

The same day that Devin set out to catch the elusive Imboden, three regiments from Col. John B. McIntosh's brigade, the First Rhode Island, the First Massachusetts, and the Sixth Ohio, all under the command of Col. Horace B. Sargent of the First Massachusetts, moved out from their camps behind the Rappahannock and rode to Orlean where they established an outpost. From there, Col. Sargent dispatched patrols to the various gaps in the Blue Ridge to seek out and destroy enemy detachments and guerilla bands. One patrol turned out to be disastrous for the Sixth Ohio, when on September 1, the Confederates ambushed about 50 of the Sixth's troopers under the command of Maj. Matthew H. Cryer at Barbee's Cross Roads. The force of about 150 Confederates attacked from both sides of the road inflicting 31 casualties, including Cryer who was shot in the knee, and losing 30 horses. Nevertheless, Sargent remained in the vicinity, his men performing their duty until September 4 when they were relieved by other regiments of McIntosh's brigade, including the First Pennsylvania. During that time the First Massachusetts and the Sixth Ohio suffered approximately 75 casualties, while the First Rhode Island lost not a man. Sargent complained that he would need the entire Cavalry Corps to picket the country properly.[135]

Orders filtered down through the system on August 28 that relieved the First Brigade Horse Artillery, commanded by Capt. James M. Robertson, then serving with Pleasonton's cavalry, and replaced it with the Second Brigade under Capt. John C. Tidball. Robertson's batteries undoubtedly required refitting, having seen significant service since replacing Tidball back on the 15th.[136] While garnering little attention the horse artillery served a vital function with the cavalry of both sides. Among the Federal batteries were some of the finest in the army. Their contributions to the success of Buford's, Gregg's, and Kilpatrick's commands should not be overlooked. Maintaining these batteries in the field and keeping them functioning at a high level required extraordinary effort, making their replacement at intervals understandable. On the other side no such replacements existed. The Confederate horse batteries served continuously; taking whatever opportunities they could to rest and refit but always knowing they were to be ready at a moment's notice.

The 30th dawned with Maj. Gen. Henry W. Halleck having something stuck in his craw. Lt. John T. Wood and Col. Tom Rosser's successful gunboat adventure of the previous week had not sat very well with the Federal General-in-Chief. He wired Meade that a naval effort was to be made to recapture the two lost boats. If, however, they made a dash for the shallow water up river toward Fredericksburg, the navy would be unable to carry out its mission. Meade was ordered to send cavalry and artillery down the north bank of the Rappahannock to destroy the boats should they attempt to escape. Halleck requested that due to the delicate nature of the operation one of Meade's "most careful officers" be placed in charge. Whether Meade paid any attention to this admonition is unknown. What he did do was select the cavalry closest to Fredericksburg – Brig. Gen. H. Judson Kilpatrick's division supported by a brigade from Buford's division that would guard Kilpatrick's rear. Additionally, troops from Maj. Gen. Gouverneur K. Warren's Corps of infantry would replace Kilpatrick's men in guarding and holding United States and Banks' fords.[137] Wood and Rosser had accomplished their task with less than 500 men. Halleck stirred up over 8,000 to do the same job.

Early on the morning of August 31, Stuart, completely unaware of Kilpatrick's soon-to-be-launched adventure down river, focused his attention on the river above and below Rappahannock Bridge. His scouts had reported that the enemy activity at the bridge had continued through the night. He also knew that a brigade of the enemy's cavalry was stationed at Amissville and that wagons had been heard moving from Warrenton to Beverly Ford. What all this amounted to, he was unwilling to state just yet, although the threat of an advance by the enemy had to be considered.[138] Meanwhile, much farther downstream, Kilpatrick's entire division trotted off toward King George Court House. September would be a very different month from August, and the Federal cavalry was about to welcome it with a loud BANG!

Notes:
1. *Philadelphia Inquirer*, August 8, 1863.
2. Carter Diary; Morrissett Diary; Collins Letter.
3. Richard Henry Watkins to Mary Watkins, August 5, 1863, Watkins Papers, 1861-1865, Mss1W3272a1-355, VHS.
4. John O. Collins to My Dear Wife, August 11, 1863, John Overton Collins Papers (Mss1C6944a), VHS.
5. *Philadelphia Inquirer*, August 17, 1863.
6. *O.R.*, Series 1, vol. 29, part 1, 66; *Washington Evening Star*, August 8, 1863.
   Note: the *Star* gave credit for the rescue to Company F of the First Maine on its way to Washington to exchange its worn out horses for fresh ones.
7. *New York Herald*, August 10, 1863.
8. *O.R.*, Series 1, vol. 29, part 2, 33.
9. Neese, *Three Years in the Confederate Horse Artillery*, 205; Bradshaw, *Diary...McVicar*, 23.
10. Charles A. Legg to Dear Parents, August 7, 1863, Charles A. Legg Letters, Book 5:31-33, Lewis Leigh Collection, USAMHI.
11. William Ramsey to Dear Cousin, August 8, 1863, William Ramsey Letters, CWMC, USAMHI.
    According to Ramsey, the civilian population suffered not only from the heat but from a shortage of food, which is not surprising considering the vast number of men occupying the farms, villages, and towns on both sides of the Rappahannock. Ramsey also claimed that the Federal commissary officers were given orders to sell small quantities of food to the civilians.
12. *O.R.*, Series 1, vol. 29, part 2, 14-15.
13. *Ibid.*, 17-18; *New York Herald*, August 10, 1863.
14. Fourth Virginia Cavalry Record Book kept by Assistant Adjutant-General Sgt. Peter J. Fontaine, Eleanor S. Brockenbrough Library, MOC.
15. Neese, *Three Years in the Confederate Horse Artillery*, 205; Bradshaw, *Diary...McVicar*, 23.
    One source asserted that the rain did bring cool breezes the next day in Warrenton. Ramsey Letter.
16. *O.R.*, Series 1, vol. 29, part 2, 18-19; Cheney Diary.
    Col. William Gamble returned to the command of his brigade, relieving Col. George H. Chapman of the Third Indiana. Chapman Diary.
17. *O.R.*, Series 1, vol. 29, part 2, 20.
    Buford's failure to locate any of Gen. Gregg's command along the Hazel may have come from the fact that the First Pennsylvania, McIntosh's brigade, that had been picketing the river was withdrawn across the Rappahannock on the 8th, encamping at Sulphur Springs, although it still picketed the Hazel with its reserve at Oak Shade. McIntosh's entire brigade pulled back to Sulphur Springs, the Thirteenth Pennsylvania doing picket duty at Jeffersonton. The two bodies of troopers may have just missed each other during the period of the First Pennsylvania's move. Lloyd, *History of the First Regiment Pennsylvania Reserve Cavalry*, 70; Sauerburger, ed., *I Seat Myself to Write You*, 167; Hand, Jr., *One Good Regiment*, 73.
    Kilpatrick's division maintained its position, guarding the lower Rappahannock.
18. James A. Jeter to Bettie, August 8, 1863, John William Holloway Papers (Mss1H72865a), VHS.
19. *O.R.*, Series 1, vol. 29, part 1, 67-68; Crowninshield, *First Regiment of Massachusetts Cavalry Volunteers*, 167-168; Lloyd, *History of the First Regiment Pennsylvania Reserve Cavalry*, 70.

20.   *O.R.*, Series 1, vol. 29, part 1, 67, part 2, 24, part 2, 33-34; Crowninshield, *First Regiment of Massachusetts Cavalry Volunteers*, 168.

    For sanitary conditions, Buford's division moved its camp to midway between Rappahannock Station and Kelly's Ford. Brig. Gen. Wesley Merritt to Col. C. Ross Smith, August 9, 1863, Telegrams Collected by the Secretary of War, Unbound, RG 107, M504, NARA.

21.   *O.R.*, Series 1, vol. 29, part 2, 22.

22.   Carter Diary; Morrissett Diary; Collins Letter; Donahue Diary.

    Gregg's Division was still encamped between Sulphur Springs and Jefferson-ton. Sauerburger, ed., *I Seat Myself to Write You*, 168; Hand, Jr., *One Good Regiment*, 73.

    Though camped near Brandy Station, elements of Jones's Brigade probably also watched the Rixeyville road. Arehart, "Diary of W. H. Arehart," 272.

23.   *Richmond Daily Dispatch,* August 11, 1863.

24.   *Ibid.*

    Even the Federals were attuned to the rumor. In his report on the cavalry fighting on August 1, Brig. Gen. John Buford mentioned specifically that he faced Stuart and that Stuart had not been relieved. *O.R.*, Series 1, vol. 27, part 1, 932.

25.   J. E. B. Stuart to My Darling Wife [Flora Stuart], August 11, 1863, Stuart Papers, 1851-1968, Mss1ST923d, Microfilm reel C621, VHS.

26.   *Richmond Daily Dispatch*, August 19, 1863.

    The source of the rumor was never divulged and neither was the identity of the letter writer ever revealed. The rumor appeared again in the August 15 issue of the *Richmond Daily Inquirer*. Other anonymous supporters came to Stuart's defense in the August 13 issue of the *Richmond Sentinel* and the August 18 issue of the *Richmond Whig*. All undoubtedly were strong advocates of their respective positions. However, the fact that such a rumor could surface at this time could only mean that some faction of those who disliked Stuart was intent on replacing him and may have been testing the waters to see the feasibility of such a move. Within the army itself, Stuart's role in the recent campaign had come under some scrutiny and criticism. A cavalry private wrote to the *Richmond Daily Examiner* on August 13 sharply criticizing Stuart for the loss of horses on the ride to Gettysburg. The paper's editor defended Stuart, stating that the army lost more horses through neglect and mistreatment. The rumblings went all the way up to members of Robert E. Lee's staff, notably Maj. Charles Marshall, who blamed Stuart for the failure of the entire campaign. Certainly Stuart may have had an inkling of what was being said and chose to ignore it until the newspaper articles forced him to acknowledge that his enemies were working against him behind the scenes. The confidence in the support of Robert E. Lee and President Davis that Stuart expressed to his wife was well founded, as nothing ever came of the matter and Stuart remained in command. *Richmond Daily Inquirer*, August 15, 1863; *Richmond Sentinel*, August 13, 1863; *Richmond Whig*, August 18, 1863; *Richmond Daily Examiner,* August 13, 1863; J. E. B. Stuart to My Darling Wife [Flora Stuart], August 11, 1863, Stuart Papers, 1851-1968, Mss1ST923d, Microfilm reel C621, VHS.

    On August 19, the *Richmond Whig* confirmed that the Hood appointment had been nothing but rumor, but on the 20th it raised its ugly head again in the *Richmond Daily Dispatch.* A writer, identified only as "Virginian," stated his surprise that anyone claimed to speak for the entire cavalry, as did the writer in the *Whig*. "Virginian" assured the readership that Hood's appointment would not be an "outrage" and that the cavalry would "follow him with pride." *Richmond Whig*, August 19, 1863.

The controversy refused to dissipate. On the 20th, a column in the *Richmond Sentinel* responded to the editor of the *Richmond Daily Examiner* who had defended the charge that Stuart's raids caused an undue loss of horses. The *Sentinel* writer claimed that the men would not neglect their horses if they could help it simply because they owned their horses and the high cost of getting another would discourage their mistreatment. The conditions of a raid were such that the men could not render the care required to keep the horses healthy. The commander needed to be aware of this and take steps to make sure the horses received the proper care and feeding. The writer stated, "It is for the commander to make all necessary provision, and not to exact more than animal endurance can bear. It is not sufficient that he be dashing and brave; he must be practical." *Richmond Sentinel,* August 20, 1863.

Obviously, these words were directed at Stuart. Certainly, the Confederate trooper had greater incentives for maintaining the health of his mount than his counterpart in blue. However, what everyone failed to understand was that Stuart had orders to follow and the safety of his men to consider. A slow pace on any of his raids could have resulted in disaster, which would have brought on severe criticism from the press – the same press that lauded the raids as triumphs. Perhaps what Stuart should have done was avoid raiding from the beginning. However, since some of Stuart's raids originated with Lee and were tied to army operations, it is difficult to see how. Though no one knew it then, Stuart had gone on his last raid. Whether it was Stuart's desire to avoid criticism, a lack of good horseflesh, the military situation that confronted the army, or the improvement of the Federal cavalry, the raiding days were over.

27. Boteler joined Stuart's staff as a voluntary aide. The exact date of his joining is unknown, although the date of his acceptance letter, August 15, is usually given. However, Chambliss's letter to Boteler is dated August 10 and states that it is in answer to a request by Boteler, who, therefore, must have joined the staff before this date. *O.R.*, Series 4, vol. 2, 718.

28. The uproar over the Richmond breech-loading carbine, a Confederate copy of the Federal Sharps carbine, began in March 1863 when 40 guns arrived at Stuart's headquarters near Culpeper Court House. The guns found their way to Capt. P. W. McKinney's Company of the Fourth Virginia, Fitz Lee's Brigade. What happened next became a point of conjecture between the men of the cavalry and officials in Richmond. According to Lt. N. D. Morris of the Fourth, the guns were tried and found wanting. Seven of the nine guns fired burst. That Morris chose to report this in the *Richmond Whig* and not through proper military channels outraged government officials and the superintendent of the Richmond Armory, Capt. William S. Downer, who strongly disagreed with Morris's claim.

Downer wrote to Col. Josiah Gorgas, Chief of Ordnance of the Confederacy, and explained that the bursting of the guns could not have happened as Morris stated, since it was impossible to overload the gun. The barrels had been tested to five times the charge of powder used in a regular load. Downer went on to explain just what must have happened, which was due to the unfamiliarity of the men with the gun. He made suggestions to avoid the problem in the future, but there was to be almost no future for the gun. Morris's letter and the reputation of the gun among the cavalry, along with the inability of the manufacturer to produce finely crafted parts that a design change demanded, doomed the weapon. Robert E. Lee delivered the final coup when he requested a new muzzle-loading model carbine for the cavalry be designed and manufactured.

Just what impact a Confederate breech-loading carbine, even in limited numbers, might have had in the cavalry clashes of the summer and fall of 1863 can never be known. A thousand such weapons in the hands of Stuart's troopers certainly would have had some impact and may have helped level the playing field a little. As it was, Lt. Morris's letter and Robert E. Lee's request kept the Confederate cavalry behind in the weapons race, a position from which they could see the backs of their enemies draw farther and farther away. William A. Albaugh III and Edward N. Simmons, *Confederate Arms* (New York: Bonanza Books, 1957), 66-91.

The problem did not all rest with Gorgas or the Richmond armory. If Confederate cavalry lacked firearms the fault could sometimes be attributed to the cavalrymen themselves and their officers. In an August 15th letter to Stuart, Robert E. Lee voiced his concern that the men did not always use what was issued them, even when the arms could give adequate service. He mentioned the 2,000 Austrian rifles sent to the cavalry before the Pennsylvania campaign. Few were ever issued and those that were had been either returned after Brandy Station or thrown away. Six hundred Enfield and Mississippi rifles had been sent to one cavalry brigade whose ordnance officer rejected them on the spot, stating that the men would not accept them. Lee intimated that if the cavalry complained about a lack of arms, the blame could not be attributed to Gorgas and his department alone. *O.R.*, Series 1, vol. 29, part 2, 648.

Lee failed to understand that rifles issued to cavalry made the men mounted infantry, at least in the eyes of the men themselves. In trying to fight the mounted battle that Brandy Station became, the rifles were more of a hindrance than a help. Their weight and size made fighting with saber and pistol all that more difficult. True they had their place in dismounted actions, but these were not the kind of fights the men or their leaders envisioned for the cavalry. The solution seemed to lie in a well-designed and well-manufactured breach-loading carbine but that would never materialize from the Confederate ordnance department.

29. The saddle issue received some attention from Col. Gorgas as well. The quartermaster's department had been manufacturing saddles based on the Jenifer design, which, according to Gorgas, had been approved by the cavalry until three months before Chambliss's letter. Whatever had happened since then went unexplained. Gorgas affirmed that all future saddles would be based on the McClellan tree. *O.R.*, Series 4, vol. 2, 720-721.

30. The horse infirmary came into being before the month expired. Capt. Benjamin S. White of Stuart's staff, who had been seriously wounded in the throat at Brandy Station on June 9, received the assignment of setting up and overseeing the infirmary. The location was the Tye River Valley in Nelson County, Virginia. By December Stuart reported that White had sent 1,210 horses, that would have otherwise been lost to the service, back to the army . Benjamin White, National Archives and Record Service, comp., *Compiled Service Records of Confederate General and Staff Officers, and Non-Regimental Enlisted Men*, Microcopy No. 331 (Washington, 1961), Roll 265; (hereafter cited as CSR); Trout, *They Followed the Plume*, 280-283.

The problem of finding replacement horses never received the attention it required from the government and continued to plague the cavalry until the end of the war materially affecting not only number of men mounted for combat, but also the morale of those that were. To lose one's horse meant service in another branch of the army or, later in the war, an assignment to the "foot dragoons." How much the fear of losing a horse impacted a trooper as he went into battle cannot be stated with any degree of certainty, but that the thought of where he would end up without his trusted steed crossed the mind of the rider should not be overlooked. Worse might have been the loss due to hard service or disease, the former increasing as the number of men available for duty decreased and much of the latter out of the control of the men altogether. As the availability of horses dwindled, troopers had to range farther and farther from the army to obtain one. The absences grew longer and the men still with their regiments shouldered an ever-increasing burden. Even in 1863 the size of some brigades had fallen to that of a strong regiment at the beginning of the conflict. That the Confederate cavalry was still able to contend at all with their well-equipped adversary is a testament to the courage and devotion to duty of the men and their officers, but the end result was inevitable.

As mentioned above, the Federal high command showed concern over the number of horses being used by the cavalry and other branches of the service. Steps had been taken to eliminate the undue stress placed on the animals through deliberate misuse and a lack of care. Oddly, in two regiments of the Federal cavalry the men owned their own horses – the Third Indiana and a Pennsylvania regiment - and were cited by one source as examples of how well the men cared for their animals compared to the rest of the cavalry, suggesting that private ownership had some advantages. *Vermont Chronicle*, August 11, 1863.

31. *O.R.*, Series 4, vol. 2, 718-720.
32. *Ibid.*, Series 1, vol. 29, part 1, 68-70; McLean, *California Sabers*, 52-53.
   The Second Massachusetts was attached to the Department of Washington under the command of Maj. Gen. Samuel P. Heintzelman. *O.R.*, Series 1, vol. 29, part 2, 133-134.
33. *O.R.*, Series 1, vol. 29, part 2, 28.
34. Allen L. Bevan to Dear Sister, August 11, 1863, Bevan Letters, CWMC, USAMHI.
35. *O.R.*, Series 1, vol. 29, part 2, 681.
   There was also an August 10 return for the Army of Northern Virginia that gave Stuart's aggregate present and absent as 19,354 officers and men, an aggregate present of 10,210, with an effective strength of 8,404. However, it did not give the number of men present but dismounted and unavailable for actual duty on the front lines. The general August return was given in the main text because this number was delineated. *Ibid.*, 636.
36. Driver, *14th Virginia Cavalry*, 25; J. L. Scott, *36th and 37th Battalions Virginia Cavalry* (Lynchburg: H. E. Howard, Inc., 1986), 6.
37. *New York Times*, August 12, 1863; Brig. Gen. John Buford to Maj. Gen. Alfred Pleasonton, August 8, 1863, Telegrams Collected by the Secretary of War, Unbound, RG 107, M504, NARA.
38. *O.R.*, Series 1, vol. 29, part 2, 25.
39. *Ibid.*, 25 and 51-52; Brig. Gen. Wesley Merritt to Colonel [C. Ross Smith] August 10, 1863, Telegrams Collected by the Secretary of War, Unbound, RG 107, M504, NARA Michael Donlon to Dear Brother, August 19, 1863, CWMC, USAMHI.
   This same order replaced Capt. John C. Tidball's Second Brigade of Horse Artillery, which was sent to report to the Artillery Reserve, with Capt. James M. Robertson's First Brigade.
40. *O.R.*, Series 1, vol. 29, part 2, 32; Hillman A. Hall, W. B. Besley, Gilbery G. Wood, eds., *History of the Sixth New York Cavalry* (Worcester: The Blanchard Press, 1908), 154-155;

Donahue Diary.

      Since the fight of August 1, portions of Jones's Brigade apparently had remained near Culpeper Court House. Part of the brigade continued to guard the Hazel River crossings while other parts drew picket duty near Stevensburg. Undoubtedly this was due to the weakness of Robertson's Brigade.

41.   *New York Herald*, August 11, 1863; Silas Wesson Diary, CWTIC, USAMHI.

42.   *Richmond Daily Examiner*, August 14, 1863.

      Some of what the scouts reported proved to be only partially correct. In a telegraph to R. E. Lee on the 22nd, Fitz Lee reported that Meade's Twelfth Corps had moved out on the 16th for Alexandria. In truth, only seven regiments, the Second Massachusetts, the Third Wisconsin, the Twenty-seventh Indiana, and the Fifth, Seventh, Twenty-ninth, and Sixty-sixth Ohio had been dispatched to Alexandria for duty in New York. Fitz Lee to Gen. R. E. Lee, August 22, 1863, Charles Scott Venable Papers, 1862-1894, SHC/UNC; *O.R.*, Series 1, vol. 29, part 2, 50 and 127.

43.   *O.R.*, Series 1, vol. 29, part 2, 35.

      The reasons behind this rearrangement can only be surmised, but may have found their origin in the strength depletion of all the units involved and a desire to improve efficiency by consolidation. Huey's conduct while in command of the brigade does not seem to have been in question. The break-up of his brigade may have been simply because he was the junior brigade commander in Gregg's division.

      The First Rhode Island and the Sixth Ohio ended up in McIntosh's brigade while the Eighth Pennsylvania became part of Col. Gregg's brigade.

44.   Carter Diary.

45.   Carter Diary; Morrissett Diary.

46.   Hall, Sixth *New York Cavalry*, 155.

47.   *O.R.*, Series 1, vol. 29, part 1, 73-74; *New York Herald*, August 15, 1863.

48.   *O.R.*, Series 1, vol. 29, part 2, 42-44; *New York Herald*, August 19, 1863.

49.   *O.R.*, Series 1, vol. 29, part 2, 44-45.

      To illicit such a response, other officers in the army besides Pleasonton must have believed that Stuart intended to make another raid. Those of the past had caused not only physical damage but also considerable consternation and embarrassment, especially when the gray cavalry made it look all too easy, which it was not. Needless to say the Confederates did nothing to suppress and probably contributed in every way they could toward fomenting such rumors.

50.   *Ibid.*, 46-47, 49-51.

      Buford's division rode through Bealton Station and Catlett's Station, encamping near Weaverville along Cedar Run. Cheney Diary; Frank Diary; Inglis Diary.

51.   *O.R.*, Series 1, vol. 29, part 2, 51.

52.   *Richmond Sentinel*, August 18, 1863.

      Bank's Dam is the same as Bank's Ford.

53.   Abraham G. Jones to Dear Parents, August 21, 1863, Abraham G. Jones Papers, Collection No. 135, ECMC/JL/ECU.

54.   Neese, *Three Years in the Confederate Horse Artillery*, 206.

55.   *O.R.*, Series 1, vol. 29, part 2, 60-61.

56.   Another source states that 3 men and 27 horses were captured. *Ibid.*, part 1, 73; Glazier, *Three Years*, 312-313; *Vermont Chronicle*, August 25, 1863; John B. Kay to My Dear Father, August 13, 1863; Kay Papers, Microfilm mf468 c, BHL/UM.

      The Seventh Michigan, Custer's brigade, reached Hartwood Church on the

12th. The rest of the brigade and Sawyer's brigade probably arrived about the same time. Andrew N. Buck to Brother and Sister, August 13, 1863, Buck Family Papers, Microfilm mf 309-311 c, BHL/UM.

57.   Hand, Jr., *One Good Regiment*, 74; *Philadelphia Inquirer*, August 21, 1863.

58.   Yoder Diary; Ressler Diary; Alvin N. Brackett to Dear Friend Hattie, September 3, 1863, Brackett Letters, Gregory A. Coco Collection, HCWRTC, USAMHI.

        One source stated that the Thirteenth Pennsylvania marched for Catlett's Station on the 16th. This could have happened if it brought up the rear of the column or accompanied the brigade's wagon train. Hand, Jr., *One Good Regiment*, 75.

59.   Sauerburger, ed., *I Seat Myself to Write You*, 170; Rawle, *Third Pennsylvania Cavalry*, 326.

60.   *O.R.*, Series 1, vol. 29, part 2, 53, part 1, 74-75; McLean, *California Sabers*, 54-55.

61.   Klement, ed., "Edwin B. Bigelow," 227; John B. Kay to Dear Brother Thomas, August 17, 1863, John B. Kay Papers, Microfilm mf468 c, BHL/UM; Harrington Diary; Charles Johnson to Dear Mother, August 16, 1863, Charles M. Johnson Letters, Collection No. Wyles Mss 36, Box 1, Folder 4, DCDL/UCSB.

62.   Smith, *"Scott's 900,"* 112.

63.   Diary of William Richard Carter, Accession #39390, Reel 2644, LV.

64.   Hugh Buckner Johnston, ed., *The Confederate Letters of William Henry Edwards of Wilson County, North Carolina* (Wilson, North Carolina: publisher unknown, 1977), no page number.

65.   John O. Collins to Dear Wife, August 17, 1863, John Overton Collins Papers (Mss1C6944a), VHS.

66.   *O.R.*, Series 1, vol. 29, part 2, 61; Frank M. Brown to Dear Father, August 30, 1863, Brown Family Papers, Box No. 85859 Aa2, BHL/UM; John B. Kay to Dear Brother Thomas, August 17, 1863; John B. Kay Papers, Microfilm mf468 c, BHL/UM; William Rockwell to My Dear Wife, August 18, 1863, Donald C. Rockwell Collection, 1862-1936, Call No. A-328, WMUARHC/WMU; *Detroit Free Press*, August 30, 1863.

67.   Ressler Diary; Yoder Diary; Charles H. Miller, *History of the Sixteenth Pennsylvania Cavalry for the Year Ending October 31st, 1863* (Philadelphia: King & Baird, Printers, 1864), 39; Tobie, *First Maine Cavalry*, 189.

68.   *O.R.*, Series 1, vol. 29, part 2, 67; *Philadelphia Press*, August 22, 1863; Lloyd, *History of the First Regiment Pennsylvania Reserve Cavalry*, 70-71.

69.   *Philadelphia Inquirer*, August 18, 1863.

70.   *Philadelphia Press*, August 22, 1863.

71.   *O.R.*, Series 1, vol. 29, part 2, 68.

72.   *Ibid.*, 69.

73.   Fortunately, saner heads prevailed this time. There is no record that Pleasonton was ordered to send out any of his regiments to investigate the supposed threat. If any men were sent, they probably numbered no more than a squadron.

74.   Lloyd, *History of the First Regiment Pennsylvania Reserve Cavalry*, 70-71.

75.   *O.R.*, Series 1, vol. 29, part 2, 74; *Lancaster Daily Evening Express*, August 22, 1863.

        The fact that Merritt filed this report indicates that he either did not go with his brigade to Alexandria or returned to the army and assumed command of the division, replacing Devin who commanded in Buford's absence.

76.   *O.R.*, Series 1, vol. 29, part 2, 72.

77.   The men of other North Carolina regiments met in Orange Court House and drafted resolutions confirming their loyalty to the army and the country. The First North Carolina, being stationed too far away, held its own meeting. Hartley, *Stuart's Tarheels*, 257.

78. John G. Barrett, *The Civil War in North Carolina* (Chapel Hill: The University of North Carolina Press, 1963), 171-172; *Richmond Sentinel*, August 26, 1863.

The situation became serious enough for Governor Zebulon B. Vance to request that Lee send him a brigade or a least a regiment of North Carolina troops to deal with the deserter problem, promising to return in short order to Lee more men than sent to him. Despite his own manpower shortage, Lee dispatched Brig. Gen. Robert F. Hoke with two infantry regiments and one cavalry squadron to Vance. The squadron came from Jenkins's (Ferguson's) Brigade, but from which regiment or battalion is unknown. Whether the squadron was detached before or after the brigade moved to the Valley could not be determined. *O.R.*, Series 1, vol. 29, part 2, 676 and 692.

79. *Richmond Sentinel*, August 26, 1863.

80. *O.R.*, Series 1, vol. 29, part 1, 76-77; Robert J. Driver, *Fifth Virginia Cavalry* (Lynchburg: H. E. Howard, Inc., 1997), 194, 212, 239; Lee A. Wallace, Jr., *A Guide to Virginia Military Organizations, 1861-1865* (Lynchburg: H. E. Howard, Inc., 1986), 44-45; Robert Brooke Jones to My Dear Wife, August 24, 1863, Jones Family Papers, 1812-1930, Mss1J735d, VHS.

81. *O.R.*, Series 1, vol. 29, part 2, 68, 72, 74.

82. *Ibid.*, 74-77.

This was probably the Eighth New York, which was encamped in the area of Bristersburg. Sgt. Jasper B. Cheney recorded in his diary that his regiment cleaned their pistols after firing them off. Cheney Diary; *Daily Union & Advertiser*, date unknown; *NYSMMVRC* at, <www.dmna.state.ny.us/historic/mil-hist.htm> December 31, 2009.

83. *O.R.*, Series 1, vol. 29, part 2, 649-651.

Lee went so far as to address the problem, in regards to Mosby, with Stuart, stating that reports indicated that while Mosby appeared to take few men on his ventures, running terrible risks as a result, other information suggested that a number of his men and officers were selling captured goods in the rear of the Confederate army. Again, so strong was his faith in the ranger chief, Lee could not believe that Mosby knew anything about it. *Ibid.*, 652-653.

84. *Richmond Sentinel*, August 26, 1863.

85. *O.R.*, Series 1, vol. 29, part 2, 62.

86. John O. Collins to My Dear Wife, August 20, 1863, John Overton Collins Papers (Mss1C6944a), VHS.

Note: This letter began on the 20th and ended with an entry for the 22nd.

87. William D. Smith to Dear Companion, August 22, 1863, William D. Smith Letters and Papers 1862-1865, WRP/DU.

88. *Richmond Sentinel,* August 20, 1863; Carter Diary; Morrissett Diary.

89. *O.R.*, Series 1, vol. 29, part 2, 82-83.

90. Glazier, *Three Years in the Federal Cavalry*, 313-314; *Vermont Watchman and State Journal,* November 13, 1863.

Besides the partisan threat, Confederate sharpshooters across the river had consistently harassed the pickets of The Fifth Michigan, Custer's brigade, stationed near the Falmouth, taking potshots at them. Under a flag of truce, Custer himself, with members of his staff, negotiated a ceasefire and soon a friendly trade in coffee, tobacco, newspapers, and conversation commenced. Harrington Diary; *Detroit Free Press,* August 30 and September 2, 1863; Charles Johnson to Dear Mother, August 23, 1863, Charles M. Johnson Letters, Collection No. Wyles Mss 36, Box 1, Folder 4, Department of Special Collections DCDL/UCSB.

91. *O.R.*, Series 1, vol. 29, part 2, 84-85; *New York Herald*, August24, 1863.

92. John Inglis to his sister, August 22, 1863, John Inglis Papers, 1862-1911, SC22716 Box 1 Folder 1, NSL.

93. Those parts of the order most affecting the cavalry were as follows:

> **1.** The allowance of spring wagons and saddle horses for contingent wants, and of camp and garrison equipage, will remain as established by circular, dated July 17, 1863.
>
> **2.** For each full regiment of infantry and cavalry, of 1,000 men, for baggage, camp equipage, &c., 6 wagons.
>
> **4.** The supply train for forage, subsistence, quartermaster's stores, &c., to each 1,000 men, cavalry and infantry, 7 wagons.
>
> To every 1,000 men, cavalry and infantry, for small-arms ammunition, 5 wagons.
>
> To each 1,500 men, cavalry and infantry, for hospital supplies, 3 wagons.
>
> To each brigade, cavalry and infantry, for commissary stores for sales to officers, 1 wagon.
>
> To each division, cavalry and infantry, for hauling forage for ambulance animals, portable forges, &c., 1 wagon.
>
> To each division, cavalry and infantry, for carrying armorers' tools, parts of muskets, extra arms and accouterments, 1 wagon.
>
> It is expected that each ambulance and each wagon, whether in the baggage, supply, or ammunition train, will carry the necessary forage for its own team.
>
> *O.R.*, Series 1, vol. 29, part 2, 85-87.

94. *Philadelphia Inquirer*, August 25, 1863.

95. Henry Norton, ed., *Deeds of Daring or History of the Eighth N. Y. Volunteer Cavalry* (Norwich: Chenango Telegraph Printing House, 1889), 73; Blackwell, *12th Illinois Cavalry*, 118; Lloyd, *History of the First Regiment Pennsylvania Reserve Cavalry*, 70-71; Hall, *Sixth New York Cavalry*, 155; Hard, *Eighth Illinois Cavalry*, 269.

96. Cheney, *Ninth Regiment, New York Volunteer Cavalry*, 128-129.

97. *O.R.*, Series 1, vol. 29, part 2, 89, 92.

98. Thomas P. Nanzig, *3rd Virginia Cavalry* (Lynchburg: H. E. Howard, Inc., 1989), 40.

99. *O.R.*, Series 1, vol. 29, part 2, 92; Rawle, *Third Pennsylvania Cavalry*, 327.

100. Ressler Diary.

101. At least one source stated that the wheat crop was excellent and plenty was to be had for man and horse. Edwards Diary.

102. Michael P. Musick, *6th Virginia Cavalry* (Lynchburg: H.E. Howard, Inc., 1990), 164; Wallace, *A Guide to Virginia Military Organizations*, 47.

103. *O.R.*, Series 1, vol. 29, part 1, 79.

104. Yoder Diary; Ressler Diary; Alvin N. Brackett to Dear Friend Hattie, September 3, 1863, Brackett Letters, Gregory A. Coco Collection, HCWRTC, USAMHI; Hand, Jr., *One Good Regiment*, 75.

105. Just how many men the Federals had in the fight is a point of debate. Mosby claimed he fought 63 while the Federals reported only 26 men accompanied the horses with each man leading three animals and that there were no other guards. *O.R.*, Series 1, vol. 29, part 1, 80; McLean, *California Sabers*, 55.

106.   *O.R.*, Series 1, vol. 29, part 1, 80; *Richmond Sentinel*, September 9, 1863.

There were other casualties, although the numbers are again in question. Mosby reported 2 killed and 3 wounded and claimed 6 enemy killed and 12 captured. Another Confederate source gave the numbers as 3 killed, 3 wounded, and 12 captured. The Federals admitted to 2 killed, 2 wounded, 1 mortally, and 7 captured or 2 killed, 3 wounded, and 9 captured, depending on the source. *O.R.*, Series 1, vol. 29, part 1, 80; James J. Williamson, *Mosby's Rangers* (New York: Ralph B. Kenyon, Publisher, 1896), 90; McLean, *California Sabers*, 56; *Boston Daily Advertiser,* August 31, 1863.

107.   *Washington Evening Star*, September 2, 1863; *Boston Daily Advertiser*, August 31, 1863; Jeffery D. Wert, *Mosby's Rangers* (New York: Simon and Shuster, 1990), 96.

108.   Some have argued that Mosby, White, and the other guerilla bands operating behind the lines had little effect on the actual strength of Meade's army as it confronted Lee and Stuart along the Rappahannock. The opinion that few of Pleasonton's cavalry were ever assigned to pursue Mosby and the others has some truth in it. Only three regiments of cavalry, the Second Massachusetts, the Thirteenth New York, and the Sixteenth New York, and one battalion of cavalry, the Maryland Battalion of the Potomac Home Guard Brigade, none of them from Meade's army, were ever permanently assigned to seek out and destroy the partisans. The effective strength of these units was probably never over 1,000 men. In this sense, officially, the partisans did not hamper the front line units by drawing any of them into a permanent assignment to hunt them.

However, the facts are that numerous patrols were constantly being sent out by Buford, Gregg, and Kilpatrick to guard lines of communications, roads and bridges, accompany supply or sutler wagons, round up possible guerillas from the civilian population, respond to supposed threats of enemy cavalry raids in rear of the army, many triggered by partisan activities, and picketing various locations in the midst of areas in which guerilla bands operated. Federal regimental histories and official correspondence confirm that cavalry from Meade's army were detailed frequently for such duties and beyond the physical strain, the stress of not knowing where the enemy might strike next took a toll on the men that is impossible to gage. Certainly, if Pleasonton had been ordered to cross the Rappahannock in strength and strike at Stuart, he could have done so. He had the numbers to do it. But, Mosby, White, and the others did occupy troopers of the Federal cavalry, wearing out both men and horses that could have been put to better use during the long hot weeks the armies confronted each other across the river. While Mosby's greatest contribution was the intelligence he gathered and passed on to Lee and Stuart, his horse-fly pestering of the enemy not only distracted his adversaries but forced them to expend manpower and horsepower in an effort to stop him – an effort that never achieved success. *O.R.*, Series 1, vol. 29, part 2, 134, 139, 239; McLean, *California Sabers*, 58; Stephen Z. Starr, *The Union Cavalry in the Civil War: Volume II, The War in the East, From Gettysburg to Appomattox, 1863-1865* (Baton Rouge: Louisiana University Press, 1981), 53-54; Virgil Carrington Jones, *Ranger Mosby* (Chapel Hill: The University of North Carolina Press, 1944), 12.

109.   *O.R.*, Series 1, vol. 29, part 2, 665; Warner, *Generals in Gray*, 166.

110.   Driver, *14th Virginia Cavalry*, 26.

The Federals did not at first realize that the brigade had gone. On the 28th, Gen. Gregg was still reporting that he faced both Jones's and Jenkins's (Ferguson's) brigades near Sperryville. *O.R.*, Series 1, vol. 29, part 2, 106.

111.   *Supp. to O.R.*, part 2, vol. 1, 767; John B. Kay to Dear Brother Dicky, August 27, 1863; John B. Kay Papers; Victor E. Comte to Dear Elise, August 24, 1863; Victor E. Comte Papers, Microfilm mf365 c, BHL/UM; *Washington Evening Star*, August 28, 1863; *New York Herald*, August 28, 1863; *Detroit Free Press*, September 2, 1863; *Detroit Advertiser and Tribune*, September 4, 1863; *Vermont Watchman and State Journal*, November 13, 1863.

      Although one of the above sources stated that a captain, lieutenant, commissary officer, and a private were captured, some of the other sources reported that a Capt. Hunter from the Thirteenth Virginia Infantry and four men belonging to the Confederate topographical department were captured in King George County while making a survey. The time of their capture corresponds with Custer's presence in the county. It is possible that all these men were taken by different regiments and not combined in any report.

      The Capt. Hunter mentioned was probably Capt. Frederick Campbell Stuart Hunter of the Thirtieth, not the Thirteenth Virginia Infantry who was listed as being captured on the 24th at Rappahannock Station. The date and location do not quite match, but dates were not always accurate and since all of the Confederate infantry had been withdrawn from along the Rappahannock, Hunter could not have been captured at Rappahannock Station. This was most likely where he was taken after his capture. What makes Hunter the prime candidate is the fact that he was born in King George County and would have been very familiar with it. *HDSACWRD*, <www.civilwardata.com> November 3, 2008.

112.   *O.R.*, Series 1, vol. 29, part 2, 103; Col. J. Irwin Gregg to Col. C. Ross Smith, August 26, 1863, Telegrams Collected by the Secretary of War, Unbound, RG 107, M504, NARA; Ressler Diary; Yoder Diary; Miller, *Sixteenth Pennsylvania Cavalry*, 39; *HDSACWRD*, <www.civilwardata.com> August 23, 2009.

      Ressler stated that Swann captured 11 horses.

113.   *O.R.*, Series 1, vol. 29, part 2, 103.

114.   Carter Diary.

115.   "Company Q" was the topic of a letter written to the *Richmond Sentinel* on August 27. The writer, "Justice," stated emphatically that while Stuart had abolished "Q", it still existed, and would continue to exist until the cause that created it was dealt with. He explained that men might be without their horses for a number of reasons and while the horses were often sent to the rear, the men were not, leaving them in limbo as far as their usefulness as cavalry was concerned. He pleaded for an understanding of the men consigned involuntarily to this much-maligned group and assured the readership that when mounted these men had been among the elite of Stuart's cavalry. All that kept them from being so again was a good horse. *Richmond Sentinel*, September 1, 1863.

116.   *Richmond Sentinel*, August 31, 1863; Nanzig, *3rd Virginia Cavalry*, 124; Warner, *Generals in Gray*, 247-248.

117.   *Richmond Whig*, August 28, 1863.

118.   J. E. B. Stuart to My Darling Wife [Flora Stuart], August 28, 1863, Stuart Papers, 1851-1968, Mss1ST923d, Microfilm reel C621, VHS.

119.   This good news helped blunt a personal loss Stuart had suffered. On the 26th, Stuart had received word of the death of his sister, Victoria, who was just 26 years old. J. E. B. Stuart to My Dear Wife [Flora Stuart], August 26, 1863, Stuart Papers, 1851-1968, Mss1ST923d, Microfilm reel C621, VHS.

      Although Stuart does not name the sister who died, it could only have been

Victoria. The death dates of his other sisters, Nancy, Bethenia, Mary, Columbia, and Virginia, do not correspond to this time. Thomas David Perry, *"The Dear Old Hills of Patrick" The Laurel Hill Reference Book* (2004), 48-49.

120. *O.R.*, Series 1, vol. 29, part 1, 92.

The Eleventh New York, also known as "Scott's Nine Hundred," was attached to the department of Washington commanded by Maj. Gen. Samuel P. Heintzelman. *O.R.*, Series 1, vol. 29, part 2, 132.

121. Only three regiments of the brigade, the First, Second, and Fourth Virginia, can be confirmed as having been sent. That the Third remained behind is based on Col. Carter's diary in which he stated that the regiment was in camp with all quiet on the 28th and 29th. The Fifth Virginia had not yet returned from assisting the Confederate Navy. Robert J. Driver, Jr., *1st Virginia Cavalry* (Lynchburg: H. E. Howard, Inc., 1991), 71; Trussell Diary; Robert J. Driver, Jr. and H. E. Howard, *2nd Virginia Cavalry* (Lynchburg: H. E. Howard, Inc., 1995), 96; Woodford B. Hackley, *The Little Fork Rangers* (Richmond, Va.: Press of the Dietz Printing Co., 1927. Reprint, with revised Index by Alice Chappelear Nichols, Stephens City, VA: Commercial Press, 1984), 87; Morrissett Diary; Carter Diary; Driver, *Fifth Virginia Cavalry*, 60.

122. Hackley, *The Little Fork Rangers*, 87.

123. *O.R.*, Series 1, vol. 29, part 2, 106.

124. The movement of Ferguson to the Valley may have been the source of the rumored raid.

Jones's Brigade was nowhere near Sperryville either. It was encamped near Culpeper Court House. Arehart, "Diary of W. H. Arehart," 274.

125. Allyne C. Litchfield to My Dear Wife, August 30, 1863, Allyne Cushing Litchfield Papers, James S. Schoff Civil War Collection, Manuscripts Division, WLC/UM.

126. *O.R.*, Series 1, vol. 29, part 2, 108.

127. *Ibid.*, 109-110.

128. Chapman Diary; Frank Diary.

129. *O.R.*, Series 1, vol. 29, part 2, 108.

130. The Sixth New York was not with the brigade at this time, having accompanied 200 sutler wagons to a camp on the shore of the Potomac Bay, two miles south of Washington. It began a return trip to Warrenton Junction on the 31st as escort for 300 sutler wagons. Hall, *Sixth New York Cavalry*, 156.

The reason for Buford's absence at this time is unknown.

131. *O.R.*, Series 1, vol. 29, part 1, 94.

132. *Ibid.*, part 2, 94-96; Cheney, *Ninth Regiment, New York Volunteer Cavalry*, 131.

The historian of the Ninth New York mistakenly thought that the brigade's original mission was to find and fight Mosby who had reportedly captured some sutler wagons.

133. Even after this debacle, the notion that a large Confederate force hovered near Leesburg could not be dissipated. A reporter for the *Washington Evening Star*, readily admitted to the fact that the only "enemy" encountered by Devin had been McCallum's company, but nevertheless persisted in the belief that Confederate cavalry was present and threatened the area. He even named the enemy, stating that Gen. Jones (Brig. Gen. William E. Jones) had a force of mostly guerillas near a point along the Blue Ridge known as "The Trap." This force varied in size from 500 to 4,000 men and was raised from men who "skulk about their homes in citizens habiliments when a large Union force may be threatening them." *Washington Evening Star*, September 3, 1863.

134. *O.R.*, Series 1, vol. 29, part 1, 95.
135. *O.R.*, Series 1, vol. 29, part 1, 91; Thomas Covert to My Dear Wife, September 2, 1863, Covert Collection, USAMHI; Sauerburger, ed., *I Seat Myself to Write You*, 174; Frederic Denison, *Sabres and Spurs: The First Regiment Rhode Island Cavalry in the Civil War, 1861-1865* (No city; The First Rhode Island Cavalry Veteran Association, 1876, Reprint, Baltimore: Butternut and Blue, 1994), 281; Rawle, *Third Pennsylvania Cavalry,* 331.
136. *O.R.*, Series 1, vol. 29, part 2, 110.
137. *Ibid.*, 110,112-113.
138. J. E. B. Stuart to General (R. E. Lee), August 31, 1863, Charles Scott Venable Papers, 1862-1894, SHC/UNC.

Chapter Four

Back to the Rapidan

Judson Kilpatrick may not have scored high on the "careful" officers list, but no one could say that he lacked enthusiasm about coming to grips with the enemy. By dawn on September 1, he was well on his way to King George Court House and by 3:00 that afternoon had driven in the Confederate outposts and was advancing on three roads. The rest of the day went equally as well. The determined Federal offensive chased the enemy across the river, leaving Kilpatrick free to place Lt. Samuel S. Elder's Battery E, Second U. S. Artillery and Lt. William D. Fuller's Battery C, Third U. S. Artillery in positions above and below Port Conway. With both the *Satellite* and *Reliance* in view on the far side of the river, the sharpshooters of the First Vermont took aim at the Confederates who were busy removing machinery from the two vessels. The graycoats skedaddled, and Kilpatrick settled back to await the ironclad that the navy had promised to send in support.

By dawn of the 2nd the ironclad had yet to arrive. After waiting an additional two hours, Kilpatrick decided to act. With part of the Sixth and Seventh Michigan, Custer's brigade, firing from along the riverbank, he opened with his artillery, riddling the *Satellite* so badly she began to take on water. The *Reliance* also took heavy damage. The enemy responded with artillery of their own. As Kilpatrick watched the bombardment from a porch at Port Conway, a Confederate shell from a gun taken off one of the gunboats landed in the yard 50 feet short of where he sat. As the general and his officers left the porch and made their way around the side of the house a fusillade of musketry tore through the trees over their heads and another shell landed in the rear of the house. Kilpatrick hurried to take himself out of range.

About 11:00, additional enemy artillery arrived and opened fire. Frustrated that the Confederates had managed to remove both guns and machinery from the boats overnight and in his inability to do further damage, Kilpatrick satisfied himself with the fact that his artillery had rendered the boats worthless to the enemy. He pulled his men back from the river and encamped at Lamb's Creek Church for the night. The next day he led his tired but triumphant men back to their camps near Hartwood Church, arriving about 9:00 in the evening.[1]

At the opposite end of the Federal line, Col. J. Irvin Gregg's concern did not center on gunboats but on the constant harassment of his men by Confederate troops who ambushed his patrols. After an August 31 evening patrol received fire from a concealed enemy force, Gregg could restrain himself no longer and dispatched the following letter.

> Headq'rs 2D Division, C. C.
> September 1, 1863
>
> Sir: My patrol was fired upon, last evening, by a concealed party of Confederate troops, near the mill between Corbin's and Newby's Cross-Roads, and one man wounded and four captured.
> If the same should again occur, I will hold the inhabitants of the country in the immediate vicinity responsible, and cause all houses, barns, or other property, to be destroyed.
> Very respectfully,
> Your obedient servant,
> J. Irvin Gregg
> Col. Com'g
> To the Officer Commanding Confederate Troops, near Gaines' Cross-Roads, Va.[2]

If Gregg expected to end hostilities with such a letter, he proved gravely mistaken. Certainly, his men would not have hesitated to ambush any Confederate column that happened to ride within carbine range. To expect less from his foes reveals his exasperation at not being able to do anything else to control the situations into which he was compelled to place his men. If he had thought the men lying in wait had been partisans, then his attempt to frighten and subdue the local populace might be understandable. But the fact that he addressed his letter to the Confederate officer commanding in the area shows that he held regular Confederate troops accountable for the actions. The local commander dutifully passed the letter up the chain of command until it reached Stuart who responded to Gregg in kind.

> Headq'rs Cavalry Division
> Army Northern Va., Sept. 3, 1863
> To Col. J. I. Gregg, Commd'g 2d Div'n Cavalry Corps, Army of the Potomac
>
> Sir – Your communication of the 1st instant, addressed to the "officer commanding Confederate troops near Gaines' X Roads, Va.," has been referred to me. It caused no surprise. I expect such from those who, baffled in legitimate warfare, seek to turn their weapons against helpless women and children and unarmed men.
> Your *threat* is harmless. For any acts such as you propose, I will now know whom to hold responsible.
> My Government knows how to protect her citizens; and

justice, though sometimes *slow,* will be *sure*, to reach the perpetrators of such barbarities as you desire to inaugurate. Our citizens
are accustomed to your bravado. Our soldiers know their duty.

    I am, Colonel
    Yours, with due respect,
    J. E. B. Stuart,
    Major General Comd'g[3]

Whether or not Gregg received Stuart's reply, he must have realized that
if he persisted in sending out his patrols, the Confederates would continue to strike
at them in any manner they could, including from ambush. No record of Gregg
burning homes, barns, or other property exists and the matter seems to have died
with the exchange of verbal pleasantries.

Gregg's short note proved to be the only Federal offensive operation on
the 1st of the month, other than Devin's fruitless excursion to Leesburg and the
rapid march of the Third Pennsylvania, McIntosh's brigade, to Orlean to support
Col. Sargent whose outposts had been driven in. Nothing further developed on either front. Meanwhile, the fear that the withdrawal of Kilpatrick's vedettes along
the Rappahannock might precipitate an enemy advance evaporated by the afternoon. Quiet reigned through much of the day, until about 7:30 in the evening when
10 to 15 of the enemy slipped across the river at Skinker's Dam and struck pickets
of the One Hundred Forty-ninth New York Infantry, killing one and putting the
remnant to flight.[4] Their work accomplished, the Confederates slipped back over
the river and peace resumed.

The 2nd did not pass as serenely. The Thirteenth Pennsylvania had ridden
out from its camp on September 1 to replace the Tenth New York, both regiments
in Gregg's brigade, Gregg's division, on outpost duty near Oak Shade. Capt. Patrick
Kane, commanding the Pennsylvanians, reported that the entire regiment numbered 195 men. These were parceled out with Lt. Joseph Roberts and 38 men at
Utz's Ford; Lt. William O'Conner and 16 men at Stark's Ford; Capt. William B. Grif-
fith and 16 men at Rixeyville Ford, and Capt. Nathaniel Sneyd and 80 men at
Corbin's Cross Roads. Capt. Kane and the remaining 45 men manned the reserve
post at Oak Shade. All was well until 10:00 on the night of the 2nd when the post
at Rixeyville Ford, suddenly found itself under attack from three sides. An enemy
force estimated at between 80 and 100 men had avoided the three-man outpost and
struck the reserve, shattering it. The Confederates wounded 1 man and made off
with 15 horses. In his report of the encounter, Capt. Kane questioned Capt. Grif-
fith's vigilance while defending his own disposition of the meager number of
troops available to him. The entire episode demonstrated that an under strength
regiment could not fulfill its duty if placed in unfavorable circumstances. Nevertheless, the Thirteenth remained on outpost duty until the 11th.[5]

Elsewhere, the blue cavalry passed the day with the usual scouting expeditions, picket duty, escort duty, marching, drilling, and resting.[6] One patrol spent

the day not in vain. The Sixteenth Pennsylvania, Gregg's brigade, left its camp near Sulphur Springs and trotted through Amissville to Sandy Hook, returning by way of Flint Hill. The expedition gathered in four prisoners, a total which some may have questioned as not being worth the effort.[7] South of the river, the Confederates maintained their routine as well with a few exceptions.[8]

Pvt. John O. Collins of the Tenth Virginia, Chambliss's Brigade, had some catching up to do. First, he needed rest, having just returned from a little jaunt into Federal lines. Second, he wanted to take the time to write a letter to his beloved wife. Fortunately, he could accomplish the latter while doing the former and set himself down to recount his adventure.

With a captain, 3 lieutenants and about 40 men, Collins rode out on a scout that resulted in nothing more than a major discomfort for all concerned. When the captain chose to start for home, Collins, displeased with the outcome thus far, requested that he and 5 other troopers be permitted to venture out on their own in an attempt to acquire a few much needed horses.[9] The captain proved willing and Collins and his small band set out. Selecting a spot where the Federals watered their horses before going on patrol, the wily Confederates, after cutting several narrow paths through briers to gain access to the stream, sat down to wait. Soon, nine Federals approached, their carbines at the ready. Undeterred, Collins and his men waited until the blue troopers were in mid-stream before jumping up and yelling for their foe's surrender. Seeing that they outnumbered the graycoats, the Federals decided to resist. The fight lasted a scarce few seconds, resulting in one Federal killed and two wounded with no Confederate casualties. The "raiders" each made off with a horse and its rider. The party's entry into camp atop fine horses with all the trimmings came as a surprise to the men of the regiment, who had given them up as captured or worse. Everything considered, Collins was quite pleased with himself and very satisfied with his booty.[10]

Two other cavalrymen clashed in the first days of September, but they both were on the same side, or were supposed to be. The personalities of Maj. Gen. J. E. B. Stuart and Brig. Gen. William E. "Grumble" Jones could not have been more incompatible. To assert that they harbored an intense dislike for each other would be an understatement. That they had managed to work together and achieved some significant successes for as long as they had could be attributed to their devotion to their duty and to the hard work of Robert E. Lee, who knew Jones's worth and struggled to keep him with the army. Lee had gone so far as to table Jones's proffered resignation before the Gettysburg campaign in an effort to buy time to resolve the problem. Now, for reasons unknown, Stuart and Jones had words. Stuart, feeling Jones had been disrespectful to a superior officer, had him arrested, and brought before a court martial. In the end, Jones would be found guilty and sent to Southwest Virginia.[11] Stuart had marked Col. Thomas L. Rosser of the Fifth Virginia, Fitz Lee's Brigade, to succeed Jones, but until Rosser received a promotion and the assignment, Col. Oliver R. Funsten would command the brigade.

Other changes in the gray cavalry loomed. Lee's August 1 letter to Jefferson Davis had finally made its way through the system and produced a major shake up of both the command structure and the organization of the mounted arm of Lee's army. The cavalry would no longer be one division but a corps. Wade Hampton and Fitzhugh Lee gained promotion to major general and would command the two newly formed divisions. To equalize the two divisions, at least in number of brigades, required the creation of a sixth brigade, which could be accomplished by a reshuffling of the regiments.[12] This was in keeping with Stuart's belief that the brigades, as presently constituted, contained more regiments, battalions, or legions than one man could effectively handle.[13] By reducing the number of units in each brigade a new brigade could be formed. Under these conditions, three new brigadier generals would be needed. However, other circumstances also came into play.

Brig. Gen. Laurence S. Baker, who had been promoted to command Hampton's Brigade in Hampton's absence, had been wounded and might not be able to return. Likewise, Col. Matthew C. Butler deserved promotion, but the terrible wound he suffered at Brandy Station on June 9 would keep him invalided for some time. Since Robert E. Lee did not want temporary command of the brigades to fall on the senior colonels, a decision was made to promote two additional colonels to brigadier generals to command the brigades of Baker and Butler until those officers could return.[14] As a result, the four brigade openings fell to Baker, Butler, Lunsford L. Lomax, and Williams C. Wickham. In the absence of Baker and Butler, James B. Gordon and Pierce M. B. Young would be promoted to command of their brigades, respectively.[15]

Among all the promotions being handed out, one man's name was surprisingly absent. Stuart certainly expected to receive a lieutenant generalcy as the Confederate Congress had declared that all corps commanders should hold that rank. In fact, in a letter to Flora dated September 4, 1863, Stuart confessed that a rumor circulating at that time had him being granted the promotion. He expressed his belief that the rumor was true and wished that Flora might be present when he received notification.[16] He included a photograph of himself in a new uniform, stating that it was of him with his new rank.[17] Such a promotion would have appeared to be automatic. But it was not to be. If Lee ever considered Stuart for promotion to lieutenant general, he never put it in writing. Though there would be a Cavalry Corps, Stuart would command it as a major general.[18]

While government officials in Richmond restructured Lee's cavalry, the war continued along the Rappahannock. September 3 came and went without causing a ripple in the river, although Stuart did attempt to make one by striking at Gregg. When Stuart's guide failed him, he returned without firing a shot.[19] Though Stuart may have been frustrated by his failure to get at the enemy, he formulated a plan based on information he had received that sent one his more daring scouts, Frank Stringfellow, on a mission behind enemy lines.

Federal Brig. Gen. Joseph J. Bartlett had his headquarters near New Baltimore in what Stuart thought an exposed position. Stuart determined to capture

Bartlett and assigned Stringfellow the task. On the night of the 4th, Stringfellow and 12 men filtered across the river and along a mountain road until coming within 200 yards of their objective. Forming his men, he brazenly led them forward toward the picket post. Knowing what Federal cavalry operated in the area, Stringfellow responded to the sentry's challenge by claiming to be a patrol of the Third Pennsylvania. Allowed to pass, he led his men to a point 20 yards from the camp. Again challenged and asked to give the countersign, Stringfellow rode forward, hoping to capture the guard. The plan failed when the man fired his musket and alerted the camp. Stringfellow, his men galloping behind him, charged into the camp, firing. The troopers riddled a large tent with bullets, scattering the members of a brass band. A melee erupted with shots flying in every direction. In the confusion, Bartlett made his escape in his underwear; horses stampeded through a neighboring camp; one of Stringfellow's men pulled down Bartlett's headquarters' flag; and the raiders made off without a scratch to a man or a horse. Despite coming home without the grand prize, Stringfellow received accolades from Stuart who had to settle for Bartlett's flag instead of the general himself.[20]

The 4th and 5th passed with neither side desiring to break the peace.[21] Capt. Robert Randolph of the Fourth Virginia, Fitz Lee's Brigade, had his fill of rest and relaxation and claimed that he had not had so little to do since the war began.[22] Pvt. Abraham G. Jones, his regiment, the Fifth North Carolina, Robertson's Brigade, still doing outpost duty from Ellis' Ford to the junction of the Rapidan and the Rappahannock, wrote home, celebrating his good health and the fact that peace reigned but lamenting that his turn to go home had not yet come.[23] These quiet days evidently gave a trooper from Hampton's command too much time to think about his situation and he left his compatriots and gave himself up to the enemy. The information he brought with him made the northern newspapers. He reported on the condition of Stuart's cavalry, stating that each man furnished his own horse and prices for mounts hovered around $1,000.00, that the only forage issued for the animals was three pounds of shelled corn or three and a half pounds of oats daily and no hay, and that throughout his brigade the "desire for peace was universal and all hope of success was gone."[24] Some men had indeed lost hope, but others stood to the colors each day and did their duty. With all the problems the gray cavalry faced, Stuart counted on these men more than ever.

A cavalryman from Buford's division also left his command on the 4th. Col. William Gamble, who had been leading the First Brigade since January, went on leave on the 2nd. Buford had been working on his replacement since the last week in August. He had sent a recommendation to Pleasonton on the 29th, offering the name of Col. George H. Chapman of the Third Indiana. Pleasonton responded the next day, agreeing to Buford's choice. Two days after Gamble's departure, Chapman assumed command.[25]

Activity picked up on the 6th. Early in the day, three patrols from the Third Pennsylvania, McIntosh's brigade, received the assignment to look for a small party of six guerillas supposed to be lurking about. Lt. William B. Rawle in command of seven men ventured out along the Salem Road. After riding about two miles, he came under attack by a force far exceeding the six men that had been reported. Charged front, right, and left by at least 20 men, Rawle fought valiantly to extricate his men from the trap. With his own horse wounded in the head and becoming unmanageable, he barely slipped past the encircling enemy and linked up with one of the other patrols from his regiment. Rawle put his loss of three men down to the sending of small parties into unknown country.[26]

Other Keystone cavalry from McIntosh's brigade had problems as well. The First Pennsylvania had resumed picket duty along Carter's Run back on the 4th and the troopers probably were looking forward to being relieved soon. Men clad in gray did indeed want to relieve them, not of their duties but of their horses, arms, and equipment. Lt. Thomas Turner of Mosby's band, leading 40 men, arrived near his target about midnight, reconnoitered, and made plans. Striking Lt. George W. Lyon's Company I picket post at 10:00 the next morning, Turner made off with 20 horses and 3 mules. Lyon and a corporal were killed in the skirmish and five men were captured. The Confederates lost one man captured. The blame for the fiasco fell on a sentry who left his post without firing a shot or giving an alarm. Placed under arrest, he awaited trial for his failure to do his duty.[27]

Near Rappahannock Station, other Federal sentinels were paying much closer attention to what was happening in their front. Capt. Hobart D. Mann of the Eighth New York reported that on the night of the 6th his sentries heard "noises like the tearing up of railroad track" and heavy wagons or artillery moving toward Brandy Station. Although he added that the enemy's lines had not changed, the sounds triggered his suspicions and he felt it important enough to report.[28] At another time such noises may have passed as "business as usual" but with all the inactivity over the past several days, Mann felt something ominous in them. If the Confederates were working on a surprise, he did not want it to be said that he had been caught napping.

Not until the 8th did anything happen to threaten the tranquility once again. Fortunately, the threat passed. The Federal scouts that crossed the river at Ballard's Dam at 2:00 in the morning managed to obtain the information they wanted without disturbing so much as a flea on one of their foe's horses. Finding an enemy cavalry brigade backed by infantry in their front, the scouts simply turned around and returned the way they came. Kilpatrick, who recorded the venture, added that his vedettes had nothing new to report, as everything remained quiet.[29]

The same claim was made on the 9th by sentries on both sides of the river. The lull lengthened, but a careful observer might have predicted that it could not last. Something had to give. That giving began on the 10th with a movement by troopers of Brig. Gen. David McM. Gregg's division. Back on the 6th when Gregg had sent in his report of the debacle at Carter's Run to Pleasonton, he noted that McIntosh had forwarded a message concerning enemy activity near Middleburg. The brigade commander thought it should be investigated. Pleasonton agreed and on the morning of the 10th, McIntosh himself led elements of the First Pennsylvania, First Massachusetts, Third Pennsylvania, Sixth Ohio, and four guns from Battery C, Second U. S. Artillery toward Salem. Splitting his force near that place, McIntosh sent Col. Horace B. Sargent of the First Massachusetts with his own regiment and the Sixth Ohio through Salem, Rectortown, and Rector's Cross Roads to a point north of Middleburg. Each of the hamlets was to be surrounded and any enemy found captured. In the meantime, McIntosh led the other regiments by way of White Plains and approached Middleburg from the south. In the end, all these elaborate preparations resulted in chasing a party of eight to ten men that managed to escape. During the expedition's return on the 11th, the Third Pennsylvania, acting as rear guard, skirmished with a small band of the enemy south of Upperville, capturing one man and two horses. Once again, a false report had launched hundreds of men and horses on a wild goose chase that netted five or six prisoners.[30] Mosby's and White's activities, both real and imagined, continued to take their toll.

At sometime on the 11th, Stuart sat down and wrote a letter to his wife stating that all was quiet. He also revealed that he was not yet a lieutenant general. A hint of resignation that he would stay a major general appeared in his words as he admitted that Lee had not brought up the subject and neither had he.[31] Nevertheless, others were taking up the cry to promote Stuart. A writer, identifying himself only as "Dyke," called for President Davis to promote Stuart as the writer knew "of no man in the Confederate army who has labored more zealously, day and night, to enhance the interest of the Confederacy than Major-General J. E. B. Stuart, who richly merits promotion."[32] Events were conspiring that would give Stuart the opportunity to labor even more for the Confederacy, but no amount of labor would bring him the lieutenant generalcy he and others thought he deserved.

North of the Rappahannock another general sat down to write a letter. Maj. Gen. George G. Meade sent his not to a lady fair but to Maj. Gen. Henry W. Halleck in Washington. Meade recorded that for the past two days his vedettes along the river from Ellis' Ford to below Falmouth noticed a change in their counterparts on the other's side. The enemy's infantry pickets had been replaced by cavalry. Additionally, two scouts had returned from a mission behind that portion of the Confederate line and had reported that Maj. Gen. Lafayette McLaws's Division, known to have been in the area, was no longer there. Rumors circulating throughout that region claimed that Lee was falling back from his positions along the Rapidan. As a result of this evidence, Meade proposed further investigation, possibly by a strong reconnaissance toward Culpeper.[33] Later that evening, Meade, having decided his course of action, made preparations to execute a major thrust across the river by ordering the Second Corps under Maj. Gen. Gouverneur K. Warren to Rappahannock Station to support the cavalry, which would be the main strike force. The commanders of the Eleventh and First Corps were also alerted to the movement and ordered to keep their commands in readiness. All this shuffling into position took place on the 12th.[34] The Cavalry Corps also prepared. Gregg, his men given orders to take four days rations and two days forage with them, would cross the Rappahannock River at Sulphur Springs and the Hazel River below Oak Shade, Buford over the Rappahannock at Rappahannock Station, and Kilpatrick further downstream at Kelly's Ford.[35]

That day saw Stuart continuing the brigade reviews that he had been holding for several days.[36] Mounted on "Highflyer," which the *Richmond Daily Dispatch's* correspondent called the general's "favorite steed," Stuart watched Jones's Brigade, commanded by Brig. Gen. Lunsford L. Lomax, go through its drills. The *Dispatch's* reporter thought the men looked like regulars, being "well armed" and "comfortably clad." Stuart raced all over the field, observing each troop. Plans had been made to review Hampton's old brigade on the 13th and Chambliss's on the 14th followed by the other brigades thereafter. A corps review was in the works as well.[37] However, the pageantry would have to be postponed indefinitely. Unexpected visitors were on their way.

That the vast movement of men, horses, and equipment north of the river failed to rouse Confederate curiosity may be attributed to the heavy rain and thunderstorm that struck the area in the afternoon of the 12th.[38] The softening of the ground may have dampened the noise. The Federals also stayed back from the fords as much as possible, hiding here and there in the rolling countryside. Fortunately, the Confederates had some warning of the impending visit. Just after midnight, Stuart received word that the enemy planned to cross the river in force at several points. He quickly made preparations and by at least an hour before daybreak his entire line had been alerted.[39] It changed nothing.

Just after daylight on the 13th, Brig. Gen. David McM. Gregg led his division across the Hazel River, Companies D, E, and F of the First Pennsylvania, McIntosh's brigade, driving back Capt. Edward A. H. McDonald's Company of the Eleventh Virginia that had been on picket and pushing ahead toward Muddy Run.[40] The Fourth and Eighth Pennsylvania, Col. Gregg's brigade, then took the lead and fought McDonald and the rest of the Eleventh that had come up to reinforce him for about half an hour. Maj. Samuel B. M. Young led Companies A and B of the Fourth Pennsylvania in a gallant charge across the run that rattled the defenders. Unable to hold on any longer, the Confederates attempted to burn the bridge over the stream before retreating, but the ever-resourceful Gregg would not be denied. His men extinguished the fire, produced wood from somewhere, replanked the bridge, and thrust ahead. McIntosh's brigade now rode to the front. The going proved more difficult now that Brig. Gen. Lunsford L. Lomax, commanding Jones's Brigade, had brought up the Seventh and Twelfth Virginia and Capt. Wiley H. Griffin's Baltimore Light Artillery. Disputing every yard of ground, Lomax retreated slowly along the road to Culpeper.[41]

In the interim, Buford had pushed out from his bridgehead with the Ninth New York spread out in the van as skirmishers. Lomax, whose attention had been focused on Gregg, soon realized that a threat loomed from the direction of Rappahannock Station when Maj. Cabell E. Flournoy, commanding the Sixth Virginia and a squadron of sharpshooters from the Ninth Virginia, fell back to Brandy Station.[42] From the heights of Fleetwood Hill the cannoneers from a section of Capt. William M. McGregor's Battery, commanded by Lt. Charles E. Ford in Capt. McGregor's absence, and a lone piece from Capt. Roger P. Chew's Battery, under Chew himself, watched the advancing Federals. After firing a number of shots, Chew quickly realized that Flournoy's retreat would allow the enemy to move around his right flank. Orders came to limber, withdraw down the hill, and take the road back toward Culpeper. In doing so, Chew soon discovered that the Federals were pushing the gray cavalry back at such a rate that the guns were in danger of being overrun. Unable to reach the road, the artillery hightailed it across the fields until out of danger. Unlimbering on the front lawn of "Auburn," the home of John Minor Botts, Chew fired one shot before limbering again and galloping to a new position at the edge of a wood.[43]

Flournoy rallied west of Brandy Station, determined to hold as long as he could or until aid arrived. That aid came from Chambliss's Brigade that had been encamped on the Bradford farm, which bordered the Botts farm. About this same time, other artillery joined the fray. Capt. Marcellus N. Moorman's Battery of the Stuart Horse Artillery and the other guns of Chew's and McGregor's batteries opened on the Federals. The Thirteenth Virginia and part of the Ninth Virginia went into line to the left of the railroad in Botts's woods while the Fifteenth Virginia, dismounted, and the rest of the Ninth, mounted, held the right. Lomax, who had ridden over from the Rixeyville Road to assess the situation, took command of the regiments north of the railroad while Lt. Col. Richard L. T. Beale of the Ninth Virginia took command of those south of the railroad. The newly formed line fell back until it took almost the same position as on the August 1 fight near the Kennedy house. It would not be there for long.[44]

Kilpatrick's two brigades with the Second New York, Davies's brigade, in the lead splashed across the river at Kelly's Ford at 6:00 that morning, chasing the Confederate vedettes back toward Stevensburg. Sending a single regiment, the First Michigan, Custer's brigade, in pursuit, Kilpatrick rode on toward Brandy Station, arriving at almost the same time as Buford who remained north of the railroad. Kilpatrick deployed Davies's brigade south of the tracks and opened fire with a section of Lt. Jacob H. Counselman's Battery K, First U. S. Artillery. The Second New York charged only to encounter deadly artillery fire that killed or wounded three men and four horses in its first blast. Unable to contend with both Buford and Kilpatrick, Lomax and Beale withdrew.[45]

Col. Peter Stagg's First Michigan, which had drawn the short straw, rode away from Kilpatrick's column toward Stevensburg. The Michiganders faced scant resistance until within a mile of the hamlet when they ran into Baker's Brigade, commanded this day by Col. James B. Gordon. Confronted with what he described as a brigade and a battery of the enemy, Stagg hesitated not a moment but deployed his men and drove the gray skirmishers back on their reserves to within pistol shot of the battery. At this juncture, Gordon had had enough of the upstart bluecoats and ordered his main line and his horse artillery, under Capt. James F. Hart, to open fire. Faced with numbers he could not handle, Stagg withdrew, falling back slowly until he reached a good defensive position. There he hung on until he communicated his situation to Custer and received orders to rejoin the brigade. Gordon was left to ponder what was happening far to his left along the railroad. The sound of battle moving farther and farther behind him indicated that he might have to fall back as well.[46]

Gregg continued to advance along the Rixeyville Road. The Seventh and Twelfth Virginia regiments and Griffin's Battery fought with the usual delaying tactics, knowing that unless they received help, nothing could stop the Federals from taking Culpeper.[47] Nearing the village about noon, the Confederates could look southeast and see the predicament they and their compatriots were in. Buford and Kilpatrick had pushed Lomax and Beale back to the woods where Stuart had held Buford on August 1. Here the Confederates tried to make another stand, but the situation deteriorated rapidly. Beale, desperately trying to hold the right of the line, watched the enemy slowly outflank him. He rode toward the center, hoping to find help that he had been told was coming. Instead, he saw the center and left giving way. Artillery fire on the far left along the Rixeyville Road also alerted him that Gregg had almost reached Culpeper. Just after giving orders for a retreat and while riding back to the right of the line, Beale received a ball in his leg, forcing him to leave the field. There was nothing else to do. As they fell back, the dismounted men of the Fifteenth Virginia faced two charges, losing some men to the enemy. A counter-charge by the Ninth Virginia drove back the Federals and rescued some of the captured men, but the blue juggernaut rolled on.[48]

The Confederates retreated over Mountain Run with elements of the Ninth Virginia crossing near the railroad bridge and others where they could. One of Chew's guns and one of Moorman's took position on a hill just across the run and east of Culpeper. Other guns from Chew's, Moorman's, and McGregor's batteries along with Griffin's, which was close at hand and still fighting Gregg, unlimbered where they could.[49] The rapid retreat of the gray cavalry left the two guns under Chew exposed when the enemy began once again to move around the flanks.[50] As senior officer, Capt. Chew ordered the two guns to limber and retreat. Pvt. Benjamin T. Holliday, Chew's Battery, who had no horse and had been riding the limber chest of his piece, received permission from Chew to meet the gun southwest of the village and started rearward on foot. He had barely covered 60 yards of ground when he heard the thundering of hooves behind him. Turning, he saw his gun overrun by charging Federal cavalry. Custer and elements of the Second New York, Fifth New York, First Vermont, and the First Michigan from both his and Davies's brigades had passed around the right of the hill, through the railroad cut where they could not be seen from the summit, and came up in rear of the gun. Chew managed to escape and Lt. James W. Thomson of Chew's Battery defiantly emptied his pistol at the bluecoats before riding away, but the gun's crew was captured. Moorman's gun and crew also fell to the jubilant Custer, who had his horse killed under him and suffered a wound during the charge.[51]

At almost the same time, Moorman came near losing another gun on another part of the field. Unlimbered near a wood line, the gun proved a tempting target, and some Federal cavalry worked its way around and charged the gun from the rear. Knowing that the gun could not be turned in time, Sgt. Lewis T. Nunnelee and his fellow cannoneers prepared to give as good account of themselves as possible. Suddenly, a small group of horsemen rode between the charging enemy troopers and the gun and opened a sharp fire from their pistols. The Federals turned and made for the wood. Nunnelee looked to see who his rescuers were and saw none other than Stuart and members of his staff, who soon rode off into the swirling fight.[52]

While Custer overran Chew's and Moorman's guns, the Seventh and Twelfth Virginia, Jones's Brigade, disengaged from Gregg and retreated southwest of Culpeper, taking a position along the road to Cedar Mountain and Locust Dale, and waited for Gregg.[53] Griffin's weary cannoneers, unable to follow the cavalry, tried to withdraw through the streets of Culpeper. Two of the battery's three guns made it, but the last, under Lt. John McNulty, did not possess the same luck. Intent on racing through the village as quickly as his tired horses would allow, McNulty was unprepared and completely defenseless when the First Vermont charged from a cross street and gobbled up the gun, McNulty, and nine cannoneers. A squadron of the Ninth Virginia, Chambliss's Brigade, assigned to protect the gun was unable to prevent the loss.[54] These men would redeem themselves later in the contest. The triumphant Federals came near duplicating their feat soon after, surprising one of Chew's other guns while it attempted to escape down the village's main street. Only the fact that the battery's horses out ran their foes' more exhausted mounts saved the piece from capture.[55]

McGregor's Battery had its own close call. Forced from its position when its cavalry supports scattered, it fell back through Culpeper, entering by one street as Federal cavalry entered from another, attempting to cut off the gun and its crew. Lt. Ford quickly divined the enemy's intentions, turned the guns into a side street, and rode into the open. Swinging the guns around, he ordered them unlimbered. As the Federals thundered in pursuit, a blast of canister greeted them. That coupled with a charge of some nearby gray troopers, saved the guns.[56]

By 1:00 the Confederates abandoned Culpeper and fell back, making a stand along the road to Pony Mountain. The Confederate horse artillery pounded the Federals as they emerged from Culpeper. The First Vermont received a heavy fire as it took position on a knoll south of the village. Custer, ignoring his wound, arrived and ordered the regiment to charge the wood bordering the road. Capt. Charles A. Adams led Companies B, C, H, and G forward and drove the enemy back to their artillery, capturing 26 prisoners. Emerging from the trees at the base of a hill, Adams's troopers looked up to see a mounted unit preparing to charge them. The Ninth Virginia had been endeavoring to form a line on the ridge overlooking the wood. On seeing the blue cavalry, the men suddenly realized that the enemy was close at hand and would have to be dealt with promptly. While attempting to form for a charge, some of the Ninth's men inadvertently rode into some briars and stirred up a hornets' nest. Hornets or Federals? The choice became easy. The Ninth lunged forward in a charge that struck the unformed Vermonters sending them back toward Culpeper. The Ninth's onslaught carried almost to the outskirts of the village, capturing 21 prisoners along the way.[57]

Col. Henry E. Davies's brigade received some rough treatment as well. Enemy artillery fire proved all too accurate and Davies sent the Fifth New York on a charge into a wood to the left of the railroad south of Culpeper. The nature of the ground broke the Fifth's formation, making it an easy target for a countercharge that drove the regiment back. The Second New York reinforced the Fifth and Davies himself led the Fifth back into the wood where he met Custer, who was also heavily engaged. Again the gray troopers surprised their foe by outflanking the Second New York's right and pushing it back. In desperation, Davies dismounted his last regiment, the First West Virginia, and sent it forward. Armed with new Spencer rifles, the West Virginians tipped the scales in favor of the Federals, forcing the Confederates out of the trees and across open ground. But Davies's men had worn themselves out. Davies received orders to halt and allow Buford's men to move to the front. He put up no argument.[58]

About the same time but a half a mile to the south of Culpeper, the Fifth Michigan came under a flanking fire from an enemy battery and sharpshooters. Orders dispatched the regiment to drive them off. Col. William D. Mann discovered that the task would not be an easy one. The Confederate skirmishers occupied positions in a thicket along a creek, the banks of which proved too steep and slippery for horses to cross. Not willing to turn back without even firing a shot, Mann dismounted about 100 men with carbines and sent them forward. Slipping and sliding down the bank of the creek, the troopers waded the stream, scrambled up the other side, and fought their way uphill against enemy fire that soon began to weaken. Not being able to halt the intrepid bluecoats the Confederate skirmishers pulled back and the horse artillery limbered up and galloped away on the road to Stevensburg.[59]

The story was the same all along the Confederate lines, too many Federals coming from too many directions. The gray cavalry withdrew to a position near the crossroads at the base of Pony Mountain where the Rosson Inn stood.[60] Along the way the fighting intensified, becoming the hottest of the day. The Confederate horse artillery concentrated its fire on Col. George H. Chapman's brigade, Buford's division, as it advanced. One shot killed seven horses in Company M of the Eighth Illinois. The Fifteenth Virginia, Chambliss's Brigade, alone charged three times, attempting to hold back Kilpatrick and Buford. Fortunately, some help had arrived from the direction of Stevensburg in the form of Gordon with Baker's Brigade and Hart's Battery. The addition of Gordon allowed Maj. Thomas C. Waller of the Ninth Virginia, now commanding the regiment in place of the wounded Beale, to again make a stand.[61] Confederate skirmishers occupied the James Inskeep house that stood near the Rosson Inn. Firing from the upper windows at the Federals to keep them at bay, they soon became the targets of the enemy's artillery. Lt. William D. Fuller unlimbered his guns and began to shell the house and surrounding area. One of the shells smashed through a wall and floor and exploded in the cellar, killing Abraham Curtis, his wife and son, and wounding his daughter. Others who had taken shelter with them escaped physical injury but had their nerves shattered.[62]

The wooded slopes of Pony Mountain afforded the Confederates an opportunity to halt the Federal onslaught. While various guns of the Stuart Horse Artillery boomed out against the enemy, dismounted troopers took shelter along fencerows and behind trees. Buford sent a dismounted line of men up the slope. At another point, the First Michigan charged up the mountain on horseback, some of the men slipping out of their saddles due to the steepness of the grade. Amidst the tangles and shadows both sides fought grimly, but after a stubborn resistance the Confederates at last gave way.[63] Stuart now pulled his forces back toward Raccoon Ford on the Rapidan.[64] The Federals pursued, but the gray troopers put up no opposition and crossed the river to safety. Davies's brigade encamped in the shadow of Pony Mountain while Custer's men bedded down three miles further south on the road to Raccoon Ford. Buford's troopers also camped between the mountain and the river.[65]

Gregg, meanwhile, engaged the Seventh, Eleventh, and Twelfth Virginia, Jones's Brigade, southwest of Culpeper. Once past the village, the First Pennsylvania, Gregg's brigade, deployed as mounted skirmishers with Companies F, E, G, D, and K stretched out to the right of the Cedar Mountain Road, Companies A, B, and C in the center bordering the road, and Companies I, L, and M to the left of the road. Company H, being without carbines, stayed on the road in support, ready to charge at a moment's notice. The regiment started forward and had not reached the first group of hills before it came under a severe fire from the enemy hidden in the trees and brush. Casualties rose rapidly. The Pennsylvanians, quickly grasping the futility of advancing further on horseback, dismounted and pressed forward on foot, supported by the entire brigade. The half-mile long line charged ahead, forcing the gray troopers back to the next range of hills where the struggle renewed. And so it went for four miles. The Keystone troopers gave way to other regiments, but the Seventh, Eleventh, and Twelfth Virginia had to fight on without aid. About 4:00 the Confederates took position on the ridges above Cedar Run. Repeated assaults failed to budge them and Gregg finally called a halt to the day's fighting. His men camped about four miles south of Culpeper. Satisfied that he had done all that could be done, Lomax withdrew the other regiments under his command to Rapidan Station on the Rapidan River and to Fry's Ford on the Robinson River. Pickets were left at Cedar Mountain and the Twelfth Virginia and a section of Chew's Battery stayed north of the river to guard Fry's Ford near Locust Dale.[66]

At 5:30, Pleasonton sent a dispatch to Meade, recounting his success, admitting to 3 men killed and 40 wounded, and confirming that Lee "had retired" across the Rapidan.[67] Indeed, Pleasonton had accomplished far more than Meade had expected. Having been concerned for what Lee might do if provoked, Meade had sent a dispatch at 2:00 in the afternoon reminding Pleasonton of the object of his reconnaissance and cautioning him not to bring on a general engagement.[68] By 8:00 that evening, Meade's tone had changed. Pleasonton's success led the army commander to state that the cavalry would hold Culpeper. In actuality, Brig. Gen. Alexander S. Webb's division of Warren's Second Corps occupied Culpeper by 5:00.[69] Meade now had confirmation that Lee had pulled back to beyond the Rapidan. For the Federal cavalry the day had been a great triumph.

The Southern troopers had nothing to celebrate save that with three brigades and four batteries of horse artillery they had fought against three divisions and at least three batteries of artillery and that most of them had lived to tell the tale. Losses were placed at 150 killed, wounded, and captured.[70] What may have stung the most was the loss of the three pieces of horse artillery. These had been lost simply because the cavalry had not been able to render the batteries' proper support. The cause of the defeat could not be laid on Stuart. Lee had placed his cavalry chieftain in a very compromising position north of the Rapidan without infantry support and was well aware of it, having cautioned Stuart that once the enemy knew no infantry lay north of the Rapidan, they would try to take Culpeper.[71] In his report to President Davis, the army commander as much as stated that Stuart had done all he could. Lee did not exhibit any surprise over the day's result.[72] As for Stuart, he broke the news of the disaster to Flora very matter-of-factly, stating that the enemy now occupied Culpeper but that he had not given it up without a fight.[73] Apparently Stuart saw the situation much as did Lee. The cavalry had been asked to hold the land between the rivers without infantry to back them up. That they had done so for several weeks could only be viewed as a success, even if the day's outcome had not been.

On the 14th, Pleasonton decided to see how far he could push Stuart and advanced toward the Rapidan. Gen. Gregg sent McIntosh's brigade against the Confederate vedettes at Cedar Mountain, chasing them back to the Robinson River.[74] South of the mountain, the brigade turned east and stopped at Mitchell's Station two miles short of Rapidan Station. Here McIntosh ordered Col. Horace B. Sargent with his own First Massachusetts, the Sixth Ohio, and the First Rhode Island, a total of 599 officers and men, to move forward to the Rapidan, drive any enemy he encountered over the river, and discover what force held the other side. Nearing the river, Sargent reached the edge of a wood and stared out over an open plain that stretched out a half-mile in front of him, sloping down to the river from which the ground inclined at a steeper angle on the other side. Both banks provided an excellent field of fire. Not knowing exactly what lay ahead, he flung out a line of skirmishers from the Sixth Ohio and the First Rhode Island, keeping the First Massachusetts in reserve.[75]

Earlier that morning, upon hearing that the Federals were advancing, Stuart, who was present, prepared to meet them. A section of Moorman's Battery had crossed the river and unlimbered on a hillock behind some fencing between "Annandale," the home of Col. Alexander G. Taliaferro, and the home of a Mr. Antrim.

Several guns from other horse batteries took position on the south bank. Cavalry accompanied Moorman over the river and spread out as skirmishers. At the sight of enemy skirmishers emerging from the wood to their front, all the artillery opened fire. If the Federals wanted the Rapidan Station crossing, they were going to have to fight for it.[76]

The noisy greeting confirmed that the Confederates were present in some strength and unwilling to be pushed any further. Sargent, believing that Gregg had not meant for him to engage so large a force, sent a dispatch explaining what he had seen, only to have his commander repeat his previous order. Resigned to what had to be done, Sargent formed a line of dismounted skirmishers in the wood and advanced into the open, engaging the Confederates at about 500 yards. Then, riding forward with his staff to a rise of ground, he observed his foe, completely oblivious to the shot and shell that fell around him. While the Federal commander proved invulnerable, the Confederate artillery fire did take a considerable toll on his men who sat their horses behind him, knowing that they could not respond as they would have liked. To do so would have meant charging across an open field into the teeth of artillery and skirmisher fire. The First Rhode Island alone lost 13 men wounded.[77]

The skirmishing dragged on throughout the afternoon, neither side willing to bring on a general engagement until near sunset. At that time, Maj. Cabell E. Flournoy of the Sixth Virginia, Jones's Brigade, apparently had had enough and approached Stuart, asking for permission to cross the river and have at the enemy.[78] Stuart gave his consent. Flournoy proceeded, crossed with his men, and formed them by squadrons for a charge. Handling his troopers with precision, Flournoy made three charges on the Federal skirmish line. The first two inflicted little damage, capturing a prisoner or two. The third, however, caught the Federals in the midst of a maneuver. The Sixth Ohio had been on the line all day and orders had come for their relief. The First Maryland (Federal), which had come forward from Mitchell's Station, replaced the Ohioans, but before the regiment could align itself properly, the movement caught the eye of Moorman's cannoneers and they opened fire. Flournoy saw his opportunity and charged. Overrunning the skirmishers, the Virginians came to grips with the unprepared Marylanders. The fight was of short duration as elements of the First Rhode Island and the First Massachusetts arrived to help drive back the gray troopers. During part of the charge, some of Moorman's shells fell among the Sixth Virginia, the only negative on a day in which Stuart's troopers and artilleryman exacted a little bit of retribution for what they had endured just 24 hours earlier.[79]

In the early morning hours further downstream, Kilpatrick approached Somerville Ford and threw out the Sixth Michigan, Custer's brigade, as skirmishers. Firing erupted almost immediately between the Michiganders and infantry from Maj. Gen. Jubal Early's Division that occupied works on the other side. Before long, four guns from Lt. Col. Thomas H. Carter's Battalion of artillery unlimbered and began shelling the enemy. Not to be outgunned, Kilpatrick ordered up Lt.

William D. Fuller's Battery C, Third U. S. Artillery and a lively artillery duel commenced. The Confederate gunners were soon under a severe fire and Carter had to bring up additional guns. As a result, the situation for the Federal artillery deteriorated rapidly. Facing at least 12 pieces of enemy artillery that held higher ground, Fuller's cannoneers and Company A of the First Ohio, lying down nearby in support of the battery, came under a plunging fire. Kilpatrick soon recognized that his artillery could not overcome the enemy's advantages in numbers and position and ordered Fuller to withdraw.[80]

Meanwhile the Sixth Michigan held on with some support from the First Vermont, the Fifth Michigan, and the First Michigan, which arrived later in the day, having earlier been in support of Fuller.[81] At first, the Vermonters received orders to charge the ford, but saner heads prevailed and instead the troopers took what shelter they could behind some log cabins. During the day, a cow wandered a bit too close and a few of the Vermont men decided to have some fresh milk. However, the Confederates protested vigorously to the Federals enjoying Southern milk and a few shots scattered the would-be milkers.[82] Nothing more transpired on Kilpatrick's front, but to his left at Raccoon Ford the sparring continued.

With Col. Thomas Devin's brigade in the lead, Buford's division set off in the morning from its camps for the ford. Some of Stuart's troopers still north of the Rapidan disputed the Federal advance. The Third Indiana, Chapman's brigade, repulsed a charge near Lime Church on one of the roads approaching the ford, but overall, the gray cavalry had not the strength to do much more than snipe at the enemy. As at Somerville Ford, the Confederates – Gordon with Baker's Brigade along with infantry support - had had considerable time to prepare for the defense of Raccoon Ford and when Buford arrived he met with immediate resistance. Riding with the Twelfth Illinois, Chapman's brigade, Buford approached the river and received a note, warning that the enemy's batteries covered the road on which he and the regiment marched. Barely had the message been delivered when a shell struck a nearby tree and dropped into the road amidst the general and his staff. A scattering to the four winds ensued as the shell's fuse burned down. The explosion sent fragments after the fleeing men, but the only casualty was an orderly's horse.[83]

Deciding that any further advance on the road would be impossible, Buford sent the Third Indiana, Eighth New York, and Twelfth Illinois, all of Chapman's brigade, forward as dismounted skirmishers. A rise in the ground above the ford provided the troopers with some shelter. However, Confederate sharpshooters had the range, making it extremely dangerous for any man to lift his head. Carbine and musket fire crackled along the line. Artillery added to the chorus as Hart's Battery of the Stuart Horse Artillery, supported by the Fifth North Carolina joined the fray. Lt. Jacob H. Counselman's Battery K, First U. S. Artillery, supported by the Eighth New York, unlimbered and answered in kind. Some of the Eighth took shelter in an old carpenter's shop, using benches as breastworks and boring loopholes in the walls through which to shoot. Lt. Richard S. Taylor quickly found that his refuge could not protect him from the enemy's deadly fire. Taylor had just fired and dropped behind a bench to reload when a bullet ripped through his loophole, nearly ending his war.[84]

Others were not so fortunate. Corp. Simeon Banks of the Third Indiana, crouching behind a log breastwork he had built between two houses, fought for five hours before fate caught up with him. He had just laid his carbine on the log to take another shot when he was struck and killed instantly. Sgt. Napoleon B. Kemper and his brother, Pvt. Thomas J. Kemper, troopers in the Twelfth Illinois, fought together on the regiment's skirmish line. Sgt. Kemper received a wound to the chest. Rushing to his brother's side, Pvt. Kemper also was struck in the chest. Both were mortal wounds. The brothers died just days apart.[85]

Civilians too could not escape the leaden hail. "Retreat," home of Confederate scout Frank Stringfellow, stood on a bluff overlooking the ford. Caught unaware by the approaching combatants, the Stringfellow family was at home and forced to take what shelter they could. Sometime during the action Frank's mother was struck in the foot. She stayed in the house until the fighting ceased when an unidentified Federal officer had her carried on a stretcher to "Sumerduck," the home of a relative. Unknown to the Federals, Mrs. Stringfellow smuggled out the family's silver under her blankets. At first her wound engendered concern that amputation might be necessary, but with the careful attentions of a Federal surgeon she recovered.[86]

Dusk brought an end to the fighting on the 14th. Meade expressed his view of the fighting to Gen. Halleck in Washington, admitting he had gained only the knowledge that the Confederates held the line of the Rapidan in strength and any attempt to force a crossing would be costly. From prisoners taken, including a member of the Forty-eighth Mississippi Infantry of Brig. Gen. Carnot Posey's Brigade, Maj. Gen. Richard H. Anderson's Division, A. P. Hill's Corps, the Federal commander postulated that Lee no longer had Longstreet's Corps with him and indeed he did not, Longstreet having left for the west on the 8th. Nevertheless, Meade felt that with what Lee had left, the southern army could hold its position. Meade also believed that although he might have an advantage in numbers, he could see no object in advancing. Such action, he wrote, would require a change in his supply base. He also thought that he did not possess the strength in numbers to lay siege to Richmond, if he could push Lee back that far. He concluded by reporting that Pleasonton would hold his position on the Rapidan and probe for a possible crossing site.[87]

In his communication to President Davis, Robert E. Lee concluded that the Federal thrust simply had been a reconnaissance-in-force but assured his chief that if it proved more he was prepared. Although Meade had hounded Stuart to the Rapidan and taken Culpeper, all the Federal commander had really gained was a change in position. The stalemate would continue. While Lee assumed great risk in detaching Longstreet, he felt confident that he could deal with anything Meade might attempt. The one thing Lee was not prepared to do was go over on the offensive – at least, not yet. All he could do for the present was wait.[88]

Although occupied with the enemy at Rapidan Station, Stuart took time during the day to order Fitz Lee's old brigade, now led by newly christened Brig. Gen. Williams C. Wickham, from its camp near Fredericksburg to Verdiersville where it could support the line of the Rapidan.[89] The reshuffling of the regiments into their new brigades would proceed over the next several days. In the meantime, the Confederates looked for opportunities to strengthen their position. Thoughts of possibly striking a blow at their adversaries across the Rapidan could be entertained but realistically could not be acted upon until the cavalry brigades regrouped and the enemy's dispositions evaluated.

Having driven all but a few pickets of Jones's Brigade across Fry's Ford on the 14th, McIntosh's troopers withdrew and encamped around Cedar Mountain with some elements pulling back in rear of Pony Mountain.[90] That same day, Kilpatrick sent Davies's brigade to cover Robertson's Ford on the Rapidan, but being misinformed as to its location, Davies sent troopers to the wrong ford. Not until the afternoon of the 15th did he realize his mistake and dispatch Capt. George V. Griggs with a portion of the Second New York to Robertson's Ford with orders to clear out any Confederates still north of the river, dig rifle pits, and connect with Gregg's left flank. The enemy did nothing to ruffle Griggs's feathers and the day passed quietly.[91]

Upstream, the 15th dawned at Rapidan Station with the opponents glaring at each other across the same ground as the day before. Some, if not all, of the Sixth Virginia withdrew across the river, but only temporarily, returning to their post after dark. Confederate artillery still covered the ground, making any Federal advance dangerous.[92] Portions of the Federal cavalry also pulled back to Cedar Mountain where Gregg's division regrouped. Elements of Warren's Second Corps replaced them.[93] The First and Third Pennsylvania, McIntosh's brigade, rode in the opposite direction, leaving their camps near Cedar Mountain at 4:00 in the morning and taking up outpost duties along the Rapidan River near Rapidan Station. The Third formed a skirmish line in support of the pickets and stayed in that formation the entire day.[94] Stuart wanted to retain command of the railroad bridge as it put a thorn in the Federals' side of which they were well aware. As long as the Confederates held the bridge, a rapid thrust over the river remained a possibility.[95]

Custer's brigade still occupied the ground on the north bank of Somerville Ford. The Sixth Michigan, supported by the First Vermont, sniped at the enemy. The Confederates did not hesitate to do likewise. An hour or two after midnight on the 15th, both regiments finally received relief and fell back.[96] The First Michigan supported the men at the ford until it withdrew at 10:00 at night.[97] Col. George Gray of the Sixth Michigan who commanded the vedettes at the ford reported that the enemy dug entrenchments throughout the day. He added that four batteries covered the ford and that his men came under volley fire repeatedly.[98] Pvt. John R. Morey of the Fifth Michigan recorded in his diary his day's experience, "This morning we get in a hollow so that they cannot shoot at us with their rifles and so they try shelling us their bombs bursting over us and passing over some rods beyond us before they burst."[99]

At Raccoon Ford, little changed from the previous day. Skirmishing interspersed with occasional artillery outbursts flared up intermittently.[100] A dismounted Sixth New York, Devin's brigade, drove toward the ford with the object of crossing if conditions permitted. They didn't. The Confederates greeted the regiment with musket and artillery fire, forcing the New Yorkers to hunker down until nightfall when they withdrew.[101] Some regiments of Buford's command drew other duties. The Eighth Illinois, Chapman's brigade, trotted down river to Morton's Ford and beyond, trying to find a weak link in the enemy's defenses. Companies F and G rode all the way to Germanna Ford, crossed and drove a weak enemy force back some distance before returning at dark.[102]

In retrospect, the day's activities showed one thing clearly, the Federal cavalry's advance had ground to a halt at the line of the Rapidan. Meade had not wanted to see the end of such a successful operation and at 9:00 in the morning, had ordered that the banks of the river be examined in the hope that a point could be discovered where the enemy had not entrenched and a pontoon bridge might be constructed.[103] Throughout the day, at least a portion of his cavalry faithfully carried out those instructions only to be rebuffed at every point, save Germanna Ford. In contrast to Meade's, Pleasonton's early morning orders to Gen. Gregg revealed a different view of the situation. They said nothing about probing for a crossing point, but instead directed that the enemy still north of the river, meaning at Rapidan Station, be driven to the south bank, if practicable, and then that an outpost line be established. Gregg made no attempt to execute this directive, being well aware of the strength of the enemy's position. In the same communication, Pleasonton also instructed Gregg to send back any spare men to collect supplies and the division's share of the newly arrived shipment of 1,000 fresh horses.[104] This Gregg could do and did. The scope of these instructions did not encompass an advance over the Rapidan. Pleasonton seemed to be content with what his cavalry had achieved and found no reason to push his luck.

Whether Brig. Gen. Henry E. Davies received Pleasonton's admonition concerning driving back the Confederates still north of the Rapidan is unknown, but he nevertheless took steps on the morning of the 16th to do just that. Davies's skirmishers advanced and chased the enemy over the Rapidan River at Robertson's Ford, except for a small contingent that held onto the Robertson house. At the second ford, the bluecoats found the going a bit rougher. Determined to keep their hold on the southern side of the ford, a Confederate infantry regiment crossed the river in support of its outposts and threw back a battalion of the Fifth New York. In this instance, however, the graycoats bit off a bit more than they could chew. A portion of the Second New York led by Capt. Charles Hasty arrived to reinforce their comrades. They soon had support from the First West Virginia and Counselman's battery. The fight quickly turned against the Confederates who broke for the ford, leaving some of their dead behind but carrying off their wounded.[105]

Confederate aggressiveness continued all day at Raccoon Ford with occasional skirmisher fire keeping everyone on both sides alert, at least until late in the afternoon. About 5:00 an increase in artillery fire that dropped shells into the camp of the Sixth New York, Devin's brigade, wounding several men, masked a rapid crossing of the ford by a part of the Seventh Louisiana Infantry from Brig. Gen. Harry T. Hays's Brigade, Maj. Gen. Jubal A. Early's Division, Lt. Gen. Richard S. Ewell's Corps. The graycoats slipped quietly through a field of standing corn, avoiding Federal pickets, and struck the reserve post of the Fourth New York, Devin's brigade, killing Capt. William Hardt and wounding or capturing about 30 men. The disaster drew the ire of superior officers, Pleasonton among them, and the regiment was stripped of its colors until such time that it proved itself worthy to be a part of the "glorious and noble First Division."[106] The pickets of the Sixth Michigan, Custer's brigade, under Lt. Don George Lovell nearly suffered the same fate, but Col. George Gray brought up the rest of the regiment backed by the Fifth Michigan and drove off the enemy.[107]

Companies G and K of the Eighth Illinois, Chapman's brigade, rode out during the day, heading for Germanna Ford. Arriving, they found an open door and crossed the river without opposition. Not having the strength to do more than look around and undoubtedly surprised at the absence of Confederate forces, they soon decided that they had learned enough and returned to safety without firing a shot.[108] The incursion apparently did not go completely unnoticed by the Confederates, who may have simply withdrawn, not wanting to bring on a fight. However, the pickets would soon return to make sure the next Federal patrol to visit would receive a different welcome.[109]

As the day waned, Meade again ordered a shifting of his troops for the following day, reflecting his desire to place his infantry in closer proximity to the enemy along the river. The Second Corps would march at daylight and relieve the cavalry pickets from Cedar Mountain to Somerville Ford. Simultaneously, the Twelfth Corps would replace the cavalry from Raccoon Ford to Morton's Ford. Pleasonton received specific instructions to assign a brigade to cover the right flank of the army and connect with the pickets of the Second Corps. He was to place two squadrons at the disposal of the commanders of the Second and Twelfth Corps and to form a portion of the cavalry to guard the army's left flank while assembling his reserve at Stevensburg.[110] In effect, the cavalry had earned a respite, and Meade took steps to provide what he could.

Unfortunately, the shift did not come soon enough for some of the troopers of Custer's brigade still watching Somerville Ford on the 16th. About noon, the 100 men of the Sixth Michigan, guarding the ford, found themselves outflanked and forced to leave their ditch and scurry rearward to avoid being gobbled up. The Confederates drove back 200 men from the Seventh Michigan under Lt. Col. Allyne Litchfield that had been in support. After advancing about a half a mile, the gray intruders ran into the Fifth Michigan, summoned by Kilpatrick to rectify the situation, which charged through the Sixth and Seventh, recovering all the lost ground and chasing the enemy back over the ford. Casualties were light, although the Seventh had one officer wounded, Capt. Robert Sproul. After the fight, the Confederates quieted down, allowing the Michigan men to look over their shoulders for the promised infantry relief that finally arrived on the 17th.[111]

Likewise, Confederate infantry assumed an increasingly larger role in guarding the various fords along the Rapidan. As a result, some of Stuart's regiments and horse batteries spent at least part of the 16th traveling to their new brigade assignments. A number of men grumbled among themselves over the changes.[112] Most of Lee's mounted arm appears to have avoided confrontation with the enemy this day. Indeed, Wickham's Brigade enjoyed a quiet restful day at Verdiersville, a growing number of men attending prayer meetings led by the Rev. Thomas N. Conrad, soon to be the regiment's next chaplain.[113] Stuart evidently took advantage of the break to do a little house hunting, writing to Flora that he had found a house and farm for sale that would suit them perfectly. He hoped to purchase it.[114] While war raged around him, he still envisioned a peaceful life sometime in the future. And, peace did indeed come for most of the cavalry of both armies, at least for two days. Then once more bugles blew and men rode to do battle.

Notes:

1.   This account has been compiled from the following sources: *O.R.*, Series 1, vol. 29, part 1, 96-99; John R. Morey to Cousin William, September 6, 1863, John R. Morey Papers, Microfilm mf363 c, BHL/UM; Victor E. Comte to Dear Elise, September 3, 1863; Victor E. Comte Papers, Microfilm mf365 c, BHL/UM; Frederick Bush to Dear Father, September 3, 1863, Christian and Frederick Bush Collection, MS 2004-22, Box 1, Folder 1, AM; Harrington Diary; Inglis Diary, Archives of Michigan; Morey Diary; *Washington Evening Star*, September 4, 1863; *Philadelphia Press*, September 4, 1863; *New York Times*, September 4 and 5, 1863; *New York Herald*, September 4 and 5, 1863; *Vermont Watchman and State Journal*, November 13, 1863.

        Gamble's brigade, Buford's division, moved from its camp along Cedar Run on the 31st in support of Kilpatrick. Gamble bivouacked for the night at Hartwood Church. On the 1st, the brigade marched to Falmouth and encamped, staying there throughout the next day and night. The Twelfth Illinois guarded the camp. The Eighth New York did picket duty along the river through the night of the 2nd, listening to several enemy bands playing across the river in Fredericksburg. On the 3rd, the brigade withdrew to Hartwood Church, returning to Weaverville on the 4th. Chapman Diary, Cheney Diary; Frank Diary; Wesson Diary; *Daily Union & Advertiser*, date unknown; *NYSMMVRC* at, <www.dmna.state.ny.us/historic/mil-hist.htm> December 31, 2009.

        Lt. George M. Gilchrist of the Third Indiana, a member of Buford's staff, wrote home that Kilpatrick had done little to earn the headlines that followed the expedition's conclusion. Gilchrist felt that Kilpatrick had bungled the operation and that the newspapers reported it as a success because Kilpatrick had the reporters in his pocket. Undoubtedly, both rivalry and jealousy played a roll in Gilchrist's view of the event. Truth be told, Kilpatrick had accomplished about all he could have under the circumstances. It is doubtful that Buford could have done much better, considering the lack of assistance from the navy. George Montfort Gilchrist to My Dear Mollie, September 10, 1863, George Montfort Gilchrist Family Papers, 1854-1921, MMC-3626, Archival Manuscript Material (Collection), LC.

2.   *Richmond Sentinel*, September 7, 1863.
3.   *Ibid.*
4.   *O.R.*, Series 1, vol. 29, part 2, 151-152.
5.   *Ibid.*, part 1, 100-101; Hand, Jr., *One Good Regiment*, 76-78.
6.   Lloyd, *History of the First Regiment Pennsylvania Reserve Cavalry*, 71; Hall, *Sixth New York Cavalry*, 156; Klement, ed., "Edwin B. Bigelow," 227; Miller, *Sixteenth Pennsylvania Cavalry*, 39; Norton, *Deeds of Daring*, 73; Pyne, *First New Jersey Cavalry*, 171; Rawle, *Third Pennsylvania Cavalry*, 327.
7.   Ressler Diary; Yoder Diary.
8.   Carter Diary; Morrissett Diary.
9.   The horse problem had not gone away for the men on the front lines or the newspapers back in Richmond. An editorial appeared in the *Richmond Daily Dispatch* on September 3, 1863, criticizing the current system by which troopers obtained their horses, meaning by purchase, not by raid from the enemy. The editor felt that unless something was done, and soon, the whole of the cavalry might be "broken up." He did not stop with chastising the government over the 40 cents a day allowance to the trooper as rental for his horse, but went further, stating that the failure to supply forage and horse shoes led directly to the problem of dismounted cavalrymen being unable to

perform their duties. Ending with a plea for the Confederate Congress to address the issue, stating boldly that the government should supply the horses, the editor concluded that if nothing were done large bodies of troopers would soon be dismounted. Thankfully, neither the troopers nor Stuart or his officers came in for any blame in the matter.

10. John O. Collins Letter, September 2, 1863, John Overton Collins Papers (Mss1C6944a), VHS.
     It is possible that this is the attack Col. J. Irvin Gregg referred to in his letter. Although the casualties are not the same in number, that is not surprising. The time and the area fit.

11. *O.R.*, Series 1, vol. 29, part 2, 771-772; McDonald, *History of the Laurel Brigade*, 168; Freeman, *Lee's Lieutenants*, III, 213.

12. When the army had returned to the Rappahannock line, Stuart's command consisted of six brigades – Hampton's (Baker), Fitz Lee's, W. H. F. Lee's (Chambliss), Robertson's, Jones's, and Jenkins's (Ferguson). That number reduced to five when Jenkins's Brigade transferred back to the Valley.

13. Freeman, *Lee's Lieutenants*, 209.

14. The only exception to this was Col. John R. Chambliss who would continue to command W. H. F. Lee's brigade as a colonel. Why Chambliss did not rate a promotion at this time is unknown.

15. On August 31, 1863, Stuart's Cavalry Division was organized as follows:

    Hampton's Brigade - Brig. Gen. Wade Hampton
      Cobb's (Georgia) Cavalry, Col. Pierce M. B. Young
      Phillips (Georgia) Cavalry, Lt. Col. William W. Rich
      Jeff. Davis (Mississippi) Legion, Lt. Col. Joseph F. Waring
      First North Carolina Cavalry, Col. James B. Gordon
      First South Carolina Cavalry, Col. John L. Black
      Second South Carolina Cavalry, Col. Matthew C. Butler
    William H. F. Lee's Brigade – Col. John R. Chambliss, Jr.
      Second North Carolina Cavalry, Col. William G. Robinson
      Ninth Virginia Cavalry, Col. Richard L. T. Beale
      Tenth Virginia Cavalry, Col. James Lucius Davis
      Thirteenth Virginia Cavalry, Col. John R. Chambliss, Jr.
      Fifteenth Virginia Cavalry, Col. William B. Ball
    Robertson's Brigade - Col. Dennis D. Ferebee
      Fourth North Carolina Cavalry, Col. Dennis D. Ferebee
      Fifth North Carolina Cavalry, Lt. Col. Stephen B. Evans
    Fitzhugh Lee's Brigade - Brig. Gen. Fitzhugh Lee
      First Battalion Maryland Cavalry, Lt. Col. Ridgely Brown
      First Virginia Cavalry, Col. Richard W. Carter
      Second Virginia Cavalry, Col. Thomas T. Munford
      Third Virginia Cavalry, Col. Thomas H. Owen
      Fourth Virginia Cavalry, Col. Williams C. Wickham
      Fifth Virginia Cavalry, Col. Thomas L. Rosser
    Jones's Brigade - Brig. Gen. William E. Jones
      Sixth Virginia Cavalry, Lt. Col. John Shac Green
      Seventh Virginia Cavalry, Col. Richard H. Dulany
      Eleventh Virginia Cavalry, Lt. Col. Oliver R. Funsten
      Twelfth Virginia Cavalry, Col. Asher W. Harman

Thirty-fifth Battalion Virginia Cavalry, Lt. Col. Elijah V. White
O.R., Series 1, vol. 29, part 2, 686-687.
On September 9, the cavalry's organization looked as follows:
First Division - Maj. Gen. Wade Hampton
    Jones's Brigade - Brig. Gen. William E. Jones (Col. O.R. Funsten)
        Sixth Virginia, Lt. Col. John Shac Green
        Seventh Virginia, Col. Richard H. Dulany
        Twelfth Virginia, Col. Asher W. Harman
        Thirty-fifth Virginia Battalion, Lt. Col. Elijah V. White
    Baker's Brigade - Brig. Gen. Laurence S. Baker (Col. John B. Gordon)
        First North Carolina, Col. James B. Gordon
        Second North Carolina, Lt. Col. William G. Robinson
        Fourth North Carolina, Col. Dennis D. Ferebee
        Fifth North Carolina, Col. Stephen B. Evans
    Butler's Brigade - Brig. Gen. M. C. Butler (Col. P.M.B. Young)
        Cobb's (Georgia) Legion, Col. Pierce M. B. Young
        Jeff. Davis (Mississippi) Legion, Lt. Col. Joseph F. Waring
        Phillips (Georgia) Legion, Lt. Col. William W. Rich
        Second South Carolina, Lt. Col. Thomas J. Lipscomb

Second Division - Maj. Gen. Fitzhugh Lee
    Rooney Lee's Brigade - Brig. Gen. William H. F. Lee
        First South Carolina, Col. John L. Black
        Ninth Virginia, Col. Richard L. T. Beale
        Tenth Virginia, Col. James Lucius Davis
        Thirteenth Virginia, Col. John R. Chambliss, Jr.
    Lomax's Brigade - Brig. Gen. Lunsford L. Lomax
        First Maryland Battalion, Lt. Col. Ridgely Brown
        Fifth Virginia, Col. Thomas L. Rosser
        Eleventh Virginia, Col. Oliver R. Funsten
        Fifteenth Virginia, Col. William B. Ball
    Wickham's Brigade - Brig. Gen. Williams C. Wickham
        First Virginia, Col. Richard W. Carter
        Second Virginia, Col. Thomas T. Munford
        Third Virginia, Col. Thomas H. Owen
        Fourth Virginia, Lt. Col. William H. Payne
    O.R., Series 1, vol. 29, part 2, 707-708.
The above chart would make it appear that on September 9 this command structure was in effect. Nothing could be further from the truth. The dates of the promotions for the new brigadiers compared to the dates from which their commissions ranked and the dates they actually assumed command of their brigades varied. Baker and Lomax had obtained their promotions on July 30, but their commissions were dated July 23. Baker took command of Hampton's Brigade immediately after Hampton was wounded and continued to lead it until his own wounding on August 1. Lomax, on the other hand, did not actually command a brigade until the reorganization in September, having no command until then even though he had held the rank of brigadier general for over a month. He did command Jones's Brigade for a short time. Butler and Wickham received their commissions on September 2 to rank

from September 1. However, Butler's wound prevented him from taking command for a lengthy period, allowing for Young's promotion. Wickham seems to have taken command upon his brigade's formation. Gordon received his commission on September 28, but only took command of his brigade on October 5. Rosser's, and Young's commissions ranked from September 28, 1863, but the actual date of their promotion was October 10 and they did not take command of their brigades until sometime after this date. The actual reorganization, meaning the shuffling of the regiments into their new brigades, was not announced until September 12 and was facilitated over the next several days, despite the fighting on the 13th. William C. Davis and Julie Hoffman, eds., *The Confederate General* (The National Historical Society, 1991), vol. 1, 53, 152, vol. 3, 6, vol. 4, 85, vol. 5, 113, vol. 6, 135, 169; Warner, *Generals in Gray*, 15, 40-41, 110, 191, 265, 335-336, 348; Carter Diary; Morrissett Diary; Donahue Diary.

When the Bristoe Station campaign began on October 9, only Gordon and Lomax were actually in command of their brigades as brigadier generals. Young commanded Butler's Brigade as a colonel. Wickham was absent, having been injured in a fall from his horse, his brigade being led by Col. Thomas H. Owen. Col. Oliver R. Funsten, not Rosser, led Jones's Brigade, Jones being under arrest. Col. John R. Chambliss continued to lead W. H. F. Lee's Brigade. Freeman, *Lee's Lieutenants*, 248; *O.R., Series 1*, vol. 29, part 1, 439 and 452.

The September 9 reorganization was itself reorganized. When the command structure was finalized, it appeared as follows:

Hampton's Division - Maj. Gen Wade Hampton
    Gordon's Brigade - Brig. Gen. James B. Gordon
      First North Carolina Cavalry, Maj. Rufus Barringer
      Second North Carolina Cavalry, Col. William G. Robinson
      Fourth North Carolina Cavalry, Col. Dennis D. Ferebee
      Fifth North Carolina Cavalry, Lt. Col. Stephen B. Evans
    Young's Brigade - Brig. Gen. Pierce M.B. Young
      First South Carolina Cavalry, Col. John L. Black
      Second South Carolina Cavalry, Col. Thomas J. Lipscomb
      Cobb's Legion, Lt. Col. William G. Delony
      Jeff. Davis Legion, Lt. Col. Joseph F. Waring
      Phillips Legion, Lt. Col. William W. Rich
    Rosser's Brigade - Brig. Gen. Thomas L. Rosser
      Seventh Virginia Cavalry, Col. Richard H. Dulany
      Eleventh Virginia Cavalry, Col. Oliver R. Funsten
      Twelfth Virginia Cavalry, Col. Asher W. Harman
      Thirty-fifth Virginia Cavalry Battalion, Lt. Col. Elijah V. White

Fitzhugh Lee's Division - Maj. Gen. Fitzhugh Lee
    Lee's Brigade - Col. John R. Chambliss, Jr.
      Ninth Virginia Cavalry, Col. Richard L.T. Beale
      Tenth Virginia Cavalry, Col. J. Lucius Davis
      Thirteenth Virginia Cavalry, Col. John R. Chambliss, Jr.
    Lomax's Brigade - Brig. Gen. Lunsford L. Lomax
      First Maryland Cavalry Battalion, Lt. Col. Ridgely Brown
      Fifth Virginia Cavalry, Lt. Col. Henry Clay Pate
      Sixth Virginia Cavalry, Lt. Col. John Shac Green

Fifteenth Virginia Cavalry, Col. William B. Ball
Wickham's Brigade - Brig. Gen. William C. Wickham
First Virginia Cavalry, Col. Richard W. Carter
Second Virginia Cavalry, Col. Thomas T. Munford
Third Virginia Cavalry, Col. Thomas H. Owen
Fourth Virginia Cavalry, Lt. Col. William H. Payne
O.R., Series 1, vol. 29, part 1, 820-821.

16. J. E. B. Stuart to My Darling One [Flora Stuart], September 4, 1863, Stuart Papers, 1851-1968, Mss1ST923d, Microfilm reel C621, VHS.

17. Unlike the Federal army where each general's rank had its own insignia, Confederate generals supposedly wore the exact same insignia whether a brigadier or a full general. Stuart's rank insignia would not change if he gained promotion to lieutenant general, allowing him to send a photograph of himself in the uniform he was currently wearing as a major general and claim he was now in the uniform of a lieutenant general.

18. Douglas Southall Freeman speculated on the reasons Lee may have had for not requesting promotion for Stuart. Freeman stated that Lee had nothing against Stuart personally. What stood in Stuart's way was the type of command he had – cavalry. Freeman felt that Lee did not equate commanding cavalry with commanding infantry. Douglas Southall Freeman, *Lee's Lieutenants* (New York: Charles Scribner's Sons, 1943), III, 211-212.

19. J. E. B. Stuart to My Darling One [Flora Stuart], September 4, 1863, Stuart Papers, 1851-1968, Mss1ST923d, Microfilm reel C621, VHS.

20. *O.R.*, Series 1, vol. 29, part 1, 102-103; *Richmond Daily Dispatch*, September 10, 1863; James Dudley Peavy, ed., *Confederate Scout: Virginia's Frank Stringfellow* (Onancock, Virginia: The Eastern Shore Publishing Co., 1956), 43-44; R. Shepard Brown, *Stringfellow of the Fourth* (New York: Crown Publisher, Inc., 1960), 211-213.

21. According to one source, Jones's Brigade attempted to raid an enemy cavalry encampment near the Hazel River but called it off when it was discovered that Federal infantry camped nearby. Neese, *Three Years in the Confederate Horse Artillery*, 207.

22. Robert Randolph to Dear Sister, September 7, 1863, Minor Family Papers, 1810-1932, Mss1M6663c. Microfilms C610-618, VHS.

23. Abraham G. Jones to Dear Brother, September 4, 1863, Abraham G. Jones Papers, Collection No. 135, ECMC/JL/ECU.

24. *New York Herald*, September 8, 1863.

25. Chapman Diary; *HDSACWRD* at, <www.civilwardata.com> August 5 and 6, 2009.

26. Rawle, *Third Pennsylvania Cavalry*, 332.

27. *O.R.*, Series 1, vol. 29, part 1, 103-104; Lloyd, *History of the First Regiment Pennsylvania Reserve Cavalry*, 71; Williamson, *Mosby's Rangers*, 91-92; Sauerburger, ed., *I Seat Myself to Write You*, 174-175; *Philadelphia Press*, September 7, 1863.

28. *O.R.*, Series 1, vol. 29, part 2, 160.

29. *Ibid.*, 161; John B. Kay to Dear Parents, September 9, 1863; John B. Kay Papers, Microfilm mf468 c, BHL/UM.

30. *O.R.*, Series 1, vol. 29, part 1, 104; Sauerburger, ed., *I Seat Myself to Write You*, 176.
    The fear of guerillas led to a squadron of the Twelfth Illinois, Chapman's brigade, receiving orders on the 10th to march to Washington. The purpose of the trek was to guard a wagon train coming back to the army with supplies. The squadron did not return until the 15th. Frank Diary.

31. J. E. B. Stuart to My Darling One [Flora Stuart], September 11, 1863, Stuart Papers, 1851-1968, Mss1ST923d, Microfilm reel C621, VHS.

Stuart admited the same to Miss Nannie Price in a letter of the same date. J. E. B. Stuart to Miss Nannie Price, September 11, 1863, Adele H. Mitchell, ed., *The Letters of Major General James E. B. Stuart* (The Stuart – Mosby Historical Society, 1990), 341-344.

32. *Richmond Daily Dispatch*, September 10, 1863.

33. *O.R.,* Series 1, vol. 29, part 2, 167.

The movement noticed by the Federals was connected to the transfer of Lt. Gen. James Longstreet's Corps from Lee's army to the west to reinforce the army of Gen. Braxton Bragg that had begun on the 8th. Freeman, *Lee's Lieutenants*, 221-223.

34. *O.R.,* Series 1, vol. 29, part 2, 169, 172.

35. Crowninshield, *First Regiment of Massachusetts Cavalry Volunteers*, 170; Hard, *Eighth Illinois Cavalry*, 270; Glazier, *Three Years in the Federal Cavalry*, 320; Gillespie, *Company A, First Ohio Cavalry*, 173; Morey Diary; Cheney Diary; Alvin N. Brackett to Dear Brother, September 12, 1863, Brackett Letters, Gregory A. Coco Collection, HCWRTC, USAMHI; Allen L. Bevan to My Dear Sister, September 21, 1863, Allen L. Bevan Letters, CWMC, USAMHI.

36. J. E. B. Stuart to My Darling One [Flora Stuart], September 11, 1863, Stuart Papers, 1851-1968, Mss1ST923d, Microfilm reel C621, VHS.

The cavalry were not the only troops undergoing reviews. On the 9th, Lee reviewed Lt. Gen. Richard S. Ewell's Second Corps. Stuart attended this review. *Richmond Daily Dispatch*, September 16, 1863.

37. The configuration of the regiments and brigades at this time is uncertain. In his letter to Flora, Stuart stated that the brigades of Wickham, Lomax, and Butler had been formed. However, the *Dispatch* reporter wrote that he saw a review of Jones's Brigade "commanded at present by Gen. Lunsford L. Lomax." Two additional sources name Lomax as the commander of Jones's Brigade in the fighting on the 13th. Another complication is the fact that although the order to realign the regiments into their new brigades was issued on the 9th and announced on the 12th, the date of its completion is unknown. Stuart's letter confirms that some but not all of the reorganization had taken place by the 11th, but he probably meant on paper, since the actual moving of the regiments had not as yet begun. Therefore, just who commanded what at this time cannot be determined. In his report of the action on the 13th, Robert E. Lee wrote that Stuart opposed three enemy cavalry divisions with three brigades, the fourth, Fitz Lee's, being near Fredericksburg. Lee's numbering of the brigades does not seem to include Robertson's Brigade or make reference to the two new brigades that would be formed from the realignment. Perhaps the Fourth and Fifth North Carolina had already joined Baker's Brigade, under Gordon. However, the Fifth Virginia was still with Fitz Lee's Brigade and did not take part in the fighting, indicating that the new alignment had not yet been completed. No Confederate officer, other than Lee, ever filed a report of the fighting on the 13th, making it extremely difficult to know exactly what happened. If this is correct then the realignment was incomplete. J. E. B. Stuart to My Darling One [Flora Stuart], September 11, 1863, Stuart Papers, 1851-1968, Mss1ST923d, Microfilm reel C621, VHS; *O.R.,* Series 1, vol. 29, part 1, 134; *Richmond Daily Dispatch*, September 15, 1863; Arehart, "Diary of W. H. Arehart," 276; H. B. McClellan, *I Rode with Jeb Stuart* (Bloomington: Indiana University Press, 1958), 373; McDonald, *History of the Laurel Brigade*, 171.

One source claimed that the Fifth Virginia and the Sixth Virginia fought side by side from the commencement of the fight on the 13th. However, in his letter of the 18th, Robert Brooke Jones, who belonged to the Fifth, stated that the cavalry near Culpeper did the fighting, inferring that he was not engaged. Grimsley, *Battles in Culpeper County*, 15-17; Robert Brooke Jones to My Dear Wife, September 18, 1863, Jones Family Papers, 1812-1930, Mss1J735d, VHS.

38.   Neese, *Three Years in the Confederate Horse Artillery*, 207-208.

39.   *O.R.*, Series 1, vol. 29, part 1, 134; Beale, *9th Virginia Cavalry*, 98; Beale, *A Lieutenant of Cavalry in Lee's Army*, 124; Trout, ed., *Memoirs*, 65; Neese, *Three Years in the Confederate Horse Artillery*, 208.

McClellan stated that a Dr. Hudgin, formerly attached to the Ninth Virginia and later a staff surgeon at cavalry headquarters, brought word of the impending attack. McClellan, *I Rode with Jeb Stuart*, 372.

Another source appears to contradict the Federals quiet approach to at least one of the crossings. According to an article in the *Philadelphia Inquirer* dated September 16, 1863, Maj. George H. Covode led a portion of the Fourth Pennsylvania toward the Hazel River crossings the night of the 12th. He encountered Confederates and drove them over the river. Maj. Covode halted his column to wait until morning before crossing. He reported that about 10:00 he heard considerable firing and interpreted it as the Confederates he had chased firing on reinforcements sent to support them. According to the article, the Federal troops advanced over the river the next morning without opposition. No official reports were filed on this incident.

40.   Sauerburger, ed., *I Seat Myself to Write You*, 177.

McIntosh's brigade crossed at the ford on the Rixeyville Road below Oak Shade. J. Irvin Gregg's brigade crossed at a ford a mile downstream. Lloyd, *History of the First Regiment Pennsylvania Reserve Cavalry*, 71.

One source stated that a Federal force consisting of about 600 cavalry and artillery crossed at Stark's Ford near the conjunction of the Thornton and Hazel rivers. It is possible that a portion of McIntosh's brigade crossed here. Frank Moore, ed., *The Rebellion Record: A Diary of American Events, Volume Seven* (New York: D, Van Nostrand, Publisher, 1864), 504.

41.   Ressler Diary; Moore, *Rebellion Record*, 504; Capt. William Hyndman, *History of a Cavalry Company: A Complete Record of Company "A," 4th Penn'a Cavalry* (Philadelphia: Jas. B. Rodgers Co., Printers, 1870), 120-121; Arehart, "Diary of W. H. Arehart," 276; Armstrong, *11th Virginia Cavalry*, 51; W. W. Goldsborough, *The Maryland Line in the Confederate Army* (Baltimore: Press of Guggenheimer, Weil & Co., 1900. Reprint, Gaithersburg, Maryland: Olde Soldier Books Inc., 1987), 286; McDonald, *History of the Laurel Brigade*, 171; *Daily National Intelligencer*, September 16, 1863; Musick, *6th Virginia Cavalry*, 48; Edward A. Green Memoir, Eleanor S. Brockenbrough Library, MOC; *Lancaster Daily Evening Express*, September 16, 1863.

The Eleventh probably reinforced McDonald during his withdrawal to Muddy Run. The remainder of the regiment may have been waiting north of Rixeyville and joined the fight before the run was crossed and the Seventh and Twelfth arrived.

42.   Although Flournoy's regiment, the Sixth, was in Jones's Brigade, the majority of which fought on the Rixeyville Road, it appears that it was picketing the fords from the junction of the Hazel and the Rappahannock rivers to at least Rappahannock Station. Below that point, the Fifteenth Virginia seems to have been guarding the fords. By the nature of the Federal advance, Flournoy fell back toward Brandy Station and not toward the rest of his brigade at Rixeyville. This caused the Sixth to fight with

Chambliss's Brigade at Brandy Station and the Botts farm. The fact that a portion of the Ninth Virginia was with Flournoy supports this view. Musick, *6th Virginia Cavalry*, 48; Fortier, *15th Virginia Cavalry*, 40.

43.   Cheney, *Ninth Regiment, New York Volunteer Cavalry*, 132; Moore, *Rebellion Record*, 504; Shreve, "Reminiscences;" Neese, *Three Years in the Confederate Horse Artillery*, 208; Trout, *Galloping Thunder*, 348-349.

44.   Moore, *Rebellion Record*, 504; Beale, *9th Virginia Cavalry*, 99.

     McClellan stated that Beale commanded W. H. F. Lee's (Chambliss's) brigade but Beale stated that Lomax did. McClellan, *I Rode with Jeb Stuart*, 372.

45.   *O.R.*, Series 1, vol. 29, part 1, 118, 120; Glazier, *Three Years in the Federal Cavalry*, 320-321; Moore, *Rebellion Record*, 504.

46.   *O.R.*, Series 1, vol. 29, part 1, 123-124; Trout, ed., *Memoirs*, 222.

47.   Green Memoir.

48.   Moore, *Rebellion Record*, 504; Beale, *9th Virginia Cavalry*, 99.

49.   Beale, *A Lieutenant of Cavalry in Lee's Army*, 124; Neese, *Three Years in the Confederate Horse Artillery*, 208; Trout, *Galloping Thunder*, 350.

50.   One source stated that the regiment ordered to protect the guns moved through a mistake in orders. *Western Democrat*, September 22, 1863.

51.   *O.R.*, Series 1, vol. 29, part 1, 112, 118-119, 129; Trout, *Galloping Thunder*, 350-351; Glazier, *Three Years in the Federal Cavalry*, 322; McDonald, *History of the Laurel Brigade*, 174.

     As with so many incidents during the war, just who captured these guns became an issue. Captain, later Colonel, Hampton S. Thomas, Assistant Adjutant and Inspector General on the staff of Gen. Gregg, wrote after the war that a charge of one of Gregg's brigades chased the Confederate cannoneers away from their guns. After the brigade had passed, another general, meaning Custer, with his staff and orderlies rode up the hill and ordered the guns hauled off the field. A newspaper article later claimed that this general captured them in a gallant charge. Thomas alleged that because Gregg would not have reporters in his camp, other officers became the darlings of the papers, getting credit that rightfully belonged to others. Despite Thomas's protest, which appeared years after the Little Big Horn, Custer has been given credit for the capture. Colonel Hampton S. Thomas, *Some Personal Reminiscences of Service in the Cavalry of the Army of the Potomac* (Philadelphia: L. R. Hamersly & Co., 1889), 15.

52.   Trout, ed., *Memoirs*, 65-66.

53.   Edward A. Green Article, *Warren Sentinel*, Eleanor S. Brockenbrough Library, MOC; Denison, *Sabres and Spurs*, 287.

54.   Goldsborough, *The Maryland Line*, 286; Ide, *First Vermont Cavalry*, 135; Beale, *9th Virginia Cavalry*, 99; *Philadelphia Inquirer*, September 18, 1863.

     Goldsborough places the number captured at ten, including McNulty, but Ide states that a total of eight men were taken prisoners. A search of the Battery's roster reveals the names of ten men captured on this date. Trout, *The Hoss*, 207-225.

     One account claimed that Custer, along with a color sergeant and four orderlies, mostly from the First Michigan were the first to take possession of the gun. *NYS-MMVRC* at, < www.dmna.state.ny.us/historic/mil-hist.htm> December 31, 2009.

55.   Neese, *Three Years in the Confederate Horse Artillery*, 21.

56.   Shreve, "Reminiscences."

57.   *O.R.*, Series 1, vol. 29, part 1, 129; Beale, *A Lieutenant of Cavalry in Lee's Army*, 126; *Vermont Journal*, September 26, 1863; *Philadelphia Inquirer*, September 18, 1863.

     Hornets seemed to be everywhere. At some point in the fighting the Sixth Ohio,

McIntosh's brigade, Gregg's division, was ordered into a stand of oak at the edge of open country. The officer assigned to placed them rode off to report his mission accomplished. While in the act of doing so, the regiment appeared in full flight from the timber. Startled the officer tried to halt the rout only to find that he could not and in fact, was forced to accompany the fleeing men. Later, the regiment's commander, Col. William Stedman, admitted that his men could stand all the shot and shell the enemy could send their way, but not hornets. Neither could the officer. Thomas, *Some Personal Reminiscences*, 15.

58.   *O.R.*, Series 1, vol. 29, part 1, 120-121.

59.   *Ibid.*, 127

The Confederates that Mann engaged may have been some of Gordon's men with Hart's Battery. Although the Confederates retreated along the road to Stevensburg, this road passes Pony Mountain, east of which lies another road that heads in the direction of Raccoon Ford. According to one source, Gordon and Hart retreated to Raccoon Ford after fighting near Pony Mountain. Trout, ed., *Memoirs*, 222.

60.   Henry Morford, *The Coward: A Novel of Society and the Field in 1863* (Philadelphia; T. B. Peterson & Brothers, 1864), 457.

While this is a novel, its information on the battle is very accurate and contains greater detail than most of the reports written on the engagement.

61.   Hard, *Eighth Illinois Cavalry*, 271; Moore, *Rebellion Record*, 504; Trout, ed., *Memoirs*, 222.

62.   *O.R.*, Series 1, vol. 29, part 1, 130; *Washington Evening Star*, September 18, 1863; *Philadelphia Inquirer*, September 21, 1863; *Washington Daily Morning Chronicle*, September 21, 1863; Thomas B. Person to Dear Sister, September 19, 1863, Southgate-Jones Family Papers, Box 1, Folder 1862-1963, WRP/DU; Morford, *The Coward*, 457-458; Mary Stevens Jones and Mildred Conway Jones, *Historic Culpeper* (Culpeper: Culpeper Historical Society, Inc., 1974) 109; Hard, *Eighth Illinois Cavalry*, 271.

Inskeep appears as Inskip in the 1860 Census. Email from Robert F. O'Neill, February 10, 2010.

Of these sources, three specifically name the man killed as a Mr. Curtis. While all these sources disagree on some of the details - one stating that one of the family was killed running through a field - they do confirm that such an incident did occur and that the fighting in and near Culpeper claimed both soldiers and civilians.

63.   *O.R.*, Series 1, vol. 29, part 1, 124; Hard, *Eighth Illinois Cavalry*, 271; Morford, *The Coward*, 457-467; *NYSMMVRC* at, <www.dmna.state.ny.us/historic/mil-hist.htm> December 31, 2009.

64.   Just when or if Stuart took command on the field is a point of conjecture. H. B. McClellan wrote that Stuart remained out of the fighting, leaving Lomax to direct Jones's and Chambliss's brigades. However, later in his text, McClellan stated that Stuart retreated to the Rapidan. Although the use of Stuart's name in this context might simply mean the Confederate cavalry in general, another source claimed that Stuart took command just before Chew lost his gun and conducted the retreat. McClellan, *I Rode with Jeb Stuart*, 373-374; McDonald, *History of the Laurel Brigade*, 173.

65.   *O.R.*, Series 1, vol. 29, part 1, 121 and 128.

66.   *Ibid.*, 134-135; Arehart, "Diary of W. H. Arehart," 276; Green Article, *Warren Sentinel*; Sauerburger, ed., *I Seat Myself to Write You*, 177; Lloyd, *History of the First Regiment Pennsylvania Reserve Cavalry*, 72-73; Neese, *Three Years in the Confederate Horse Artillery*, 212; Allen L. Bevan to My Dear Sister, September 21, 1863, CWMC, USAMHI.

Federal forces advancing along the railroad stopped at Mitchell's Station. *O.R.*,

Series 1, vol. 29, part 1, 132; *Richmond Whig*, September 16, 1863.

The Robinson River was also known as Robertson's River. The change in name occurred around this time. Maps from the period reflect this fact, some using Robertson's and others Robinson. The same holds true for the ford near Locust Dale, which is called Robertson's Ford on some maps and Fry's Ford on others. For clarity, regarding the river, Robinson will be used in all instances. Fry's Ford will be used in place of Robertson's Ford.

67.   *O.R.*, Series 1, vol. 29, part 1, 112.

Pleasonton's actual loss was greater than he first reported. One source gave the names of 66 wounded. Another partial listing totaled 1 killed and 31 wounded. A third source stated that 24 men were captured. *Philadelphia Inquirer*, date unknown; *New York Herald*, September 15, 1863; *Philadelphia Press*, September 19, 1863.

68.   *O.R.*, Series 1, vol. 29, part 2, 175.

69.   *Ibid.*, part 1, 132, and part 2, 175.

70.   *Richmond Whig*, September 16, 1863.

The horse artillery alone suffered 39 casualties, most of them captured. Trout, *Galloping Thunder*, 351-352.

71.   *O.R.*, Series 1, vol. 27, part 3, 1075.

72.   *Ibid.*, vol. 29, part 1, 134-135.

73.   J. E. B. Stuart to My Darling One [Flora Stuart], September 16, 1863, Stuart Papers, 1851-1968, Mss1ST923d, Microfilm reel C621, VHS.

74.   The section of Chew's Battery and the Twelfth Virginia that had encamped north of the river overnight withdrew over the ford about 9:00 on the morning of the 14th and took a position on the south side, guarding the crossing. According to one report, some of Jones's cavalry that had remained on the north side when the Federals pulled back to Cedar Mountain at the end of the day's fighting on the 13th were still there on the 15th. This could have been a squadron of the Twelfth Virginia that stayed north of the river on the 14th when the rest of the regiments and Chew's Battery retreated across the river. *O.R.*, Series 1, vol. 29, part 1, 122; Arehart, "Diary of W. H. Arehart," 276; Neese, *Three Years in the Confederate Horse Artillery*, 212.

Lt. Isaac H. Ressler of the Sixteenth Pennsylvania, Gregg's brigade, Gregg's division, wrote that his regiment rode to Raccoon Ford and fought there before withdrawing to Culpeper Court House for the night where the regiment went on picket duty. Ressler Diary.

75.   *O.R.*, Series 1, vol. 29, part 1, 116-118; Denison, *Sabres and Spurs*, 287-288; Crowninshield, *First Regiment of Massachusetts Cavalry Volunteers*, 172-173.

76.   *Richmond Daily Dispatch*, September 17, 1863; Trout, ed., *Memoirs*, 66; Denison, *Sabres and Spurs*, 287.

The regiment to which the skirmishers belonged cannot be determined exactly. The Confederate regiments present were the Seventh Virginia, the Eleventh Virginia, and the Sixth Virginia. According to one source, the Sixth did not cross the river until near sunset. Another source claimed that the Ninth Virginia made a charge during the fighting, but the Ninth was at Raccoon Ford and not at Rapidan Station. The skirmishers most likely belonged to the Seventh Virginia, as this regiment had one man killed on this day. Donahue Diary; Crowninshield, *First Regiment of Massachusetts Cavalry Volunteers*, 172-174; Beale, *9th Virginia Cavalry*, 100; Robert K. Krick, *9th Virginia Cavalry* (Lynchburg: H. E. Howard, Inc., 1982), 28; Robert L. Armstrong, *7th Virginia Cavalry* (Lynchburg: H. E. Howard, Inc., 1992), 134.

The additional artillery probably came from Griffin's and McGregor's batteries of horse artillery. Trout, *Galloping Thunder*, 719.

77. *O.R.*, Series 1, vol. 29, part 1, 116-118; Denison, *Sabres and Spurs*, 288; *Richmond Daily Dispatch*, September 17, 1863.

Sargent reported his loss at 3 killed, 22 wounded, and 4 missing. *O.R.*, Series 1, vol. 29, part 1, 117.

78. The terms under which Stuart allowed Flournoy to take his regiment over the river are unclear. Sources appear to disagree as to whether Stuart gave permission to attack or just to make a demonstration. *Daily Richmond Examiner*, September 16, 1863; Musick, *6th Virginia Cavalry*, 49; Moore, *Rebellion Record*, 505.

79. *O.R.*, Series 1, vol. 29, part 1, 117; Crowninshield, *First Regiment of Massachusetts Cavalry Volunteers*, 172-174; Moore, *Rebellion Record*, 505; Musick, *6th Virginia Cavalry*, 49; Donahue Diary; *Daily Richmond Examiner*, September 16, 1863.

80. *O.R.*, Series 1, vol. 29, part 1, 119, 126, 422; Morey Diary; John B. Kay to My Dear Afflicted Parents and Brothers, September 9, 1863; John B. Kay Papers, Microfilm mf468 c, BHL/UM; Gillespie, *Company A, First Ohio Cavalry*, 176; Moore, *Rebellion Record*, 505.

Kay misidentified the ford as Fry's (Robertson's) Ford, but did state that the ford was on the Rapidan. Fry's Ford is on the Robinson and the Sixth Michigan was nowhere near there. Kay's description of the fight and the artillery shelling confirms what occurred at Somerville Ford.

Carter reported 6 killed and 17 wounded, a grim testament to Fuller's accuracy before he withdrew. Company A, First Ohio, lost not a man.

81. The Seventh Michigan also supported part of the battery until the night of the 14th when it withdrew to a point near the Somerville Ford road where it encamped until the 15th. *O.R.*, Series 1, vol. 29, part 1, 127.

82. *Ibid.*, 128; Hoffman, *First Vermont*, 137.

The commander of the Fifth Michigan, Col. Russell A. Alger, reported that he marched to Raccoon Ford and arrived there about 10:00 in the morning. He made no mention of having been diverted to Somerville Ford. However, if he followed the Sixth Michigan, which also marched toward Raccoon Ford before being sent to Somerville Ford, Alger may not have realized at the time he wrote his report that he actually had fought at Somerville Ford. *O.R.*, Series 1, vol. 29, part 1, 125.

83. Cadwallader Jones Iredell to unknown addressee, September 15, 1863, Cadwallader Jones Iredell Papers, 363-Z, Folder 1, Correspondence 1862-1863, SHC/UNC; Abraham G. Jones to unknown addressee, September 16, 1863, Abraham G. Jones Papers, Collection No. 135, ECMC/JL/ECU; Hard, *Eighth Illinois Cavalry*, 271-272; *New York Herald*, September 18, 1863.

The Ninth, Tenth, Thirteenth, and Fifteenth Virginia regiments had also retreated to the ford and also may have engaged the Federals.

Lime Church is now St. Paul's Episcopal Church. Jones, *Historic Culpeper*, 127.

84. *O.R.*, Series 1, vol. 29, part 1, 130; Chapman Diary; Cheney Diary; Abraham G. Jones to Dear Brother Ellick, September 20, 1863, Abraham G. Jones Papers, Collection No. 135, ECMC/JL/ECU; Hard, *Eighth Illinois Cavalry*, 272; Trout, ed., *Memoirs*, 222; *New York Herald*, September 18, 1863; *Daily Union and Advertiser*, September 22, 1863; NYS-MMVRC at, <www.dmna.state.ny.us/historic/mil-hist.htm> December 31, 2009.

85. Blackwell, *12th Illinois Cavalry*, 123; Hard, *Eighth Illinois Cavalry*, 272.

86. Hard, *Eighth Illinois Cavalry*, 272; Brown, *Stringfellow of the Fourth*, 223-225, 297; *New York Herald*, September 18, 1863; Jones, *Historic Culpeper*, 101.

Of course, just who fired the ball or shell fragment that wounded Mrs. Stringfellow became a matter of contention. A Northern newspaper stated that the wound was from a "Minié ball from a rebel sharpshooter." Other sources place the blame on Federal artillery, shelling the Confederates. On this occasion, since the Federal artillery was firing from the same side of the river on which "Retreat" stood and the Confederates were firing toward the house, the errant projectile would appear to have been of Southern origin.

87. *O.R.,* Series 1, vol. 29, part 2, 179-180.

88. *Ibid.,* part 1, 135.

89. Trussell Diary; Morrissett Diary; Carter Diary.

The move did not include the Third Virginia, which remained behind until all commissary stores had been moved and the brigade wagon train had arrived from Port Royal. Carter Diary.

90. *O.R.,* Series 1, vol. 29, part 1, 121-122; Rawle, *Third Pennsylvania Cavalry,* 335; Crowninshield, *First Regiment of Massachusetts Cavalry Volunteers,* 177; Denison, *Sabres and Spurs,* 289.

91. *O.R.,* Series 1, vol. 29, part 1, 121-122; Neese, *Three Years in the Confederate Horse Artillery,* 212.

Just what ford Davies's first sent his troopers to cannot be determined. Davies himself admitted to his confusion of the fords and their names. His report indicates that Griggs was to hold both fords, which suggests that they were close to each other. *O.R.,* Series 1, vol. 29, part 1, 122.

92. Donahue Diary; Trout, ed., *Memoirs,* 66.

93. Denison, *Sabres and Spurs,* 289.

94. Rawle, *Third Pennsylvania Cavalry,* 335.

95. *O.R.,* Series 1, vol. 29, part 2, 191.

96. *Ibid.,* part 1, 128.

One source would seem to indicate that part of the relief consisted of the Fifth Michigan. Pvt. Frank M. Brown of the Fifth wrote home on the 16th, stating that he was at Somerville Ford. Frank M. Brown to Dear Mother, September 16, 1863, Brown Family Papers.

97. *O.R.,* Series 1, vol. 29, part 1, 121-122.

98. *Ibid.,* part 2, 189

99. John R. Morey Diary, John R. Morey Papers, Microfilm mf363 c, BHL/UM.

100. *O.R.,* Series 1, vol. 29, part 1, 130; Cheney Diary; Inglis Diary.

101. Norton, *Deeds of Daring,* 73; Hall, *Sixth New York Cavalry,* 157.

102. Hard, *Eighth Illinois Cavalry,* 273.

During this time, the Seventeenth Pennsylvania had been performing other duties north of the Rappahannock. After participating in the fighting on the 13th, the regiment had been ordered back over the river and went on picket. By the night of the 14th, the men found themselves in line of battle at Brentsville, and on the following day after half a day's march, fought with the enemy until night. Just exactly what enemy the Pennsylvanians encountered cannot be determined, but probably local guerillas faced them. This is another instance of a front line regiment having to be dispatched to secure an area in the army's rear. Sergeant Joseph E. McCabe, "Itinerary of the Seventeenth Regiment, Pennsylvania Volunteer Cavalry," in *History of the Seventeenth Regiment Pennsylvania Volunteer Cavalry,* compiled by Henry P. Moyer (Lebanon: Sowers Printing Company, 1911), 333.

103. *O.R.*, Series 1, vol. 29, part 2, 189.

Meade took steps to consolidate his cavalry's gains, ordering the Twelfth Corps to Stevensburg, the First Corps to a point midway between Stevensburg and Culpeper, the Second and Fifth Corps to Culpeper, the Third Corps to a position between Stone-House Mountain and Culpeper, and the Sixth Corps to Stone-House Mountain. The Eleventh Corps was to guard the Rappahannock bridges, Catlett's Station, and Bristoe Station. The Artillery Reserve moved forward to camp near the Fifth Corps, while the cavalry took up the duty of picketing the front and flanks. Meade's headquarters moved to Culpeper. *O.R.*, Series 1, vol. 29, part 2, 193-194.

104. *O.R.*, Series 1, vol. 29, part 2, 188.

At 1:30 on the morning of the 16th, Gregg received an order directing him to hold Cedar Mountain as long as possible and that Gen. Warren would support him at Fox Mountain to Gregg's right and rear. This order seems to indicate that an enemy advance was expected on the Federal army's right flank and indeed, dispatches from Meade to both the Third and Sixth Corps commanders stated that such an advance was already taking place, which it wasn't. Again, rumors of any advance by Lee threw a scare into the Federal high command. *O.R.*, Series 1, vol. 29, part 2, 197.

105. *O.R.*, Series 1, vol. 29, part 1, 122, 129-130.

The Confederate unit involved in this fight probably came from Brig. Gen. Harry T. Hay's Brigade of infantry made up of the Fifth, Sixth, Seventh, Eighth, and Ninth Louisiana. The brigade was stationed in the area between Rapidan Station and Raccoon Ford during this time.

106. *O.R.*, Series 1, vol. 29, part 1, 114; Hall, *Sixth New York Cavalry*, 157; Hard, *Eighth Illinois Cavalry*, 273; Cheney Diary; Inglis Diary; *Richmond Enquirer*, September 22, 1863; *NYSMMVRC* at, <www.dmna.state.ny.us/historic/mil-hist.htm> December 31, 2009.

Hardt had placed men in the cornfield but they had been driven out by Confederate sharpshooters. When the Ninth New York replaced the Fourth later that night, Capt. Timothy Hanley ordered the cornstalks knocked down to allow for a clear view of the area from which the surprise had come.

For the whole regiment to suffer for the lapse of a few seemed an injustice to the men of the regiment and the brigade. Attempts were made to have a court of inquiry look into the incident. A court was ordered but never convened. Eventually the Secretary of War was apprised of the matter, and he reversed the order on January 6, 1864. Pleasonton had already returned the colors on the 4th. There is reason to believe that the man standing in the way of resolving the situation was John Buford. With his passing, the circumstances changed and the cavalry and the regiment moved on. *NYSMMVRC* at, <www.dmna.state.ny.us/historic/mil-hist.htm> February 24, 2009; Notes supplied by Robert F. O'Neill.

107. *Grand Rapids Daily Eagle*, October 1, 1863.

108. Hard, *Eighth Illinois Cavalry*, 273.

109. Morrissett Diary.

110. *O.R.*, Series 1, vol. 29, part 2, 198.

111. Allyne C. Litchfield to My Dear Wife, September 17, 1863, Allyne Cushing Litchfield Papers, James S. Schoff Civil War Collection, Manuscripts Division, WLC/UM; William Rockwell to My Dear Wife, September 18, 1863, Donald C. Rockwell Collection, 1862-1936, Call No. A-328, WMUARHC/WMU.

The identity of the attacking Confederate force is unknown, but it was most likely infantry.

112. Donahue Diary; Neese, *Three Years in the Confederate Horse Artillery*, 213; William Taylor My Dear Mother, September 17, 1863, Taylor Family Papers, 1751-1902, Mss1T2197a, VHS.

113. Richard Henry Watkins to Mary Watkins, September 19, 1863, Watkins Papers, 1861-1865, Mss1W3272a1-355, VHS; Nanzig, *3rd Virginia Cavalry*, 102.

114. J. E. B. Stuart to My Darling One [Flora Stuart], September 17, 1863, Stuart Papers, 1851-1968, Mss1ST923d, Microfilm reel C621, VHS.

Chapter Five

Toward Bristoe Station

Meade spent September 17 and 18 exploring his options, finally concluding that he had few. On the 17th, he sent his chief engineer, Maj. James C. Duane, to examine the Rapidan from Raccoon Ford to Germanna Ford. The major never got close enough to Raccoon Ford to investigate, the enemy having 11 cannon looming over the crossing. At Morton's Ford, he met with greater success and reported that only a small rifle pit overlooked the ford, although campfire smoke beyond it indicated the presence of at least a regiment of Confederates. A small force that Duane estimated to be ten men guarded Germanna Ford and he liked the prospects of throwing a pontoon bridge over the river at this location.[1]

Though Maj. Duane's assessment of conditions at two of the three fords appeared to be somewhat favorable, Meade's fortitude wavered. The day after he received his engineer's report, he cabled Washington and stated his case. He felt that any advance would require a risk he was unwilling to take without solid backing from his superiors, meaning Maj. Gen. Henry W. Halleck and President Lincoln. Explaining further, Meade cited the enemy's heavily fortified positions along the Rapidan, pointing out that the best prospect of crossing lay at Morton's Ford. Even then, he recounted, a crossing would bring on a major engagement that would result in heavy casualties. Should he prevail, he feared that he did not have the strength to follow up the victory and pursue Lee to Richmond. He closed with, "I can get a battle out of Lee under very disadvantageous circumstances, which may render his inferior force my superior, and which is not likely to result in any very decided advantage, even in case I should be victorious."[2]

Meade's trepidation that even in victory he might fail to gain any advantage over Lee signaled his true state of mind. He had gained more from his cavalry's advance on the 13th and 14th than he undoubtedly had expected. Now with another river between him and his foe, he could not bring himself to risk anything more. The fear of Lee gaining any advantage, though the Confederate army had been reduced by one third, dealt a more crippling blow than all of Lee's artillery could have delivered. Meade was willing to settle for stalemate once more, unless the burden of making the decision as to what to do could be placed on Halleck's and Lincoln's shoulders.

However, neither Halleck nor Lincoln lent assistance to their troubled army commander. Their responses mirrored each other in many respects. They had no intention of making decisions from afar and both dismissed Richmond as a target, stating unequivocally that the destruction of Lee's army, not the capture of Richmond, should be Meade's goal. Lincoln went further, reminding Meade that if Lee, while acting on the defensive, could hold Meade in check and in effect place him on the defensive, then the Federal army, which outnumbered Lee's army three to two, could hold its lines with less men. The unveiled threat to reduce Meade's strength if he would not use his men to somehow strike at Lee should have signaled to Meade that Lincoln had grown tired of a status quo war. It also meant, as Halleck wrote, "You are free to exercise your own judgment on this subject."[3]

While Halleck and Lincoln crafted their responses to Meade, Kilpatrick explored ways to get at the enemy even though his troopers had been relieved of outpost duty along the river by the Second Corps on the 17th. On the following day he sent a lone scout across the Rapidan a mile below Raccoon Ford. The intrepid trooper crept through the Confederate infantry's picket line, slipped past another line of men a quarter mile behind the ford, and explored the area up to two miles beyond. He observed a division of infantry moving down river and learned that the troops on duty at Ely's Ford, comprising dismounted cavalry and a brigade of infantry, expected an attack at any time.[4] Nothing came of the scout's efforts and Kilpatrick's men enjoyed a peaceful day in camp.[5]

Pleasonton's other two divisions actually moved away from the enemy. Buford fell back to Stevensburg - Devin's brigade on the 17th and Chapman's on the 18th. The Twelfth Corps replaced Buford's vedettes along the Rapidan.[6] Gen. Gregg pulled back from near Rapidan Station on the 18th with McIntosh's brigade encamping near Culpeper Court House and Col. Gregg's brigade near Cedar Mountain.[7] If Meade decided to do something more, he would need his cavalry. Although some of the regiments still performed outpost duty at points from near Rapidan Station to Germanna Ford on the Rapidan and to United States Ford on the Rappahannock, most had the opportunity to rest and recuperate their strength while their commander-in-chief made up his mind what to do next. For seven Federals the waiting grew to be too much and they gave themselves up to the Fourth Virginia pickets at Germanna Ford on the 18th.[8] Those possessing a greater resolve bided their time and gathered strength for when the struggle would inevitably resume.

Like Meade, Robert E. Lee also communicated with his superiors, only in his case that meant just one man, President Davis. On the 18th, Lee wrote two letters, informing the president that except for the Eleventh Corps the Federal army now lay between the Rappahannock and the Rapidan. He also expected an advance across the Rapidan at Morton's Ford. Lee reported that he thought Meade had been receiving reinforcements and hoped that his own army might be able to be increased, especially if Federal troops had been withdrawn from the coastal areas of Virginia and North Carolina. Preparations had already been made should the Confederate army be forced to fall back by sending all surplus supplies to Orange Court House and Charlottesville.[9] Still not feeling able to assume the offensive, Lee could only wait on his adversary.

While his commander contemplated possible future events, Stuart addressed one of the recent past. The fighting of the 13th and 14th, but particularly of the former date, had taken a toll on the gray cavalry. More importantly, it had revealed a problem that had to be addressed with alacrity. Stuart had seen three guns of his prized horse artillery fall into enemy hands and the blame could be laid at the boots of the cavalry. Four days after the disaster, Stuart issued General Order No. 3,

> Officers immediately in command on the battle-field will be held to strict accountability for the safety of artillery operating with their commands. They will see that a sufficient support of cavalry sharpshooters is in every case specially charged with its support and protection at all hazards.
> By command of Maj. Gen. J. E. B. Stuart[10]

The inference was obvious. The gray troopers had failed to protect the artillery; failed to stand when they had to stand; and failed to look out for their comrades in arms, who were looking out for them. With this order, Stuart made it quite clear that his artillery had to be protected in all circumstances. In the future, he wanted no repetition of what happened on the 13th.

Stuart also addressed other problems. An order sent out on the 19th required that an accounting be made of all government issued arms and accouterments as well as any that had been turned in for repairs. Furthermore, any future requisitions for arms and other ordnance material must include the number required and the number on hand. The days of haphazard record keeping and waste were over. As the Confederacy's supplies diminished, everyone needed to make an effort toward conservation.[11]

During the time Meade contemplated his next move, his army's vedettes continued to brush up against those of the enemy. On the 19th, the Sixteenth Pennsylvania, Gregg's brigade, Gregg's division, stationed on the army's far right near Wayland's Mill on Crooked Run, drove across the stream, sending the enemy scurrying over the Robinson River. Pleased with their efforts the Pennsylvanians pulled back and formed a new outpost line toward Fox Mountain.[12] Near the other end of the river line, companies G and H of the Eighth New York, Chapman's brigade, Buford's division, acted as guard for Brig. Gen. Henry J. Hunt, who was on a scouting mission along the Rapidan. At Germanna Ford the intrepidity of some of Hunt's escort overcame common sense. According to Lt. Jasper B. Cheney of the Eighth New York, four of his 12 man party saw about a dozen enemy pickets on the other side of the river and "charged through the river without orders and captured five men and five horses and some arms and equipments without the loss of a single man killed or wounded."[13] The prisoners came from the Fourth Virginia, Wickham's Brigade, Fitz, Lee's Division and the attack stirred up excitement throughout the immediate vicinity, causing Wickham's Brigade to move out in response. The New Yorkers skedaddled back over the river before suffering any repercussions from their escapade and nothing more came of the incident.[14]

Throughout the day and again the following day, the Federal Signal Corps intercepted Confederate signals from Clark's Mountain. Robert E. Lee had been informed that Pleasonton's cavalry had been relieved of picket duty along the Rapidan by Meade's infantry and that part of the cavalry apparently had been shifted to the Federal army's right. Lee felt this move might be an attempt to flank his army.[15] Indeed on the 20th, Meade took steps to implement such a plan by ordering two divisions of his cavalry out on a reconnaissance-in-force of the area between the Robinson and Rapidan rivers from Madison Court House and Burtonsville to Fry's and Barnett's fords. The mission was to ascertain the force of the enemy in the area, discover the number and serviceability of the roads and fords, especially the road leading from Burtonsville to Orange Court House, and examine the ground at the fords for suitable crossing points. Pleasonton chose Buford's and Kilpatrick's divisions for the task.[16]

At this time, Stuart's cavalry held positions along the Rapidan and Robinson rivers with Fitz Lee's Division concentrated around Verdiersville, watching some of the Rapidan and Rappahannock fords, and Hampton's Division stationed near Orange Court House but guarding the fords of the Robinson from its junction with the Rapidan up to Madison Court House. Even before Lee received word of the Federal shift to his left flank, Stuart had taken steps to provide some warning should the enemy advance over the Robinson. As early as the 17th, Stuart had sent Lt. Thomas Marshall of the Twelfth Virginia, Jones's Brigade, now under Col. Oliver R. Funsten, with eight men to Madison Court House to observe the enemy. On the 21st, Col. Thomas B. Massie brought up the rest of the regiment. Brig. Gen. Laurence S. Baker's Brigade, led by Col. Dennis D. Ferebee of the Fourth North Carolina, encamped between Orange Court House and Rapidan Station, as did Brig. Gen. Matthew C. Butler's Brigade, temporarily commanded by Col. James B. Gordon, and Capt. James F. Hart's Battery of horse artillery.[17] Capt. Marcellus N. Moorman's Battery, which had been picketing the Robinson River at Locust Dale, was encamped on the farm of a Dr. Slaughter between Locust Dale and Barnett's Ford on the Rapidan.[18] The stage was set, waiting only the lifting of the curtain.

With Kilpatrick's division in the lead, the Federal cavalry column moved out between 7:00 and 8:00 on the morning of the 21st, riding through Culpeper Court House and James City toward the Robinson River. Crossing the stream at Russell's Ford, the blue troopers scattered or scooped up Confederate pickets belonging to Funsten's Brigade and thundered toward Madison Court House. The Fifth Michigan, Custer's brigade, charged into the town, forcing the Confederates back along the road leading to Orange Court House. The day growing late, Kilpatrick's division occupied the town while Buford's men encamped between it and the Robinson.[19]

At 7:30 on the morning of the 22nd, Buford wrote a dispatch to Pleasonton outlining his plans for the day. Due to the greater distance that Kilpatrick's division had to cover, Kilpatrick had already left, moving in the direction of Wolftown with orders to cross the Rapidan and proceed downstream to Liberty Mills. Buford's own division would split, with Chapman's brigade advancing along the Gordonsville pike in the hope of connecting with Kilpatrick at Liberty Mills. Devin's brigade would also split, sending the Sixth New York and a section of artillery to Locust Dale while the remainder of the brigade took the road to Barnett's Ford. After he had rendezvoused with Kilpatrick, Buford hoped to concentrate his forces between the Robinson River and Barnett's Ford by day's end. He gave no indication that he believed he would have any difficulty carrying out his mission, despite acknowledging that the enemy's cavalry occupied the area through which he intended to move and that a small infantry force guarded Liberty Mills.[20] At about 10:00, Buford watched Chapman trot out from Madison Court House down the road to Liberty Mills and Devin ride off along the road to Barnett's Ford.[21]

Leading Chapman's column, the Third Indiana encountered no opposition until near Jack's Shop when it ran into Stuart's advance guard, Company F of the First North Carolina, Gordon's Brigade, led by Lt. Noah P. Foard, who had orders to charge the enemy on sight.[22] Without hesitation, Foard's men drew their sabers and went at the bluecoats. Maj. William H. Cheek, temporarily in command of the First while Lt. Col. Thomas Ruffin was having a shoe nailed to his horse's hoof, was about to follow Foard with the rest of the 130 men of the regiment when Stuart cautioned him to take care and avoid a possible ambush. Indeed, Foard's charge had driven the enemy back into an open field where the Third Indiana's dismounted skirmishers lined a wooden fence and fired a volley at the oncoming Tarheels, bringing Foard's charge to a halt. Veering to his left, Foard attempted to reach the shelter of some rolling ground and wood, only to have his horse killed under him as he attempted to leap a fence. Defiantly, he took the time to cut away his saddle and bridle and carried them from the field as minié balls zipped past him.[23]

Behind the gallant lieutenant, Cheek moved forward, but heeding his commander's advice and on seeing Foard repulsed, ordered his men to sheath their sabers, take up their carbines, and fire. Foard's men also had abandoned their sabers and answered the Hoosiers' fire with their pistols as best they could but soon realized that their position was untenable and retreated to join Cheek. Unsure of what to do next, Cheek rode back to Stuart, who ordered the regiment dismounted and deployed in the field on the right of the road less than 100 yards from the enemy. Sending Capt. William H. H. Cowles with Companies A and H, still mounted, to hold the left flank, Cheek led the rest of the regiment in a charge that forced the bluecoats back through the pines into another open field where mounted troopers reinforced them. In the meantime, Cowles barely had arrived on the flank when he also ordered his men to dismount and threw them forward as skirmishers. Now the whole regiment including Cheek, whose horse had been shot from under him, fought on foot.[24]

The Third Indiana soon received additional reinforcements in the form of the Eighth Illinois and the Eighth New York. Leaving their horses behind, the men of the two regiments moved through the wood and tangled with the enemy skirmishers.[25] The Confederates also fed in more men from the other regiments of the North Carolina brigade and from Ferebee's Brigade.[26] The fighting escalated. Capt. Alexander B. Andrews of Company B, First North Carolina, fell into the arms of Maj. Cheek, shot through his left lung. The wound was feared mortal, but the captain would survive.[27] The Second South Carolina, Gordon's Brigade, lay in a small depression, safe from most carbine and pistol fire and from artillery rounds that arced overhead. Their time of leisure proved short-lived. The regiment's commander, Lt. Col. Thomas J. Lipscomb, rode forward, exposing himself needlessly. A bluecoat sharpshooter almost made him pay for his rashness, grazing his head with a bullet. The colonel ignored the enemy's fire and ordered Company G of his regiment to advance across an open field, which was done with some loss.[28] Soon, the feeding in of men on both sides stabilized the lines. For the present, the fight had become a standoff.

During the time Chapman started grappling with Stuart, Kilpatrick's brigades continued their march begun so early that morning. Crossing the Rapidan at Simm's and Burton's fords and turning southeast, the blue column, led by Custer's brigade, under Col. Edward B. Sawyer of the First Vermont in Custer's absence, rode toward Liberty Mills without opposition.[29] On nearing that place, however, Kilpatrick ran into infantry and artillery that blocked his further advance. He also heard the sound of firing from across the river in his rear. Kilpatrick withdrew from the infantry and ordered his trailing brigade under Brig. Gen. Henry E. Davies to cross the river at White's Ford and strike the enemy's flank and rear.[30] Davies sent the Second New York followed by a battery of horse artillery and then the Fifth New York over the Rapidan and along a wood-lined road so narrow that the men rode just two abreast. Davies planned to intersect the Gordonsville Pike behind Stuart, cutting off his retreat to Liberty Mills.[31]

The stalemated action between Chapman and Stuart lasted about three hours until the blue cavalry managed to outflank the Confederates, forcing them back through Jack's Shop toward Liberty Mills.[32] After retreating about a mile, the intermingled regiments of Ferebee's and Gordon's brigades came to a hill in open country. Crowning its summit, guns of Hart's, McGregor's, and Moorman's batteries had been posted to sweep the ground in every direction.[33] The troopers quickly grasped the situation. Their line of retreat had been cut and as if to verify that fact, bullets began to fly at them from what seemed like every point of the compass. Stuart could be seen sitting on his proud bay, Highflyer, next to McGregor's guns, pointing first one way then another as the enemy came into his view. Though Davies had managed to thrust the Second New York into Stuart's path, his position proved precarious. Almost immediately he came under fire from enemy artillery. To hold on he would need help from Chapman and Kilpatrick.[34]

Faced with Federals in his front and rear, and indeed the terms "front" and "rear" held little meaning for the Confederates at the moment, Stuart had only one choice – break through Kilpatrick and reach Liberty Mills. To hold Chapman at bay, Stuart launched several charges in support of the Second South Carolina, Gordon's Brigade, which had been fighting a rear-guard action during the retreat. Capt. Leonard Williams of the Second had seen his men continually outflanked during the retreat. At times he fought enemy sharpshooters in his front, flank, and rear. He joined in the charge that Stuart ordered, hoping to gain time for his fellow troopers to deal with Kilpatrick.[35]

The charges succeeded in temporarily halting Chapman's advance. Now Stuart unleashed the Phillips Legion, Cobb's Legion, and the Fourth North Carolina on Kilpatrick. On the receiving end of the attacks was the Second New York. A dismounted company of the regiment under Capt. Willard Glazier had deployed to the right of the pike while a mounted contingent led by Maj. Samuel McIrvin and Capt. Charles Hasty held the pike itself. Captains John F. B. Mitchell's and Obediah J. Downing's squadrons took position to the left of the road in front of a post and rail fence that ran at right angles to the pike.[36]

Kilpatrick and Davies had accompanied the Second New York as it advanced to the pike. The former rode with Maj. McIrvin as he led his squadron forward in a charge against the oncoming Confederates. A short distance down the road, Kilpatrick drew off to the side and cheered on McIrvin as he led his men by. The blue troopers collided with the Seventh Virginia, Funsten's Brigade, that had counter-charged. In the brief but violent melee that followed, the Seventh hurled back McIrvin and his men, wounding the major in his shoulder, unhorsing, and capturing him. Capt. Hasty, surrounded, fought until wounded and taken prisoner. Others fell into the hands of the enemy and the rest retreated to the wood, rallying there. The Seventh attempted pursuit, but Mitchell's and Downing's men sent them scurrying back to their supports. Again the Seventh charged, only to be hurled back once again. However, the desperate ferocity of the Confederate attacks, added to the Federal artillery's failure to find a position where it could unlimber and the Fifth New York's inability to deploy in support of its sister regiment, convinced Kilpatrick that he could not prevent Stuart from breaking through. He ordered Davies to hold his position until the artillery and the Fifth could be safely withdrawn. The job fell to the Second New York alone.[37]

Meanwhile, Lt. Col. Thomas Marshall, commanding the Seventh Virginia, saw the impossibility of driving the Federals from their position solely through frontal assault. While he consulted with Stuart, the horse artillery opened fire on the New Yorkers with grape and canister. Marshall returned to his men and, now joined by the Twelfth Virginia in the center and the Eleventh Virginia on the left, took position on the far right. The Eleventh and Twelfth struck the blue line straight on while the Seventh rolled up the New Yorkers' flank. Mitchell and Downing watched their men fall back to the post and rail fence that now trapped a large number of them. Some Confederates attempted to round up prisoners. Among them was Sgt. John W. Green of the Eleventh, who rode up to two Federals at the fence and demanded their surrender. Instead, they raised their carbines. Green attempted to fire his pistol but it misfired, and he was shot and killed. Others from the Twelfth dismounted and tore sections of the fence down, allowing troopers from their regiment and the Seventh and Eleventh to push the Second New York back to and down the White's Ford road, opening the pike. The graycoats rapid advance cut off Glazier and his lone company. Keeping his head, the captain managed to elude the Confederates, who were more intent on reaching Liberty Mills than capturing wayward bluecoats, and led his men to safety.[38] Stuart rode on to Liberty Mills and a renewal of the contest with Kilpatrick.

During the dramatic action on the pike, Devin made his way almost peacefully toward Barnett's Ford. Not until he neared the river did he encounter any serious resistance. The Ninth New York threw out skirmishers and moved forward. Devin brought up his artillery and opened fire on enemy wagons across the river. Suddenly two guns of a Confederate battery, still north of the river, appeared. The section belonged to Moorman's Battery of horse artillery under Lt. John J. Shoemaker that had been encamped on the Dr. Slaughter farm. Earlier that morning, the advance of the Sixth New York drove back elements of Funsten's Brigade from Locust Dale. Shoemaker had opened fire without moving his guns from where they had been parked for the night. Before long, however, the sound of Devin's column approaching Barnett's Ford alerted Shoemaker to the fact that he could be cut off. He limbered and headed for the ford.[39]

On arriving at Barnett's, Shoemaker, whose only support came from a handful of cavalry, attempted to take a position north of the ford and hold back Devin's column, but the Ninth New York's skirmishers closed in and opened a hot fire, causing Shoemaker to retreat rapidly to the ford. Crossing and turning to the right he led his section to the crown of a high hill. From there the strength of the Northern squadrons could be seen. Shoemaker greeted the bluecoats with shot and shell. Hoping to target the battery's crew, the Ninth's skirmishers worked their way close to the ford only to discover that enemy infantry held the opposite bank in force. A second dismounted squadron from the Ninth entered the fray but failed to gain any advantage, although one of the Ninth's sharpshooters managed to hit Lt. Col. Henry Rogers of the Thirteenth North Carolina Infantry, Brig. Gen. Alfred M. Scales's Brigade, Maj. Gen. Cadmus M. Wilcox's Division, A. P. Hill's Corps, in the head, a wound that disabled him from further service. The New Yorkers held on until about 10:00 that night before pulling back.[40] Devin had successfully reached his target but like Kilpatrick and Chapman he failed to deliver a fatal blow.

Late in the afternoon, Stuart safely crossed the Rapidan at Liberty Mills and turned immediately upstream to confront part of Sawyer's brigade, which faced some Confederate infantry across a stream. On arriving the First North Carolina, Gordon's Brigade, moved to the left of the infantry, throwing forward Company K under Capt. John H. Addington as an advance guard. Emerging from a wood that had shielded them from sight, the Tarheels came under an accurate artillery fire. Immediately in front of them stood the Seventh Michigan that had crossed the run to develop the enemy. Dismounting one of their companies while the others remained mounted in support, the Michiganders soon discovered that the gray cavalry outflanked them. Seeing his advantage, Stuart ordered a charge, which was executed with some élan.[41] The Seventh skedaddled as best it could across the bridge. Recognizing he could do nothing more, Sawyer pulled back his artillery while his cavalry peppered the North Carolinians with carbine fire from across the stream that had brought the Tarheel's charge up short. With daylight fading, Stuart called an end to the fight. Sawyer fell back and with Davies, who had been in support, crossed the Rapidan, and camped with Devin's brigade between Providence Church and Barnett's Ford.[42]

While Hampton's Division struggled with Buford and Kilpatrick, Wickham's and Lomax's brigades of Fitz Lee's Division received orders to march via Orange Court House and Liberty Mills and join Stuart at Barboursville. The troopers mounted up early and started off, but any expectations of joining Stuart in time to aid him that day were wishful ones. The long ride stretched through the morning and afternoon, the weary cavalrymen not encamping until near 10:00 at night.[43] All understood that the next day they would have the same opportunity to meet the foe as had Hampton's Division that day.

On the morning of the 23rd, Buford's and Kilpatrick's men stirred from their bivouacs and headed back toward the Robinson River. The Sixth New York, Devin's brigade, had the easiest trek. Having been near Locust Dale, the regiment simply held its position until it united with the brigade that had pulled back from Barnett's Ford about 10:00 and marched for Locust Dale. The second squadron of the Ninth New York acted as rearguard. Its commander, thinking that Devin would withdraw to Madison Court House and cross the river at Russell's Ford, mistakenly rode on toward Madison Court House. The capture of a courier sent to locate Devin's column alerted the squadron in time for it to turn around and find the right road just before the enemy blocked its path. It reached Fry's Ford safely and crossed without further incident.[44]

Kilpatrick's column ran into greater difficulty. The First Michigan, Sawyer's brigade, under Lt. Col. Peter Stagg, bringing up the rear of the column, reached Good Hope Church and discovered that the troops ahead of it had stopped for breakfast. Stagg's vedettes, a mile to his rear, reported the Southerners advancing in large numbers. As the division began to move on toward the river, aiming for Smoot's Ford, Stagg received orders to hold the Confederates back because Kilpatrick planned to halt the column for an hour once it reached the crossing.[45] Even though he promised reinforcements, Kilpatrick displayed a complete lack of appreciation for Stagg's predicament. The Confederates continued to push ahead aggressively. When a frontal attack failed to budge Stagg, Stuart swung around one flank. The reinforcements promised Stagg failed to materialize. Instead, Kilpatrick had trotted off toward the ford, leaving his rear guard high and dry. Only some quick action by Stagg prevented his men from being cut off. He made for the ford post-haste, still skirmishing with his stubborn pursuers. Near the ford, Stagg saw a welcomed sight, a brother regiment, the Fifth Michigan, drawn up to support him. Federal artillery opened fire from the northern bank and under its protection both regiments withdrew.[46] After crossing the river, Buford eventually made his way back to Stevensburg to watch the lower fords of the Rapidan above its junction with the Robinson while Kilpatrick watched the fords of the Robinson.[47]

Having been unable to strike more than glancing blows at his retreating adversaries, Stuart reestablished his outpost line along the Robinson with elements of Hampton's Division, taking the rest back toward Rapidan Station.[48] Wickham's and Lomax's brigades from Fitz Lee's Division trekked all the way back to Orange Court House, not encamping until 11:00 at night.[49]

Typically, both sides claimed victory. The Confederates rejoiced that they had stopped what they thought to have been a raid on Gordonsville and possibly Charlottesville and inflicted considerable casualties on the enemy.[50] Stuart received praise for wresting "the victory from this very superior force of Yankees, by his indomitable pluck and perseverance."[51] Even Lee expressed his satisfaction with what Stuart accomplished.[52] The Federals saw their expedition a success. Buford touted that all the goals of the reconnaissance had been met and Stuart given a good thumping besides.[53] The truth lay somewhere between the two views.

Even as the cavalry of both armies attempted to catch their collective breaths on the 24th, Maj. Gen. Henry W. Halleck telegraphed Meade, inquiring whether the army commander contemplated any immediate movement against Lee and that if he did not to prepare the Eleventh and Twelfth Corps to withdraw to Washington. Meade replied that he had no plans.[54] His lack of any offensive operations over several weeks, other than those executed by the Federal cavalry prompted the decision to move troops to where someone would make better use of them. Unfortunately, no cavalry would leave the Army of the Potomac, meaning that Stuart's weary troopers would have to stay alert and prepared for anything. Lee warned Stuart that Meade's next thrust would be at the other end of he line. He had yet to learn about the withdrawal of the two corps.[55]

The same day Stuart returned from pursuing his foe, he addressed the horse shortage problem in one of his brigades. While fighting may have been intermittent, the business of managing Lee's mounted arm confronted the cavalry chieftain on a daily basis. This time he ordered a reduction of transportation in Funsten's Brigade. Only four wagons per regiment would be allowed – one for regimental headquarters; one for company officers' baggage; and two for cooking utensils. All others had to be turned into the quartermaster, excepting forages and ambulances. Attrition continued to grind away at Stuart's command.[56]

Over the next few days, Meade quietly shifted the Eleventh and Twelfth Corps toward Washington. The task was not a simple one since some of the Twelfth's regiments stood outpost duty from Somerville Ford to Stringfellow's Ford on the Rapidan with the corps's main body near Raccoon Ford. Any overt activity would alert Lee to the move. Nevertheless, not until the 28th did Lee have any idea that two corps had disappeared from his front. In fact, for a time Lee believed that Meade was receiving reinforcements in order to build up a large numerical advantage. When at last Lee learned the truth, the information did not come from Stuart but from a source in the Shenandoah Valley.[57]

162

On the surface, it would appear that Stuart failed in his duty to discover such a large enemy troop movement. However, this circumstance once again reflects the impact of a physical obstruction on cavalry operations. The Rapidan River stood between the opposing forces with both sides guarding all the fords. The heavy concentration of troops behind the river prevented any deep penetration even if a small force could cross the river. A single individual might get through, but two legs can only cover so much ground. Furthermore, units constantly shifted hither and thither behind the lines. Differentiating the movement of a corps from a regiment changing its campsite became a near impossibility for one man or a group of men. Even if Stuart had crossed the river with a small force and had managed to dodge his way through the Federal encampments, only a stroke of incredible luck would have allowed him to discover the detachment of the Twelfth Corps and its destination. He then would have had to have the same luck to return with his information. Such is too much to ask of the gods of war.

During the days in which Meade saw a portion of his army decamp and trudge off to fight in the west, the cavalry of both sides spent time recovering from their two-day brawl among the pines. While the 24th had been spent in marching back to camps - the Confederates to either the Orange Court House area or in the case of Wickham's Brigade to Verdiersville, and the Federals to Culpeper Court House or Stevensburg – the 25th passed quietly, excepting for those on outpost duty and a portion the Fifth New York that clashed with a sizable body of the enemy at the Hazel River Bridge.[58] Gregg's division had had almost no contact with the enemy while Buford and Kilpatrick clashed with Stuart. McIntosh's brigade had been camped near Culpeper Court House, some of its regiments doing picket duty near Rapidan Station. On the 22nd the brigade rode to Stevensburg and then back to Culpeper on the 23rd. Col. Gregg's brigade had performed much the same duty but near Thoroughfare and Fox mountains. The next day the entire division saddled up, trotted to the Rappahannock, and crossed. Its assignment was to replace a division of the Eleventh Corps, guard the railroad, and look out for guerillas. Encamping for the night on the road to Bealton Station, on the 25th the division renewed its march, stretching out its regiments and eventually covering the countryside from Deep Run in the east to Rappahannock Station to the west and Kettle Run and Bristoe Station in the north. It would stay in this area until October 9.[59]

Stuart's troopers settled further into their customary activities on the 26th. While some men took up the onerous outpost duty, others lay in camp. A 36-man contingent of the Third Virginia, Wickham's Brigade, Fitz Lee's Division, under Lt. Charles R. Palmore trotted off to Fredericksburg to relieve Lt. Thomas H. Hall's troopers who had been watching their foes across the river. However, the men of Companies A, D, G, and E used their time to look over their new Richmond-made carbines that just had been issued the previous day. Time would tell if the weapons could stand the strain of service in the field. The seemingly never ending reshuffling of units among the newly constituted brigades affected the Maryland Battalion, which had been attached to Wickham's Brigade, as it joined Lomax's Brigade.[60]

How long the quiet would reign remained to be seen.

The front-line calm did not encompass newspapers. With little transpiring in Lee's army, the pundits once again rose up to commentate on the state of Stuart's cavalry. Over the next several days, articles appeared in various Richmond papers, focusing on the mounted arm. The *Richmond Whig and Public Advertiser* made amends for previous negative statements about Stuart by eating some crow, admitting that the reasons for the cavalry's decline could not be laid at Stuart's boots but rather at the feet of "the authorities," who were "neglecting" the cavalry. Stuart received credit for having done "all in his power to make this important area of service all that it could be."[61] Two articles appeared in the October 1 editions of the *Whig* and the *Enquirer*, each dealing in its own way with the problems faced by the Southern horse. One writer took umbrage at the words "fell back" used by an editor in regard to how Stuart fought the enemy on several occasions. A spirited defense of Lee's cavalry chief that reached back to the fight at Brandy Station on June 9 explained the various actions taken by Stuart during the engagements mentioned, concluding that a "great injustice has been done both Stuart and his command."[62] The second article attempted to rouse farmers throughout the South to do everything in their power to sustain the cavalry by contributing money in order that the gallant "Old Dominion Dragoons" (Company B, Third Virginia) might be able to remount a number of its men so that they could stop the raids on farmers conducted by enemy cavalry.[63] The effectiveness of the plea is unknown.

Stuart reacted to the articles defending him as one might expect. After having endured considerable abuse from the press, he relished every word written in his support, even sending a copy of the *Whig* article to Flora.[64] His gallant conduct and quick reactions that had brought him out of the trap at Jack's Shop had not hurt his reputation among his men. However, he also was concerned about the public's perception of him. Those not in the ranks could not see what transpired on the battlefields and relied on reporters and editors to supply them with information. Among this group, Stuart had not faired well for some time. The change seen in these articles seemed to indicate that the negative opinions were at least diminishing.

However, not all of the articles reflected positive views. One scathingly rebuked everyone from Lee down for the condition of the cavalry, citing the odds it had to face, the supplies it never saw, the raw recruits sent to replace good men lost through red tape or short-sightedness, the horses disabled for want of horseshoes and nails, lack of bridles, or poorly constructed saddles, and the incompetence or greed of supply officers and headquarters personnel. Bitterness oozed from every line and while the article evidenced some exaggeration, a ring of truth echoed throughout. The writer did not name or accuse Stuart directly but certainly held the commander of the cavalry accountable as far as what he had the power to change and had failed to. Lee, Stuart, and others in the army and the government knew many of these things, but the ability to rectify them lay beyond their power. The Confederacy's capacity to meet the needs of its soldiers in the field diminished daily. That the cavalry should not suffer as did every other branch of the army and indeed the civilian population was unrealistic.[65]

On the 26th the First Vermont, which had been detached from Custer's brigade, ran afoul of an enemy raiding party that attacked the First's picket post at Richard's Ford on the Rappahannock.[66] A lieutenant and 16 men fell victim to a band of Confederates that apparently had crossed the river near its junction with the Rapidan and proceeded on foot to the road leading from Stafford Court House that passed through Hartwood Church. Coming upon the Vermonters, the raiders killed one man and captured the lieutenant and 13 others. The ruckus failed to alert the Eighth New York, Chapman's brigade, Buford's division, guarding the other side of the ford, and the enemy made off with their captures. In his report of the incident, Lt. Col. Addison W. Preston, commanding the First Vermont, stated that he sent out scouting parties after the raiders but to no avail. He further revealed that guerillas frequently skirmished with his patrols and concluded with an almost audible sigh of relief that his men would be replaced that very night by the Sixth and Ninth New York regiments of Devin's brigade.[67]

Col. Preston's emotions probably turned from relief to frustration when the two regiments failed to arrive. Nor did they turn up the morning of the 27th. By the afternoon, the telegraph wires were humming. Buford replied to an inquiry from Pleasonton's Chief-of-Staff, Col. C. Ross Smith, explaining that the regiments had started the morning of the 26th and he had not heard from them since. He then quickly changed the subject to report that all was quiet from Richard's to Morton's fords. Had Col. Preston been consulted, he may have had a dissenting opinion. Eventually the New Yorkers showed up and the Sixth replaced the First Vermont at Richard's Ford while the Ninth did the same for the Eighteenth Pennsylvania, Davies's brigade, Kilpatrick's division, at United States Ford.[68]

Although Buford asserted that all was well along his stretch of the river and while Preston could have provided convincing evidence to the contrary, the actual situation encompassed both points of view. During the day vedettes on both sides of the river seemed more inclined to comradeship or at least peaceful co-existence, crossing the water to exchange newspapers, tobacco, coffee, and stories. However, the relaxed atmosphere belied the fact that the two sides were still enemies. Night wrought a change in temperament and bushwhacking, raiding, and other exchanges of unpleasantries held sway. Guerilla bands and regular cavalry roamed behind enemy lines. Many of the regular Confederate cavalrymen who participated in raiding wanted only to capture horses and equipment, frequently allowing their owners to go free. Guerillas were another matter and the Federals hunted them down at every opportunity. Apparently the peace Buford touted depended on the time of day one made his observation.[69]

Raids of outposts and patrols plagued the other end of the Union line as well. On the 27th the Acting Assistant Quartermaster for Meade's Third Corps, Lt. Henry R. Williams, received a serious wound when attacked by what was reported to be regular Confederate cavalry. Williams's commander, Maj. Gen. William H.

French, in writing Pleasonton about the incident, named Lt. William B. Tidwell of the Second North Carolina, Ferebee's Brigade, and 12 of his men as the group responsible. He further claimed that the enemy had a force of cavalry behind the Sixth Corps that sent scouting parties at regular intervals behind his lines. French obviously wanted something done. Kilpatrick received orders to reconnoiter behind the Sixth Corps and dispatched Capt. Henry Grinton with Companies B, F, H, and M of the Second New York, Davies's brigade, to the Rixeyville area. Leaving half his men to picket the Hazel River, Grinton led the rest on a scout, crossing the river at Browning's Ford and riding to the Sperryville Pike. Other than information that the men who attacked Lt. Williams were guerillas headquartered nearby and not the Second North Carolina nothing was gained.[70]

Mosby's operations behind Federal lines continued to spread fear and consternation among soldiers and civilians alike. On the 28th the *Washington Evening Star* reported that Mosby led 150 men on a raid to Alexandria to capture Col. D. H. Dulany, military aide to Francis H. Pierpont, governor of West Virginia. The article was a wealth of misinformation and reflected the effect Mosby had on the populace and the press. He did make the raid, but it was to capture Pierpont, not his aide, and he had about five men with him, including Col. Dulany's son, French, who rode with Mosby. Discovering Pierpont was not at home the target became Col. Dulany, who was not overly pleased to see his son on this occasion.[71]

Across the Rapidan, Stuart's regiments dealt not with guerillas or partisans, but something nearly as bad – inspectors. Wickham's Brigade stood before Stuart's new Assistant Inspector General, Lt. Col. George St. Leger Grenfell, on the 28th, as had some brigades in the days before and others would after, and an inspection by Grenfell was no parade ground picnic. A professional soldier of fortune, he had been assigned to Stuart's staff by Robert E. Lee in the hope that his expertise might have an impact on both the cavalry and the horse artillery. The comments by a few of the troopers who faced Grenfell's cold eye testify that he did his job well. Regrettably, he did not mesh with the rest of Stuart's staff and was relieved of his duties late in December.[72]

Except for such disagreeable interruptions, life in the gray cavalry's camps adhered to the usual routines. Every once in awhile, the men experienced the excitement of moving their camps for reasons such as better grazing for their mounts. However, ulterior motives may have been at work in some instances. The same day the Third Virginia, Wickham's Brigade, faced the implacable Lt. Col. Grenfell orders came, from whom is not entirely clear, to move camp.[73] Having endured the inspector's harsh gaze once, someone may have determined to relocate the regiment to a place where it might not so easily be found. If the ploy worked, the men undoubtedly rewarded their ingenious comrade in an appropriate manner.

Pleasonton's troopers also engaged in camp moving and inspections from time to time, but unlike Stuart's men, they additionally traipsed around after phantom Confederates.[74] The rumor mill sent a portion of Col. Gregg's brigade, still encamped near Catlett's Station, out on the 29th in search of two North Carolina regiments reputed to be near Amissville. As with almost all such expeditions, the enemy failed to materialize and the village's inhabitants reported that none had been there.[75] The patrol returned to camp and with their other comrades-in-arms watched September close out peacefully.

Except for a scout conducted by a squadron of the Twelfth Virginia, Funsten's Brigade, Hampton's Division, that netted two Federal prisoners, Stuart's cavaliers did nothing to disturb the tranquility of the last days of the month. The lack of activity permitted Stuart to address a problem that had been growing for some time. In a September 30th letter to Adjutant and Inspector General Samuel Cooper, the cavalry commander admitted that his reports of battles and engagements were a year behind and offered as a reason his constant attention to current operations that left him little time for writing reports. While his staff already had an adjutant, he requested that another be appointed and offered the name of Capt. John Esten Cooke, a prewar novelist and relative of Stuart's through marriage who was serving on the staff as Ordnance Officer. Cooper agreed to the appointment but not to Stuart's request for the promotion of Cooke to major. The official date of Cooke's transfer did not come until October 27. By that date, a number of events had occurred that added several reports to Cooke's workload.[76]

As uneventful as was the last day of September, the first day of October was filled with activity from near the Potomac to the Robinson. Lt. Col. Elijah V. White and his Thirty-fifth Virginia Cavalry Battalion shattered the calm by attacking Camp Beckwith near Lewinsville, which was located about three miles north of Fairfax Court House. With 50 men, White approached the camp along the Dranesville road, dodged the enemy's pickets by using a wood road or path through a wood that had been left unguarded, and just after midnight struck the camp. So unexpected was White's appearance that the Federals failed to fire a single shot. Company B of the Sixteenth New York took the brunt of the onslaught, suffering 2 killed, 2 wounded, and 10 captured along with 51 horses and their equipment. An infantry detachment had 1 man wounded and 10 taken prisoners. Thirteen horses belonging to the quartermaster department also fell into White's hands. At the same time, another 50 men from White's command under Lt. William F. Dowdell clashed with Capt. Samuel C. Means of the Independent Virginia (Union) Rangers about five miles outside of Harpers Ferry, wounding 3, capturing 5, and scooping up another 8 horses and their equipment.[77]

Further south near Warrenton, Capt. Robert J. McNitt, commanding 100 troopers of the First Pennsylvania, McIntosh's brigade, Gregg's division, ran afoul of what he reported to be a strong mounted force of the enemy. A lively skirmish ensued until both sides decided that neither had any advantage at which time the Confederates withdrew along the Greenwich road after inflicting a loss of two men wounded on the Federals while themselves having one man captured. Shortly after the fight, McNitt joined forces with 100 men from the First Maryland (Union), also from McIntosh's brigade, under Maj. Charles H. Russell, who took command and rode on to Warrenton. The column had no further contact with the enemy on the road or in the town.[78]

Although most of Stuart's cavalry lounged in their camps on the 1st, at least two contingents managed to get in a little exercise. Wickham's Brigade, Fitz Lee's Division, once again roused itself and marched to a new campsite near Orange Spring. The mundane event became a topic for diaries throughout the brigade when Gen. Wickham's horse fell, severely bruising the general's left leg.[79] Meanwhile, a part of the Seventh Virginia, Funsten's Brigade, Hampton's Division, also did some moving about. Eight men stole across the Robinson River and descended on an enemy outpost, taking three prisoners. Their intrepidity received further reward in the capturing of eight fully equipped horses. Stuart, himself, wrote a rather truncated report of the incident, evidently having found the exploit worthy of his personal attention and perhaps not wanting to burden Cooke with additional work.[80]

On a rainy October 2, the men of Buford's division, guarding the Rappahannock from Falmouth to Kelly's Ford, received some welcomed news. They were to be relieved. At the same time, the men of Gen. Gregg's division received bad news. They were the relief. Orders arrived for Col. Gregg to send his brigade to Bealton Station from where he would establish an outpost line from Kelly's Ford upstream to Freeman's Ford and included an admonishment to keep an eye on Sulphur Springs and the road to Warrenton. Col. Sargent, still in command of the First Brigade, moved his men from Catlett's Station and Bristoe Station to Hartwood Church and took over the picketing duties downstream from Kelly's Ford on the 3rd and 4th. He left behind the Third Pennsylvania to guard the railroad bridge over Kettle Run.[81] In his diary Pvt. John R. Morey explained how he and other men from Kilpatrick's division spent their afternoon, "About noon Officers' Call blows and every man in the regiment that wants to go has permission to go to a great horse race between Gen. Kilpatricks [sic] horse Monitor and a battery horse from the third [sic] Army Corps which resulted in the battery horse beating him three successive times."[82] What affect this had on the general's temperament over the next few days is unknown.

Company A of the First Virginia, Wickham's Brigade, also found itself doing picket duty but along the Rapidan at Skinker's Ford and on the Wycoff farm above Culpeper Mine Ford. The rainy miserable weather did not sit well with the men or with Col. Chambliss's boys. As water filled the bottom of the latter's tents, they bailed out as best they could. Still, water was better than lead or iron. Diary entries echoed each other in recording that all was quiet.[83] Private John O. Collins of the Tenth Virginia sought shelter under his little fly and wrote a letter to his wife, lamenting, "We are not getting enough to eat yet or for our horses either [.] [W]e cant [sic] keep up cavalry this winter unless they feed the horses better for they are going down evry [sic] day."[84] For men throughout the ranks, the situation was the same.

The 3rd passed uneventfully.[85] The following day brought only minor activity, including the interception of a semaphore message from one of Stuart's colonels that indicated that rations for the men had not as yet arrived. Collins, and presumably his horse, had to go hungry for at least another day. Confederate artillery lobbed a few shells at the enemy near Somerville Ford to which the Federals chose not to reply. The only real operation conducted by cavalry resulted from Pleasonton ordering Gen. Davies to send out a patrol to examine the upper road from Culpeper Court House to Madison Court House. The First West Virginia drew the duty almost immediately after a brigade review conducted by Kilpatrick. Capt. Hugh P. Boon and his men left at 5:00 in the afternoon and rode toward James City, turning south about a mile and a half from that place. After covering another eight miles on a road so narrow at points that the troopers could only proceed in single file, Boon ran into Confederate vedettes about two miles north of the Robinson River. The enemy retreated across the river where they had a strong reserve force. Boon fell back, not wishing to bring on any kind of engagement. His report on the road and the surrounding terrain, which featured thick woods and numerous small runs, indicated that any attempted advance would meet with great difficulty. If Pleasonton had considered an offensive movement over this road, the results of the scout had to have been greatly disappointing. Indeed, it appeared that any offensive move would be heavily resisted as the enemy presented a strong front and had been seen fortifying the crossing at Fry's Ford downstream from where Boon had scouted.[86]

While his patrol ran into enemy pickets, Kilpatrick ran into a more refined, though no less resistant, Confederate in the form of a daughter of the owner of the farm where he had his headquarters. While Kilpatrick conducted his review, the fair lady took it upon herself to serenade the staff officers who had not accompanied their general. Her song selection raised eyebrows, but her charms warded off any protests. Having finished a rousing rendition of "The Bonnie Blue Flag," she was in the midst of "Dixie" when the general returned. Kilpatrick promptly had her arrested and incarcerated in the smokehouse. There she stayed for half a day. Then Kilpatrick had her brought to him and told her that she could either go back to "prison" or sing the "Star-Spangled Banner." Coyly, she protested that she did not know the song, but Kilpatrick would have none of it. In the end, she sang - possibly off key - and secured her release.[87] Elsewhere, the war ground on.

A movement of portions of Meade's Sixth Corps on October 5, though not offensive in nature, set off a flurry of messages between several of Robert E. Lee's Signal Corps stations. The Federal shuffling about caused one Confederate alarm gun to be fired and sent ripples of speculation throughout the army. Just after 6:00 in the evening, the need for accurate information as to what Meade might be up to sent Fitz Lee on a scouting mission, not across the Rapidan but up the side of Clark's Mountain. In a brief message to Stuart, Fitz stated that he saw nothing that would indicate a general advance of the enemy. All the rumors ended and everyone settled down for a night's rest.[88]

For the troopers of Kilpatrick's division spit and polish became the order of the day. A review ordered by Gen. Pleasonton caused extra work for the rank and file, but the newspapers relished in the pomp. Pleasonton praised his cavalrymen and received their cheers even while the business of the war intruded upon the scene. Dispatches brought to Kilpatrick during the review from the Second New York, Davies's brigade, reported what was believed to be a movement by the enemy. Kilpatrick pocketed the messages until Pleasonton finished receiving his accolades and then set about discovering the true nature of the situation. The next day Kilpatrick ascertained that an enemy column had marched toward Madison Court House and encamped. Nothing more came of the matter.[89]

While Pleasonton held his review, some of the Confederates across the river spent their time drilling. The Third Virginia, Wickham's Brigade, Fitz Lee's Division, held mounted drill in the morning, dismounted in the evening, and dress parade once a day throughout the 4th, 5th, 6th, 7th, and 8th. Certainly, other regiments did the same.[90] Fitz Lee's brigades held the right of the Confederate line and Hampton's the left. Stuart's troopers stretched out from somewhere near Fredericksburg to beyond Madison Court House. With little happening along this extended line, other than a few quick strikes across the river after dark, the days were being put to good use. The men, it seems, had two daytime options, neither of which were their choice – stand picket duty or drill. In between these periods of forced labor, they could attend to their horses and equipment, write letters, and relax in general. Eating occurred only if rations could be found.

Federal cavalry stretched equally as far along the rivers as Stuart's. Kilpatrick held the far right along the Robinson; Buford held the center; and Gregg guarded the railroad and the left. Pleasonton continued his reviews, visiting Kilpatrick's division on the 8th and Buford's on the 9th. Buford had reviewed his command just the day before.[91] During these days, guerilla attacks and raiding persisted. On the evening of the 6th, guerillas struck a patrol of the Third Pennsylvania, McIntosh's brigade, Gregg's division, two miles out from Catlett's Station on the road to Bristoe Station. Of the five-man patrol, two fell into enemy hands and three suffered wounds. The regiment sent out both mounted and dismounted men in an attempt to track down the perpetrators, but they had vanished into the night.[92]

On the night of the 7th-8th, amidst a muffling rain, a raiding party from the Seventh Virginia, Funsten's Brigade, Hampton's Division, attacked an outpost of Company C of the Seventh Michigan, Custer's brigade, Kilpatrick's division, at Utz's Ford on the Robinson River. Sgt. Andrew N. Buck of the Seventh Michigan gave an accounting of the attack, "At 2 A.M. a party of some 40 rebs crossed over evaded our pickets – surprised the reserve taking some five men and 18 horses killing Sgt. E. A. Cook of Co. C. You see the secesh understand perfectly the country about here and know how to strike. A reb rode up to Sgt. Cook after he was mortally wounded and asked if he was wounded. A Corp. replied for the Sgt. Saying he was when the reb added 'we did not intend to hurt anyone; our intention was to capture.'"[93] In addition to Sgt. Cook, the Michiganders suffered one wounded and six captured. The Virginians also scooped up 22 fully equipped horses. On the morning of the 8th, the enemy struck Kilpatrick's pickets at Russell's Ford on the Robinson, killing one before retreating back over the river. In retaliation, Kilpatrick sent parts of the Fifth New York, Davies's brigade, and the

Fifth Michigan, Custer's brigade, across the river at Russell's Ford. They rode all the way to Madison Court House, encountering only a few vedettes, and then withdrew.[94] Such *petite guerre*, which ground away at both armies, was about to end, however.

Gen. Braxton Bragg's victory over Maj. Gen. William S. Rosecrans at Chickamauga, thanks in part to Lee's dispatching Longstreet's Corps to reinforce Bragg's army, prompted Lee to suggest that Confederate forces advance against the enemy in all quarters. On his own front, Meade's lack of offensive activity opened the door for Lee's own push. On October 9, Lee set the wheels in motion by ordering Stuart to swing around Meade's right flank. The Bristoe Station campaign had begun.[95]

Notes:
1.	*O.R.*, Series 1, vol. 29, part 2, 201.
2.	*Ibid.*, 201-202.
3.	*Ibid.*, 206-208.
4.	*Ibid.*, 198, 202-203; Harrington Diary.
5.	Morey Diary.
6.	Cheney Diary; Wesson Diary; Frank Diary; Inglis Diary; Hall, *Sixth New York Cavalry*, 158; Cheney, *Ninth Regiment, New York Volunteer Cavalry*, 133; Hard, *Eighth Illinois Cavalry*, 273.
7.	Ressler Diary; Allen L. Bevan to My Dear Sister, September 21, 1863, Allen L. Bevan Letters, CWMC, USAMHI; Sauerburger, ed., *I Seat Myself to Write You*, 178; Denison, *Sabres and Spurs*, 289; Rawle, *Third Pennsylvania Cavalry*, 335.
8.	Cheney Diary; Inglis Diary; Ressler Diary; Hall, *Sixth New York Cavalry*, 156; Miller, *Sixteenth Pennsylvania Cavalry*, 39; Cheney, *Ninth Regiment, New York Volunteer Cavalry*, 132; Lloyd, *History of the First Regiment Pennsylvania Reserve Cavalry*, 74; Rawle, *Third Pennsylvania Cavalry*, 335; Morrissett Diary; Theophilus F. Rodenbough, Henry C. Potter, and William P. Seal, *History of the Eighteenth Regiment of Pennsylvania Cavalry*, (New York: Wynkoop Hallenbeck Crawford Co., 1909), 44.

	The First Vermont crossed the Rappahannock at the railroad bridge, doing picket duty at points along the river that included Richard's Ford and also guarding against guerillas. Hoffman, *First Vermont*, 137-138; *O.R.*, Series 1, vol. 29, part 1, 198.

	This movement may have brought forth a reaction from Stuart. Pvt. William H. Arehart of the Twelfth Virginia, Jones's Brigade, encamped along the Robinson River, recorded in his diary that at 5:00 on the 17th, his brigade received orders to march toward Culpeper. After covering 20 miles, the brigade camped on the Madison Court House and Culpeper road. Sometime after 10:00 the next morning, Stuart ordered them back and the brigade camped near Madison Court House on the night of the 18th. Arehart, "Diary of W. H. Arehart," 277.
9.	*O.R.*, Series 1, vol. 29, part 2, 730-731.
10.	*Ibid.*, 729.
11.	Fourth Virginia Cavalry Headquarters Book kept by Sgt. Maj. Charles L. Mosby, Eleanor S. Brockenbrough Library, MOC.
12.	Miller, *Sixteenth Pennsylvania Cavalry*, 39-40
13.	Jasper B. Cheney Diary, CWTIC, USAMHI.
14.	Cheney Diary; Norton, *Deeds of Daring*, 73-74; Morrissett Diary; Carter Diary.

	The five men captured were Pvt. William H. Davis, Pvt. Thomas H. Fisher, Pvt. M. H. McCoy, Pvt. A. S. Moss, and Pvt. William S. Moss. Kenneth L. Stiles, *4th Virginia Cavalry*, (Lynchburg: H. E. Howard, Inc., 1985), 107, 110, 125, 127; Morrissett Diary.
15.	*O.R.*, Series 1, vol. 29, part 2, 209-211.
16.	*Ibid.*, part 1, 140, and part 2, 215-216; Gillespie, *Company A, First Ohio Cavalry*, 177.

	Gregg's troopers remained in their camps and on picket. However, Capt. Joseph J. Gould of the First Rhode Island, McIntosh's brigade, drew a different duty. Along with about 100 men, he was detached and ordered to report to Fifth Corps headquarters for picket and courier duty. On the 12th of October he left to return and was attacked near Warrenton, losing almost 50 of his men as prisoners. He and the remainder managed to escape. Ressler Diary; Denison, *Sabres and Spurs*, 290, and 292-293.
17.	Brooks, ed., *Stories*, 189; Hartley, *Stuart's Tarheels*, 264-265; Edward A. Green Memoir,

Eleanor S. Brockenbrough Library, MOC; Abraham G. Jones to Dear Brother Ellick, September 20, 1863, Abraham G. Jones Papers, Collection No. 135, ECMC/JL/ECU; *Fayetteville Observer*, October 5, 1863; Trout, ed., *Memoirs*, 67; Survey of Culpeper and a part of Madison counties, Virginia, Civil War Maps, Library of Congress, www.loc.gov/index.html.

       Hereafter, for the sake of clarity and brevity, Jones's Brigade will be referred to as Funsten's Brigade, Baker's Brigade will be referred to as Ferebee's Brigade, and Butler's Brigade will be referred to as Gordon's Brigade until the actual commanders assumed their commands.

18.   Trout, ed., *Memoirs*, 67.

19.   Chapman Diary; Cheney Diary; Frank Diary; Inglis Diary; Morey Diary.

       Morey stated that the first battalion of his regiment, the Fifth Michigan, dismounted and cleared the town.

       Buford's and Kilpatrick's divisions were still encamped near Stevensburg on the morning of the 21st. Norton, *Deeds of Daring*, 73-74; Hall, *Sixth New York Cavalry*, 158; Klement, ed., "Edwin B. Bigelow," 227; *New York Times*, October 3, 1863.

       The Eighteenth Pennsylvania, Davies's brigade, and the First Vermont, Custer's brigade, did not take part in the reconnaissance, being assigned to picket duty near Hartwood Church at the far end of the line above the Rappahannock. On the 21st, portions of these regiments conducted a reconnaissance several miles below Falmouth. Rodenbough, *Eighteenth Regiment of Pennsylvania Cavalry*, 44; O.R., Series 1, vol. 29, part 2, 221.

20.   O.R., Series 1, vol. 29, part 1, 140-141.

21.   *Washington Daily Morning Chronicle*, September 28, 1863.

22.   Hard, *Eighth Illinois Cavalry*, 274; *Fayetteville Observer*, October 5, 1863; Colonel W. H. Cheek, "Additional Sketch Ninth Regiment (First Cavalry)," *Histories of the Several Regiments and Battalions from North Carolina in the Civil War 1861-65*, 1, edited by Walter Clark, (Raleigh: E. M. Uzzell, 1901. Reprint, Wendell, North Carolina: Broadfoot's Bookmark, 1982), 452.

       A portion of Funsten's Brigade withdrew before Chapman's advance and supplied Stuart with accurate information on what he faced. *Fayetteville Observer*, October 5, 1863.

23.   Fred C. Foard Reminiscences, Fred C. Foard Papers, Accession No. PC.500, North Carolina State Archives, Raleigh, NC, USA; Cheek, "Additional Sketch Ninth Regiment," 452; Hartley, *Stuart's Tarheels*, 265.

24.   *Fayetteville Observer*, October 5, 1863; *Daily National Intelligencer*, September 26, 1863; Cheek, "Additional Sketch Ninth Regiment," 452-453.

25.   Hard, *Eighth Illinois Cavalry*, 274; *Boston Daily Advertiser*, September 26, 1863.

26.   *Fayetteville Observer*, October 1, 1863; Cheek, "Additional Sketch Ninth Regiment," 453; Paul B. Means, "Additional Sketch Sixty-third Regiment (Fifth Cavalry)," *Histories of the Several Regiments and Battalions from North Carolina in the Civil War 1861-65*, 3, edited by Walter Clark, (Goldsboro: Nash Brothers, 1901), 573.

27.   *Fayetteville Observer*, October 5, 1863; Mays, "Sketches," 103; Cheek, "Additional Sketch Ninth Regiment," 453; Manarin, *North Carolina Troops*, 19.

28.   Mays, "Sketches," 103.

29.   Buford reported that Kilpatrick crossed the Rapidan at Simm's (also spelled Sim's) and White's fords and another ford one and a half miles above Liberty Mills. If Buford was referring to Kilpatrick's crossing of the Rapidan from north to south, he

would appear to be in error. White's Ford is several miles down stream from Simm's Ford and Kilpatrick would have had to ride right past Stuart's flank above Jack's Shop and down the pike to reach the road that led to White's. Another source stated that he crossed at Burton's and Simm's fords. This seems more accurate, as Burton's is the next ford to Simm's and the same road that accesses the Simm's Ford road also accesses Burton's Ford road. *O.R.,* Series 1, vol. 29, part 1, 141; *New York Times,* October 3, 1863; C. S. Dwight, *Survey of Culpeper and a part of Madison counties, Virginia* (Library of Congress, Map collections:1500-2004, *http://memory.loc.gov/cgi bin/query/D?gmd:4:./temp/~ammem_pMTx:* (accessed March 24, 2009).

Concerning the third-named ford, Buford may have been referring to Brooking's or Brookin's Ford (also known as Garnett's Ford) and may have been talking about Kilpatrick's south to north crossing when Kilpatrick attempted to block the road to Liberty Mills in Stuart's rear. Davies stated that he crossed at White's Ford with the Second and Fifth New York and his artillery and sent the First West Virginia across the river at a ford lower downstream, to get in Stuart's rear. The latter regiment clashed with some Confederates and according to Davies, took 17 prisoners. This must have been at Brooking's Ford, which was nearer to Liberty Mills. *O.R.,* Series 1, vol. 29, part 1, 141; Boudrye, *Fifth New York Cavalry,* 77; Klement, ed., "Edwin B. Bigelow," 229; Dwight, *Survey.*

30.   *O.R.,* Series 1, vol. 29, part 1, 141-142.

31.   *Ibid.,* 141-142; Glazier, *Three Years in the Federal Cavalry,* 326.

32.   *Washington Daily Morning Chronicle,* September 28, 1863; *Fayetteville Observer,* October 1, 1863; Mays, "Sketches," 103.

33.   *Fayetteville Observer,* October 5, 1863.

       Seven guns from three batteries were engaged. Capt. James F. Hart's Battery had four guns in the fight; Capt. William M. McGregor's had two; and Capt. Marcellus N. Moorman's had one. Trout, *Galloping Thunder,* 720, n 6.

34.   *Fayetteville Observer,* October 5, 1863; Shreve, "Reminiscences;" *O.R.,* Series 1, vol. 29, part 1, 141-142; Glazier, *Three Years in the Federal Cavalry,* 326.

       Stuart's horse, Highflyer or Highfly, was shot during the engagement. J. E. B. Stuart to My Darling Wife [Flora Stuart], October 25, 1863, Stuart Papers, 1851-1968, Mss1ST923d, Microfilm reel C621, VHS.

35.   Douglas, *A Boot Full of Memories,* 282; Mays, "Sketches," 103-104.

36.   Brooks, ed., *Stories,* 193-194; *New York Times,* October 2, 1863; Glazier, *Three Years in the Federal Cavalry,* 326.

37.   *New York Times,* October 2, 1863; *Richmond Daily Enquirer,* October 1, 1863; *O.R.,* Series 1, vol. 29, part 1, 142.

38.   *Richmond Daily Enquirer,* October 1, 1863; *Western Democrat,* October 6, 1863; McDonald, *History of the Laurel Brigade,* 176; *Manuscript of Edward Allen Hitchcock McDonald, History of the Laurel Brigade,* William Thomas Leavell and Edward Allen Hitchcock McDonald Papers, 1831-1932, Box 14, Rare Book, Manuscript, and Special Collections Library, WRP/DU; *New York Times,* October 2, 1863; *O.R.,* Series 1, vol. 29, part 1, 142; Glazier, *Three Years in the Federal Cavalry,* 327.

       Somewhere in the fighting Lt. Col. William G. Delony of Cobb's Legion, Gordon's Brigade, received a wound in his leg. During Stuart's withdrawal to the river he stopped at a house to rest and receive attention to his wound from Surgeon Henry S. Bradley, the Legion's assistant surgeon. Advancing Federals captured both men. Delony would die in a hospital in Washington City on October 2. *Fayetteville Observer,*

October 5, 1863; *Richmond Daily Enquirer*, September 28, 1863; Robert K. Krick, *Lee's Colonels*, (Dayton: Morningside House, Inc., 1991)117.

39. Cheney, *Ninth Regiment, New York Volunteer Cavalry*, 133; Trout, ed., *Memoirs*, 67; Shoemaker, *Shoemaker's Battery*, 54.

> The historian of the Sixth New York, Devin's brigade, Buford's division, claimed to have fought with the Twelfth Virginia Cavalry, Funsten's Brigade, near Locust Dale. Other sources place the Twelfth with Stuart at Jack's Shop. Writers have claimed that elements of both the Eleventh and Twelfth Virginia were on picket along Robinson River on the 21st and were driven back to Madison Court House by Buford's advance. That a portion of the Eleventh or Twelfth retreated along the road to Locust Dale and opposed the Sixth New York's advance on the 22nd must be considered a possibility. Hall, *Sixth New York Cavalry*, 158; McDonald, *History of the Laurel Brigade*, 176; Armstrong, *11th Virginia Cavalry*, 53; Green Article, *Warren Sentinel*.

40. Cheney, *Ninth Regiment, New York Volunteer Cavalry*, 133; Trout, ed., *Memoirs*, 67; *Richmond Daily Enquirer*, September 24, 1863; Krick, *Lee's Colonels*, 325.

41. Two sources confirmed that the First and Fifth North Carolina, Ferebee's Brigade, participated in the charge. Indeed, Stuart may have launched the entire brigade at the Federals. Thomas B. Person to Dear Mother, September 29, 1863, Southgate-Jones Family Papers, Box 1, Folder 1862-1963, WRP/DU; Abraham G. Jones to Dear Parents, September 24, 1863, Abraham G. Jones Papers, Collection No. 135, ECMC/JL/ECU.

42. *O.R.*, Series 1, vol. 29, part 1, 141-142; J. E. B. Stuart to Mrs. J. E. B. Stuart, September 26, 1863, Stuart Papers, 1851-1968, Mss1ST923d, Microfilm reel C621, VHS; Allyne C. Litchfield to My Dear Wife, September 24, 1863, Allyne Cushing Litchfield Papers, James S. Schoff Civil War Collection, Manuscripts Division, WLC/UM; *Fayetteville Observer*, October 5, 1863; Klement, ed., "Edwin B. Bigelow," 229.

> Apparently a controversy arose between Stuart and Maj. Gen. Cadmus M. Wilcox over what Stuart felt was Wilcox's failure to aid him in opposing Sawyer, leaving all the fighting to Stuart's weary troopers. Wilcox believed that Stuart had given R. E. Lee the idea that Wilcox had not cooperated with Stuart, telling Lee that Wilcox would not interrupt his men cooking their rations to send them forward. On the 26th, Wilcox wrote Stuart claiming that he had not sent his two small infantry regiments into the fight not because they were cooking but rather that, being on foot, they could not hope to catch Sawyer's mounted men. Wilcox went further, claiming to have examined the ground over which the Tarheels charged and finding a fence that the North Carolinians could not have crossed. What all this amounted to was Wilcox wanting to make sure his command was not maligned and that Lee understood what happened from his perspective. In writing Stuart, Wilcox showed his respect for the cavalry chief and his desire to straighten out the "misunderstanding" between them. Unfortunately, the eventual outcome of the situation is unknown. Maj. Gen. Cadmus M. Wilcox to Maj. Gen. J. E. B. Stuart, September 26, 1863, Henry Brainerd McClellan Papers, Mss2M1324b, VHS.

43. Milton B. Steele Diary, Eleanor S. Brockenbrough Library, MOC; Trussell Diary; Carter Diary; Morrissett Diary; Donahue Diary; Richard Henry Watkins to Mary Watkins, September 24, 1863, Watkins Papers, 1861-1865, Mss1W3272a1-355, VHS.

44. *Richmond Daily Enquirer*, September 28, 1863; Cheney, *Ninth Regiment, New York Volunteer Cavalry*, 134; *O.R.*, Series 1, vol. 29, part 2, 224.

45. *Richmond Daily Enquirer*, September 28, 1863.

> Smoot's Ford was also known as Hume's Ford.

O.R., Series 1, vol. 29, part 1, 142-143; Morey Diary.

      Several sources stated that Buford's brigades marched all the way back to their camps at Stevensburg. Cheney Diary; Frank Diary; Inglis Diary

47.   According to a member of his staff who wrote a letter home, Buford reestablished his headquarters at Stevensburg by the 24th. A trooper of the Fifth Michigan, Custer's brigade, wrote home from James City on the 30th and Kilpatrick in a *Philadelphia Weekly Times* article stated that he was on the army's right front at James City. George Montfort Gilchrist to My Dear Mollie, September 24, 1863, George Montfort Gilchrist Family Papers, 1854-1921, MMC-3626, Archival Manuscript Material (Collection), LC; Frank M. Brown to Dear Father, September 30, 1863, Brown Family Papers, Box No. 85859 Aa2, BHL/UM; *Philadelphia Weekly Times*, August 23, 1879.

48.   As of the 29th, the First North Carolina, Ferebee's Brigade, was still encamped on the Madison County side of the Rapidan at Barnett's Ford, indicating that Stuart maintained a presence between the two rivers for at least a week after the fight at Jack's Shop. Cadwallader Jones Iredell to unknown addressee, September 15, 1863, Cadwallader Jones Iredell Papers, 363-Z, Folder 1, Correspondence 1862-1863, SHC/UNC.

49.   *O.R.*, Series 1, vol. 29, part 2, 225; Carter Diary; Morrissett Diary; Donahue Diary.

50.   Casualties vary according to the source. Southern newspapers claimed a loss of 125 to 400, according to one newspaper, with at least 100 killed or wounded, according to another. A third put the loss at 10 killed and 40 wounded, and 30 captured and a fourth at less than 70. A North Carolinian's assessment may have been closer to the truth, estimating the loss for those troopers who confronted Chapman as 92 out of 500 engaged. Enemy losses were 115 captured and 100 killed and wounded. *Richmond Daily Dispatch*, September 24, 1863 and September 25, 1863; *Richmond Daily Enquirer*, September 26, 1863 and September 28, 1863; *Fayetteville Observer*, October 5, 1863.

      Northern newspapers claimed that Buford's total lost was 1 killed and 25 wounded. Estimates of enemy casualties ranged from 40 to 50 killed and 75 captured by Chapman, 50 captured by Kilpatrick, and 30 to 40 killed and wounded and another 60 captured by Devin. *New York Herald*, September 25, 1863; *New York World*, September 25, 1863; *New York Tribune*, September 25, 1863.

      In actuality, Stuart filed no report, making it difficult to estimate his losses, although the intensity of the fighting would seem to place them between 100 and 150 men. Davies placed his loss at 1 killed, 10 wounded, and 73 missing. Stagg gave his as 3 wounded and 14 missing. Chapman failed to file a report but the Eighth Illinois's regimental historian stated that the regiment suffered 11 wounded, 1 mortally, and the chronicler for the Third Indiana listed 1 killed and 6 wounded. *O.R.*, Series 1, vol. 29, part 1, 142-143; Hard, *Eighth Illinois Cavalry*, 274; Pickerill, *Third Indiana Cavalry*, 96.

51.   *Richmond Daily Enquirer*, October 1, 1863.

      That the Federals significantly outnumbered Stuart's cavalry is debatable. Considering what portions of Buford's and Kilpatrick's forces were engaged at any given time, it would seem that the two sides were fairly equal.

      Not everyone was willing to applaud Stuart's performance. Capt. Walter G. MacRae of the Seventh North Carolina Infantry wrote home that Stuart had received a severe drubbing, scrambling across the Robinson River in disarray, and that the Federal cavalry frequently came out on top in fights with Stuart. MacRae's view was undoubtedly shared by others, but how wide spread such feelings were throughout the army cannot be known. Walter G. MacRae to Dear Brother, September 26, 1863, Hugh MacRae Papers, 1817-1943, Box 3 - Letters 1862-1878, Folder - Letters 1862-1863, WRP/DU.

52. *O.R.*, Series 1, vol. 29, part 2, 742-743.
53. *Ibid.*, part 1, 141.
54. *Ibid.*, 147.
55. *Ibid.*, part 2, 743.
56. R. H. Woodward to William Taylor, September 24, 1863, Taylor Family Papers, 1751-1902, Mss1T2197a, VHS.

    This order was probably implemented throughout the cavalry.
57. *O.R.*, Series 1, vol. 29, part 2, 227, 753-754.
58. Trussell Diary; Steele Diary; Carter Diary; Morrissett Diary; Donahue Diary; Klement, ed., "Edwin B. Bigelow," 229; Norton, *Deeds of Daring*, 74; Hall, *Sixth New York Cavalry*, 158; Glazier, *Three Years in the Federal Cavalry*, 328; Boudrye, *Fifth New York Cavalry*, 77-78.

    Lomax's Brigade encamped near Orange Court House until the 26th when it returned to its old camp near Raccoon Ford. Elijah S. Johnson Diary, Elijah S. Johnson Papers, 1862-1907, Mss2J6314B-MFC 598, VHS.
59. *O.R.*, Series 1, vol. 29, part 2, 268; Ebenezer S. Johnson to Dear Brother, September 24, 1863, Ebenezer S. Johnson Letters, Earl Hess Collection and CWMC, USAMHI; Allen L. Bevan to Dear Sister, September 29, 1863, Allen L. Bevan Letters, CWMC, US-AMHI; Albinus R. Fell to Diana, October 10, 1863, CWMC, USAMHI; Ressler Diary; Sauerburger, ed., *I Seat Myself to Write You*, 179; Pyne, *First New Jersey Cavalry*, 172; Lloyd, *History of the First Regiment Pennsylvania Reserve Cavalry*, 74; Rawle, *Third Pennsylvania Cavalry*, 335; Tobie, *First Maine Cavalry*, 192; Miller, *Sixteenth Pennsylvania Cavalry*, 40; Hand, Jr., *One Good Regiment*, 79.

    This movement of an entire division of cavalry for the purpose of securing a rear area from the threat of guerillas demonstrates once again the impact of Mosby's and the other partisans' operations on Meade's forces.

    The various sources given above show that the regiments of the division seemed to be scattered in all directions. From McIntosh's brigade the First Rhode Island started off at Catlett's Station and by October 9 was near Falmouth. The First New Jersey encamped at Bristoe Station. The First Pennsylvania remained near Catlett's and the Third Pennsylvania encamped on Kettle Run. The Sixth Ohio was stationed at Warrenton Junction. In Col. Gregg's brigade the First Maine stayed close to Bealton Station while the Sixteenth Pennsylvania watched Deep Run near Morrisville.
60. Carter Diary; Musick, *6th Virginia Cavalry*, 50; Robert J. Driver, Jr., *First and Second Maryland Cavalry, C.S.A.* (Charlottesville: Howell Press, Inc., 1999), 63.
61. *Richmond Whig and Public Advertiser*, September 29, 1863.
62. *Richmond Whig*, October 1, 1863.

    Not to be outdone, a private from Company B of the Ninth Virginia, Chambliss's Brigade, had enough time on his hands to pen an extensive article railing against the editors' use of the phrase "our cavalry fell back" and its application to Virginians especially. In conclusion, the trooper stated, "that Gen. Stuart has the entire confidence of his command." *Richmond Enquirer*, October 2, 1863.
63. *Richmond Enquirer*, October 1, 1863.
64. J. E. B. Stuart to Mrs. J. E. B. Stuart, October 3, 1863, Stuart Papers, 1851-1968, Mss1ST923d, Microfilm reel C621, VHS.
65. *Richmond Whig*, October 2, 1863.
66. The rest of Custer's brigade continued to do picket duty about James City and along the Robinson. *Allegan Journal*, October 12, 1863.

67.   *O.R.*, Series 1, vol. 29, part 1, 198.

68   *Ibid.*, part 2, 234; Cheney, *Ninth Regiment, New York Volunteer Cavalry*, 135; Hall, *Sixth New York Cavalry*, 158; Norton, *Deeds of Daring*, 74; Inglis Diary.
      Chapman's Brigade also picketed this section of the river along with Devin's regiments. In addition to doing picket duty at Richard's Ford on the Rappahannock, a part of the Eighth New York also was stationed at Germanna Ford. Cheney Diary.

69.   Cheney, *Ninth Regiment, New York Volunteer Cavalry*, 135; *Philadelphia Press*, October 3, 1863.
      Cheney especially cited a portion of the Fourth Virginia, Wickham's Brigade, Fitz Lee's Division, that had been acting as a partisan band north of the Rappahannock. A report filed by Buford mentioned that the Prince William Company of cavalry was fully mounted and stationed at Stafford Court House. This company was indeed part of the Fourth Virginia and originated in Prince William County that bordered Stafford County on the north. Its men would have had some familiarity with the area, allowing them to operate behind enemy lines with some impunity. *O.R.*, Series 1, vol. 29, part 2, 235.

70.   *O.R.*, Series 1, vol. 29, part 1, 198-199; Glazier, *Three Years in the Federal Cavalry*, 328; Manarin, *North Carolina Troops*, 107.
      Gen. French gave the name of the commander of the enemy's force as Lt. Tidball and that of his command as the Independent North Carolina Cavalry. The only officer whose name is reasonably close was Tidwell who was in the Second North Carolina.
      Browning's Ford was also known as Starke's Ford.

71.   *Washington Evening Star*, October 1, 1863; Williamson, *Mosby's Rangers*, 93-94; Wert, *Mosby's Rangers*, 98.
      French was apparently a nickname. The son's real name was Daniel F. Dulany.

72.   Trout, *Plume*, 157-162; Stephen Z. Starr, *The Life of a Soldier of Fortune: Colonel Grenfell's Wars* (Baton Rouge: Louisiana State University Press, 1971), 99, 107-112; Walter Lord, ed., *The Fremantle Diary* (Boston: Little, Brown and Company, 1954), 119-120; Carter Diary; Morrissett Diary; Richard Henry Watkins to Mary Watkins, September 28, 1863, Watkins Papers, 1861-1865, Mss1W3272a1-355, VHS.
      Chambliss's Brigade was inspected on October 1. Edwards Diary.

73.   Carter Diary; Richard Henry Watkins to Mary Watkins, September 28, 1863, Watkins Papers, 1861-1865, Mss1W3272a1-355, VHS.

74.   Klement, ed., "Edwin B. Bigelow," 229.

75.   *O.R.*, Series 1, vol. 29, part 2, 236-237; Brig. Gen. David McM. Gregg to Col. Alfred Gibbs, October 1, 1863, Telegrams Collected by the Secretary of War, Unbound, RG 107, M504, NARA.

76.   Arehart, "Diary of W. H. Arehart," 278; J. E. B. Stuart to Gen. Samuel Cooper, September 30, 1863, Stuart Papers, 1851-1968, Mss1ST923d, Microfilm reel C621, VHS; Trout, *Plume*, 92.

77.   *O.R.*, Series 1, vol. 29, part 1, 200-204; *Washington Evening Star*, October 5, 1863; John E. Divine, *35ᵗʰ Battalion Virginia Cavalry* (Lynchburg: H. E. Howard, Inc., 1985), 39-40.
      The Sixteenth New York was attached to the Department of Washington under the command of Maj. Gen. Samuel P. Heintzelman. *O.R.*, Series 1, vol. 29, part 2, 134.
      The Independent Virginia (Union) Rangers, also known as the Loudoun Rangers, was attached to the department of West Virginia under the command of Brig. Gen. Benjamin F. Kelly. *O.R.*, Series 1, vol. 29, part 2, 139.

78.   *O.R.*, Series 1, vol. 29, part 1, 204; Brig. Gen. David McM. Gregg to Col. J. Irvin Gregg, September 29, 1863, Telegrams Collected by the Secretary of War, Unbound, RG 107,

M504, NARA; Sauerburger, ed., *I Seat Myself to Write You*, 181.

The identity of the Confederate forces engaged is unknown. Col. Horace B. Sargent, commanding Gen. Gregg's First Brigade, who filed the report, stated that the Confederates had 100 to 150 men. Neither Mosby nor White had such a force in the area and there are no records to indicate that any portion of Stuart's cavalry was stationed in the vicinity. McNitt probably faced a small band of local guerillas that attacked from ambush, hiding their actual strength by using various cover. Certainly the source of the enemy's numbers came from McNitt who undoubtedly greatly overestimated what he faced. In such exaggerations lay the root cause of the detachment of significant portions of Pleasonton's cavalry to patrol rear areas of the army. Gregg's entire division was engaged in guarding the railroad and surrounding areas, a task better suited for Meade's infantry, for almost three weeks in response to guerilla activities that were often overblown.

79. Trussell Diary; Steele Diary; Carter Diary; Morrissett Diary.

80. *O.R.*, Series 1, vol. 29, part 1, 204-205.

Col. Thomas M. Garrett, commanding Brig. Gen. Robert D. Johnston's Brigade, reported that on the night of October 1, Lt. Plato Durham of the Twelfth North Carolina Infantry also crossed the Rapidan and struck Federal cavalry pickets, killing one, wounding one, and capturing one man, eight horses, and nine saddles and bridles. This attack was separate from that of the Seventh Virginia.

81. *Ibid.*, part 2, 242-243; Brig. Gen. David McM. Gregg to Col. J. Irvin Gregg, October 1, 1863, Telegrams Collected by the Secretary of War, Unbound, RG 107, M504, NARA; Cheney Diary; Rawle, *Third Pennsylvania Cavalry*, 336; Hall, *Sixth New York Cavalry*, 159.

One trooper from the Sixth New York, Devin's brigade, Buford's division, had a close call on the 2nd when captured by four of the enemy reputedly from the Fourth Virginia, Wickham's Brigade, and the Ninth Virginia, Chambliss's Brigade. The graybacks took his horse and equipment, along with some personal effects, then marched him for several miles before releasing him, much to his relief. Hall, *Sixth New York Cavalry*, 159.

82. John R. Morey Diary, John R. Morey Papers, Microfilm mf363 c, BHL/UM.

One source claimed that Kilpatrick was a very active participant in such contests, racing as many as ten times a day. William Rockwell to My Dear Wife, October 10, 1863, Donald C. Rockwell Collection, 1862-1936, Call No. A-328, WMUARHC/WMU.

John Esten Cooke claimed that Kilpatrick was racing his favorite mare, Lively, on a race course at James City in the days before Stuart's advance on October 9. *Philadelphia Weekly Times*, October 10, 1885.

83. Steele Diary; Carter Diary; Morrissett Diary' Arehart, "Diary of W. H. Arehart," 279.

84. John O. Collins to My dear Wife, October 2, 1863, John Overton Collins Papers (Mss1C6944a), VHS.

85. The *New York Times* reported that 600 Confederate infantry attempted to storm across Germanna Ford only to be repulsed with severe loss by 100 of Buford's men on picket there. Other than this reference, no record of this action can be found. With such a large number of men engaged, the fight should have been recorded in various regimental histories or other newspapers. That it was not would appear to indicate that the reporter received false information. *New York Times*, October 6, 1863.

86. *O.R.*, Series 1, vol. 29, part 2, 259-260; William Wilkin Diary, CWMC, USAMHI; David R. Trego to Dear Brother, October 3, 1863, David R. Trego Papers, Box No. 86662 Aa1,

BHL/UM; *New York Herald*, October 7, 1863; Andrew N. Buck to Intimate Brother and Sister, October 6, 1863, Buck Family Papers, Microfilm mf 309-311 c, BHL/UM. Gilbert Chapman to Janie, October 4, 1863, Gilbert W. Chapman Letters, MS/Chamberlain Family Collection, Burton Historical Collection, Detroit Public Library (hereafter cited as BHC/DPL).

88.   *O.R.*, Series 1, vol. 29, part 2, 257-259.

89.   *New York Tribune*, October 9, 1863; *New York Times*, October 25, 1863; Andrew N. Buck to Intimate Brother and Sister, October 6, 1863, Buck Family Papers, Microfilm mf 309-311 c, BHL/UM; Klement, ed., "Edwin B. Bigelow," 230.

One reporter commented on the condition of the horses, stating that if "any want of freshness or spirit were discernible" it should be attributed "to the immense amount of picket duty" performed by the cavalry, causing it to "never have time to recruit condition for an onset against the enemy with the greatest efficiency." The astute observation held true for the mounted service of both armies. *New York Tribune*, October 9, 1863.

90.   Carter Diary; Johnson Diary.

In a letter he wrote on the 7th from his camp near Rapidan Station, Sgt. Abraham G. Jones of the Fifth North Carolina, Ferebee's Brigade, stated that Brig. Gen. James B. Gordon had assumed command of his brigade which consisted of the First, Second, Fourth, and Fifth North Carolina. Jones mentioned that he had heard that Gordon was a good man and a brave officer. Abraham G. Jones to Dear Parents, October 7, 1863, Abraham G. Jones Papers, Collection No. 135, ECMC/JL/ECU.

91.   Cheney Diary; Cheney, *Ninth Regiment, New York Volunteer Cavalry*, 136; Gillespie, *Company A, First Ohio Cavalry*, 180.

One source gives the date of Buford's review as the 7th and that of Pleasonton as the 8th. Inglis Diary.

92.   *O.R.*, Series 1, vol. 29, part 1, 209; Rawle, *Third Pennsylvania Cavalry*, 336.

93.   Andrew N. Buck to Intimate Brother and Sister, October 8, 1863, Buck Family Papers, Microfilm mf 309-311 c, BHL/UM.

94.   *O.R.*, Series 1, vol. 29, part 1, 211 and part 2, 265; Christian or Frederick Bush to Dear Brother, October 9, 1863, Christian and Frederick Bush Collection, MS 2004-22, Box 1, Folder 1, AM; Rawle, *Third Pennsylvania Cavalry*, 211; William O. Lee, comp., *Personal and Historical Sketches and Facial History of and by Members of the Seventh Regiment Michigan Volunteer Cavalry 1862-1865* (Detroit: 7th Michigan Cavalry Association, 1902), 134; Allyne C. Litchfield to My Dear Wife, October 8, 1863, Allyne Cushing Litchfield Papers, James S. Schoff Civil War Collection, Manuscripts Division, WLC/UM; *Washington Daily Morning Chronicle*, October 17, 1863.

95.   *O.R.*, Series 1, vol. 29, part 2, 780 and part 1, 439.

Maps

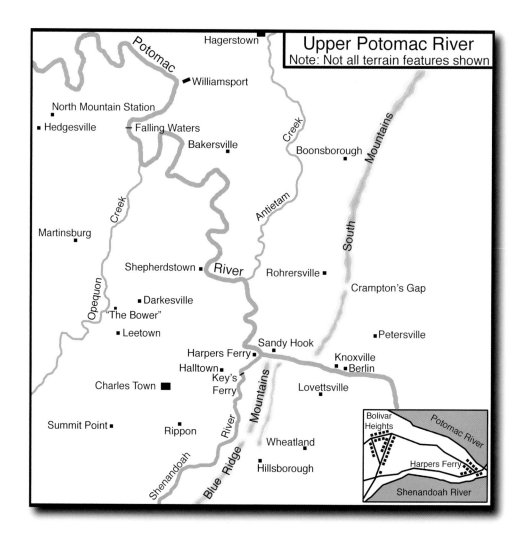

Upper Potomac River
Note: Not all terrain features shown

Potomac

Hagerstown

Williamsport

North Mountain Station

Hedgesville

Falling Waters

Bakersville

Creek

Boonsborough

Mountains

South

Antietam

Martinsburg

Creek

Shepherdstown

River

Rohrersville

Crampton's Gap

Opequon

Darkesville

"The Bower"

Leetown

Sandy Hook

Petersville

Harpers Ferry

Knoxville

Halltown

Berlin

Key's
Ferry

Charles Town

Lovettsville

Summit Point

Rippon

Mountains

Wheatland

Shenandoah

Blue Ridge

River

Hillsborough

Bolivar
Heights

Potomac River

Harpers Ferry

Shenandoah River

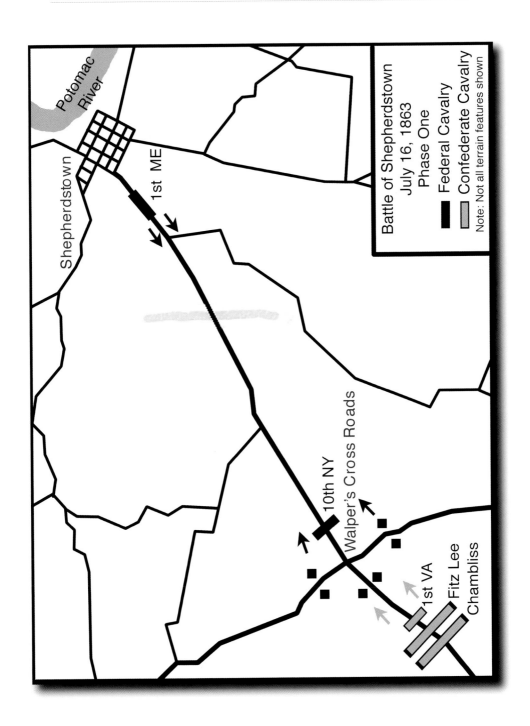

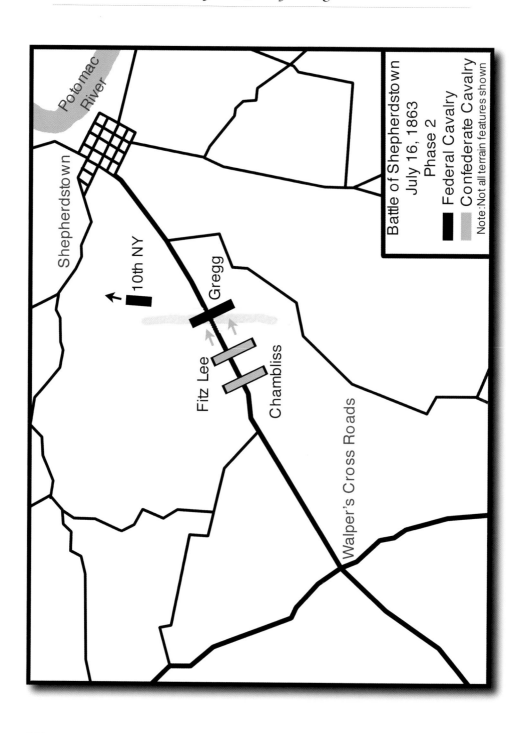

Battle of Shepherdstown
July 16, 1863
Phase 2

Federal Cavalry
Confederate Cavalry
Note:Not all terrain features shown

Potomac River

Shepherdstown

10th NY

Gregg

Fitz Lee

Chambliss

Walper's Cross Roads

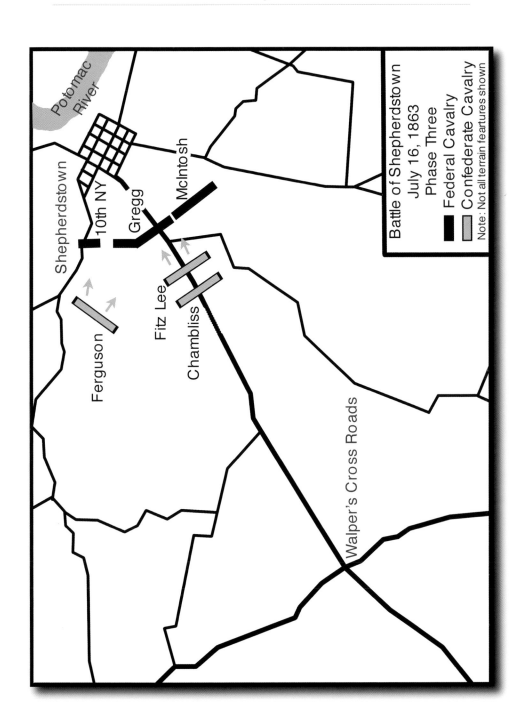

Battle of Shepherdstown
July 16, 1863
Phase Three

Federal Cavalry
Confederate Cavalry
Note: Not all terrain features shown

Potomac River

Shepherdstown

10th NY

Gregg

McIntosh

Ferguson

Fitz Lee

Chambliss

Walper's Cross Roads

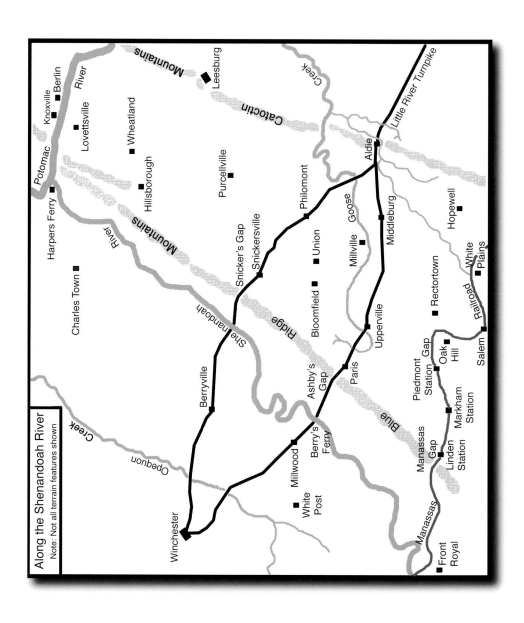

Along the Shenandoah River
Note: Not all terrain features shown

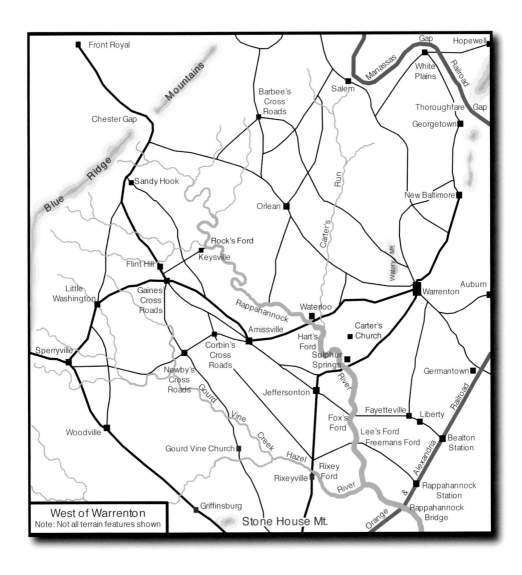

Front Royal

Mountains

Chester Gap

Blue Ridge

Sandy Hook

Barbee's Cross Roads

Salem

Manassas

Gap

Hopewell

White Plains

Railroad

Thoroughfare Gap

Georgetown

New Baltimore

Orlean

Carter's Run

Rock's Ford

Keysville

Flint Hill

Watery Mt.

Little Washington

Gaines Cross Roads

Rappahannock

Waterloo

Warrenton

Auburn

Amissville

Carter's Church

Sperryville

Corbin's Cross Roads

Hart's Ford

Sulphur Springs

Germantown

Newby's Cross Roads

Jeffersonton

River

Gourd

Vine

Creek

Fox's Ford

Fayetteville

Liberty

Railroad

Woodville

Gourd Vine Church

Hazel

Lee's Ford

Freemans Ford

Alexandria

Bealton Station

Rixey Ford

Rixeyville

River

Rappahannock Station

&

Rappahannock Bridge

Griffinsburg

Stone House Mt.

Orange

West of Warrenton
Note: Not all terrain features shown

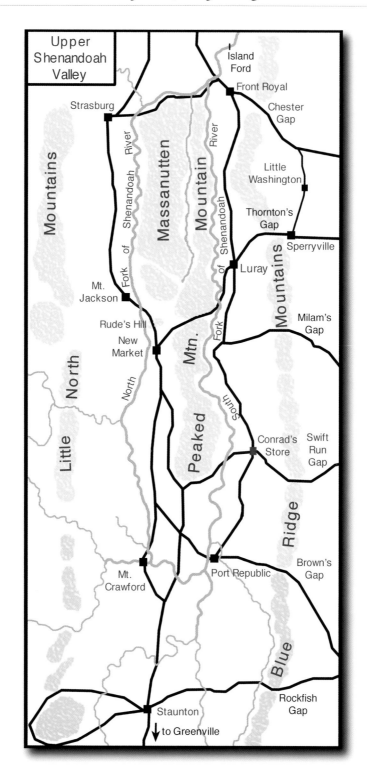

Upper
Shenandoah
Valley

Island
Ford

Front Royal

Strasburg

Chester
Gap

Mountains

River

Shenandoah

of

Fork

Massanutten

River

Mountain

Shenandoah

of

Fork

Little
Washington

Thornton's
Gap

Sperryville

Luray

Mountains

Mt.
Jackson

Milam's
Gap

Rude's Hill

New
Market

North

Mtn.

Fork

South

Little North

Peaked

Conrad's
Store

Swift
Run
Gap

Ridge

Mt.
Crawford

Port Republic

Brown's
Gap

Blue

Rockfish
Gap

Staunton

to Greenville

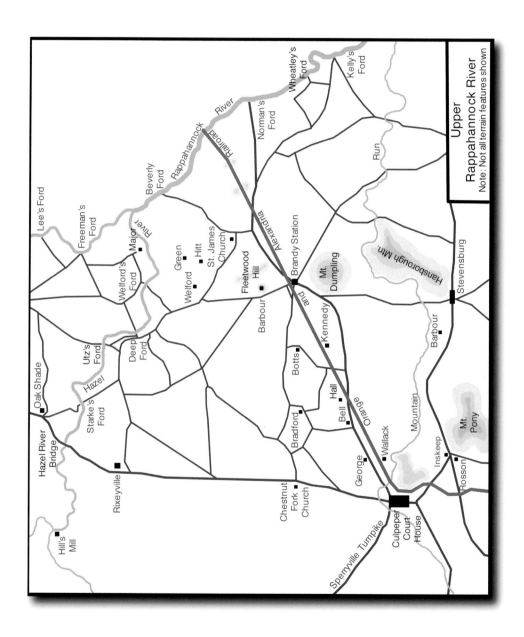

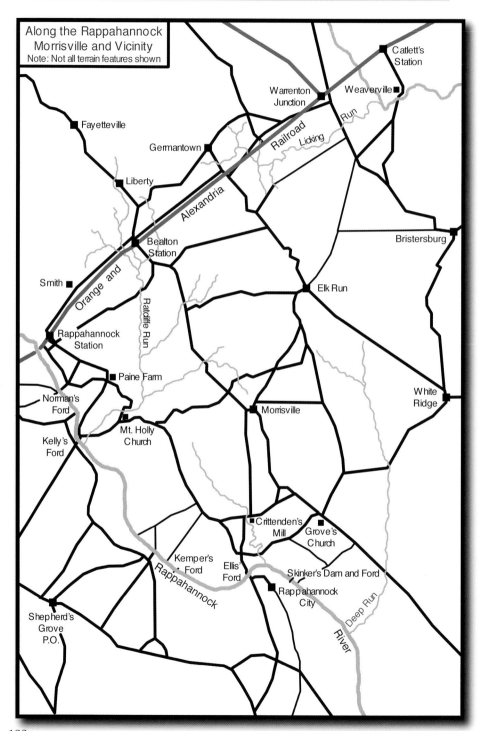

Along the Rappahannock
Morrisville and Vicinity
Note: Not all terrain features shown

Catlett's Station

Weaverville

Warrenton Junction

Licking Run

Fayetteville

Germantown

Railroad

Liberty

Bristersburg

Alexandria

Bealton Station

Elk Run

Smith

Orange and

Ratcliffe Run

Rappahannock Station

Paine Farm

White Ridge

Norman's Ford

Morrisville

Kelly's Ford

Mt. Holly Church

Crittenden's Mill

Grove's Church

Kemper's Ford

Ellis' Ford

Skinker's Dam and Ford

Rappahannock

Rappahannock City

Deep Run

Shepherd's Grove P.O.

River

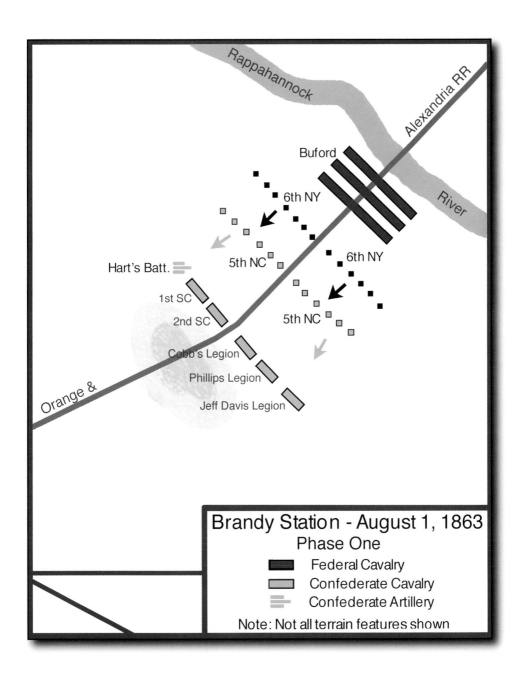

Rappahannock

Alexandria RR

River

Buford

6th NY

5th NC

Hart's Batt.

1st SC

2nd SC

6th NY

5th NC

Cobb's Legion

Phillips Legion

Jeff Davis Legion

Orange &

Brandy Station - August 1, 1863
Phase One

■ Federal Cavalry
□ Confederate Cavalry
≡ Confederate Artillery

Note: Not all terrain features shown

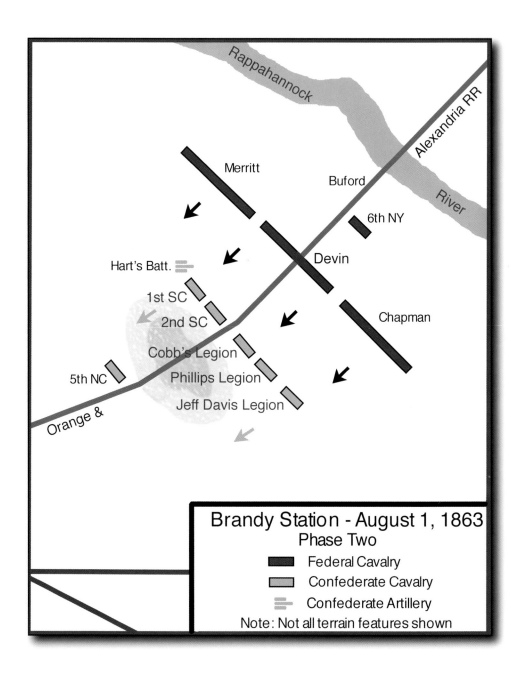

Brandy Station - August 1, 1863
Phase Two

- Federal Cavalry
- Confederate Cavalry
- Confederate Artillery

Note: Not all terrain features shown

Maps

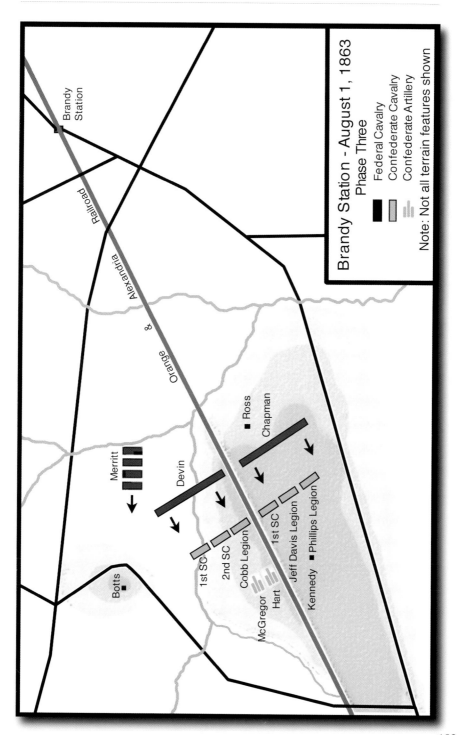

Brandy Station - August 1, 1863
Phase Three

Federal Cavalry
Confederate Cavalry
Confederate Artillery

Note: Not all terrain features shown

Brandy Station

Railroad

Alexandria

& Orange

Ross

Chapman

Merritt

Devin

Botts

1st SC

2nd SC

Cobb Legion

McGregor

Hart

1st SC

Jeff Davis Legion

Kennedy

Phillips Legion

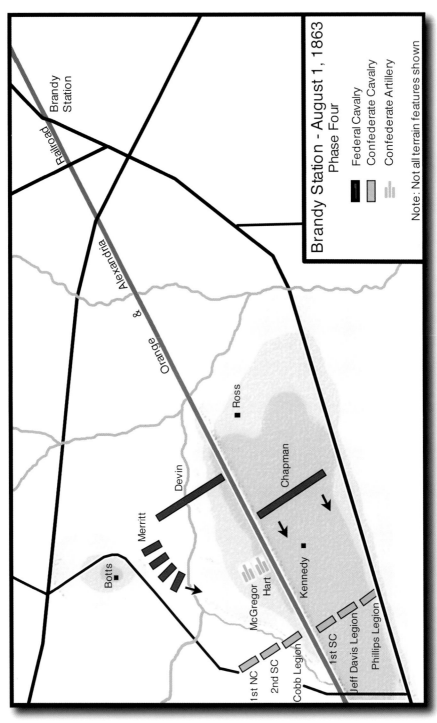

Brandy Station - August 1, 1863
Phase Four

Federal Cavalry
Confederate Cavalry
Confederate Artillery

Note: Not all terrain features shown

Brandy Station

Railroad

Alexandria & Orange

Ross

Devin

Chapman

Merritt

Botts

McGregor

Hart

Kennedy

1st NC

2nd SC

Cobb Legion

1st SC

Jeff Davis Legion

Phillips Legion

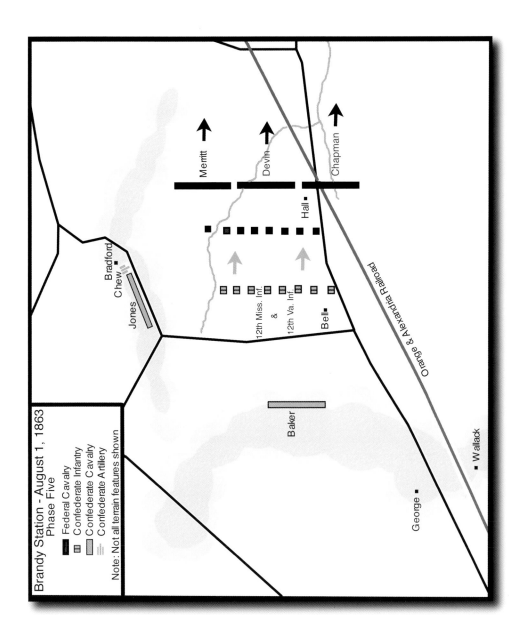

Brandy Station - August 1, 1863
Phase Five

- ■ Federal Cavalry
- ▥ Confederate Infantry
- ▬ Confederate Cavalry
- ▦ Confederate Artillery

Note: Not all terrain features shown

Bradford
Chew
Jones
Merritt
Devin
Chapman
Hall
12th Miss. Inf.
&
12th Va. Inf.
Bell
Baker
Orange & Alexandria Railroad
George
Wallack

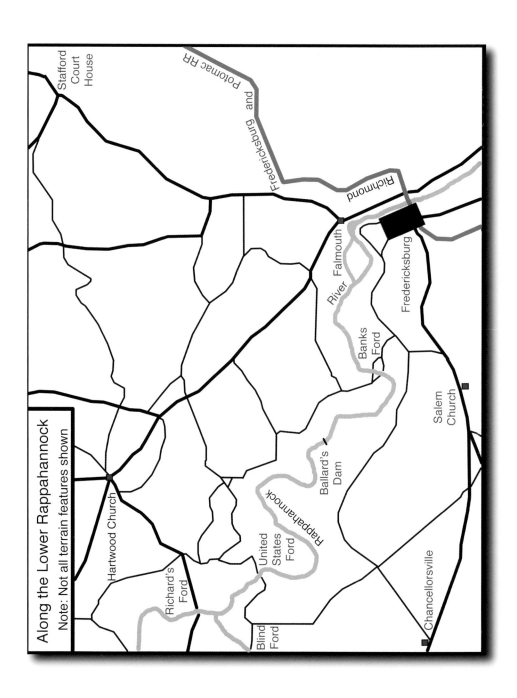

Along the Lower Rappahannock
Note: Not all terrain features shown

Stafford Court House

Fredericksburg and Potomac RR

Richmond

Falmouth

River

Banks Ford

Fredericksburg

Salem Church

Ballard's Dam

Rappahannock

Hartwood Church

United States Ford

Richard's Ford

Chancellorsville

Blind Ford

Maps

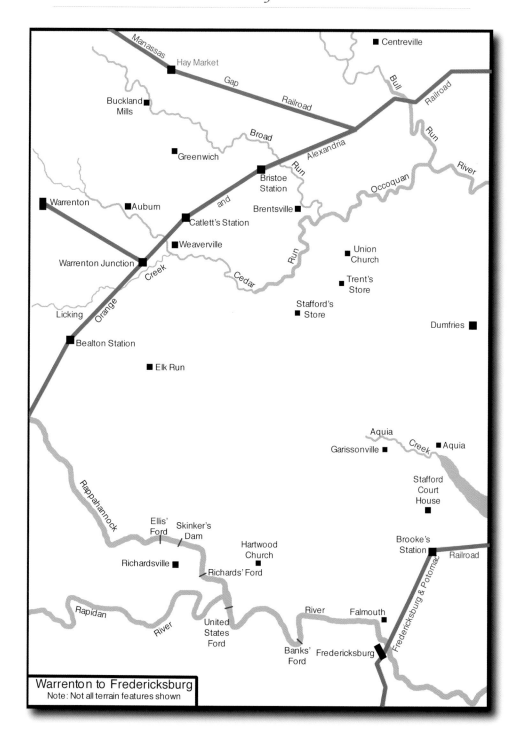

Centreville

Manassas

Hay Market

Gap

Railroad

Buckland Mills

Broad

Bull

Railroad

Alexandria

Run

Greenwich

Run

River

Bristoe Station

Occoquan

Warrenton

Auburn

and

Brentsville

Catlett's Station

Weaverville

Union Church

Run

Warrenton Junction

Creek

Cedar

Trent's Store

Stafford's Store

Dumfries

Licking

Orange

Bealton Station

Elk Run

Aquia

Aquia

Garissonville

Creek

Stafford Court House

Rappahannock

Ellis' Ford

Skinker's Dam

Hartwood Church

Brooke's Station

Railroad

Richardsville

Richards' Ford

Fredericksburg & Potomac

Rapidan

River

River

Falmouth

United States Ford

Banks' Ford

Fredericksburg

Warrenton to Fredericksburg
Note: Not all terrain features shown

197

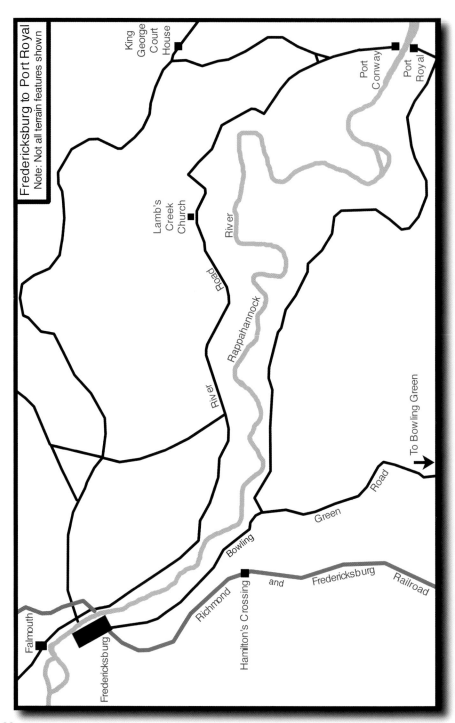

Fredericksburg to Port Royal
Note: Not all terrain features shown

King George Court House

Port Conway

Port Royal

Lamb's Creek Church

River

Road

River

Rappahannock

To Bowling Green

Green Road

Bowling

Falmouth

Fredericksburg

Richmond

Hamilton's Crossing

and

Fredericksburg

Railroad

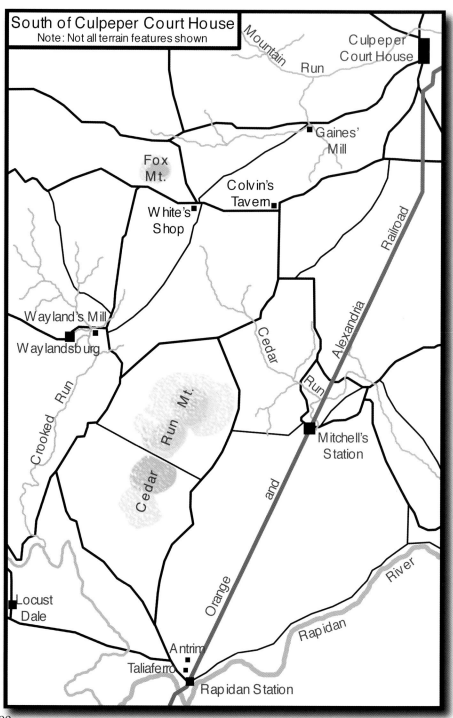

South of Culpeper Court House
Note: Not all terrain features shown

Mountain Run

Culpeper Court House

Gaines' Mill

Fox Mt.

Colvin's Tavern

White's Shop

Railroad

Wayland's Mill

Waylandsburg

Cedar

Run

Alexandria

Crooked Run

Cedar Run Mt.

Mitchell's Station

and

Orange

River

Locust Dale

Rapidan

Antrim

Taliaferro

Rapidan Station

Maps

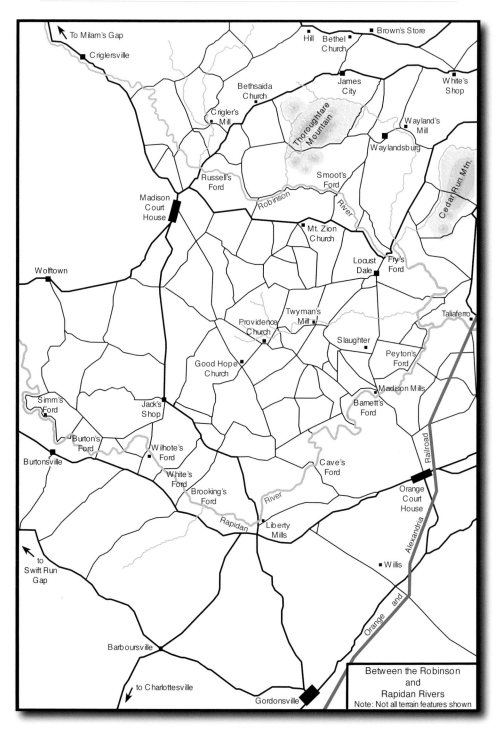

To Milam's Gap

Criglersville

Hill   Bethel
Church

Brown's Store

Bethsaida
Church

James
City

White's
Shop

Crigler's
Mill

Thoroughfare
Mountain

Wayland's
Mill

Waylandsburg

Cedar Run Mtn.

Russell's
Ford

Smoot's
Ford

Robinson   River

Madison
Court
House

Mt. Zion
Church

Wolftown

Locust
Dale

Fry's
Ford

Twyman's
Mill

Taliaferro

Providence
Church

Slaughter

Peyton's
Ford

Good Hope
Church

Madison Mills

Simm's
Ford

Jack's
Shop

Barnett's
Ford

Burton's
Ford

Wilhote's
Ford

Cave's
Ford

Railroad

Burtonsville

White's
Ford

Orange
Court
House

Brooking's
Ford

River

Rapidan

Liberty
Mills

to
Swift Run
Gap

Willis

Orange   and   Alexandria

Barboursville

Between the Robinson
and
Rapidan Rivers

Note: Not all terrain features shown

to Charlottesville

Gordonsville

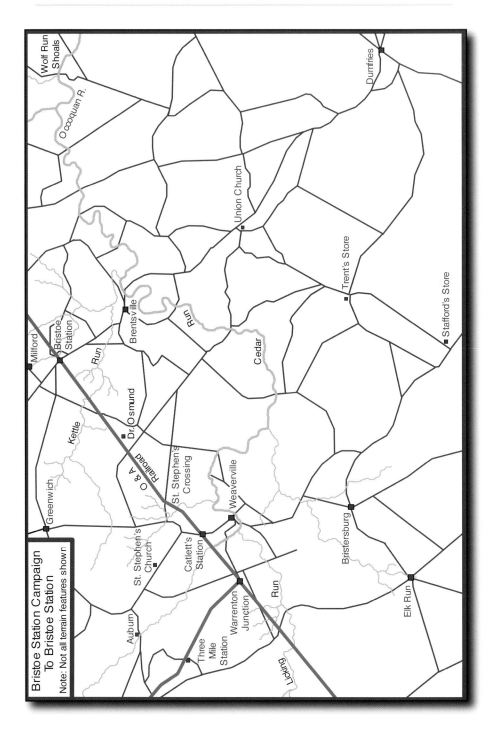

Bristoe Station Campaign
To Bristoe Station
Note: Not all terrain features shown

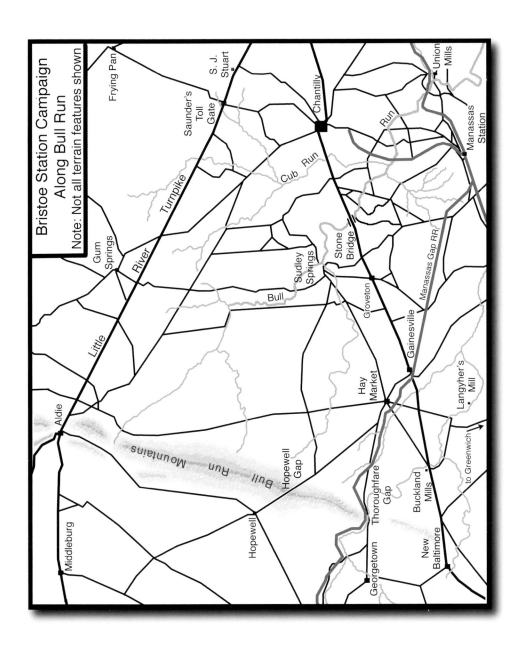

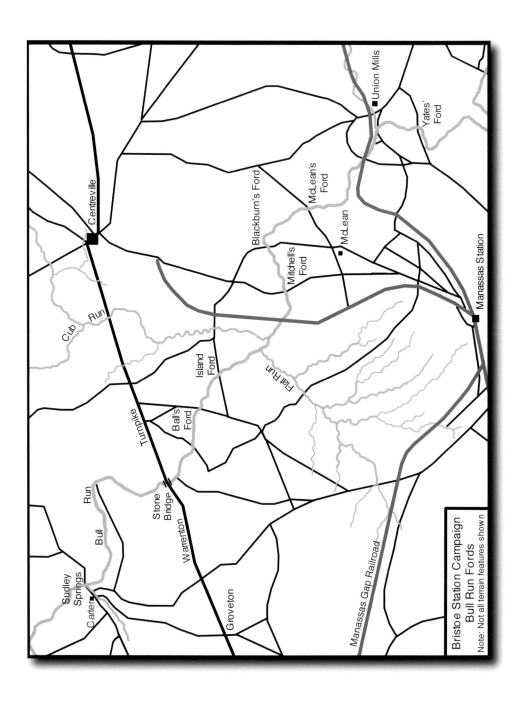

Bristoe Station Campaign
Bull Run Fords
Note: Not all terrain features shown

Maps

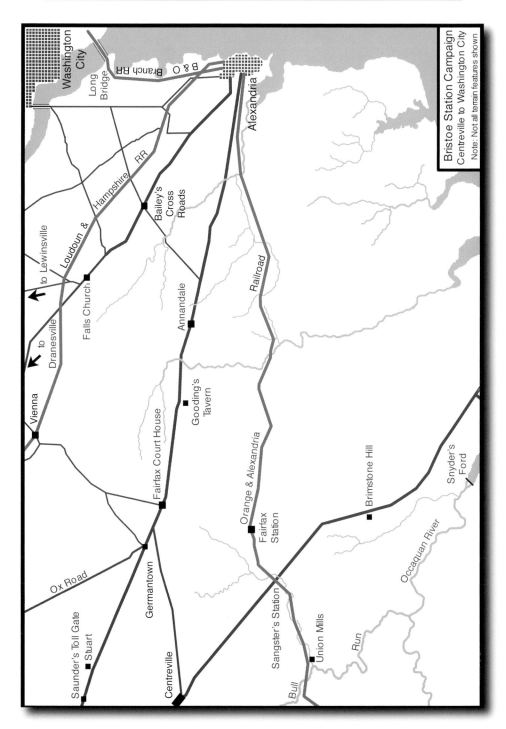

Bristoe Station Campaign
Centreville to Washington City
Note: Not all terrain features shown

Washington City

Long Bridge

B & O Branch RR

Alexandria

Loudoun & Hampshire RR

Bailey's Cross Roads

to Lewinsville

Falls Church

to Dranesville

Annandale

Railroad

Vienna

Fairfax Court House

Gooding's Tavern

Orange & Alexandria

Brimstone Hill

Snyder's Ford

Fairfax Station

Occaquan River

Ox Road

Germantown

Sangster's Station

Union Mills

Run

Saunder's Toll Gate

Stuart

Centreville

Bull

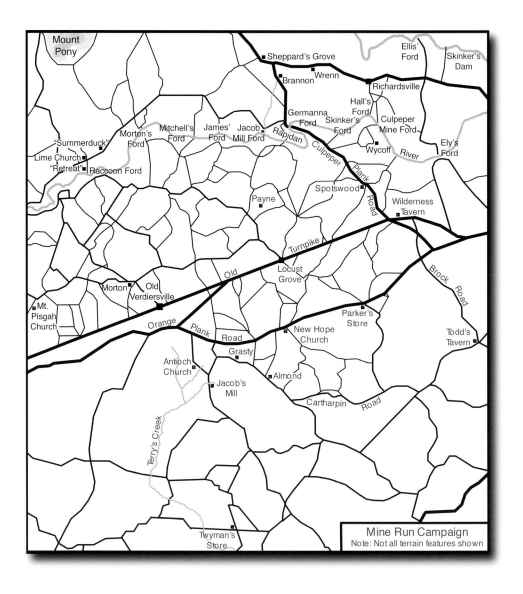

Mine Run Campaign
Note: Not all terrain features shown

Chapter Six

The Bristoe Station Campaign

The 9th of October dawned with both armies maneuvering against the other. Despite his desire to strike at the enemy as soon as possible, Lee quickly found himself one step behind his foe. At 6:30 that morning, Meade put his cavalry in motion, ordering Gen. Gregg to march day and night and concentrate at Culpeper Court House, Kilpatrick to watch the Madison Court House and Woodville road as well as all the roads leading to Culpeper Court House, and Buford, in cooperation with Maj. Gen. John Newton, commanding the First Corps, to force a passage over the Rapidan at Germanna Ford and uncover Morton's Ford.[1] Reports filtered in to Meade about a weakening of the enemy's outpost lines, the withdrawal of artillery from earthworks, and the movement of heavy forces toward Madison Court House. Davies received orders from Kilpatrick to take his entire brigade to Criglersville on the far right of the line.[2] Whatever Lee proposed to do, Meade planned to be prepared for it.

As the day wore on additional reports came in and new orders were sent out. Davies received a message that an enemy column halted and encamped about two miles from Madison Court House. He was ordered to make camp and, under the admonition to maintain vigilance, throw out pickets from two of his regiments from Russell's Ford to Griffinsburg, keeping his two other regiments and Capt. Samuel S. Elder's Battery E, Fourth U. S. Artillery at Brown's Store near James City. Another communication directed Custer to maintain a careful watch over his vedettes along the river from Russell's Ford downstream to the mouth of Crooked Run, make sure that all his men had two days rations for themselves and one day's forage for their horses, and be prepared to move at any time.[3]

Amidst all this commotion, plans were completed for the crossing of the Rapidan on the 10th. Meade's headquarters notified Fifth Corps commander, Maj. Gen. George Sykes, and Sixth Corps commander, Maj. Gen. John Sedgwick, to be prepared to support the operation with Sykes massing under the cover of a wood near the headquarters of Newton's First Corps and Sedgwick moving his corps to and then along the river in conjunction with the march of Newton and Buford on the other side.[4] Finally, at 7:00 in the evening, Meade telegraphed Maj. Gen. Henry W. Halleck back in Washington City, informing him of the enemy's movement toward Madison Court House and his own plans to force a crossing of the Rapidan at Germanna and Morton fords. Admitting that Lee's intentions had yet to become clear, Meade felt sure that he had placed his army in a position to meet any contingency.[5] The next move belonged to Robert E. Lee.

At the United States Military Academy cadets learned about strategy and grand tactics by studying the various great captains of war. Among those illustrious soldiers, Napoleon Bonaparte ranked high on the list. Lee had used the campaigns of Napoleon as models for his own operations against several of the Army of the Potomac's commanders on a number of occasions. This plan proved no different. Using a natural obstacle, the Rapidan River, to mask his movement, Lee swung his army around Meade's extended right flank, hoping to place himself in his enemy's rear where he could either force Meade into retreat or draw him into a battle on ground of Lee's own choosing. As with Napoleon, the cavalry would play an important role by screening the movement and seizing important points such as fords, towns, and crossroads. Napoleon had Murat. Lee had Stuart.

Lee had begun his movement on the 8th by shifting Maj. Gen. Richard H. Anderson's and Maj. Gen. Henry Heth's divisions of Lt. Gen. A. P. Hill's Corps from near Peyton's Ford and Rapidan Station to beyond Orange Court House and within two miles of Cave's Ford on the Rapidan River. On the 9th Maj. Gen. Cadmus M. Wilcox's Division left its camp near Barnett's Ford and fell in behind Anderson and Heth as they waded across the Rapidan at Cave's Ford and marched for Madison Court House. Lt. Gen. Richard S. Ewell's Corps, led by Maj. Gen. Robert E. Rodes's Division, followed by Maj. Gen. Edward Johnson's and Maj. Gen. Jubal A. Early's divisions, passed Orange Court House, crossed the river at Barnett's Ford, and swung south of Hill's Corps onto the road to Madison Court House. Progress proved painfully slow, the troops limited to narrow circuitous paths in an effort to conceal the movement from enemy observers north of the Rapidan. The troops made camp wherever night found them.[6]

With the brigades of Brig. Gen. James B. Gordon, Col. Pierce M. B. Young, and Col. Oliver R. Funsten, Stuart had marched to the right of the infantry and gone into camp about a mile short of Madison Court House on the night of October 9. Vedettes from Young's and Funsten's brigades watched the Robinson River from its mouth to Criglersville, where the infantry was to cross the next day.[7] The troopers had been warned not to fraternize with the enemy. After dark a picked body of men crossed the river under orders to capture the Federal signal station on Thoroughfare Mountain that overlooked the Confederate line of march. At 3:00 the next morning, Stuart detached Funsten's Brigade and the Second North Carolina from Gordon's Brigade to act as advance guard for Lee's infantry under Ewell and Hill.[8] Funsten reported to Gen. Hill at Crigler's Mill and screened the march of his column until Gen. Ewell ordered him to occupy Griffinsburg on the Culpeper-Sperryville pike and hold it if possible. At 10:00 that night Funsten ran into the enemy's outposts about a half mile outside of the village. Deciding to go no further, he camped for the night.[9]

While Funsten screened the infantry, Stuart, with Gordon in the lead and Young following, crossed the river at Russell's Ford and pushed on toward James

City. In the van rode Lt. William A. Benton with Company A of the Fourth North Carolina.[10] On the north bank, Benton scattered the outposts of the Fifth New York, Davies's brigade, forcing the bluecoats to leave their breakfast of mutton, sweet potatoes, and coffee, and driving them back about a mile to their reserves, which were also routed. The New Yorkers continued their retreat until they reached Bethsaida Church. Here the One Hundred Twentieth New York Infantry under Capt. Abram L. Lockwood, which had camped at the church the night before, quickly formed a line to make a stand. Lt. James L. Daughdrill of the Jeff Davis Legion made a reconnaissance and reported the presence of infantry to Stuart.[11]

Lockwood deployed his 211 men in a small wood and waited, having been promised support from Companies C and D of the Fifth New York stationed behind him. Stuart threw Gordon straight at the foot soldiers while swinging Young around their left flank. Gordon advanced a dismounted force, keeping most of his command on their horses, while Lt. Col. John D. Twiggs led the First South Carolina of Young's Brigade against Lockwood's flank and rear. The Fifth New York failed to come to Lockwood's aid, leaving the infantry to fight on its own. Almost surrounded, Lockwood could only watch as the enemy overwhelmed his men. One hundred and fourteen officers and men fell into Stuart's hands. The others scattered or retreated hurriedly along the road to James City.[12]

Stuart, wasting no time in following up on his success, pushed on. Upon approaching James City he paused to ascertain just exactly what confronted him and discovered that in addition to Kilpatrick's two brigades, a substantial infantry force, which turned out to be part of Brig. Gen. Henry Prince's infantry division of Maj. Gen. William H. French's Third Corps, and six pieces of artillery, blocked the road. Kilpatrick withdrew through the village, took a position on a ridge near Bethel Church, and waited. Stuart knew he faced odds too great to challenge and chose not to attack in force, though he did harass the enemy with Gordon's Brigade in front and Young's on the flank. Two guns from Capt. Wiley H. Griffin's Baltimore Light Artillery of the Stuart Horse Artillery also engaged the enemy's attention by firing intermittently. Soon Capt. James F. Hart's Battery, commanded this day by Lt. Edwin L. Halsey, unlimbered in support of Griffin.[13] Stuart took time to write to R. E. Lee and inform him of the situation, stating that the cavalry would hold its position until the enemy infantry had cleared the road and then outflank James City.[14] In the meantime, Stuart set about to engage the attention of the enemy without bringing on a general fight.

The skirmishing lasted throughout the afternoon. At about 3:00, Custer arrived with his brigade and Lt. Alexander C. M. Pennington's Battery M, Second U. S. Artillery, which soon unlimbered and opened fire on Confederates holding a wood to the right of the town. Sitting back-to-back with his adjutant, Maj. Henry B. McClellan, dictating dispatches, Stuart became tired and stretched out on the ground, as did McClellan. Scarcely had they done so when a shot from the enemy's battery passed over them, so close that they could feel the windage. Striking the ground just feet behind them, the shell exploded but harmed no one. Had the two men been sitting up they would have been struck and killed.[15]

The bombardment continued until 4:00 in the afternoon when Maj. John E. Clark with a battalion of the Fifth Michigan, Custer's brigade, made a dash for a section of Hart's guns that had been advanced almost beyond its supports, coming within 200 yards of them. Capt. Robin Ap. C. Jones of the First South Carolina with 50 men strategically posted behind a stonewall delivered a telling volley that along with a blast of canister from the guns compelled the enemy to make a hasty retreat. After that, desultory artillery and skirmisher fire echoed across the countryside until darkness fell.[16] Stuart had accomplished all that had been asked of him in driving back the enemy from the Robinson and neutralizing the signal station atop Thoroughfare Mountain.[17] As the sun set he might have wondered if Fitz Lee had fared as well at the other end of the line.

Unlike Kilpatrick, who had been the anvil for Stuart's hammer, Buford struck at Fitz Lee first. Taking his two brigades, Chapman's and Devin's, Lt. Edward B. Williston's Battery D, Second U. S. Artillery, and Lt. Edward Heaton's Battery B/L, Second U. S. Artillery, Buford rode out from his camp near Stevensburg at 8:30 in the morning toward Germanna Ford on the Rapidan River. Arriving at noon, Buford made the necessary arrangements for crossing the ford and by 1:00 the Eighth New York, Chapman's brigade, splashed over the river in the face of pickets from the First Maryland of Lomax's Brigade that guarded the river from Germanna to Mitchell's fords. The Marylanders quickly retreated after losing 13 men from Company E as prisoners. Turning his column upstream, Buford marched for Morton's Ford, scooping up additional prisoners as he went and skirmishing with dismounted sharpshooters from the Fifth Virginia who slowed but could not stop his progress. Night had fallen by the time he reached the entrenchments closest to the ford. These the Confederates had abandoned, falling back to other works nearby. Buford encamped for the night and waited to hear from Newton.[18]

The remainder of Fitz Lee's Division spent most of the day virtually unaware of Buford's incursion. On the night of the 9th, Wickham's Brigade, under the command of Col. Thomas H. Owen of the Third Virginia, camped on the farm of Jeremiah Morton about three miles southeast of Somerville Ford. Not until the evening of the 10th did Owen learn that the Federals had crossed the river and by then he could offer no assistance to Lomax.[19] Col. John R. Chambliss's Brigade had drawn the duty of guarding Stuart's and the army's rear as it advanced over the Robinson. Leaving its camp near Raccoon Ford on the 9th, the brigade, following Ewell's and Hill's infantry, crossed the Rapidan at Peyton's Ford and camped for the night at the Madison house just south of the ford. The next morning, the brigade retraced its hoof prints back to its old camp where it spent the night.[20] The 11th would see both brigades drawn into the conflict.

While Kilpatrick and Buford tussled with Stuart and Lomax respectively, Gen. Gregg maintained his watch along the Rappahannock below its junction with the Rapidan. However, the growing threat to the army's right flank soon caused Meade to send for Gregg's division. Col. John P. Taylor, now commanding Gregg's

First Brigade, received orders at 2:00 on the morning of the 10th to pull back his vedettes from their posts that stretched over 40 miles and concentrate at Kelly's Ford on the Rappahannock. Eight hours later the brigade, except for portions of the First New Jersey and the Sixth Ohio, had arrived and halted to await further instructions.[21] Meade through Pleasonton also sent orders to Gen. Gregg, who had his headquarters with Col. J. Irvin Gregg's Second Brigade, to place himself on the Culpeper-Sperryville pike in support of Kilpatrick's right flank. The brigade had left Bealton Station at 5:00 on the morning of the 10th and by 11:00 had reached Culpeper Court House where further instructions directed it to Wayland Mills that lay southeast of James City. The sound of fighting at that place alerted Gen. Gregg to the fact that Kilpatrick was under attack. Col. Gregg halted his march at the Kirby house near Fox Mountain on the road from Culpeper to James City and encamped for the night, after sending out pickets from the First Maine along the road leading to the mill and some from the Sixteenth Pennsylvania to Cedar Run or Slaughter's Mountain.[22]

By the morning of the 11th, Robert E. Lee's offensive had succeeded not only in dislodging Meade from his positions on the right of his line but also in threatening his infantry camps around Culpeper Court House. As a result the Federal commander issued orders for the movement of his army on the 11th. The Third Corps was to watch the Rappahannock from Sulphur Springs to Freeman's Ford; the Second Corps to take position on the Third's left from Freeman's to Beverly Ford; the Fifth Corps to the left of the Third from Beverly to Rappahannock Station; the Sixth Corps left of the Fifth from Rappahannock Station toward Kelly's Ford; the First Corps at Kelly's Ford extending to its right to link with the left of the Sixth Corps. The Third and Fifth Corps, along with the cavalry, were also charged with covering the army's withdrawal. Kilpatrick was to cover the retreat to Culpeper Court House and from there, follow the infantry along the railroad to Rappahannock Station. Gregg was ordered to follow the Third Corps to Sulphur Springs.[23] Meade had held Culpeper since September 13th when the Federal cavalry had driven Stuart across the Rapidan. Now Lee could take it back. The Confederate commander's plan for the 11th focused on following up his success on the 10th by liberating Culpeper Court House.[24]

Of the three Federal cavalry divisions, Gregg's would have the easiest day. Taylor's brigade, minus the Third Pennsylvania, crossed the Rappahannock at Kelly's Ford and rode toward Brandy Station. Near there a staff officer handed Taylor orders, sending him back over the river at Rappahannock Station and on to Sulphur Springs. He spent the day in the saddle and never saw a single gray trooper. Likewise, Col. Gregg's brigade, minus the Thirteenth Pennsylvania, left its bivouac at Fox Mountain early in the morning and trotted off to Culpeper Court House, where it received orders to proceed via Rixeyville to Sulphur Springs, and encamped for the night between Jeffersonton and the springs.[25] The men of the brigade never laid eyes, much less sabers, on their foe. The division's easy day did not epitomize that of the other two divisions of Pleasonton's cavalry or of Stuart's.

At 1:00 on the morning of the 11th, Stuart wrote to Lee giving the disposition of his forces. Young's Brigade held the road from James City to Russell's Ford where Maj. William H. Cheek, Gordon's Brigade, with a dismounted battalion was stationed. To Young's left, the rest of Gordon's Brigade held the road from the residence of William Hill, where Stuart had his headquarters, to James City and Brown's Store. Funsten's Brigade still guarded Ewell's front. Stuart expressed concern over what his next move should be, fearing that Young might be attacked and driven back in the morning. Such a circumstance would threaten the Confederate lines of communication through Madison Court House. If such an attack occurred Gordon could aide Young, but it would delay the army's supply train and slow Lee's movement. In the end, all Stuart could do was wait for the morning. [26]

At 7:00 in the morning, Kilpatrick acted on the orders that had reached him during the night. Custer's brigade, minus the First Vermont and Lt. William Egan's section of Pennington's battery that had been assigned to Davies's brigade that morning, trotted off along the road to Colvin's Tavern. Davies used the James City road, riding through Gaines' Mill. To protect his northwestern flank Kilpatrick ordered the First West Virginia, Davies's brigade, to retire down the Culpeper-Sperryville pike. Davies rode along unmolested and reached Culpeper about noon. He ordered the First Vermont and Lt. Egan's section of artillery to rejoin Custer south of town. Davies also ordered the Second New York to scout back along the road the brigade had just traveled to ascertain the proximity of the enemy. Meanwhile, Custer arrived and reunited with the First Vermont and Lt. Egan's section of artillery on a hill just outside of Culpeper. Although Kilpatrick could count himself lucky that he had been able to withdraw from James City without alerting the Confederates, he knew that Stuart soon would be in hot pursuit and made preparations to greet him.[27]

Sometime after dawn, the gray cavalry found that their adversaries had disappeared during the night. Leaving Young's Brigade at James City to guard the army's flank, Stuart led Gordon's Brigade to Griffinsburg where he found Funsten's Brigade already skirmishing with the enemy. Sending the Eleventh Virginia under Lt. Col. Mottrom D. Ball to Rixeyville to determine the enemy's line of retreat, Stuart marched with Funsten down the Culpeper-Sperryville pike toward Culpeper Court House. Gordon rode on Stuart's right, intersecting the pike at Stone House Mountain. The cavalry's rapid advance caught the One Hundred and Sixth New York Infantry marching parallel to the right of the gray cavalry and attempting to rejoin its sister regiments from Col. Benjamin F. Smith's Third Brigade, Third Division, of the Third Corps. Not wanting to allow what appeared to be an isolated infantry regiment to escape, Stuart turned to Lt. George Baylor, commanding Company B of the Twelfth Virginia, and ordered him to charge. Although somewhat surprised, Baylor led his 50 men forward. Maj. Andrew N. MacDonald, commanding the One Hundred and Sixth, had made every effort to drive through the Confederate skirmishers to his front only to see his formation broken up by the dense underbrush. He soon realized that a greater threat lay on his left flank when he noticed cavalry coming at him. He brought his men into line on a rise of ground. They fired a volley that passed completely over the heads of Baylor and his troopers who returned fire with their pistols, killing Capt. James S. Peach, but were prevented from using their sabers on the New Yorkers because of an intervening ditch. Stuart was more than satisfied with Baylor's effort even though MacDonald succeeded in escaping and reuniting with his own forces.[28]

As the Confederates neared Culpeper, Kilpatrick started to consolidate his command under the gaze of his commander, Maj. Gen. Alfred Pleasonton.[29] Kilpatrick ordered Custer to retreat through the town, cross Mountain Run, and take position on the the George house hill. Davies also reached the hill but not before nearly losing two of his regiments. The First West Virginia had not yet arrived. Word reached Davies that the regiment was two miles outside of town with the enemy close on its hooves. The Fifth New York under Maj. John Hammond galloped off to support its brother regiment. Together the West Virginians and the New Yorkers slowed the Confederate advance until coming in sight of the town where Lt. Pennington's battery, now unlimbered and ready for action on the heights, opened fire over their heads, covering the final stages of their retreat.[30] Soon after these regiments reached safety, the Second New York in the act of retiring after having reconnoitered the James City road found itself outflanked and under attack by overwhelming numbers. Nearly cut off, the squadron careened through Culpeper. Its commander, Capt. George V. Griggs, had been killed and his second in command, Lt. William B. Shafer, wounded and taken prisoner. It fell to Sgt. Lewis Barker to save the men. This he did by leading them in a charge that broke through the enemy with the loss of only five men. With the return of the Second New York, Kilpatrick could begin his retreat to the Rappahannock.[31]

On nearing the town, Stuart discovered that the enemy's infantry had withdrawn toward the Rappahannock, leaving cavalry alone to face him. Supported by artillery on the hills behind them, the blue troopers attempted to check the Southerners' advance. Gordon's Brigade rode straight at the enemy, the Fourth North Carolina having the greatest success, driving its opponents back toward the Wallack house but losing Col. Dennis D. Ferebee with a wound to his foot. Capt. William H. H. Cowles of the First North Carolina took possession of the courthouse in Culpeper.[32] Despite these victories, the Federal artillery's position proved too dangerous to challenge head on. Recognizing this, Stuart advanced Capt. Wiley H. Griffin's Battery to occupy the enemy and, taking Gordon's and Funsten's brigades, the latter having only two regiments, the Seventh and the Twelfth Virginia, swung around by the left flank past Chestnut Fork Church on the Rixeyville road and the Bradford and Botts farms to attack the Federal rear.[33] Even as Stuart maneuvered to strike at Kilpatrick, events elsewhere now contributed to make the day most interesting for all concerned.

As the drama between Kilpatrick and Stuart played out through the morning hours, another one unfolded between Buford and Fitz Lee along the Rapidan. Buford had dutifully carried out his part of Meade's plan to advance over the river.

During the night of the 10th, he waited to hear from First Corps commander, Maj. Gen. John Newton, who had orders to move his command across the river at Morton's Ford and link with him. Buford, completely unaware that Meade had altered his plans due to Lee's offensive, finally received word at 7:00 on the morning of the 11th that his commander-in-chief had "changed the program" and Newton would not be joining him. However, the information had not come through official channels, so Buford remained in the dark as to "what course to pursue." Finally, orders reached him, but to his surprise they were ones telling him not to cross the river at all and to return and cross the Rappahannock at Kelly's Ford. Lacking anything else to go on, Buford decided to retreat over the Rapidan and head for the Rappahannock. To gain a little breathing room, he attacked with Devin's brigade, driving back the Confederate forces holding the second line of entrenchments. Simultaneously, he started Chapman's brigade across the river. At first all appeared to go smoothly, but problems soon developed.[34]

Col. Thomas L. Rosser's Fifth Virginia opposed Buford's early morning advance but could not stop it until Lomax came up with the rest of his brigade and the Twentieth North Carolina Infantry under the command of Col. Thomas F. Toon and five companies of the Twelfth North Carolina Infantry under Col. Henry E. Coleman, both from Brig. Gen. Robert D. Johnston's Brigade.[35] Lomax reoccupied the inner entrenchments and began threatening Buford's left flank. Buford might have been able to execute his withdrawal more rapidly but for a problem with the ford, which had to be repaired. This slowed the crossing to a crawl. To cover the operations at the ford Buford threw out skirmishers and brought up two guns. As the morning lengthened the fighting intensified. Some of Devin's skirmishers occupied a barn and opened a withering fire on the Confederates. Adjutant John T. Gregory of the Twelfth North Carolina Infantry led 20 volunteers in an assault on the barn, routed the enemy, and held it against a counter-attack, earning the compliments of his brigade commander. Later, Chambliss rode up with his brigade and one gun from Capt. Roger P. Chew's Battery, which unlimbered about 1,000 yards from the enemy's guns. The artillery duel that immediately developed finally ended an hour later when the Federals limbered up and rode for the ford. Under the cover of Chew's fire, Lomax charged. By this time Chapman's brigade had crossed the river and so had a large portion of Devin's. Lt. Edward B. Heaton's Battery B/L, Second U. S. Artillery and Lt. Edward B. Williston's Battery D, Second U. S. Artillery took position on the heights across the river and covered Devin's rear guard, consisting of the Sixth and Ninth New York regiments, that met Lomax's charge and repulsed it long enough to withdraw, although both regiments suffered a number of casualties.[36] Buford's day had just begun.

Fitz Lee had arrived at Raccoon Ford earlier that morning and recognized an opportunity to trap the Federal cavalry between two forces. After sending Lomax and Chambliss downstream on the south side of the river, he crossed to the north bank Owen's Brigade and Col. Thomas M. Garrett with the remaining infantry from Johnston's Brigade, intending to move north and catch Buford in the act of crossing the river at Morton's Ford. Unfortunately for Fitz Lee's plan, Buford became aware of it in time to send Chapman with the Eighth and Twelfth Illinois and the Third Indiana, which had completed crossing the river, and a battery of artillery along the north bank to intercept Owen. The two forces collided near the Stringfellow house just north of the ford. Fitz Lee immediately commanded Owen to charge the Federal battery before ascertaining the strength or position of the enemy cavalry. Obediently, Owen led Col. Richard W. Carter's First Virginia and Owen's own Third Virginia under Lt. Col. William R. Carter in an attack up the road while the Second and Fourth Virginia deployed in the fields to the left of the road to support the assault and Capt. James Breathed's First Stuart Horse Artillery that was unlimbering nearby. Fitz Lee's rashness in ordering the charge soon bore bitter fruit when he realized that the enemy battery had far more support than he had supposed and he sent a rider to recall Owen. The Federal artillery dealt harshly with Breathed as well. The first shot tore the arm off a cannoneer at the Whitworth gun and cut the right wheel in two.[37]

The First and Third Virginia had nearly reached the enemy's dismounted skirmishers when the courier delivered Fitz Lee's order. Attempting a change of front in the face of an aggressive enemy often brought disaster. As expected, in this instance the blue cavalry, on seeing the disorder in the Confederate ranks, opened fire, adding to the confusion. However, Owen proved worthy of the challenge and soon had things in hand again. He quickly dismounted the sharpshooters from the First and Third Virginia, posted them along a fence line, and formed the rest of the two regiments, still mounted, with sabers drawn in support of Breathed. The sharpshooters from the Second and Fourth Virginia deployed in a wood to protect the left flank. Nevertheless, encouraged by what he perceived as a golden opportunity to capitalize on his enemy's mistake, Chapman thrust forward his skirmish line, threatening Breathed's guns. Owen countered with the mounted portion of the Fourth Virginia. Riding up to Capt. William B. Newton, who commanded the regiment at this time, to give the order, Owen's horse was shot from under him. At Capt. Newton's direction, Sgt. James Churchill Cooke dismounted and gave his horse to Owen, who then turned to Newton and ordered him to charge the Eighth Illinois's skirmishers. Unperturbed, the Illinoisians delivered a telling volley that killed Newton, mortally wounded Capt. Phillip D. Williams of Company A, and broke up the attack. Shortly thereafter, the appearance of Col. Garrett's infantry forced Chapman to fall back, although he gave ground grudgingly.[38]

Having successfully crossed the river and held Fitz Lee at bay, Buford began a withdrawal toward Brandy Station. Minor skirmishing along the way gained in intensity until near Stevensburg where Buford united his two brigades and made a stand to protect wagons passing through the hamlet on their way to Kelly's Ford. He did not have to wait long. Fitz Lee came up and prepared to attack. Owen filed to the left across a flat plain toward the Barbour house and charged alternately with the Third, Second, and Fourth Virginia, assigning the First Virginia to protect Breathed's Battery. The Federal artillery on the only rise of ground in the area rained a deadly fire of shot and shell on the oncoming graycoats. Capt. Jesse Irvine of the Second Virginia lost his leg and had his horse killed. Lt. Col. William R. Carter of the Third Virginia had his horse killed beneath him and became a prisoner when the enemy counter-charged. Fortunately, the Second Virginia, which had failed to come to the Third's support when a shell exploding over it disordered the ranks, rallied in time to push back the enemy and rescue Carter. Finally, Garrett appeared with his infantry brigade and advanced against Buford's left. Initially successful, Garrett soon found himself in danger of being outflanked on his right, forcing Lt. Col. William S. Davis's Twelfth North Carolina Infantry to change front and attack this new threat. Suddenly, Lomax and Chambliss came up on the infantry's right. Chew's Battery, supported by the Tenth Virginia, unlimbered and opened fire. One of its shells exploded amidst the enemy hitting three men and four horses. In the meantime, Chambliss led the Ninth and Thirteenth Virginia forward. The Federals finally gave way, but Buford had managed to hold on until all the wagons had crossed Mountain Run before breaking off the fight and riding for Brandy Station where other adventures awaited him.[39]

To the northwest, Stuart with Funsten's and Gordon's brigades crossed the Rixeyville road at Chestnut Fork Church and moved ahead rapidly in the direction of Brandy Station, hoping that he might arrive in time to secure Fleetwood Hill.[40] However, that plan began to unravel. Kilpatrick, being all too aware of Stuart's intentions, had skillfully used his artillery to gain time for his brigades to withdraw from the George house hill northwest of Culpeper. The Federal cavalry marched rapidly toward Brandy Station with Custer to the left of the road and Davies to the right. Stuart's parallel route brought him in sight of Kilpatrick's retiring column at Slaughter Bradford's house. Noticing what appeared to be a detached portion of the enemy, Stuart sent Lt. Col. Thomas Ruffin at the head of the First North Carolina, Gordon's Brigade, down on it. The Tarheels' onslaught scooped up a number of prisoners, causing Custer to move his artillery to the front of his column for greater protection. Hurriedly, he rode on.[41]

Approaching the station, Kilpatrick soon realized that as rapidly as he had retreated from Culpeper, Buford, despite his clashes with Fitz Lee, had pulled back even faster from the Rapidan. In doing so Buford had reached Brandy Station in time to encounter the rear of the Fifth Corps, making its way to the Rappahannock, but before Kilpatrick arrived. Here, for the first time, Buford learned of the army's change of position and to his shock, that Kilpatrick still faced the enemy somewhere in the direction of Culpeper. Buford hunkered down to hold the line of retreat open for the Third Division.[42]

In following Buford's force to Brandy Station, Fitz Lee found himself in a position to deal the Federal cavalry a damaging blow. Lomax, with Chew's Battery in tow, arrived first and sent Col. Thomas L. Rosser's Fifth Virginia and Col. Julien Harrison's Sixth Virginia charging through Brandy Station, taking possession of the railroad and momentarily thwarting Buford's plan to hold it until Kilpatrick could reach him. Lomax also ordered the Fifteenth Virginia to cut off some ambulances coming along the railroad from the direction of Culpeper. Maj. Charles R. Collins, leading the regiment, crossed the railroad to intercept them. Following in the wake of Lomax's Brigade, Owen's Brigade reached the station and advanced beyond it in the direction of Beverly Ford. Fitz Lee now had two brigades interposed between Buford and the oncoming Kilpatrick. Unfortunately, the Confederates were completely unaware of the latter's presence – a circumstance that would change abruptly.[43]

Kilpatrick knew that only a bold front could extricate him from the predicament in which he found himself. He formed his two brigades into columns of squadrons by regiments and moved forward with Davies's brigade still on the right and Custer's still on the left. Then, throwing caution to the wind, Kilpatrick pushed Custer's brigade to the front. Custer's time had come. Sabers drawn, he led the First and Fifth Michigan forward in a charge, leaving Sixth and Seventh Michigan to deal with the enemy in his rear. That enemy, Stuart, now stood poised to wreak havoc on Kilpatrick. The Twelfth Virginia, Funsten's Brigade, led by Col. Thomas B. Massie, now charged in between Custer and Davies, threatening to cut Kilpatrick's division in half. Stuart prepared to seize the moment, forming the Fourth and Fifth North Carolina, Gordon's Brigade, to advance in support of the Twelfth. Davies had other ideas. Capt. Samuel S. Elder's Battery E, Fourth U. S. Artillery unlimbered and opened fire on Owen's and Lomax's regiments. While the Second New York held the rear and the First West Virginia's repeating rifles raked the Twelfth Virginia, Davies sent the First Vermont across the railroad to his right and then turned his attention to Stuart on his left. At the head of the Eighteenth Pennsylvania, he charged into the flank of the North Carolinians, catching them in column of fours in a sunken road. Thundering over a rise in the ground that shielded them from view, the Pennsylvanians shattered the Tarheels, sending them reeling from the field in a rout that Stuart and Gordon with their pistols drawn could not stop. Fortunately, the Seventh Virginia, Funsten's Brigade, that had earlier taken the wrong road at Chestnut Fork Church came up, struck the Pennsylvanians in their flank, and sent them flying, killing several, wounding Maj. Harvey B. Van Voorhis and capturing him and 32 others. But Gordon was done for the day and Stuart's opportunity lost.[44]

The first of Fitz Lee's regiments to feel the weight of Kilpatrick's presence was the Fifteenth Virginia. As Maj. Collins rode forward to intercept the ambulances, he noticed a strong force coming from the wood near the Botts farm and turned down the railroad to ascertain its strength, which he estimated to be at least a brigade. Almost immediately, a portion of the enemy column, which turned out to be the First Vermont, broke off, crossed the railroad in front of Collins and advanced toward him. Throwing forward his skirmishers to screen his main body, he pulled back toward the station where he rallied on Chew's Battery. Fitz Lee also had discovered the unwanted visitors on his flank and rear. Lomax and Owen scarcely had begun to form their brigades to face Buford, who occupied Fleetwood Hill, when Kilpatrick made his entrance onto the field. Coming under severe fire

After Gettysburg

from Elder's Battery near the Kennedy farm and Buford's artillery stationed on the Fleetwood Hill and seeing Custer's Michiganders thundering down on their left and rear, Fitz Lee's brigades hastened to escape certain destruction. Buford now committed some of his regiments to hurry the Confederates on their way and the swirling mass of men and horses rushed back through and past the station down the road to Stevensburg.[45]

Galloping ahead of the blue-gray melee in a desperate attempt to reach his battery in time rode Capt. Roger P. Chew. He had moved forward in the wake of the Fifth and Sixth Virginia's charge to locate a position for his guns. Now all thought of that had vanished. He reached his men sitting their horses alongside the road to Stevensburg and yelled at Gunner George M. Neese to unlimber and fire in the hope that the cavalry would rally. Neese unlimbered but had no real target. The fight taking place not more than 100 yards to his front in a strip of wood prevented him from firing in that direction for fear of doing as much damage to his own cavalry as to the enemy's. Nevertheless, he had to fire if only to provide some encouragement for Fitz Lee's hard-pressed troopers. Swinging his gun to the left, Neese let off a few rounds out across some open pastureland. Soon after, the gray cavalry rallied and Buford pulled back, but the opportunity to cut off and destroy a large part of Kilpatrick's division had been lost. Buford and Kilpatrick had now linked their forces and were taking position northwest of Brandy Station below Fleetwood Hill.[46]

After his troopers regrouped about 400 yards to the rear, Lomax prepared to deal with both Kilpatrick and Buford. With the brigade's sharpshooters and the First Maryland Battalion in a wood near the station, the Fifth, Sixth, and Fifteenth Virginia, were soon charging all over the field and being met by the Federals with equal fervor. Having at first acted as support for Chew's Battery, which now targeted the large number of enemy troopers and did excellent execution, the Fifteenth Virginia under Maj. Collins moved forward, hoping to capture some of the confused masses in his front. Before Collins could reach them, however, the enemy opened a concentrated fire from skirmishers on his right flank and he turned to attack them. At that moment the Fifth Virginia charged obliquely through the Fifteenth, which, despite the breaking of its line, still successfully drove the enemy back on his supports. Withdrawing into a wood to reform his command, Collins came under a heavy fire from the opposite side of the railroad. Again, he charged and threw back his foes until attacked by two bodies of the enemy, one on each flank. With the help of another regiment he repulsed the Federals and pulled back to reform. In all, the Fifth, Sixth, and Fifteenth made five or six charges before the blue cavalry finally withdrew. The Sixth lost Col. Harrison to a thigh wound during one of its charges. In the intense fighting, the troopers of the First Maryland, fighting on foot, advanced and retreated several times, once being surrounded and forced to fight hand to hand, using their pistols instead of their long arms.[47]

Once Kilpatrick formed on Buford's right, the Federals too charged here and there, buying time for the infantry and the wagon train to reach Rappahannock Station. Custer led several charges across the fields. One came up short in front of a ditch, forcing the blue troopers to retire in some disorder. Thinking to take advantage of this, a body of Confederates emerged from a wood and swept forward to outflank a section of Elder's battery. The Fifth New York, Davies's brigade, and Companies B and H of the First Vermont, Custer's brigade, intervened and held the enemy in check long enough for the battery to limber and take a new position.[48]

The confused fighting also swallowed up Chambliss's Brigade, which arrived while Lomax and Owen were already heavily engaged. Leaving the Tenth Virginia to support Chew's Battery on the Stevensburg Road and coming on to the field with the Ninth and Thirteenth Virginia, Chambliss saw a large force of the enemy to the left of the station. He immediately ordered the Ninth Virginia, led this day by Maj. Thomas Waller, to charge. The Ninth successfully routed the enemy's sharpshooters from the wood near the station and on its hooves came Maj. Joseph E. Gillette and the Thirteenth, which struck at the force supporting the sharpshooters. Both Waller and Gillette suffered wounds in the action and a number of men were killed or wounded.[49] The Tenth did not escape the fight, becoming drawn into the charges and counter-charges from friend and foe alike. At one point, 15 of its dismounted men joined in a forward movement only to find themselves surrounded by the enemy when the Confederates had to retreat. For a time they fought hand to hand but realized the hopelessness of their position and laid down their arms. In a letter to his wife from Old Capitol Prison in Washington, Pvt. John O. Collins, one of the captured troopers, recounted that he had been struck with a saber but was unhurt. His friend Pvt. James Scott had been scooped up with him after trying to hide around a building. A few shots fired under the house had quickly brought his surrender.[50]

The result of all this fighting boiled down to Buford and Kilpatrick united atop Fleetwood Hill, with the latter to the right of the former. The heights soon bristled with the guns of Elder's, Pennington's, Heaton's, and Williston's batteries. Stuart and Fitz Lee, having linked during the free-for-all brawl around the station, could see the futility of assaulting such a position. Stuart did what he could, at one point galloping up to Chew's Battery and requesting a rifled piece. Gunner Neese limbered his gun and dashed off with Stuart toward the hill on which the Barbour house stood. The position allowed Neese to enfilade the Federal artillery on Fleetwood Hill. Unlimbering near the house, Neese opened fire and quickly drew the attention of four of the enemy's guns that turned in his direction. Before he had fired his third shot, a 12-pound ball rocketed through a nearby shed, sending glass and wood splinters flying, and struck the gun carriage, shattering two spokes and effectively placing the gun out of action for the remainder of the day. The shock of the striking ball knocked down three men but only hurt one, Pvt. Benjamin F. Reily, who lost an eye from a wood splinter.[51]

Still not willing to give up, Stuart settled on a flanking maneuver, shifting Fitz Lee with Lomax's and Chambliss's brigades around the left toward St. James

Church. The day waned and Pleasonton began to withdraw toward the Rappahannock. Stuart pressed Buford's left flank and made demonstrations against his front but not enough to impede the Federal cavalry's march. By 8:00 that night Buford and Kilpatrick had crossed the river and gone into camp. Never having gotten close enough to strike at the retreating blue columns, Fitz Lee settled down for the night with Lomax encamping at Welford's Ford on the Hazel River and Chambliss near Beverly Ford. Owen, Funsten, and Gordon pulled back near the Botts farm below Brandy Station and camped as did Chew's Battery. Young's Brigade, which had missed the day's festivities, stayed encamped at James City for another night.[52]

The fighting on the 11th tested the mettle of both cavalries. Buford's and Kilpatrick's withdrawals had more to do with Meade's frame of mind and the orders he issued than Stuart's aggressiveness or the Confederate cavalry's prowess. Not knowing what Lee might be up to, other than an apparent effort by the Southern commander to place his army on his flank and rear, Meade, in one sense, took the saber out of Pleasonton's hand and placed his cavalry in an unfavorable position.[53] Forced to cover the retreating infantry corps, Pleasonton just barely managed to avoid a disaster and scurry over the Rappahannock. Knowing his enemy was committed to a withdrawal and having Lee's infantry at his back if not on the battlefield, Stuart could afford to go over to the offensive without worrying that his adversaries might turn and come at him with everything they had. From dawn to dusk, Buford and Kilpatrick committed their regiments to one task – get back over the Rappahannock. Stuart committed his regiments to stopping them or at least inflicting on them so much damage that they would cease to be operational for the near future. In the end, Pleasonton succeeded and Stuart failed. The fighting demonstrated that the troopers of both sides were more than willing to slug it out with each other and at the close of the day, both could point to moments of triumph and disaster. However, even in retreat the Federal cavalry, including the attached horse artillery, showed that it had a lethal sting. It had improved in every area from the days when the mere sight of a plume seemed to send it reeling. These bluecoats were one tough, nasty bunch and no one knew that better than the boys in gray. Equally, Stuart could point with pride to the accomplishments of his cavalrymen. They had liberated Culpeper and witnessed their enemy disappear across the Rappahannock. However, this fact had to be tempered with the understanding that their foe would have retreated anyway. In effect, all that Stuart's troopers accomplished was to accelerate the process. The deterioration of the gray cavalry's numbers, horses, and equipment coupled with the vast improvement of their enemy meant only one thing. If Pleasonton had wanted to remain south of the Rappahannock, he could have. The events of the next day made this fact very clear to the Confederates when the enemy returned in force.

Robert E. Lee's infantry followed the cavalry to Culpeper Court House and spent the night near there. Lee planned to follow up on his success thus far by marching north and then sweeping east to catch Meade's army as it trooped along the Orange and Alexandria Railroad. The gray cavalry would again screen the movement. As a result, Stuart had his couriers up and riding hard early on the morning of the 12th.[54] A dispatch reached Young at James City, ordering him to Culpeper Court House where he would guard the army's quartermaster and commissary stores and wait for further orders. Another reached Funsten, sending him with his brigade to the front of Ewell's infantry on the road through Rixeyville. Stuart took Gordon's Brigade and Fitz Lee's Division, minus Col. Thomas L. Rosser's Fifth Virginia and one gun from Chew's Battery left behind to hold Fleetwood Hill should the Federals decide to renew the contest of the previous day, and rode on the infantry's right flank, crossing the Hazel River at Starke's Ford and marching for Fox's Ford on the Rappahannock.[55]

The day began equally early for Gen. Gregg's division encamped around Sulphur Springs. About midnight Gregg received orders to send a scouting party toward Little Washington and Sperryville to ascertain the enemy's movements. Col. Charles H. Smith and his First Maine, Col. Gregg's brigade, drew the duty and well before sunrise the men of the regiment mounted their horses and set out on what turned out to be a four-day mission.[56] Gen. Gregg ordered the other regiments of Col. Gregg's brigade across the Rappahannock, leaving the Thirteenth Pennsylvania south of the river to picket beyond Jeffersonton toward Rixeyville and to support the First Maine should it have to return quickly. Around 10:00 in the morning, the advance of Lt. Col. Mottrom D. Ball's Eleventh Virginia that had rejoined Funsten that morning drove the vedettes of Capt. Patrick Kane's Company E of the Thirteenth into the village. Positioned behind a stonewall that encircled a church, the Thirteenth frustrated Ball's dismounted men in their efforts to drive the bluecoats out. Finally, mounting his men, Ball charged from the right flank, succeeded in dislodging the enemy's sharpshooters, and chased them down the road to the ford. Meanwhile, across the river Gen. Gregg ordered Col. Gregg to send a regiment to the Thirteenth's relief. The Fourth Pennsylvania, with Col. Gregg following, crossed the river and headed for Jeffersonton. A half mile from that place, the Keystone Staters encountered their brother regiment retiring. Col. Gregg immediately set about to recover the village.[57]

Wasting no time, Col. Gregg ordered Maj. Michael Kerwin of the Thirteenth Pennsylvania to retake the village, which he did with a dismounted attack, while Capt. Alender P. Duncan with one dismounted squadron of the Fourth Pennsylvania charged from the right. The Confederates lost several men killed and wounded, causing Stuart to rethink his approach. Leaving Ball and the Eleventh Virginia to contend with the Federals in Jeffersonton, Stuart bypassed the village by sending Lt. Col. Thomas A. Marshall with the Seventh Virginia to the left and rear of the village and Funsten with Lt. Col. Thomas B. Massie's Twelfth Virginia to the right and rear. Back at Jeffersonton, Ball ordered his men to mount their horses and charged down the road and into the village several times before dislodging the Pennsylvanians. At this moment, Funsten, having captured a great many of the Pennsylvanian's led horses, launched the Twelfth against their flank. Gregg resisted stubbornly until being informed that the Seventh Virginia had cut the road to the springs in his rear. Learning this fact by some means, the Pennsylvanians broke and could not be rallied. As Gregg accompanied his men rearward, trying to escape the trap, the Tenth New York came up only to receive a deadly flanking fire that compelled it to retreat behind a hill where it opened fire to assist Gregg's withdrawal. Additional covering fire came from two squadrons of the Eighth Pennsylvania, located at the bridge and the ford, and one gun from Lt. Horatio B. Reed's Battery A, Fourth U. S. Artillery under Reed himself that moved forward from the battery's position along the Fayetteville road. The battery had been firing in support of Gregg from the time it could see the enemy. This intervention permitted Gregg to extricate his other two regiments and retreat across the river, but not before suffering a large number of killed, wounded, and captured. The Twelfth Virginia followed up the enemy, driving it to the river.[58] The loss of Jeffersonton meant that the First Maine was on its own.

Stuart pushed his advantage. Under the fire of supporting artillery, he dismounted some of his men and along with some infantry from Brig. Gen. Stephen D. Ramseur's Brigade of Maj. Gen. Robert E. Rodes's Division of Ewell's Corps moved down to the river and opened fire. Then he ordered the Seventh and Eleventh to cross further upstream at Hart's Ford in an effort to outflank the Federals. During this time, Col. Gregg had made preparations to contest any further advance. On crossing the ford, he had allowed the two, shattered Pennsylvania regiments to retreat and had dismounted the Tenth New York and the Sixteenth Pennsylvania, spread them out along the river, and added two squadrons of the Eighth Pennsylvania. Reed's lone gun stayed in position to lend what support it could. These men soon felt the weight of the Southern rifle and artillery fire and fell back. Seeing his opportunity, Stuart turned to Lt. George Baylor of the Twelfth Virginia and ordered him to charge across the bridge with his company. As before, Baylor wasted no time in questioning his commander. He charged, followed by the other companies of the regiment. Unfortunately, on reaching the bridge, Baylor found that the planks had been taken up. Without pause, he led his men down to the ford and across. Backed by Ewell's infantry, delayed momentarily until the bridge planks were re-laid, Stuart drove Gregg past the hotel at Sulphur Springs. Here the Twelfth collided with troopers from Col. John P. Taylor's First Brigade that had advanced from near Warrenton. Col. Gregg had begun to shift his regiments toward the threatened fords downstream, turning over the defense of the springs and the points above to Taylor.[59]

Maj. Hugh Janeway led the First New Jersey, the foremost regiment of Taylor's brigade, forward and into a hornet's nest.[60] Capt. James Hart's squadron took to the wood on the right of the road and began to dispute the enemy's advance. The regiment's commander, Lt. Col. John W. Kester, who had been detached to serve on Gen. Gregg's staff this day, fell hard to the earth when a shell fragment struck his horse while he attempted to deliver a message to Col. Gregg. Kester would be just one of the many casualties this day. Hart's troopers soon received help from Janeway, who committed a second squadron under Maj. John H. Lucas. Intending to deploy dismounted on Hart's left, Lucas came over a rise of ground directly into the oncoming Twelfth Virginia. Not waiting to form, he charged, driving the Twelfth and its supporting infantry back beyond the hotel. Regrouping his men, Lucas formed a dismounted skirmish line and began to withdraw. Janeway met a second advance by the Confederates with a charge by another squadron led by Lieutenants Samuel Craig, William Hughes, and John Kinsley. A section of Capt. Joseph W. Martin's Sixth New York Light Battery unlimbered and added its metal to the fray. Janeway's aggressiveness caused the Confederates to pause until near sundown, when they renewed their efforts against Janeway's right flank, causing the First to withdraw. As darkness fell, the Confederates pressed forward in an effort to rout their foe. In this they proved unsuccessful, though inflicting 30 casualties and capturing 170 horses. Among the fallen was Maj. Lucas, shot in the head and killed. Taylor withdrew toward Fayetteville and reunited with Gregg's brigade, encamping along the road between that place and Warrenton for the night. After Taylor's and Gregg's retreat, Stuart waited until sufficient infantry had crossed the river before ordering Funsten and Gordon, who had come up to the front of the infantry column, to march toward Warrenton. Skirmishing continued into the night until the two brigades occupied the town.[61]

For most of Fitz Lee's Division, the day passed on the march. Crossing the Rappahannock at Fox's Ford, some of Lee's troopers bivouacked there while others trotted on toward Sulphur Springs, encamping for the night between that place and Warrenton.[62] However, for Rosser's Fifth Virginia left behind on Fleetwood Hill, the day had proved more interesting, thanks to Meade's decision to send Buford back over the Rappahannock.

Events transpired quickly at Meade's headquarters early on the 12th. At 9:50, a report came in, informing Meade that no Confederates appeared to be opposite the ford at Rappahannock Station and that some force of cavalry and a battery occupied Fleetwood Hill.[63] At 10:15, Meade sent for Maj. Gen. John Sedgwick, commander of the Sixth Corps, and by noon had given him orders to conduct a reconnaissance-in-force toward Brandy Station, taking his own corps, the Fifth Corps, and Buford's division, and to seize Fleetwood Hill. Any intention of the enemy to give battle there and Meade would back Sedgwick up with the rest of the army. If the enemy retreated, Sedgwick was to send Buford on alone toward Culpeper Court House to ascertain the force holding that place. By noon Buford was over the river and riding south toward Fleetwood.[64]

By 2:00, Buford's advance had driven in Rosser's outposts. After three or four rounds from Chew's lone gun, Rosser decided that the bluecoats meant business and began a gradual withdrawal toward Culpeper. He dispatched a courier to Col. Pierce M. B. Young whose brigade had been ordered to Culpeper by Stuart to ask for support and then halted about two miles west of Brandy Station to make a brief stand and gain time for Young to come up. Chew threw a few shells into the railroad cut at Buford's oncoming troopers who simply ignored them, knowing they far outnumbered their foe. Rosser fell back another two miles to near Culpeper and found Young's dismounted brigade and parts of Hart's and Moorman's batteries of horse artillery in position on the George house hill. Spread out over a mile in length with Lt. Col. Thomas J. Lipscomb's Second South Carolina on the right, Lt. Col. John D. Twiggs's First South Carolina in the center, and Lt. Col. Joseph F. Waring's Jeff Davis Legion on the left, Young prepared to aid Rosser and protect the valuable commissary and quartermaster stores in the town. Considering the strength of the opposition, their task looked formidable.[65]

Rosser's skirmishers passed through Young's thin line, which immediately delivered a volley along with the artillery. Recognizing that the Confederates had received reinforcements of unknown size, Buford unlimbered a battery and soon the thunder of guns echoed across the fields around Culpeper for the second day in a row. The skirmishing continued until dusk when Buford fell back to Brandy Station to camp for the night. Rosser and Young undoubtedly breathed a sigh of relief and did all they could to convince Buford that he had made a wise choice by lighting a large number of campfires and bringing up a band to play as if they had not a care in the world. The histrionics had little to do with Buford's decision to withdraw. With three corps at his back, Buford could have brushed the gray cavalry aside and taken Culpeper, doing untold damage to Lee's plans and perhaps ending the campaign right then and there. However, Meade's orders held sway and indeed, Buford had accomplished all that had been asked of him. He also took the time to collect a few wounded that had been left behind and overlooked or ignored by the Confederates and to bury a number of dead. Despite the success of the venture, the Federal stay south of the Rappahannock was brief.[66]

By 8:00 that night, Meade had received Sedgwick's report on what the reconnaissance-in-force had revealed about the enemy south of the Rappahannock. Not finding Lee where he was willing to fight him, Meade informed Gen. Halleck in Washington that Lee might slip around the Army of the Potomac and get between it and the capital. About 9:00, Meade received word from Gen. Gregg informing him of the fighting at Sulphur Springs. The confrontation persuaded Meade to escape before Lee could spring his trap. Fifteen minutes later, Meade ordered Sedgwick's force, including Buford, back across the Rappahannock. The cavalry roused itself from its short slumber at 1:30 in the morning and marched for the river, following the infantry. Over the next hour Meade scrambled to shift his army to meet the new threat to his right flank, sending the First Corps to Warrenton Junction; the Second Corps to Fayetteville; the Third Corps, then near Freeman's Ford, to turn and face toward Sulphur Springs and Warrenton; the Fifth Corps to Beverly Ford; and the Sixth Corps to Rappahannock Station. Kilpatrick's command, which had not been engaged all day due to its condition from the previous day's fighting, had moved back near Hartwood Church and Bealton Station where it guarded the army's wagon train and watched fords on the lower Rappahannock.[67] Neither the infantry nor the cavalry would stay where they were for very long.

Fifty minutes after midnight on the 13th Meade issued new marching orders. The First Corps was to leave Warrenton Junction and march five miles along the railroad toward Bristoe Station as soon as either the Fifth or Sixth Corps reached Warrenton Junction; the Second and Third Corps were to move to Three Mile Station on the Warrenton Branch Railroad, fronting on Warrenton; the Fifth and Sixth Corps were to take position at Warrenton Junction, looking toward Warrenton. Meade directed the cavalry to protect the flank of the army facing Lee and detail a sufficient guard for the army's supply train as it moved from Weaverton. The information obtained by Sedgwick and the Stuart/Gregg fight at Jeffersonton, allowed Meade to correctly deduce Lee's position and intention. Indeed, Lee planned to reunite his two corps at Warrenton. Stuart would place his regiments between Lee and Meade, which, as events unfolded, proved to be quite an unsafe location.[68]

At 10:00 in the morning Stuart received a message from Lee directing him to make a reconnaissance toward Catlett's Station. Stuart selected Lomax's Brigade for the mission, supporting him with Funsten's and Gordon's brigades. Lomax rode as far as Auburn. On discovering that the enemy occupied Warrenton Junction in force he halted to await Stuart's arrival with the other two brigades. Reaching Auburn, Stuart determined to continue on to Catlett's Station, leaving Lomax at Auburn to guard his rear. After dispatching a scouting party under his chief engineering officer, Capt. William W. Blackford, toward Three Mile Station, Stuart rode on to St. Stephen's Church. Just south of the church with a clear view toward Catlett's Station, he made two valuable discoveries. First, he realized that Meade was retreating to Manassas and second, a large portion of the Federal army's supply train stood in park between Warrenton Junction and Catlett's Station. Knowing that Lee would put such valuable information to immediate use, Stuart wrote a dispatch to Lee at 3:30 in the afternoon and selected Maj. Andrew R. Venable, the cavalry's inspector-general, to carry it back to Lee. The major galloped off toward Auburn. What he found changed Stuart's mission from one of reconnaissance to one of survival.[69]

Venable certainly expected to find Lomax at Auburn, but he didn't. Instead, he ran into infantry from Col. Charles H. T. Collis's First Brigade and Col. P. Regis De Trobriand's Third Brigade of Maj. Gen. David B. Birney's First Division of Maj. Gen. William H. French's Third Corps that had advanced along the road from Warrenton Junction to Auburn and had skirmished with Lomax for possession of the crossroads. Not even Fitz Lee's arrival with the other brigades of his division altered the fact that Auburn could not be held and sometime between 3:00 and 4:00, Fitz Lee pulled Lomax out of the unequal contest and withdrew toward Warrenton, effectively closing Stuart's escape route. Venable hurried off a courier to Stuart with the news of his discovery, detoured around Birney, and rode on to Lee, giving him the information Stuart had gathered and advising him of his cavalry chieftain's situation. Meanwhile, Venable's courier reached Stuart and as if to reinforce the shocking news the messenger brought, Capt. Blackford galloped in and reported to Stuart, confirming that the road to Auburn had fallen into enemy hands.[70]

Stuart now faced three choices. He could ignore his rear, bring up his seven guns, and attack the wagon park and nearby enemy troops; he could turn and try to slip by the blocking troops or fight his way through them; or he could conceal his force and wait until Lee, having hopefully received Stuart's dispatch, advanced the army and opened the road. Sometime after 9:00 in the evening, Stuart decided to move back to Auburn and see what awaited him there. In the growing darkness his advance began to skirmish with the enemy near the hamlet, convincing him that he had little choice but to conceal his command and wait the dawn. Selecting a wooded ravine to his right, Stuart dismounted his troopers, posted men with the wagon teams and artillery horses to keep them quiet, and settled down for a long, nerve-wracking, intensely cold night. Through the dark hours, six volunteers wormed their way through the Federal encampments, some so close that voices could be heard, in an effort to get word to Lee of Stuart's whereabouts.[71] All arrived safely. Not so for enemy couriers, as several fell into Stuart's hands, their dispatches informing him that the enemy knew nothing of the gray cavalry's location.[72]

Relieved that his position had not been discovered, Stuart waited through the night. Lee had ordered a portion of Ewell's Corps to Stuart's relief, but by dawn on the 14th the rescuers had yet to appear. Stuart knew nothing of this, but as the day brightened, slowly dispersing the dense fog that had aided the Confederates in their concealment, the welcome sound of gunfire broke the silence. Believing the fighting to be Lee coming to his rescue, Stuart ordered Maj. Robert F. Beckham, commander of the horse artillery, to wheel his seven guns - three from McGregor's Battery, two from Griffin's Battery, and two from Chew's Battery – into position atop a rise and to open fire. Beckham's barrage fell on Col. Nelson A. Miles's First Brigade of Col. Paul Frank's First Division of Maj. Gen. Gouverneur K. Warren's Second Corps, temporarily under the command of Brig. Gen. John C. Caldwell, and catching the infantrymen with their arms stacked and boiling their morning coffee. The One Hundred Twenty-fifth New York Infantry of Brig. Gen. Joshua T. Owen's Brigade, Third Division, Second Corps, in the act of crossing Flower Brook that powered Auburn's grist and saw mills, came under the same fire. Chaos engulfed the bluecoats, but only momentarily. Miles and Frank quickly rode among their men, rallying them and forming a battle line facing Catlett's Station. Caldwell soon had his own artillery blasting away and his troops maneuvering to get at his foe's flanks. The One Hundred and Twenty-sixth New York Infantry quickly joined its brother regiment, the One Hundred Twenty-fifth, threw out a line of skirmishers, and pushed forward toward the road. None of this escaped Stuart's attention. Nor did the fact that the firing he had interpreted as Lee coming to his rescue had died away.[73] The enemy's artillery soon compelled Stuart to withdraw his guns from the unequal contest, leaving only the dismounted cavalrymen to hold the line. About the same time, Gordon became aware of the danger to his left flank that extended across the road to Catlett's Station, Stuart's only escape route, and ordered Col. Thomas Ruffin with the First North Carolina to charge. Successful at first, the Tarheels soon faced numbers they could not oppose and retreated, leaving Ruffin mortally wounded and a prisoner. Gordon watched the regiment recoil and met Capt. William H. H. Cowles who had taken over command of the regiment after

Ruffin's fall and given the order to retreat when no support came up. Cowles galloped up to talk to Gordon in order to ascertain what to do next. As they discussed their options, a fragment of shell struck Gordon in the face. The errant missile only scratched his nose, however, and he ignored it thereafter.[74]

Ruffin's charge, though repulsed, achieved its objective, maintaining Stuart's exit route. Seizing the moment, Stuart sent his wagons and artillery across a hastily built bridge over the millrace and onto the road the Federals had used to reach Auburn. Gordon attended to the enemy before him, and Funsten's Brigade, dismounted and fighting as sharpshooters, formed the rear guard and was the last over the bridge. A number of enemy stragglers became prisoners. Stuart halted his column on the road over which the Federals had marched the previous evening and rode on to find Lee. Caldwell made no effort to pursue, having another problem to worry about in the form of advancing Confederate infantry from the direction of Warrenton. The belated distraction assured Stuart's escape from what could have been a disaster. The loss of two brigades, seven guns, and his cavalry chief probably would have brought Lee up short and certainly would have curtailed operations for the immediate future. As it turned out, Lee kept moving forward.[75]

While Stuart played at hide-and-seek, Fitz Lee's brigades had done little more on the 13th than what they had done on the 12th - march. Moving from their camps near Fox's Ford and Sulphur Springs, Fitz Lee led his troopers through Warrenton and down the road toward Catlett's Station where he encountered Lomax, scuffling with the enemy. Several regiments from Lomax's, Owen's, and Chambliss's brigades, dismounted, deployed in a wood, and skirmished with the Federals until the bluecoat infantry appeared and grape shot began to whistle overhead, causing the gray troopers to fall back toward Warrenton and encamp for the night. Fitz Lee sent a message to his uncle, Gen. R. E. Lee, admitting that he could go no further until the enemy left his front, which probably would not happen until morning.[76]

Young and Rosser, still keeping watch over the commissary and quartermaster stores at Culpeper, awoke on the 13th to find that Buford and his accompanying infantry had vanished during the night. A portion of Young's Brigade followed the railroad toward the river, capturing about 30 prisoners and confirming that the Northerners had actually abandoned their offensive. At sunset, Young led his regiments to Rixeyville and camped there for the night.[77]

The Federal cavalry accomplished a number of tasks on the 13th, none of which had to do with fighting their mounted foe. Encamped on the north side of the Rappahannock near Rappahannock Station, Buford spent most of the day resting his weary men, not having finished crossing the river until near daylight. Orders from Pleasonton had reached him sometime after 11:00 the previous night, instructing him to "cover the flank and rear of the trains of the army tomorrow on their march to Centreville by way of Brentsville." Hours passed as the trains moved on. Finally between 1:00 and 3:00 in the afternoon, Buford moved out and made his way to Warrenton Junction where he camped.[78] Buford's third brigade, Brig. Gen.

Wesley Merritt's, finally rejoined the army, having been sent for by Meade on the 10th. Merritt left his camp near Washington City on the morning of the 11th, reached Fairfax Court House on the 13th, and linked up with the army near Bristoe Station on the 14th.[79]

Gen. Gregg's weary division left its camp near Fayetteville on the morning of the 13th and marched in rear of the Second Corps toward Auburn, arriving there about 9:00 that night. Gregg camped in front of the Second Corps, picketing the roads on his left flank. He deployed the entire Tenth New York, Col. Gregg's brigade, on the road leading to Warrenton where he knew the enemy lay. Kilpatrick's division also spent the day marching. Davies started for Fayetteville early in the morning and relieved one of Gen. Gregg's brigades from outpost duty. Later in the day, he marched for Buckland Mills, reaching there about 11:00 at night. After throwing out pickets toward Warrenton, Greenwich, and Centreville his men encamped. Custer, guarding the army's right flank and rear, also shifted eastward. Col. Edward B. Sawyer of the First Vermont received orders at 3:00 on the morning of the 13th to have his regiment and the Fifth Michigan, also under his command, collected at Morrisville by daylight. As soon as his men assembled, he marched for Bealeton Station to link with the rest of the division. Custer then marched east and about 10:00 arrived near Gainesville and camped for the night.[80]

After Stuart escaped early on the 14th, he took Funsten's and Gordon's brigades and shifted to the right of the army, moving toward Bristoe Station. Unfortunately, complications arose. Skirmishers from Maj. Gen. Robert E. Rodes's Division of Ewell's Corps swung out from the division's line of march. A column of infantry followed them, forcing Stuart further to the right. The detour prevented Stuart from reaching Bristoe until after dark. How much his presence might have mitigated Hill's disastrous attack cannot be known. However, the skirmishers certainly prevented him from being where he thought he should have been.[81] Young's Brigade had spent the night of the 13th at Rixeyville, but in the morning Young received instructions directly from Robert E. Lee to proceed to Bealeton Station. Arriving there, the troopers rested until evening when another order put them on the march to rejoin Stuart near Bristoe Station.[82] Fitz Lee's brigades drew the army's left flank, marching through New Baltimore, Buckland, and Gainesville toward Bristoe Station, camping for the night near Langyher's Mill on Broad Run.[83]

Like the infantry, the Federal cavalry wound its way north over various routes, trying to guard the army's flanks and supply trains. Buford roused his regiments at 3:00 in the morning, but slow moving wagons delayed the cavalry's departure from Warrenton Junction until 9:30. Reaching Brentsville, Buford discovered parked wagons by the hundreds with no effort being made to move them. With the Southern horse nipping at his hooves, Buford tried persuading the few quartermasters he could find to get the train moving, but not a wagon budged until near dark, when the fighting at Bristoe Station could be seen. The wagons finally began to move at about 7:00.[84] Through the night they wound their way northward. After the firing at Bristoe died down, an unknown force attacked Buford's vedettes near Brentsville, but the Eighth Illinois, Chapman's brigade, helped drive them back and nothing more developed. The blue cavalry occupied the village through the night. Buford ordered his troopers to stand to horse, parts of the Sixth New York, Devin's brigade, and Eighth New York, Chapman's brigade, doing guard duty while the other regiments of the division lay in line of battle in the rain without fires, supper, or sleep. The last wagon crossed Broad Run about daylight.[85]

With the rumor of Stuart being within their lines filtering its way through the regiments of the Second Cavalry Division, Gen. Gregg's troopers had stood to horse through the night of the 13th. At 5:00 on the morning of the 14th, Confederate infantry began to press against the outposts of the Tenth New York, Col. Gregg's brigade, and those of Taylor's brigade. Maj. M. Henry Avery and the troopers of the Tenth battled against long odds. Capt. George Vanderbilt's squadron, forming the advance picket force, retired, delaying the enemy until Avery had time to form the remainder of the regiment. When Vanderbilt's line appeared 300 yards distant, Avery sent a second squadron to its support. The reinforcements managed to push the enemy back a short distance, but then had to retreat. To gain more time Avery launched Lt. Thomas W. Johnson with the Fifth Squadron in a saber charge that again halted the enemy's advance, although the gallant lieutenant fell wounded and was captured. Avery continued his retreat under the protection of Capt. Joseph W. Martin's battery, reaching Catlett's Station where he rejoined his brigade.[86]

While Avery skirmished with the gray infantry, Taylor's brigade, with the exception of one regiment, dismounted and formed a line along the crest of a ridge to hold the Confederates in check and prevent them from reaching the wagon trains. Gregg's brigade, minus the Tenth New York, left their coffee still boiling and formed behind Taylor in reserve, masked behind a hill. Martin's battery now added its support to Taylor, as did Lt. Horatio B. Reed's Battery A, Fourth U. S. Artillery. Once the wagons moved out of danger, Taylor and Gregg fell back over the Walnut Branch of Cedar Creek, the former taking position about a half a mile beyond while the latter continued on to Saint Stephen's Crossing. The Sixteenth Pennsylvania, Gregg's brigade, held the creek crossing long enough to allow Lt. Reed's guns and its brother regiments to withdraw, but in the fighting lost Lt. Col. John K. Robison, who was wounded. The enemy followed on the hoofs of the Sixteenth and took possession of the main road, nearly cutting off Lt. George Brown's section of Martin's battery, which withdrew through a heavy enemy fire that inflicted a number of casualties in the First Massachusetts, Taylor's brigade, acting as its support. Taylor could not hold his new line for long. The Confederates brought up a battery and opened on the brigade's right rear. The First Pennsylvania, acting as rearguard, took a pounding but, refusing to break, marched off in fine style and fell back toward Bristoe Station.[87]

Reaching Kettle Run, the sound of heavy infantry fighting could be heard coming from the direction of Bristoe Station. Just after Taylor's brigade, now in advance of Gregg's, crossed the bridge over the run, Confederate infantry opened fire from a dense thicket on the cavalry's left flank. The First Pennsylvania replied, holding its position until the rest of the brigade, with the exception of the rear guard under Maj. Hugh H. Janeway of the First New Jersey, passed the danger point. Taylor placed his brigade to the left and left rear of Brig. Gen. John C. Caldwell's infantry division, holding the left flank of the Federal line along the railroad. However, the Confederates sent a brigade across the railroad, cutting off Janeway. Taylor called on Capt. James H. Leeman, commanding a squadron of the Sixth Ohio, to charge through the enemy and inform Janeway of his situation. The bold move caught the confederates off guard and Leeman not only reached Janeway but also freed 15 prisoners from the Second Corps along the way, capturing their guard as well. Janeway had formed his skirmishers into a column of fours and prepared to attempt to cut his way through to the ford when Col. Gregg arrived and ordered him to follow his brigade across the railroad and form as skirmishers to the right of the Sixteenth Pennsylvania's skirmishers. Here Gregg fought until dark, protecting the Second Corps's hospital. When the fighting ceased, both brigades withdrew to Brentsville where they helped Buford protect the army's wagon train.[88]

Judson Kilpatrick's Third Division roused itself from its camps near Buckland Mills and Gainesville early on the 14th. As Davies's brigade prepared to move out toward Sudley Springs, a column of Confederate infantry appeared, forcing the Eighteenth Pennsylvania, acting as rear guard, into action. The fighting, which began about 10:00 in the morning, proved of short duration, and Davies moved through Gainesville toward Sudley Springs, although without Capt Enos J. Pennypacker of the Eighteenth who was captured.[89] Custer's troopers traveled the shorter distance, marching from near Gainesville in the direction of Sudley Springs. About 3:50 in the afternoon, Kilpatrick moved the division back toward Gainesville where he skirmished with an enemy column marching from Hay Market to Gainesville. Darkness brought an end to the fight and the two brigades camped between Groveton and Sudley Springs for the night.[90]

During this day, the actions of the cavalry from both armies pivoted around Bristoe Station where the infantry of the two armies clashed. Although Lee had hoped to strike at Meade while the Army of the Potomac's wagon trains and infantry hurried north to avoid being caught in a trap, the Confederate commander-in-chief did not want what happened at Bristoe Station. In his eagerness to deliver a crippling blow to the Federal army before it could escape, A. P. Hill bungled badly. In close pursuit of his foe, Hill marched along the road from Greenwich to Bristoe Station and came within sight of the station. Observing what he thought to be the Meade's Third Corps that in reality was part of the Fifth Corps, Hill promptly made preparations to attack it south of Broad Run. As the brigades of Maj. Gen. Henry Heth's Division formed their battle lines and advanced, Hill suddenly realized that more of the enemy lay to his right along the railroad. Hill ordered Maj. Gen. Richard H. Anderson to hurry forward two brigades to support Heth's right flank, but before Anderson's troops could get into position, Hill, fretting over the delays and fearful that his prey would escape, committed Heth to battle. The brigades of Brig. Gen. John R. Cooke and Brig. Gen. William W. Kirkland advanced toward Broad Run, unknowingly exposing their flanks to Maj. Gen. Gouverneur K. Warren's Second Corps lying hidden behind the railroad embankment. Cooke and Kirkland had no alternative but to swing around and try to dislodge Warren from his position. The effort was futile. The brigades were decimated. During the inevitable withdrawal, five guns of Maj. David G. McIntosh's battalion of artillery were captured. Although Lee would send his cavalry in pursuit of Meade, for all intents and purposes any chance he had of delivering a crushing blow to the Federal army died at Bristoe Station.[91]

Notes:

1.   *O.R.*, Series 1, vol. 29, part 2, 268; Chapman Diary; Cheney Diary; Ressler Diary; Hand, Jr., *One Good Regiment*, 80.

   According to Buford's report, the order was not received until 7:20 that night, a delay of over 12 hours.

2.   *O.R.*, Series 1, vol. 29, part 2, 269.

3.   *Ibid.*, 270 and part 1, 384 and 389.

   One of the regiments picketing the Griffinsburg to Woodville road was the First West Virginia. Wilkin Diary.

4.   *O.R.*, Series 1, vol. 29, part 2, 272-274.

5.   *Ibid.*, 276.

   Recognizing his need for every cavalryman available to him, at 12:20 in the afternoon of the 10th, Meade dispatched orders for Brig. Gen. Wesley Merritt, commanding the Reserve Brigade, consisting of the First, Second, and Fifth United States and the Sixth Pennsylvania Cavalry, then stationed near Washington, recruiting and refitting, to rejoin the army as quickly as possible. The troopers prepared to march and stood to horse by 5:00 on the evening of the 10th. However, specific orders did not reach Merritt until 7:00 on the morning of the 11th when the brigade moved out, passing through Washington, over Long Bridge, and camping for the night near Bailey's Crossroads. On the 13th, the brigade proceeded to Fairfax Court House and rejoined the army the following day near Bristoe Station. *Ibid.*, 353 and part 2, 283; Gracey, *Annals of the Sixth*, 198.

6.   *O.R.*, Series 1, vol. 29, part 1, 410 and 417; *Richmond Whig*, October 17, 1863.

7.   *O.R.*, Series 1, vol. 29, part 1, 457; *Richmond Whig*, October 17, 1863.

   Young commanded Brig. Gen. Matthew C. Butler's brigade, while Funsten led Brig. Gen. William E. Jones's brigade.

8.   Funsten did not have his entire force with him. White's Battalion, the Thirty-fifth Virginia Battalion, continued its operations in Loudoun County and a company of the Twelfth Virginia had been assigned scouting duties in Rappahannock County. Additionally, on the morning of the 10th, Stuart detached two squadrons from the Seventh Virginia and Twelfth Virginia for special duty, leaving them to guard the infantry. *Ibid.*, 455; Green Memoir; Arehart, "Diary of W. H. Arehart," 280.

9.   *O.R.*, Series 1, vol. 29, part 1, 455; Hartley, *Stuart's Tarheels*, 276.

10.   *O.R.*, Series 1, vol. 29, part 1, 439-440 and 460.

11.   *Ibid.*, 328, 440, 457-458, and 460; *Washington Daily Morning Chronicle*, October 17, 1863; *National Tribune*, February 11, 1892; Brooks, ed., *Stories*, 196.

   Col. William R. Brewster, commander of the Second Brigade, Second Division, Third Corps, who had been ordered to support Kilpatrick, had sent Lockwood forward.

12.   *O.R.*, Series 1, vol. 29, part 1, 328 and 440; *Richmond Daily Dispatch*, October 27, 1863; Daniel Branson Coltrane, *The Memoirs of Daniel Branson Coltrane: Co. I, 63rd Reg., N. C. Cavalry, C. S. A.*, (Raleigh, N. C.: Edwards & Broughton Company, 1956), 21.

   Gen. Prince did attempt to send aid to Lockwood by ordering forward Lt. Col. Waldo Merriman with the Sixteenth Massachusetts Infantry. The regiment had covered scarcely a mile when word arrived that Lockwood had been routed. *O.R.*, Series 1, vol. 29, part 1, 319.

13.   *O.R.*, Series 1, vol. 29, part 1, 319 and 440; Trout, ed., *Memoirs*, 223; Trout, *Galloping Thunder*, 366.

14. J. E. B. Stuart to General [R. E. Lee], October 10, 1863, Charles Scott Venable Papers, 1862-1894, SHC/UNC.

15. *O.R.*, Series 1, vol. 29, part 1, 389; *Philadelphia Weekly Times*, June 7, 1879; *Philadelphia Weekly Times*, October 10, 1885; John Esten Cooke, *Wearing of the Gray* (New York: E. B. Treat and Company, 1867. Reprint, Millwood, New York: Kraus Reprint Co., 1977), 255.

16. *O.R.*, Series 1, vol. 29, part 1, 440 and 458; Trout, ed., *Memoirs*, 223; *Philadelphia Weekly Times*, June 7, 1879.
      Stuart placed the number of skirmishers behind the wall at 150. The number used here comes from Young's report as it seems more accurate, considering the size of the regiments at this time.

17. The Confederates failed to capture the signal station but succeeded in driving off the men who took their equipment with them. *New York Tribune*, October 12, 1863.

18. *O.R.*, Series 1, vol. 29, part 1, 347-348 and 465-466; Chapman Diary; Cheney Diary; Driver, *Maryland Cavalry*, 63; Driver, *5th Virginia Cavalry*, 62.
      Buford captured a total of 65 prisoners. *O.R.*, Series 1, vol. 29, part 2, 280.

19. *O.R.*, Series 1, vol. 29, part 1, 471; Steele Diary; Carter Diary.
      Wickham had been seriously injured on October 1 during the march to relocate his brigade's camp. The brigade will be referenced as Owen's Brigade until the return of Wickham to command.

20. Beale, *9th Virginia Cavalry*, 100; *Richmond Daily Dispatch*, October 27, 1863.

21. *O.R.*, Series 1, vol. 29, part 1, 360; Albinus R. Fell to Diana, October 10, 1863, Albinus R. Fell Letters, CWMC, USAMHI; Denison, *Sabres and Spurs*, 292; Pyne, *First New Jersey Cavalry*, 173; Edward G. Longacre, *Jersey Cavaliers: A History of the First New Jersey Cavalry, 1861-1865* (Hightstown: Longstreet House, 1992), 172.
      The First New Jersey had been sent on a reconnaissance to the Northern Neck of Virginia and marched 25 miles before couriers reached them with orders to return. The regiment would rendezvous with the brigade at 2:00 on the morning of the 11th.
      The Sixth Ohio was still north of the Rappahannock at Crittenden's Mills southeast of Morrisville, having just been relieved of picket duty near Warrenton Junction.
      One source stated that Taylor assumed command of McIntosh's brigade on October 8, but he probably had been leading the brigade since the 1st when McIntosh left. The brigade will be referenced as Taylor's Brigade for the remainder of this work as McIntosh did not return to the Army of the Potomac until May 1864. Lloyd, *History of the First Regiment Pennsylvania Reserve Cavalry*, 138-139; HDSACWRD at, <www.civilwardata.com> August 5, 2009.

22. *O.R.*, Series 1, vol. 29, part 1, 365 and 369, and part 2, 286; Alonzo J. Sawyer Diary, CWMC, USAMHI; Ressler Diary; Tobie, *First Maine Cavalry*, 192-193; Hyndman, *History of a Cavalry Company*, 123.
      Some confusion exists as to the role of the Tenth New York in the early part of this campaign. On the 9th the regiment, commanded by Maj. M. Henry Avery, picketed the Rappahannock River from Freeman's Ford to Sulphur Springs. Receiving orders at his headquarters at Liberty to concentrate with the other regiments of the brigade at Bealton Station, Avery could not pull in his vedettes quickly enough to move out that night. He reached the station the next morning, found the brigade had already departed, and finally joined Gregg at Culpeper, arriving at 4:00 in the afternoon. If Avery's report is accurate then Gregg did not advance to Fox Mountain until after 4:00. However, Col. Gregg stated that he left Culpeper immediately after receiving orders to support Kilpatrick at 11:00 on the morning of the 10th and en-

camped at Fox Mountain for the night. Avery made no mention of going on to Fox Mountain but reported that he camped at Culpeper on the night of the 10th. Gen. Gregg recorded that the brigade was encamped at Culpeper on the morning of the 11th, meaning that was where it had camped for the night.

Obviously, the brigade could not be camped both at Fox Mountain and Culpeper on the night of the 10th unless it was divided and the records do not indicate that. Col. Gregg's report and accounts from the Fourth Pennsylvania, the Eighth Pennsylvania, and the First Maine all state that these regiments encamped at Fox Mountain on the night of the 10th while Gen. Gregg's and Maj. Avery's reports claim that the brigade encamped at Culpeper that night. The historian for the Sixteenth Pennsylvania recorded that his regiment camped at Fox Mountain on the night of the 9th, but this appears to be a dating error. With the information available, it is at present impossible to place the location of Tenth New York for the night of the 10th. *O.R.*, Series 1, vol. 29, part 1, 356, 365, and 369, and part 2, 286; Tobie, *First Maine Cavalry*, 192-193; Hyndman, *History of a Cavalry Company*, 123; Miller, *Sixteenth Pennsylvania Cavalry*, 40.

In his diary, Pvt. John Dollar of the Eighth Pennsylvania of Col. Gregg's brigade claimed that his regiment fought at James City with Kilpatrick. John Dollar Diary, HCWRTC, USAMHI.

23. *O.R.*, Series 1, vol. 29, part 2, 286-287.

Sulphur Springs was also known as Warrenton Springs and White Sulphur Springs.

24. *Ibid.*, part 1, 410.

25. *Ibid.*, part 1, 356, 361, and 365; Richard N. Griffin, ed., *Three Years a Soldier: The Diary and Newspaper Correspondence of Private George Perkins, Sixth New York Independent Battery 1861-1864* (Knoxville: University of Tennessee Press, 2006), 141; Ressler Diary; Sawyer Diary; Denison, *Sabres and Spurs*, 292; Pyne, *First New Jersey Cavalry*, 173-174; Lloyd, *History of the First Regiment Pennsylvania Reserve Cavalry*, 74; Hyndman, *History of a Cavalry Company*, 123-124; Miller, *Sixteenth Pennsylvania Cavalry*, 40; Tobie, *First Maine Cavalry*, 193; *New York Times*, October 21, 1863.

In his report, Gen. Gregg stated that the Second Brigade left Culpeper to ride to Rixeyville, while Col. Gregg recorded the brigade marched from Fox Mountain to Sulphur Springs. In his history of the First Maine, Edward P. Tobie provides an explanation for this apparent dilemma. He wrote that the brigade did indeed camp at Fox Mountain just after dark on the 10th and awoke at 3:00 on the morning of the 11th to ride to Culpeper Court House. From there it proceeded to Sulphur Springs.

The Third Pennsylvania from Col. Gregg's brigade remained on guard along the railroad near Catlett's Station as did the Thirteenth Pennsylvania from Taylor's brigade. Rawle, *Third Pennsylvania Cavalry*, 336.

26. J. E. B. Stuart to General [R. E. Lee], October 11, 1863, Charles Scott Venable Papers, 1862-1894, SHC/UNC.

27. *O.R.*, Series 1, vol. 29, part 1, 381, 385, 390, and 393; Klement, ed., "Edwin B. Bigelow," 231.

28. *O.R.*, Series 1, vol. 29, part 1, 338-339 and 441; George Baylor, *Bull Run to Bull Run or Four Years in the Army of Northern Virginia* (Richmond: B. F. Johnson Publishing Company, 1900. Reprint, Washington, D. C.: Zenger Publishing Co., Inc., 1983), 163-164; John Esten Cooke, *Mohun or The Last Days of Lee and His Paladins* (New York: F. J. Huntington and Company, 1869. Reprint, Charlottesville: Historical Publishing Co., Inc., 1936), 77-78; *Philadelphia Weekly Times*, October 10, 1885; *National Tribune*, June 16,

1892; *HDSACWRD* at, <www.civilwardata.com> October 27, 2009.

Once again various views of this incident exist. MacDonald's report asserts that he lost 3 killed, 10 wounded, and 25 missing. He stated that he inflicted three times the killed and wounded on the enemy than his command suffered. However, both Stuart and Baylor claimed that not a man or horse was lost in the charge. The casualty records for the Twelfth Virginia appear to verify this. *National Tribune*, June 16, 1892; *HD-SACWRD* at, <www.civilwardata.com> April 25, 2009 and October 27, 2009.

29. That Pleasonton was with Kilpatrick at Brandy Station can be confirmed, but he had to have been with Kilpatrick before that and probably had his headquarters at Culpeper. *Philadelphia Inquirer*, October 15, 1863.

30. *O.R.*, Series 1, vol. 29, part 1, 381, 385, and 441; Boudrye, *Fifth New York Cavalry*, 79.

31. *O.R.*, Series 1, vol. 29, part 1, 385.

32. Stuart, Gordon, and McClellan stated that Ferebee of the Fourth North Carolina suffered a wound in his foot during this attack. Other sources give the date as October 13 or the place as Bristoe Station. However, the Fourth was not engaged on the 13th, spending the day marching and eventually being trapped at Auburn, and was nowhere near Bristoe Station. *Ibid.*, 441 and 460; Manarin, *North Carolina Troops*, 266; Krick, *Lee's Colonels*, 137; Colonel W. P. Shaw, "Fifty-Ninth Regiment (Fourth Cavalry)," *Histories of the Several Regiments and Battalions from North Carolina in the Civil War 1861-65*, 3, edited by Walter Clark, (Goldsboro: Nash Brothers Book and Job Printers, 1901. Reprint, Wendell, North Carolina: Broadfoot's Bookmark, 1982), 465; *Philadelphia Weekly Times*, June 7, 1879; *Western Democrat*, November 10, 1863.

33. *O.R.*, Series 1, vol. 29, part 1, 393 and 441.

34. *Ibid.*, 348; Chapman Diary; Cheney Diary.

According to one source, Meade sent two orderlies to Buford with new orders. Neither got through and both were presumed captured. *Philadelphia Inquirer*, October 14, 1863.

35. *O.R.*, Series 1, vol. 29, part 1, 415.

Johnston's Brigade was part of Maj. Gen. Robert E. Rodes's Division of Lt. Gen. Richard S. Ewell's Corps.

36. *Ibid.*, 415, 463, and 465; Neese, *Three Years in the Confederate Horse Artillery*, 217; Bradshaw, *Diary...McVicar*, 27-28; Trout, *Galloping Thunder*, 721n37; Hall, *Sixth New York Cavalry*, 160; Cheney, *Ninth Regiment, New York Volunteer Cavalry*, 136.

At some point during the fighting Lomax had his horse killed under him. *Richmond Daily Dispatch*, October 16, 1863.

37. *O.R.*, Series 1, vol. 29, part 1, 348, 415, 463, and 471; Blackwell, *12th Illinois Cavalry*, 124; Francis Halsey Wigfall to Louis T. Wigfall, October 23, 1863, Wigfall Family Papers, MMC-3183, Manuscript Division, LC.

Garrett's infantry was composed of the Fifth North Carolina under Lt. Col. John W. Lea, the Twenty-third North Carolina under Capt. Frank Bennett, and five companies of the Twelfth North Carolina led by Lt. Col. William S. Davis.

One source stated that a ditch impassible to mounted troops caused the recall. Grimsley, *Battles in Culpeper County*, 20.

38. *O.R.*, Series 1, vol. 29, part 1, 348 and 471; Blackwell, *12th Illinois Cavalry*, 124; Hard, *Eighth Illinois Cavalry*, 278; *Richmond Sentinel*, October 19, 1863; *Richmond Dispatch*, November 2, 1902.

In Cooke's *Dispatch* account he incorrectly dated the action as having occurred on November 11, 1863. He further recorded that he had several freshly killed hares attached to his saddle that he did not have time to remove. Owen used his horse throughout the remainder of the day, during which the hares came loose and were lost. Almost 40 years later, Cooke still bemoaned his lost rations.

39. *O.R.*, Series 1, vol. 29, part 1, 348, 416, 463, 465, 471, and 474; *Richmond Daily Dispatch*, October 21, 1863; Grimsley, *Battles in Culpeper County*, 20; Carter Diary; Bradshaw, *Diary...McVicar*, 28-29; "The Second Virginia Cavalry in the War, 1861-1865," Irving P. Whitehead Papers, Alderman Library, University of Virginia.

40. *O.R.*, Series 1, vol. 29, part 1, 442-443.

41. *Ibid.*, 390, 443, and 460; Means, "Additional Sketch Sixty-third Regiment (Fifth Cavalry)," 576; Hartley, *Stuart's Tarheels*, 280.

 The exact time this incident occurred is uncertain. McClellan clearly stated that the North Carolinians' attack occurred simultaneously with the charge of the Twelfth Virginia on a different target. Means claimed that after the charge the First North Carolina found itself ahead of Custer's column. Stuart reported that the two charges were separate attacks, the one occurring at the Bradford house and the other near the Botts house. Gordon reported that he ordered the charge on the enemy's rear guard, while Funsten reported that the Twelfth Virginia was at the front of the column. The two attacks could not have been coordinated, though the possibility exists that they occurred simultaneously by accident. McClellan, *I Rode with Jeb Stuart*, 380; *Philadelphia Weekly Times*, June 7, 1879; *O.R.*, Series 1, vol. 29, part 1, 443, 455 and 460.

 The regiment receiving the Tarheels' charge appears to have been the Seventh Michigan under Col. William D. Mann. *O.R.*, Series 1, vol. 29, part 1, 390.

42. *O.R.*, Series 1, vol. 29, part 1, 348-349 and 381.

43. *Ibid.*, 465, 468, and 469; Donahue Diary.

44. *O.R.*, Series 1, vol. 29, part 1, 386, 390, 394, 443, 455, and 460; Means, "Additional Sketch Sixty-third Regiment (Fifth Cavalry)," 576; Hartley, *Stuart's Tarheels*, 281-282; Coltrane *Memoirs*, 22; McDonald, *History of the Laurel Brigade*, 182-183; Rodenbough, *Eighteenth Regiment of Pennsylvania Cavalry*, 44; Andrew N. Buck to Brother and Sister, October 12, 1863, Buck Family Papers, Microfilm mf 309-311 c, BHL/UM; Dexter M. Macomber Diary, Clarke Manuscripts, Clarke Historical Library, Central Michigan University (hereafter cited as CHS/CMU); *Philadelphia Weekly Times*, June 7, 1879; *Detroit Advertiser and Tribune*, October 27, 1863.

45. *O.R.*, Series 1, vol. 29, part 1, 465 and 471; Carter Diary; Hall, *Sixth New York Cavalry*, 161; Cheney, *Ninth Regiment, New York Volunteer Cavalry*, 136; *Philadelphia Weekly Times*, February 7, 1880.

46. *O.R.*, Series 1, vol. 29, part 1, 465 and 468; Donahue Diary; Neese, *Three Years in the Confederate Horse Artillery*, 217.

47. *O.R.*, Series 1, vol. 29, part 1, 349; 463, 465, 467, 468, and 469; Donahue Diary; Allyne C. Litchfield to My Dear Wife, October 12, 1863, Allyne Cushing Litchfield Papers, James S. Schoff Civil War Collection, Manuscripts Division, WLC/UM; *Richmond Daily Examiner*, October 14, 1863.

48. *O.R.*, Series 1, vol. 29, part 1, 386 and 394; *National Tribune*, February 11, 1892 and November 3, 1892.

 Frederic C. Newhall claimed that Pleasonton ordered that no charge be made because of the ditch. According to this account, the Federal cavalry walked up to the ditch and the Confederate cavalry on the other side simply withdrew without offering the slightest resistance. How Pleasonton knew the ditch was there and why Kilpatrick, Custer, and numerous regimental commanders reported participating in several charges were not explained. *Philadelphia Weekly Times*, August 30, 1879

49. *O.R.*, Series 1, vol. 29, part 1, 474.

50. John O. Collins Letter, October 14, 1863, John Overton Collins Papers (Mss1C6944a), VHS; War Record of Doctor James McClure Scott, Sarah Travers Lewis (Scott) Papers, Mss7:1SCO845:1, VHS.

51. *O.R.*, Series 1, vol. 29, part 1, 381 and 444; Neese, *Three Years in the Confederate Horse Artillery*, 220; Bradshaw, *Diary...McVicar*, 29; Trout, *The Hoss*, 56.

52. *O.R.*, Series 1, vol. 29, part 1, 349, 444, 456, 458, 469, and 474; Arehart, "Diary of W. H. Arehart," 280; Hartley, *Stuart's Tarheels*, 282; Neese, *Three Years in the Confederate Horse Artillery*, 221.

     Casualties for the day's fighting are difficult to calculate. No two sources agree. The fact that not all units included specific daily losses in their reports, preferring to provide casualty statistics for the entire campaign, does not help. For example, Federal losses on the 11th ranged between 70 and 225 killed, wounded, captured, or missing, depending on the source. Allowing for unreported casualties, it would appear that Buford and Kilpatrick lost somewhere around 250 men. Stuart reported handing in to the provost marshal 565 prisoners on the 11th, not all of which were cavalry. Confederate losses are equally hard to compute with a low of 75 and a high of about 210 killed, wounded, captured, or missing. The first number is unreasonable and the last figure also seems too low due to a number of regiments not reporting. The Confederate losses were probably closer to, and more than likley over, 300. *O.R.*, Series 1, vol. 29, part 1, 376, 389, 395, 453, 456, 460, 469, 474, *Washington Evening Star*, October 12, 1863; *Milwaukee Daily Sentinel*, October, 20, 1863; *Richmond Enquirer*, October 13, 1863; *Daily Richmond Examiner*, October 19, 1863; HDSACWRD at, <www.civilwardata.com> May 30-June 6, 2011; and information supplied by Bryce Suderow.

     Lt. Col. John Shac Green of the Sixth Virginia reported that his regiment camped for the night near Beverly Ford. *O.R.*, Series 1, vol. 29, part 1, 468.

     Part of Chambliss's Brigade may have been camped near Welford's Ford as one source stated that the third squadron of the Ninth Virginia picketed just below the Welford house that night. Edwards Diary.

     According to one source, Company E of the Twelfth Virginia guarded Starke's Ford further up the Hazel River. Green Article, *Warren Sentinel*.

     Capt. Obadiah J. Downing of the Second New York with the 50 skirmishers under his command became cut off during the fighting and could not rejoin the regiment in time to cross the Rappahannock at Kelly's or Ellis' fords. He kept his head, concealed his men overnight, led them over the river at Richard's Ford the next day, and reunited with his regiment. He did not lose a man. *O.R.*, Series 1, vol. 29, part 1, 388.

53. F. C. Newhall, who was a captain on Pleasonton's staff at the time of the battle, made this point in an article printed in the August 30, 1879, issue of the *Philadelphia Weekly Times*.

54. In addition to sending his couriers out, Stuart ordered his provost marshal, Lt. Garland M. Ryals, to arrest John Minor Botts, stating in the order that Ryals should "send him to Richmond," and that "charges will be forwarded from these headquarters as soon as practical." Ryals was admonished not to allow Botts to "annoy General Lee, but keep him as a prisoner of State."

     Ryals took Botts to Culpeper Court House and detained him there from 10:00 in the morning to 5:00 at night when Botts was released, no charges having been made against him.

The arrest infuriated Botts who wrote a letter that ended up in Northern newspapers though it was purportedly written to the *Richmond Daily Examiner*. This paper eventually published excerpts from the letter taken from the Northern newspapers. Botts insisted that he had been arrested without charge and that officers of the high command had turned the army against him and allowed his property to be destroyed. He cited the destruction of his garden, yard, cornfields, fencing, and 30 hogs. He inquired "if such power can be exercised by General Stuart with impunity – with whom and where does the power stop? To how low a grade of military authority does it descend?" Botts hinted at what may have instigated the arrest, stating that while General Meade had not eaten at his home, he had invited him to do so and would do so again if the opportunity arose, "without consulting Stuart on the subject."

Whether the invitation caused the arrest is unknown, as Stuart does not appear to have commented on it at any later time. A Northern newspaper claimed it occurred because Botts violated his parole of neutrality. Botts had been arrested in Richmond sometime before March 22, 1862, and held for several weeks until a court of inquiry was convened in April. On the 25th of that month, a general order released him under a parole of honor to a location in the interior of his own choosing, with the consent of The War Department. The parole restricted his travel to a five-mile radius from where he chose to live and ordered him to refrain from expressing opinions that were damaging or detrimental to the Confederate government. Having this previous arrest on his records made him a target whenever Confederate forces visited the area. Stuart's arrest of Botts may have been a reminder that neither the government nor the army had forgotten his earlier "indiscretion."

    O.R., Series 2, vol. 2, 1545-1547; *Richmond Daily Examiner,* December 1, 1863; *New York Times*, November 1, 1863.

55.   *O.R.*, Series 1, vol. 29, part 1, 410, 444, 446, 456, 458, 460, and 463.

    Stuart believed that even if the Federals crossed the Rappahannock and moved toward Culpeper, Lee's march north would soon force them to abandon their purpose. For this reason, he chose to leave only a token force to hold Fleetwood Hill.

56.   The advance of Lee's infantry along the Rixeyville road cut off the First Maine. Its subsequent adventures deserve some attention.

    Col. Smith led the regiment through Gaines' Cross Roads without opposition, though a few guerillas hovered about the column. Leaving Capt. Paul Chadbourne at the crossroads, Smith trotted on to Little Washington, stationing a second company along the road between that place and the crossroads. He then selected 100 troopers riding the best horses and dispatched them toward Sperryville under the command of Lt. Col. Stephen Boothby and Maj. George M. Brown. Smith also sent Lt. William Harris and 12 men back to Gregg with the information obtained thus far.

    Boothby and Brown returned near sunset with nothing to report. Smith then retraced his hoofprints to Gaines' Cross Roads where he sent Capt. Chadbourne and his well-rested company ahead to report the latest findings to Gregg. Smith intended to camp at Amissville for the night but on approaching the village discovered that A. P. Hill's Corps blocked his route. He found a young black boy of 14 willing to guide him through the woods and across the fields, sometimes over hogpaths, toward Orlean. However, the boy could only take him part way and Smith had to secured another guide to take him to Orlean and on to Waterloo, which also had to be bypassed because of the presence of the enemy.

    Beyond Waterloo, and acting on the belief that a part of the Federal army was at Warrenton, Smith openly rode down the pike. Nearing the town, the column's advance encountered a cavalry camp to one side of the road and halted to determine what should next be done. Without informing his commander, Maj. Sidney W. Thaxter rode into the camp and called out, demanding to know the identity of the regiment. A reply of "the Twelfth" failed to satisfy the major who inquired further, asking to know which "Twelfth" it was. No sooner had the answer of "the Twelfth Virginia" been given than Thaxter vacated the camp and reported to a stunned Smith.

Ordering a fence along the roadside torn down, Smith led his troopers cross country in the dead of night, marching by star-light until he came to a large plantation where he secured another guide who took the wayward regiment to New Baltimore. Arriving there, the men of the First Maine turned in the direction of Gainesville and out of immediate danger. Along the way, Smith paused for an hour to rest his men and horses at which time he dispatched Maj. Brown with orders to find Meade or Gregg or someone in authority and make a report. The information proved of great value to Meade who had not known of the location of Lee's infantry for two days. Smith eventually rejoined his brigade on the morning of the 16th. Tobie, *First Maine Cavalry*, 193-199; Sawyer Diary.

It should be noted that one source stated that 180 men of the First Maryland (Union) accompanied the First Maine. This could not be confirmed from any other source. *New York Times*, October 21, 1863.

57. *O.R.*, Series 1, vol. 29, part 1, 356, 365, 445 and 456; McDonald, *History of the Laurel Brigade*, 185; Michael Dougherty, *Prison Diary of Michael Dougherty, Late Co. B. 13thPa., Cavalry* (Bristol, Pa.: Charles A. Dougherty, Printer, 1908), 1; Hand, Jr., *One Good Regiment*, 82-83; Hyndman, *History of a Cavalry Company*, 124-125; *Washington Daily Morning Chronicle*, October 17, 1863.

58. *O.R.*, Series 1, vol. 29, part 1, 365, 370-372, and 456; Dollar Diary; Baylor, *Bull Run to Bull Run*, 167-168; McDonald, *History of the Laurel Brigade*, 186-187; Dougherty, *Prison Diary*, 1; Hyndman, *History of a Cavalry Company*, 125-127; Green Memoir; *Washington Daily Morning Chronicle*, October 17, 1863.

The extent of the disaster can be determined from the loss of 127 men in the two regiments, according to one Northern source, 300, according to another, or 500 from a third. The Confederates reported capturing between 425 and 450 prisoners. Either way the losses were significant. *O.R.*, Series 1, vol. 29, part 1, 456; Green Memoir; Dougherty, *Prison Diary*, 1; Hyndman, *History of a Cavalry Company*, 126.

Both Hyndman and Dougherty were captured. The former suffered a wound, being shot in the right ear, the ball coming out in the back of the head. The latter was awarded the Medal of Honor for his heroic actions in driving the enemy from a building and holding it for several hours. Hand, Jr., *One Good Regiment*, 81 and 84; Beyer and Keydel, eds., *Deeds of Valor*, 553.

59. *O.R.*, Series 1, vol. 29, part 1, 365, 368, 370, 372, and 456; Ressler Diary; Dollar Diary; Brooks, ed., *Stories*, 200; Baylor, *Bull Run to Bull Run*, 169; *New York World*, October 15, 1863; *Richmond Sentinel*, October 27, 1863.

60. Gen. Gregg reported that two regiments were sent forward, but Col. Taylor mentioned only the First New Jersey. *O.R.*, Series 1, vol. 29, part 1, 357 and 361.

61. *Ibid.*, 357, 361, 446, 457, and 460; Pyne, *First New Jersey Cavalry*, 176-183; Longacre, *Jersey Cavaliers*, 173-175.

Stuart lost 33 killed or wounded. Gregg suffered a loss of 20 killed, 126 wounded, and 400 missing or captured. *O.R.*, Series 1, vol. 29, part 1, 457; Dyer, Frederick H., *A*

Compendium of the War of the Rebellion, (Des Moines, Iowa: The Dyer Publishing Company, 1908), 924.

Janeway's troopers entered the contest with scarcely three carbine rounds per man due to their ammunition becoming unserviceable from the recent rains. Considering the odds they faced, this fact makes their performance quite remarkable.

On the morning of the 12th, the First Massachusetts bid farewell to its colonel, Horace B. Sargent, who was transferred to the army of Maj. Gen. Nathaniel P. Banks. Crowninshield, *First Regiment of Massachusetts Cavalry Volunteers*, 179.

62.   *O.R.*, Series 1, vol. 29, part 1, 463, 468, and 472.

The division appears to have been spread out from south of Warrenton, past Sulphur Springs, to near Fox's Ford.

63.   *Ibid.*, part 2, 295.

64.   *Ibid.*, 296-297, and part 1, 349; Chapman Diary; Cheney Diary; Frank Diary.

The Second Corps was to march to Rappahannock Station, cross behind the Sixth, but remain massed near the river.

65.   *O.R.*, Series 1, vol. 29, part 1, 349, 446, and 458-459; J. E. B. Stuart to General [R. E. Lee], October 12, 1863, Charles Scott Venable Papers, 1862-1894, SHC/UNC; Neese, *Three Years in the Confederate Horse Artillery*, 221-223; Brooks, ed., *Stories*, 201; Trout, ed., *Memoirs*, 69-70 and 223; *Philadelphia Weekly Times*, June 7, 1879.

66.   *O.R.*, Series 1, vol. 29, part 1, 349, 446, and 458-459; Neese, *Three Years in the Confederate Horse Artillery*, 221-223; Brooks, ed., *Stories*, 201; Cheney Diary; Hard, *Eighth Illinois Cavalry*, 279; Pickerill, *Third Indiana Cavalry*, 98; *Philadelphia Weekly Times*, June 7, 1879.

67.   *O.R.*, Series 1, vol. 29, part 2, 292-294, 298-300, and part 2, 386 and 391; Hall, *Sixth New York Cavalry*, 162; Klement, ed., "Edwin B. Bigelow," 231; *Washington Daily Morning Chronicle*, October 13, 1863; Macomber Diary.

At 9:30 Meade sent a dispatch to Maj. Gen. Gouverneur Warren ordering him to move his command to Warrenton Junction, fronting on Warrenton. Then at 10:15 he ordered Warren to Fayetteville, fronting Sulphur Springs.

One source stated that Kilpatrick had been sent to watch the lower Rappahannock fords because a large force of the enemy was rumored to have crossed the river at Falmouth. *Washington Daily Morning Chronicle*, October 13, 1863.

68.   *O.R.*, Series 1, vol. 29, part 1, 410 and 447, and part 2, 302-303.

69.   *Ibid.*, part 1, 447; J. E. B. Stuart to General [R. E. Lee], October 13, 1863, Charles Scott Venable Papers, 1862-1894, SHC/UNC.

Stuart misnamed the church in his report as Saint Andrew's Church, but it was in fact St. Stephen's. Carl R. Schmal, "Enemy Back of You! J. E. B. Stuart's Close Call at Aunurn in October 1863," *Fauquier*, vol. 8, no. 1, (Spring1995): 39.

70.   *O.R.*, Series 1, vol. 29, part 1, 311-312, 447, 463, and 466.

71.   The names of these intrepid men were: Pvt. Robert W. Goode, Company G, First Virginia Cavalry, one of Stuart's couriers; Pvt. H. Hillery "Crockett" Eddins, Company B, Twelfth Virginia Cavalry; Pvt. Richard C. Baylor, Company B, Twelfth Virginia Cavalry; Sgt. Ashton M. Chichester, McGregor's Battery, Stuart Horse Artillery; and Sgt. C. P. Shurley, McGregor's Battery, Stuart Horse Artillery. Stuart stated that six men performed the feat but gave the names of only five. *O.R.*, Series 1, vol. 29, part 1, 453; Dennis E. Frye, *12th Virginia* Cavalry (Lynchburg: H. E. Howard, Inc., 1988), 108 and 124; Driver, *1st Virginia Cavalry*, 178; Trout, *The Hoss*, 132 and140.

72.   *O.R.*, Series 1, vol. 29, part 1, 447-448; Cadwallader Jones Iredell to unknown ad-

dressee, October 23, 1863, Cadwallader Jones Iredell Papers, 363-Z, Folder 1, Correspondence 1862-1863, SHC/UNC.

73.   According to one source, shots from Stuart's guns landed among Ewell's advance troops who retreated. McClellan, *I Rode with Jeb Stuart*, 393.

74.   *O.R.*, Series 1, vol. 29, part 1, 253-254, 256, 258-265, 267-276, 299-300, 303-304, 448, 461; Ezra D. Simons, *A Regimental History: The One Hundred and Twenty-fifth New York State Volunteers*, (New York: Ezra D. Simons, Publisher, 1888), 157-158; Baylor, *Bull Run to Bull Run*, 173; Schmahl, "Enemy Back of You!" 41-42; Freeman, *Lee's Lieutenants*, 258; Cheek, "Additional Sketch Ninth Regiment," 456; Coltrane, *Memoirs*, 24-25; Trout, *Galloping Thunder*, 374 and 772 n54; *New York Herald*, October 16, 1863.

75.   *O.R.*, Series 1, vol. 29, part 1, 254, 448; McClellan, *I Rode with Jeb Stuart*, 392; Freeman, *Lee's Lieutenants*, 259.
       Apparently, Lomax's account of what had occurred once Stuart had ridden on to St. Stephen's Church satisfied the cavalry chief. In his own report of the incident his reference concerning what Lomax had encountered signified that his subordinate had done all that could have been expected of him until Fitz Lee had ordered his withdrawal. *O.R.*, Series 1, vol. 29, part 1, 448 and 466.

76.   *O.R.*, Series 1, vol. 29, part 1, 463, 467-468, 470, 472, and 475; Steele Diary; Trussell Diary; Donahue Diary; Carter Diary; Fitzhugh Lee to General R. E. Lee, October 13, 1863, Charles Scott Venable Papers, 1862-1894, SHC/UNC.

77.   *O.R.*, Series 1, vol. 29, part 1, 459.
       The location of Rosser's Fifth Virginia is somewhat puzzling. Pvt. Robert B. Jones wrote a letter to his wife on the 13th, recording that he was at Culpeper Court House. He mentioned that he wrote hurriedly, a possible indication that the regiment would soon me moving. George M. Neese's section of Chew's Battery had moved to Rixeyville on the night of the 12th after Buford withdrew to Brandy Station. This appears to have been executed independent of any cavalry accompanying the section, even though it had been attached to Rosser. Considering these facts and the actions of Young's Brigade, Rosser probably accompanied Young's Brigade on its march to Rixeyville on evening of the 13th. Robert Brooke Jones to My Dear Wife, October 13, 1863, Jones Family Papers, 1812-1930, Mss1J735d, VHS; Neese, *Three Years in the Confederate Horse Artillery*, 223.

78.   *O.R.*, Series 1, vol. 29, part 1, 349-350; Cheney Diary; Frank Diary; Pickerill, *Third Indiana Cavalry*, 98-99; Norton, *Deeds of Daring*, 75; Hall, *Sixth New York Cavalry*, 162; Hard, *Eighth Illinois Cavalry*, 279; Cheney, *Ninth Regiment, New York Volunteer Cavalry*, 138.
       In his report, Buford cited a copy of Pleasonton's order that is dated October 13, 1863, and timed at 11:00 in the evening. He then goes on to explain his actions before his movement to Warrenton Junction. Either Buford copied the date incorrectly in his report or Pleasonton misdated it. All the other records mentioned above state that the division moved out from the river early in the afternoon of the 13th, well before the time given on the order.

79.   *O.R.*, Series 1, vol. 29, part 1, 353; Gracey, *Annals of the Sixth*, 198.
       Merritt recorded that he rejoined the army near Bristoe "about" the 13th. Gracey stated it was the 14th. The brigade apparently did not rejoin Buford immediately. All of Merritt's messages were sent either to Col. C. Ross Smith, Chief of Staff, or Charles C. Suydam, Pleasonton's Assistant Adjutant General, at Cavalry Headquarters and not to Buford. *O.R.*, Series 1, vol. 29, part 1, 351-353.

80.   *O.R.*, Series 1, vol. 29, part 1, 357, 361, 366, 368, 386, 391, and 396; Denison, *Sabres and Spurs*, 305; Hand, Jr., *One Good Regiment*, 84; Rodenbough, *Eighteenth Regiment of Pennsylvania Cavalry*, 44; Klement, ed., "Edwin B. Bigelow," 231; Asa B. Isham, *An Historical Sketch of the Seventh Regiment Michigan Volunteer Cavalry*, (New York: Town Topics Publishing Company, 1893), 34; Allyne C. Litchfield to My Dear Wife, October 16, 1863, Allyne Cushing Litchfield Papers, James S. Schoff Civil War Collection, Manuscripts Division, WLC/UM; *Vermont Watchman and State Journal*, December 4, 1863.

81.   *O.R.*, Series 1, vol. 29, part 1, 449 and 461.

82.   *Ibid.*, 459.

83.   *Ibid.*, 463 and 472; Steele Diary; Donahue Diary; Carter Diary.

84.   A colorful story appeared in the *New York World* that told of Buford being so frustrated in his inability to persuade the quartermasters and teamsters to move that he unlimbered a rifled gun and fired a few rounds up the road high over the wagons. Supposedly, this awoke the sleeping teamsters who finally began to move their wagons, thinking the enemy was close behind them. This account could not be confirmed from any other source. *New York World*, October 19, 1863.

85.   *O.R.*, Series 1, vol. 29, part 1, 350; Cheney Diary; Frank Diary; Pickerill, *Third Indiana Cavalry*, 99; Norton, *Deeds of Daring*, 75; Hall, *Sixth New York Cavalry*, 163; McCabe, "Itinerary of the Seventeenth Regiment, Pennsylvania Volunteer Cavalry," 333; Hard, *Eighth Illinois Cavalry*, 279-280; Cheney, *Ninth Regiment, New York Volunteer Cavalry*, 138-139.

86.   *O.R.*, Series 1, vol. 29, part 1, 361, 366, and 368-369; Denison, *Sabres and Spurs*, 305.
     The Third Pennsylvania of Taylor's Brigade received orders to report to Gen. Buford at 7:00 on the morning of the 14th and accompanied the wagon train to Bristoe Station, arriving about 6:00 in the evening. It spent the night on picket. Rawle, *Third Pennsylvania Cavalry*, 336.

87.   *O.R.*, Series 1, vol. 29, part 1, 358, 361 and 366; Ressler Diary; Hand, Jr., *One Good Regiment*, 85; Lloyd, *History of the First Regiment Pennsylvania Reserve Cavalry*, 74-75; Griffin, ed., *Three Years a Soldier*, 142; Miller, *Sixteenth Pennsylvania Cavalry*, 40; *New York Herald*, October 19, 1863.

88.   *O.R.*, Series 1, vol. 29, part 1, 350, 358, 361-362, and 366; Pyne, *First New Jersey Cavalry*, 189-191 and 193; Longacre, *Jersey Cavaliers*, 176-177; Miller, *Sixteenth Pennsylvania Cavalry*, 40.
     Janeway had with him a part of his regiment and troopers from other regiments that had acted as skirmishers on the column's flank during the brigade's crossing of Kettle Run. Most of the First New Jersey, led by Capt. William W. Gray, crossed the run below the railroad bridge and not at the ford where the rest of the brigade had crossed.
     Gen. Gregg accompanied Col. Gregg's brigade.

89.   *O.R.*, Series 1, vol. 29, part 1, 386; Rodenbough, *Eighteenth Regiment of Pennsylvania Cavalry*, 44.

90.   *O.R.*, Series 1, vol. 29, part 1, 376 and 396; Klement, ed., "Edwin B. Bigelow," 231; J. H. Kidd, *Personal Recollections of a Cavalryman* (Ionia: Sentinel Printing Company, 1908), 211.

91.   *O.R.*, Series 1, vol. 29, part 1, 426-427, 429, and 430-433; William W. Hassler, "The Slaughter Pen at Bristoe Station," *Civil War Times Illustrated*, vol. 1, no. 2, (May 1962): 8-13 (hereafter cited as *CWTI*); Freeman, *Lee's Lieutenants*, 242-247.
     Hill's loss amounted to 143 killed, 773, wounded, and 445 captured.

Chapter Seven

Return to the Rappahannock

The Federal army's retreat along the Orange and Alexandria Railroad culminated in its concentration at Centreville as Meade had ordered on the night of the 13th.[1] As the weary infantry trudged to the positions assigned to the various corps, the blue cavalry carried out its duty of guarding the marching columns' flanks and rear and the precious wagon trains. The early morning fog on the 15th clouded not only men's vision but also their minds. Buford, having seen the last wagon safely across Broad Run, watched as the rolling column moved on toward the crossing of Cedar Run. Once across this obstacle, Buford felt certain that his charges would be safe from the small enemy cavalry force following them at a respectable distance. Indeed, the Eleventh Virginia, the lone regiment dispatched by Stuart toward Brentsville to monitor the enemy cavalry in that area, had no intention of trying to interfere with the withdrawal. However, Buford received a shock when he learned that by some error the wagons had marched circuitously and crossed back over Cedar Run onto the enemy's side. Fortune smiled in that when the Confederate cavalry did advance, Buford still occupied a position that allowed him to protect the wayward wagons as they now raced for Bull Run. Controlling the fords along that stream now became vital.[2]

Early in the morning, Jeb Stuart, under orders to make a "bold demonstration" so the enemy would think all of Lee's army was in pursuit, roused his troopers from their bivouacs near Bristoe Station and started out for Manassas Junction with Fitz Lee's Division and Hampton's Division, minus Young's Brigade, still on its way from Bealeton Station, and the Eleventh Virginia from Funsten's Brigade. Gordon's Brigade led the march and on reaching the junction, drove in pickets belonging to Col. George C. Burling's Sixth New Jersey Infantry of Brig. Gen. Gershom Mott's Third Brigade, Second Division, Third Corps and with support from Fitz Lee pressed on to McLean's Ford on Bull Run. On nearing the ford, Mott bolstered the retreating pickets by committing the rest of the Sixth New Jersey Infantry and Lt. Col. John P. Dunne's One Hundred Fifteenth Pennsylvania Infantry. Resistance stiffened, forcing Gordon back. The success was short-lived. Stuart fed in the dismounted brigades of Lomax, Owen, and Chambliss and drove Burling and Dunne over the run and into rifle pits on the north bank where a portion of Col. William J. Sewell's Fifth New Jersey Infantry reinforced them.[3]

Mott recognized that the gray cavalry intended to capture the ford and ordered a section of Lt. Francis W. Seeley's Battery K, Fourth U. S. Artillery, under Lt. Frank G. Smith, to open fire. Instead, Smith began to withdraw, stating that he feared losing his guns. Shocked, Mott repeated the order, and Smith fired several rounds before again limbering. This time Mott allowed him to go because a section of Capt. O'Neil W. Robinson's Fourth Battery, Maine Light Artillery arrived. The section had few men, and Mott detailed some of his infantry to be horse holders so the drivers could assist in serving the guns. Worse, no officer accompanied the guns, and the sergeant in charge had been wounded on the way. Mott's aide-de-camp, Capt. Joseph W. Crawford took command and soon had one gun blasting away. Mott remained cool and calm in the face of Stuart's onslaught. When the regiments in the rifle pits began to run out of ammunition, he replaced them with elements of the Fifth and Eighth New Jersey Infantry. Repeated assaults by the gray cavalry reached the run, only to be driven back. Stuart decided to up the ante.[4]

Seeing the stiff resistance of Mott at McLean's Ford, Stuart shifted Chambliss's Brigade upstream toward Mitchell's Ford and called on Maj. Robert F. Beckham, who brought up four guns of the Stuart Horse Artillery, one from Capt. Roger P. Chew's Battery and three from Capt. James Breathed's, that took position at the edge of a wood near the McLean house. Chambliss threw out his dismounted skirmishers under the command of Capt. Thomas Haynes. They quickly reached the ford, taking possession of the rifle pits on the south bank but went no further. Capt. Frank Rich with a detachment of Col. Clinton D. MacDougall's One-Hundred Eleventh New York Infantry held the opposite bank and refused to budge. The Federals had been driven as far as they would allow. Still Chambliss persisted. Capt. Haynes soon became a victim of the standoff. Forced to stay mounted to cover his extended line, Haynes became a target for every enemy musket he passed. One shot found its mark, and his grieving men carried him from the field with a wound that disabled him for life.[5]

To all the skirmisher fire, Chew and Breathed added the shot, shell, and canister of their four guns. Any thought Beckham or his gunners had of dominating the field disappeared when Capt. George E. Randolph of the First Rhode Island Artillery, Chief of Artillery for the Third Corps, galloped up with another section of Robinson's battery, placed it to the left of Mott's line, and moved the section already engaged to a redoubt on a hill overlooking Blackburn's Ford that lay downstream from Mitchell's. When these four guns opened fire, Chew and Breathed, occupying an open position on flat ground, took a terrible pounding. Beckham, his horse killed beneath him, had to leave the field. One gun had its axle shot in two. Although both sides had an equal number of guns, the superior positions of Robinson's two sections and the crossfire these guns could deliver far outmatched Chew and Breathed. As senior officer left on the field, Chew ordered Breathed's other two guns to limber to the rear, covering the move with his lone piece that somehow managed to avoid obliteration until it too could withdraw.[6]

Sometime during the fight at McLean's Ford, Stuart received word that portions of the enemy's wagon train had yet to cross Bull Run. This was Buford's wandering wagon train, and Stuart wanted it badly. He assigned Gordon the task of attacking Buford in front while he rode with Funsten's Brigade in an effort to get between the enemy and Yates' Ford downstream from McLean's. While Stuart maneuvered, Gordon, supported by guns of the Stuart Horse Artillery Battalion, engaged in a dismounted fight with the Third Pennsylvania, acting as rearguard for Devin's brigade.[7] Try as he might, Gordon could make little headway due to the dense thickets that shielded his foe and a makeshift barricade that had been constructed across the road. He brought up his artillery and pounded the Third but to little avail. At one point the Seventeenth Pennsylvania struck at Gordon's flank, dislodging him and allowing the Federals to gain a moment's respite. Unfortunately, the Seventeenth had to retreat, almost carrying back the Third. But the stubborn bluecoats rallied. Fitz Lee brought up a portion of Lomax's Brigade. Still, the Pennsylvanians held. When Stuart finally arrived about dark, he launched the Twelfth Virginia against the barricade and briefly celebrated success when the enemy retreated. Tearing down the barrier Gordon rushed ahead only to run into a deadly volley from the Keystone Staters. Twice more the gray cavaliers charged with equal results. Finally, the wagons reached safety, and the Third withdrew across the ford under sporadic artillery fire, leaving Gordon with only a few prisoners and not a single wagon.[8]

Kilpatrick, already safely ensconced behind Bull Run, sat out the day's fighting, although Custer, ever aggressive, could not sit idle while a fight raged just three miles to his left. In the afternoon, he ordered newly returned Maj. James H. Kidd to take his Sixth Michigan on a scout across the run toward Gainesville to establish the strength of the enemy there. Kidd trotted off, made his observations, and returned, informing his commander that the enemy occupied the village in force, something Custer probably could have guessed from all the commotion going on east of his position. Had Kidd's regiment been cut off and destroyed or captured, Custer would have had many questions to answer, but his luck, already becoming legendary, held.[9]

Night found the cavalry of both armies scattered hither and yon after a day of marching and fighting. Buford camped along the road to Fairfax Station for the night. Merritt's Reserve Brigade, under Col. Alfred Gibbs of the Nineteenth New York, operating independently of Buford, marched from Sudley Springs and bivouacked near Centreville. Gen. Gregg's division had preceded Buford's across Bull Run, but Taylor's brigade had turned back to assist in repulsing Stuart. It arrived too late, and Taylor returned the way he had come. Most of his brigade encamped near Fairfax Station, but a part of it guarded Wolf Run Shoals on the Occoquan River. Col. Gregg's troopers spent the night near Fairfax Station, although he had vedettes from the Sixteenth Pennsylvania out as far as Union Mills. Kilpatrick maintained his watch on the army's right flank along Bull Run with Davies camped near the Stone Bridge on the Warrenton Turnpike, picketing at New Market, Groveton, and on the road toward Aldie, and Custer on the old battlefield near the turnpike. Stuart's troopers spent the night along Bull Run and around

Manassas Junction. Young's Brigade rejoined Stuart during the night.[10]

During the 15th, while Stuart clashed with retreating Northern cavalry and supply trains, Robert E. Lee took out his frustration over Meade's escape on the Orange and Alexandria Railroad. His infantry would spend this day and the next two tearing up the tracks from Cub Run to the Rappahannock, leaving the cavalry to deal with the enemy. From his headquarters at Centreville, Meade had spent the 15th moving his corps around like chess pieces to defend Bull Run, Cub Run, the Occoquan, and the roads to the west. Even before all of his cavalry and wagons had safely crossed Bull Run, he assigned his mounted divisions to watch the various fords and roads in front of the infantry. Gregg would watch the upper fords of the Occoquan, using Taylor's brigade, while portions of Col. Gregg's brigade covered the lower fords on Bull Run. Buford drew the lower Occoquan. Kilpatrick would picket along the upper Bull Run to New Market and toward Aldie on the Little River Turnpike. At these various positions, Pleasonton's cavalry would await Stuart's advance.[11]

Unfortunately for the Southern cavalry chief's plans, the weather on the 16th did not cooperate. Rain fell in torrents and runs rose. The majority of the Federal cavalry held to their camps, trying to get some rest on the muddy ground. But Stuart pressed on. Leaving Fitz Lee's Division in the vicinity of Manassas, he rode out in the morning with Hampton's Division, a section of Capt. Marcellus N. Moorman's Battery, and one gun from Capt. Wiley H. Griffin's toward Groveton, hoping to cross Bull Run above Sudley Springs and maneuver to the rear of Centreville. Near Groveton he heard Confederate infantry pickets clashing with the Fifth New York, Davies's brigade, but did not become engaged himself. Davies's troopers drove the graybacks as far as Gainesville before returning to their camp. Stuart managed to get across a swollen Bull Run late in the day and bivouacked at Stone Castle. As darkness swallowed the day, Brig. Gen. Thomas L. Rosser rode into the camp of Funsten's Brigade, formerly Jones's, and took command.[12]

Undoubtedly aided rather than hampered by the weather conditions, one other Confederate force struck a blow, albeit a small one, on the 16th. John Mosby had not taken an active role in Lee's offensive operations. With Federal troops marching back and forth and up and down roads in every direction, Mosby chose to keep a low profile. But amidst the day's downpour he led Company A of his Rangers from its camp near Frying Pan to S. J. Stuart's house on the Little River Turnpike near Chantilly. Near here he corralled 40 prisoners and 64 horses and mules, all part of a wagon train that had delivered supplies to the Sixth Corps. The escapade aroused the ire of Brig. Gen. Michael Corcoran, whose brigade of infantry located at Fairfax Court House had the responsibility of guarding the area. Corcoran could do little more than send out infantry the next day in a hopeless effort to run down the raiders. Mosby left his captures with Company B and struck again, this time on the Ox Road from Frying Pan to Germantown, taking nine men and their horses at a picket post. This constant buzzing around the outskirts of the army did little to affect Meade, whom Mosby had pestered the previous two months, but enough to draw some attention from those troops in the Department of Washington. The Gray Ghost would be heard from again in the future.[13]

On the 17th, Stuart resumed his march around the right flank and toward the rear of the Federal army, reaching the Little River Turnpike three miles east of Aldie and riding on through Gum Springs to Frying Pan.[14] Not far beyond this point, the leading squadron from Young's Brigade charged an enemy outpost, capturing a number of men. Young threw out a dismounted line of sharpshooters and became engaged with an infantry regiment from Maj. Gen. John Sedgwick's Sixth Corps. Meade had assigned Sedgwick to guard the Little River Turnpike at Saunder's Toll Gate. To protect his right flank, Sedgwick had pushed out troops along the road to Frying Pan. The Jeff Davis Legion played a conspicuous role in the two-hour skirmish that followed. Stuart broke off the fight at sundown, feeling that he had learned all he could about the disposition of the troops in front of him, and because he had received a message stating that Lee wanted to see him. The division retreated along the same roads it had advanced and camped near the Little River Turnpike for the night. Stuart's excursion had a decided affect on Meade, who shifted Buford's division from his left to his right and rear, with Chapman's brigade being stationed at Fairfax Court House and Devin's at Chantilly. Buford had reported from his headquarters at Brimstone Hill that the Occoquan ran 15 feet deep, that he had secured the only ferryboat, and that the lowest ford, Snyder's, was impassable. Now he ordered his men to saddle up and left the job of holding the Occoquan to Gregg, who received orders to stretch his men out to cover the stream below Wolf Run Shoals. In doing so the Third Pennsylvania briefly skirmished with an unknown force on the other side of the stream. The Sixteenth Pennsylvania drew picket duty as well, but the only enemy met was hunger as the men went without food.[15]

Kilpatrick, still watching the upper Bull Run, decided to probe for the enemy on his front and flank. While Custer's brigade lay in camp all day, Davies's, then camping on the Carter farm near Sudley Springs and picketing toward Hay Market, Thoroughfare Gap, and from Bull Run to the Little River Turnpike, sent out scouting parties to the gap and Aldie. Had they been sent earlier they may have crossed sabers with Stuart, but all they turned up was information that Stuart had passed through the area. As he had done on the 16th, Davies once again dispatched the Fifth New York of his brigade to harass the Confederate vedettes on the Warrenton Pike. A squadron of the First Virginia had its outposts near Bull Run. These fell back so rapidly that no skirmish line could be formed to meet the onrushing New Yorkers. The Virginians raced down the pike until arriving near Gainesville where the Fourth Virginia's pickets alerted Maj. Robert Randolph, commanding the Fourth, who prepared to meet the enemy. Col. Thomas H. Owen with the rest of the brigade arrived and threw out skirmishers, but Davies had accomplished all he wanted and withdrew. Owen reestablished his outposts at Groveton. The brigade encamped on the Ellis farm along Broad Run. Lomax's Brigade again managed to avoid contact with the enemy, moving from Manassas to Gainesville and camping there.[16]

Late in the afternoon Merritt's Reserve Brigade, still under Col. Gibbs, pushed across Bull Run at Blackburn's Ford under orders to occupy Manassas Junction. Gibbs moved cautiously toward the Orange & Alexandria Railroad until he ran into Chambliss's outposts near Manassas about 9:00. Earlier in the day, Chambliss had been ordered to move forward and encamp in rear of Manassas Junction. Leaving his position on the road between Manassas and Brentsville, he arrived in the early evening and almost immediately his vedettes clashed with Gibbs's advance. By the light of burning railroad ties, a skirmish erupted. Companies G and H of the Ninth Virginia under the command of Lt. Nicholas E. Davis guarded the road to the ford supported by another squadron. Initially the Federals drove Davis back, but he gathered a few men around him and charged, giving his regiment time to form. The charge succeeded but Davis was killed. The regiment, now mounted, became engaged. However, Chambliss, rather than be drawn into a heavy fight, followed orders and retreated toward Bristoe Station. He need not have worried. Gibbs pulled back as well. Chambliss's troopers stood to horse all night near the station.[17]

Stuart awoke on the morning of the 18th and marched with Hampton's Division from near the Little River Turnpike to Gainesville where the division rested and he received word of the army's retreat toward the Rappahannock River. In the evening, he moved the division above Hay Market to obtain forage and supplies, camping on the road for the night. During the day, Stuart's scouts or spy network, operating at peak efficiency, informed the cavalry chieftain that Kilpatrick's division could be advancing toward him at any time. Indeed, Kilpatrick had received orders at 3:00 that afternoon to press forward on the Warrenton Pike and feel out the enemy. He complied, sending Davies's brigade along the pike and Custer's brigade, with the First Vermont in the lead, up the road from Sudley Springs to Hay Market. At about 5:00 just beyond Groveton, Davies ran into Lt. John M. Jordan's Company C of the Third Virginia, picketing the road, and pushed it back to Gainesville where Capt William M. Field's squadron reinforced Jordan. Stuart quickly learned of the attack and, concerned that his own position might be threatened, ordered Young's Brigade to mount up in a pouring rainstorm, ride through, and secure Hay Market. However, with darkness falling, the Federals chose to call it a day and encamped about a half mile short of Gainesville, Custer having joined Davies on the pike. Young's patrols soon confirmed that the road to Gainesville was still open, and everyone settled in for the night. They would need all the sleep they could get.[18]

Fitz Lee's Division drew other duties. In the morning, Lomax marched from Gainesville to Bristoe Station, assigning the Fifteenth Virginia to guard the ford over Broad Run at Milford upstream from the station. Owen's Brigade shifted from the Ellis farm to Langyher's Mill, although the Fourth Virginia, replacing the Third, remained on guard duty at Gainesville. Chambliss, whose vedettes had stayed north of Broad Run, held the point where the road crossed the stream near Bristoe Station. Before long, they would be entertaining visitors.[19]

Brig. Gen. Wesley Merritt, having just rejoined the Reserve Brigade, had concerns about his army's right flank. Stationed at Manassas Junction, he sent out patrols toward Thoroughfare Gap and in the morning, personally led a reconnaissance along the railroad toward Bristoe Station. About a mile from the station, the Sixth Pennsylvania encountered the pickets of Chambliss's Brigade. These slowly retreated, crossing Broad Run where Chambliss had formed the brigade's other regiments under the protective guns of Chew's Battery, which calmly waited for the Northerners to come into range. When the bluecoats appeared Chew opened fire. Chambliss's and Lomax's skirmishers added their fire to the barrage. Merritt fed in the Fifth United States but quickly became convinced that if he wanted to go any further it would require considerably more effort than what he had expended thus far. He decided to fall back to Manassas Junction and report what he had found. Chambliss's troopers fell back across Kettle Run and camped for the night.[20]

Gregg's division spent the 18th accomplishing a variety of tasks. From their various positions along Bull Run, most of the division's regiments converged on Fairfax Station, taking the opportunity while there to secure rations. At least one regiment maintained a watch on the lower Bull Run. Maj. M. Henry Avery's Tenth New York picketed from Union Mills to a point five miles downstream. If Gregg thought his troopers would be able to enjoy a respite, he erred grievously. At 12:15 in the afternoon, he received orders to march north to Vienna and join forces with Col. Charles R. Lowell, Jr., commanding the Second Massachusetts, which was attached to the Department of Washington. The reason for the conjunction centered on the Federals' ever-present fear of an enemy cavalry raid in the army's rear. Stuart had not only caused Meade to move Buford, but now Gregg. For whatever reason Gregg took his time complying, and at 11:30 that night a dispatch arrived directing him to stop his column and that new orders would be forthcoming.[21]

During the 17th and the 18th, reports from various sources convinced Meade that Lee's offensive had run its course. However, he advised his superiors in Washington that until he knew something definite about Lee's location, his own army had to maintain its present position. By 10:00 on the night of the 18th he had enough information to convince himself to move forward and issued marching orders for the following day. The First Corps would move forward from Centreville to Hay Market; the Second Corps would cross Bull Run at Mitchell's and Blackburn's fords and march on the north side of the railroad to Milford on Broad Run; the Third Corps would leave its position at Union Mills, march on the south side of the railroad, and take position on Broad Run opposite Bristoe Station; the Fifth Corps was directed to march by way of Island Ford on Bull Run, through Hay Market to Groveton; the Sixth Corps would follow the First and stop at Gainesville for the night; Buford and Gregg drew wagon train guard duty at the fords of Bull Run. That left Kilpatrick to divine the whereabouts of the enemy to the front, and the orders that he received at daylight the next morning directed him to continue to advance as far as possible on the pike toward Warrenton.[22]

On the 19th, Meade's whole army lurched forward in pursuit of Lee. Infantrymen, cavalrymen, and artillerymen wiped the sleep from their eyes, ate breakfast, if they had any rations and the time, formed lines and columns, and headed south. Judson Kilpatrick's division, the van of the army, started earlier than most. The troopers were in for a long, long day. Confederate vedettes from Young's Brigade, Hampton's Division, gave up Gainesville to the Sixth Michigan, Custer's brigade, without a struggle. In the village, Kilpatrick learned that a large force of the enemy under Stuart himself had split with one column riding toward Warrenton and the other to Hay Market. To verify this information and to guard his flanks as he advanced, Kilpatrick sent the First West Virginia, Davies's brigade, under Maj. Harvey Farabee toward Hay Market to watch his right and the Seventh Michigan, Custer's brigade, under Col. William D. Mann to Greenwich to protect his left. Both regiments quickly reported that Stuart had withdrawn along the pike in the direction of Buckland Mills. Kilpatrick moved forward, chasing Stuart's rear guard, consisting of one regiment of Young's Brigade, over Broad Run at Buckland Mills. Stuart threw out sharpshooters from Rosser's and Gordon's brigades, Hampton's Division, along the run and in the village and unlimbered his artillery.[23]

As Stuart deployed his forces, he sent word to Fitz Lee, ordering him to come to Buckland Mills. During the early morning, Lee had withdrawn Owen's Brigade from along Broad Run at Langyher's Mill and Lomax's and Chambliss's brigades from Milford and Bristoe Station through Catlett's Station to Auburn. On receiving Stuart's orders, Lee concocted a plan to entrap Kilpatrick and sent word to Stuart, who immediately saw the opportunity for what it was and assented. Still, Stuart had to hold the line along the run to give Fitz Lee time to move into position.[24] The question remained as to how long Stuart could hold out. Fortunately, the heavy rain of the previous night had made the run impassable except for the bridge and a ford a mile down stream.[25]

Leading Kilpatrick's column, Custer came up to Broad Run a little before 10:00 and quickly realized that the depth of the stream and its steep, wooded banks limited his opportunities to advance except across the bridge. Even more serious for Custer, Stuart had no intention of providing the Federals with easy access to it. Small arms fire erupted, and a piece of artillery could be seen in a position that covered the bridge and the open ground approaching it. Maj. James H. Kidd of the Sixth Michigan, first on the scene, dismounted a portion of his regiment and sent it forward to engage the Confederate sharpshooters. Custer with his staff and escort arrived and foolishly stopped in the middle of the open road. Stuart's artillery seized the moment and dropped a shell into the middle of the group. The often-faulty Confederate ammunition on this occasion worked perfectly, exploding and scattering the group but remarkably not harming anyone. Once more, Custer's luck held sway.[26]

Delaying no longer than it took to order up the rest of his brigade, Custer replied to Stuart's challenge by spreading out the rest of the Sixth Michigan to cover his center across the pike, with the Fifth Michigan to the right, and the Seventh Michigan to the left. The First Michigan and the First Vermont formed the reserve. He also placed Lt. Alexander C. M. Pennington's Battery M, Second U. S. Artillery on the high ground at "Cerro Gordo", the home of the Hunton family. Pennington, his guns flanking both sides of the house, targeted the woods and hamlet on the other side of the run that teemed with skirmishers and replied to the enemy artillery. The morning wore away as the two sides battled each other across the stream. Davies came up and concealed his men in the wood to the left of the pike, ready to cross as soon as Custer cleared the way. That was the problem. Stuart would not budge.[27]

As noon approached Custer received good news. The Seventh Michigan had discovered a ford at Kinsley's Mill downstream from the bridge, crossed the run, and moved down on Stuart's right flank.[28] Custer now made a bold attack on the bridge and succeeded in gaining the other side, chasing the Confederate skirmishers from Buckland Mills. Unknown to Custer, Stuart had decided to follow Fitz Lee's plan and with his flank threatened gave up the bridge and the hamlet to lure Kilpatrick into the trap already forming for him. Custer's "victorious" troopers chased the Confederates about a mile. At first Stuart put up some resistance in order to withdraw his skirmishers. Lt. John J. Shoemaker's section of Moorman's Battery opened fire from a hill about a mile down the road to New Baltimore on one of Custer's mounted squadrons, but eventually Stuart allowed himself to be chased in the hope that the Federals would follow. But Custer would not be the one to pursue Stuart down the pike. It was now about noon. The Michigan Brigade's commander ordered his men to the side of the road where they could enjoy a quick lunch. Kilpatrick took the opportunity to halt his column for an hour until the scouting parties that he had sent to Auburn and Thoroughfare Gap returned. Davies's men may also have seized the moment to dig into their haversacks for a bite to eat. When the scouting parties reported no enemy in sight at either location, Davies's brigade, with Kilpatrick and his staff bringing up the rear, took the lead and trotted off toward New Baltimore. As Kilpatrick rode away, he ordered Custer to follow.[29]

Davies encountered Stuart's rear guard skirmishers about a mile from Buckland Mills, probably near the same place Custer had advanced to before pulling back. The Federals had no trouble moving ahead and passed through New Baltimore to the hills beyond. From all indications, Kilpatrick might have felt that he could reach Warrenton before the close of the day. Davies learned from some helpful citizen that Fitz Lee had turned off to the right in the direction of Thoroughfare Gap. That important piece of information would soon prove false because back toward Buckland Mills, Fitz Lee had introduced himself to Custer. The sound of artillery fire in his rear alerted Davies that something was amiss. Shortly, an officer from Kilpatrick's staff arrived, confirmed that the enemy had struck the column's left and rear, and ordered Davies to halt where he was and await further instructions.[30]

Earlier that morning, Fitz Lee had left Auburn with Owen's Brigade in the lead followed by Chambliss's and then Lomax's. He also had with him portions of Breathed's, McGregor's, and Chew's batteries. At first moving northeast along the road between Auburn and Greenwich, Fitz Lee swung off the road and rode almost due north across country. As Owen's Brigade on the right moved forward, the Second Virginia scooped up pickets belonging to the Seventh Michigan that had been once more sent toward Greenwich and then took position with its brother regiments on the hills overlooking Buckland Mills. What greeted Fitz Lee's eyes surprised him. Between the Confederates and the bridge over Broad Run stood Custer's brigade. Custer had just given the order to saddle up. With the Fifth Michigan in the lead he set off to join Davies, but everything changed in a matter of minutes. As a precautionary measure, before proceeding, Custer directed Maj. Kidd to throw out his men 500 yards to the left of the road facing the wood that covered the hill overlooking the pike and hold there until the other regiments of the brigade had passed. Kidd complied and Custer started out along the pike. As the Sixth Michigan, in column of fours, approached within 300 yards of the wood, Capt. Don G. Lovell, riding next to Kidd, called his commander's attention to a mounted man just outside of the wood to their front. At first Kidd thought that the unknown rider might belong to the Seventh Michigan, but Lovell pointed out that the man wore a gray uniform. Kidd questioned Lovell's conclusion until a shot from the rider's pistol confirmed the analysis. The fight for the Buckland Mills bridge was on.[31]

Fortunately for Kilpatrick and Davies, Custer had not gone too far. He came back to Kidd and deployed his brigade facing south about 200 yards from the pike, placing the Fifth and Seventh Michigan to the right of Kidd, who had formed a skirmish line, and the First Vermont in support of a gun from Pennington's battery on the extreme left.[32] The First Michigan acted as a reserve and protected the other five guns of Pennington's battery, under Lt. Carle A. Woodruff, which were located about 50 yards to the right and rear of the single gun's position. The Confederate battle line, consisting of dismounted men, most of them from Owen's Brigade, now emerged from the wood and began to increase the pressure on Custer, who thought he faced enemy infantry. Breathed's Battery opened fire, beginning yet another furious encounter with its great antagonist, Pennington's battery. The two had linked up in several brawls already and this one proved no different. Neither side gave an inch. Breathed got the worst of it – one gun dismounted, driver Hayward Tripplett's lower leg badly mangled, causing the amputation of his foot, Lieutenants Philip P. Johnston and Daniel Shanks wounded, and six horses killed. Chew's Battery joined the fray, but Pennington could not be moved by artillery fire alone. Additional help would be needed.[33]

The booming cannon to the northeast galvanized Stuart to action. Having lured his adversaries to within a few miles of Warrenton, he now turned on them with a vengeance, determined to crush Kilpatrick between his own forces and Fitz Lee's. The blow could have been devastating had Davies not acted on his own initiative. Having been told by Kilpatrick's staff officer to wait for additional orders, Davies became increasingly alarmed at the growing intensity of the artillery fire in his rear. He reached the conclusion that to linger in his present position might not be his best choice. Directing the Second New York that had been in the forefront of his advance to hold its ground for a time before following the rest of the brigade, Davies turned back toward Buckland Mills. His decision proved fortuitous. With Gordon's Brigade in the center, Young's on the left, and Rosser's on the right, Stuart struck. Initially, he found the going difficult as the New Yorkers put up a stiff resistance only to be overwhelmed by the charge of Maj. Rufus Barringer at the head of the First North Carolina, Gordon's Brigade. The Second rallied, only to be broken again. And so the regiments careened up the pike.[34]

Meanwhile, Custer fought valiantly to give Davies time to reach the bridge. Pennington's lone gun failed to halt Owen's skirmishers and its capture appeared imminent. Lt. Stephen A. Clark, commanding Company L of the First Vermont, acted promptly. Taking several men with him into the wood to the left of the gun, Clark and his company began to fire their pistols rapidly into the air while yelling at the top of their lungs. The noise caused the Confederates to slow down long enough for Pennington to withdraw his gun and rejoin the battery, although he lost three or four horses in the process. All down the line, Custer's force faced an equally aggressive enemy. The Fifth Michigan, under Col. Russell A. Alger, stretched to the breaking point on the right in an effort to hold the pike open until Davies arrived, found itself slowly being driven back. At the other end of the line the Sixth Michigan, with almost empty ammunition pouches, battled desperately to hold a fence line . His battery reunited, Pennington quickly grasped the situation. If the enemy placed a gun on the hill he had just vacated, his battery would be decimated. He ordered his cannoneers to limber their pieces and fell back, hoping to find another position where he could make a stand. He found none and galloped over the bridge, placing two guns in position and opening a fire that effectively slowed the Confederates' pursuit and covered Custer's retreat.[35]

Grudgingly, Custer's right flank gave way and Fitz Lee crossed the pike effectively cutting off Davies from the bridge. Knowing he could do no more, Custer began to withdraw his regiments. The First Vermont, the Seventh Michigan, the Sixth Michigan, and the Fifth Michigan crossed the bridge. The First Michigan brought up the rear while Pennington's two guns pounded away over their heads. Not all of the troopers reached the bridge in time. Lt. Col. Addison Preston and a number of troopers of the First Vermont, finding themselves cut off, used the ford at the Kinsley millrace downstream from the bridge. Maj. John E. Clark and a portion of his battalion of the Fifth Michigan, consisting of Companies B, E, G, and K, did not fare as well, becoming separated from the other companies of the regiment. Being dismounted and unable to reach their horses, Clark and his men fell prisoners to the Fourth Virginia, Owen's Brigade. Still Custer fought to hold the bridge from the other side. His men, their carbine ammunition almost exhausted, resorted to their pistols to keep the gray cavalry at bay.[36]

Davies learned of Custer's withdrawal late in the afternoon when he arrived on the ridge about a mile from Buckland Mills and saw Fitz Lee's troopers swarming over the ground between him and Broad Run. Ordering the Fifth New York under Maj. John Hammond to fan out on the column's right flank and hold the enemy in check, Davies looked for a way to save his brigade. Stuart already had taken one option off the table by driving the Second New York past the junction with the Thoroughfare Gap Road just beyond New Baltimore. Then he had dispatched Young's Brigade around Davies's flank hoping to surround the bluecoats, but Stuart had advanced so rapidly that he passed the point where he had instructed Young to attack. Faced with the enemy on his front, right, and rear, Davies coolly directed his wagons, artillery, and the column of troopers off the pike to his left, instructing them to move across country and to cross Broad Run somewhere above Buckland Mills. A charge by the First West Virginia and the Second New York led by Capt. John F. B. Mitchell blunted Stuart's pursuit and gained precious time for the fording of the run above its hairpin turn. Here some of the wagons, ambulances, and caissons became stuck and fell into Confederate hands along with several horses and a few prisoners. The weary blue cavalrymen then made their way over fields and through wood toward Hay Market. The artillery, under the careful guidance of Surgeon Henry Capehart of Davies's staff, who was familiar with the area, also reached safety. But Davies's day was not yet done.[37]

Neither Stuart nor Fitz Lee was willing to let Kilpatrick go just yet. Stuart gathered together elements of Gordon's and Rosser's brigades, including some from the Seventh and Eleventh Virginia that had somewhat dispersed during the attack, and pursued Davies toward Hay Market. Fitz Lee, whose troopers had crossed the Buckland Mills bridge in Custer's wake and at the ford at Kinsley Mill, pushed up the pike toward Gainesville. Kilpatrick understood his predicament well enough to know that he would need assistance in stopping the gray cavalry from doing more damage to his already hard pressed division. He communicated with Maj. Gen. John Newton, commanding the First Corps, who ordered Third Division commander Brig. Gen. John R. Kelly to aid Davies. Kelly in turn detailed Col. Edwin H. Webster's Seventh Maryland Infantry of the Third Brigade to move out on the road from Hay Market through Thoroughfare Gap. Webster, whose regiment already had been designated for outpost duty on that road and the one to Leesburg, had 125 men under Capt. John Makechney on the gap road, one and a half miles from Hay Market.[38]

Webster just had seen to the posting of a chain of outposts between the two roads when firing erupted on his left. A gallop of about a mile brought him where he could see that Makechney had his hands full. Stuart had caught up with Davies's rear guard and was driving it through the Seventh Maryland's pickets. Makechney's men fought amid the growing darkness and Davies's disorganized troopers in a desperate effort to save themselves as much as their mounted compatriots. Capt. Samuel S. Elder's Battery E, Fourth U. S. Artillery, supported by Col. Edmund L. Dana's One Hundred Forty-third Pennsylvania Infantry joined the fray. Makechney conducted a successful withdrawal and concentration of his men on the road that helped stiffen resistance. Nevertheless, Stuart struck again about 8:00 in the moonlight, having worked some of his men between the road and Broad Run on the left where the Seventh had failed to post vedettes. The Confederates almost succeeded in surrounding Makechney's small command, but the arrival of the First Maryland Infantry under Lt. Col. John W. Wilson stabilized the line and halted the enemy, although skirmishing sputtered on and off until 10:00 that night.[39]

Meanwhile, Fitz Lee nipped at Custer's hooves. Pennington had limbered his two guns and retreated up the pike. His place was taken by some of Fitz Lee's guns that hurried the blue cavalry along in their flight with a few shots at their rear guard. Col. Owen then ordered the Third Virginia at the head of his column to charge, followed by the Second and First Virginia. The chase continued. Pennington took position on the left about a mile and a half from the bridge. Then, after receiving orders, he fell back through a line of Sixth Corps infantry skirmishers deployed in a wood and unlimbered again, but his day was done and he did not fire. Through these skirmishers also passed Custer's exhausted men. When Owen came up, the Federal infantry greeted him with a volley that ended further pursuit. As the night deepened, the troopers, blue and gray, and their horses found what food, drink, and rest they could. After almost 12 hours of marching and fighting Stuart could claim a victory, and Kilpatrick could breathe a sigh of relief that his defeat was not the disaster it could have been.[40]

For the rest of Meade's mounted arm the day passed relatively peacefully. Merritt left Manassas Junction and as he had done on the 18th moved forward to Bristoe Station. This time he encountered no enemy and rode on to Catlett's Station. He pushed a patrol two miles farther and on encountering enemy outposts, pulled back, and camped at Catlett's for the night.[41] Buford's division, dutifully covering the army's wagon train, marched through Centreville and the old Bull Run battlefield, halting between Groveton and Hay Market for the night.[42] Gregg also guarded wagons. Taylor's brigade marched from Fairfax Station to Union Mills, then to Centreville, and finally toward Gainesville, encamping for the night along Cub Run. The First New Jersey drew the duty of scouting south of Manassas toward Brentsville before rejoining the brigade that night. Col. Gregg's brigade assisted in watching the precious wagons. His regiments' camps stretched from Centreville to Fairfax Station to Manassas Junction.[43]

By the 19th, Robert E. Lee's infantry, after having thoroughly dismantled most of the railroad from Cub Run back toward the Rappahannock by destroying bridges, burning ties, and carrying away all the iron it could transport, had again reclaimed the defensive lines along the river. Stuart's success against Kilpatrick allowed the Confederate cavalry to withdraw towards the Rappahannock at a leisurely pace on the 20th. Fitz Lee retraced his hoof prints back to Auburn and then rode through Three Mile Station to Beverly Ford, crossing the river and encamping near Dr. Green's home.[44] Hampton's Division under Stuart fell back through Warrenton with only a force of enemy infantry following him. Moorman's Battery unlimbered south of the town, expecting a possible attack. When it failed to materialize, the cannoneers limbered their guns and plodded on to Sulphur Springs, crossing the Rappahannock there, and proceeding over the Hazel.[45] Their day ended at 8:00 when they reached their old camp near Rixeyville. The cavalry, badly in need of supplies, followed the battery over the Rappahannock and camped for the night. Chew's Battery crossed at Beverly Ford, the water being so high that the men carried their ammunition across in their arms.[46]

For Meade the 19th closed under a cloud of rumors. Kilpatrick reported that Ewell's and Hill's infantry were at Warrenton, a fact that he could not possibly have known. Another report claimed that Stuart had 8,000 cavalry near Snicker's Gap and was preparing for another raid into Maryland via Williamsport or Berlin and still another that Longstreet's Corps had returned to Lee and another invasion across the Potomac, with Washington City as the goal, was imminent. Meade was cautioned to "prepare for the storm."[47] As a result the army inched forward from Gainesville to Warrenton on the 20th, finding no Confederates and no railroad. Merritt pulled back from Catlett's Station to Bristoe Station to protect the men working on the reconstruction of the railroad and to cover the area back to Bull Run. He would be engaged in this work through the 23rd.[48] Most of Buford's division mounted a reconnaissance from Hay Market through Thoroughfare Gap. On reaching Georgetown, the Sixth New York and the first two squadrons of the Ninth New York, both regiments belonging to Devin's brigade, trotted on to White Plains and then turned toward Warrenton. The other regiments of the division rode from Georgetown through New Baltimore toward Warrenton. The only enemy encountered was a lone Mosby scout captured at White Plains along with some sutler's stores.[49] Still guarding the supply trains, Gregg's regiments marched from their various camps to Bull Run, camping there for the night.[50] Kilpatrick's exhausted troopers held to their camps between Gainesville and Groveton, recuperating.[51]

With the re-establishment of the Rappahannock as the boundary between the two armies, Lee's offensive, for all intents and purposes, came to an end. While the soldiers of both sides certainly felt the effects of their strenuous exertions during the twelve days of marching and fighting, the cavalry in particular suffered greatly. In a letter to his wife on October 25, Capt. Richard H. Watkins of the Third Virginia, Owen's Brigade, wrote, "A great many horses played out on our last campaign and nearly one half of my company will have to get fresh ones. Some are talking about going into infantry the price of horses is so high. And I fear that unless our horses are better many will be compelled to change their branch of service."[52] Stuart drew official attention to the hardships faced by his horses in his report stating, "The matter of greatest concern to me during this short and eventful campaign was the subject of forage for the horses."[53] The men too had gone without rations. Private William C. Corson, also of the Third Virginia, recounted in an October 23 letter to his wife, Jennie, "Our cavalry suffered more for something to eat than on any previous occasion during the war. We were three days and nights without a morsel of anything to eat save a few grapes and haws."[54] Compounding the problem was the fact that the country being almost desolate, nothing could be scavenged.

The Federals suffered equally. At one time the Ninth New York, Devin's brigade, had but eight to ten fit horses per company. Large numbers of dismounted troopers made their way from the front to the dismount camp in search of another horse. The First Massachusetts, Taylor's brigade, Gregg's division, went from the 12th to the 16th without rations being issued. Rest and refitting should have been given the highest priority and for some this was the case. For others, the dreaded picket duty and patrolling loomed before them. The war dragged on, and they had to fight it.[55]

Despite whatever success Stuart might have thought had been achieved, he still had his critics. The *Richmond Whig* managed to see catastrophe amidst victory. Even as Lee maneuvered Meade back toward Washington and Stuart chased Pleasonton here and there, the worst was prophesized. In an editorial column the writer praised Stuart for his victories and his captures of the enemy's men and horses – all accomplished even though the cavalry had "to feed their horses on weeds and pay a dollar a piece for horse shoe nails." The good news proved too good. Too many "Yankees" taken. Too much food required to feed them. Flour prices skyrocketing as a result. No room for them. "Our cavalry are reaping a large crop of laurels, but, at the same time, they are scaring the good people of Richmond out of their senses. The laws of hospitality demand that our 'Yankee guests' be fed first of all . . . But if the prisoners keep on coming; the meal tub and the flour barrel will soon give out . . . and if somebody don't make haste to stop Stuart and his men from hauling in the cod-fish gentry, the consequences will be fatal."[56]

A member of the Eleventh Virginia Cavalry attempted to come to Stuart's rescue. In a long letter to the *Richmond Sentinel*, he wrote in part, "Let me add in closing, in view of aspersions lately made, that Gen. Stuart has, throughout these late dangerous scenes, conducted himself so nobly as to put down all slanders, and endear himself more than ever to his command. His coolness in difficulty, his perfect fearlessness, his boldness in the face of dangers, and his kind and gentle manner to his troops, and his inspiring confidence in himself, have won the highest praise even from those who spoke ill of him before."[57] For this trooper, at least, Stuart had demonstrated his abilities and added to his reputation. His conduct and his successes proved his worth as Lee's cavalry chieftain. Apparently, however, in the future, he would have to capture fewer of the enemy or ask his own men to eat less. Since many of them had already gone three days without rations, a little longer shouldn't hurt.

On the other hand, the Federal cavalry reaped praise. "The services of the cavalry corps under Major-Gen. Pleasonton cannot be too highly appreciated and the division commanders, Gens. Buford, Gregg and Kilpatrick, executed their delicate and arduous duties with the most admirable coolness, decision, and skill." The fact that Pleasonton's forces had been roughly handled on at least three occasions failed to affect the view of the press or the public. But within the ranks of Davies's brigade festered some animosity toward Kilpatrick over the debacle at Buckland Mills. Not even a party thrown by Kilpatrick could gloss over the fact that something had misfired and someone was responsible, whether the press or the public recognized it or not.[58]

Recovery continued on the 21st even as Stuart's hungry troopers manned familiar outposts along the Rappahannock. The brigades by necessity began to scatter to both accomplish the task of guarding the river line and so that the horses could find grazing. From Flint Hill to Dr. Welford's and nearby Mrs. Major's farms to near Brandy Station, the gray troopers began the process of healing body, mind, and spirit.[59] Stuart eventually totaled up the cost of the campaign – 56 killed and 334 wounded. The horse artillery lost 2 killed and 16 wounded. He estimated the number missing at less than 45, which probably did not included a trooper of the First Virginia who deserted on the 22nd. There may have been others who could take no more of the hard duty and privation, but most stayed in the depleted ranks, including those having no horse. One such man was Pvt. Cincinnatus J. Ware, who wanted to send his family some much needed money but had to purchase a horse. They would receive the funds only if he could not find a horse to purchase. Such were the decisions faced by the men of Stuart's command.[60]

North of the river Buford's division concentrated around Warrenton with the Chapman's brigade northwest of the town and Devin's brigade about one and a half miles south of it.[61] Gregg's division guarded supply trains that wound their way over the Warrenton Turnpike. Then Taylor's brigade rode to Gainesville and through Thoroughfare Gap to New Baltimore, bivouacking about a mile from Warrenton on the Waterloo pike. Col. Gregg's brigade escorted a wagon train through Gainesville, encamping near Warrenton for the night.[62] As they had the day before, Kilpatrick's troopers kept to their camps, continuing to recover from their grueling fight on the 19th.[63] Merritt still guarded the railroad repair crews.[64] As he watched his cavalry carry out it various duties, Pleasonton, like Stuart, calculated the expense of the campaign – 73 killed, 312 wounded, and 866 missing.[65] These losses coupled with the vast number of men who had been dismounted translated into more work for those still in the ranks. The veterans already knew this unpleasant truth. The newer men were about to learn it.

On crossing the Rappahannock, Robert E. Lee's infantry had encamped on both sides of the Orange & Alexandria Railroad with Ewell's Corps on the right and Hill's on the left. Sufficient troops maintained a watch over the various fords along the river at Rappahannock Bridge and further downstream, the idea being that they would delay the enemy until support could come up. To better facilitate his plan, Lee decided to fortify a portion of the north bank of the river near the railroad bridge. He laid down a pontoon bridge, built an earthwork large enough for four guns, and dug rifle pits on both sides of the earthwork, angling back toward the river. Federal fortifications south of the river were turned around to face north and positions for guns also constructed. A brigade of infantry and four guns occupied the works north of the river. Lee realized that the line of the Rapidan held greater defensive advantages, and if Meade should threaten the Rappahannock by any other means than direct assault, the Confederate commander would have to fall back and occupy the works his army had held before the Bristoe campaign, but he hoped to hold this line in an effort to discourage Meade from advancing any further.[66]

On the 22nd, most of Stuart's cavalry maintained their posts of the previous day with one exception.[67] In support of Lee's plan of operations, Chambliss's Brigade rode out from its camps and across the pontoon bridge. Its mission was to watch the enemy and act as an early warning system for the infantry north of the river. About a mile beyond the bridge, Chambliss halted, threw out his skirmishers, and almost immediately ran into the Second Pennsylvania, under Lt. Col. Joseph P. Brinton, of Gregg's brigade stationed near Bealton Station. Gregg's regiments were stretched out along a line from near Sulphur Springs through Fayetteville to the station. Brinton had orders to establish an outpost line from Freeman's Ford to Kelly's Ford. The skirmish lasted only a short time, Chambliss withdrawing toward the river, as the Second received reinforcements in the form of the First Maine. Although casualties were light, one especially grieved the Pennsylvania regiment as well as Kilpatrick. Maj. Charles F. Taggart of the Second, who had served on Kilpatrick's staff, took a terrible wound to the knee that required amputation. He failed to recover and died on the 24th. Pleasonton followed up the enemy's retreat by sending a small party to reconnoiter the line of the railroad to Rappahannock Station, but Chambliss had done all the falling back he was going to do for the day, and the scouts turned back after verifying that the railroad had been destroyed at least as far as Ratcliffe's Run.[68] Further up river at Waterloo, the First Rhode Island, Taylor's brigade, exchanged pleasantries, not lead, with the Fourth Virginia, Owen's Brigade. Gen. Gregg also confirmed that the enemy held the crossing at Sulphur Springs. The other regiments of his division either settled into their camps of the 21st like the First New Jersey, moved their camp like the Third Pennsylvania, or finished wagon escort duty and finally established camp like the First Maine and the Sixteenth Pennsylvania.[69]

Buford's and Kilpatrick's regiments remained stationary.[70] The infantry of Meade's army did the same with the First Corps stationed at Georgetown; the Second between Warrenton and Warrenton Junction; the Third at Catlett's Station with one brigade at Bristoe Station; the Fifth at New Baltimore; and the Sixth at Warrenton.[71] By all indications, the army appeared to be settling in for a time while the work of reconstructing the railroad continued unabated. Its completion would figure prominently in any plans Meade might formulate. The supply trains maintained their reputation for being slow and vulnerable to attack. The Confederate force north of the river at Rappahannock Station was a minor thorn at present. Supplies were what the army needed after its arduous efforts since the 9th.

As a result, Meade's supply line proved to be a tempting target for the partisans operating behind the Federal lines. Always on the lookout for easy pickings, Lt. Frank Williams of Mosby's Rangers could not help but scoop up a number of horses he found peacefully grazing in a field near Fairfax Court House. Not surprisingly, elements of the First District of Columbia Cavalry and the Second Massachusetts under Maj. Everton J. Conger started in pursuit. Williams and his men had been scouting since the previous day and stopped to rest their weary horses. The advantage then passed to Conger, who came up on the band through a heavy wood and surprised them. In the action that followed only Williams managed to escape and that by deserting his horse and taking refuge in the trees. One of the rangers, Charles Mason, was killed and three others - Jack Barnes, Ed Stratton, and Robert M. Harrover were captured. The episode proved that operating behind the lines, even for such successful units as Mosby's Rangers, proved a dangerous game.[72]

With both armies stationary, Stuart took time on the 23rd to conduct some overdue business. The recent losses in men and horses prompted him to bring up the subject of reinforcements and in a letter addressed to Gen. Samuel Cooper, the Confederacy's Adjutant and Inspector General, Stuart revisited the order regarding the transfer of the Eighth and Fourteenth Virginia to his command. Issued on October 8, the order had not been carried out, the two regiments continuing with their commands as part of Maj. Gen. Samuel Jones's Department of Western Virginia and East Tennessee. Endorsed and forwarded by Lee, who felt that some emergency would arise, as it always seemed to do, that would keep the regiments right where they were, the request met with immediate opposition. Gen. Jones responded by addressing the matter in a letter to Secretary of War James A. Seddon, explaining the necessity of leaving the two regiments in his department. Seddon forwarded the letter to Lee. Not to be outdone, Lee countered with another letter to Cooper, reiterating Stuart's arguments and adding that the terrain in which the regiments were stationed was not conducive to cavalry operations. The effort proved useless and the regiments stayed put. Stuart would simply have to deal with Pleasonton with those troops already in hand.[73]

Circumstances also forced Stuart to broach another subject he had hoped to rectify through other means. The capture of Brig. Gen. William H. F. "Rooney" Lee while recovering from wounds sustained at the battle of Brandy Station on June 9, had left Lee's Brigade in the capable hands of Col. John R. Chambliss of the Thirteenth Virginia. Stuart had made every effort to have "Rooney" Lee exchanged, but the Federals declined. Wanting to solidify his command and reward Chambliss for his service, Stuart wrote to Gen. Cooper requesting that Chambliss be promoted to brigadier general and placed permanently in command of the brigade he now led. As he had on numerous other occasions, Stuart recognized talent and tried to reward it.[74]

Throughout the Confederate cavalry's bivouacs quiet reigned except for the men of Chambliss's command. About 11:00 in the morning, the Second Pennsylvania, Gregg's brigade, Gregg's division, again came calling. Pickets of the Ninth Virginia met them below Bealton Station. Reinforced by the First Maine, the Federals forced Chambliss back to the fortifications at the Rappahannock Bridge. Here the gray infantry appeared in strength the Federal cavalry could not match and they in turn began to withdraw. Chambliss followed and by 2:00 in the afternoon all had returned to their starting points. The whole exercise wore out men and horses and gained nothing.[75] Taylor's brigade, Gregg's division, performed a variety of duties. The First Rhode Island maintained its outposts near Waterloo. The Third Pennsylvania had dress parade in the morning, during which a pitch was made to the troopers to re-enlist. The response proved underwhelming. The other regiments had similar experiences.[76]

The day passed for the other two divisions of Pleasonton's cavalry in a like manner. In Buford's division, Devin's brigade uprooted itself from its camp near Warrenton about 1:00 in the afternoon and rode through Fayetteville to Liberty, encamping there for the night. Devin did push one regiment as far as Bealton Station.[77] Chapman's brigade held to its camps and outposts.[78] Merritt's Reserve Brigade still guarded the railroad work crews, but on this wet, cold, and miserable day saddled up in the morning and took an excursion to Gainesville. The day-long circuitous ride brought them round again to their morning camp at Manassas Junction at 9:00 that evening, making the whole trek, conducted past and through the camps of various infantry units, inexplicable to the men.[79] Kilpatrick's men continued the work of recovery in their camps near Hay Market and Gainesville. For some boredom became their new enemy, that and the awful weather that drew choral complaints.[80]

However, even the mundane could be deadly. On the night of the 23rd, a train carrying 126 condemned horses from Kilpatrick's division left Gainesville around 11:00. The horses' riders, under the command of Capt. Obediah J. Downing of the Second New York, Davies's brigade, scattered among the 17 cars on their way to the dismount camp, acted as guard for the cargo. The hurried reconstruction of the railroad had not allowed for a switch at Gainesville, so the train had to run backwards toward Washington, a fact that figured prominently in what followed. Five miles from the station while negotiating a curve at a high speed, the engine tore the tracks from the rotted ties and tumbled down a steep embankment, dragging nine cars with it. The troopers, riding on top of the cars were thrown in every direction, some being buried under the wreckage when it at last came to rest. About 25 men were injured, several of whom later died. Fifty horses were killed outright or had to be shot. Capt. Downing, his own mount among the casualties, walked back to Gainesville for help. The darkness of the night hindered rescue operations and not until dawn was the extent of the catastrophe known.[81]

Even as the rescue parties tore through the train wreckage on the cold and stormy morning of the 24th, Devin's brigade stirred from its camp at Liberty and marched to a point below Bealton Station. Devin then advanced the Sixth and the Ninth New York toward the Rappahannock with the idea of driving the enemy's vedettes across the river and establishing his own there. Successful at first, the New Yorkers encountered tougher resistance close to the fortifications that guarded the pontoon bridge. At this juncture, Confederate infantry, supported by cavalry, poured from the works and followed Devin, who withdrew rapidly and did not really engage, back to Liberty. That accomplished, the graybacks in turn pulled back to their former position.[82]

The skirmish stirred up a hornets' nest of activity north of the river. Buford's other brigade, Chapman's, saddled up and then unsaddled when the crisis passed. Col. Gregg's brigade, Gregg's division, also heard the bugle call of "Boots and Saddles," roused itself, and formed a line of battle only to learn that the enemy had withdrawn. To verify that all was well, a squadron of the Sixteenth Pennsylvania made a reconnaissance to Beverly Ford late in the afternoon and followed that up with picket reserve duty.[83] Elsewhere the Third Corps commander, Maj. Gen. William H. French, received orders to send a brigade to support the cavalry, and Maj. Gen. George Sykes's Fifth Corps shifted to Auburn. All the other corps were instructed to be prepared to march at a moment's notice.[84] Even Kilpatrick's troopers made ready to march, although the orders never came.[85] The only cavalry that avoided being put in the saddle was Merritt's, which, after its previous day's trek, stayed in camp.[86] The whole brouhaha demonstrated that Meade still had concerns about Lee striking again north of the Rappahannock.

Stuart's cavalry, other than Chambliss, stirred scarcely a hoof. The men continued to guard the various fords, replacing each other in turn. For some this meant crossing the river, but most just watched from the southern side.[87] Very little changed on the 25th. The quartermasters finally had time to distribute clothing while the men went through a daily routine of roll calls, horse grazing, fire starting, cooking their meager rations, and employing all sorts of small activities that helped pass the time. Troopers came and went on horse requisition duty, all the while worrying whether or not they could get a new mount and sustain one if they did.[88] Letter writing also occupied many a soldier's time including Stuart's. He wrote to his wife about several topics. One of these focused on Gen. Lee's congratulations on the cavalry's role in the recent campaign. The rumor that he would soon be a lieutenant general also had arisen again as had the one concerning him being replaced by Gen. John B. Hood. The latter came through the lines with a comment by Federal Maj. Gen. John Sedgwick, who reputedly said that he hoped it was true.[89]

Among Pleasonton's command the subject of horses drew attention as well. In a communication sent to Meade's chief of staff, Pleasonton submitted two reports, one from Gen. Buford and the other from Gen. Gregg. Both men presented the condition of their divisions as being dire. Buford had 2,000 men and horses but only half could be labeled as fit for arduous duty. Disease had increased, and the lack of transport made it extremely difficult to feed his animals. Gregg echoed Buford. The Second Division's horses were in poor condition as well, due to a lack of forage. No hay had been issued for two weeks. Kilpatrick's report came in later in the day but reiterated the same facts. Hoof disease and swelled tongue ran rampant, affecting 200 horses in just four days. Additionally, Kilpatrick complained about his missing men. Many, he thought, had taken off to the dismount camp where they quickly learned to "appreciate the easy life." Pleasonton took the opportunity to recommend that dismounted men not go to the dismount camp for horses but remain with their commands and that the horses be brought to them. Meade agreed. The suggestion eventually drew a response from Maj. Gen. George Stoneman, who was at the time in command of the dismount camp. Stoneman argued that he would require about 150 men who knew what they were doing to move 500 horses and that he was already short handed, trying to deal with the

16,000 unserviceable horses under his charge.[90] There the matter stood. What remained was a choice between two evils. Both options had drawbacks and neither could address the real problem – the cavalry had been used hard. From this time until the army entered into its winter encampment, nothing would change.

Indeed, it didn't. Duty still called. In Buford's division, Devin's brigade moved from Liberty and established an outpost line from Morrisville on the left to Bealton Station on the right. Nothing of the enemy was seen or heard.[91] Chapman's troopers pulled themselves onto their mounts and marched through Germantown to Liberty and Fayetteville, encamping at and between both villages for the night.[92] In Gen. Gregg's division, Taylor's brigade had the luxury of staying put in its camp near Waterloo but still performed its duties along the Rappahannock. The Third Pennsylvania, which had relieved the First Rhode Island from picket duty near Waterloo the day before was on as friendly terms with its opponents as the Rhode Islanders had been. Col. Gregg's brigade held to its camps around Fayetteville. A small patrol from the Sixteenth Pennsylvania drew fire from Confederate vedettes at Beverly Ford, illustrating that not all Pennsylvanians were on good terms with the enemy.[93] Kilpatrick received no marching orders this day. His men recovered in their camps as they had done since the 20th, except for those dispatched to the assistance of their comrades at the site of the train derailment.[94] Merritt maintained his position at Manassas Junction.[95]

The 25th became an important day for one of the batteries of Federal horse artillery that had accompanied and fought with Pleasonton's cavalry through several campaigns. Lt. Alexander C. M. Pennington's Battery M, Second U. S. Artillery received a new battle flag covered with the names of the 31 engagements it had participated in since the beginning of the war. Manufactured by Tiffany and costing $125.00, the flag was made of red satin with a gold bullion border. Over the chenille-work crossed cannon were the letters "U. S." and "M" in needlework. All the battle names were also done in needlework. Attached to a silver mounted staff, topped with a silver spear point, the flag would in the future, fly over one of the finest batteries in the Federal army. The Confederate horse artillery was already quite familiar with Pennington's 3-inch ordnance rifles and with the way the battery fought. The battery would only add to its reputation and that of its commander.[96]

Although Lee had successfully, for the moment, wrecked the railroad from Rappahannock Station to Bull Run, his men had not been able to bring off all the iron, which the South desperately needed, when they retreated. On the 26th, they were still engaged in collecting and transporting it over the river.[97] The necessity of protecting the men performing this vital task precipitated yet another clash with Federal cavalry. Infantry from Brig. Gen. James A. Walker's and Brig. Gen. George H. Steuart's brigades of Maj. Gen. Edward Johnson's Division of Ewell's Corps pushed out along the railroad toward Bealton Station, encountering pickets of the Fourth New York and the Seventeenth Pennsylvania, Devin's brigade, Buford's division, east of the railroad. The rapid advance cut off part of the Seventeenth, which had been watching Kelly's Ford. The squadron eventually would manage to rejoin the regiment. Devin responded to the enemy by sending in the Sixth and the Ninth New York. Still the Confederates came on, forcing back the vedettes from the Sixteenth Pennsylvania of Col. Gregg's brigade west of the railroad. Buford fed Chapman's brigade into the fray, sending the Eighth Illinois to support the Sixteenth. He intended to draw the enemy into a wood near Germantown where Col. Benjamin F. Smith's infantry brigade of Maj. Gen. William H. French's Third Corps awaited. Walker and Steuart failed to fall into the trap, holding their position. Buford now brought up a section of Lt. Edward B. Williston's Battery D, Second U. S. Artillery to which the Confederates replied in kind. The entire day's skirmishing amounted to little as the Federals gave up ground and not much else. Casualties were few. The firing died away late in the afternoon.[98]

As usual the Confederate offensive brought a small avalanche of orders from Meade's headquarters. Maj. Gen. John Newton, commanding the First Corps, was to hold himself in readiness to reinforce French if required. French was instructed not to advance but to hold his position at Bealton Station. A courier's dispatch caused Merritt's cavalry brigade to saddle up, prepare to move from Manassas Junction to Bealton Station, connect with Buford's left, and keep Buford informed of the enemy's approach. Col. Gregg expressed concern for his outposts from Freeman's Ford to Beverly Ford. So great was his concern that he feared he would soon be without a command. Signal officers on Watery Mountain reported that it took one enemy column 40 minutes to pass one point. The Second, Fifth, and Sixth Corps commanders were placed on alert and the wagon trains ordered to prepare to head rearward. Only Kilpatrick avoided the alert due to the condition of his men.[99] Through all this commotion, Lee's men hauled railroad iron back to the Rappahannock unmolested.

While Buford and Gregg tussled with the gray intruders, Stuart's cavalry maintained the status quo, except for a few regiments that moved their camps.[100] Stuart took the time to craft a well-deserved letter of appreciation to Col. Oliver R. Funsten for the commendable manner in which he had exercised command of "Grumble" Jones's Brigade in the interim between Jones's leaving and Rosser's arrival. Funsten had indeed performed more than adequately. He would have to be satisfied with Stuart's letter, as he would never rise to the rank of brigadier general.[101]

The movement of Meade's army southward opened up more opportunities for John Mosby to strike at the supply trains winding their way along the roads behind the front lines. Between 8:00 and 9:00 on the night of the 26th, Mosby at the head of 50 men swooped down on the middle of a train of about 40 to 50 artillery wagons about two miles from New Baltimore. The Twelfth Illinois, guarding the train, with squadrons positioned at the beginning and end of the column, could not reach the threatened teamsters before the partisans had unhitched over 145 horses and mules and disappeared with them and some prisoners, including Lt. Lauriston L. Stone, commissary of the artillery reserve, into the night.[102]

Mosby stayed active over the next few days, causing the usual turmoil among teamsters, guards, and sutlers traveling or standing watch on the roads between Washington and the army. The ever-evolving circumstances made for some unusual occurrences. A Dr. Osmund, whose home lay between Catlett's Station and Bristoe Station, played host, willingly or unwillingly, to officers and men of both sides. On one occasion, some Confederates were captured in his house by a Federal patrol one night and early the next morning some Federals were captured there by the Confederates.[103] This tit-for-tat type of warfare was nothing new to an area that had seen the armies of both sides march through and occupy it repeatedly. Getting used to it was another matter.

On the morning of the 27th, Buford advanced Devin's brigade to determine the disposition of the enemy to his front. With the Ninth New York fanned out as skirmishers, Devin moved forward and soon discovered that the Confederates had retreated once again to the river, but still held a position with their left in rear of the Smith house and their right at Rappahannock Station. Nothing of any other significance occurred during the last hours of the day. Chapman's brigade resumed picket duty, the Eighth New York having the honor of the day's watch. Merritt's brigade at last rejoined Buford, marching all night through very disagreeable weather before reaching Germantown at 4:00 in the morning where the regiments made camp.[104] Gen. Gregg's division guarded fords as well. Some of the First Maine, Col. Gregg's brigade, replaced the Sixteenth Pennsylvania at Beverly Ford. In Taylor's brigade the First New Jersey relieved the Third Pennsylvania at the ford below Waterloo. The First Pennsylvania kept watchful eyes on the ford at Sulphur Springs.[105] Except for a patrol of 40 men from the First West Virginia, Davies's brigade, that spent the night of the 26th in a useless ride, Kilpatrick's troopers simply added another day to their recovery schedule.[106]

Across the watery divide, the Confederate cavalry kept an eye on the bluecoat pickets, performed the usual camp routines, and attended to such other mundane tasks as court martial duty. Captains Richard H. Watkins and Jones R. Christian, the latter formerly attached to Stuart's headquarters, found Sgt. James H. Owen of the Third Virginia, Owen's Brigade, Fitz Lee's Division, guilty of being absent without leave, breaking him to the ranks, having him forfeit one month's pay, closely confining him, and putting him on the ring four hours each day for ten days.[107] A hard punishment for a veteran soldier already once wounded. But, discipline had to be maintained, and men had to be kept in the ranks.

October 28 was a day that many diarists summed up with a modicum of words, almost all pertaining to lying around in their camps. However, some found other things to do. In Fitz Lee's Division, the Sixth Virginia, Lomax's Brigade, moved its camp to the Botts farm. Troopers from the Third Virginia, Owen's Brigade, after drawing corn at Brandy Station, replaced those of its brother regiment, the Second Virginia, on guard at Rappahannock Bridge. The Fifteenth Virginia, Lomax's Brigade, rode to Jeffersonton and guarded the crossing near Waterloo.[108] The same kind of exchanges occurred over the river as the First Maine, Gregg's brigade, Gregg's division, relieved one of its brother regiments; the Fifth

United States, Merritt's brigade, Buford's division, took the place of the Sixth New York, Devin's brigade, Buford's division, near Elk Run; and the Eighth Illinois, Chapman's brigade, Buford's division, also left the comforts of camp to watch the enemy.[109] In a communication with Pleasonton's chief of staff, Col. C. Ross Smith, Buford gave his division's position as being camped on both sides of the road from Warrenton to Falmouth with his left being near Kelly's Ford and his right connecting with Gen. Gregg near Beverly Ford. He also reported that the enemy still held Rappahannock Station with infantry and that their line was three quarters of a mile long.[110] The fighting of the 26th had changed nothing.

The next two days passed in much the same manner. Even the newspapers found nothing to write about from the front other than that the reconstruction of the railroad had reached Catlett's Station. About the only cavalry activity to occur on the 30th involved Capt. Benoni Lockwood of the Sixth Pennsylvania, Merritt's brigade, Buford's division. With two engineer officers from Meade's staff, he ventured out on a reconnaissance, penetrated the enemy's outpost lines, and scouted along the river, noting the position of the enemy's forces and gathering other valuable information. The three returned safely at 10:00 on the morning of the 31st. The tiny expedition was a harbinger of greater things to come in the near future. In addition to sending out the patrol, on the 29th Meade shifted some of his infantry corps, moving the Third into position south of Warrenton Junction on the heights overlooking Licking Run and the Fifth to Three Mile Station.[111]

On the last day of the month everyone awoke to a rainy morning. Cold weather set in during the day. In Buford's division, Devin's brigade, stretched out along the road from Bealton Station to Morrisville, was joined by Merritt's, which rode to Elk Run, halfway between the station and Morrisville. Both brigades picketed toward Kelly's and Ellis' fords. Chapman's brigade moved not a hoof, although some of the men pushed pens and pencils around, working on muster rolls. Several of Gen. Gregg's troopers also focused on muster rolls and at least the First Maine, Gregg's brigade, bade welcome to the paymaster bearing two months pay. The Third Pennsylvania, Taylor's brigade, stood inspection - an unpleasant ordeal, considering the weather. For the others, the day passed, as had the previous few, quietly. The men of Kilpatrick's command, long idle, finally gathered themselves and marched, some more than others. The First West Virginia, Davies's brigade, made it only as far as Manassas Junction, but the Eighteenth Pennsylvania, Davies's brigade, and the First Vermont, Custer's brigade, reached Bristoe Station.[112]

End of the month activities also occupied some of Stuart's regiments. Lt. John Joseph Downman, acting ordnance officer for Brig. Gen. Williams C. Wickham's Brigade, still commanded by Col. Owen, had the dreaded duty of inventorying the ordnance and ordnance stores for his regiment, the Fourth Virginia. His reports revealed that the Fourth carried a variety of arms, including Sharps rifles, Sharps carbines, Merrill carbines, Burnside rifles, Gallagher rifles, and Army and Navy revolvers. The same held true for other regiments throughout the cavalry. Supplying ammunition for such an eclectic collection of arms tested the Confederate ordnance department on a daily basis.[113]

For at least one grayback, the month ended on a high note. Pvt. Elijah Johnson of the Fifteenth Virginia, Lomax's Brigade, Fitz Lee's Division, had been on outpost duty near Jeffersonton for two days. Men assigned to such duty, necessary as it was, seldom welcomed it with joy, but Johnson felt differently and hoped that he could remain where he was indefinitely. The company of several neighboring girls and a bounty of food, the latter somehow overlooked by other troopers who had passed through the area, caused him to wish for a lengthy stay - a couple of months stay. It was not to be. As October closed, so did Johnson's picket duty. For him it was back to camp and whatever rations the commissary could scrounge up and deliver – if they had the transport. He could always hope that he would get back to his paradise, but the Federals would have more to say about that than his own officers.[114]

Notes:
1. *O.R.*, Series 1, vol. 29, part 2, 306-307 and part 1, 10.
2. *Ibid.*, part 1, 350, 362, and 449.
3. *Ibid.*, 330, 350, 449, 461, 463, 466-468, 470, 472, and 475.

     The effectiveness of Stuart's "bold demonstration" this day would not convince all of the officers of the Army of the Potomac that Lee marched hard upon their heels. At least one, Maj. Gen. Gouverneur Warren, commanding the Second Corps, came to the conclusion late in the afternoon that "all that is going on in my front is mere humbug." He urged Meade that Lee could be whipped in a fair fight and wanted to push forward. Unfortunately, Meade still thought otherwise. *O.R.*, Series 1, vol. 29, part 2, 328-329.
4. *O.R.*, Series 1, vol. 29, part 1, 330-331.
5. *Ibid.*, 302 and 475; Edwards Diary; Beale, *9th Virginia Cavalry*, 102-103; *New York Herald*, October 20, 1863.
6. *O.R.*, Series 1, vol. 29, part 1, 330-331; 340, and 472; Neese, *Three Years in the Confederate Horse Artillery*, 225-228; Bradshaw, *Diary...McVicar*, 30; Francis Halsey Wigfall to Louis T. Wigfall, October 23, 1863, Wigfall Family Papers, MMC-3183, Manuscript Division, LC.
7. Just which guns of the battalion fought here cannot be determined accurately. Stuart stated that Beckham fought here and he may have, this being later in the day than the fight at McLean's Ford, giving the horse artillery commander time to acquire another horse, but Stuart doesn't record which batteries were engaged. When he left Bristoe Station, Stuart had Breathed's, McGregor's, Griffin's, and Chew's batteries with him. Hart's and Moorman's accompanied Young's Brigade. Three guns of Breathed's Battery and one gun from Chew's fought at McLean's, leaving two guns from Chew's and all of McGregor's and Griffin's to fight at Yates' Ford. It would appear that one or both of the latter were engaged here. Trout, *Galloping Thunder*, 375.

     For several weeks, the Third Pennsylvania had been attached to Brig. Gen. Henry D. Terry's division of the Sixth Corps. Relieved of that duty on the evening of October 12, the regiment had orders to report to the nearest cavalry command, which turned out to be Devin's. Rawle, *Third Pennsylvania Cavalry*, 345; *Philadelphia Weekly Times*, January 20, 1883.

     According to one account, the Federals gained some precious time by sending Corp. Andrew J. Speese of the Third Pennsylvania forward with a flag of truce fashioned with a newspaper as no white cloth could be found. Speese reportedly inquired as to what troops faced his regiment since it was raining and the troopers all wore ponchos covering their uniforms. On being told that the men were from Gordon's North Carolina Brigade, Speese stated that before the fighting began, Gen. Buford wanted to talk to Gordon about some wounded men lodged in the house nearby. The Confederate emissary dutifully rode off to seek Gordon, who, when he arrived, sent a message back to Speese that he was ready to talk to Buford. At that juncture, Speese revealed that the whole story had been a ploy to gain time to put all the Third's men into position. The disgruntled grayback trotted off to inform his commander that he had been duped. This story could not be confirmed from other sources. *Philadelphia Weekly Times*, January 20, 1883.
8. *O.R.*, Series 1, vol. 29, part 1, 350, 449-450, 461, and 466; Baylor, *Bull Run to Bull Run*, 175; McCabe, "Itinerary of the Seventeenth Regiment, Pennsylvania Volunteer Cavalry," 333; Hard, *Eighth Illinois Cavalry*, 280; Pickerill, *Third Indiana Cavalry*, 99; Hall,

Sixth New York Cavalry, 163; Rawle, *Third Pennsylvania Cavalry*, 336-337, 353-354; *Philadelphia Weekly Times*, January 20, 1883.

   According to two sources, at sometime during the morning, the First Maine, which had not as yet rejoined Col. Gregg's brigade, received orders to cross Bull Run on a reconnaissance toward Manassas Junction. Just when the First Maine conducted its foray cannot be determined nor can the ford where it crossed the run. Because it was acting independently of the brigade it could have joined in the fighting at any of the fords, although this would not explain the orders to go on a reconnaissance. Supposedly, after exchanging a few shots with the Confederates, the regiment withdrew, making a brief stand when reinforced south of the run. A charge by the enemy convinced the Mainers to put the stream between themselves and their belligerent foe. Regimental Surgeon Horace Stevens, who had wanted to hear the buzzing of "minnie" balls past his ears but had been convinced by Col. Charles H. Smith not to cross the run abruptly lost all his curiosity when a spent bullet struck the horse of Hospital Steward Samuel C. Lovejoy who had accompanied him. The pair hurriedly abandoned their "post." The regiment rode back to Fairfax Station where it joined the brigade the next day. Tobie, *First Maine Cavalry*, 206; Sawyer Diary.

9.   *O.R.*, Series 1, vol. 29, part 1, 390; Macomber Diary.

10.   *O.R.*, Series 1, vol. 29, part 1, 350, 353, 362, 382, 386-387, 391, 459, 463, 468, and 475; Pyne, *First New Jersey Cavalry*, 193-194, Kidd, *Personal Recollections*, 211; Glazier, *Three Years in the Federal Cavalry*, 342; Gracey, *Annals of the Sixth*, 199; Ressler Diary; Carter Diary.

   Gibbs led the brigade until the 18th.

11.   *O.R.*, Series 1, vol. 29, part 1, 362, 369, 387, 391, and 411, and part 2, 324-326 and 335; Pyne, *First New Jersey Cavalry*, 194; Lloyd, *History of the First Regiment Pennsylvania Reserve Cavalry*, 76; Rawle, *Third Pennsylvania Cavalry*, 358.

   The First New Jersey picketed the Occoquan at Wolf Run Shoals as did the First Pennsylvania. The Third Pennsylvania picketed along both Bull Run and the Occoquan.

12.   *O.R.*, Series 1, vol. 29, part 1, 387, 450, 457, 459, 463, 466, and 475, and part 2, 335; Cheney Diary; Frank Diary; Wilkin Diary; Ressler Diary; Morrissett Diary; Edwards Diary; Johnson Diary; Donahue Diary; Carter Diary; Shoemaker, *Shoemaker's Battery*, 58-59; Trout, ed., *Memoirs*, 71 and 224; Steele Diary; Green Article, *Warren Sentinel*; Boudrye, *Fifth New York Cavalry*, 83; Lloyd, *History of the First Regiment Pennsylvania Reserve Cavalry*, 76; *New York Herald*, October 20, 1863.

   A possibility exists that a part or all of Hart's Battery accompanied Stuart, but this cannot be confirmed from any other source.

   Lomax's Brigade appears to have spent the day in camp. One source stated that the Sixth Virginia moved about two miles northwest of Manassas and encamped for the night. A Fifteenth Virginia trooper claimed to have remained near Manassas all day. Lomax probably spread out his regiments between Manassas and New Market to watch various fords on Bull Run.

   Chambliss's Brigade bivouacked on the road between Brentsville and Manassas Junction.

   Owen's Brigade seems to have been spread out between Manassas Junction and Gainesville with the First and Third Virginia at Manassas and the Fourth at Gainesville. The position of the Second Virginia cannot be established.

13. *O.R.*, Series 1, vol. 29, part 2, 344-345; Williamson, *Mosby's Rangers*, 98-99; Wert, *Mosby's Rangers*, 103; *New York Times*, October 20, 1863.

    Mosby's escapades were not the only problem faced by the supply officers in Washington city and Meade's army. Sometimes the Confederates had nothing to do with supplies not arriving where they should. On the 10th, 1,600 horses and mules moved out from the remount camp and headed for the Army of the Potomac. On the 18th, 391 of them arrived. The rest were reported as missing along the way. With the army in desperate need of horses, such incompetence must have enraged Meade as well as Stoneman, who had charge over the remount camp. Maj. Gen. George Stoneman to Maj. Gen. George G. Meade, October 10, 1863, and Lt. John W. Spangler to Lt. Col. Sawtelle, October 18, 1863, Telegrams Collected by the Secretary of War, Unbound, RG 107, M504, NARA.

14. An outpost of the Eighteenth Pennsylvania, Davies's brigade, Kilpatrick's division, stationed on the Little River Turnpike may have discovered Stuart's advance toward Gum Springs. A sergeant reported his post being cut off by a cavalry force coming through the wood to the right of the road, forcing him to take his men cross county to Gum Springs where he hoped to join other pickets. However, on reaching this point, he found that the enemy had driven these men back. The sergeant then led his men back along the road from Gum Springs to the Warrenton Turnpike and gave his report. Citizens in the area stated that the Confederates belonged to Col. Elijah V. White's command but in fact, may have been part of Stuart's column, securing his flank while the rest of the division marched to Frying Pan. *O.R.*, Series 1, vol. 29, part 2, 340.

15. *O.R.*, Series 1, vol. 29, part 1, 450-451 and 459, and part 2, 324, 340 and 344-345; Brooks, ed., *Stories*, 205; Cheney Diary; Ressler Diary; Hard, *Eighth Illinois Cavalry*, 281; Hall, *Sixth New York Cavalry*, 163; Cheney, *Ninth Regiment, New York Volunteer Cavalry*, 139; Brig. Gen. John Buford to Maj. Gen. Alfred Pleasonton, October 17, 1863, Telegrams Collected by the Secretary of War, Unbound, RG 107, M504, NARA; *Philadelphia Inquirer*, October 20, 1863.

    Buford received his orders late on the evening of the 17th and did not comply until the following day. Chapman sent at least two regiments, the Eighth Illinois and the Eighth New York, up the Little River Turnpike toward Aldie, but no enemy was encountered. The camps of the two brigades seem to have been spread out along the road between Chantilly and Fairfax Court House.

16. *O.R.*, Series 1, vol. 29, part 1, 387 and 472; Steele Diary; Morrissett Diary; Carter Diary; Donahue Diary; Johnson Diary; Klement, ed., "Edwin B. Bigelow," 232; Boudrye, *Fifth New York Cavalry*, 83; Rodenbough, *Eighteenth Regiment of Pennsylvania Cavalry*, 44; Glazier, *Three Years in the Federal Cavalry*, 342.

    Davies committed at least the Fifth New York to the advance. The Eighteenth Pennsylvania spent the day picketing Bull Run and scouting toward Aldie. The Second New York reportedly picketed, scouted, and patrolled on either side of the run. The actions of the First West Virginia cannot be determined. The idea that Davies sent just the Fifth New York against the Confederates at Groveton should be considered in that the regiment could have easily pushed back the few pickets at Groveton and continued down the turnpike until encountering the Fourth Virginia near Gainesville, withdrawing when opposition stiffened.

17. *O.R.*, Series 1, vol. 29, part 1, 450 and 475, and part 2, 335; Edwards Diary; Gracey, *Annals of the Sixth*, 199; Beale, *9th Virginia Cavalry*, 103; *New York Herald*, October 20, 1863.

18. *O.R.*, Series 1, vol. 29, part 1, 382, 387, 391, 396, 451, 459, and 998; Carter Diary; Morrissett Diary; Wilkin Diary; Macomber Diary; Allyne C. Litchfield to My Dear Wife, October 20, 1863, Allyne Cushing Litchfield Papers, James S. Schoff Civil War Collection, Manuscripts Division, WLC/UM; *New York Herald*, October 21, 1863; *Vermont Chronicle*, November 7, 1863.

   In his report, Kilpatrick misdated the order for his advance on the 18th as the 19th. Both Davies and Custer correctly date it as the 18th as do all other sources.

19. *O.R.*, Series 1, vol. 29, part 1, 451, 459, 467-468, 470, 472, and 475; Edwards Diary.

20. *O.R.*, Series 1, vol. 29, part 1, 351-352 and 475, and part 2, 347 and 997-998; Neese, *Three Years in the Confederate Horse Artillery*, 229; Edwards Diary; Johnson Diary; Donahue Diary; Gracey, *Annals of the Sixth*, 199-200.

   Col. Alfred Gibbs of the Nineteenth New York commanded the brigade until sometime during the 18th when Merritt assumed command.

   A discrepancy exists between Merritt's dispatches and his report of his actions on the 17th and 18th. In the former, he stated that he advanced on Bristoe Station on the 17th and was repulsed by artillery. However, in the latter he mentioned advancing only as far as Manassas on the 17th and then going on to Bristoe Station on the 18th. Chambliss also misdated this action as being on the 17th. Considering that all other sources cited above give the day of the fight at Bristoe as the 18th, Merritt must have misdated his dispatches and Chambliss's memory must have failed him when he wrote his report on the 24th. The most convincing evidence comes from Edwards's diary, which was written as the events unfolded.

21. *O.R.*, Series 1, vol. 29, part 1, 362 and 369, and part 2, 348-349; Ressler Diary; Sawyer Diary; Pyne, *First New Jersey Cavalry*, 194; Miller, *Sixteenth Pennsylvania Cavalry*, 40; Rawle, *Third Pennsylvania Cavalry*, 337; Denison, *Sabres and Spurs*, 307.

   The above sources all confirm that Gregg's regiments marched to Fairfax Station. One confirms that it went as far as Fairfax Court House where it encamped at 11:00 that night. None claim that a march to Vienna was begun.

   Some of Buford's regiments also moved back to Fairfax Court House. Those known to have done so were the Eighth Illinois, the Eighth New York, and the Seventeenth Pennsylvania. Other regiments, notably the Ninth New York, marched to Chantilly. The chronicler of the Sixth New York mentions both places. What appears evident is that Buford's division lay between Fairfax Court House and Chantilly. As mentioned previously, early in the morning the Eighth Illinois and the Eighth New York, scouting out the Little River Turnpike toward Aldie, failed to encounter the enemy. Cheney Diary; Hall, *Sixth New York Cavalry*, 163; Cheney, *Ninth Regiment, New York Volunteer Cavalry*, 139; Hard, *Eighth Illinois Cavalry*, 281; McCabe, "Itinerary of the Seventeenth Regiment, Pennsylvania Volunteer Cavalry," 333.

22. *O.R.*, Series 1, vol. 29, part 1, 382, and part 2, 349.

23. *Ibid.*, part 1, 382, 387, 391, 397, 451, and 459; Kidd, *Personal Recollections*, 213; *New York Times*, October 23, 1863.

   In his report, Col. Edward B. Sawyer of the First Vermont claimed to have attacked a heavy skirmish line, supported by at least a brigade, and caused it to flee from the field even after the enemy "had thrown his whole strength" into it, implying that he faced the whole brigade with only a battalion of his regiment. Sawyer even quoted Custer's report that stated, "The First Vermont Cavalry, under Colonel Sawyer, deserve great credit for the rapidity with which they forced the enemy to retire." Unfortunately, the whole episode is fictitious. Young's Brigade, which acted as rear guard, used only one regiment to protect the rear of the column and this unit retired gradually as the Federals advanced. No stands were made until they reached Broad Run at Buckland Mills. Furthermore, the Sixth Michigan led Custer's advance, not the First Vermont. Finally, Custer was referring to the First Vermont's actions on the afternoon and evening of the 18th, not the morning of the 19th.

Young reported that his brigade acted as rearguard during the withdrawal from Gainesville and stated that he did not participate in the fighting at the bridge. He must have passed through and taken position on the hill about a mile from the run.

Just which batteries of horse artillery Stuart had with him can only be partially determined. Since Lt. John J. Shoemaker's section of Moorman's Battery and a single-gun section of Griffin's Baltimore Light Artillery had accompanied Stuart to Frying Pan, they would have been with him at Buckland Mills. Hart's Battery was also attached to Hampton's Division. Sgt. Lewis T. Nunnelee of Moorman's Battery stated in his reminiscences that his section, Shoemaker's, crossed the run, rode over the county line, and unlimbered on a hill to await the enemy's advance. He mentioned opening fire from this position after the sharpshooters were engaged. He fired on a squadron of enemy cavalry at which time the enemy's artillery opened fire. In the history of his battery, Hart records being involved in the pursuit but not in the opening stages of the fight. That leaves Griffin. If Stuart deployed any artillery in the immediate vicinity of the village, it probably would have been from Griffin's Baltimore Light Artillery. Trout, ed., *Memoirs*, 71-72 and 224.

24. According to James H. Kidd, who commanded the Sixth Michigan in the fight, in a meeting with Fitz Lee in 1881, Lee blamed his attack's lack of complete success on Stuart for fighting at Broad Run and not falling back quickly enough. Lee felt that Kilpatrick could have been destroyed if Stuart had followed Lee's plan with greater alacrity. The problem with this colorful reminiscence is that Fitz Lee did not propose his plan until after Stuart had stopped at the run and sent for Fitz Lee to join him. Only then did Lee suggest attempting to lure Kilpatrick into a trap. Furthermore, Stuart had to delay the Federals long enough for Lee to arrive and get into position to launch his attack. If Lee did indeed express such a view to Kidd, he was being most unkind to his former commander. Kidd, *Personal Recollections*, 226;

25. *O.R.*, Series 1, vol. 29, part 1, 382 and 451; McClellan, *I Rode with Jeb Stuart*, 393; Blackford, *War Years With Jeb Stuart*, 241.

Stuart reported that during his retreat along the pike, before reaching Buckland, he had sent Fitz Lee word to guard his, Stuart's, right flank. Later in his report, as he took up position along Broad Run, Stuart stated that he had ordered Fitz Lee to come to Buckland and support him. Finally, Stuart mentions that a dispatch arrived from Fitz Lee about the time Kilpatrick was trying to get around Stuart's flanks, suggesting the plan to withdraw and trap Kilpatrick between the two Confederate divisions. Stuart then responded to Fitz Lee's suggestion, informing him that he would withdraw along the pike and wait for Fitz Lee's signal to turn and attack. In the space of a couple of hours, four messages, three from Stuart to Fitz Lee and one from Fitz Lee to Stuart, passed between these two men in which a plan was created and agreed to. The trust the two had in each other is evident, as is the ability to extemporize in the face of an aggressive enemy.

26. *O.R.*, Series 1, vol. 29, part 1, 391; Stephen Fonzo, *A Documentary and Landscape Analysis of the Buckland Mills Battlefield*, prepared for the Buckland Preservation Society and submitted to the National Park Service American Battlefield Protection Program,

March 11, 2008, 2 and 5; Kidd, *Personal Recollections*, 214; J. E. B. Stuart to General [R. E. Lee], October 19, 1863, Charles Scott Venable Papers; *New York Times*, October 23, 1863; *Detroit Free Press*, October 30, 1863.

27.   *O.R.*, Series 1, vol. 29, part 1, 382; Fonzo, *Buckland Mills Battlefield*, 2 and 25; Kidd, *Personal Recollections*, 214; *Supp. to O. R.*, part 1, vol. 5, 591; Trout, ed., *Memoirs*, 71.

        One source stated that Capt. Samuel S. Elder's Battery E, Fourth U. S. Artillery also was engaged at this time, but from what position is unknown. *New York Times*, October 23, 1863.

28.   The lieutenant colonel of the Seventh Michigan recorded that as his regiment returned from Greenwich and was about to attack Stuart's flank, it was fired upon by its own artillery, resulting in one man losing his foot and having his horse killed and causing the regiment to take cover in a hollow until the mistake could be corrected. Allyne C. Litchfield to My Dear Wife, October 20, 1863, Allyne Cushing Litchfield Papers, James S. Schoff Civil War Collection, Manuscripts Division, WLC/UM.

29.   *O.R.*, Series 1, vol. 29, part 1, 382, 387, 391, and 451; Kidd, *Personal Recollections*, 215; Trout, ed., *Memoirs*, 71; *New York Times*, October 23, 1863.

        If Kilpatrick was being forthright in his report, and not just attempting to cover up a lack of vigilance, and he really did send a scouting party to Auburn, then some unknown officer failed miserably in the execution of his orders. Fitz Lee's entire division rested near Auburn and then moved toward Buckland Mills. While the time of the departure of Kilpatrick's patrols is unknown, they probably left either while Custer fought Stuart across Broad Run or immediately after Custer had succeeded in crossing. Either way, the idea that a patrol moving from the vicinity of Buckland Mills toward Auburn could somehow have missed three brigades of cavalry and artillery moving from Auburn to Buckland Mills stretches credibility to the breaking point. Since Kilpatrick stated that both patrols returned before he advanced down the pike, the fact that the officer in command of the detachment sent to Auburn failed to find any of the enemy either reveals a severe case of myopia or gross incompetence.

        In his report, Custer boasted that when his men took Buckland Mills they forced Stuart to abandon a dinner that just had been placed before him and that some of Custer's men enjoyed the repast in Stuart's place. Not to be outdone, Capt. John Esten Cooke of Stuart's staff recorded in his diary entry for October 27, 1863, that Kilpatrick had been seated at the dinner table when Stuart's guns opened fire, announcing his attack in conjunction with Fitz Lee's, and that Kilpatrick hurriedly left without partaking of a single bite. One or both of stories may be apocryphal, but since neither Custer nor Cooke had access to the other's writings at this time, they could not have been attempting to upstage each other. If factual, the stories simply illustrate the rapidly changing events on this day. *O.R.*, Series 1, vol. 29, part 1, 391; Diary of John Esten Cooke, MSS 5295, Clifton Waller Barrett Library of American Literature, Special Collections, UV.

        Another version of the story exists. According to Brig. Gen. Pierce M. B. Young, Stuart had breakfasted at "Cerro Gordo" that morning but left before the Federals approached. Young then took his place at the table and was eating when a shell burst over the house, causing him to leave hurriedly and race for the bridge. He managed to escape. Custer arrived and was told by the two Hunton sisters who had prepared and served the meal, that Stuart and Young had just left. Supposedly Custer took Young's breakfast and asked the two ladies to have something prepared for him for dinner. When Fitz Lee attacked and Custer retreated past the house, he called to the sisters that he had taken Young's breakfast and so Young could have his dinner. Again, separating fact from fiction is impossible. As with the Custer/Cooke version of events, the story presents a vivid account of the day's varying fortunes. John Toler, "Old Roommates' Chance Encounter at Buckland Mill," *Fauquier County Historical Society Newsletter*, vol. 24 no. 1, (2002): 3-4.

30.   *O.R.*, Series 1, vol. 29, part 1, 382, 387, and 391; Kidd, *Personal Recollections*, 218 and 222; *Philadelphia Weekly Times*, August 23, 1879.

        Kilpatrick recorded that he first learned of Fitz Lee's approach from a scouting patrol that he sent toward Auburn. This could not have been the patrol previously mentioned since Kilpatrick clearly stated that the two patrols he had sent out earlier had returned before he rode from Buckland Mills toward New Baltimore. All of his subsequent actions stemmed from this second patrol's report. He supposedly halted Davies and sent out the Seventh Michigan to discover just what the unknown column was. However, the Seventh Michigan was attached to Custer's brigade and not Davies's. Kilpatrick was accompanying Davies and had left Custer at Buckland Mills, meaning that the Seventh was not at Kilpatrick's disposal. Neither Davies nor Custer mentioned the Seventh being dispatched on such a mission. Maj. Kidd of the Sixth Michigan alludes to the fact that the Seventh scouted in the direction of Greenwich not Auburn. His account confirms that the appearance of the lone rider was the first indication that the enemy was present on Custer's flank. Had a patrol found Fitz Lee as Kilpatrick asserts, then Kidd would not have been taken by surprise as he certainly was. Custer reported that he was informed that the enemy was approaching from the direction of Greenwich not Auburn. Kilpatrick also claimed that his scouting party mistook Fitz Lee's Division for Brig. Gen. Wesley Merritt's brigade, which he supposed was moving from Catlett's Station to Auburn. Unfortunately, Kilpatrick's account of events does not agree with the facts and, as with his previous statement that he had sent a scouting party toward Auburn, which somehow managed to miss seeing all of Fitz Lee's force, appears to be an attempt to persuade Pleasonton, to whom the report was addressed, that he had taken all the necessary steps to protect his flanks when in fact he had not.

31.   *O.R.*, Series 1, vol. 29, part 1, 466-468, 470, 473, and 475; Kidd, *Personal Recollections*, 218-220; Karla Jean Husby, comp., *Under Custer's Command: The Civil War Journal of James Henry Avery* (Washington, D.C.: Brassey's, 2000), 53.

32.   Some accounts claimed that Pennington had two guns on the flank, but his report clearly stated that he took only one gun with him. *Supp. to O. R.*, part 1, vol. 5, 591; Kidd, *Personal Recollections*, 221; S. A. Clark, "Buckland Mills," *Maine Bugle*, vol. 4, no. 2, (April 1897): 109.

33.   *O.R.*, Series 1, vol. 29, part 1, 391; Fonzo, *Buckland Mills Battlefield*, 4; H. H. Matthews, "Part XIV Continued (The Bristoe Campaign)," *St. Mary's Beacon*, Thursday, May 11, 1905; Trout, *Galloping Thunder*, 377; Neese, *Three Years in the Confederate Horse Artillery*, 230.

        The exact location of the five guns of Pennington's Battery is in question. One source claimed that they occupied a position on the right of Custer's line that stretched three fourths of a mile beginning near Broad Run on the left. However, Pennington wrote that after the enemy's skirmishers appeared on the left, he placed his battery in a position to meet their attack and opened fire on them before taking one gun from the battery and moving only 50 yards to the front and left, where he unlimbered on a hill that gave him an excellent field of fire, leaving the rest of the battery in place. This would indicate that his battery was much closer to the bridge and not on the right of Custer's line. Clark, "Buckland Mills," 109; *Supp. to O. R.*, part 1, vol. 5, 591.

A source indicated that the Confederate skirmishers and Breathed's Battery took position "in the face of shot and shell" meaning that Pennington opened fire before Breathed did. Pennington also stated that he opened fire on the enemy's skirmishers and then an enemy battery opened in reply. If so then Stuart may have launched his attack after hearing Federal artillery and not Fitz Lee's. *O.R.*, Series 1, vol. 29, part 1, 473; *Supp. to O. R.*, part 1, vol. 5, 591.

34. *O.R.*, Series 1, vol. 29, part 1, 387, 451; Glazier, *Three Years in the Federal Cavalry*, 346; Lieutenant-Colonel W. H. H. Cowles, "Auburn Mills," *Histories of the Several Regiments and Battalions from North Carolina in the Civil War 1861-65*, 1, edited by Walter Clark, (Raleigh: E. M. Uzzell, Printer and Binder, 1901), 458; Hopkins, *The Little Jeff*, 177; *Daily Charlottesville*, March 3, 1895.

In his account of the fighting, Capt. W. H. H. Cowles claimed to have led the charge from the beginning. However, he did not command the regiment at the beginning of the fight. Maj. Rufus Barringer led the initial assault until his horse, Black Shot, fell with him into a building while passing through New Baltimore. At this point, Cowles rode to the front and led the regiment forward.

35. *O.R.*, Series 1, vol. 29, part 1, 391-392; *Supp. to O. R.*, part 1, vol. 5, 592; Clark, "Buckland Mills," 110; Hubard Jr., *Memoirs of a Virginia Cavalryman*, 111; *Vermont Chronicle*, November 7, 1863; *New York Times*, October 23, 1863.

36. *O.R.*, Series 1, vol. 29, part 1, 391-392; Clark, "Buckland Mills," 110; Fonzo, *Buckland Mills Battlefield*, 5; Kidd, *Personal Recollections*, 222; *New York Times*, October 23, 1863; *Detroit Free Press*, October 24, 1863.

In a postwar article, Pvt. William B. Conway claimed that he demanded the surrender of a major, possibly Clark, who refused on the grounds that Conway was not a commissioned officer. A cocked pistol to the major's head gained Conway the officer's sword. Conway also stated that many of the prisoners were drunk and that they refused to move rapidly to the rear, hoping to be rescued. *Richmond Times Dispatch*, October 12, 1902.

37. *O.R.*, Series 1, vol. 29, part 1, 387, 452, and 459; Henry Coddington Meyer, *Civil War Experiences under Bayard, Gregg, Kilpatrick, Custer, Raulston, and Newberry, 1862, 1863, 1864*, (New York: Knickerbocker Press, 1911), 67; *Richmond Sentinel*, October 29, 1863; Douglas, *A Boot Full of Memories*, 291.

H. B. McClellan wrote that some of Davies's men escaped across the bridge with Custer, indicating that some had rushed ahead of the column. McClellan does not explain how he knew this occurred, so some doubt must be attached to the claim. McClellan, *I Rode with Jeb Stuart*, 395.

38. *O.R.*, Series 1, vol. 29, part 1, 231-235, 452; Fonzo, *Buckland Mills Battlefield*, 54, n98; *Richmond Sentinel*, October 29, 1863.

39. *O.R.*, Series 1, vol. 29, part 1, 232-235.

Before Stuart's 8:00 attack, he crossed words with a Federal officer who was with Makechney at that time. The unknown officer, searching for Webster, rode out into the darkness and up to Stuart's vedettes. He inquired where he could find Webster. Stuart called him forward and asked him "if Gen. Stuart would not do as well." The officer's answer was not recorded and Stuart soon sent his men forward. *Richmond Sentinel*, October 29, 1863.

40. *O.R.*, Series 1, vol. 29, part 1, 473; *Supp. to O. R.*, part 1, vol. 5, 592; Hubard Jr., *Memoirs of a Virginia Cavalryman*, 112; Carter Diary; *New York Times,* October 23, 1863.

   The extent of Stuart's success has been disputed from the firing of the last shot of the day. One source claimed that Kilpatrick "reported personally at headquarters and received the thanks of both Gens. Meade and Pleasonton for the able manner in which he had discharged the important duty that had been entrusted to him, and the skill he displayed in extricating his command from the most trying positions in which a command can be placed." As for Stuart, he claimed in his report of the campaign, written four months later, "Kilpatrick's division seemed to disappear from the field of operations for more than a month." The truth is harder to get at.

   Kilpatrick offered as a reason for his surprise that he understood his flank to be protected by other portions of the army, undoubtedly meaning Merritt who reached Catlett's Station during Meade's advance. However, Kilpatrick's own or at least his scouting parties' lack of vigilance led directly to the surprise. In an 1879 article for the *Philadelphia Weekly Times*, Kilpatrick stated that he "had been deceived by the scouts," which, if taken literally, is virtually an accusation of treason or at least cowardice in the face of the enemy. The conclusion is simpler. Stuart baited the hook and Kilpatrick bit on it.

   Casualties can shed some light on the extent of Kilpatrick's discomfiture. His command suffered 12 killed, 52 wounded, and 199 captured to Stuart's 9 killed, 30 wounded, and 3 captured. Kilpatrick also lost a few wagons, including Custer's headquarters wagon. By anyone's accounting, the blue cavalry had suffered a humiliation they would not soon forget.

   O.R., Series 1, vol. 29, part 1, 452; Clark, "Buckland Mills," 110; Fonzo, *Buckland Mills Battlefield*, 110; *New York Times,* October 22, 1863; *New York Times,* October 23, 1863; *Philadelphia Weekly Times*, August 23, 1879.

41. *O.R.*, Series 1, vol. 29, part 1, 353; Gracey, *Annals of the Sixth*, 200.

   Just whose pickets Merritt's troopers ran into is unknown.

42. Cheney Diary; Frank Diary; Hall, *Sixth New York Cavalry*, 163; Cheney, *Ninth Regiment, New York Volunteer Cavalry*, 139; Hard, *Eighth Illinois Cavalry*, 281; Blackwell, *12th Illinois Cavalry*, 127; McCabe, "Itinerary of the Seventeenth Regiment, Pennsylvania Volunteer Cavalry," 333.

43. Pyne, *First New Jersey Cavalry*, 194-195; Rawle, *Third Pennsylvania Cavalry*, 358; Miller, *Sixteenth Pennsylvania Cavalry*, 40; Denison, *Sabres and Spurs*, 308; Ressler Diary; Sawyer Diary; Tobie, *First Maine Cavalry*, 207.

44. *O.R.*, Series 1, vol. 29, part 1, 452, 464, 473, and 475; Steele Diary; Trussell Diary; Carter Diary; Morrissett Diary; Edwards Diary; Beale, *9th Virginia Cavalry*, 104; Neese, *Three Years in the Confederate Horse Artillery*, 231.

45. The crossing of the Hazel was not without a bit of adventure. Two ladies from Warrenton, not wishing to remain behind within Federal lines, had secured a ride south in Stuart's ambulance. As the wagon crossed the river it became wedged between two rocks. No amount of pulling by the mules could free it. Seizing on their only recourse, General Stuart, Colonels Pierce M. B. Young and Bradley T. Johnson, and Capt. Cadwallader J. Iredell, along with a few others, dismounted into the waist deep water and pushed at the wheels for about a half an hour before finally dislodging the wagon. The hazards of rescuing fair damsels are limitless. Cadwallader Jones Iredell to unknown addressee, October 23, 1863, Cadwallader Jones Iredell Papers, 363-Z, Folder 1, Correspondence 1862-1863, SHC/UNC.

46. *O.R.*, Series 1, vol. 29, part 1,459 and 461; Trout, ed., *Memoirs*, 72; Neese, *Three Years in the Confederate Horse Artillery*, 231; Bradshaw, *Diary...McVicar*, 31; J. E. B. Stuart to General [R. E. Lee], October 20, 1863, Charles Scott Venable Papers, 1862-1894, SHC/UNC.

      Pvt. Edward Green stated that his regiment, the Twelfth Virginia, returned all the way to Brandy Station on the 20th. Green Memoir; Green Article, *Warren Sentinel*.

      Robert E. Lee requested that Stuart provide a brigade of cavalry to cover the removal of iron from the railroad over the Rappahannock. The brigade was to be positioned near the railroad with pickets at Catlett's Station. Just which brigade Stuart assigned to this duty, and there is no indication that he did, is unknown. *O.R.*, Series 1, vol. 29, part 2, 794-795.

47. *O.R.*, Series 1, vol. 29, part 2, 355-359.

      The fear that Stuart might make another raid into Maryland may not have been as ridiculous as it sounded. In his congratulatory note to Stuart for his defeat of Kilpatrick, Lee wrote, "It is not my design for you to advance or to cross the Potomac, but to withdraw on the line formerly designated, when you think it advantageous to do so." This suggests that Stuart may have been entertaining the idea of following up his great success with another venture behind the Federal army. In any event, Lee's words of praise came laced with words of caution and a reminder of previous orders. There would be no raid. Meade could have rested easy if he had known. *O.R.*, Series 1, vol. 29, part 2, 794.

48. *O.R.*, Series 1, vol. 29, part 1, 353 and part 2, 358.

49. Inglis Diary; Cheney Diary; Hard, *Eighth Illinois Cavalry*, 281; Cheney, *Ninth Regiment, New York Volunteer Cavalry*, 139; Hall, *Sixth New York Cavalry*, 163; McCabe, "Itinerary of the Seventeenth Regiment, Pennsylvania Volunteer Cavalry," 333; *Philadelphia Inquirer*, October 22, 1863; *New York Times*, October 22, 1863.

      One source reported that Buford encountered some enemy skirmishers that retired as he pushed forward. This cannot be verified from Confederate sources. *New York Herald*, October 22, 1863.

      On the 19th the Second Pennsylvania, which had been acting as provost guard under Brig. Gen. Marsena R. Patrick, received orders to report to Gen. Gregg for assignment to Col. Gregg's brigade. The First Maryland (Union) was detailed to Gen. Patrick as provost guard. Samuel Penniman Bates, *History of the Pennsylvania Volunteers, 1861-1865*, (Harrisburg: B. Singerly, state printer, 1869-1871), Vol. 3, 323; *Philadelphia Inquirer*, October 20, 1863.

50. *O.R.*, Series 1, vol. 29, part 1, 362 and 369; Ressler Diary; Sawyer Diary; Pyne, *First New Jersey Cavalry*, 195; Rawle, *Third Pennsylvania Cavalry*, 358; Miller, *Sixteenth Pennsylvania Cavalry*, 40; Denison, *Sabres and Spurs*, 308; Tobie, *First Maine Cavalry*, 207.

51. Wilkin Diary; Hoffman, *First Vermont*, 150; Rodenbough, *Eighteenth Regiment of Pennsylvania Cavalry*, 44.

      The First Vermont did change its camp from near Gainesville to Groveton. It remained at the latter place until the 24th when it returned to its old campsite at Gainesville.

52. Richard Henry Watkins to My Precious Mary, October 25, 1863, Watkins Papers, 1861-1865, Mss1W3272a1-355, VHS.

53. *O.R.*, Series 1, vol. 29, part 1, 452.

54. William Clark Corson to My Dear Jennie, October 23, 1863, William Clark Corson Papers 1861-1865, Mss1c8184a1-64, VHS.

Two other sources confirm the three days without rations for the Fourth Virginia, Owen's Brigade, and the Fifteenth Virginia, Lomax's Brigade. Morrissett Diary; Johnson Diary.

55. Cheney, *Ninth Regiment, New York Volunteer Cavalry*, 139; Crowninshield, *First Regiment of Massachusetts Cavalry Volunteers*, 182; *New York Herald*, October 22, 1863.

One source estimated the loss of horses in Pleasonton's cavalry as 3,500. Since Pleasonton began the campaign with 12,126 men and horses "Present for duty equipped," the loss constituted almost 30%. *O.R.*, Series 1, vol. 29, part 1, 226; *New York Times*, October 24, 1863.

In addition to the bone-numbing fatigue that crippled many mounts, Brig. Gen. Wesley Merritt reported that a large number of the 471 disabled horses in his command had fallen victim to "hoof-rot" that could disable a horse in a single day. *O.R.*, Series 1, vol. 29, part 1, 353.

56. *Richmond Whig*, October 17, 1863.

Even the Northern press took shots at Stuart. A correspondent for the *New York Times* wrote, "Stuart commanded the cavalry in person on that day [Buckland Mills], but, as he is under a cloud just now with Virginians, Hampton, who is the rising man, gets all the credit, little or great as that may be, for the Buckland Mills affair." Facts - Hampton had not been in the field since Gettysburg - had little impact on those who wanted to criticize Stuart. *New York Times*, October 29, 1863.

57. *Richmond Sentinel*, October 29, 1863.

58. *New York Times*, October 20, 1863; Kidd, *Personal Recollections*, 226; Allyne C. Litchfield to My Dear Wife, October 22, 1863, Allyne Cushing Litchfield Papers, James S. Schoff Civil War Collection, Manuscripts Division, WLC/UM.

59. Carter Diary; Edwards Diary; Steele Diary; Arehart, "Diary of W. H. Arehart," 281; Trout, ed., *Memoirs*, 72; Neese, *Three Years in the Confederate Horse Artillery*, 231; Hopkins, *The Little Jeff*, 177; McDonald, *History of the Laurel Brigade*, 203.

60. *O.R.*, Series 1, vol. 29, part 1, 454; Steele Diary; Cincinnatus J. Ware to My Dear Bess, October 23, 1863, Hughes-Ware Family Papers, Collection #37961, Correspondence Box 1, Folder 10, LV.

61. Inglis Diary; Cheney Diary; Hard, *Eighth Illinois Cavalry*, 281; Cheney, *Ninth Regiment, New York Volunteer Cavalry*, 139; Hall, *Sixth New York Cavalry*, 163; McCabe, "Itinerary of the Seventeenth Regiment, Pennsylvania Volunteer Cavalry," 333.

The Eighth New York had remained behind to do picket duty around Fairfax Station. Norton, *Deeds of Daring*, 75.

The Twelfth Illinois continued to guard wagon trains along the Warrenton turnpike. Blackwell, *12th Illinois Cavalry*, 127.

One source reported that artillery and cavalry skirmished with the enemy at Sulphur Springs, but since none of the Federal cavalry reached this location on the 21st, the report appears to have been false. *New York Herald*, October 22, 1863.

62. Ressler Diary; Sawyer Diary; Sauerburger, ed., *I Seat Myself to Write You*, 182; Pyne, *First New Jersey Cavalry*, 195; Rawle, *Third Pennsylvania Cavalry*, 358; Denison, *Sabres and Spurs*, 309; Tobie, *First Maine Cavalry*, 207.

63. Wilkin Diary; Hoffman, *First Vermont*, 150; Rodenbough, *Eighteenth Regiment of Pennsylvania Cavalry*, 44.

The above diarist recorded that his regiment, the First West Virginia, moved camp about a half mile. At this time the regiment had only about 100 men ready for duty. The writer's company had ten.

64. *O.R.,* Series 1, vol. 29, part 1, 353.

65. *Ibid.,* 343.

66. *Ibid.,* 611; *Supp. to O. R.,* part 1, vol. 5, 617-618.

67. Carter Diary; Morrissett Diary; Donahue Diary.

68. *O.R.,* Series 1, vol. 29, part 2, 368; Ressler Diary; Sawyer Diary; Beale, *9th Virginia Cavalry,* 104-105; Edwards Diary; *Philadelphia Inquirer,* October 26, 1863; *New York Times,* October 26, 1863.

69. *O.R.,* Series 1, vol. 29, part 2, 368; Denison, *Sabres and Spurs,* 309; Pyne, *First New Jersey Cavalry,* 195; Rawle, *Third Pennsylvania Cavalry,* 358; Ressler Diary; Sawyer Diary; Tobie, *First Maine Cavalry,* 207.

70. Inglis Diary; Cheney Diary; Hall, *Sixth New York Cavalry,* 164; McCabe, "Itinerary of the Seventeenth Regiment, Pennsylvania Volunteer Cavalry," 333; Hard, *Eighth Illinois Cavalry,* 281; Cheney, *Ninth Regiment, New York Volunteer Cavalry,* 139; Wilkin Diary; Rodenbough, *Eighteenth Regiment of Pennsylvania Cavalry,* 44.

71. *O.R.,* Series 1, vol. 29, part 2, 368.

72. *Ibid.,* part 1, 494; Williamson, *Mosby's Rangers,* 100-101.

73. *O.R.,* Series 1, vol. 29, part 2, 778, 800, 807-810, and 819-820.

74. J. E. B. Stuart to General [Samuel Cooper], October 23, 1863, Stuart Papers, 1851-1968, Mss1ST923d, Microfilm reel C621, VHS.

The government in Richmond responded slowly to Stuart's request. Not until January 27, 1864, was Chambliss promoted, his commission to date from December 19, 1863. Davis and Hoffman, eds., *The Confederate General,* vol.1, 173.

75. Carter Diary; Morrissett Diary; Donahue Diary; Edwards Diary; Sawyer Diary; Tobie, *First Maine Cavalry,* 207.

76. Denison, *Sabres and Spurs,* 309; Rawle, *Third Pennsylvania Cavalry,* 337.

77. *O.R.,* Series 1, vol. 29, part 2, 377; Inglis Diary; Hall, *Sixth New York Cavalry,* 164; McCabe, "Itinerary of the Seventeenth Regiment, Pennsylvania Volunteer Cavalry," 333.

78. Cheney Diary; Hard, *Eighth Illinois Cavalry,* 281; Blackwell, *12th Illinois Cavalry,* 127.

79. *O.R.,* Series 1, vol. 29, part 1, 353; Gracey, *Annals of the Sixth,* 200.

80. Wilkin Diary; Rodenbough, *Eighteenth Regiment of Pennsylvania Cavalry,* 44.

81. *New York Times,* October 26 and 28, 1863.

Since Lee's infantry had torn up all the track south of Bull Run, burning the ties, the fact that the ties used in the reconstruction were rotted would seem to indicate that they had been stored out in the elements for a considerable time. In the rush to rebuild the railroad, proper inspections probably had not been made of all the material used, resulting in these rotted ties being laid down. The speed of the train certainly contributed to the accident, as did the placement of the engine at the rear of the train. All of these factors contributed to the disaster.

Some of the regiments whose troopers were aboard the train were the Eighteenth Pennsylvania, the Second New York, and the Fifth New York.

82. *O.R.,* Series 1, vol. 29, part 2, 377; Inglis Diary; Sawyer Diary; Hall, *Sixth New York Cavalry,* 164; Cheney, *Ninth Regiment, New York Volunteer Cavalry,* 139; *New York Times,* October 26, 1863; *Philadelphia Inquirer,* October 26, 1863.

Just which of Chambliss's regiments supported the infantry is difficult to determine. The Ninth Virginia had been pulled back to its camp, leaving either the Tenth or the Thirteenth Virginia to perform the duty. Devin recorded that he faced a brigade of cavalry in addition to infantry. *O.R.,* Series 1, vol. 29, part 2, 378; Edwards Diary.

83. Cheney Diary; Sawyer Diary; Ressler Diary; Sauerburger, ed., *I Seat Myself to Write You*, 183.

    Gen. Gregg reported that Taylor's picket posts extended from Waterloo to Fox's Ford with Col. Gregg's stretching from there to Beverly Ford. He expressed concern that if the enemy pushed beyond Fayetteville, he would have to withdraw his pickets from Fox's Ford. The stabilizing of the lines in the afternoon alleviated this situation. *O.R.*, Series 1, vol. 29, part 2, 378-379.
84. *O.R.*, Series 1, vol. 29, part 2, 379-380.
85. Wilkin Diary.

    Kilpatrick did send a note to Pleasonton's chief of staff, Lt. Col. C. Ross Smith, informing him that a report had been received about either White or Mosby being near Thoroughfare Gap. Kilpatrick had ordered Davies to use a regiment to reconnoiter the area. *O.R.*, Series 1, vol. 29, part 2, 380.
86. Gracey, *Annals of the Sixth*, 201.
87. Carter Diary; Morrissett Diary; Donahue Diary; Edwards Diary; Steele Diary; Arehart, "Diary of W. H. Arehart," 282; Trout, ed., *Memoirs*, 72; Neese, *Three Years in the Confederate Horse Artillery*, 231.
88. Richard Henry Watkins to My Darling, October 25, 1863, Watkins Papers, 1861-1865, Mss1W3272a1-355, VHS.
89. J. E. B. Stuart to My Darling Wife, October 25, 1863, Stuart Papers, 1851-1968, Mss1ST923d, Microfilm reel C621, VHS.
90. *O.R.*, Series 1, vol. 29, part 2, 382-382, 400-402.
91. Inglis Diary; Cheney, *Ninth Regiment, New York Volunteer Cavalry*, 139; *Washington Daily Morning Chronicle*, October 29, 1863.
92. Cheney Diary; Hard, *Eighth Illinois Cavalry*, 281; Hall, *Sixth New York Cavalry*, 164.
93. Ressler Diary; Rawle, *Third Pennsylvania Cavalry*, 338 and 359; Denison, *Sabres and Spurs*, 309-310; Tobie, *First Maine Cavalry*, 207.
94. Wilkin Diary; Hoffman, *First Vermont*, 150; Rodenbough, *Eighteenth Regiment of Pennsylvania Cavalry*, 44.
95. Gracey, *Annals of the Sixth*, 201.
96. *New York Times*, October 26, 1863.
97. *Philadelphia Inquirer*, October 26, 1863.
98. *O.R.*, Series 1, vol. 29, part 2, 385-390; Inglis Diary; Cheney Diary; Ressler Diary; Hall, *Sixth New York Cavalry*, 164; McCabe, "Itinerary of the Seventeenth Regiment, Pennsylvania Volunteer Cavalry," 333; Cheney, *Ninth Regiment, New York Volunteer Cavalry*, 139; Hard, *Eighth Illinois Cavalry*, 281-282; *Washington Daily Morning Chronicle*, October 29, 1863; *Philadelphia Inquirer*, October 31, 1863.

    One source reported that Lt. Edward Heaton's Battery B/L, Second U. S. Artillery was engaged. The only casualty registered by the artillery was in Williston's battery. While this does not eliminate Heaton's participation, it confirms Williston's. *Washington Daily Morning Chronicle*, October 29, 1863; *Philadelphia Inquirer*, October 31, 1863.

    Two sources stated that the Confederates had both cavalry and infantry present. Just which regiments of cavalry were represented is difficult to ascertain. Both the First and the Fourth Virginia had one casualty each reported on this day, one at Bealton Station and one at Warrenton. That portions of these regiments participated in the skirmish must be considered. Driver, *1st Virginia Cavalry*, 164; Stiles, *4th Virginia Cavalry*, 111; *HDSACWRD* at, <www.civilwardata.com> August 9, 2009; *Wash-*

ington Daily Morning Chronicle, October 29, 1863.

After fighting most of the day, at 4:00 in the afternoon, the Sixth New York of Devin's brigade was sent six miles down river to Elk Run where it camped and went on picket duty. Hall, *Sixth New York Cavalry*, 164.

99. *O.R.*, Series 1, vol. 29, part 2, 385-390; Rodenbough, *Eighteenth Regiment of Pennsylvania Cavalry*, 44.
100. Johnson Diary; Carter Diary; Morrissett Diary; Donahue Diary; Arehart, "Diary of W. H. Arehart," 282.
101. *O.R.*, Series 1, vol. 29, part 2, 802-803.
102. *Ibid.*, part 1, 495; Blackwell, *12th Illinois Cavalry*, 127; *Washington Evening Star*, October 28, 1863; *Washington Daily Morning Chronicle*, October 29, 1863; *New York Herald*, November 1, 1863; *HDSACWRD* at, <www.civilwardata.com> August 10, 2009.

According to one account Lt. Stone had upon his person a considerable amount of government funds that also fell into Mosby's hands or those of some of his men. No mention of such funds can be found in Mosby's report. *New York Herald*, November 1, 1863.

103. *New York Times*, October 31, 1863.
104. *O.R.*, Series 1, vol. 29, part 2, 392-393; Inglis Diary; Cheney Diary; Gracey, *Annals of the Sixth*, 201; Cheney, *Ninth Regiment, New York Volunteer Cavalry*, 139.
105. Ressler Diary; Rawle, *Third Pennsylvania Cavalry*, 338 and 359; Sauerburger, ed., *I Seat Myself to Write You*, 183.
106. Wilkin Diary; Rodenbough, *Eighteenth Regiment of Pennsylvania Cavalry*, 44.

One of Kilpatrick's men did not have a quiet time in camp recuperating. Lt. Theodore A. Boice of the Fifth New York, Davies's brigade, rode out from camp and into the arms of what was reported to be a party of Mosby's men. Taken prisoner, the crafty Boice dropped his hat and in the process of retrieving it, pulled a gun from his boot and made his escape in a hail of lead. Struck five or six times he survived his wounds and returned to duty, eventually becoming lieutenant colonel of the regiment. *Wyoming Mirror*, date unknown; *NYSMMVRC* at, <www.dmna.state.ny.us/historic/mil-hist.htm>; *HDSACWRD* at, <www.civilwardata.com> December 31, 2009.

107. Carter Diary; Morrissett Diary; Donahue Diary; Nanzig, *3rd Virginia Cavalry*, 121.
108. Carter Diary; Morrissett Diary; Donahue Diary; Edwards Diary; Steele Diary; Johnson Diary; Neese, *Three Years in the Confederate Horse Artillery*, 231-232.
109. Inglis Diary; Cheney Diary; Ressler Diary; Sawyer Diary; Wilkin Diary; Hall, *Sixth New York Cavalry*, 164; McCabe, "Itinerary of the Seventeenth Regiment, Pennsylvania Volunteer Cavalry," 333; Hard, *Eighth Illinois Cavalry*, 282.
110. *O.R.*, Series 1, vol. 29, part 2, 395-396.
111. *Ibid.*, 397-398; Gracey, *Annals of the Sixth*, 201; *Philadelphia Inquirer*, October 31, 1863.
112. *O.R.*, Series 1, vol. 29, part 2, 403; Cheney Diary; Ressler Diary; Sawyer Diary; Wilkin Diary; Gracey, *Annals of the Sixth*, 201; McCabe, "Itinerary of the Seventeenth Regiment, Pennsylvania Volunteer Cavalry," 333; ; Rawle, *Third Pennsylvania Cavalry*, 338; Hoffman, *First Vermont*, 150; Rodenbough, *Eighteenth Regiment of Pennsylvania Cavalry*, 45.
113. Fourth Virginia Cavalry Records Book, Eleanor S. Brockenbrough Library, MOC; Stiles, *4th Virginia Cavalry*, 107.
114. Johnson Diary.

Chapter Eight

From the Rappahannock Toward Mine Run

"It is still quiet." For any reporter worth his weight in printer's ink, such a lead-in for an article he was submitting to his editor might have proved a death knell for his job. The addition of "There has not been any firing on our front for the last three days," would not have helped his case. Nevertheless, when there was no news fit to print - there was no news fit to print.[1] Such was the case for the reporter of the *New York World* on November 1. However, two of his compatriots, L. A. Hendricks and George A. Hart, from the *New York Herald*, had a unique method of circumventing the dearth of copy. While visiting at a house in Auburn on the night of October 31, they became prisoners of John Mosby. The Gray Ghost permitted them to write letters home. The enterprising Mr. Hart, ever true to his calling, used the opportunity not to write to loved ones but to his paper, describing his capture in detail and his treatment at the hands of the partisan chieftain. Hart's story appeared in the November 27 issue of his paper. When there is news fit to print, even when you are the one making it, print it.[2]

Though quiet may have reigned, even down to an agreement between vedettes not to break the peace, it did not mean that everyone not standing picket duty sat around idle. Buford reported that he had advanced his outpost line to within carbine range of the enemy's with his right at Beverly Ford and his left stretching halfway down to Kelly's Ford where it bent back and extended to the Bealton Station/Morrisville Road. He added that Merritt's brigade ran its picket line from Elk Run to Morrisville, meaning that it faced eastward and not southward, though nothing had been reported from that area other than guerilla activity.[3] Gen. Gregg's division held the right of the line above Beverly Ford. A report that the enemy had advanced against the pickets of the Sixteenth Pennsylvania of Gregg's brigade that watched Freeman's Ford sent the First Maine out on a scout to investigate. The whole episode turned out to be nothing, at least as far as anyone could discover, and the troopers returned at dark, a bit frustrated no doubt.[4] The men of the First West Virginia, Davies's brigade, Kilpatrick's division, somehow came to the conclusion that further campaigning would not occur and began to fix up their camp at Manassas Junction for permanent residence through the coming winter. To their shock, the evening brought orders to prepare to move at 7:00 in the morning. The rest of the division would also saddle up - its target Catlett's Station. The time had come to get back into the fight, if there was to be one.[5]

After Gettysburg

South of the Rappahannock, Stuart's regiments watched the fords, spent time in camp, and did a little scouting. Owen's Brigade made plans for a jaunt over the river. Two hundred troopers from the Fourth Virginia and 50 from the Third, all under the command of Capt. Robert Randolph of the Fourth, crossed the river at Freeman's Ford in the face of the Sixteenth Pennsylvania's pickets of Gregg's division and dashed down stream, recrossing at Beverly Ford under the noses of Buford's. Randolph suffered no loss and attributed it to the fact that the enemy disappeared before he could make contact. This "raid" was undoubtedly the disturbance that brought out the First Maine, which obviously arrived after the Confederates had departed. Just what Randolph accomplished by his scout, other than the knowledge that Federal vedettes could retreat rapidly and that his horses could still carry his men, must not have amounted to much. It could not have been worth the effort considering that no prisoners had been taken. If gathering information had been the objective, Randolph had failed miserably.

Besides the failure of Randolph to accomplish anything, Stuart suffered two other losses. The first had been brewing for sometime but came to a head when Gen. Robert E. Lee issued an order detaching all Maryland units from their current organizations and sending them to Hanover Junction where they would be formed into the Maryland Line under Col. Bradley T. Johnson. This would take the First Maryland Cavalry and Capt. Wiley H. Griffin's Baltimore Light Artillery away from Stuart. The reorganization of Maryland forces thrilled some and angered others. Stuart could not have been overly pleased with it as it robbed him of two fine units at a time when his cavalry continued to erode from a variety of causes.[6] Stuart's second defeat came fittingly on the 2nd when Lee answered Stuart's letter concerning the inspector reports on the horse artillery. They had not been favorable and in fact, were severely critical of the condition of some of the batteries' equipment. Stuart had pleaded "hard service," which was indeed true, but Lee stood firm about the lack of care given to the harnesses and other leather accouterments as well as admonishing the men of Capt. Roger P. Chew's Battery for not washing their guns and equipment even after being in camp for over a week. Lee concluded by stating that he understood Stuart and the horse artillery's officers would take the necessary steps to correct the problems.[7]

Stuart rallied from these setbacks and wrote to his wife, Flora, on a variety of subjects, including naming his third child. The little girl had been born on October 9 at the beginning of the recent campaign. In the midst of the marching and fighting, he had taken time to write and suggest a name, Virginia Pelham. Now he wanted to know if Flora agreed with his selection. He also revealed plans for a cavalry review on the 4th or 5th. The disparagement of his leadership of the cavalry by some individuals persisted. He encouraged her to rise above it. Stuart revealed his view of the war when he addressed the problem of the boxes containing their possessions left behind in St. Louis when the family came from his post out west to join the Confederacy. He wanted them brought to Baltimore where he could get them during the army's next advance north. His most recent success may have played a significant role in forming this overly optimistic view of the how the war was progressing for the South.[8]

The cavalry under Stuart's command persevered in their duty of observing the enemy and protecting the fords. They also engaged in scouting expeditions in the hope either of securing prisoners who might shed some light on doings north of the Rappahannock or booty. The First Virginia set out on the 2nd to accomplish these goals but returned empty-handed.[9]

This day brought the completion of the repairs to the railroad all the way to Warrenton Junction. The damage of the campaign, at least the material damage to the Army of the Potomac's supply line, now repaired, Meade looked around for a way to get at his adversary. He envisioned nothing that would bring "any probability of success" by a direct advance on Lee via Rappahannock Bridge or Kelly's Ford. He also ruled out turning the enemy's left because of the broken country, the bad roads, and the necessity of either abandoning his line of communication or leaving a significant portion of his army behind to protect it. That left only Lee's right toward Fredericksburg. He planned to throw his army across the river at Bank's Ford and Fredericksburg, which meant a change of base, forcing Lee to come to him. He wrote to Gen. Halleck seeking his and President Lincoln's consent for his plan.[10] While Meade muddled through the details of such a move and waited for a reply from his superiors, his cavalry continued to keep an eye, or two, on Stuart.

Gen. Gregg's division maintained its outpost line above Beverly Ford. In Gregg's brigade, the Second Pennsylvania replaced the Sixteenth Pennsylvania at Freeman's Ford, very much aware of the day's previous incursion by the enemy.[11] The Third Pennsylvania, Taylor's brigade, drew the same duty elsewhere, allowing its brother regiment, the First Rhode Island, to return to camp. Unfortunately, for the newly arrived Keystone Staters, the day brought another visit from the enemy. This time the Confederates proved quicker than the bluecoats, crossing the river somewhere between Waterloo and Sulphur Springs, breaking through another regiment's picket line at Carter's Church, and scooping up three members of the Third before disappearing back over the river at Waterloo.[12] Buford's troopers replicated the actions of Gregg's only at different locations and without losing any men to the enemy. The Eighth New York guarded the crossing at Rappahannock Station. Its brother regiment, the Ninth New York, which had relieved the Seventeenth Pennsylvania on the 1st, watched the river south of Morrisville near Ellis' Ford.[13] Kilpatrick's division stayed at Catlett's Station.[14] Those troopers of Pleasonton's cavalry that had no duty used the time in camp to acquire that which they needed most – rest, although some acquired it while tending to letter writing, equipment repair, and a myriad of other mundane tasks that required only a modicum of exertion.[15]

Nothing much changed on the 3rd on either side of the river, although Meade did receive an answer to his proposed offensive and base shift. Neither Halleck nor Lincoln approved. Meade stepped back to square one.[16] An alarm late in the day roused Kilpatrick's men from their repose about midnight and hurried them off in the direction of Falmouth. Word had come that a Confederate force of 600 cavalry had crossed the river at Fredericksburg with the intent of destroying part of the newly reconstructed railroad and scouring the country for whatever could be had. A ride of over 30 miles took the regiments through Stafford Court House to Falmouth. Pvt. Victor E. Comte of the Fifth Michigan wrote to his wife, Elsie, what happened when the column encountered the enemy, "It appears that the Rebels weren't any too anxious holding a great reception for us. Instead of waiting for our visit they ran away to the other side of the river. There they fired a few shots but as our rifles reach farther than their muskets they had enough sense to retire to their strongholds at Fredericksburg Heights."[17] The Federals then fell back to Hartwood Church and camped for the night.[18] Another rumor had caused a full division of cavalry to go on an exhausting march that could have been avoided had time been taken to verify the report. Even worse, the order for the reconnaissance-in-force had come from Meade, demonstrating that he still feared even the smallest threat to his supply line. What damage he thought a rapidly moving mounted force of 600 men could actually do to the railroad, which was guarded for almost its entire length, is unknown. But, since such a force never existed, a more cautious response to such "reports" was wanted of the high command. Buford's and Gregg's divisions attended to the same dull routines as on the previous days, although the guerilla activity finally got to Wesley Merritt. Exasperated by the hit-and-run tactics and the fact that the perpetrators melted into the countryside like gophers into their holes, he determined to strike a blow. Knowing that some of the male civilian population of Prince William County made up the bands his men fought, he ordered the rounding up of all men within the area of his command and sent them to army headquarters to be dealt with by the Provost Marshal General. The arrests failed to resolve the situation, but Merritt undoubtedly felt he had to do something, regardless of how futile it might be.[19]

Despite the blue cavalry's sweep through the countryside, guerillas made their presence known. While riding with three other men, Lt. Theodore M. Sage, regimental quartermaster of the Sixth Pennsylvania, was shot from ambush on the road between Morrisville and Elk Run. His loss was deeply felt throughout the regiment and the brigade. Another tragedy was barely averted when, while visiting the Sixth's picket line, Gen. Merritt was fired on by guerillas. Had he been wounded or killed on the Sixth's watch, the regiment would have been devastated.[20]

Stuart's plan for a Cavalry Corps review began to take shape on the 4th when at least two brigades, Gordon's and Lomax's, held reviews in preparation. Others, like Rosser's, spent the day on the march toward the review site - the Botts Farm once again. Some regiments underwent individual inspections to ensure that all was in readiness.[21] Feelings toward the review ranged from Capt. Cadwallader J. Iredell of the First North Carolina, Gordon's Brigade, who thought he would have a grand time to Capt. Richard H. Watkins of the Third Virginia, Owen's Brigade, who wrote to his wife that he would rather be home with his children.[22] A canvas of the troopers of Stuart's command probably would have shown that the majority of the men sided with Watkins.

Amidst all the buffing and polishing, one commander had the authority to ignore the preparation and the review. John Mosby spent several days taking the war to the enemy. He conducted a raid in the area of Catlett's Station on the 3rd through the 5th, capturing five men, including an adjutant, and six horses. Mosby thought he had killed another officer. Lt. Timothy Hedges of the Second New York, Kilpatrick's acting commissary of subsistence, ran into Mosby while riding between St. Stephen's Church and Auburn. The young officer evidently had no intention of being taken prisoner and in the struggle received a wound so grave, the ball penetrating his back and passing through his lungs, that Mosby reported that he had been killed. Hedges, however, survived.[23]

Held on the John Minor Botts farm and under the eyes of Robert E. Lee, Gov. John Letcher of Virginia, and a host of others, the grand Cavalry Corps review on the 5th permitted Stuart to show off his victorious legions for all to see, including, undoubtedly, some enemy observers. Lee, Stuart, Gov. Letcher, and their staffs rode among the assembled regiments and horse artillery batteries before taking position on a rise of ground. Then the cavalry and artillery passed in review and finally conducted mock charges. No mock battle as had been conducted on June 8 took place, but after the troopers and artillerymen marched past the high command, they returned and galloped by, sabers drawn with Stuart and staff at the head, in an earthshaking charge. The death of one man and the serious injuring of several others marred the day's festivities.[24] After the sound of the last mock charge died away, the brigades separated and rode back to their assigned positions and the real war.

North of the Rappahannock, Alfred Pleasonton also had a review of sorts. Over the course of several weeks, he had received numerous complaints from his subordinate officers concerning the condition of horses being supplied to them and the lack of forage. After reviewing everything, he acted. In a letter to Brig. Gen. Seth Williams, Assistant Adjutant General of the Army, Pleasonton voiced his dissatisfaction concerning the remounts supplied by the Dismounted Camp and the process of forwarding them to the cavalry. He offered a solution for the remount problem, but not for the shortage of forage. What he recommended basically eliminated Maj. Gen. George Stoneman's command and placed resupplying of the cavalry into Meade's hands by establishing depots within the limits of the army. Stoneman responded, effectively countering Pleasonton's arguments. He also discussed the forage problem, which was not under his control, stating that the condition of the horses he forwarded to the army mattered little if they did not get hay, citing the fact that Gen. Gregg's Second Division, specifically Col. J. Irvin Gregg's brigade, had not received forage for 21 days. Army command addressed the problem in its usual manner, issuing an order that once again trimmed down the number of horses and mules each branch of the army would be allowed. It also established the amounts of hay and grain each animal was to receive but mentioned not a word of how the forage and grain was to be supplied on a regular basis, which was the real problem.[25] As if all this scribbling had actually solved their various troubles, Pleasonton, Stoneman, and army command turned their attention back to fighting the Confederates, especially those who had been causing chaos behind the front lines.

General Orders Number 42 called attention to the recent upsurge in losses of personnel, animals, and equipment to the roving bands of partisans and guerillas infesting the region between the Army of the Potomac and Washington City. The order had nothing to do with sending out patrols, marching here and there in search of a ghostly foe, or rounding up every able bodied man of Southern leanings in the area. Instead it targeted the officers and men under Meade's command. Recognizing that the actions of the officers and men often put them in danger, Meade established rules of conduct that were to be followed henceforth. The social visiting of families within the scope of army operations and riding for pleasure were strictly forbidden. In the transmitting of orders or the conducting of public business all care was to be taken by the men not to become unnecessarily exposed to attack.[26] The order intended to change behavior that originated with the officers and men themselves, and while such behavior could be changed, the lure of a warm hearth, a lovely young lady, a home cooked meal, and a moment's respite from duty would always be irresistible temptations for some - a fact that Meade certainly knew all too well.

During the time Pleasonton wrote his letter, his cavalry went on about their business. Devin's brigade of Buford's division moved its camp below Bealton Station with the Sixth New York going on picket below Morrisville near Ellis' Ford.[27] In Gregg's division Taylor's brigade saw the First Pennsylvania relieve the Third Pennsylvania on picket near Waterloo while in Gregg's brigade the First Maine replaced the Sixteenth Pennsylvania at Freeman's Ford. Other regiments also changed places.[28] Kilpatrick's weary troopers rode from Hartwood Church to their camp at Catlett's Station, completing their fruitless scouting expedition.[29] At army headquarters, however, something stirred that would bear fruit in abundance.

In his report of the November 7 disaster at Rappahannock Bridge, Robert E. Lee explained his reason for retaining a force on the north bank of the river. "With the view of deterring him [Meade], if possible, from advancing farther into the interior this winter, I caused the works he had constructed on the north side of the river, near the bridge, to be converted into a *téte-de-pont*, to defend a pontoon bridge, which we had laid down at this point, constructing at the same time lines of rifle-pits on each side of the stream."[30] Certainly the advantage Meade held by having easy access to the Rappahannock Bridge area and the high ground on the north bank in the vicinity of Kelly's Ford preyed on Lee's mind. The various offensive thrusts the Federal army had conducted over the river at these two points since August reinforced Lee's reasoning, which appeared sound, but appearances can be deceiving.[31]

Since the close of the Bristoe Station campaign Meade had done very little about this thorn in the side of his army. All that changed on the November 6.

Meade issued orders affecting the entire army. He directed the First, Second, and Third Corps, designated the "left column" under Maj. Gen. William H. French, toward Kelly's Ford. The Fifth and Sixth Corps, designated the "right column" under the command of Maj. Gen. John Sedgwick, moved toward Rappahannock Station. The cavalry also received its assignment - Buford's division to shift to the right flank and cross the river at the upper fords; Kilpatrick's division to position itself on the left flank and cross at Ellis' or Kemper's ford; Gregg's division to be held in reserve, guarding the wagon train between Bealton Station and Morrisville.[32] The commander-in-chief left no doubt as to his intentions, specifically stating in separate orders to Sedgwick and French that he wanted them to drive the enemy from the fortifications north of the river and follow up on their success by crossing the river and moving toward Brandy Station.[33]

While the 6th became a day of preparation for Pleasonton's cavalry, the routine duties of picketing and scouting also needed to be conducted. Merritt wrote Buford that he had sent a officer to the Paine house near Kelly's Ford the previous day who returned to report that only a few vedettes could be observed. However, the morning of the 6th brought an enemy incursion of unknown strength that drove back Merritt's pickets. With the Confederates now north of the river at Kelly's, Merritt, who knew by this time of the planned advance, questioned whether they should be allowed to stay. Wisely, Buford told him that the small force meant little and that he should let them alone.[34] The rest of Buford's division and those of Kilpatrick's and Gregg's did no marching, holding to their camps until after midnight.[35]

No knowledge of the impending blow filtered across the river to Lee, Stuart, or any other officer. Not even those north of the river manning the *téte-du-pont* had the slightest indication of what Meade intended. Had the Confederates been alert they may have acquired a sense of what was coming, but circumstances favored Meade. Maj. Gen. Jubal Early had received orders on the 5th to relieve the troops in the fortifications and did so on the 6th, sending Brig. Gen. Harry T. Hays's Brigade, commanded by Col. Davidson B. Penn of the Seventh Louisiana Infantry, to replace Brig. Gen. James A. Walker's Brigade. During such an exchange, troops become more vulnerable and while Meade would not attack this day, his army's movements would have been more difficult to detect, the Confederates being distracted with their own.[36]

Stuart's cavalry had its own adjusting to do, as the brigades took up their positions once again after the grand review.[37] Rosser's Brigade and a section of Chew's Battery left their camp at the Major house south of Rixeyville, crossed the Hazel River, rode through Amissville, and reached Gaines' Cross Roads, encamping a mile west of it. The move took them away from what would be the theater of operations the next day. Stuart would not have allowed this had he any knowledge of the enemy's plans.[38] Those cavalrymen who had reached their camps on the evening of the 5th, spent the 6th as they had the days before the review. Everything seemed peaceful, but the Third Virginia, Owen's Brigade, received orders to pack two days' rations and be prepared to move out at a moment's notice. Capt.

George H. Matthews's squadron went out on picket, being reinforced later by Capt. William M. Field's squadron. The brigade was encamped near the farm of Reuben Hitt that lay south of Beverly Ford.[39] Whatever the Third prepared for would never occur. Visitors were coming.

For the Confederates, the morning of the 7th passed without anything transpiring that would have caused any alarm. Then about noon the Federals in the form of Maj. Gen. William H. French's infantry began to push beyond Mount Holly Church where they had arrived about midnight, driving back Confederate pickets. Arriving at Kelly's Ford, the blue infantry pushed across and engaged the Second and Thirtieth North Carolina Infantry regiments of Brig. Gen. Stephen D. Ramseur's Brigade, Maj. Gen. Robert E. Rodes's Division, Ewell's Corps. Unable to offer much in the way of resistance, those of Ramseur's two regiments who could fell back. Many of their comrades who had been stationed along the river became prisoners. The superiority of the Federal artillery in number and position prevented Rodes from bringing up additional troops. He quickly noticed that the enemy drove to his left in the direction of Rappahannock Bridge and not along the Stevensburg Road. By evening, his line stretched from Wheatley's Ford to Mountain Run. French, satisfied in acquiring a foothold on the south bank, spent the evening hours and the night bringing reinforcements over the river.[40] As Lee had feared, the enemy had been able to use the advantages of the ground at Kelly's Ford to force a crossing. Worse awaited the Confederate army at Rappahannock Bridge.

Maj. Gen. John Sedgwick's troops approached the Confederate skirmish line about 3:00 in the afternoon, forcing the enemy skirmishers into their rifle pits. A heavy artillery duel commenced amidst the continuing fire of the infantry. Meanwhile, Maj. Gen. Jubal Early crossed the river, scouted the advancing Federals, and determined to reinforce Col. Penn with most of Brig. Gen. Robert F. Hoke's Brigade under Col. Archibald C. Godwin. After consulting with Lee, Early concluded that no further troops needed to be sent and as night loomed, both generals felt confident that no further assaults would be made and if one was made that it could be repulsed with the troops at hand. Then at dusk, two brigades of Brig. Gen. David A. Russell's division under Colonels Emory Upton and Peter C. Ellmaker stormed the works. The fight lasted only long enough for the Federals to charge over the fortifications and accept the surrender of those graycoats that could not get away. So rapid had been the attack that the artillery on the south bank could not fire in time, nor could it sweep the interior of the fortifications for fear of hitting Penn's and Godwin's troops. Over 1,600 men were either killed, wounded, or captured, along with four pieces of artillery, caissons, ammunition, small arms, and the pontoon bridge that spanned the river. Only about 600 total from both brigades managed to get across the river. Penn and Godwin became prisoners and Gen. Hays, who had arrived in time to cross the river and get himself surrounded, escaped when his horse bolted and carried him to safety.[41] The disaster stunned Lee and the army while Meade's men rejoiced at the ease of their victory.

In all the fighting, the cavalry of both armies did little. Buford's division pulled back its outposts from the river and marched for Sulphur Springs, where it bivouacked for the night after stopping in a cornfield along the way to feed the horses.[42] The regiments of Gen. Gregg's division pulled in their vedettes, left their camp, and marched through Fayetteville and Liberty to Bealton Station, encamping there for the night. Taylor's brigade, following Col. Gregg's, stopped at the station.[43] Kilpatrick's division left Catlett's Station at 3:00 in the morning and rode to Grove's Church above Ellis' Ford, arriving about the time the fighting opened at Kelly's Ford. The First Vermont, Custer's brigade, continued on to guard Ellis' ford.[44]

The Southern cavalry played even less of a role in the day's actions, holding to its camps or its posts along the upper portions of the Rappahannock above the bridge and along the Hazel River. Only after recognizing the extent of the disaster and what it portended did the cavalry begin to react. Orders came very late in the day to begin breaking up camps throughout the brigades. Baggage packed up and sent to the rear, the troopers prepared to face the enemy the next day.[45] Rosser's Brigade, far out on the left of the army at Gaines' Cross Roads, received orders about midnight to saddle up and return. The next day would be one of movement for the brigade and much of Stuart's cavalry.[46]

Buford's troopers had an early morning bugle call on the 8th. Orders called for the men to be ready to move at 4:00. With Chapman's brigade in the lead, the division crossed the Rappahannock at Sulphur Springs, chasing before them a few enemy vedettes. The column rode through Jeffersonton to Rixey's Ford on the Hazel River where the Tenth Virginia, Chambliss's Brigade, skirmished with the Third Indiana before falling back toward Rixeyville. Buford continued to advance, but about four miles from Culpeper Court House, the Third, now dismounted, encountered stiffer opposition in the form of infantry from Maj. Gen. Cadmus Wilcox's Division of Hill's Corps. The Hoosiers soon received reinforcements. The Eighth Illinois arrived and with them Col. Chapman who ordered Capt. John M. Waite to charge with his mounted squadron. The captain tried to explain to the near-sighted colonel that infantry lay ahead, but Chapman, who could not see them, repeated his order. Waite galloped forward only to be brought up short by a murderous fire. Falling back, he dismounted his men, formed a line, supported by a mounted Eighth New York, and held on. Buford brought up Lt. Edward B. Williston's Battery D, Second U. S. Artillery and Lt. John H. Butler's Battery G, Second U. S. Artillery, which gave and took fire throughout the fight. Butler received such a severe wound in his heel from a shell fragment that his foot had to be amputated at the ankle. Merritt, on the right, also came to grips with the enemy, the Sixth Pennsylvania suffering the most. After an hour and a half, Wilcox withdrew as darkness brought an end to the fighting. Leaving the Sixth to picket the field, the regiments of the two brigades encamped for the night while Devin's men lay down north of the Hazel River.[47]

Judson Kilpatrick had his men mounted and moving about dawn. Crossing the Rappahannock at both Kemper's and Ellis' fords, leaving the First Michigan, Custer's brigade, to guard the latter, he pressed on toward Stevensburg. Initially facing only the Second South Carolina, Young's Brigade, Hampton's Division, the Federals soon ran up against the rest of the brigade. A heavy skirmish erupted with Capt. James F. Hart's Battery adding the thunder of its guns to the staccato of small arms fire. A flanking column of dismounted skirmishers from the Fifth New York, Davies's brigade, caused Hart to limber and retreat to a position near the hamlet. Gordon's Brigade, Hampton's Division, came up and formed a line with Young's. Suddenly, a cheer echoed up and down the ranks. Having recovered from the wound he had received at Gettysburg, Wade Hampton rode onto the field to take command of his division for the first time. Renewed in spirit if not in numbers, Gordon's and Young's troopers held on until dusk when the firing died away. Hampton fell back through Stevensburg, leaving it to Kilpatrick. The men of both sides encamped for the night.[48]

Gregg's two brigades separated at Bealton Station. Taylor's brigade, with the exception of the First New Jersey, which received the assignment of accompanying the prisoners taken in the assault on the 7th to Washington, marched off to Rappahannock Station while Col. Gregg's brigade trotted off to Morrisville.[49]

The Federal infantry also advanced from the bridge at Rappahannock Station toward Brandy Station. Owen's and Lomax's brigades, Fitz Lee's Division, watched them, the former from near Brandy Station and the latter from Fleetwood Hill. The remaining section of Chew's Battery, the other being with Rosser, took position with Owen's Brigade. A portion of Capt. Marcellus N. Moorman's Battery supported Lomax. All kept watch toward the Rappahannock. At some point Chambliss's Brigade, Fitz Lee's Division, arrived to assist in what all knew would soon happen. They did not have to wait long. Both Sedgwick and French sent columns toward Brandy Station. As the infantry came into view, the artillery and cavalry began to skirmish with the forward elements. Inevitably, all three brigades had to fall back. They held on for a time on Kennedy House hill, but soon withdrew toward Culpeper before which the Confederate infantry busily dug entrenchments that extended from near Chestnut Fork Church, across the railroad behind the Hall house, and on down to Mt. Pony. The enemy followed the cavalry and skirmished briefly with the gray infantry before darkness ended the day's fighting.[50]

Despite all the entrenching the Confederate infantry did in front of Culpeper Court House, Lee had no intention of getting caught with a river at his back. His columns quickly and quietly wound their way to the fords of the Rapidan and crossed, leaving Stuart's cavalry once again to cover the withdrawal. As a result, the 9th became a day of maneuvering and minor confrontations for the cavalrymen of both armies. Fitz Lee's Division left Culpeper early in the day and rode west on the Sperryville pike amidst the first snowfall of the season. The brigades turned south before reaching Griffinsburg and encamped for the night around Bethel Church near Brown's Store.[51] Hampton's Division fell back toward the Rapidan in the face of the slow Federal advance.[52]

Chapman's and Merritt's troopers of Buford's command roused themselves from their slumber, left their bivouac north of Culpeper Court House, and on discovering that their opponents from the previous day had disappeared, rode for Brandy Station. On arrival, Buford found the Sixth Corps already in possession of the place. He then turned his regiments toward Rappahannock Station where he rendezvoused with Devin's brigade and set about resupplying his men.[53]

Other than those men required for outpost duty, Kilpatrick planned for his victorious troopers to rest for most of the day. However, the tempting target of Pony Mountain loomed in the distance and by 11:30 in the morning, Alfred Pleasonton began playing with the idea that Kilpatrick could occupy it with a little help from the infantry. Sending an inquiry up the chain of command, Pleasonton had his answer by noon. A division of the Third Corps left Brandy Station in the afternoon and marched off toward Stevensburg. Kilpatrick, ever impatient, did not wait for it to arrive. Knowing he would have support if he needed it, he called on Custer's brigade and sallied forth, leaving Davies behind to prepare for a move back across the Rappahannock the next day. The Confederates offered virtually no resistance, and Kilpatrick had his prize late in the afternoon without having to share any of the glory with the infantry.[54]

In Gen. Gregg's division, Taylor's brigade stayed at Rappahannock Station doing the unwelcomed task of wagon escort duty. Col. Gregg's brigade moved down to the area around Kelly's Ford and Mount Holly Church. The orders came to unsaddle, giving some of the men the impression that they would encamp there for some time.[55]

On the 10th, Meade's army reacted to the orders issued on the 9th. The Second, Third, and Sixth Corps, and part of the Fifth hunkered down south of the Rappahannock centering on Brandy Station and stretching from Welford Ford on the Hazel River to Kelly's Ford on the Rappahannock. A brigade of the Fifth Corps and all of the First Corps would be left north of the Rappahannock.[56] Pleasonton's cavalry also executed orders received the previous day. The troopers of the First Maine and the Sixteenth Pennsylvania of Col. Gregg's brigade, Gregg's division, put their saddles back on their horses and marched through Morrisville to Hartwood Church where their pickets watched the roads leading to United States and Richard's fords and Falmouth. The Fourth Pennsylvania, Gregg's brigade, placed vedettes at Elk Run. The brigade's other regiments took station at Morrisville. Taylor's brigade, Gregg's division, left Rappahannock Station for Fayetteville. Establishing headquarters there, Taylor carried out his instructions by sending the First Pennsylvania to picket Sulphur Springs and the Sixth Ohio to Freeman's Ford. After spreading some of his other regiments out to Waterloo and up to Warrenton, his line stretched 75 miles in length.[57] Buford left his camp near Rappahannock Bridge and reoccupied Culpeper Court House. Merritt, after patrolling to within a half a mile of Cedar Run Mountain, established his outpost line before falling back to Culpeper Court House. Chapman's brigade picketed toward Rapidan Station. The Sixth New York, Devin's brigade, drew the assignment of going out on patrol but ran into nothing and came back. In the town, the troopers found officers' trunks and supplies of winter clothes that had been left behind in the log cabin winter quarters that some of Lee's infantry had built.[58] Kilpatrick's cavalry remained at Stevensburg with orders to guard the Rapidan River to the left of Rapidan Station.[59]

Stuart's cavaliers filled the day with marching. Fitz Lee's brigades left their bivouacs about Bethel Church and Brown's Store and crossed the Robinson River. Some regiments encamped between the Robinson and the Rapidan while others continued over the Rapidan into Orange County. On the way, Owen's Brigade dropped off the Fourth Virginia at Mt. Zion Church to watch the fords nearby while the other regiments and the section of Chew's Battery rode on and encamped on the farm of Dr. Slaughter. Hampton's Division retreated over the Rapidan and began its march along the south bank of the river to take position on the army's right flank.[60]

The activities of the next several days centered on marching, finding permanent campsites for the winter, patrolling, establishing outpost lines, and foraging. Buford sent the First and Sixth squadrons of the Ninth New York from Devin's brigade on a scout through James City to the Robinson River on the 11th. The haul included two mail carriers, the knowledge that no Confederates lingered north of the river, and that the Fourth Virginia, Owen's Brigade, Fitz Lee's Division, picketed the south side. The presence of the Federals at Smoot's Ford brought out Company B of the Fourth to support its vedettes, but nothing happened other than the bluecoats left their own pickets from the Fourth New York, Devin's brigade, Buford's division, on the north side of the ford. The Eighth Illinois, Chapman's brigade, Buford's division, rode down along the railroad to Rapidan Station, discovering only a few of the enemy left behind as scouts. The First United States Cavalry, Merritt's brigade, Buford's division, trotted out on a reconnaissance to the Robinson River with orders to cross if practicable, and a regiment from Devin's brigade was sent toward Madison Court House.[61] Buford wanted to know what his adversaries were doing. In truth, they were doing very little. Most of Fitz Lee's Division crossed the Rapidan, the brigades pitching their camps in various locations around Orange Court House.[62] Hampton's Division continued marching toward the right flank of the army.[63] If Buford had concerns that Stuart's cavalry might cross the river, he needn't have worried.

Gregg's Division maintained its vigilance about Hartwood Church. In Col. Gregg's brigade, the First Maine came off outpost duty and returned to Morrisville where Companies A and H drew brigade supply train guard duty at Bealton Station. The Sixteenth Pennsylvania marched through Morrisville to Elk Run to relieve the Fourth Pennsylvania on picket duty there. The Thirteenth Pennsylvania reported to Meade's headquarters where it received the assignment of guarding the army's cattle herd. The duties of Taylor's brigade mirrored those of Gregg's, without all the guard duty, the First Pennsylvania went on outpost duty between Sulphur Springs and Rappahannock Station, its brother regiments either going or coming off picket.[64] Kilpatrick's division kept an eye on the Rapidan and Robinson fords.[65]

On the 12th George A. Custer's temper got the best of him, and he wrote a scathing letter to Capt. Charles C. Suydam, Assistant Adjutant-General of the Cavalry Corps, regarding horses supplied to his command from the Dismounted Camp. Some of his men had returned the previous day on horses in worse condition than those sent to the camp for rehabilitation. Of 40 troopers from the Seventh Michigan who rode from the camp to the army only 23 arrived. The other mens' horses broke down on the way. Custer stated that his command ". . . suffers about as much from the influences and effect of the Dismounted Camp as it does from the weapons of the enemy." He concluded with a devastating quip, "It is an actual fact that there are men in my command who have been captured by the enemy, carried to Richmond, and rejoined my command in less time than it frequently requires for men to proceed to the Dismounted Camp and return mounted." Pleasonton used the opportunity to express his displeasure in an addendum before forwarding the letter. Gen. Stoneman, still in command of the Dismounted Camp, received the unwelcome notes and responded with equal vitriol, claiming that "I have understood that Custer's brigade are great horse-killers, and it is very likely that the seventeen horses were used up as stated, though they were considered serviceable when they left the depot." As in the past, the verbal assaults failed to bring victory to either side. In actuality, both failed to recognize that as long as the cavalry had to execute the strenuous duties required of it by the exigencies of the war, the horse problem would not go away. Indeed, no solution to it really existed.[66]

The real war continued. Lt. William T. Boyd's and Capt. George H. Matthews's squadrons of the Third Virginia, Owen's Brigade, Fitz Lee's Division, crossed the Robinson River with a forage train, looking for corn, and returned at 11:00 at night with four wagonloads. The Fourth Virginia, Owen's Brigade, came off picket duty and another regiment took its place. A threat to another portion of the outpost line brought out the Third Virginia in force, but the Federals had no intention of crossing the river and all returned to normal. The other regiments of Fitz Lee's Division held to the same routine of the previous day, although the Sixth Virginia, Lomax's Brigade, and Moorman's Battery of horse artillery shifted their camps to a better location.[67] Hampton's Division took position to watch the fords of the lower Rappahannock down toward Fredericksburg. A section of Chew's battery camped nine miles from Fredericksburg on the road to Spotsylvania Court House.[68]

The Federal cavalry spent the day settling into its camps and switching regiments on outpost duty. In Buford's Division, Col. William Gamble returned to take command of the First Brigade, Col. Chapman going back to his regiment, the Third Indiana. The Eighth New York spent some time paroling prisoners.[69] Gregg's Division guarded the lower Rappahannock fords from its headquarters at Morrisville. Some of the First Maine, Gregg's brigade, drew the mundane duty of escorting broken down mules from the brigade to Bealton Station while 20 to 30 men from the Sixteenth Pennsylvania, Gregg's brigade, went on picket, as did troopers from its brother regiment, the First Pennsylvania. The First Rhode Island, Taylor's brigade, moved its camp to Fayetteville, doing picket toward Warrenton.[70] Kilpatrick's brigades maintained their watch of the Rapidan fords from their camps at

Stevensburg. The First Vermont, Custer's brigade, having returned from prisoner escort duty, moved to Raccoon Ford and picketed seven miles of the river from that point for the next three days.[71]

So quiet had the front become that on the 13th members of Company B, of the First North Carolina, Gordon's Brigade, Hampton's Division, had the time to compose a letter to Gov. Zebulon Vance on behalf of Pvt. William J. Smith, who by profession was a shoemaker. Thirty-one of his comrades signed the letter requesting that Smith be sent home where it was felt he could be of greater service to his country. Their plea fell on deaf ears, and Smith stayed with the army, although someone did notice his talent, appointing him as saddler for the regiment in January 1864.[72] Elsewhere, Capt. William M. Field's and Lt. John A. Chappell's squadrons of the Third Virginia, Owen's Brigade, Fitz Lee's Division, conducted another foraging expedition over the Robinson. Then the regiment moved its camp to Mt. Zion Church, relieving its brigade brother, the Fourth Virginia. The Sixth Virginia, Lomax's Brigade, Fitz Lee's Division, did some foraging of its own toward James City, encountering enemy cavalry from Buford's command on the road between James City and Madison Court House. A brief chase resulted with no loss on either side.[73] Hampton's brigades settled into their camps. The attached section of Chew's Battery, however, had a bit of adventure. Encamped in a clearing nine miles southwest of Fredericksburg, a few of the men attempted to smoke out one of the local rabbits for supper and inadvertently set fire to the pine brush that housed the animal. In moments, the gunners thoughts of rabbit stew vanished, replaced by a fight to save their harnesses and equipment from the roaring flames. Their loss proved minimal. The rabbit's fate is unknown.[74]

The Federals also stirred a little. Besides their run in with the Sixth Virginia, Buford's scouting parties also discovered Confederate infantry pickets on the north side of the river at Rapidan Station. The rest of the division conducted routine soldierly activities.[75] Gen. Gregg's command suffered loss at the hands of guerilas when five troopers from the First Rhode Island, Taylor's brigade, picketing near Warrenton, were captured. Otherwise the day passed uneventfully.[76] It did not do so for the Second New York of Davies's brigade, Kilpatrick's Division. Lt. Col. Otto Harhaus took a small force down to Morton's Ford on the Rapidan and "made as much show" in front of the enemy as he could. Meanwhile Capt. Obadiah J. Downing took his portion of the regiment to Mitchell's Ford and did the same. At both locations, the Confederates displayed an interest, even firing on Harhaus's men, and showed sufficient strength to repel any small force that might attempt to cross. The remainder of Kilpatrick's command carried out routine duties or rested in camp.[77]

Buford's finding of Confederate infantry north of the Rapidan sparked Pleasonton to action on the 14th. He ordered Buford to mount a reconnaissance as soon as possible to confirm the exact whereabouts of the enemy around Rapidan Station. For some, the urgency of the dispatch may have foreshadowed a renewal of activity, but for others, the monotonous repetition of going on and off picket duty persisted. The Ninth New York, Devin's brigade, relieved its brother regiment, the Fourth New York, near James City. Another of Devin's regiments, the Sixth New York, came off duty and returned to camp. The Eighth New York, Gamble's brigade, went on picket near the Rapidan.[78] A change of a different sort had occurred in Kilpatrick's division. Its commander trotted off to Washington City on court martial duty, leaving the division in the capable hands of Gen. Custer, whose brigade command passed to Col. Charles H. Town of the First Michigan. During the day, Davies conducted an inspection of his outpost line along the Rapidan and came to the conclusion that the Confederate infantry pickets had been replaced by cavalry and the infantry moved back from the river. Pleasonton ordered additional reconnaissances to confirm Davies's findings.[79] A large detail from the First Maine, Gregg's brigade, Gregg's division, occupied themselves with escorting wagons from Morrisville to Warrenton Junction. The Third Pennsylvania, Taylor's brigade, Gregg's division, and several other regiments did picket duty or rested in camp.[80] Nothing disturbed the quiet south of the rivers.[81]

The reconnaissances Pleasonton ordered on the 14th had Custer's and Buford's troopers up bright and early on the 15th. Custer wasted little time in sending a dismounted Sixth Michigan and First Vermont, Town's brigade, to probe toward Raccoon Ford. They found an alert enemy that greeted them with artillery fire. The Sixth fell back only to have the Confederates send three companies down to the river to harass them with small arms fire. The advance of the First and Fifth Michigan, Town's brigade, at Morton's Ford had greater success, driving the enemy back from the river into their prepared works on higher ground and forcing them to rely on their artillery to contain the bluecoats. Custer, who accompanied the First, brought up a section of Battery M, Second U. S. Artillery, and a duel erupted during which Custer personally fired two shots. His advance caused the Confederates to bring up a heavy column of infantry that Custer estimated to be a division. Davies pushed forward to Mitchell's and Germanna fords, finding the former strongly defended by infantry. The heavy rains had made the river impassable, so all Custer could do was guess the situation on the other side.[82]

Buford conducted his own operation on the right flank. Devin's brigade set out toward James City, sweeping through the hamlet and turning south to the Robinson River where it encountered the vedettes of the Third Virginia, Owen's Brigade, Fitz Lee's Division, on the south bank. Gamble's brigade reconnoitered toward Rapidan Station and discovered Confederate infantry entrenched on the north side with infantry and artillery visible south of the river.[83] Buford's findings confirmed that Lee had some infantry close to the Rapidan north of Orange Court House with a force of cavalry of unknown strength south of the Robinson in Madison County. Coupled with what Custer had discovered and what the signal officer stationed on Pony Mountain had been able to see, Meade had a much clearer picture of his foe's location and that Lee's force was stationary.[84]

Gregg's Division sat idle on the 15th, except for picketing, wagon train escorting, and camp moving - the First Maine, Gregg's brigade, having its camp flooded out overnight by a heavy thundershower. Part of the idleness was somewhat distasteful. The Third Pennsylvania and several other regiments, including the First Rhode Island, of Taylor's brigade formed a hollow square to watch the depressing ceremony attached to the drumming out of service of two of the Third's men for desertion. A shaving of half of the men's heads, beards, and mustaches preceded the branding of the left hip with the letter "D."[85]

The only Southern cavalry that may have been involved with the day's action would have been portions of Hampton's Division stationed along the lower Rapidan. This would have been Gordon's or Young's brigades, Rosser's being deployed along the Rappahannock. Any participation, however, would have been minimal, as all Federal reports indicated the Confederate infantry's presence in strength. Fitz Lee's brigades stayed in their camps. The horse artillery battalion began gathering together on the farm of Col. John Willis south of Orange Court House.[86]

The 16th passed routinely for the cavalry of both armies, although Col. John P. Taylor, Gregg's Division, conducted an inspection of his brigade's outposts. He reported quiet all along his line except for the consistent attacks of guerillas every night after dark. Gregg added to the report, stating that he had been forced to completely ring Warrenton in an effort to cut off communication between the inhabitants and the guerillas. That action precipitated attacks from front and rear, the loss of men from an attack on the First Pennsylvania proving that fact quite effectively.[87] Buford reported quiet on his front as well and that Custer's division had withdrawn to its old position after its advance the previous day. Buford intended to extend his left flank to Somerville Ford to link with Custer.[88]

Stuart's cavaliers stirred little until the 17th, when Owen's Brigade, Fitz Lee's Division, roused from its camp with orders to go to the Valley to reinforce Brig. Gen. John D. Imboden's command in its fight to contain Brig. Gen. William W. Averell's force after its victory at Droop Mountain on the 6th. Owen led his four regiments through Madison Court House to Criglersville where they camped for the night. The expedition ended abruptly when word came that Averell had retreated on his own. Owen led his troopers back to their camps between the Robinson and the Rapidan the next day.[89] Tranquility reigned elsewhere, as Stuart's men enjoyed a lull that many undoubtedly hoped would lead to the conclusion of operations for the year.

Across the rivers, the Federal cavalry went about its daily tasks that included some patrolling. Maj. Seymour B. Conger of the Third West Virginia, Devin's brigade, Buford's division, with about 100 men rode off down the Sperryville pike on a scout. He confirmed that the Confederates from the Valley had not crossed the mountains in weeks and that some of Fitz Lee's troopers regularly reconnoitered around Sperryville. The value of the reconnaissance received a boost with the capture of five prisoners and between 150 to 200 cattle, a welcomed sight to any soldier's eyes.[90] Like their counterparts in gray, the Federal troopers belonging to regiments guarding the various fords on the three rivers concluded to leave well enough alone, staying in their camps, exchanging vedettes as necessary, guarding wagons, and just resting.[91]

Wade Hampton had been out of action since July and on his return to the cavalry wasted little time getting back into it. Early on the morning of the 18th, the Eighteenth Pennsylvania, Davies's brigade, Custer's division, under the command of Capt. Marshall S. Kingsland, was camped at the crossroads that led to Ely's and Germanna fords and charged with watching Ely's Ford.[92] During the night of the 17th, orders arrived for the regiment to supply a detail to accompany Lt. Edward W. Whittaker, an aide-de-camp to Gen. Kilpatrick, and Capt. Horace W. Dodge of the Fifth Michigan, Town's brigade, on a reconnaissance to Ely's Ford by way of Germanna Ford. Sixty men were assigned the duty. Capt. Kingsland also received instructions to withdraw his main reserve toward Stevensburg, leaving 50 men at the crossroads. When Whittaker and Dodge arrived, they found all in readiness and marched off toward Germanna Ford. The rest of the Eighteenth prepared to eat breakfast and move out. Suddenly shots rang out on the Ely's Ford road and although the troopers of the Eighteenth made an attempt to form a line, Hampton's troopers quickly overran the camp. The Confederates had made their unexpected appearance after Hampton bluffed his way over Ely's Ford by putting men dressed in Federal overcoats in the front ranks of Gordon's Brigade to fool the Eighteenth's pickets.[93] The shattered Eighteenth fell back along the Stevensburg road. Meanwhile Whittaker, who had ridden about two miles down the Germanna Ford road, heard the sound of the fighting at the crossroads and turned around. He ran into one of the North Carolina regiments drawn up and waiting for him. Unable to offer battle to so large a force, Whittaker took shelter in the wood, tried to hold on, but was forced to scatter. Back at the crossroads Hampton, facing the Second New York, Davies's brigade, and the rallied remnants of the Eighteenth, decided he had achieved all he could and splitting his force, retreated to Ely's and Germanna fords to make his escape. At the latter, he almost scooped up Capt. Luke McGuinn and part of the Fifth New York, Davies's brigade, stationed there, but the wary McGuinn retreated down river.[94]

The lightning attack netted Hampton about 50 men captured, including the Eighteenth Pennsylvania's assistant surgeon, George W. Withers. Eighty-three horses, ten mules, one ambulance, one hospital wagon, one army wagon, one forge, and the Eighteenth's flag were also taken. A payroll officer complete with payroll fell into the hands of the Fifth North Carolina. Kingsland could have faced censure, but his commander, Davies, argued that the captain was not responsible due to the circumstances. Kingsland's two saber cuts and his brave actions during the fight supported Davies's position. The Eighteenth also suffered the loss of Lt. Roseberry Sellers, who had accompanied Whittaker's column and was killed in the fight along the Germanna Ford road.[95]

At the same time Hampton conducted his attack, another Confederate force crossed the Rapidan below Raccoon Ford in an attempt to capture a contingent of the First Michigan, Town's brigade, Custer's division, under Maj. Melvin Brewer stationed at the ford. Crossing under the cover of darkness, the graycoats waited in a ravine until dawn to attack. The delay allowed Brewer to get wind of their presence and prepare for them. After a two-hour skirmish that gained the intruders nothing, they retreated back over the river. Later in the day, as the Seventh Michigan, Town's brigade, replaced the First, the enemy opened fire with artillery, but no casualties resulted. Similar probing occurred up and down the river line. The Federals reasoned that Lee simply wanted to locate the position of Meade's army. If true, the Confederate commander knew little more at the end of the day than he did at its beginning.[96]

The Federals did some scouting of their own, Buford sending the Sixth Pennsylvania, Merritt's brigade, toward James City. It brought back a few prisoners after which the regiment returned to outpost duty with its brother regiments along the division's line from James City to Cedar Run.[97] Gen. Gregg's division, still stretched out from Warrenton past Waterloo to Ellis' Ford, maintained its outpost line and performed the same duties it had been doing. In Gregg's brigade, the First Maine and the Second Pennsylvania replaced the Sixteenth Pennsylvania on picket duty. At least one regiment, the Third Pennsylvania, Taylor's brigade, had gone without rations for two days. The railroad having nearly been finished to Culpeper Court House, such shortages must have puzzled the men.[98]

Although peace reigned along the lines over the next several days, the war and other things progressed. On the 19th, Pvt. Benjamin F. Joyner of the Second Virginia, Owen's Brigade, Fitz Lee's Division, somehow ended up in the hands of Buford's cavalry. He brought the interesting information that Maj. Gen. Harry Heth's Division of infantry occupied Madison Court House.[99] Behind Federal lines, troopers drew clothing, wrote letters, welcomed the payroll officer, fought boredom, paroled prisoners, and went on and off outpost duty.[100] Custer tried again to discover the strength of the Confederates at Germanna, Ely's, Hall's, Humphrey's, and Urquhart's fords, sending an officer to investigate and report. The officer brought back information regarding the practicality of each ford for infantry and wagons, as well as the fords' defenses. What Meade did with the information remained to be seen.[101]

The 20th passed in like manner for most of the cavalry of both armies. While the vast majority of the men stayed in camp, a few were called to go through the motions of picketing and scouting. The Sixteenth Pennsylvania, Gregg's brigade, Gregg's division, rode down to Ellis' and Kelly's fords but saw no graybacks. The Eighth New York, Gamble's brigade, Buford's division, drew picket duty as did three squadrons from the Ninth New York, Devin's brigade, Buford's division. The Eighteenth Pennsylvania, Davies's brigade, Custer's division, guarded Germanna Ford.[102]

On the 21st, two deserters provided Kilpatrick, now returned and once again in command of his division, information about the position of Ewell's and Hill's infantry and Hampton's Division. He felt confident enough to advise Meade as to the strength of Lee's army as well.[103] On this day, a very sick John Buford left the army for Washington City. His illness, which proved to be typhoid fever, had worsened to the point that he could no longer carry out his duties. Brig. Gen. Wesley Merritt took over as division commander. Col. Alfred Gibbs of the Nineteenth New York assumed command of the Reserve Brigade.[104]

The rain that cascaded down drenched everything and forced all but the most necessary operations to a standstill, except for John Mosby, who found the rain good cover for a raid on a wagon train belonging to the First Pennsylvania, Taylor's brigade, Gregg's division, near Fayetteville. With about 75 of his men, he swept down on 30 men guarding 5 wagons and although the attack did not go quite as planned, the escort escaping, the wagons fell into his hands. Unfortunately, only a few of the medical supplies the wagons contained could be brought off, along with 12 prisoners, 10 horses, and 17 mules. Detachments from the First Pennsylvania and its brother regiment, the Sixth Ohio, camped nearby, mistook the partisans, who were dressed in blue overcoats, as friends and not until they were fired upon did they recognize their adversaries. The First pursued close to Thoroughfare Gap, capturing 2 of the rangers, but went no further as darkness ended the chase.[105]

The activity of Mosby's partisans and other guerilla bands aside, the relative calm of the previous days in regards to any kind of significant offensive operations from either Meade or Lee and the cessation of thrusts over the rivers by the cavalry of the two armies seemed to herald that both sides had concluded to draw the curtain over the hostilities for the year. For those who thought this to be the case, a rude awakening loomed. As early as the 20th, Meade had written to Halleck, informing him that the recent rains had damaged the railroad, but that as soon as it could be fixed and the army supplied, he intended to turn Lee's right by advancing over Germanna and Ely's fords, the same fords Custer's scout had examined.[106]

Notes:

1. *New York World*, November 2, 1863.
2. Williamson, *Mosby's Rangers*, 104 and 437-440.
3. *New York Times*, November 5, 1863; *O.R.*, Series 1, vol. 29, part 2, 407; Inglis Diary; Cheney Diary; Gracey, *Annals of the Sixth*, 201; Cheney, *Ninth Regiment, New York Volunteer Cavalry*, 139.
4. Ressler Diary; Sawyer Diary.
5. Wilkin Diary; Hoffman, *First Vermont*, 150; Gillespie, *Company A, First Ohio Cavalry*, 188; Rodenbough, *Eighteenth Regiment of Pennsylvania Cavalry*, 45.
6. Driver, Jr., *First and Second Maryland Cavalry*, 65; Trout, *Galloping Thunder*, 375.
7. *O.R.*, Series 1, vol. 29, part 2, 816.

    Capt. James F. Hart's Battery also underwent inspection and its condition became the content of another letter from Lee to Stuart on November 4. The lack of morning reports and maintaining proper records among other shortcomings, including improper equipment and the poor condition of the horses, Lee partly blamed on the absence of Capt. Hart, but the message came through clearly. The problems needed to be addressed and quickly. *O.R.*, Series 1, vol. 29, part 2, 820-821.
8. J. E. B. Stuart to My Darling One [Flora Stuart], July 18, 1863, Stuart Papers, 1851-1968, Mss1ST923d, Microfilm reel C621, VHS.
9. Steele Diary.
10. *O.R.*, Series 1, vol. 29, part 2, 409.
11. Ressler Diary.
12. Rawle, *Third Pennsylvania Cavalry*, 338 and 359.
13. Cheney Diary; Cheney, *Ninth Regiment, New York Volunteer Cavalry*, 139; Inglis Diary;
14. Wilkin Diary; Rodenbough, *Eighteenth Regiment of Pennsylvania Cavalry*, 45.
15. Sawyer Diary; Hall, *Sixth New York Cavalry*, 165; McCabe, "Itinerary of the Seventeenth Regiment, Pennsylvania Volunteer Cavalry," 333; Rodenbough, *Eighteenth Regiment of Pennsylvania Cavalry*, 45.
16. *O.R.*, Series 1, vol. 29, part 2, 412.
17. Victor E. Comte to Dear Elise, November 6, 1863; Victor E. Comte Papers, Microfilm mf365 c, BHL/UM.
18. *O.R.*, Series 1, vol. 29, part 2, 413 and 415; Wilkin Diary; Gillespie, *Company A, First Ohio Cavalry*, 188; Rodenbough, *Eighteenth Regiment of Pennsylvania Cavalry*, 45; Hoffman, *First Vermont*, 150; Andrew N. Buck to Own Brother and Sister, November 9, 1863, Buck Family Papers, Microfilm mf 309-311 c, BHL/UM.

    As far as can be determined, no regular Confederate cavalry had been sent to Fredericksburg, so the identity of the "cavalry" encountered by Kilpatrick is unknown. A reporter for the *New York Herald* asserted that the enemy proved to be "straggling guerilla bands." He also claimed that during the return march, guerillas attacked Kilpatrick's wagon train, capturing a sergeant, four men, four mules, and a wagon. *New York Herald*, November 6, 1863.
19. Cheney Diary, Inglis Diary; Ressler Diary; Sawyer Diary; *New York Herald*, November 6, 1863.

    The Fourth New York and a squadron of the Seventeenth Pennsylvania relieved the Ninth New York on picket duty near Morrisville. Cheney, *Ninth Regiment, New York Volunteer Cavalry*, 139.

    The Sixth Pennsylvania, Merritt's brigade, Buford's division, picketed at Kelly's Ford, Hartwood Church, and Morrisville. Gracey, *Annals of the Sixth*, 202.

20. Gracey, *Annals of the Sixth*, 202-204.
21. Cadwallader Jones Iredell to unknown addressee, November 4, 1863, Cadwallader Jones Iredell Papers; Beverly Barrier Troxler and Billy Dawn Barrier Auciello, ed., *Dear Father: Confederate Letters Never Before Published: A Collection of Letters Written to Mathias Barrier of Mt. Pleasant, North Carolina from His Two Sons, Rufus Alexander Barrier and William Lafayette Barrier,* (North Billerica, MA: Autumn Printing, 1989), 114; Donahue Diary; Johnson Diary; Armstrong, *7th Virginia Cavalry*, 60; Carter Diary.
22. Cadwallader Jones Iredell to unknown addressee, November 4, 1863, Cadwallader Jones Iredell Papers; Richard Henry Watkins to My Precious One, November 4, 1863, Watkins Papers, 1861-1865, Mss1W3272a1-355, VHS.
23. *O.R.*, Series 1, vol. 29, part 1, 550; *New York Herald*, November 7, 1863.
24. Carter Diary; Donahue Diary; Edwards Diary; Morrissett Diary; Steele Diary; Trout, ed., *Memoirs*, 73; Neese, *Three Years in the Confederate Horse Artillery*, 233-234; Driver, *10th Virginia Cavalry*, 50; Armstrong, *11th Virginia Cavalry*, 60; *Richmond Whig*, November 13, 1863; *The People's Press*, December 3, 1863.

At this time, according to the return for October, Stuart's cavalry had an effective total present of 7,917 men, with an aggregate present of 9,767, and an aggregate present and absent of 17,786. Pleasonton's cavalry had 11,190 present for duty, with an aggregate present of 13,687, and an aggregate present and absent of 27,263. *O.R.*, Series 1, vol. 29, part 2, 405 and 811.
25. *O.R.*, Series 1, vol. 29, part 2, 418-422.
26. *Ibid.*, 423.
27. Inglis Diary; Cheney, *Ninth Regiment, New York Volunteer Cavalry*, 140.

One source stated that during the night, the enemy attempted to capture pickets belonging to the Third Indiana, Chapman's brigade, Buford's division, near Rappahannock Station. The Confederates most likely belonged to the infantry stationed in the fortifications north of the river. *Philadelphia Press*, November 10, 1863.
28. Ressler Diary; Sawyer Diary; Rawle, *Third Pennsylvania Cavalry*, 338 and 359.
29. Wilkin Diary; Gillespie, *Company A, First Ohio Cavalry*, 188; Rodenbough, *Eighteenth Regiment of Pennsylvania Cavalry*, 45.
30. *O.R.*, Series 1, vol. 29, part 1, 610.
31. Freeman, *Lee's Lieutenants*, 3, 264.
32. *O.R..*, Series 1, vol. 29, part 2, 425-426.
33. *Ibid.*, part 2, 426-428.
34. *Ibid.*, part 2, 424-425.
35. Cheney Diary; Inglis Diary; Ressler Diary; Sawyer Diary; Wilkin Diary; Hall, *Sixth New York Cavalry*, 165; McCabe, "Itinerary of the Seventeenth Regiment, Pennsylvania Volunteer Cavalry," 333; Rodenbough, *Eighteenth Regiment of Pennsylvania Cavalry*, 45; Rawle, *Third Pennsylvania Cavalry*, 338; Denison, *Sabres and Spurs*, 310; Cheney, *Ninth Regiment, New York Volunteer Cavalry*, 140.
36. *O.R.*, Series 1, vol. 29, part 1, 618.
37. One of two things may have occurred. Some cavalry could have been left on picket, supported by infantry, or all the cavalry could have been withdrawn and the pickets been replaced by infantry. The latter does not appear to have been the case. Such activity probably would have drawn the attention of the Federal cavalry pickets and been reported. No reports reflecting this were found. If the Confederate cavalry pickets were left in position, as seems most likely, they would have undoubtedly been told not to bring on any kind of engagement.

38.   Neese, *Three Years in the Confederate Horse Artillery*, 234; Bradshaw, *Diary...McVicar*, 32; Armstrong, 11th Virginia Cavalry, 60.

　　　　One source stated that the Eleventh Virginia, Rosser's Brigade, had been sent to Gaines' Cross Roads on October 26. Very likely the brigade was also sent at this time, coming back for the review and then returning on November 6. Hawse Diary.

39.   Carter Diary; John A. Holtzman Diary, in Hackley, *The Little Fork Rangers*, 88.

40.   *O.R.*, Series 1, vol. 29, part 1, 555-556 and 630-633.

41.   *Ibid.*, 574-575 and 613; Freeman, *Lee's Lieutenants*, 3, 263-267; Martin T. McMahon, "From Gettysburg to the Coming of Grant," *Battles and Leaders of the Civil War* (The Century Company, 1884. Reprint, New York: Thomas Yoseloff, Inc., 1956), 4, 87.

　　　　This surprise has never been connected with Stuart. The debacle belonged to the infantry alone. Despite having held a review just two days previously, Stuart never received blame for not knowing that an attack was coming. As far as can be determined, he had no men north of the river. Whatever scouting missions, if any, had been undertaken by the infantry commanders north of the river to keep the pulse of the Union army's activities, they failed to discover the coming attack as did the local guerillas or Mosby's men. Meade appears to have formulated and executed his plan in such a small time frame as to render it very difficult to have gathered intelligence about it. Not even a scout by Early himself just hours before the assault revealed anything that caused undue alarm in the Confederate high command. Apparently, neither Early nor the other officers involved appear to have been censured. Strangely, this surprise is never equated with the one Stuart suffered on June 9 for which he has been accused of not knowing that the enemy was coming, even though he wasn't on the north side of the river.

42.   Cheney Diary; Inglis Diary; Hall, *Sixth New York Cavalry*, 165; McCabe, "Itinerary of the Seventeenth Regiment, Pennsylvania Volunteer Cavalry," 333; Hard, *Eighth Illinois Cavalry*, 280; Cheney, *Ninth Regiment, New York Volunteer Cavalry*, 139; Gracey, *Annals of the Sixth*, 204; *O.R.*, Series 1, vol. 29, part 2, 430.

　　　　The chronicler of the Eighth Illinois mistakenly gave the day of the march as the 8th and the historian of the Sixth Pennsylvania wrote that the division marched on the 6th. Both have the destination as Sulphur Springs but erred as to the date.

43.   Ressler Diary; Sawyer Diary; Sauerburger, ed., *I Seat Myself to Write You*, 185; Denison, *Sabres and Spurs*, 310; Pyne, *First New Jersey Cavalry*, 196; Rawle, *Third Pennsylvania Cavalry*, 338 and 359; Tobie, *First Maine Cavalry*, 208; Lloyd, *History of the First Regiment Pennsylvania Reserve Cavalry*, 77; Griffin, ed., *Three Years a Soldier*, 142; *O.R.*, Series 1, vol. 29, part 2, 432 and 441.

44.   Wilkin Diary; Gillespie, *Company A, First Ohio Cavalry*, 188; Husby, comp., *Under Custer's Command*, 54; Hoffman, *First Vermont*, 150; Andrew N. Buck to Own Brother and Sister, November 9, 1863, Buck Family Papers, Microfilm mf 309-311 c, BHL/UM; *Vermont Chronicle*, November 21, 1863.

　　　　Kilpatrick at first reported that he engaged and drove back two regiments from Hampton's Division at Grove Church. No evidence could be found that any Southern cavalry were in the area. He later attributed the opposition his men encountered to "bushwhackers." *O.R.*, Series 1, vol. 29, part 2, 429 and 432.

45.   Carter Diary; Donahue Diary; Morrissett Diary; Hartley, *Stuart's Tarheels*, 301.

46.   Neese, *Three Years in the Confederate Horse Artillery*, 234; Armstrong, *11th Virginia Cavalry*, 60.

47. Hard, *Eighth Illinois Cavalry*, 282-283; Gracey, *Annals of the Sixth*, 204-205; Chapman Diary; Cheney Diary; Inglis Diary; *Supp. to O.R.*, part 1, vol. 5, 621; *O.R.*, Series 1, vol. 29, part 1, 636; *New York Herald*, November 11, 1863; *New York World*, November 11, 1863; *Daily Union & Advertiser*, date unknown; NYSMMVRC at, <www.dmna.state.ny.us/historic/mil-hist.htm> December 31, 2009.

    One source claimed that the Thirty-fifth Virginia, Rosser's Brigade, harassed Buford's column as it advanced. Considering that on this day Rosser marched from Gaines' Cross Roads to Culpeper Court House, probably on the road through Newby's Cross Roads and past Gourd Vine Church, along the right flank of Buford's advance, the possibility exists that the Thirty-fifth may have made contact with Buford's right flank at some point. However, no corroborative evidence could be found to support this. Hall, *Sixth New York Cavalry*, 165.

48. *O.R.*, Series 1, vol. 29, part 2, 433; Wilkin Diary; Gillespie, *Company A, First Ohio Cavalry*, 189-190; Boudrye, *Fifth New York Cavalry*, 84-85; Hartley, *Stuart's Tarheels*, 301; Douglas, *A Boot Full of Memories*, 298; Means, "Additional Sketch Sixty-third Regiment (Fifth Cavalry)," *Histories of the Several Regiments and Battalions from North Carolina in the Civil War 1861-65*, 3, 584; *Vermont Chronicle*, November 21, 1863; *Vermont Watchman and State Journal*, December 4, 1863; *Wyoming Mirror*, date unknown; *NYS-MMVRC* at, <www.dmna.state.ny.us/historic/mil-hist.htm>.

    Hampton had reported for duty in Richmond on the 3rd and had been ordered to report to Robert E. Lee for assignment. On the 8th he received orders from Lee to report to Stuart and assume command of his division. *O.R.*, Series 1, vol. 29, part 2, 817 and 828.

49. Ressler Diary; Sawyer Diary; Denison, *Sabres and Spurs*, 310; Pyne, *First New Jersey Cavalry*, 196; Rawle, *Third Pennsylvania Cavalry*, 338 and 359; Tobie, *First Maine Cavalry*, 208; Lloyd, *History of the First Regiment Pennsylvania Reserve Cavalry*, 77; Griffin, ed., *Three Years a Soldier*, 142.

50. *O.R.*, Series 1, vol. 29, part 1, 614 and part 2, 437-438; Carter Diary; Donahue Diary; Morrissett Diary; Bradshaw, *Diary...McVicar*, 32; Shoemaker, *Shoemaker's Battery*, 60; Krick, *9th Virginia Cavalry*, 30; Trout, ed., *Memoirs*, 73; Trout, *Galloping Thunder*, 388.

    The section of Chew's Battery that had accompanied Rosser's Brigade to Gaines' Cross Roads had quite an adventure. Starting at dawn, the section arrived at Culpeper Court House where it remained until near sunset when orders arrived sending it to Stevensburg. While on the march word came that the enemy already had possession of that place and that the section should return to Culpeper Court House. A mile from the town a dispatch altered the section's course yet again, this time to Brandy Station. After a mile trek, the darkness and the exhaustion of the horses forced the section to encamp near the Wallack house. The possibility exists that Rosser's Brigade made the same odyssey. Neese, *Three Years in the Confederate Horse Artillery*, 234-235.

51. Carter Diary; Donahue Diary; Edwards Diary; Morrissett Diary; Trussell Diary; Bradshaw, *Diary...McVicar*, 32; Trout, ed., *Memoirs*, 73-74; Shoemaker, *Shoemaker's Battery*, 60-61.

52. Hawse Diary; Neese, *Three Years in the Confederate Horse Artillery*, 236; Trout, ed., *Memoirs*, 225.

    Just where the various brigades went cannot be determined. Neese recorded that his section of Chew's Battery retreated along the Orange and Alexandria Railroad to within a mile of Rapidan Station where he camped for the night. Some portion of

Hampton's Division undoubtedly accompanied him, but Neese failed to record the name of the brigade. Hawse, who was in the Eleventh Virginia, Rosser's Brigade, wrote that he fell back to the Robinson River, so this brigade probably rode with Chew's section. The possibility exists that Gordon's and/or Young's brigades did the same. However, Kilpatrick did report that his pickets encountered enemy cavalry vedettes three miles from Raccoon Ford on the 9th, so part of Hampton's Division may have crossed the Rapidan at Raccoon or Somerville fords. *O.R.*, Series 1, vol. 29, part 2, 439.

53. Chapman Diary; Cheney Diary; Inglis Diary; Hard, *Eighth Illinois Cavalry*, 283; Cheney, *Ninth Regiment, New York Volunteer Cavalry*, 140.
54. *O.R.*, Series 1, vol. 29, part 2, 439-442; Husby, comp., *Under Custer's Command*, 54; Gillespie, *Company A, First Ohio Cavalry*, 190; *New York World*, November 11, 1863.
55. Ressler Diary; Sawyer Diary; Rawle, *Third Pennsylvania Cavalry*, 338 and 359.
56. *O.R.*, Series 1, vol. 29, part 2, 440-441.
57. *O.R.*, Series 1, vol. 29, part 2, 441; Ressler Diary; Sawyer Diary; Tobie, *First Maine Cavalry*, 209; Rawle, *Third Pennsylvania Cavalry*, 338 and 359-360.
58. *O.R.*, Series 1, vol. 29, part 2, 441 and 445; Cheney Diary; Inglis Diary; Gracey, *Annals of the Sixth*, 205; Cheney, *Ninth Regiment, New York Volunteer Cavalry*, 140.
59. *O.R.*, Series 1, vol. 29, part 2, 441; Rodenbough, *Eighteenth Regiment of Pennsylvania Cavalry*, 45
60. Carter Diary; Donahue Diary; Edwards Diary; Morrissett Diary; Neese, *Three Years in the Confederate Horse Artillery*, 236; Trout, ed., *Memoirs*, 74; Shoemaker, *Shoemaker's Battery*, 61; Driver, *1st Virginia Cavalry*, 75; Driver and Howard, *2nd Virginia Cavalry*, 102.
61. *O.R.*, Series 1, vol. 29, part 2, 446 and 926; Carter Diary; Morrissett Diary; Cheney, *Ninth Regiment, New York Volunteer Cavalry*, 140-141.
62. Richard Henry Watkins to My Own Dear Mary, November 11, 1863, Watkins Papers, 1861-1865, Mss1W3272a1-355, VHS; Trout, ed., *Memoirs*, 74; Bradshaw, *Diary...McVicar*, 32.
63. Neese, *Three Years in the Confederate Horse Artillery*, 236-237.
    Neese's section of Chew's Battery, attached to one of the brigades of the division, marched along the Orange Plank Road, turning north on the Brock Road and encamping for the night where Wilderness Run crossed the Culpeper Plank Road. While the route of Hampton's Division cannot be verified, the section undoubtedly marched with one of the brigades.
64. Ressler Diary, Sawyer Diary; Hand, Jr., *One Good Regiment*, 87; Rawle, *Third Pennsylvania Cavalry*, 338 and 360; Sauerburger, ed., *I Seat Myself to Write You*, 187.
65. Wilkin Diary.
66. *O.R.*, Series 1, vol. 29, part 2, 448-9.
67. Carter Diary; Donahue Diary; Morrissett Diary; Richard Henry Watkins to My Own Dear Mary, November 11, 1863, Watkins Papers, 1861-1865, Mss1W3272a1-355, VHS; Trout, ed., *Memoirs*, 74.
68. Hawse Diary; Neese, *Three Years in the Confederate Horse Artillery*, 237.
69. Cheney Diary; Inglis Diary; Hard, *Eighth Illinois Cavalry*, 284.
70. Ressler Diary; Sawyer Diary; Ebenezer S. Johnson to Dear Mother, November 13, 1863, Ebenezer S. Johnson Letters, Earl Hess Collection and CWMC, USAMHI; Rawle, *Third Pennsylvania Cavalry*, 338 and 360; Denison, *Sabres and Spurs*, 310; Tobie, *First Maine Cavalry*, 208.

Sometime around the 12th, a number of ambitious Confederates who had more energy than they knew what to do with, cut down most of the telegraph poles from near Hartwood Church to Falmouth. One source attributed it to regular cavalry, but no record of any of Hampton's regiments, which would have been the closest, having crossed the river could be found. More likely the mischief could be laid at the hoofs of guerillas. Ebenezer S. Johnson to Dear Mother, November 13, 1863, Ebenezer S. Johnson Letters, Earl Hess Collection and CWMC, USAMHI.

71. Wilkin Diary; Rodenbough, *Eighteenth Regiment of Pennsylvania Cavalry*, 45; Hoffman, *First Vermont*, 150.

A newspaper reported that Kilpatrick clashed with Confederate cavalry under Stuart at Mitchell's Station on the morning of the 12th. This action could not be verified from any other source. *Philadelphia Press*, November 14, 1863.

72. Governor's Papers – Zebulon Baird Vance, 1862-1865, 1877-1879, Box GP 168, Folder 11/10 – 14/63; Manarin, *North Carolina Troops*, 26.

73. Carter Diary; Donahue Diary; Morrissett Diary; Brig. Gen. John Buford to Lt. Col. C. Ross Smith, November 13, 1863, Telegrams Collected by the Secretary of War, Unbound, RG 107, M504, NARA.

74. Neese, *Three Years in the Confederate Horse Artillery*, 237-238.

75. Brig. Gen. John Buford to Lt. Col. C. Ross Smith, November 13, 1863, Telegrams Collected by the Secretary of War, Unbound, RG 107, M504, NARA; Cheney Diary; Inglis Diary; Hard, *Eighth Illinois Cavalry*, 284.

76. Denison, *Sabres and Spurs*, 310; Ressler Diary; Sawyer Diary; Rawle, *Third Pennsylvania Cavalry*, 338 and 359.

77. *O.R.*, Series 1, vol. 29, part 2, 451-452; Wilkin Diary.

78. Maj. Gen. Alfred Pleasonton to Brig. Gen. John Buford, November 14, 1863, Telegrams Collected by the Secretary of War, Unbound, RG 107, M504, NARA; Cheney Diary; Inglis Diary; Cheney, *Ninth Regiment, New York Volunteer Cavalry*, 141; Hall, *Sixth New York Cavalry*, 166.

79. *Baltimore Sun*, November 19, 1863; *O.R.*, Series 1, vol. 29, part 1, 676 and part 2, 453.

Hereafter, Kilpatrick's division will be referenced as Custer's division, until Kilpatrick's return to command.

Custer's brigade will be referred to as Town's brigade for the same time period.

80. Ressler Diary; Sawyer Diary; Rawle, *Third Pennsylvania Cavalry*, 360.

81. Carter Diary; Donahue Diary; Morrissett Diary.

The Fourth Virginia came off picket and moved to Twyman's Rainy.

82. *O.R.*, Series 1, vol. 29, part 2, 459 and 462; Wilkin Diary; Victor E. Comte to Dear Elise, November 17, 1863; Comte Papers, Microfilm mf365 c, BHL/UM; *New York Times*, November 18, 1863; *New York Herald*, November 23, 1863; *New York World*, November 18, 1863; *Baltimore Sun*, November 19, 1863; *The Detroit Free Press*, November 20, 163.

83. *O.R.*, Series 1, vol. 29, part 2, 460-461; Brig. Gen. John Buford to Lt. Col. C. Ross Smith, November 15, 1863, Telegrams Collected by the Secretary of War, Unbound, RG 107, M504, NARA; Cheney Diary.

84. *O.R.*, Series 1, vol. 29, part 2, 460-461.

85. Alvin N. Brackett to Dear Friend Hattie, November 15, 1863, Brackett Letters; Ressler Diary; Sawyer Diary; Rawle, *Third Pennsylvania Cavalry*, 338; Denison, *Sabres and Spurs*, 310.

Denison recorded the punishment as having occurred on the 12th, but this appears to be an error.

86.   Carter Diary; Donahue Diary; Edwards Diary; Morrissett Diary; Neese, *Three Years in the Confederate Horse Artillery*, 238; Trout, ed., *Memoirs*, 74.
87.   *O.R.*, Series 1, vol. 29, part 2, 467-468; Sauerburger, ed., *I Seat Myself to Write You*, 188; *New York Herald*, November 19, 1863; *Washington Daily Morning Chronicle*, November 26, 1863; Rawle, *Third Pennsylvania Cavalry*, 338-339.
      A patrol from the First Maine, Gregg's brigade, that routinely checked on Kemper's Ford conducted a small raid that caused a furor within the command. During the patrol, the corporal in charge who had taken command when the sergeant became sick allowed his men to pilfer a number of cabbages from a woman's garden near the ford. On discovering the theft, the lady reported it to headquarters, launching an investigation. The culprits appeared to be from Company G, but when the sergeants were called in and questioned, not one knew anything about it, nor did the sergeant who had been ill reveal that he had not been on duty that night. Thus the raid became one of the more successful adventures in regimental lore. Tobie, *First Maine Cavalry*, 209-210.
88.   Brig. Gen. John Buford to Lt. Col. C. Ross Smith, November 16, 1863, Telegrams Collected by the Secretary of War, Unbound, RG 107, M504, NARA.
      The Eighth Illinois relieved the Eighth New York on picket duty. Cheney Diary.
89.   Carter Diary; Morrissett Diary; Trussell Diary; Richard Henry Watkins to My Darling Mary, November 20, 1863, Watkins Papers, 1861-1865, Mss1W3272a1-355, VHS.
      There are some anomalies in some of the diary entries. Carter recorded that the brigade was headed for Swift Run Gap. Criglersville is on the way to Milam's Gap not Swift Run Gap. Trussell wrote that the march took place on the 17th, but he may have been simply recording the return march date. He also indicated that the target might have been Luray, which would have meant passing through Thornton's Gap that lay north of Swift Run Gap. Watkins wrote that his regiment, the Third Virginia, was actually camped in a gap, although he failed to mention which one.
90.   Brig. Gen. John Buford to Lt. Col. C. Ross Smith, November 16, 1863, Telegrams Collected by the Secretary of War, Unbound, RG 107, M504, NARA; Hall, *Sixth New York Cavalry*, 166; *Washington Daily Morning Chronicle*, November 26, 1863.
91.   Cheney Diary; Inglis Diary; Ressler Diary; Sawyer Diary; Wilkins Diary; Frank M. Brown to Dear Father, November 18, 1863, Brown Family Papers, Box No. 85859 Aa2, BHL/UM; Sauerburger, ed., *I Seat Myself to Write You*, 188.
      A furor erupted in the camp of the Fifth Michigan, Town's brigade, Custer's division, when the men drew their pay and discovered that they had been docked for winter clothing issued to them. They had been told to throw away their winter clothes the previous spring on the promise that the articles would be replaced free. Other discrepancies emerged. One man, who had kept a careful record of what he had been issued, was charged for a pair of trousers he had never received, while another paid for boots never issued to him. Such dealings angered the men to such an extent that the safety of the officers was threatened. A shady-dealing quartermaster sergeant escaped harm only because he had left on a furlough. Victor E. Comte to Dear Elise, November 17, 1863, Victor E. Comte Papers, Microfilm mf365 c, BHL/UM; Frank M. Brown to Dear Father, November 18, 1863, Brown Family Papers, Box No. 85859 Aa2, BHL/UM.
92.   Several locations for the camp are possible – one at Sheppard's Grove, one near the Brannon house, and one near the Wrenn house. The latter location is the shortest distance to the fords and was probably the site of the camp.

The Eighteenth at this time numbered approximately 140 men present for duty. The picket force at Ely's Ford numbered fifteen men. *New York Times*, November 23, 1863.

93. According to one source only two regiments participated in the attack, the First and Fifth North Carolina. Means, "Additional Sketch Sixty-third Regiment (Fifth Cavalry)," *Histories of the Several Regiments and Battalions from North Carolina in the Civil War 1861-65*, 3, 584-585.

94. *O.R.*, Series 1, vol. 29, part 1, 655-657; Frank M. Brown to Dear Father, November 19, 1863, Brown Family Papers, Box No. 85859 Aa2, BHL/UM; Means, "Additional Sketch Sixty-third Regiment (Fifth Cavalry)," *Histories of the Several Regiments and Battalions from North Carolina in the Civil War 1861-65*, 3, 584-585; Rodenbough, *Eighteenth Regiment of Pennsylvania Cavalry*, 45; Boudrye, *Fifth New York Cavalry*, 85; *New York Times*, November 23, 1863; *Vermont Watchman and State Journal*, December 4, 1863.

95. *O.R.*, Series 1, vol. 29, part 1, 657; Means, "Additional Sketch Sixty-third Regiment (Fifth Cavalry)," *Histories of the Several Regiments and Battalions from North Carolina in the Civil War 1861-65*, 3, 584; Rodenbough, *Eighteenth Regiment of Pennsylvania Cavalry*, 45; *New York Times*, November 23, 1863.

96. *O.R.*, Series 1, vol. 29, part 2, 471; *New York Times Supplement*, November 21, 1863; *New York Times*, November 23, 1863; *Philadelphia Press*, November 23, 1863.

    Considering that the Confederate infantry guarded the fords, they most likely conducted these operations.

97. Gracey, *Annals of the Sixth*, 201;

98. Ressler Diary; Rawle, *Third Pennsylvania Cavalry*, 339; *Daily National Intelligencer*, November 18, 1863; *Philadelphia Press*, November 23, 1863.

99. Brig. Gen. John Buford to Maj. Gen. Andrew A. Humphreys, November 19, 1863, Telegrams Collected by the Secretary of War, Unbound, RG 107, M504, NARA.

    Buford labeled Joyner a deserter but another source claimed he was captured. Driver and Howard, *2nd Virginia Cavalry*, 236.

100. Cheney Diary; Inglis Diary; Ressler; Sawyer Diary; Wilkin Diary; Hall, *Sixth New York Cavalry*, 166; Rodenbough, *Eighteenth Regiment of Pennsylvania Cavalry*, 45; Rawle, *Third Pennsylvania Cavalry*, 339.

    The Third Pennsylvania, Taylor's brigade, Gregg's division, stood picket at Fox's Ford, stretching its line toward Rappahannock Station and Sulphur Springs. The Fourth New York, Devin's brigade, Buford's division, relieved its brother regiment the Sixth New York.

101. *O.R.*, Series 1, vol. 29, part 2, 474-475.

    Apparently, engineer officers accompanied by 20 troopers from the Fifth Michigan conducted another scouting expedition from the 19th to the 23rd and surveyed the entire Rapidan River line, supplying Meade with much more detailed information than the officer from Custer could have gathered in one day. Perhaps Custer's officer brought back preliminary findings from this expedition. Victor E. Comte to Dear Elise, November 23, 1863, Victor E. Comte Papers, Microfilm mf365 c, BHL/UM.

102. Carter Diary; Donahue Diary; Ressler Diary; Sawyer Diary; Wilkin Diary; Hall, *Sixth New York Cavalry*, 166; Rodenbough, *Eighteenth Regiment of Pennsylvania Cavalry*, 45; Rawle, *Third Pennsylvania Cavalry*, 339; Brig. Gen. John Buford to Lt. Col. C. Ross Smith, November 20, 1863, Telegrams Collected by the Secretary of War, Unbound, RG 107, M504, NARA.

103. *O.R.*, Series 1, vol. 29, part 2, 476.

104.   Hard, *Eighth Illinois Cavalry*, 280; *HDSACWRD*, <www.civilwardata.com> November 23, 2009; *O.R.*, Series 1, vol. 29, part 1, 665; *New York Times*, November 25, 1863.
        Hereafter, Buford's division will be referenced as Merritt's division, and Merritt's brigade will be referred to as Gibbs's brigade.

105.   *O.R.*, Series 1, vol. 29, part 1, 659-660; Williamson, *Mosby's Rangers*, 107-110; Lloyd, *History of the First Regiment Pennsylvania Reserve Cavalry*, 77-78; Sauerburger, ed., *I Seat Myself to Write You*, 189; *Philadelphia Press*, November 23, 1863.

106.   *O.R.*, Series 1, vol. 29, part 2, 473-474.

Chapter Nine

From Mine Run to Winter Quarters

While Meade calmly waited and planned, Lee did the same. Though the commander-in-chief of the Army of Northern Virginia felt some sense of security behind his river-line defenses, he understood both their strengths and weaknesses and took steps in the event that Meade tried to alter the status quo. Both Ewell and Hill had their instructions, although Ewell had given up his command to Maj. Gen. Jubal A. Early due to illness. "Old Jube" would have to be on the alert and up to the task, if Meade attempted anything, since Ewell's Corps, being on the right and closer to the foe, would be the first to feel the weight of the enemy's advance. So, Meade waited on the railroad and Lee waited on Meade. In the meantime, the cavalry persevered.[1]

The 22nd brought the first step in Meade's planned offensive when he ordered the First Corps under Maj. Gen. John Newton to concentrate at Rappahannock Station, leaving one division to guard the railroad back to the bridge over Bull Run above Manassas Junction. Newton had received word on the 20th that such a move was in the planning stage and now he was to carry it out. To assist Brig. Gen. John R. Kenly, whose division would be given the task of guarding the railroad, a contingent of cavalry from Gregg's division would be provided. The First Rhode Island drew the duty and left on the 23rd.[2] Besides Newton's order, Meade also called for a meeting of his corps commanders at 1:00 on the afternoon of the 23rd, a sign that something might be in the wind. Gregg's division received orders to prepare to move at 6:00 that same morning, each man carrying three days' rations and two days' forage.[3] For the cavalry, the opening of a new campaign meant only one thing, more hard riding and fighting. One man looked to alleviate some of the former.

Like many other officers in Pleasonton's cavalry, Col. William D. Mann of the Seventh Michigan, Custer's brigade, Kilpatrick's division, had concerns about the constant wear and tear on the horses in his command. He had developed what he believed to be a solution. Sgt. Andrew N. Buck of the colonel's regiment explained about Mann's passion in a November 23 letter to his brother and sister, "The 'Buggy brigade' is fully engaging the attention of Col. Mann . . . who is now in Washington pressing his petions [sic] backed with Custer's and Kilpatrick's signatures. . . . This peculiar arm of the service allows the soldiers to ride in covered wagons with steel springs – each wagon to contain ten men being drawn by four horses. The men are to be armed with Spencer's repeating rifle crowned with a sabre bayonet – their business being to skirmish and charge on foot – thus reliev-ing the cavalry from any dismounted duty – a duty always unwelcomed." Mann proposed to organize at least a regiment of cavalry that rode in wagons. The men would be able to carry more ammunition than the regular cavalryman and thus be able to skirmish with the enemy for longer periods. With only four horses pulling each wagon, six horses would be eliminated that would otherwise be required for the same number of men. The unit also could be used to guard wagon trains, free-ing infantry of that duty and offering greater security because of their rapid-fire weapons. Mann believed that the wagons could go wherever the artillery went, meaning the horse artillery that accompanied the cavalry, and prove to be an asset.[4] Unfortunately, even if approved, such a unit would take time to organize, so for the present one man on one horse would have to do. The other regiments of Kil-patrick's and Buford's divisions endured the usual duties but with the added bur-den of rain and mud.[5]

President of the Confederacy, Jefferson Davis, arrived at Orange Court House on the afternoon of the 21st to visit Lee and the army. He spent the rest of the day at Lee's headquarters. His itinerary for the next few days included attend-ing church services with Lee on Sunday, the 23rd, and reviewing Early's and Hill's infantry on the following days.[6] His presence would somewhat distract Lee from the military situation at hand. If Meade's plan became operational, the President would have the opportunity to see his army in action. Stuart's cavalry did not ap-pear on the review list, a circumstance that probably disappointed some and elated others. The lack of preparing for such an event did not mean that the men had noth-ing to do, although they came close. Had it not been for taking turns on picket, doing nothing would have been the majority of the men's pastime. The Third Vir-ginia, Owen's Brigade, Fitz Lee's Division, assumed watch over the fords of the Robinson north of Mt. Zion Church, relieving one of its brother regiments. Such changes occurred along the river line wherever the cavalry was stationed.[7]

On the 23rd, Meade issued orders for the movement of the army on the 24th. The various corps would move to cross the Rapidan at Germanna, Jacob's Mill, and Culpeper Mine fords, forcing a crossing if necessary, while Kilpatrick continued to guard the Rapidan fords and Merritt watched the army's right.[8] How-ever, Gen. Gregg's division already had orders from the 22nd and proceeded to execute them. Before sunrise, the brigades drew in their vedettes and prepared to march. Taylor's brigade moved to Bealton Station and then toward Morrisville. Gregg's brigade, temporarily under the command of Col. Pennock Huey of the Eighth Pennsylvania, concentrated at Morrisville.[9]

Lee's army focused its attention on President Davis. On the 22nd he had at-tended the Episcopal Church in Orange Court House and heard an excellent sermon by Brig. Gen. and Rev. Dr. William N. Pendleton, Lee's artillery chief. Officers of all ranks dropped by Lee's headquarters to pay their respects. The 23rd brought a ride up Clark's Mountain with Lee to observe the Federal army, at least those portions that were visible.[10] In the Southern army's camps, the 23rd mirrored the previous days.

312

Orders flashed throughout Meade's army early on the 24th, postponing the planned movement because of the heavy rain. Pleasonton hurried off the same order to Gregg, who stood poised to thrust across the Rapidan. Indeed, his command had marched to Ellis' Ford, where it crossed the Rappahannock and rode on to Ely's Ford on the Rapidan. Here one regiment from Huey's brigade crossed the river, driving in pickets belonging to Rosser's Brigade, Hampton's Division, before Gregg received the message, cancelling the movement sometime before noon. He immediately pulled back. Huey's brigade encamped at Richardsville and Taylor's at Rappahannock City near Ellis' Ford.[11] Elsewhere, Kilpatrick's division heard "Boots-and-Saddles" at 6:00 in the morning and was on the march when the dispatch reached them, countermanding the offensive. Fortunately, they had not ridden very far and returned to camp.[12] The day also brought Gen. Kilpatrick news that his wife had died at West Point. Because of Meade's proposed operation, he could not leave the army. Gen. Davies telegraphed his father in New York to do all he could for the family.[13]

Merritt's division carried out its function of guarding the army's right flank even as the campaign ground to a muddy halt. The withdrawal of the infantry in preparation for the offensive left the vedettes from Devin's brigade isolated and open to attack. A number of them stationed out on the Culpeper Court House/Sperryville road fell into enemy hands, causing Devin to send a patrol of 17 men out to look for them. These ran into about 60 troopers from the First Virginia, Owen's Brigade, Fitz Lee's Division, and had to retreat hastily, losing a few men captured. Devin now ordered Maj. Seymour B. Conger of the Third West Virginia with 100 men from his regiment and the Sixth New York to disperse the enemy. Just beyond Griffinsburg where the road crosses the Hazel River, Conger ran into the Confederates and in the sharp skirmish that followed, Lt. John E. Hoffman of the Third was killed and two men from the Sixth were wounded. The Sixth finally broke through and chased their foes up into the mountains where they disappeared into the trees.[14]

The rain that doomed Meade's movement also shortened President Davis's visit. The gray infantry escaped the reviews, except for the band of the Eleventh Mississippi Infantry that had to endure the spit and polish when it played for Davis on the evening of the 23rd. The next morning the president boarded a train for Richmond with Gen. Stuart, who accompanied Davis to Gordonsville.[15] Back in the army's camps, everyone tried to keep dry.

Meade's commanders fine tuned their plans and kept a critical eye on the conditions of the roads throughout the 25th. The extra time meant finishing the construction of bridges over Mountain Run and repairing some of the roads from Brandy Station toward the three fords of the Rapidan that the army planned to use. A Custer scout checked Germanna Ford and found that the Confederates had made no changes in their defenses, except that two small rifle pits were being dug. Gen. Gregg had his division up at 4:00 in the morning. Breakfasted, the troopers saddled at 11:00 and waited to move out. At 2:00 in the afternoon, orders came to unsaddle and encamp. The Tenth New York, Huey's brigade, drew outpost duty. Not being in the van of the army, the men of Merritt's and Kilpatrick's divisions sat in their camps, excepting those on outpost duty, waiting for mother nature to dry the roads.[16]

Later in the day, Robert E. Lee received word from two of his scouts that something stirred in the Federal army - the First Corps had been issued eight days rations; Gen. Gregg's division of cavalry was in the act of crossing the Rappahannock at Ellis' Ford; and infantry moved along the railroads. Piecing these facts together with what he could glean from the Washington newspapers, Lee concluded that Meade intended to move against him and immediately wrote President Davis to inform him of that fact. However, Lee gave Davis no inkling of his plan of action, only warning, "every precaution should be taken to avoid disaster."[17] While Lee waited to see what Meade intended, his army spent the 25th as it had the previous week, watching the fords and lying around in its camps. In the cavalry, the Fourth Virginia, Owen's Brigade, Fitz Lee's Division, drew four days rations and prepared to go on picket, relieving its brigade brother, the Third Virginia.[18] The brigade's other regiments lounged in camp, waiting their turn at the onerous duty. Fitz Lee's other two brigades, Chambliss's and Lomax's, stationed around Orange Court House, did much the same, as did Hampton's Division along the upper Rapidan. All seemed quiet.

At 4:00 on the morning of the 26th, Thanksgiving Day, a circular from Meade's headquarters informed the army's corps commanders that they were to execute their orders of the 23rd at 6:00 in the morning. The Fifth Corps was the first infantry over the Rapidan, crossing at Culpeper Mine Ford at 10:30 followed by the First Corps that only managed to get one division over the river. The Second Corps was to cross at Germanna Ford. The Third Corps, directed to cross over at Jacob's Mill Ford and to be followed by the Sixth Corps, ran into difficulty when Brig. Gen. Henry Prince, commanding the Second Division, failed to start on time and did not reach the ford until noon. This delay slowed the whole advance, as Meade ordered the Fifth Corps to halt its march and held back the Second Corps from crossing until the progress of the Third Corps could be determined. Not until 1:30 in the afternoon did the Second Corps cross the river, driving off pickets from Rosser's Brigade, Hampton's Division. The Fifth Corps finally lumbered forward at 3:00. The move to turn Lee's right had begun with a bit of a stumble for the infantry. Not so the cavalry.[19]

Gen. Gregg's division splashed over Ely's Ford, Huey's brigade in the van. Once across, the Tenth New York took the advance. Encountering no enemy, Gregg slowed his march to match that of the Fifth Corps that had crossed the Rapidan on his right at Culpeper Mine Ford. At 8:00 in the evening, he encamped at the headwaters of the Po River on the road from Parker's Store to Spotsylvania Court House and picketed toward Parker's Store. The First New Jersey, Taylor's brigade, bringing up the rear of the column, spread out its vedettes to link with those from the Fifth Corps.[20]

Custer, now in command of the division in Kilpatrick's absence, moved his brigades from their camps to Morton's Ford on the Rapidan for the purpose of making a demonstration to occupy the Confederates' attention. Custer's brigade, under Col. Charles H. Town of the First Michigan, took position at the ford while Davies's brigade rode upstream to Raccoon Ford. As Davies approached the ford along the river road, Confederate artillery opened fire on his column, forcing him to drift to his right and follow the wood line until he reached his intended position near the ford. There he found a picket force from Town's brigade, contending with enemy sharpshooters who occupied several houses on the north bank of the river. The Confederate works on the south bank, being higher, completely dominated the ford. Nevertheless, Davies brought up a section of Lt. Edward Field's Battery E, Fourth U. S. Artillery that took position on the only sheltered place on the north bank and began shelling the enemy's works on the other side of the river. Eight of the enemy's guns immediately replied and a spirited duel commenced, lasting until the Confederates placed two additional guns to Field's right that rendered the Federal artillery's position untenable. Davies withdrew Field and the fighting died down to occasional skirmisher fire. At Morton's Ford, several lines of enemy entrenchments laid out on high ground in nearly a semicircle and overlooking the ford confronted Custer, who had stayed with his old brigade. Several guns and masses of infantry could be seen occupying the works. At 10:00 in the morning, Custer, hearing artillery fire down river, brought up Lt. Alexander C. M. Pennington's Battery M, Second U. S. Artillery and opened fire. The bombardment continued throughout the day without any measurable results. However, Custer achieved his goal, which was to occupy the enemy's attention from the real crossings downstream. The day ended at both fords with no gains on either side for all the powder and shot expended.[21]

Merritt's division played its part in the drama as well. Devin's brigade left its camp on the James City road and rode to Culpeper Court House, occupying the town and placing vedettes all around it, sealing it off from the surrounding country. He also sent out patrols to Brandy Station. Gibbs's Reserve Brigade received orders to proceed to Ely's Ford and guard the army's supply trains. Gibbs rode as far as Stevensburg, encamping there for the night. Gamble's brigade drew the same duty and left its camps near Culpeper Court House, trotted through Stevensburg, and camped on the road between that place and Richardsville. Pleasonton's cavalry had had a good day, achieving all that had been asked of it.[22]

Receiving reports from his observers on Clark's Mountain, once the morning fog dissipated, Robert E. Lee reacted to Meade's offensive as soon as he determined its direction, ordering Early's Corps to march to Locust Grove along the Old Turnpike while Hill's Corps moved down the Plank Road. Stuart alerted his division commanders to the Federal advance. At the time, Rosser's Brigade, Hampton's Division, was posted toward Fredericksburg while Hampton's other two brigades, Young's and Gordon's, were encamped around Twyman's Store. Stuart ordered Hampton to be ready to support his outposts at Ely's and Germanna fords. Rosser moved toward Chancellorsville to do just that, but at about 8:00 news came from his vedettes of the enemy's crossing at Ely's Ford, and he rode toward Todd's Tavern instead. Hampton left Twyman's Store late in the day for the Plank Road. Fitz Lee was directed to leave one brigade to cover the fords of the upper Rapidan and take the other two to relieve the infantry at Morton's and Raccoon fords. Chambliss's Brigade took position at Mt. Pisgah Church; Lomax's Brigade moved to Morton's Ford; and Owen's Brigade rode to Raccoon Ford. Owen, being on the extreme left flank and watching the Robinson River fords near Mt. Zion Church, did not begin his march until 10:00 at night, crossing the Rapidan at Barnett's Ford and moving over slippery roads in intense cold. Nevertheless, Owen and Lomax arrived at their assigned positions about 4:00 in the morning, allowing the infantry to withdraw.[23]

The movement of the vast Federal army necessarily left parts of it vulnerable to attack. While Lee was not in position to do so, one Confederate force was. When reports reached him of Meade's offensive, John Mosby assembled his command at Rectortown. A scouting expedition led by the partisan chief himself revealed a tempting target – a large wagon park at Brandy Station guarded by infantry. Mosby decided to attack it that night and did so, carrying off over 130 mules and horses and 15 wagons and burning another 19 wagons loaded with oats.[24] Among the vast storehouse of Federal supplies, such a loss made only a minor dent, but the attack ably demonstrated that for all the troops Meade had assigned to guard his wagon trains, it wasn't enough. In truth, the number required to completely neutralize Mosby and the other partisans and guerillas operating against Meade's supply lines would have greatly reduced the number of men available for offensive operations. Aggravating as it was, Meade had to accept such losses, hope that the steps he had taken would minimize them, and move on. Lee was his target, not Mosby.

A somewhat frustrated Meade, who had expected to be in position to attack Lee early on the 27th, instead found his army with several miles to go before even hoping to engage the enemy. He issued marching orders at 12:15 in the morning, giving Pleasonton the vague instructions to "direct a force of that arm [the cavalry] to move in advance on the roads in front of the army." For Gregg this meant fronting the Fifth Corps and he did so by marching from his camp through Parker's Store toward New Hope Church where at 11:00 Taylor's brigade, Companies K and L of the Third Pennsylvania having the advance, brushed against two dismounted squadrons of skirmishers, one each from the Second and Fifth North Carolina, Gordon's Brigade, Hampton's Division. A mounted Fourth North Carolina and the other squadrons of the Second and Fifth backed the skirmishers. Stuart, a bit angered by what he considered the Tarheels' late arrival, had wanted to meet the enemy farther up the road and earlier in the day but now made the best of the situation, though encumbered by a lack of carbine and rifle ammunition and missing Young's Brigade that had not yet arrived.[25]

On contact with the enemy, Taylor dismounted Captain Charles Treichel's squadron of the Third Pennsylvania in the wood near the New Hope Church and with Lt. William F. Potter's squadron, all under the command of Capt. Walter S. Newhall, Acting Assistant Adjutant-General of the brigade, charged across the open ground, pushing Gordon's skirmishers back into the trees on the opposite side of the clearing. Newhall now deployed Treichel and Potter to the left of the Plank Road with Treichel's right flank on the road. The remainder of the Third dismounted and formed a line to the left of the road back at the church. A squadron from the First Massachusetts under Capt. Benjamin W. Crowninshield dismounted and deployed as skirmishers on the right of the road. Stuart ordered two guns of Capt. James F. Hart's Battery of horse artillery to unlimber and open fire. In response the squadrons of the Third Pennsylvania at the church moved to the right flank of the First Massachusetts and the whole line charged, driving back Gordon's line a considerable distance. Though giving ground, Gordon fought determinedly and held on until Brig. Gen. Henry H. Walker's Brigade, Maj. Gen. Henry Heth's Division, Hill's Corps, arrived. Walker relieved Gordon's line, brought Taylor's advance to a halt, and drove the Federal cavalry back. Gordon's troopers now split, one portion under Gordon going to Walker's right and the other under Capt. William H. H. Cowles, moving to the left toward the Turnpike. Walker found the Federal cavalry a hard nut to crack. His skirmishers advanced 700 yards ahead of his brigade line and were without support. Taking advantage of the situation, Taylor fed in all of the First Massachusetts right into Pennsylvanians' line. The Third, whose ammunition had all but given out, declined to go to the rear. Instead, they borrowed cartridges from the First Massachusetts's troopers and fought on. However, the two regiments could not go forward and indeed, were struggling to maintain their position. Fortunately, their earlier advance had opened the way for the First New Jersey and the First Pennsylvania to deploy in their midst. The latter regiment had remained mounted for a time in case the Confederates launched a mounted charge, but now it, along with the First New Jersey, the Third Pennsylvania, and the First Massachusetts, swept forward on foot. The charge broke Walker's skirmish line, swept around both flanks, and netted 28 prisoners from the right of the line, mostly from the Fifty-fifth Virginia Infantry.[26]

Stuart replied by committing Hampton with Young's Brigade, which had come up at last. Taylor countered with a section of Capt. Joseph W. Martin's Sixth New York Independent Battery. The fighting escalated. Lt. William F. Potter's squadron of the Third Pennsylvania on the far left took position along the unfinished railroad bed with Lt. Samuel S. Green and several troopers occupying a tobacco barn where they took up the role of sharpshooters. Here the Third fought stubbornly until Walker committed a third of his brigade as skirmishers along the entire front and Young came down on the Third's flank, dislodging Green from the barn and chasing back the whole blue line. Stuart soon committed two guns from the Rowan Artillery and four from the Branch Artillery of Maj. John C. Haskell's Artillery Battalion, under the command of Lt. John R. Potts. In the heavy artillery duel that followed, Martin's first section of the Sixth New York Battery used up three chests of ammunition and withdrew, being replaced by another section of the battery. Against the increased enemy force and under heavy artillery fire, Taylor could barely hold on much less advance. Realizing that his cavalry had done all it could and with only the Sixth Ohio left in reserve and Confederate infantry increasing the pressure against his line, he decided to call it a day and fell back about 4:00, allowing units from the Pennsylvania Reserves of the Fifth Corps to take up the fight. Capt. Frank C. Gibbs's Battery L, First Ohio Light Battery took over for Martin's Battery and immediately took a pounding from Potts, suffering several casualties. Nevertheless, the Federal infantry stabilized the situation and the fighting soon died away. After dark, Walker withdrew and Young's Brigade took his place.[27]

During all this fighting, Rosser's Brigade of Hampton's Division was not idle. From his camp at Todd's Tavern, Rosser dispatched scouts to reconnoiter the flank of Gregg's division and ascertained that he could not attack it with any hope of success. Unwilling, however, to permit the enemy to escape unscathed, he decided to let the blue troopers pass him by and attack the First and Fifth Corps wagon train that followed. Moving down the Brock Road, Rosser struck the train at the intersection of the Plank and Brock roads. The Twelfth Virginia turned right and the Seventh Virginia to the left, moving along the road until they ran into resistance. Opening a harassing fire to occupy the attention of the infantry guarding the train, the two regiments slowly fell back to the crossroads, keeping the enemy at bay and allowing Rosser with the Eleventh Virginia to slip in among the wagons. He succeeded in destroying about 40 wagons and brought off another 8, loaded with supplies, plus 7 ambulances, 230 mules and horses, and 95 prisoners. He left behind a frazzled and panicked column of teamsters, bewildered and frustrated infantry officers, and a blocked road that would take some hours to clear. The brigade's loss amounted to two killed and three wounded. Rosser fell back to Todd's Tavern to camp for the night. Here, he received orders to rejoin the division.[28]

Like Gregg's division and the Fifth Corps, the rest of Meade's army prepared to step off early in the morning with the intent of striking whatever enemy they might find ahead of them. With that in mind, at about 1:00 in the morning at Morton's and Raccoon fords, Custer learned that the infantry that had opposed him the day before had abandoned their works, leaving a much weaker force of cavalry, which came from Fitz Lee's Division, to contest any advance. The information prompted Custer to act as soon as possible. Just after daylight, a portion of Town's brigade with the Seventh Michigan in the lead, crossed at Morton's Ford while Davies moved the Second and Fifth New York over the river at Raccoon Ford at 9:00. Town occupied the entrenchments previously held by the gray infantry and patrolled over two miles beyond the ford. Davies managed only a half a mile. Late in the day Lomax deployed his men as skirmishers and pressed Town until he withdrew across the ford. Owen did the same to Davies with the same result. Except for a futile attempt by a small force from Owen's command to regain the rifle pits near the river, by dark all was as it had been at dawn.[29]

Merritt's troopers saw nothing of the enemy. The division, with the Ninth

New York, Devin's brigade, bringing up the rear, rode through Stevensburg and joined the wagon trains of the First and Sixth Corps after a five-mile march. Acting as the train's guard, the column moved on toward Richardsville, establishing a large wagon park near Ely's Ford before camping for the night. Pickets from Devin's brigade took up their posts toward Stevensburg and Brandy Station, the Sixth New York being stationed at Germanna Ford. The Eighth New York, Gamble's brigade, watched Ellis' Ford on the Rappahannock.[30]

Meade's infantry also clashed with the enemy on the 27th, notably at Payne's farm where Maj. Gen. Edward Johnson's Division, Early's Corps, blocked the advance of Maj. Gen. William H. French's Third Corps. Near Locust Grove on the Turnpike, Brig. Gen. Harry Hays confronted Maj. Gen. Gouverneur K. Warren's Second Corps, halting its progress toward the high ground west of Mine Run. Meade had hoped that French would link with Warren and make a concerted effort against Lee, but once again Brig. Gen. Henry Prince, Third Corps, bungled his assignment. A thoroughly disgusted Meade pondered his options overnight. While he had failed to deal a major blow against the enemy, he now knew where Lee was and decided to attack with the First, Second, and Sixth Corps the next day at dawn. During the night orders were sent, troops were shifted, and preparations were made. Come the light, the Federals attacked. They hit nothing. Lee had withdrawn in the darkness to a line on the heights west of Mine Run that Meade had hoped to seize. Meade would spend the 28th studying the enemy's line and contemplating his next move.[31]

In the wake of the non-battle, Pleasonton's cavalry had little to do. Gregg's division held its previous position on the army's flank with Taylor's tired brigade falling all the way back to Wilderness Tavern, dropping off the Third Pennsylvania and the First Massachusetts to guard Parker's Store along the way. Huey's brigade settled in around New Hope Church, except for the First Maine. Just before dark on the 27th, six companies of the regiment under Lt. Col. Stephen Boothby rode off to the right to open communications with army headquarters. At dusk, they ran into a force of unknown strength, which opened fire. Boothby tried to force his way through but the darkness and the determination of his foe persuaded him to fall back. The next morning Col. Charles H. Smith led the entire regiment down the same road. On reaching the scene of the previous night's fight, a sentry dressed in blue stepped forward. Smith soon discovered that Boothby had been fighting with a Federal regiment, not a Confederate one. The infantry had thought they were skirmishing with a Confederate cavalry patrol. The mystery solved Smith led his men on to headquarters where they received orders sending them halfway back along the road they had just taken where they went on picket.[32]

The two other divisions of Federal cavalry continued to man their posts. Along the Rapidan, Custer again threw Town's brigade across the river at Morton's Ford. It skirmished throughout the day with Lomax's troopers but did not attempt to advance as far as it had on the 27th. Lomax made his move at dusk, striking the Federal line hard enough to eventually cause Town to fall back over the ford. Davies contented himself with defending his side of Raccoon Ford, opening fire whenever a target presented itself. Owen had no intention of crossing but replied to Davies's fire throughout the day to confirm his presence and intention to dispute the ground should Davies show any interest in crossing.[33] Most of Merritt's division stayed in their camps around Richardsville, guarding the army's supply train. A portion of the Sixth Pennsylvania, Gibbs's brigade, shifted down the Rapidan to picket the river toward its junction with the Rappahannock. Nothing occurred to disturb Merritt's troopers other than a depletion of their rations. The Ninth New York drew supplies from the wagon train that lay conveniently at hand, a welcomed anomaly.[34]

When Lee had withdrawn during the night of the 27th, Hampton's Division had pulled back to a position on the Catharpin Road between the Grasty and Almond farms where Rosser's Brigade joined it. The division had no contact with the enemy throughout the 28th but that night Stuart, whose headquarters was at Verdiersville, received orders from Lee to swing around the Federal army's left and rear and conduct a reconnaissance to ascertain the enemy's "position and situation." Stuart immediately sent word to Hampton to supply his men with ammunition and to be prepared to move at dawn. He then rode to Hampton's headquarters. Not finding Hampton there, Stuart took Rosser's Brigade and started down the Catharpin Road, leaving orders for Gordon's and Young's brigades to follow when Hampton arrived.[35]

Before reaching the junction of the Catharpin Road and the road to Parker's Store, Stuart's scout, Pvt. Channing M. Smith of the Fourth Virginia Cavalry, Owen's Brigade, Fitz Lee's Division, arrived with vital information. The camp of the Third Pennsylvania and the First Massachusetts lay unsuspectingly ahead. Stuart moved forward with Rosser to attack it. Since the fighting on the 27th, the Third and the First had received forage but no ammunition and had about one cartridge per man. Lt. William F. Potter's squadron of the First was posted about a half mile east of the store with Capt. Alexander M. Wright's squadron another half mile beyond. Four squadrons of the Third were at Parker's Store in a clearing north of the buildings and along the edge of the wood with horses saddled and in line, but the First Massachusetts, which was behind the Third and closest to the Plank Road, was unsaddled. Lt. Col. Edward S. Jones of the Third had command of the post and believed that vedettes from Huey's brigade at New Hope Church watched the roads south of the store. However, Lt. William B. Rawle and 19 men of Company A of the Third were stationed on the Plank Road as a reserve to a lone picket that Rawle had placed, against Jones's orders, on a wood road that intersected the Plank Road about a quarter mile west of the store. Other troopers stood duty at the railroad cut on the main road to the store. They were among the first to feel the weight of Rosser's onslaught.[36]

About noon, Capt. Daniel C. Hatcher, commanding Rosser's advance, led Company A of the Seventh Virginia forward, striking the Federal pickets, capturing several, and driving the remnants back to the reserve on the Plank Road. Here

Hatcher encountered his first stiff opposition, as a number of the blue troopers took to the wood on the flanks and opened an annoying fire. The mounted members of the reserve also gave an excellent account of themselves and Hatcher and the Seventh became confused. The narrowness of the road over which they had approached greatly limited the arrival of reinforcements. Hatcher's charge faltered but gained time for both the Thirty-fifth Virginia Battalion under Lt. Col. Elijah V. White and Lt. Col. Thomas B. Massie's Twelfth Virginia, to form and attack, Massie the front and White the flank, of the Federal line. The Third Pennsylvania did all it could to stem the tide with little help from the First Massachusetts. Their one carbine round soon exhausted and their pistols emptied, the two regiments soon gave way, many of the troopers retreating north into the wood and along a narrow road and leaving their camp and all their equipment and belongings to Rosser. Others, including Capt. Alexander M. Wright, Lt. William B. Hezlep, and a number of their men, became prisoners. Those left galloped east on the Plank Road toward Wilderness Tavern.[37]

After a brief firefight, Lt. Rawle had led the rest of his men west, down the Plank Road toward New Hope Church in search of help from Huey's brigade. He found it in the form of the Second Pennsylvania, under Col. Joseph P. Brinton, that had been on outpost duty west of the church. The Second started back up the road with the Sixteenth Pennsylvania, the First Maine, and a section of Lt. Rufus King's Battery A, Fourth U. S. Artillery, right behind it. Meanwhile, those portions of the Third Pennsylvania that had retreated east along the Plank Road ran into the outposts of the First Pennsylvania, causing that regiment to form a line across the road and send for help to the First New Jersey, which, after some confusion as to the road on which the attack was occurring, moved to reinforce the First.[38]

Back at Parker's Store, Rosser's triumphant troopers stood in awe of the booty that stretched out before them. Here lay plunder worthy of being plundered and many of the men, giving way to hunger, need, or plain avarice, helped themselves. Their moment of elation ended abruptly when Col. Brinton at the head of the Second Pennsylvania, backed by the Sixteenth, thundered into their midst, causing many to drop their spoils and reach for their carbines, pistols, or sabers. The Confederates' disorganized state did not permit them to offer much resistance, but they fought hard and held long enough for Stuart, who had accompanied Rosser, to size up the situation. He quickly recognized the importance of the unfinished railroad cut that lay several hundred yards south of the Plank Road. If the Federals pushed troops along it they could come between Rosser and his escape routes, effectively cutting off the brigade and possibly destroying it. He ordered Rosser to withdraw immediately across the cut and form a line facing Parker's Store. That accomplished, Stuart sent an urgent order to Hampton to bring up Gordon and Young.[39]

Wade Hampton had not had a good morning. He had received Stuart's initial orders about the reconnaissance-in-force at 4:00 in the morning and had taken steps to implement his instructions. Having been absent when Stuart reached his headquarters, Hampton had been playing catch-up all morning and didn't like it one bit. He resented Stuart's taking Rosser's Brigade off without leaving him specific instructions. Hampton felt he had been left out of the loop. He tagged along with Gordon's and Young's brigades as they tagged along after Rosser's, receiving directions as to which road to take from couriers along the way. When Stuart's dispatch reached him, asking for immediate support, Hampton set aside his anger and rushed Gordon to the front.[40]

The Tarheels had three miles to cover over a muddy, slippery road. At the start of their ride, Hampton directed them onto a road that intersected the Plank Road about a mile east of Parker's Store and to the right of Rosser's line. On arriving, Gordon dismounted the Second North Carolina and part of the Fifth North Carolina, threw his skirmishers forward, and deployed one gun from Capt. James F. Hart's Battery of horse artillery under Lt. Francis M. Bamberg that almost immediately opened fire on a column of mounted men on the Plank Road near the store. Bamberg's third shot found its mark, scattering the troopers. Gordon followed up the shot by charging with the Second and Fifth, leaving the First North Carolina to guard Bamberg's gun. Rosser's men joined in the assault. Driving the blue cavalry that had taken position in the railroad cut back over the Plank Road, Gordon's troopers came upon the same scene as had Rosser's men earlier – a camp full of loot. Again the Confederates paused, allowing the blue cavalry time to rally and charge up the Plank Road into Rosser's and Gordon's men who began falling back over the railroad. In the fighting, Gordon's horse was shot beneath him. At this juncture, Young arrived. Dismounting Cobb's Legion and Phillips's Legion on the left of Rosser's line, he charged into the Federals' right flank. The enemy broke and Young followed up his success by pursuing the Federals with a mounted First South Carolina. Stuart left Gordon to hold Parker's Store and moved with Young, backed by Rosser, along the Plank Road toward New Hope Church. Near that place, Huey had his artillery positioned, covering the road for a considerable distance. Young halted his troopers. Stuart soon received a message informing him that Meade's infantry had stretched southward from the turnpike and reached the Catharpin Road. Calling off Young, Stuart led his weary men over a country road toward Dr. Almond's farm on the Catharpin Road. Hampton, in the van of the column, captured a prisoner who informed him that the Federal Second Corps occupied the road. Stuart swung his column to the left, detouring around the enemy's flank, and arrived safely within his own lines at Antioch Church where he encamped for the night at about 2:00 in the morning.[41]

The expedition yielded about 100 prisoners, their arms and equipment, a large quantity of stores, and a single wagon and team. As to the information garnered, Stuart discovered that Gregg's cavalry division guarded Meade's left rear, a fact that Rosser had discovered two days previously. These results had to be measured against a loss of about 5 killed and 20 to 30 wounded or captured. The two Federal regiments encamped at Parker's Store suffered the most in men and material, Gen. Gregg admitting to 8 killed, 43 wounded, and 54 captured. He claimed that the enemy's loss was just as great.[42] He may have been trying to assuage his feelings, considering that he had put two of his regiments in harm's way with only a single cartridge round per man, and this after having two days to resupply them. The terrain lent itself to defense and had the Third Pennsylvania and First Massachusetts possessed sufficient ammunition, Rosser's initial attack over a very narrow road could have been met and very possibly been completely defeated, forcing the brigade back on its reinforcements, which would have had great difficulty coming to its aid. In the end, despite the tangle of wood, the two sides found enough open ground to claw at each other for several hours, inflicting minor damage and changing the military situation not at all.

While Hampton's and Gregg's divisions fought among the trees, Fitz Lee's and Custer's contented themselves with watching each other across the Rapidan. Neither made any move to cross, although the men maintained lines of battle in the entrenchments. Only occasional shots between pickets marred the peaceful scene.[43] Devin's brigade, Merritt's division, under orders to guard the army's wagon trains and cover the approaches to Ely's Ford on the Rapidan, uprooted itself from its camp near Richardsville, crossed over the ford, posted the Sixth and Ninth New York regiments on the road to Chancellorsville, and established a heavy picket on the road to Wilderness Tavern. Gamble's and Gibbs's brigades remained on duty around the immense wagon park near Richardsville.[44]

On the night of the 28th, Gen. Warren had proposed to Meade to allow the Second Corps to pull out of its position in line and try to outflank Lee's right. Meade acquiesced. Warren's move and his subsequent scouting of Lee's line took up most of the 29th and no attack materialized. The only success enjoyed by the Second Corps came from causing Stuart to detour around Warren's left flank to get back to Confederate lines. Meade again postponed the battle, deciding to try a double envelopment using the Third Corps on the right and the Second on the left the next morning.[45]

Lee's soldiers spent the night of the 29th digging, throwing up breastworks, and constructing abatises. By the morning of the 30th, they felt certain that if Meade attacked he would pay a high price for every foot of ground he attempted to take. All the noise made in the construction of the new line of entrenchments alerted Warren to what might confront his infantry if they advanced. He decided to take a look. What he saw convinced him that the position could not be carried and he informed Meade, who cancelled the attack. Moreover, he advised not to pursue any further operations along the present front, suggesting instead a move to the left that would have meant a change of base. Meade would have none of it and spent the rest of the day and all of December 1, contemplating what to do next. Across the line, Lee waited, hardly believing that after all of Meade's efforts his opponent would abandon his offensive without a major confrontation. Equally shocked, the officers and men of the Army of the Potomac awaited their commander's decision.[46]

While Lee and Meade stared at each other across Mine Run, their cavalry prepared for whatever might transpire. Stuart pulled back Hampton's Division from Antioch Church, dismounting and positioning it across Terry's Creek and in advance of Jacob's Mills at right angles to Warren's line. Hart's Battery occupied a hill that would permit it to enfilade the Federal infantry if it attacked Lee's line. Hart's guns did not fire a shot all day, but Capt. Marcellus N. Moorman's Battery of horse artillery managed to engage the enemy when some of Hampton's troopers skirmished with Federal infantry. This continued throughout the day until 4:00 in the afternoon, when Capt. Charles J. Raine's Battery replaced Moorman's. Other portions of Hampton's Division scouted the flank as far as Spotsylvania Court House. Rosser placed vedettes on the road below Chancellorsville.[47]

Taylor's brigade, Gregg's division, learned from its experience the previous day and concentrated all its regiments at Parker's Store. In what must have been a *déjà vu* experience, an unknown force drove in the Third Pennsylvania's outposts in the afternoon. Fortunately, the Confederates, about 50 in number, were only on one of Stuart's scouting missions and nothing more developed.[48] Huey's brigade maintained its post on the Plank Road near New Hope Church. Reinforcements for Gregg's division appeared in the form of Devin's brigade, Merritt's division, that reported to Gregg at Wilderness Tavern, thus allowing Taylor's concentration at Parker's Store. Devin picketed from Taylor's left on the Plank Road to Merritt's right at Ely's Ford.[49]

Fitz Lee and Custer carried on with their contest at Raccoon and Morton's fords. Firing erupted from time to time. Davies once again crossed the river at Raccoon Ford but after a sharp skirmish fell back. His intent was to keep the Confederates from occupying rifle pits on the bank of the stream. In this he proved successful, but Owen's troopers contented themselves with holding the entrenchments further back from the ford. Everyone could report that they had accomplished their mission.[50]

The infantry stalemate lasted throughout the first part of December, but Meade made plans to break it – not by an advance but by a retreat. Orders from army headquarters soon alerted the various commands to the withdrawal. Pleasonton's cavalry gathered itself to guard the infantry as it made its way back to the fords of the Rapidan. Gregg's division, aided by two infantry brigades from the Third Corps, watched the roads to Ely's, Culpeper Mine, and Germanna fords. Huey's brigade with Col. William Blaisdell's infantry brigade covered Ely's Ford. Taylor's brigade and Col. Benjamin F. Smith's infantry brigade took up their post at Culpeper Mine Ford, with the First Pennsylvania stationed at Wilderness Tavern. Devin's brigade, Merritt's division, protected the approaches to Germanna Ford, but Devin also sent the Seventeenth Pennsylvania out on the road from Chancellorsville to Ely's Ford. Gibbs's brigade, Merritt's division, already watched these fords from the other side of the river. Gamble's brigade, Merritt's division, still hovered over the wagon train at Richardsville, not at all a safe duty, the Eighth Illinois losing one man mortally wounded, another seriously wounded, and four prisoners to an attack by guerillas even as the vast Federal army snaked rearward.[51]

Hampton's Division lifted not a hoof all day, holding the same position as on the previous day.[52] Custer and Fitz Lee maintained their stare down at Morton's and Raccoon fords. Davies managed to push men across the river at Raccoon Ford, advancing to a hill where they met with firm resistance and withdrew. Town kept to his side of the river. The big excitement of the day on the opposite bank came when Brig. Gen. William C. Wickham, now recovered from his riding accident, returned to his command, relieving Col. Owens.[53]

Lee's turn to be shocked came on December 2 when the Confederate army awoke to find the Army of the Potomac gone. Stuart rode forward with A. P. Hill to observe an enemy that they quickly discovered wasn't there. Stuart hurried off Rosser's brigade in pursuit, leaving orders for an again absent Hampton to follow with Gordon and Young. Stuart reached New Hope Church at 10:00. A mile beyond he learned that some of the enemy had turned off toward the Turnpike. He sent scouts in that direction and pushed on toward Parker's Store. Arriving at the store at 10:45, he received information that the Second, Third, and Sixth Corps had marched toward Ely's Ford. Cutting across to the Turnpike with Young's Brigade, he continued on until he struck the road to Germanna Ford at Mrs. Spotswood's house. Along the way, the gray cavalry overtook a number of stragglers, but otherwise Meade escaped without any damage. Stuart moved forward to Culpeper Mine Ford and observed that the enemy held the ford in strength. He advised Lee that he would reconnoiter the upper fords in the hope that something could be done. Nothing could. Realizing this, Stuart sent Rosser back toward Fredericksburg to resume his picketing duties in that area and dispatched Gordon and Young to take up their familiar posts as well. Fitz Lee made only minor adjustments, such as sending the Fourth Virginia, Wickham's Brigade, to watch Somerville Ford, but otherwise his men just ogled the enemy, through binoculars if they had them.[54]

Pleasonton's cavalry followed the blue infantry back over the Rapidan. Gregg's division crossed at Ely's, Culpeper Mine, and Germanna fords, bivouacking around Richardsville. Having brought up the rear of the column that crossed at Ely's and after skirmishing briefly with some of Stuart's cavalry, the First Maine, Huey's brigade, drew the duty of guarding the road to Ely's Ford. In Taylor's brigade, the Third Pennsylvania crossed at Culpeper Mine Ford, rode on through Richardsville, and picketed toward Ellis' Ford on the Rappahannock. The First New Jersey watched Culpeper Mine Ford.[55] Devin's brigade, Merritt's division, crossed the river at Germanna Ford where the Sixth New York, acting as rear guard, scrapped with some enemy cavalry at about 4:00 in the afternoon. A detachment of the Fourth New York, sent to keep communications open between the Third and Fifth Corps, also tangled with the enemy, suffering one killed, one wounded, two captured, and two missing. The brigade encamped near the ford for the night.[56] To make room for the retreating army, Gamble's and Gibbs's brigades, Merritt's division, minus Devin's brigade, left their camps around Richardsville and marched to Culpeper Court House, stopping briefly at Stevensburg on the way. On arrival, scouts rode out in all directions to reconnoiter the countryside. At dark, the Sixth

Pennsylvania, Gibbs's brigade, established an outpost line beyond the one held before the beginning of the campaign. The Nineteenth New York, Gibbs's brigade, relieved it on the morning of the 3rd.[57] Custer's division, hearing of the army's withdrawal, expectantly awaited the end of their vigil.[58]

Meade's best-laid plans for defeating Lee's army came to naught along the banks of Mine Run. In the end, the failures of his subordinates to carry out orders contributed greatly to what had appeared to be a plan that had a reasonable chance of success. Meade shouldered some of the responsibility, as well he should have, considering that he had not allowed for those contingencies of war that always arose when campaign plans became operational. Although Meade's movement over the Rapidan had gained a quick advantage over Lee, the precautions the Confederate commander-in-chief had taken and the ineptitude of some of Meade's officers allowed him to recover. But Lee too erred, and his subordinates also failed him at a crucial juncture. The belief that Meade would not withdraw without a fight lulled Lee into a wait-and-see mentality, rendered him unprepared to take the offensive, even on a limited scale, to follow up Meade's retreat, and to strike at the blue columns before they all disappeared over the Rapidan. However, the responsibility did not lie with Lee alone. Early and Hill missed a golden opportunity to demonstrate that they possessed some initiative, waiting instead on Lee to sound the clarion call. Although the Confederates rejoiced in their "victory," they briefly endured a case of the "what-might-have-beens" as expressed by Sgt. James W. Biddle of the First North Carolina in a December 5 letter to his father, "If Gen. Lee had only attacked them Tuesday instead of waiting for Meade to make the attack, he would have demolished the Yankee Army."[59]

Stuart emerged from the campaign with if not a glowing then certainly a solid performance record. He had rushed to the front as soon as he learned of the Federal army's incursion and had done all he could to oppose it. On the army's left, his troopers held two vital fords so that Early's infantry could leave their posts and meet the oncoming enemy. He battled on the right to delay the Federal drive down the Plank Road, and when the lines stabilized, he struck the flank and rear of the enemy. Overall, the Army of Northern Virginia's cavalry had performed well. What marred this accomplishment was the friction between Stuart and Hampton that became evident in the after-action-reports of the two men. Although Stuart commanded all the cavalry, Hampton commanded his division, a fact that Stuart basically ignored for much of the campaign. He provided reasons, none of which were very strong. Hampton resented that Stuart bypassed him and even failed to keep him informed of the operations the division was conducting. Stuart had not been working in the two-division organization very long, and Hampton had not been present during most of that time. Nevertheless, Stuart got off on the wrong hoof with Hampton by not considering his subordinate's position. A burr had been placed under the saddle of the Confederate cavalry's command structure. How much irritation it would cause remained to be seen.

Except for Gregg's division, the Federal cavalry virtually sat out the campaign. Pleasonton shuffled papers; Custer watched two fords; and Merritt guarded wagon trains. Certainly the terrain in which the army operated limited cavalry from doing very much. Gregg spent his time stuck on one road, staring into the brush and waiting to be attacked. Taylor's fight on the 27th proved to be the Cavalry Corps shining moment while the scrap at Parker's Store nearly became a disaster due to the splitting of the brigade and the failure to resupply it with ammunition. Gen. Gregg had been charged with guarding too great an area with the force he had at hand. He did his best but as a result, placed one of his brigades in harm's way. The subsequent addition of Devin's brigade from Merritt's division revealed that Pleasonton and Meade realized their error. The too-little-too-late adjustment came just in time for the army's withdrawal. Had Devin been assigned to Gregg earlier, Stuart may not have been so free to operate.[60]

Custer's division received good news on the 3rd. They no longer had to spend their days shadow boxing Fitz Lee at Raccoon and Morton's fords. At least most of them didn't. The First Vermont, Town's brigade, drew the duty of guarding Morton's Ford while the Fifth New York, Davies's brigade, took up its post at Raccoon Ford. The other regiments pulled back to their old camps near Stevensburg and had just begun to settle in when the bugle blew and everyone mounted up again. Reports stated that a heavy enemy force had crossed the river but on the column's arrival, it turned out that jumpy pickets had triggered the alarm, and the regiments returned once more to camp.[61] Merritt's division stayed at Culpeper Court House. Devin's brigade rejoined the division there, leaving the Sixth New York to watch Germanna Ford. The Ninth New York encamped a mile out on the Sperryville Pike and began building winter quarters.[62] The Federal army's vast wagon park around Richardsville had disappeared, leaving Gregg's division to guard the fords. Gregg sent scouting parties to Morrisville, Hartwood Church, and United States Ford but in a communication to Pleasonton stated that his force could not picket or watch the lower fords on the Rappahannock.[63]

If Gregg concerned himself that Stuart's cavalry might cross the river, he need not have worried. The gray cavalry had had enough of winter campaigning. The brigades of Hampton's and Fitz Lee's divisions longed for their camps as much as their blue counterparts. Fitz Lee's Division shifted back toward Orange Court House and Madison County. Wickham's Brigade started from Raccoon Ford at 11:00 in the morning and marched all day, crossing the Rapidan at Peyton's Ford, reaching its old camp at Twyman's Mill in Madison County, and resuming its picketing of the Robinson River. Lomax's Brigade left Morton's Ford and rode to its former camp between Barnett's and Peyton's fords on the north side of the Rapidan. Chambliss moved from Mt. Pisgah Church to Madison Mills on the Rapidan.[64] Hampton's Division also scattered. Young's Brigade began a long ride that took it from near the Rappahannock to Waller's Tavern a few miles north of the North Anna River. The brigade crossed the river the next day and camped about five miles from Frederick's Hall Station on the Virginia Central Railroad. Gordon's Brigade received the assignment of guarding the fords along the Rapidan, even though its camp at Milford Station on the Richmond, Fredericksburg, and Potomac Railroad lay 30 miles from Ely's Ford and the other fords of the river. On the 5th, Rosser took up his old post at Hamilton's Crossroads on the railroad north of Gordon's camp. By all appearances both armies had agreed to end campaigning for the year.[65]

On the 4th, Gen. Gregg reported his division's disbursement to Pleasonton. Taylor's brigade camped at Sheppard's Grove Post Office, picketed Germanna and Jacob's Mill fords, and linked with Custer's division, which watched the upper Fords of the Rapidan, at Mitchell's Ford. Huey's brigade, still at Richardsville, guarded the lower fords of the Rappahannock.[66] Everything changed on the 5th when Pleasonton ordered Gen. Gregg to move one of his brigades to Brandy Station in the event that it might be needed to guard the army's right. Gregg chose Taylor's brigade, which moved out on the 6th to Brandy Station. Huey's brigade drew back from the Rappahannock, rode to Taylor's brigade's just abandoned camp at Sheppard's Grove Post Office, and took up the picketing of the lower Rapidan.[67]

During these same days, Custer's division, still encamped at Stevensburg, observed the enemy between Mitchell's and Somerville fords, linking with Merritt's division at the latter. Merritt's brigades stretched from Somerville Ford along Cedar Run for a mile and a half beyond Gaines' Mill below Stone House Mountain to a point on the Rixeyville road near Muddy Run. Merritt had already started sending out patrols to discover where his enemy lay. The Sixth Pennsylvania, Gibbs's brigade, drew one of them, riding to Cedar Mountain; the Ninth New York, Devin's brigade, another, marching out beyond Griffinsburg.

While Custer reported the scare of the 3rd to be nothing more than a probe by the enemy to test his outposts, a more serious incursion happened on the 5th when the Confederates crossed in some force at Somerville Ford and burned a house and some haystacks used as cover by the blue cavalry's vedettes while watching their foe. Intermittent skirmishing also occurred throughout the 5th at Raccoon Ford. That same day Merritt reported the enemy's construction of a pontoon bridge on the Rapidan between Morton's and Raccoon Ford. Custer, whose troopers patrolled this area, could not verify Merritt's report, admitting only to being harassed by a Confederate infantry regiment that crossed, not on a bridge, however, and drove in his outpost line but were quickly repulsed.[68] Pleasonton's cavalry stretched from the junction of the Rapidan and the Rappahannock, along the Rapidan, and back up to near Rixeyville. The settling-in period necessitated these days of alarms and adjustments until routines could be established.

On the 4th, the Federal signal station on Pony Mountain confirmed that Stuart's cavalry had taken up its old positions at Morton's, Raccoon, and Somerville fords, as well as at Rapidan Station, the mouth of the Robinson River, and the fords near Locust Dale in Madison County.[69] Indeed, Stuart's cavaliers had resumed all their old posts, but other than picket duty, the men's thoughts began to turn toward winter quarters or home. From the 5th through the 10th very little happened to disturb the tranquility anywhere along the lines.[70] However, not everyone had his mind solely on the coming winter. At least one officer turned his attention to the coming campaign season in the spring. On the 7th, Wade Hampton expressed his thoughts in a letter to Robert E. Lee. Hampton wanted to winter Rosser's Brigade in the Valley and Gordon's and Young's brigades in North Carolina. He also looked ahead to when Matthew C. Butler would return to resume the command of his brigade, now under Young, by suggesting that a new brigade be formed for Young. In effect, Hampton's plan would take all of his brigades away from the army, leaving Fitz Lee's Division alone to watch the enemy. For himself, Hampton asked for a temporary transfer to the west to serve with Gen. Joseph E. Johnston, who had offered him a command. Hampton's concern for his men was genuine. The wear and tear of campaigning and the lack of forage for the horses had devastated his regiments, but they were no worse off than Fitz Lee's brigades. However, his request for a transfer showed that something might have been grating on the South Carolinian - his relationship with Stuart. Hampton had only just returned to the army and was now asking to be sent from it. How Stuart viewed his subordinate's request is unknown, but Lee's response to Hampton's letter is. The division and its commander would stay with the Army of Northern Virginia.[71]

At this time, the Federal cavalry occupied themselves in much the same manner, preparing winter quarters, picketing, and riding out on patrols. On the 6th Merritt sent a scouting party toward Madison Court House. It first stopped at Thoroughfare Mountain where the officer in command could observe the enemy's dispositions quite clearly. They revealed nothing out of the ordinary. Two days later, Merritt wrote to cavalry headquarters concerning the citizens of Culpeper County. In a word, they were starving. He acknowledged that most of them would refuse to take the oath of allegiance and would do everything in their power to aid the enemy whenever and however they could. Nevertheless, he felt they should be given provisions. Pleasonton forwarded the communication to Meade.[72] Amidst the chaos, there rose a voice of reason and a heart of compassion. Gregg's and Custer's divisions mirrored Merritt's in their activities.[73]

The 10th of December brought changes. Custer received orders from cavalry headquarters to replace Gen. Gregg's vedettes along the lower Rapidan, allowing Gregg to move Huey's brigade to Bealton Station and Taylor's to Warrenton. The next day Pleasonton, unhappy with the arrangement, wrote to Meade suggesting that both brigades be concentrated at Warrenton and that Custer change his position to guard the area between Bealton Station and Morrisville. Pleasonton further proposed that one of Merritt's three brigades be placed at Stevensburg and that infantry assist Merritt in guarding the fords of the Rapidan and Culpeper Court House. Nothing immediately came of these plans or of Pleasonton's hint that new cavalry regiments stationed at the depot in Washington be drawn on to replace those regiments in the army that would soon be leaving either because of the end of their service or to recruit. Gregg carried out his orders on the 11th and 12th, placing Taylor's brigade at Warrenton and Huey's at Bealton about a mile out on the Morrisville Road. The Sixteenth Pennsylvania guarded the road.[74]

Merritt's division finally received orders to put up winter quarters. Some regiments, like the Ninth New York, Devin's brigade, began almost immediately, while others, like its brother regiment, the Sixth New York, doing picket duty on the Sulphur Springs Road, would not get started for over a week.[75] Custer's troopers also began to build winter quarters. In Davies's brigade, the Eighteenth Pennsylvania started their huts on the 11th, the First West Virginia on the 19th, and the Fifth New York on the 23rd. Relations with the enemy had softened to the point that the vedettes exchanged newspapers, coffee, and tobacco, visiting each other across the river frequently.[76] An undeclared truce wafted on the cold winter winds.

Stuart's troopers also thought of constructing winter quarters.[77] Fitz Lee made preparations to move two of his brigades, Chambliss's and Wickham's, relieved from outpost duty by Lomax's Brigade, back to Charlottesville. Lomax's regiments would take a one-month turn at watching the Robinson River after which those of another brigade would replace them. This process began on the 10th, but the following day Fitz Lee received new orders. Word came that a Federal force under Brig. Gen. Jeremiah C. Sullivan was moving up the Valley, threatening Staunton. A portion of the Second Corps under Jubal Early set out for Staunton, and Stuart ordered Fitz Lee to take two of his brigades, Chambliss's and Wickham's, and march from Charlottesville through Brown's Gap to Mt. Crawford. From the 10th to the 23rd, Lee's weary, cold, rain-soaked troopers trekked over 300 miles in pursuit of an enemy they never managed to catch. The exercise in futility exhausted men and horses.[78] During these days, Lomax's Brigade shifted its camp from Madison County to Orange County where it began to construct winter quarters.[79]

Most of Hampton's Division held close to their camps, unless they stood picket duty or happened to be in Rosser's Brigade. On the 16th, Rosser received orders to take his brigade to the Valley to intercept part of the Federal raiding force. He left his camp at Hamilton's Crossing, taking his brigade to Fredericksburg, bivouacking there until crossing the Rappahannock at dusk, and encamping five miles beyond about midnight. The next morning, in a driving cold rain, he marched north, reaching and fording the Occoquan at Wolf Run Shoals. The column rode on toward Sangster's Station on the Orange and Alexandria Railroad. Between 7:00 and 8:00 in the evening, the brigade reached a small stream that was rapidly rising. Intermittent lightning flashes revealed a stockade on the other side, guarding the approach to a railroad bridge. Those same flashes revealed Rosser's presence to a sentry who opened fire, alerting the stockade's garrison of about 50 men from Company I of the One Hundred Fifty-fifth New York Infantry. Rosser ordered the Seventh Virginia under Col. Richard H. Dulany to charge, but only a single squadron under Capt. Daniel C. Hatcher managed to hit the ford and splash across the raging stream. Seeing that Dulany would not be able to reinforce Hatcher, Rosser sent his next regiment, the Eleventh Virginia under Lt. Col. Mottrom D. Ball to Hatcher's support. The Eleventh received the full fury of the defenders' fire that killed Capt. Mordecai B. Cartwell and wounded several men and horses. Despite a stout resistance, the infantry force could not keep Rosser from taking the stockade and setting fire to the bridge. After attending to the wounded, the column pushed on toward Centreville. A Federal force, consisting of some cavalry and infantry, under the command of Lt. Col. William De Lacy of the One Hundred Sixty-fourth New York Volunteer Infantry, pursued, but on making contact with Rosser's rear guard, De Lacy's cavalry broke at the first volley and charged back into the infantry. By the time De Lacy rallied his men, Rosser had moved off. An effort was made to catch him but the officer in charge of the cavalry could not make his men understand his orders as they spoke only German and he didn't.[80]

Rosser arrived at Upperville on the morning of the 18th and after a pause of about an hour resumed his march to Berry's Ferry on the Shenandoah River. Finding the river too high to cross, Rosser rode upstream to Front Royal and camped. His command had ridden for 36 hours and covered 90 miles. On the morning of the 19th, the brigade pushed on to Luray but still could not cross the raging river. Marching on to Conrad's Store on the 20th, Rosser's regiments struggled across a still swollen river and entered the Valley. The enemy raiders having escaped through Thornton's Gap, the brigade was permitted to encamp for a week to recover from its grueling expedition.[81]

On the 16th, the Federal cavalry's officer corps suffered its greatest loss since the death of Brig. Gen. George D. Bayard almost exactly a year earlier and arguably since the beginning of the war when Brig. Gen. John Buford lost his battle with typhoid fever.[82] The news of his death filtered down through the ranks, causing shock and sorrow to all. Buford's value to the Army of the Potomac's Cavalry Corps cannot be underestimated. He brought a steadiness and confidence to his command and inspired his men without gaudy attire or boisterous announcements. His knowledge of cavalry and how it could and should be used was unsurpassed in the Federal army. That such a man as Alfred Pleasonton achieved overall command of the cavalry and not Buford was a travesty that now could no longer be rectified. Not only would Buford be missed, he would never be replaced, leaving a vacuum that other men, many of them with significant ability, attempted but failed to fill.

Buford's former troopers, encamped at Warrenton and Bealton Station, carried on without their inspiring leader. On the 14th the Ninth New York, Devin's brigade, set out on a guerilla hunt, returning on the evening of the 15th empty handed. Two days later it relieved its brother regiment, the Sixth New York, on outpost duty on the Sulphur Springs Road. On the 20th, another of the brigade's regiments, the Fourth New York took over. Patrols continued to scour the countryside for the enemy. The 16th saw Merritt push one party to within two miles of Rapidan Station where it struck enemy infantry pickets that fell back on their reserves. He sent another toward Waylandsburg, this time encountering no one. The vedettes on duty on the Sperryville Road received a visit from about 30 of the enemy who dashed down on them, capturing one man before an alert reserve galloped to their rescue. No friendly exchanges between pickets on this end of the line.[83]

Rosser's raid not only stirred up troops near Washington City but Pleasonton's cavalry as well. Taylor's brigade, Gregg's division, received orders on the 18th to send two regiments toward Salem and New Market to cut off Rosser and engage him. Taylor was advised to "pitch into them and whip them, as their horses will be tired out." Taylor complied and dispatched two regiments that patrolled all the way to Manassas Gap. Along the way, they discovered that Rosser had made his escape. The regiments returned to Warrenton.[84]

"Boots and Saddles" rang out over the camps of Gen. Gregg's regiments on the 21st. Another attempt was to be made to intercept Rosser, this time in the Valley. Troopers from the First Maine and the Second, Eighth, and Sixteenth Pennsylvania, all from Huey's brigade, under Col. Charles H. Smith of the First Maine mounted up and rode from Bealton Station to Warrenton where the First New Jersey and the Sixth Ohio from Taylor's brigade were to join them. Due to orders not having arrived in time, Taylor's two regiments were not ready. The expedition delayed its departure until the next day when the two wayward regiments received orders to rendezvous with Smith at Amissville. On the 22nd, Smith advanced on Amissville. The Sixteenth Pennsylvania charged a small group of the enemy near the hamlet, capturing one. Marching on to Gaines' Cross Roads, the Sixteenth encountered another party of Confederates, scattering them into the mountains. Meanwhile, the First New Jersey and the Sixth Ohio, having arrived at Amissville to find Smith had moved on, returned to their camps. Smith proceeded through Sperryville and Thorton's Gap to within four miles of Luray and encamped. During the night, a small party of the enemy brushed against Smith's outposts, causing no casualties.[85]

At daybreak on the 23rd, Smith rode for Luray, the Second Pennsylvania dispersing a small picket force stationed on the road. A larger body of the enemy, about 30 in number, made a stand right outside the town, but the Keystone Staters chased the graycoats through Luray, taking several prisoners. Here Smith, learning that Rosser had passed through two days previously, decided to turn back but not before putting the torch to a tannery and a factory that manufactured various leather goods for the Confederate army. On the return trip, five more tanneries went up in flames and smoke. At Little Washington the column's advance guard attacked an enemy patrol, killing one and capturing another. Bivouacking for the night, the next day the regiments returned to their old camps, arriving after dark.[86] Though Smith failed to catch his prey, he more than made up for it in the destruction of material that the South could ill afford to lose.

While Smith burned tanneries, on the 24th, Gen. Gregg dispatched Maj. Hugh H. Janeway of the First New Jersey with that regiment and 250 men from the Third Pennsylvania, all from Taylor's brigade, on a scout to Salem in the hope of bagging Mosby. However, the elusive partisan declined to make himself available, although two men allegedly of his command became Janeway's guests for the next day's festivities.[87]

Pleasonton's Third Division welcomed back Judson Kilpatrick who returned on the 20th. He had little to do with most of his troopers immersed in erecting their winter quarters. The regiments took turns standing guard and must have been elated when on the 22nd, Meade ordered that the First Corps would support the cavalry in this duty.[88]

While the weather curtailed campaigning against the enemy, the Federal government opened up a campaign of sorts against its own soldiers. The expiration of many of the troopers' enlistments loomed, sending chills up and down the spines of the high command that had nothing to do with the cold weather. The thought of hundreds of men leaving the ranks and severely crippling the strength of the army spurred the government to launch a major assault, tendering all kinds of incentives - $402.00, an immediate 35 day furlough, an additional 30 day furlough the following August, and if three–fourths of the men in a regiment with less than 15 months to serve would reenlist, the regiment would be declared a "Veteran Regiment" and be permitted to wear a special chevron on their sleeve - all to induce reenlistment for three additional years of service. The offer certainly tempted the men. The results of the proposal varied. In the Third Pennsylvania, Taylor's brigade, Gregg's division, the arduous duty trumped all and only 75 men signed on for another three years. In the First Maine, Huey's brigade, Gregg's division, a large number reenlisted. The Sixth New York, Devin's brigade, Merritt's division, became the first to reenlist as a regiment. And so it went throughout the cavalry. In the end, the government's efforts achieved enough success so that it could be assured that a sufficient number of veterans would stay in the ranks.[89]

Another rumor of a raid behind the lines elicited a flurry of back-and-forth telegrams between Meade's Headquarters and Washington. Supposedly, a woman reported that 5,000 Confederate cavalry intended to sweep down on the Orange and Alexandria Railroad at various points and destroy bridges and tracks. This time, however, Meade failed to jump, stating, "I doubt that the enemy can spare 5,000 cavalry for a raid" and taking only the precaution of alerting the troops guarding the railroad to be on the lookout.[90] This calm reaction illustrated his growing understanding of the gray cavalry's actual capabilities. The fear Stuart's cavaliers once struck was dissipating.

Christmas came and went for Fitz Lee's brigades. Chambliss and Wickham spent the day marching from Greenville to Staunton in the Valley while Lomax's troopers stuck to their picket duty on the Robinson River. A few soldiers, probably infantry, found something else to do. About 100 men descended on Orange Court House, looted a number of sutlers' tents, and carried off anything of value, including an estimated $20,000.00 in Confederate currency, $500.00 in gold, and eight to ten gold and silver watches. The cavalry was too busy for such frivolities.[91] For Hampton's men, erecting winter quarters and thoughts of home occupied hands and minds. Like activities occurred throughout the Federal cavalry. Those who could attended Christmas services, such as the one held in the Episcopal Church in Warrenton. Others worked at constructing their winter living quarters. The Eighth New York, Gamble's brigade, Merritt's division, enjoyed saddling up at 10:00 in the morning and marching out a mile from its camp at which point it promptly turned around and marched back again. Some men in the First West Virginia, Davies's brigade, Kilpatrick's division, managed to secure a supply of spirits and proceeded to get drunk. The men of the Third Pennsylvania, Taylor's brigade, Gregg's division, did not and endured a day of sobriety. Troopers of the Ninth New York, Devin's brigade, Merritt's division, drew vedette duty as did the Fifth Michigan, Custer's brigade, Kilpatrick's division. One hundred men each from the First Pennsylvania and the First New Jersey, Taylor's brigade, Gregg's division, under Capt. Jeremiah Newman of the former regiment, set off at night on a reconnaissance to Salem, bagging two guerillas before returning the next day.[92]

December limped to a cold, wet end. Rain cascaded down four of the last six days of the month. Mud reigned supreme.[93] Cavalrymen blue and gray carried on with what needed to be done, though all the while longing for an end of the doing. Routine dominated the hours, although there were still surprises. On the 26th, Gamble's brigade, Merritt's division, moved its camp three miles closer to the enemy near Cedar Mountain and went through the process of erecting winter quarters all over again. It held this position into the new year.[94] A Mosby alert rang out on the 28th, sending Lt. Col. John W. Kester of the First New Jersey, Taylor's brigade, Gregg's division, and 500 men off to Rector's Cross Roads in the hope of capturing the elusive partisan. Returning on the following day, Kester could boast of having bagged 100 Confederate uniforms and eight horses. Unfortunately, neither the uniforms nor the horses were filled with Mosby or any of his men. Though the two forces clashed, the blue cavalry's horses, worn out from their trek, could not catch those of their foe.[95] On the final day of the month and year, Meade ordered Pleasonton to send a division of cavalry to the Valley in an effort to cut off the Confederate force under Jubal Early near Winchester. So for Gregg's division, under the temporary command of Col. Taylor, the new year would begin with another long ride.[96]

In the Valley, Fitz Lee disbanded some of his regiments and portions of others for the winter. Those that had not been disbanded drew a new assignment on the 31st. Instructed to scour Hampshire and Hardy counties for supplies, Lee set out on January 1.[97] Lomax's Brigade, left behind to guard the Robinson, held fast through the end of the year.[98] So too did Gordon's and Young's brigades of Hampton's Division, watching the Rapidan and Rappahannock. Rosser's Brigade continued to serve with Early in the Valley through the year's end and beyond.[99]

A year of hard campaigning came to a close for the cavalry of both armies. Whether marching, resting in camp, picketing, caring for their horses, or going on furlough, the troopers knew that the war would continue for the foreseeable future. They huddled in the cold, dreamed of hearth and home, and waited for their next orders. They would come, sooner or later. Then "Boots and Saddles" would sound and they would ride out once more. Such was the life of a cavalryman.

Notes:
1.   *O.R.*, Series 1, vol. 29, part 2, 473-474; Freeman, *Lee's Lieutenants*, 269.

        An ulcer had developed on Ewell's amputated leg, incapacitating him. *Richmond Daily Dispatch*, November 27, 1863.

        Hereafter, Ewell's Corps will be referenced as Early's Corps.
2.   *O.R.*, Series 1, vol. 29, part 2, 474 and 477; Denison, *Sabres and Spurs*, 310.
3.   *O.R.*, Series 1, vol. 29, part 2, 477; Ressler Diary; Sawyer Diary.
4.   Andrew N. Buck to Brother and Sister, November 23, 1863, Buck Family Papers, Microfilm mf 309-311 c, BHL/UM.
5.   Cheney Diary; Inglis Diary; Hall, *Sixth New York Cavalry*, 166; Gracey, *Annals of the Sixth*, 207.
6.   *Richmond Daily Dispatch*, November 26 and 27, 1863.
7.   Carter Diary; Donahue Diary.
8.   *O.R.*, Series 1, vol. 29, part 2, 480-481.
9.   *O.R.*, Series 1, vol. 29, part 1, 811 and part 2, 479; Ressler Diary; Sawyer Diary; Rawle, *Third Pennsylvania Cavalry*, 362; Lloyd, *History of the First Regiment Pennsylvania Reserve Cavalry*, 78; Hand, Jr., *One Good Regiment*, 88.

        Huey originally had been instructed to cross the Rappahannock at United States Ford below the junction of the Rappahannock and the Rapidan, but felled trees prevented it.

        Hand recorded that the movement occurred on the 24th, but all other records show that it happened on the 23rd.

        Since Huey commanded the brigade into the new year, Gregg's brigade will be referenced as Huey's for the remainder of this work.
10.   *Richmond Daily Dispatch*, November 27, 1863.
11.   *O.R.*, Series 1, vol. 29, part 1, 903 and part 2, 479; Ressler Diary; Sawyer Diary; Rawle, *Third Pennsylvania Cavalry*, 362 and 365; Lloyd, *History of the First Regiment Pennsylvania Reserve Cavalry*, 78; Hand, Jr., *One Good Regiment*, 88; *New York Herald*, November 27, 1863.

        Gregg's dispatch dated November 23 at 12:30 in the afternoon appears to be misdated. It should read the 24th. All other sources put the advance over the Rappahannock on the 24th.
12.   Wilkin Diary; Rodenbough, *Eighteenth Regiment of Pennsylvania Cavalry*, 46; Boudrye, *Fifth New York Cavalry*, 85.
13.   [Brig. Gen.] H. E. Davies, Jr. to Hon. H. E. Davies, November 24, 1863, Telegrams Collected by the Secretary of War, Unbound, RG 107, M504, NARA.

        Kilpatrick left the army on the 25th when Meade's advance was postponed, leaving Custer in command of the division and Col. Charles H. Town of the First Michigan in command of Custer's brigade. From that date the division will be referenced as Custer's and his brigade as Town's. *Philadelphia Press*, December 7, 1863; HDSACWRD, <www.civilwardata.com> November 25, 2009; *O.R.*, Series 1, vol. 29, part 1 676.
14.   *O.R.*, Series 1, vol. 29, part 2, 660; Hall, *Sixth New York Cavalry*, 166; Hard, *Eighth Illinois Cavalry*, 284; *Richmond Sentinel*, November 27, 1863.

        The *Sentinel* article places the skirmish on the 25th, but this appears to be an error as all the other sources agreed that it occurred on the 24th. The article stated that a Lt. Duncan Commanded the Confederate force. No Lt. Duncan served in the First Virginia.

15. *Richmond Daily Dispatch*, November 27, 1863.
16. *O.R.*, Series 1, vol. 29, part 1, 809 and part 2, 484-488; Ressler Diary; Sawyer Diary; Rodenbough, *Eighteenth Regiment of Pennsylvania Cavalry*, 46; Rawle, *Third Pennsylvania Cavalry*, 362 and 365; Hall, *Sixth New York Cavalry*, 166.

    According to one source, some of Merritt's vedettes advanced against the Confederate pickets along Crooked Run north of the Robinson on the night of the 25th. This may have been done so that Merritt could then withdraw them and concentrate his command at Culpeper Court House the next day. William P. Hill to My Dear Sister, November 26, 1863, Hill Family Papers, 1787-1945, Mss1H5565aFA2, Microfilm reels C334-337, VHS.

17. *O.R.*, Series 1, vol. 29, part 2, 846.

    Lomax had Lt. Virgil Weaver with about 35 men from the Sixth Virginia operating over the Rappahannock. On the 25th, Weaver reported to Lomax from a position 300 yards from the Licking Run Bridge below Bealton Station. Fitz Lee sent Company C of the Fourth Virginia, Owen's Brigade, known as the Little Fork Rangers or the Culpeper Troop, to operate behind Federal lines in Culpeper County during this time. What information these scouts supplied to Robert E. Lee is unknown. Fitzhugh Lee to Gen R. E. Lee, November 29, 1863, Charles Scott Venable Papers, 1862-1894, SHC/UNC.

18. Carter Diary; Morrissett Diary.
19. *O.R.*, Series 1, vol. 29, part 1, 687, 694, 737, and 794; Dr. Jay Luvaas and Col. Wilbur S. Nye, "The Campaign That History Forgot," *CWTI*, vol. 8, no. 7, (November 1969): 18; *New York World*, November 28, 1863.
20. *O.R.*, Series 1, vol. 29, part 1, 806 and 809 and part 2, 480; Ressler Diary; Sawyer Diary; Pyne, *First New Jersey Cavalry*, 198; Allen L. Bevan to My Dear Sister, December 7, 1863, Allen L. Bevan Letters, CWMC, USAMHI; Lloyd, *History of the First Regiment Pennsylvania Reserve Cavalry*, 78-79; Rawle, *Third Pennsylvania Cavalry*, 365; Crowninshield, *First Regiment of Massachusetts Cavalry Volunteers*, 183; Tobie, *First Maine Cavalry*, 210-211; Sauerburger, ed., *I Seat Myself to Write You*, 190.
21. *O.R.*, Series 1, vol. 29, part 1, 811-816; *Philadelphia Press*, December 7, 1863.

    The First West Virginia, Davies's brigade, was detailed to guard the fords between Germanna and Morton's while the Sixth Michigan, Town's brigade, was detached to Somerville Ford with orders to patrol the fords above that point.

22. Hard, *Eighth Illinois Cavalry*, 284; Norton, *Deeds of Daring*, 75.
23. *O.R.*, Series 1, vol. 29, part 1, 831, 898, 903-904, and 907; Luvaas and Nye, "The Campaign That History Forgot," 18-19; Augustine S. Hughes to Dear Mother, December 1, 1863, Hughes-Ware Family Papers, Collection #37961, Correspondence Box 1, Folder 10, LV; Carter Diary; Donahue Diary; Johnson Diary; Morrissett Diary; William H. Arehart, "Diary of W. H. Arehart," *The Rockingham Recorder* 2 (January, 1954): 1, 26; Neese, *Three Years in the Confederate Horse Artillery*, 239-240 ; Trout, ed., *Memoirs*, 74; McDonald, *History of the Laurel Brigade*, 204-205; Baylor, *Bull Run to Bull Run*, 180.

    Capt. Richard H. Watkins of the Third Virginia, Owen's Brigade, received orders to take command of his regiment's wagon train and all the dismounted men and those with unserviceable horses. On the 29th, Stuart ordered him to take all the dismounted men and those with unserviceable horses in Fitz Lee's Division and guard all governmental property at Orange Court House. This amounted to about 300 men. Richard Henry Watkins to My Own Dear Mary, December 1, 1863, Watkins Papers,

1861-1865, Mss1W3272a1-355, VHS.

24. Williamson, *Mosby's Rangers*, 111-114; Wert, *Mosby's Rangers*, 109; *New York World*, November 28, 1863; *Richmond Daily Dispatch*, November 30, 1863.

   Depending on the source, the loss varies between 132 and 167 horses and mules.

25. *O.R.*, Series 1, vol. 29, part 1, 806 and 898; *New York Times*, November 30, 1863; *Spirit of the Ages*, December 14, 1863.

26. *O.R.*, Series 1, vol. 29, part 1, 897-898; *Supp. to O.R.*, part 1, vol. 5, 632-33; Rawle, *Third Pennsylvania Cavalry*, 365-367; Lloyd, *History of the First Regiment Pennsylvania Reserve Cavalry*, 79-81; Crowninshield, *First Regiment of Massachusetts Cavalry Volunteers*, 184; Pyne, *First New Jersey Cavalry*, 199-201.

   One squadron of the First Pennsylvania deployed as skirmishers on the right where the fighting was not as intense. Allen L. Bevan to My Dear Sister, December 7, 1863, Allen L. Bevan Letters, CWMC, USAMHI.

27. *O.R.*, Series 1, vol. 29, part 1, 794, 807-808, 899; *Supp. to O.R.*, part 1, vol. 5, 634-636; Sauerburger, ed., *I Seat Myself to Write You*, 190; Rawle, *Third Pennsylvania Cavalry*, 368-369; Griffin, ed., *Three Years a Soldier*, 155-156; Hopkins, *The Little Jeff*, 181.

   Huey's brigade, Gregg's division, followed Taylor's brigade forward but did not become engaged, allowing the Fifth Corps infantry to pass by it and reach the front. After the fighting had died away, Huey's brigade encamped in rear of the infantry. Sawyer Diary.

   One source stated that skirmishers from Gordon's Brigade also relieved the infantry after dark. *Wilmington Journal*, December 24, 1863.

   Infantry marching along the same road prevented Huey's brigade from reaching the scene of the action at places, forcing the cavalry to ride in single file. *Philadelphia Weekly Times*, July 1, 1882.

28. *O.R.*, Series 1, vol. 29, part 1, 904; McDonald, *History of the Laurel Brigade*, 204-205; Baylor, *Bull Run to Bull Run*, 180-181; Arehart, "Diary of W. H. Arehart," 26; Hawse Diary; Green Memoir; Green Article, *Warren Sentinel*; *Richmond Daily Dispatch*, November 30, 1863; *Daily State Journal*, December 1, 1863.

   Hawse mistakenly dated the attack as having occurred on the 28th.

   Arehart totaled the booty at 8 wagons, 10 ambulances, and 250 mules.

29. *O.R.*, Series 1, vol. 29, part 1, 813-816 and 907; Carter Diary; Donahue Diary; Johnson Diary; Morrissett Diary; Wilkin Diary; Andrew N. Buck to Brother and Sister, December 11, 1863, Buck Family Papers, Microfilm mf 309-311 c, BHL/UM; Gillespie, *Company A, First Ohio Cavalry*, 190; Boudrye, *Fifth New York Cavalry*, 86; *Richmond Daily Dispatch*, November 30, 1863; *Wyoming Mirror*, date unknown; NYSMMVRC at, <www.dmna.state.ny.us/historic/mil-hist.htm>.

   Custer reported that he engaged infantry from Hill's Corps, but Hill was nowhere near either ford, and the closest any of Early's infantry got to the fords was in the fighting near the Payne farm. Only Fitz Lee's cavalry were engaged at the fords.

30. *O.R.*, Series 1, vol. 29, part 1, 804-806; Inglis Diary; Gracey, *Annals of the Sixth*, 208; Hall, *Sixth New York Cavalry*, 167; Hard, *Eighth Illinois Cavalry*, 284-285; Norton, *Deeds of Daring*, 75.

31. Luvaas and Nye, "The Campaign That History Forgot," 30.

32. Ressler Diary; Sawyer Diary; Rawle, *Third Pennsylvania Cavalry*, 369; Tobie, *First Maine Cavalry*, 211-213; Crowninshield, *First Regiment of Massachusetts Cavalry Volunteers*, 186; Pyne, *First New Jersey Cavalry*, 205; Lloyd, *History of the First Regiment Pennsylvania Reserve Cavalry*, 81; *Philadelphia Weekly Times*, July 1, 1882.

33. *O.R.*, Series 1, vol. 29, part 1, 815-816; Carter Diary; Johnson Diary; Morrissett Diary; Wilkin Diary; Fitzhugh Lee to Gen [R. E. Lee], November 28, 1863, Charles Scott Venable Papers, 1862-1894, SHC/UNC; Andrew N. Buck to Brother and Sister, December 11, 1863, Buck Family Papers, Microfilm mf 309-311 c, BHL/UM; Gillespie, *Company A, First Ohio Cavalry*, 190; *New York World*, November 29, 1863.

An increased enemy presence at Barnett's Ford on the 27th caused Fitz Lee to strengthen the pickets there. Fitzhugh Lee to Gen [R. E. Lee], November 28, 1863, Charles Scott Venable Papers, 1862-1894, SHC/UNC.

34. Inglis Diary; Gracey, *Annals of the Sixth*, 208; Hall, *Sixth New York Cavalry*, 167; Cheney, *Ninth Regiment, New York Volunteer Cavalry*, 141.

35. *O.R.*, Series 1, vol. 29, part 1, 899-902; Arehart, "Diary of W. H. Arehart," 26-27.

36. *O.R.*, Series 1, vol. 29, part 1, 899; Rawle, *Third Pennsylvania Cavalry*, 370.

37. *O.R.*, Series 1, vol. 29, part 1, 905; McDonald, *History of the Laurel Brigade*, 206-207; Baylor, *Bull Run to Bull Run*, 181; Rawle, *Third Pennsylvania Cavalry*, 372-373; Crowninshield, *First Regiment of Massachusetts Cavalry Volunteers*, 187.

38. *O.R.*, Series 1, vol. 29, part 1, 807; Ressler Diary; Sawyer Diary; Rawle, *Third Pennsylvania Cavalry*, 372; Lloyd, *History of the First Regiment Pennsylvania Reserve Cavalry*, 81-82; Pyne, *First New Jersey Cavalry*, 205-207; Tobie, *First Maine Cavalry*, 213-214; *Philadelphia Weekly Times*, July 1, 1882.

Lt. Col. Stephen Boothby and Companies H and I of the First Maine, Huey's brigade, Gregg's division, just had come back from a reconnaissance of the Confederates' battle line.

39. *O.R.*, Series 1, vol. 29, part 1, 899-900; McDonald, *History of the Laurel Brigade*, 206-207; Baylor, *Bull Run to Bull Run*, 181.

40. *O.R.*, Series 1, vol. 29, part 1, 899, 901-902.

All or part of the Jeff Davis Legion under Lt. Col. Joseph F. Waring remained behind on picket.

41. *Ibid.*, 900, 902-903, 906-907; James W. Biddle to My Dear Pa, December 5, 1863, Samuel S. Biddle Papers and Letters, Box 2, Folder 1863-1864, Rare Book, Manuscript, and Special Collections Library, Duke University (hereafter cited as RBMSCL/DU; Theodore Stanford Garnett, *Riding With Stuart: Reminiscences of an Aide-de-Camp*, ed. Robert J. Trout, (Shippensburg: White Mane Publishing Company, 1994), 19; McSwain, *Crumbling Defenses*, 67-68; *Wilmington Journal*, December 24, 1863.

42. *O.R.*, Series 1, vol. 29, part 1, 807, 900, 903, and 907.

43. *Ibid.*, 813, 815-816, and 907; Carter Diary; Morrissett Diary; Wilkin Diary.

44. *O.R.*, Series 1, vol. 29, part 1, 804-806; Inglis Diary; Hall, *Sixth New York Cavalry*, 167; Cheney, *Ninth Regiment, New York Volunteer Cavalry*, 141.

Cheney gave the date of the crossing as the 30th, but all other sources agreed that it was the 29th.

45. *O.R.*, Series 1, vol. 29, part 1, 696-697; Luvaas and Nye, "The Campaign That History Forgot," 31-32.

Warren received 300 cavalry to assist him in his maneuver. The Sixteenth Pennsylvania, Huey's brigade, Gregg's division, drew the duty of marching in the rear of the infantry to push stragglers forward. The regiment encamped near New Hope Church for the night. Ressler Diary.

46. *O.R.*, Series 1, vol. 29, part 1, 698 and 829; Luvaas and Nye, "The Campaign That History Forgot," 34-35.

Federal skirmishers did advance about 500 yards across Mine Run on the extreme left of their line. Capt. William W. Blackford, Stuart's engineer officer, discovered this movement. Enemy artillery also deployed on a hill on Grasty's farm. Stuart informed Lee of these facts at 9:40 in the morning. J. E. B. Stuart to General [R. E. Lee], November 30, 1863, Charles Scott Venable Papers, 1862-1894, SHC/UNC.

47. *O.R.*, Series 1, vol. 29, part 1, 895 and 900; Arehart, "Diary of W. H. Arehart," 27; Trout, ed., *Memoirs*, 75 and 226; Shoemaker, *Shoemaker's Battery*, 63-64.

      Capt. Raine was killed in the action that followed.

48. Rawle, *Third Pennsylvania Cavalry*, 364 and 379; Lloyd, *History of the First Regiment Pennsylvania Reserve Cavalry*, 82.

49. *O.R.*, Series 1, vol. 29, part 1, 805 and 807; Hall, *Sixth New York Cavalry*, 167; Cheney, *Ninth Regiment, New York Volunteer Cavalry*, 141.

      Cheney gave the date of the move to Wilderness Tavern as December 1, but all other sources agree that it was November 30.

50. *O.R.*, Series 1, vol. 29, part 1, 815; Carter Diary; Wilkin Diary; Boudrye, *Fifth New York Cavalry*, 85.

      The First Rhode Island, Taylor's brigade, Gregg's division, which had been left behind to help guard the railroad, lost eight men to an attack by an unknown force of guerillas at Beverly Ford. By a ruse, two pickets were lured out of the reserve camp and then marched to the picket post. With two men dressed in blue out in front and coming from the direction of their camp, the men at the post allowed them to approach and were soon made prisoners. Lt. Thomas Turner of Mosby's Rangers used this exact type of ruse on November 27 near the Hazel River to capture a like number of men. The possibility exists that these two incidents are the same and that one of the two chroniclers misdated the event. Denison, *Sabres and Spurs*, 314-315; Williamson, *Mosby's Rangers*, 114-115.

51. *O.R.*, Series 1, vol. 29, part 1, 805 and 807; Inglis Diary; Allen L. Bevan to My Dear Sister, December 7, 1863, Allen L. Bevan Letters, CWMC, USAMHI; Hard, *Eighth Illinois Cavalry*, 285; Hall, *Sixth New York Cavalry*, 167; Lloyd, *History of the First Regiment Pennsylvania Reserve Cavalry*, 82.

52. *O.R.*, Series 1, vol. 29, part 1, 900.

53. *Ibid.*, 813 and 815-816; Carter Diary; Morrissett Diary.

54. *O.R.*, Series 1, vol. 29, part 1, 900; Carter Diary; Morrissett Diary; Arehart, "Diary of W. H. Arehart," 27; J. E. B. Stuart to General [R. E. Lee], December 2, 1863, 10 A.M., 10:45 A.M., and 3 P.M., Charles Scott Venable Papers, 1862-1894, SHC/UNC; *Philadelphia Weekly Times*, June 8, 1878.

      Stuart was incorrect about the three corps crossing at Ely's Ford. None of the infantry crossed there. However, the Second and Third Corps did cross at nearby Culpeper Mine Ford. *O.R.*, Series 1, vol. 29, part 2, 531.

55. *O.R.*, Series 1, vol. 29, part 1, 809-811 and part 2, 529 and 532; Ressler Diary; Sawyer Diary; Tobie, *First Maine Cavalry*, 215; Rawle, *Third Pennsylvania Cavalry*, 364 and 379; Crowninshield, *First Regiment of Massachusetts Cavalry Volunteers*, 188; Pyne, *First New Jersey Cavalry*, 209.

      The Sixteenth Pennsylvania, Huey's brigade, replaced the First Maine on picket later in the day. Ressler Diary.

56. *O.R.*, Series 1, vol. 29, part 1, 805; Hall, *Sixth New York Cavalry*, 167; Cheney, *Ninth Regiment, New York Volunteer Cavalry*, 141.

      The Ninth New York crossed the river at Jacob's Mill with Confederate cavalry close behind it and rejoined the brigade at Germanna Ford. Cheney, *Ninth Regiment,*

New York Volunteer Cavalry, 141; Inglis Diary.

57. *O.R.*, Series 1, vol. 29, part 1, 806; Gracey, *Annals of the Sixth*, 210; Hard, *Eighth Illinois Cavalry*, 285.

58. Boudrye, *Fifth New York Cavalry*, 87.

59. James W. Biddle to My Dear Pa, December 5, 1863, Samuel S. Biddle Papers and Letters, Box 2 Folder 1863-1864, RBMSCL/DU.

    Critics of Meade quickly harangued against him for not bringing Lee to battle. Most of the army, however, sided with their commander. His unwillingness to sacrifice them in what most likely would have been a severe mauling endeared him to them. He had not tried to recoup a bad situation with their blood. *New York World*, December 25, 1863.

60. The placement of Custer can be somewhat explained in that Pleasonton feared that Fitz Lee might cross the Rapidan, turn the Federal army's right, and attack the supply trains. Although Custer on occasion throughout the campaign acted aggressively, he had no intention of forcing a major crossing, a fact Fitz Lee well understood. Had a single division of infantry backed Custer, things might have become very interesting on the Confederate army's left, especially after Early withdrew his infantry. A greater threat to that quarter might have had a significant effect on what transpired at Payne's farm and along Mine Run. *O.R.*, Series 1, vol. 29, part 1, 802.

    Leaving an entire division of cavalry – two if you include Custer holding the fords on the upper Rapidan and protecting the army's far right - to guard wagons that never crossed the river into enemy territory requires some explanation. Merritt's thirteen regiments sat around Richardsville for most of the campaign doing nothing more than picket duty until Devin crossed the Rapidan on the 30th – to do more picket duty. What possessed Meade to eliminate one-third of his cavalry from active operations? One reason could have been a belief that the terrain did not allow cavalry to maneuver. Another could have been that he felt his supply trains were in danger. Considering this, only three possible threats present themselves – Fitz Lee, Mosby's Rangers, and guerillas. Custer neutralized Fitz Lee. That left Mosby and the other forces operating behind the Federal army. In Meade's initial orders dated the 23rd, he assigned Merritt's division to cover the army's movement on the right. Those orders change on the 27th to guarding the wagon train. This was one day after Mosby's raid on the wagon park near Brandy Station. Throughout the campaign guerillas continued their attacks, making their presence felt. The possibility must be considered that Mosby's attack and the efforts of other guerillas persuaded Meade to hold back Merritt's division to guard the wagon trains instead of utilizing it with the army. *O.R.*, Series 1, vol. 29, part 2, 481 and 496.

61. *O.R.*, Series 1, vol. 29, part 2, 539; Hoffman, *First Vermont*, 151; Rodenbough, *Eighteenth Regiment of Pennsylvania Cavalry*, 46; Boudrye, *Fifth New York Cavalry*, 87.

62. *O.R.*, Series 1, vol. 29, part 1, 805; Cheney, *Ninth Regiment, New York Volunteer Cavalry*, 142; Hall, *Sixth New York Cavalry*, 167.

63. *O.R.*, Series 1, vol. 29, part 2, 538; Ressler Diary; Sawyer Diary; Rawle, *Third Pennsylvania Cavalry*, 364; Lloyd, *History of the First Regiment Pennsylvania Reserve Cavalry*, 82.

64. Carter Diary; Morrissett Diary; Donahue Diary; Green Memoir; Green Article, *Warren Sentinel*; Robert Brooke Jones to My Own Dear Wife, December 4, 1863, Jones Family Papers, 1812-1930, Mss1J735d, VHS; Neese, *Three Years in the Confederate Horse Artillery*, 242; Robert J. Driver, Jr., *10th Virginia Cavalry* (Lynchburg: H. E. Howard, Inc., 1992), 50.

65. Orrin Ellis Diary, CWTIC, USAMHI; Hawse Diary; Arehart, "Diary of W. H. Are-hart," 27; Hopkins, *The Little Jeff*, 181; Troxler and Auciello, ed., *Dear Father: Confederate Letters Never Before Published*, 116; Means, "Additional Sketch Sixty-third Regiment (Fifth Cavalry)," *Histories of the Several Regiments and Battalions from North Carolina in the Civil War 1861-65*, 3, 586; McDonald, *History of the Laurel Brigade*, 208; Baylor, *Bull Run to Bull Run*, 183-184.

    The Fourth North Carolina later moved to Guiney's Station on the Richmond, Fredericksburg, and Potomac Railroad. The Fifth North Carolina shifted to Frederick Hall Station on the Virginia Central Railroad on December 5 and later in the month to Guiney's Station to join the Fourth. Thomas J. Gardner to My Dear Cousin Caroline, December 21, 1863, Caroline Gardner Papers, 1857-1864, WRP/DU; Jerome H. Fuller to Dear Billy, December 22, 1863, Southgate-Jones Family Papers, Box 1, Folder 1862-1863, WRP/DU; Manarin, *North Carolina Troops*, 265 and 370.

66. On December 2, Meade ordered the Fifth Corps to Rappahannock Station and assigned it the duty of guarding the railroad. A detachment of cavalry was to be attached to assist the infantry in this mission. The First Rhode Island from Taylor's brigade and the Fourth Pennsylvania from Huey's brigade were ordered to report for this duty. They served in this capacity for the remainder of the year. *O.R.*, Series 1, vol. 29, part 2, 536; Denison, *Sabres and Spurs*, 326.

67. *O.R.*, Series 1, vol. 29, part 2, 541 and 543-544; Ressler; Diary; Sawyer Diary; Allen L. Bevan to My Dear Sister, December 7, 1863, Allen L. Bevan Letters, CWMC, USAMHI; Sauerburger, ed., *I Seat Myself to Write You*, 190; Lloyd, *History of the First Regiment Pennsylvania Reserve Cavalry*, 82.

68. *O.R.*, Series 1, vol. 29, part 2, 542, 544-546; Gracey, *Annals of the Sixth*, 207; Hall, *Sixth New York Cavalry*, 168; Rodenbough, *Eighteenth Regiment of Pennsylvania Cavalry*, 46; Cheney, *Ninth Regiment, New York Volunteer Cavalry*, 142.

69. *O.R.*, Series 1, vol. 29, part 2, 542.

70. Carter Diary; Donahue Diary; Edwards Diary; Hawse Diary; Morrissett Diary; Green Memoir; Green Article, *Warren Sentinel*.

71. *O.R.*, Series 1, vol. 29, part 2, 862-863; Samuel J. Martin, *Southern Hero: Matthew Calbraith Butler*, (Mechanicsburg: Stackpole Books, 2001), 80.

72. *O.R.*, Series 1, vol. 29, part 2, 549 and 551.

    These rations were issued and accepted by the populace. *Richmond Daily Dispatch*, December 29, 1863.

73. Pvt. William D. Wilkin of the First West Virginia, Davies's brigade, Custer's division, made his own little scout across the Rapidan on the 6th. He shared a chew of tobacco that he obtained from one of the Confederate pickets and spent some time talking before returning to his side of the river. Wilkin Diary.

    The Seventh Michigan, Town's brigade, Custer's division, picketed Somerville Ford. Andrew N. Buck to Brother and Sister, December 11, 1863, Buck Family Papers, Microfilm mf 309-311 c, BHL/UM.

    The First Maine, Huey's brigade, Gregg's division, guarded Ely's, Ellis', and Skinker's fords from the 7th through the 10th. On the 8th, a patrol rode to Richard's Ford on the Rappahannock. The Sixteenth Pennsylvania, Huey's brigade, picketed Germanna Ford on the Rapidan River from the 6th to the 9th when its brother regiment, the Eighth Pennsylvania, relieved it. Ressler Diary; Sawyer Diary; Tobie, *First Maine Cavalry*, 221.

74. *O.R.*, Series 1, vol. 29, part 2, 554-555; Ressler Diary; Sawyer Diary; Sauerburger, ed.,

I Seat Myself to Write You, 190; Rawle, *Third Pennsylvania Cavalry*, 364, 380, and 388; Crowninshield, *First Regiment of Massachusetts Cavalry Volunteers*, 183; Tobie, *First Maine Cavalry*, 221; Lloyd, *History of the First Regiment Pennsylvania Reserve Cavalry*, 82.

In Huey's brigade, the First Maine relieved the Sixteenth Pennsylvania from picket duty on the 14th.

75. Inglis Diary; Hall, *Sixth New York Cavalry*, 168; Cheney, *Ninth Regiment, New York Volunteer Cavalry*, 142.

On the 9th, 100 men from the Ninth New York escorted two ladies 20 miles out on the Warrenton/Sperryville Pike to move their fathers' families inside Federal lines. The expedition lasted two days. The families took the oath of allegiance and later went north to stay with relatives. Although a humane effort, this occurred at a time when the cavalry was trying to recuperate from all its arduous duties over the past several months.

76. Wilkin Diary; Rodenbough, *Eighteenth Regiment of Pennsylvania Cavalry*, 46; Boudrye, *Fifth New York Cavalry*, 88; *New York Times*, December 10, 1863; *New York World*, December 25, 1863.

77. As of December 10, the strength of Stuart's cavalry was 17,239 aggregate present and absent – 9,381 aggregate present – 8,095 present for duty. *O.R.*, Series 1, vol. 29, part 2, 866.

78. *O.R.*, Series 1, vol. 29, part 1, 970-972; Richard Henry Watkins to My Own Dear Mary, December 20, 1863, Watkins Papers, 1861-1865, Mss1W3272a1-355, VHS; Carter Diary; Donahue Diary; Edwards Diary; Morrissett Diary; Trussell Diary; Hubard Jr., *Memoirs of a Virginia Cavalryman*, 127.

The Third Virginia did not leave on the 10th with the rest of Wickham's Brigade, remaining on picket duty until relieved by Lomax's Brigade on the 11th.

Lee's itinerary was as follows: left Charlottesville on the 14th; through Brown's Gap to Mt. Crawford on the 15th, encamping six miles from Staunton; to Staunton and then back to near Mt. Crawford on the 16th; through Staunton to Lexington on the 17th, arriving at dawn on the morning of the 18th; camped at Collierstown at the base of Little North Mountain the night of the 18th; started over the mountain, recalled, and marched toward Buchanan, encamping between that place and Fincastle on the 19th; arrived at Fincastle and marched for Covington on the 20th; reached Covington, found enemy gone, rode through Callaghan's, turned toward Warm Springs, and arrived at Goshen on the 23rd or 24th.

79. Donahue Diary; Robert Brooke Jones to My Own Dear Wife, December 15, 1863, Jones Family Papers, 1812-1930, Mss1J735d, VHS; Driver, *5th Virginia Cavalry*, 68; Musick, *6th Virginia Cavalry*, 52; Fortier, *15th Virginia Cavalry*, 53.

80. *O.R.*, Series 1, vol. 29, part 1, 982-984; Hawse Diary; Arehart, "Diary of W. H. Arehart," 29; Leavell - McDonald Papers; Editor, "Gallant Virginians at Sangster's Station," *Confederate Veteran*, (hereafter cited as *CV*) 22 (1914): 265; McDonald, *History of the Laurel Brigade*, 208-212; *New York World*, December 19, 1863; *New York Times*, December 25, 1863; *Richmond Daily Dispatch*, December 29, 1863.

The bridge was saved, the fire being extinguished by the Federal infantry. *O.R.*, Series 1, vol. 29, part 1, 983; Maj. Gen. Christopher C. Auger to Maj. Gen. George G. Meade, December 18, 1863, Telegrams Collected by the Secretary of War, Unbound, RG 107, M504, NARA.

81. Leavell - McDonald Papers; Arehart, "Diary of W. H. Arehart," 29-30; McDonald, *History of the Laurel Brigade*, 212-213; Baylor, *Bull Run to Bull Run*, 186; *Wilmington Journal*, December 31, 1863.

82. Bayard was mortally wounded by a shell fragment on December 13, 1862, at the head-quarters of Maj. Gen. William B. Franklin near Fredericksburg and died the next day. Ezra J. Warner, *Generals in Gray*, (Baton Rouge: Louisiana State University Press, 1964), 26.

83. *O.R.*, Series 1, vol. 29, part 1, 985-986; Inglis Diary; Brig. Gen. Wesley Merritt to Maj. Gen. Andrew A. Humphreys, December 16, 1863, Telegrams Collected by the Secretary of War, Unbound, RG 107, M504, NARA; Hall, *Sixth New York Cavalry*, 168.

On the 21st, Gamble left and Chapman again assumed command of the First Brigade. *HDSACWRD*, <www.civilwardata.com> December 23, 2009.

84. *O.R.*, Series 1, vol. 29, part 2, 567 and 569.

85. *Ibid.*, part 1, 987-988; Ressler Diary; Sawyer Diary; Tobie, *First Maine Cavalry*, 225-229; *Washington Evening Star*, December 29, 1863.

In his report, Col. Smith stated that the enemy who fired on his pickets during the night belonged to the command of Maj. Harry W. Gilmor, but although Gilmor was in the area, he did not claim to have made any contact with Smith's column, stating that he learned of Smith's presence after the Federals had passed through Luray. Colonel Harry Gilmor, *Four Years in the Saddle*, (New York: Harper & Brothers, Publishers, 1866. Reprint, Baltimore, Maryland: Butternut and Blue, 1987), 135.

86. *O.R.*, Series 1, vol. 29, part 1, 988-989; Dollar Diary; Ressler Diary; Tobie, *First Maine Cavalry*, 225-229;Sawyer Diary; Hand, Jr., *One Good Regiment*, 90.

87. Rawle, *Third Pennsylvania Cavalry*, 384.

88. *O.R.*, Series 1, vol. 29, part 2, 575; Victor E. Comte to Dear Elise, December 27, 1863; Victor E. Comte Papers, Microfilm mf365 c, BHL/UM; Rodenbough, *Eighteenth Regiment of Pennsylvania Cavalry*, 46.

89. Inglis Diary; Sawyer Diary; Thomas Covert to My Dear Wife, December 21, 1863, Covert Collection, USAMIH; Rawle, *Third Pennsylvania Cavalry*, 390; Tobie, *First Maine Cavalry*, 222; Cheney, *Ninth Regiment, New York Volunteer Cavalry*, 143-144; Hall, *Sixth New York Cavalry*, 168-169; Gillespie, *Company A, First Ohio Cavalry*, 191.

Some states offered an additional monetary bonus.

The chronicler of the Eighth Illinois, Gamble's brigade, Merritt's division, recorded that his regiment received an offer of $300.00, a 30 day furlough, and free transportation to Illinois and back. All was contingent, however, on the reenlistment of two-thirds of the regiment. That number was reached. Hard, *Eighth Illinois Cavalry*, 288.

90. *O.R.*, Series 1, vol. 29, part 2, 583-584.

91. Carter Diary; Donahue Diary; Morrissett Diary; Trussell Diary; Robert Brooke Jones to My Own Dear Wife, December 23, 1863, Jones Family Papers, 1812-1930, Mss1J735d, VHS; *Richmond Daily Dispatch*, December 29, 1863.

92. Inglis Diary; Sawyer Diary; Wilkin Diary; Victor E. Comte to Dear Elise, December 27, 1863; Victor E. Comte Papers, Microfilm mf365 c, BHL/UM; Sauerburger, ed., *I Seat Myself to Write You*, 196; Lloyd, *History of the First Regiment Pennsylvania Reserve Cavalry*, 83; Rawle, *Third Pennsylvania Cavalry*, 384.

93. Inglis Diary; Sauerburger, ed., *I Seat Myself to Write You*, 198; Rawle, *Third Pennsylvania Cavalry*, 384; Tobie, *First Maine Cavalry*, 229; Gracey, *Annals of the Sixth*, 211.

94. Cheney Diary; Hard, *Eighth Illinois Cavalry*, 288.

95. *O.R.*, Series 1, vol. 29, part 2, 588-589.

On the 30th, Gen. Pleasonton requested that the uniforms be sent to his head-quarters for use in a special project he had in mind. Details of what the uniforms were used for are unknown. Capt. Enos B. Parsons, Jr. to Col. J. P. Taylor, December 30, 1863, Telegrams Collected by the Secretary of War, Unbound, RG 107, M504, NARA.

96. *O.R.*, Series 1, vol. 29, part 2, 592-593; Rawle, *Third Pennsylvania Cavalry*, 384; Crowninshield, *First Regiment of Massachusetts Cavalry Volunteers*, 193; Tobie, *First Maine Cavalry*, 229-230.

   The division, minus two regiments left on picket at Warrenton, left on January 1 and made it as far as Front Royal where an unfordable Shenandoah River brought the expedition to a halt. Taylor led his command back to Warrenton, arriving on January 4. *O.R.*, Series 1, vol. 33, 10-11.

97. *O.R.*, Series 1, vol. 33, 7-8; Carter Diary; Trussell Diary; Richard Henry Watkins to My Precious Mary, December 30, 1863, Watkins Papers, 1861-1865, Mss1W3272a1-355, VHS; Baylor, *Bull Run to Bull Run*, 186; Driver, *1st Virginia Cavalry*, 76; Driver and Howard, *2nd Virginia Cavalry*, 104 and 107.

   Lee managed to round up some supplies but concluded upon his return that there was little to be gleaned from people who had been living in occupied enemy territory for months.

98. Donahue Diary.

99. McDonald, *History of the Laurel Brigade*, 215-221.

Bibliography

Manuscripts:
Archives of Michigan
       Christian and Frederick Bush Collection, MS 2004-22, Box 1, Folder 1
Central Michigan University
       Clarke Historical Library
              Clarke Manuscripts
                     Dexter M. Macomber Diary
Detroit Public Library
       Burton Historical Collection
              MS/Chamberlain Family Collection
                     Gilbert W. Chapman Letters
Duke University
       William R. Perkins Library
              Rare Book, Manuscript, and Special Collections Library.
                     Samuel S. Biddle Papers and Letters, Box 2, Folder 1863-1864
                     Confederate Veterans Papers
                            Reminiscences of the War by W. A. Curtis. Box 4 of 4,
                                    Folder - Reminiscences Undated
                     Caroline Gardner Papers, 1857-1864
                            Thomas J. Gardner Letters
                     William Thomas Leavell and Edward Allen Hitchcock McDonald Papers,
                       1831-1932, Box 14
                                    Manuscript of Edward Allen Hitchcock McDonald,
                                    History of the Laurel Brigade
                     Hugh MacRae Papers, 1817-1943, Box 3 - Letters 1862-1878, Folder – Letters 1862-1863
                     William D. Smith Letters and Papers 1862-1865
                     Southgate-Jones Family Papers, 1794-1982, Box 1, Folder 1862-1863
East Carolina University
       Joyner Library
              East Carolina Manuscript Collection
                     Abraham G. Jones Papers, Collection No. 135
Handley Library, Winchester Virginia
       Jasper Hawse Diary
Indiana Historical Society
       Civil War Diary of George H. Chapman
Jefferson County Museum
       Roger Preston Chew Papers
              George W. Shreve, "Reminiscences in the History of The Stuart Horse Artillery, C.S.A."
Library of Congress
       C. S. Dwight. Survey of Culpeper and a part of Madison counties, Virginia. Library of Congress, Map collections: 1500-2004. http://memory.loc.gov/cgibin/-query/D?gmd:4:./temp/~ammem_pMTx:: (accessed March 24, 2009).

E. N. Gilpin Papers
    Samuel J. B. V. Gilpin Diary, MMC-1906
George H. Stuart Collection, MMC-3248
George Montfort Gilchrist Family Papers, 1854-1921, MMC-3626
    Martin Oviatt Diary, Microfilm 21,640-1P
    Martin Oviatt Papers, 1863-1865
Louis Trezevant Wigfall Papers, MMC-3183
Library of Virginia
    Diary of John Carroll Donahue
    Diary of Thomas William Brown Edwards
    Diary of William Richard Carter
    Hughes-Ware Family Papers, Collection #37961, Correspondence Box 1, Folder 10, LV
        Augustine S. Hughes Letters
        Cincinnatus J. Ware Letters
    Major Daniel A. Grimsley, Battles in Culpeper County, Virginia, 1861-1865
Museum of the Confederacy
    Eleanor S. Brockenbrough Library
        Diary of Lawson Morrissett, Fourth Virginia Cavalry
        Edward A. Green Memoir
        Edward A. Green Newspaper Article *(Warren Sentinel)*
        Fourth Virginia Cavalry Record Book
        Fourth Virginia Cavalry Headquarters Book
        Leonard Williams Letters, Second South Carolina Cavalry
        Lewis T. Nunnelee Papers, History of a Famous Company of the War of Rebellion
            (So Called) Between the States (Lynchburg Battery)
        Milton B. Steele Diary, First Virginia Cavalry
        Thomas William Trussell Diary, First Virginia Cavalry
National Archives (Compiled Service Records)
    Compiled Service Records of Confederate General and Staff Officers, and Non-Regimental
        Enlisted Men, Microcopy No. M331, Roll 265
National Archives and Records Administration
    Telegrams Collected by the Secretary of War, Unbound, RG 107, M504
New York State Library
    John Inglis Papers, SC22716 Box 1 Folder 1
        John Inglis Diary
        John Inglis Letters
North Carolina State Archives
    Fred C. Foard Papers, PC.500
        Fred C. Foard Reminiscences
    Governor's Papers – Zebulon Baird Vance, 1862-1865, 1877-1879, Box GP 168, Folder 8/1 – 4/63
University of California at Santa Barbara
    Donald C. Davidson Library
        Department of Special Collections
            Charles H. Johnson Letters, Wyles Mss 36, Box 1, Folder 4
University of Michigan
    Bentley Historical Library
        Brown Family Papers, Box No. 85859 Aa2
        Buck Family Papers, Microfilm mf 309-311 c
        David R. Trego Papers, Box No. 86662 Aa1
        John B. Kay Papers, Microfilm mf468 c
        John R. Morey Papers, Microfilm mf363 c
        Victor E. Comte Papers, Microfilm mf365 c
    William L. Clements Library
        Manuscripts Division
            James S. Schoff Civil War Collection
                Allyne Cushing Litchfield Papers
                Clark-Whedon Papers

Bibliography

University of North Carolina at Chapel Hill
>> Wilson Library
>>> Southern Historical Collection
>>>> Cadwallader Jones Iredell Papers, 363-Z, Folder 1, Correspondence 1862-1863
>>>> Charles Scott Venable Papers, 1862-1894
University of Virginia
>> Alderman Library
>>> Irving P. Whitehead Papers
>>>> "The Second Virginia Cavalry in the War, 1861-1865"
>> Clifton Waller Barrett Library of American Literature
>>> Special Collections
>>>> Diary of John Esten Cooke, MSS 5295,
>> The Albert H. Small Special Collections Library
>>> Charles R. Phelps Letters (#2920),
U. S. Army Military History Institute
>> Civil War Miscellaneous Collection
>>> Abner B. Frank Diary
>>> Albinus R. Fell Letters
>>> Allen L. Bevan Letters
>>> Alonzo J. Sawyer Diary
>>> Earl Hess Collection
>>>> Ebenezer S. Johnson Letters
>>> Michael Donlon Letters
>>> William Ramsey Letters
>>> William Wilkin Diary
>> Civil War Times Illustrated Collection
>>> Isaac H. Ressler Diary
>>> Jasper B. Cheney Diary
>>> Orrin Ellis Diary
>>> Silas Wesson Diary
>> Covert Collection
>>> Thomas Covert Letters
>> Harrisburg Civil War Roundtable Collection
>>> Gregory A. Coco Collection
>>>> Alvin N. Brackett Letters
>>> John Dollar Diary
>> Lewis Leigh Collection
>>> Charles A. Legg Letters, Book 5:31-33
>> Ronald D. Boyer Collection
>>> Jonah Yoder Diary
Virginia Historical Society
>> Elijah S. Johnson Papers, 1862-1907, Mss2J6314B-MFC 598
>> Henry Brainerd McClellan Papers, Mss2M1324b
>>> Maj. Gen. Cadmus M. Wilcox to Maj. Gen. J. E. B. Stuart, September 26, 1863
>> Hill Family Papers, 1787-1945, Mss1H5565aFA2, Microfilm reels C334-337
>>> William Powell Hill Letters
>> James Ewell Brown Stuart Papers, 1851-1968, Mss1ST923d,
>>> Microfilm reel C621
>> John Overton Collins Letters, Mss1C6944a
>> John William Holloway Papers
>>> James A. Jeter Letter, Mss1H72865a
>> Jones Family Papers Mss1J735d
>>> Robert Brooke Jones Letter
>> Minor Family Papers, 1810-1932, Mss1M6663c. Microfilms C610-618
>>> Robert Randolph Letters
>> Richard Henry Watkins Papers
>> Sarah Travers Lewis (Scott) Papers
>>> War Record of Doctor James McClure Scott, Mss7:1SCO845:1

Taylor Family Papers, 1751-1902, Mss1T2197a
> September 17, 1863, Letter of William Taylor
> September 24, 1863, Letter of R. H. Woodward
> William Clark Corson Papers 1861-1865, Mss1c8184a1-64

Western Michigan University
> Donald C. Rockwell Collection, 1862-1936
> > William H. Rockwell Letters, Call No. A-328
> Western Michigan University Archives & Regional History Collection
> > Dr. Allan Giddings Collection, 1859-1876, Call No. A-333
> > George Harrington Diary

Newspapers:

Allegan Journal (Allegan, Michigan)
Baltimore Sun
Boston Daily Advertiser
Chicago Tribune
Daily Charlottesville (Charlottesville, North Carolina)
Daily Morning News (Savannah, Georgia)
Daily National Intelligencer (Washington City)
Daily State Journal (Raleigh, North Carolina)
Daily Union & Advertiser (Rochester, New York)
Detroit Advertiser and Tribune
Fayetteville Observer (Fayetteville, North Carolina)
Grand Rapids Daily Eagle (Grand Rapids, Michigan)
Lancaster Daily Evening Express (Lancaster, Pennsylvania)
National Tribune (Washington, D.C.)
New Haven Daily Palladium
New York Herald
New York Times
New York Tribune
New York World
North Carolina Presbyterian
People's Press, The (Salem, North Carolina)
Philadelphia Inquirer
Philadelphia Press
Philadelphia Weekly Times
Richmond Daily Dispatch
Richmond Daily Examiner
Richmond Daily Inquirer
Richmond Sentinel
Richmond Whig
Spirit of the Ages (Raleigh, North Carolina)
St. Mary's Beacon
Vermont Chronicle (Bellows Falls, Vermont)
Vermont Journal
Vermont Watchman and State Journal (Montpelier, Vermont)
Warren Sentinel
Washington Daily Morning Chronicle
Washington Evening Star
Weekly State Journal (Raleigh, North Carolina)
Western Democrat (Charlotte, North Carolina)
Wilmington Journal (Wilmington, North Carolina)
Wyoming Mirror (Warsaw, New York)

Articles and Unpublished Manuscripts:

Arehart, William H. "Diary of W. H. Arehart." *The Rockingham Recorder*, vol. 1, no. 3, (December, 1947): 195-215, Vol. 1, no. 4, (December 1948): 271-282, Vol. 2, no. 1, (January 1954): 23-31.

Cheek, Colonel W. H. "Additional Sketch Ninth Regiment (First Cavalry)," *Histories of the Several Regiments and Battalions from North Carolina in the Civil War 1861-65*, 1. Edited by Walter Clark.

Raleigh: E. M. Uzzell, 1901. Reprint, Wendell, North Carolina: Broadfoot's Bookmark, (1982): 444-487.

Clark, S. A. "Buckland Mills." *Maine Bugle*, vol. 4, no. 2, (April 1897): 108-110.

Cowles, Lieutenant-Colonel W. H. H. "Auburn Mills," *Histories of the Several Regiments and Battalions from North Carolina in the Civil War 1861-65*, 1. Edited by Walter Clark. Raleigh: E. M. Uzzell, Printer and Binder, 1901: 454-459.

Editor. "Gallant Virginians at Sangster's Station," *Confederate Veteran*, 22 (1914): 265.

Hassler, William W. "The Slaughter Pen at Bristoe Station." *Civil War Times Illustrated*, vol. 1, no. 2, (May 1962): 8-13.

Klement, Frank L., ed. "Edwin B. Bigelow: A Michigan Sergeant in the Civil War." *Michigan History* 38 (1954): 193-239.

Luvaas, Dr. Jay and Col. Wilbur S. Nye. "The Campaign That History Forgot." *Civil War Times Illustrated*, vol. 8, no. 7, (November 1969): 11-42.

Mays, Samuel Elias. "Sketches from the Journal of a Confederate Soldier." *Tyler's Quarterly Historical and Genealogical Magazine* 5 (1923): 95-127.

McMahon, Martin T. "From Gettysburg to the Coming of Grant." *Battles and Leaders of the Civil War*, 4. The Century Company, 1884. Reprint, New York: Thomas Yoseloff, Inc., (1956): 81-94.

Means, Paul B. "Additional Sketch Sixty-third Regiment (Fifth Cavalry)." *Histories of the Several Regiments and Battalions from North Carolina in the Civil War 1861-65*, 3. Edited by Walter Clark. Goldsboro: Nash Brothers, 1901. Reprint, Wendell, North Carolina: Broadfoot's Bookmark, 1982.

Naisawald, L. VanLoan. "Stuart as a Cavalryman's Cavalryman." *Civil War Times Illustrated*, 1, (February 1963): 6-8, 42-46.

Shaw, W. P. "Fifty-Ninth Regiment (Fourth Cavalry)," *Histories of the Several Regiments and Battalions from North Carolina in the Civil War 1861-65*, 3. Edited by Walter Clark. Goldsboro: Nash Brothers Book and Job Printers, 1901. Reprint, Wendell, North Carolina: Broadfoot's Bookmark, (1982): 456-472.

Schmahl, Carl R. "Enemy Back of You! J. E. B. Stuart's Close Call at Auburn in October 1863." *Fauquier*, vol. 8, no. 1, (Spring 1995): 34-42.

Toler, John. "Old Roommates' Chance Encounter at Buckland Mill." *Fauquier County Historical Society Newsletter*, vol. 24 no. 1, (2002): 3-4.

Books, Pamphlets and Websites

Albaugh III, William A. and Edward N. Simmons. *Confederate Arms*. New York: Bonanza Books, 1957.

Armstrong, Richard L. *7th Virginia Cavalry*. Lynchburg: H. E. Howard, Inc., 1992.

_____ . *11th Virginia Cavalry*. Lynchburg: H. E. Howard, Inc., 1989.

Barrett, John G. *The Civil War in North Carolina*. Chapel Hill: The University of North Carolina Press, 1963.

Bates, Samuel Penniman. *History of the Pennsylvania Volunteers, 1861-1865*. Harrisburg: B. Singerly, state printer, 1869-1871.

Bayard, George D., Owen Jones, John P. Taylor. *History of the First Regiment Pennsylvania Reserve Cavalry*. Philadelphia: King & Baird, Printers, 1864.

Baylor, George. *Bull Run to Bull Run or Four Years in the Army of Northern Virginia*. Richmond: B. F. Johnson Publishing Company, 1900. Reprint, Washington, D. C.: Zenger Publishing Co., Inc., 1983.

Beale, G. W. *A Lieutenant of Cavalry in Lee's Army*. Baltimore: Butternut and Blue, 1994.

Beale, R. L. T. *History of the 9th Virginia Cavalry in the War Between the States*. Amissville: American Fundamentalist, 1981.

Beyer, Walter F. and Oscar F. Keydel, eds. *Deeds of Valor: How American Heroes Won the Medal of Honor*. Detroit: The Perrien-Keydel Company, 1906.

Blackford, W.W. *War Years With Jeb Stuart*. New York: Charles Scribner's Sons, 1945.

Blackwell, Jr., Samuel M. *In the First Line of Battle: The 12th Illinois Cavalry in the Civil War*. Dekalb: Northern Illinois University Press, 2002.

Boudrye, Rev. Louis N. *Historic Records of the Fifth New York Cavalry, First Ira Light Guard*. Albany: S. R. Gray, 1865.

Bradshaw, Ada Bruce Desper, ed. *The Civil War Diary of Charles William McVicar*. no publisher, 1977.

Brooks, U. R., ed. *Stories of the Confederacy*. Columbia: The State Company, 1912.

Brown, R. Shepard. *Stringfellow of the Fourth*. New York: Crown Publisher, Inc., 1960.

Cheney, Newel. *History of the Ninth Regiment, New York Volunteer Cavalry, War of 1861 to 1865*. Jamestown: Martin Merz & Son, 1901.

Committee on Regimental History. *History of the Sixth New York Cavalry (Second Ira Harris Guard), Second Brigade – First Division – Cavalry Corps, Army of the Potomac, 1861 to 1865.* Worcester: The Blanchard Press, 1908.

Coltrane, Daniel Branson. *The Memoirs of Daniel Branson Coltrane: Co. I, 63rd Reg., N. C. Cavalry, C. S. A.* Raleigh, N. C.: Edwards & Broughton Company, 1956.

Cooke, John Esten. *Wearing of the Gray.* New York: E. B. Treat and Company, 1867. Reprint, Millwood, New York: Kraus Reprint Co., 1977.

_____. *Mohun or The Last Days of Lee and His Paladins.* New York: F. J. Huntington and Company, 1869. Reprint, Charlottesville: Historical Publishing Co., Inc., 1936.

_____. *Robert E. Lee.* New York: G. W. Dillingham Co., Publishers, 1899.

Cooke, Philip St. Geo. *Cavalry Tactics: or Regulations for the Instruction, Formations, and Movements of the Cavalry of the Army and Volunteers of the United States.* Philadelphia: J. B. Lippincott, 1862.

Crowninshield, Benjamin W. *A History of the First Regiment of Massachusetts Cavalry Volunteers.* Boston: Houghton, Mifflin and Company, 1891.

Davis, William C. and Julie Hoffman, eds. *The Confederate General.* The National Historical Society, 1991.

Dawson, John Harper. *Wildcat Cavalry: A Synoptic History of The Seventeenth Virginia Cavalry Regiment of The Jenkins-McCausland Brigade in The War Between the States.* Dayton: Morningside House, Inc., 1982.

Denison, Frederic. *Sabres and Spurs: The First Regiment Rhode Island Cavalry in the Civil War, 1861-1865.* No city, The First Rhode Island Cavalry Veteran Association, 1876. Reprint, Baltimore: Butternut and Blue, 1994.

Dickinson, Jack L. *16th Virginia Cavalry.* Lynchburg: H. E. Howard, Inc., 1989.

Divine, John E. *35th Battalion Virginia Cavalry.* Lynchburg: H. E. Howard, Inc., 1985.

Dougherty, Michael. *Prison Diary of Michael Dougherty, Late Co. B. 13th Pa., Cavalry.* Bristol, Pa.: Charles A. Dougherty, Printer, 1908.

Douglas, David G. *A Boot Full of Memories: Captain Leonard Williams, 2nd South Carolina Cavalry.* Camden: Gray Fox, 2003.

Driver, Jr., Robert J. *1st Virginia Cavalry.* Lynchburg: H. E. Howard, Inc., 1991.

_____. *5th Virginia Cavalry.* Lynchburg: H. E. Howard, Inc., 1997.

_____. *10th Virginia Cavalry.* Lynchburg: H. E. Howard, Inc., 1992.

_____. *14th Virginia Cavalry.* Lynchburg: H. E. Howard, Inc., 1988.

_____. *First and Second Maryland Cavalry, C.S.A.* Charlottesville: Howell Press, Inc., 1999.

Driver, Jr., Robert J. and H. E. Howard. *2nd Virginia Cavalry.* Lynchburg: H. E. Howard, Inc., 1995.

Dyer, Frederick H. *A Compendium of the War of the Rebellion* Des Moines, Iowa: The Dyer Publishing Company, 1908.

Fonzo, Stephen. *A Documentary and Landscape Analysis of the Buckland Mills Battlefield.* Buckland Preservation Society - submitted to the National Park Service American Battlefield Protection Program, March 11, 2008.

Fortier, John. *15th Virginia Cavalry.* Lynchburg: H. E. Howard, Inc., 1993.

Freeman, Douglas Southall. *Lee's Lieutenants.* New York: Charles Scribner's Sons, 1943.

Frye, Dennis E. *12th Virginia Cavalry.* Lynchburg: H. E. Howard, Inc., 1988.

Garnett, Theodore Stanford. *Riding With Stuart: Reminiscences of an Aide-de-Camp.* Edited by Robert J. Trout. Shippensburg: White Mane Publishing Company, 1994.

Gillespie, Samuel L. *A History of Company A, First Ohio Cavalry, 1861-1865.* Washington C.H., Ohio: publisher unknown, 1898.

Gilmor, Colonel Harry. *Four Years in the Saddle.* New York: Harper & Brothers, Publishers, 1866. Reprint, Baltimore, Maryland: Butternut and Blue, 1987.

Glazier, Captain Willard. *Three Years in the Federal Cavalry.* New York: R. H. Ferguson & Company, Publishers, 1874.

Goldsborough, W. W. *The Maryland Line in the Confederate Army.* Baltimore: Press of Guggenheimer, Weil & Co., 1900. Reprint, Gaithersburg, Maryland: Olde Soldier Books Inc., 1987.

Gracey, Samuel L. *Annals of the Sixth Pennsylvania Cavalry.* Lancaster, Ohio: Vanberg Publishing, 1996.

Griffin, Richard N., ed. *Three Years a Soldier: The Diary and Newspaper Correspondence of Private George Perkins, Sixth New York Independent Battery 1861-1864.* Knoxville: University of Tennessee Press, 2006.

Grimsley, Major Daniel A. *Battles in Culpeper County, Virginia, 1861-1865.* Culpeper: Raleigh Travers Green, publisher, 1900.

Bibliography

Hackley, Woodford B. *The Little Fork Rangers*. Richmond, Va.: Press of the Dietz Printing Co., 1927. Reprint, with revised Index by Alice Chappelear Nichols, Stephens City, VA: Commercial Press, 1984.

Hall, Hillman A., W. B. Besley, Gilbery G. Wood, eds. *History of the Sixth New York Cavalry*. Worcester: The Blanchard Press, 1908.

Hand, Jr., Harold. *One Good Regiment: The Thirteenth Pennsylvania Cavalry 1861-1865*. No city: Trafford Publishing, 2000.

Hard, M.D., Abner. *History of the Eighth Illinois Cavalry Regiment Illinois Volunteers, During the Great Rebellion*. Dayton: Morningside Bookshop, 1996.

Hartley, Chris J. *Stuart's Tarheels: James B. Gordon and His North Carolina Cavalry*. Baltimore: Butternut and Blue, 1996.

Hewett, Janet B., Noah Andre Trudeau, and Bryce A. Suderow. *Supplement to the Official Records of the Union and Confederate Armies*. Wilmington, NC: Broadfoot Publishing Company, 1994.

Historical Data Systems' American Civil War Research Database at, www.civilwardatacom

Holland, James C. ed. *Military Operations in Jefferson County Virginia (Now West Virginia) 1861-1865*. Henry Kyd Douglas Camp, No. 199, Sons of Confederate Veterans, 2004.

Hubard Jr., Lt. Robert T. *The Civil War Memoirs of a Virginia Cavalryman*. Edited by Thomas P. Nanzig. Tuscaloosa: The University of Alabama Press, 2007

Husby, Karla Jean, comp. *Under Custer's Command: The Civil War Journal of James Henry Avery*. Washington, D.C.: Brassey's, 2000.

Hyndman, Capt. William. *History of a Cavalry Company: A Complete Record of Company "A," 4th Penn'a Cavalry*. Philadelphia: Jas. B. Rodgers Co., Printers, 1870.

Kidd, J. H. *Personal Recollections of a Cavalryman*. Ionia: Sentinel Printing Company, 1908.

Ide, Horace K. *History of the First Vermont Cavalry Volunteers in the War of the Great Rebellion*. Edited and additional material by Elliott W. Hoffman. Hightstown: Longstreet House, 1992.

Isham, Asa B. *An Historical Sketch of the Seventh Regiment Michigan Volunteer Cavalry*. New York: Town Topics Publishing Company, 1893.

Johnston, Hugh Buckner, ed. *The Confederate Letters of William Henry Edwards of Wilson County, North Carolina*. Wilson, North Carolina: publisher unknown, 1977.

Jones, Mary Stevens and Mildred Conway Jones. *Historic Culpeper*. Culpeper: Culpeper Historical Society, Inc., 1974.

Jones, Virgil Carrington. *Ranger Mosby*. Chapel Hill: The University of North Carolina Press, 1944.

Krick, Robert K. *9th Virginia Cavalry*. Lynchburg: H. E. Howard, Inc., 1982.

_____. *Lee's Colonels*. Dayton: Morningside House, Inc., 1991.

Lee, William O., comp. *Personal and Historical Sketches and Facial History of and by Members of the Seventh Regiment Michigan Volunteer Cavalry 1862-1865*. Detroit: 7th Michigan Cavalry Association, 1902.

Longacre, Edward G. *The Cavalry at Gettysburg*. Rutherford: Fairleigh Dickinson University Press, 1986.

_____. *Jersey Cavaliers: A History of the First New Jersey Cavalry, 1861-1865*. Hightstown: Longstreet House, 1992.

Longstreet, James. *From Manassas to Appomattox*. Philadelphia: J. B. Lippincott, 1896. Reprint, Secaucus, New Jersey: The Blue and Gray Press, 1984.

Lord, Walter, ed. *The Fremantle Diary*. Boston: Little, Brown and Company, 1954.

Manarin, Louis H. *North Carolina Troops 1861 – 1865 – A Roster, Volume II Cavalry*. Raleigh: North Carolina Office of Archives and History, 2004.

Martin, Samuel J. *Southern Hero: Matthew Calbraith Butler*. Mechanicsburg: Stackpole Books, 2001.

McCabe, Sergeant Joseph E. "Itinerary of the Seventeenth Regiment, Pennsylvania Volunteer Cavalry." In *History of the Seventeenth Regiment Pennsylvania Volunteer Cavalry*. Compiled by Henry P. Moyer. Lebanon: Sowers Printing Company, 1911.

McClellan, H. B. *I Rode with Jeb Stuart*. Bloomington: Indiana University Press, 1958.

McDonald, William N. *History of the Laurel Brigade*. No city: Published by Mrs. Kate S. McDonald, 1907. Reprint, Arlington, Virginia: R. W. Beaty, Ltd., 1969.

McSwain, ed., Eleanor D. *Crumbling Defenses or Memoirs and Reminiscences of John Logan Black, Colonel C. S. A.* Macon: J. W. Burke Company, 1960.

Meyer, Henry Coddington. *Civil War Experiences under Bayard, Gregg, Kilpatrick, Custer, Raulston, and Newberry, 1862, 1863, 1864*. New York: Knickerbocker Press, 1911.

Miller, Charles H. *History of the Sixteenth Pennsylvania Cavalry for the Year Ending October 31st, 1863*. Philadelphia: King & Baird, Printers, 1864.

351

Mitchell, Adele H., ed. *The Letters of Major General James E. B. Stuart.* The Stuart – Mosby Historical Society, 1990.

Moore, Frank, ed. *The Rebellion Record: A Diary of American Events, Volume Seven.* New York: D, Van Nostrand, Publisher, 1864.

Moore, Henry Woodbury and James Washington Moore, *Chained to Virginia While Carolina Bleeds.* Columbia, South Carolina: Henry Woodbury Moore, M. D., 1996.

Morford, Henry. *The Coward: A Novel of Society and the Field in 1863.* Philadelphia; T. B. Peterson & Brothers, 1864.

Musick, Michael P. *6th Virginia Cavalry.* Lynchburg: H.E. Howard, Inc., 1990.

Nanzig, Thomas P. *3rd Virginia Cavalry.* Lynchburg: H. E. Howard, Inc., 1989.

Neese, George M. *Three Years in the Confederate Horse Artillery.* New York: The Neale Publishing Co., 1911. Reprint, Dayton, Ohio: Press of Morningside Bookshop, 1983.

New York State Military Museum and Veterans Research Center at, < www.dmna.state.ny.us/historic/mil-hist.htm>

Norton, Henry, ed. *Deeds of Daring or History of the Eighth N. Y. Volunteer Cavalry.* Norwich: Chenango Telegraph Printing House, 1889.

Peavy, James Dudley, ed. *Confederate Scout: Virginia's Frank Stringfellow.* Onancock, Virginia: The Eastern Shore Publishing Co., 1956.

Perry, Thomas David. *"The Dear Old Hills of Patrick" The Laurel Hill Reference Book.* 2004.

Pickerill, W. N. *History of the Third Indiana Cavalry.* Indianapolis: Aetna Printing Co., 1906.

Pyne, Henry R. *The History of the First New Jersey Cavalry.* Trenton: J. A. Beecher, Publisher, 1871.

Rodenbough, Theophilus F., Henry C. Potter, and William P. Seal. *History of the Eighteenth Regiment of Pennsylvania Cavalry.* New York: Wynkoop Hallenbeck Crawford Co., 1909.

Sauerburger, ed., Dona Bayard. *I Seat Myself to Write You a Few Lines: Civil War and Homestead Letters from Thomas Lucas and Family.* Bowie, Maryland: Heritage Books Inc., 2002.

Scott, J. L. *36th and 37th Battalions Virginia Cavalry.* Lynchburg: H. E. Howard, Inc., 1986.

Shoemaker, John J. *Shoemaker's Battery.* Gaithersburg: Butternut Press, no date.

Simons, Ezra D. *A Regimental History: The One Hundred and Twenty-fifth New York State Volunteers.* New York: Ezra D. Simons, Publisher, 1888.

Slocum, Charles Elihu. *The Life and Services of Major-General Henry Warner Slocum.* Toledo, Ohio: The Slocum Publishing Company, 1913.

Smith, Thomas West. *The Story of a Cavalry Regiment: "Scott's 900," Eleventh New York Cavalry.* Chicago: W. B. Conkey Company, 1897.

Starr, Stephen Z. *The Life of a Soldier of Fortune: Colonel Grenfell's Wars.* Baton Rouge: Louisiana State University Press, 1971.

_____. *The Union Cavalry in the Civil War: Volume II, The War in the East, From Gettysburg to Appomattox, 1863-1865.* Baton Rouge: Louisiana University Press, 1981.

Stiles, Kenneth L. *4th Virginia Cavalry.* Lynchburg: H. E. Howard, Inc., 1991.

Thomas, Colonel Hampton S. *Some Personal Reminiscences of Service in the Cavalry of the Army of the Potomac.* Philadelphia: L. R. Hamersly & Co., 1889.

Tobie, Edward P. *History of the First Maine Cavalry 1861 - 1865.* Boston: Press of Emery & Hughes, 1887.

Trout, Robert J. *They Followed the Plume.* Mechanicsburg: Stackpole Books, 1993.

_____. *The Hoss: Officer Biographies and Rosters of the Stuart Horse Artillery Battalion.* Myerstown: JebFlo Press, 2003.

_____., ed. *Memoirs of the Stuart Horse Artillery Battalion: Moorman's and Hart's Batteries.* Knoxville: The University of Tennessee Press, 2008.

Troxler, Beverly Barrier and Billy Dawn Barrier Auciello, ed. *Dear Father: Confederate Letters Never Before Published: A Collection of Letters Written to Mathias Barrier of Mt. Pleasant, North Carolina from His Two Sons, Rufus Alexander Barrier and William Lafayette Barrier.* North Billerica, MA: Autumn Printing, 1989.

U. S. War Department. *The War of the Rebellion: The Official Records of the Union and Confederate Armies.* Harrisburg, PA: National Historical Society, 1971.

Wallace, Jr., Lee A. *A Guide to Virginia Military Organizations, 1861-1865.* Lynchburg: H. E. Howard, Inc., 1986.

Warner, Ezra J. *Generals in Gray.* Baton Rouge: Louisiana State University Press, 1959.

_____. *Generals in Blue.* Baton Rouge: Louisiana State University Press, 1964.

Wert, Jeffery D. *Mosby's Rangers.* New York: Simon and Shuster, 1990.

Williamson, James J. *Mosby's Rangers.* New York: Ralph B. Kenyon, Publisher, 1896.

Index

Index

Index

Notes